THINKING SOCIOLOGICALLY

AN INTRODUCTION TO THE DISCIPLINE

William C. NesSmith

Florida Community College at Jacksonville

Harcourt Brace College Publishers

Fort Worth Philadelphia San Diego New York Orlando Austin San Antonio
Toronto Montreal London Sydney Tokyo

Publisher	Ted Buchholz
Executive Editor	Chris Klein
Developmental Editor	John Haley
Project Editors	Sarah E. Hughbanks, Nancy Lombardi
Production Manager	Cynthia Young
Art Director	Jim Dodson
Picture Editor	Sandra Lord

ISBN: 0-15-500830-7

Library of Congress Catalog Card Number: 94–75868

Address editorial correspondence to:
Harcourt Brace College Publishers
301 Commerce Street, Suite 3700
Fort Worth, TX 76102

Address orders to:
Harcourt Brace & Company
6277 Sea Harbor Drive
Orlando, FL 32887–6777
1-800-782-4479 or 1-800-433-0001 (in Florida)

Printed in the United States of America

4 5 6 7 8 9 0 1 2 3 048 9 8 7 6 5 4 3 2 1

PREFACE

For years, like other college teachers, I have been advising my students that the modern postindustrial society and the global economy pose special demands, especially for people just entering the labor market. Those who can comprehend, analyze, and manipulate sophisticated information will be at an advantage pursuing their goals, as well as better citizens. Today more than ever, teaching must go beyond merely transmitting knowledge. Sociology students must not only acquire knowledge of the discipline but also learn to apply it and to think sociologically. I hope this book will help toward that end.

This intention to help students think in a more sophisticated way is certainly not a new idea among textbook authors. But unlike most introductory textbooks, which present the discipline's concepts and theories in an encyclopedic form, *Thinking Sociologically* uses what might be called a context approach. Each section of a chapter focuses on a topic, usually framed as a question, that serves as a context or vehicle for *applying* sociological concepts and theories. The result is something closer to "sociology in action" rather than merely "sociology on display."

This book is organized around three goals:

1. Questions and topics *engage the reader's interest* and give her or him a sense of purpose: reading actively to discover, for example, What happens in the classroom, sociologically speaking? or Why do gangs get started?

2. Each chapter section introduces sociological *concepts and theories as useful, relevant tools*. For example, social change theories explore the question, Is change good for developing nations? Concepts such as diffusion, innovation, and social movements help students understand change in modernizing Japan. And demographic tools contrast the populations of Mexico and the United States. In this approach, students put sociology to use by answering practical questions and exploring specific issues.

3. In the end, I hope all this will provide the reader with a *model for thinking sociologically*. Also toward this end, each chapter features special boxes. The Research Boxes give students the chance to "look over the shoulder" of researchers as they use the tools of social science to investigate questions such as, Is a less satisfying marriage the price of parenthood? Who gets into Harvard? Critical Thinking Boxes encourage students to consider the intricacies underlying such questions as, What is human? What price equality? Do old people have a duty to die?

INSTRUCTIONAL MATERIALS AND LEARNING RESOURCES
For the Instructor

Instructor's Manual A complete resource for more effective instruction using *Thinking Sociologically*, prepared by Linda Shelly. Includes learning objectives, chapter outlines, lecture suggestions, ideas for class discussions, audiovisual resources, and sections dealing with research methods and critical thinking skills.

Test Bank This comprehensive test item file prepared by James E. Floyd of Macon College includes over 2,000 multiple-choice, true–false, and essay questions, completely keyed to the text and learning objectives from the Study Guide and Instructor's Manual. Includes test items from the Study Guide for professors who wish to reinforce students' use of that learning resource.

Social Issues **Quarterly Report Videos**   From the MacNeil/Lehrer PBS television series entitled *Social Issues*. Topics include: The Global Culture Clash, Crime and Social Justice, Health Care, and The State of American Schools. Contact your local Harcourt Brace representative for details.

The *Sociological Imagination* Video Segments   Instructors may select from 12 video segments developed from the Dallas County Community College District telecourse in introductory sociology. All programs are 26 minute clips from the actual telecourse and highlight relevant subject matter.

Computerized Test Bank   Available in IBM® and Macintosh® formats, EXAMaster™ software allows you to create tests using fewer keystrokes. Easy-to-follow screen prompts guide you step-by-step through test construction. EXAMaster™ gives you three ways to create tests:

EasyTest™ lets you create a test from a single screen. It compiles a test using questions you've chosen from the database, or randomly selects questions based on the parameters you specify.

FullTest™ gives you a whole range of options for test creation. With FullTest™, you may:

- select questions as you preview them on screen
- edit existing questions, or add your own questions
- add or edit graphics (in MS-DOS version)
- link related questions, instructions, and graphics
- have questions randomly selected from a wider range of criteria
- create your own criteria on two open keys
- block specific questions from random selection
- print up to 99 different versions of the same test and answer sheet

RequesTest™ is for the instructor without access to a computer. You may call our Software Support Line and order tests that conform to your criteria. We'll compile the test and either mail or fax it to you within 48 hours.

Overhead Teaching Transparencies   Classroom lectures will be enhanced with this collection of 54 full-color transparencies that illustrate sociological concepts. All contain information to supplement (not duplicate) material in the textbook.

Sociology Videodisc   The videodisc addresses social issues, how behavior mandates social change, and explains the theories presented in the text.

For the Student

Study Guide   Prepared by the text author, the Study Guide contains learning objectives, chapter overviews, key terms, and review tests, including multiple-choice, matching, true–false, and short-answer questions. Many test items also appear in the test bank to reinforce student use of the study guide.

SimCity™ Software Introducing an educational version of SimCity™ software geared to sociology using environmental, economic, or geographical variables to teach the volatile nature of sociology. This software allows the user to create his or her own society, an experience instructors and students will find invaluable.

Socialstat Software A new program written by Dean Savage and Jesse Reichler of City University of New York, Queens College, that presents an easy-to-use introduction to data analysis. Clear graphics make running frequency distributions, histograms, and scatterplots an exciting endeavor.

ACKNOWLEDGMENTS

Although writing a textbook is a solitary task, it is one that cannot be accomplished without the assistance, advice, and input of others. I owe a debt of gratitude to my colleagues whose comments, criticisms, and suggestions helped to shape this work:

Roger Barnes, Incarnate Word College

Foster Chason, Chattanooga State Community College

Sarah Coleman, Mohawk Valley Community College

James E. Floyd, Macon College

James Glynn, Bakersfield College

Michael Goslin, Tallahassee Community College

Charlotte Gottwald, York College

Michael Horton, Pensacola Junior College

Billie Laney, Central Texas College

John K. Lay, Butler County Community College

Elizabeth Meyer, Pennsylvania College of Technology

Monica Seff, University of Texas at Arlington

Joseph Walsh, Bucks County Community College

All textbook authors owe a debt of gratitude to the researchers and theorists who build the disciplines. In addition to these people, I wish to thank Chris Klein and John Haley at Harcourt Brace for their perceptive guidance and gracious help. And I owe special thanks to Margaret Butler, whose diligent research and clerical assistance helped me to actually enjoy this project; surely no author has ever been blessed with a more industrious and supportive assistant. Veronica Perillo lent her experienced hand in the clerical work, and my daughter, Vanessa, helped with the research. And through it all, my wife, Maureen, offered her invaluable encouragement and advice, as always.

CONTENTS

Preface   iii

Chapter 3   Social Interaction   62

Chapter 4   Socialization   96

Chapter 5   Deviance   122

Chapter 6   Social Stratification   158

Chapter 7   Racial and Ethnic Minorities   198

Chapter 8   Gender and Age   232

Chapter 9   Family   266

Chapter 10   Economic and Political Institutions   300

Chapter 13   Populations and Communities   410

Chapter 14   Social Change   444

Thinking Sociologically

SOCIOLOGY AND SCIENCE

WHY STUDY SOCIOLOGY?

Anyone assigned to read this book has the right to ask, "What will I get out of it?" One problem that immediately arises in answering this question is that sociology's most important benefits are not concrete or easily measured. Body builders can record the results of their efforts in inches and in striking photographs. Typing students can measure progress in words per minute. Of course, sociology students can identify a number of sociological facts they remember, but facts are only part of sociology's potential reward: an enhanced way of perceiving the social world.

Unlike sociology students, who acquire an enhanced mindset, body builders get concrete, observable results from their efforts.

Beneath the Surface

First, consider the "common sense" notion that women receiving welfare have a higher birthrate than other women. This is the sort of thing everyone "simply knows," right? Surely, there's no need for a sociological study to confirm the obvious. As it turns out, one study found that this "fact" is not always true. The welfare women in the study actually had a substantially *lower* birthrate than women in general (Rank, 1989). Moreover, the longer the women remained on welfare, the less likely they were to have more children. Interviews also revealed that these women desired to get off welfare, and that they fully realized they were not stable enough, financially or otherwise, to accept the responsibility of another baby. This study may not be the last sociological word on the matter, but it should cause us to question some of our assumptions about women on welfare.

Consider also the seemingly obvious prediction that people who begin drinking early in life are more likely to eventually abuse alcohol. Researchers, however, find that when children are exposed to drinking in a strong family-controlled setting with well-defined guidelines, they are actually *less* likely to become problem drinkers (Hafen and Brog, 1983; Lo and Globetti, 1991). And while it might seem that living together before marriage helps a couple test their compatibility, thus lowering the probability of divorce, sociologists find that cohabitation actually *raises* the chances for eventual divorce (DeMaris and Rao, 1992).

These cases illustrate the first benefit of the sociological perspective: It can take us beneath the surface of mere "common sense" beliefs about human social relationships. Its revelations are based on information that is more carefully and systematically collected than is true of our everyday observations. In this way, sociology gives us more reliable, accurate information about how the social world actually works.

The people around us look less familiar and more interesting when observed from unusual angles. Various body features take on new significance when viewed from new perspectives. Similarly, when we use sociology's several perspectives, the familiar can become intriguing, and previously unnoticed details of our social world are brought into focus.

Sociological imagination: the ability to perceive relationships between personal experience and the broader social environment.

Several Perspectives

Another benefit of studying sociology is illustrated by the use of multiple curriculum programs or "tracks" (such as college preparatory, vocational, and business) in many U.S. high schools. Is this the best way to provide for the different needs of students? The answer is both yes and no, because we can view the high school from more than one perspective. From one viewpoint, the high school's task is to fit students with different abilities and career goals into the most appropriate track. From another, however, the tracking system is a device for keeping lower-class children in the lower class. These opposing views may cause us to question whether the high school is a gateway to opportunity or an instrument of oppression. This consideration of new and alternative viewpoints is another benefit of studying sociology.

The Sociological Imagination

Another question reveals yet one more benefit: Does the job market influence the probability that young people will engage in delinquency? It is easy to guess that this is so, and in fact researchers find that a lack of job opportunities can be one of the social forces that "tip the balance" for some juveniles to engage in crime (Allan and Steffensmeier, 1989). In other words, delinquency can be seen as at least partly the result of broad social forces rather than simply one's character or personal circumstances. Similarly, sociologists usually cite "neighborhood effects" rather than the personal traits of residents when explaining high poverty rates in inner cities (Osterman, 1991b). This view illustrates what C. Wright Mills called the **"sociological imagination,"** in which an individual's situation is explained in terms of broad social and historical events and trends (1956).

According to Mills, if we are to more fully understand people—including ourselves—we must see them as caught in social forces beyond their personal control.

The sociological imagination helps us see how broad social forces and historical events affect us as individuals.

THE SOCIAL SCIENCES

Sociology	The study of human social relationships; in other words, what society is like, and what happens when humans interact, as in gangs, families, and other groups.
Psychology	The study of individuals, their behavior, and mental processes, including behavioral disorders, personality formation, and perceptions.
Economics	The study of the production and distribution of goods and services, including different kinds of systems organized to accomplish these basic tasks, such as capitalism or socialism, as well as more specific aspects of those systems, such as money, business organization, and labor.
Political science	The study of power and its uses, including government and voting.
Anthropology	The study of human culture and physical variations. Cultural anthropology deals with the different ways that various peoples adapt to their environments; physical anthropology focuses on racial differences among prehistoric and contemporary humans.
History	The scientific study of the past.

Figure 1-1

All sciences are attempts to discover facts about reality. The natural sciences explore the physical world; the social sciences focus on the world of human existence. Sociology fits into this category as one of these scientific studies of our social surroundings.

Graduating with skills that the job market does not need, for example, can affect our employment opportunities for years to come. And we have all felt the reverberations of the women's liberation movement at home and in the workplace, in our love relationships and careers. Likewise, U.S. government policies regarding Vietnam and Kuwait altered the personal pathways of hundreds of thousands of people. Such seemingly remote events as the introduction of the time-release birth control implant and new child-care legislation can alter our own choices and life-scripts. The sociological imagination prompts us to acknowledge the links between such broad social trends and our personal histories.

These cases illustrate three aspects of the enhanced social viewpoint sociology offers and prepare the way for a definition of **sociology:** the scientific study of human society and social behaviors. As we will see next, the benefits of sociology flow from its scientific nature.

Sociology: the scientific study of human society and social behaviors.

HOW IS SOCIOLOGY DIFFERENT FROM "COMMON SENSE"?

As we have seen, "common sense" notions are often contradicted by sociological research. Consider a few more examples. "As soon as a childless couple adopt a child, they are likely to finally get pregnant." Actually, this is not true, but many of us hold such beliefs because we wish to detect order even where there is none (Gilovich, 1991). "A personal interview enables admissions officers at elite colleges to make much better predictions about which students will succeed." Again, research finds otherwise, but people usually believe what they want to believe. "Basketball players get the 'hot hand,' and are exceptionally likely to hit the next few shots." In fact, they are more likely to hit a basket if they have missed their previous two or three shots, but people tend to be more impressed by data that seem to confirm such a belief than by evidence that contradicts it.

Thomas Gilovich describes these beliefs as "illusions of everyday life." Starting with the disciplined scientific approach, we will now begin to see how sociology probes beneath the surface of such "common sense" illusions.

The Scientific Attitude

Empirical data: information based on observation and experience.

Ever since the earliest sociologists began retreating from intellectual flights of fancy they have been obligated, like other scientists, to generate **empirical data:** evidence that can be observed or experienced by others. Unlike the subjective feelings and thoughts of our everyday thinking, numbers, videotapes, recorded interviews and other empirical evidence can be scrutinized and evaluated by other people. Indeed, when they cannot offer evidence that others can see, smell, hear, taste, or touch, sociologists and other scientists cannot pretend to offer answers, only possibilities.

Inference: reasoning from evidence, or from the known to the unknown.

Theories: logical, well-supported explanations about how facts are related.

Of course, possibilities can be useful in themselves. Certainly there is a place in sociology for taking a well-directed leap from the evidence to possible explanations. In fact, an important part of scientists' work involves **inference,** which in simple terms is reasoning from the known to the unknown. Inference allows scientists to generalize from specific data to universal laws and to build **theories:** logical, well-supported explanations about how facts are related. Such generalizing and theory-building exist as faint glimmers in our everyday "common sense" thinking, but they lie at the heart of the scientific endeavor. Without them, sociology and the other sciences could offer us only a mountain of facts.

Objectivity: maintaining clear, undistorted, and accurate perceptions free of emotions or biases.

Another intellectual demand placed on scientists is **objectivity,** perceiving the world clearly and accurately, and not allowing one's own emotions or biases to distort perceptions. This requires considerable mental discipline and can produce an internal, emotional struggle. Picture the researchers who rode with police officers in order to observe the field testing of a new arrest policy regarding wife batterers (Ferraro, 1989). Indeed, the report mentions the difficulty observers experienced in maintaining a completely open mind, an unemotional view of the husbands and their actions. It dryly notes that, "In most cases, observers did not attempt to influence police behavior, even when they disagreed with decisions" (p. 64).

The Goals of Researchers

As nonscientists, we put our minds to work in limitless ways, from savoring a moment of love to deciding which job to take, from enjoying the humor of a joke to formulating insults. The scientific approach, however, has a more limited focus: determining what is, has been, will be, and why. Any one of four goals guides the scientific researcher in this quest: description, explanation, control, and prediction.

Description The most fundamental goal for a scientist, and one that accounts for much of our everyday thinking, is to describe or record what occurs. For nonscientists, description is likely to be a simple matter of verbally recreating a situation for someone else. Scientific description, however, requires much greater precision and lays the groundwork for more ambitious goals. For example, Thomas DiPrete and David Grusky (1990) picture in detail how the door to the job market opened wider during

Sociologists sometimes use inference to take a leap from established fact to the unknown.

the 1970s as the federal government increased its affirmative action and training programs. As these efforts diminished during the 1980s, the door to the job market closed somewhat. Such descriptions cannot only illuminate portions of the social world for us, they can suggest avenues of further research, such as investigating why the job market door closed and when it might open again.

Explanation   At times we all want to know why something happened. While we sometimes explain events in terms of "fate" or "luck" or "that's just the way it goes," scientific explanation begins with **determinism,** the assumption that every phenomenon is determined or caused by something else. In other words, nothing "just happens;" every occurrence is the consequence, or effect, of some cause. To explain why something happens, then, is to establish a cause–effect relationship. For example, Paul

Determinism: the assumption that every phenomenon has a cause.

Drew and Elizabeth Holt (1988) explain why a person who is complaining to another may employ idiomatic, proverbial, or other figurative expressions such as "It's gone to pot" or "I'm left between the devil and the deep blue sea." They found that speakers use such expressions when they receive little sympathy for their complaint. They are intended to draw the complaint to a more forceful conclusion and elicit more support from the listener.

Control   Our own efforts to control our surroundings usually focus on extremely local concerns, such as the people in our household. For larger matters, such as improving our nation's schools, we often turn to scientists, whose broader data bases and more generally applicable theories enable them to deal with problems in universal terms.

For scientists, control often means changing the environment in such a way as to try to solve some problem, such as poverty, crime, or discrimination. Douglas Massey (1990), for example, shows how rising poverty rates can lead to greater racial segregation, which helps transform some neighborhoods into areas of high crime, poor schools, and family disintegration. He concludes that policies to help minorities will fail unless they focus on "racial discrimination and prejudice in the housing market" (p. 354). Sometimes such research can open the way to eventually control or change the situation.

Prediction   We can use hunches, astrology, or our own limited experience to predict the consequences of our plans and actions, or we can rely on the huge storehouse of empirical, objectively analyzed, statistically organized information of science. For example, Arland Thornton (1991) uses such data to show that when women marry young or are pregnant at marriage, their own children are likely to marry early or cohabitate. In fact, a growing body of research demonstrates that our own marital experiences can predict to some extent those of our children. Policymakers can use such information to anticipate future marriage trends and perhaps even welfare needs.

The Scientific Method

"Should I keep my child in kindergarten for another year?" Our everyday efforts to answer such questions rarely follow a conscious strategy or plan. The discipline of science, on the other hand, requires that a set of procedures more or less follows a logical sequence called "the scientific method." This formal process as described in most textbooks does not always precisely reflect how real research is done. Rather than a clean, orderly sequence, real-world research is sometimes a mire of insufficient data, blindspots, uncooperative respondents, and too little time and money. Still, the formal model we explore here offers insight into the underlying strategy that directs actual research efforts. To illustrate, we will apply one of several possible versions of the scientific method to the question posed above.

Defining the Problem and Reviewing the Research Literature   Panayota Mantzicopoulos and Delmont Morrison (1992) found that previous research amply demonstrated that retention in elementary school has few positive, and significant negative, consequences for children. The more specific case of *kindergarten* retention, however, had not been fully explored. In other words, their review of the relevant research literature revealed a gap in the body of knowledge. To close that gap, and provide a more reliable basis for parents and teachers to make decisions, Mantzicopoulos and Morrison defined their research problem as the impact kindergarten retention has on academic achievement and behavior through the second grade.

Hypothesis   The researchers next developed a **hypothesis,** a statement that reaches beyond available knowledge. A hypothesis is essentially an informed guess about the relationships between two or more **variables,** characteristics that vary from one individual, group, or time to another. This guess, however, should be solidly founded on the existing fund of knowledge. Since the rest of the research process is essentially the testing of the hypothesis, it must be a statement that can be tested with existing methods and resources.

The variables in the hypothesis must be operationally defined, that is, described in such a way that they can be clearly identified and precisely measured. This helps ensure that only relevant data will be collected. In our example, previous research had suggested strongly to Mantzicopoulos and Morrison that kindergarten retention would result in lower scores on a specified academic achievement test by the end of the second grade and would not reduce specified behavioral problems. The researchers used this as the basis of their hypothesis, which included specifications such as student behavior problems that were defined according to a previously developed "Revised Behavior Problem Checklist."

Research Design   After defining the problem and formulating an hypothesis, the scientist decides what data to collect and how. There are several methods available for collecting data—experiment, survey, observation, and use of secondary sources—and they will be described in detail later in this chapter. Based largely on the demands of the hypothesis, Mantzicopoulos and Morrison chose the experiment for gathering data about achievement and behavior problems.

Collection of Data   The actual gathering of evidence, whether in the form of administering questionnaires or running an experiment, may be done by the scientist, students, trained professionals, or members of the community. The scientist is responsible for ensuring that the data collected are appropriate and that the collectors did

Hypothesis: a statement depicting the expected relationship between two or more variables; an informed guess about such a relationship.

Variables: characteristics that vary from one individual, group, or time to another.

Scientific data gathering must be disciplined; only accurate, unbiased information should be used. Precise measurement is not always possible.

not bias or distort the data. Objectivity and empiricism are of primary importance. In their study, Mantzicopoulos and Morrison matched 53 children retained in kindergarten with 53 of their peers who advanced to elementary school. The two groups had nearly identical background characteristics (sex, race, and so on). Teachers rated the students' behavior patterns and administered achievement tests to both groups.

Data Analysis Once the data are collected, the scientist faces the task of searching for patterns that support or cast doubt upon the hypothesis. Many sociologists deal with large bodies of quantitative (that is, numerical or measurable) data, and must use statistical tests in their analyses. These tests tell the researcher the probability that chance or outside factors were responsible for the patterns and tendencies shown in the data. The tests give some specified degree of assurance—for example, 99 percent—that if many other observations were conducted the same patterns and tendencies would be found. Mantzicopoulos and Morrison found that at the end of the second year in kindergarten the retained students displayed a significant academic advantage over the group that went on to elementary school, but by the end of the second grade the latter group had pulled ahead. The probability that chance was responsible for the between-group differences was .01 percent.

Forming a Conclusion The last step of the scientific research model, logically enough, is formation of a conclusion, based on the data analysis and aimed at the hypothesis. If the researcher guessed wrong—if the hypothesis is not supported by the collected data—the problem can be redefined, or the hypothesis refined, and the process can begin again. If the data support the hypothesis, it can be accepted. This acceptance, however, remains tentative until other scientists have replicated the study and found similar results.

Even when the collected data support the hypothesis, researchers typically describe their success in cautious terms. For example, Mantzicopoulos and Morrison conclude that "the results of the present study are, in general, consistent with those obtained by other investigators. . . . Thus, it can be reasonably claimed that kindergarten retention was not helpful to children in the short interval of this study" (p. 196). But they also note that "the behavioral outcomes were much more difficult to interpret" (p. 195).

Elsewhere in this and other chapters are depictions of the scientific attitude at work. They are offered as encouragement to the reader to assimilate this empowering, disciplined way of thinking about the social world.

APPLYING THE SOCIOLOGICAL IMAGINATION TO SOCIOLOGY'S FOUNDERS

The sociological imagination enables us to see the relation between individuals' lives and their historical and social contexts. The nineteenth-century founders of sociology were undoubtedly products of their historical era, yet they also helped shape the academic currents of the present century. As they shaped sociology into a science, these men

How Do We Kid Ourselves?

Thomas Gilovich (1991) explains why, without the safeguards of the scientific attitude, we are more likely to face frustration in our everyday efforts to solve problems and answer questions. Why, for example, does rewarding a child's excellent behavior so often seem to be directly followed by less admirable behavior? We can explain this frustrating pattern in terms of the "regression effect," the tendency for extremes to be followed by a return to normalcy rather than continued extreme performance. Ignoring the fact that highs do not usually continue for very long, we tend to see continuity or coherence where there are actually only periodic peaks. Thus corporation executives optimistically—and dangerously—bet that the company's stellar performance indicates an upward trend of success instead of a brief high likely to be followed by a drop. Parents who reward their child's extraordinarily good behavior feel discouraged when it inevitably (but probably only temporarily) deteriorates. One danger in our "common sense" thinking, then, is to expect or perceive order and continuity when they do not exist.

Another trap of "common sense" is that we tend to more readily accept evidence that seems to confirm our beliefs than that which contradicts them. This is why, Gilovich argues, people tend to believe that their dreams accurately predict the future: We acknowledge only the few instances when dreams seem to have come true and ignore the multitude that have not.

Just as unflattering is our tendency to believe simply what we want to believe. As Gilovich explains, "for things we want to believe, we ask only that the evidence not force us to believe otherwise—a rather easy standard to meet" (p. 58). Thus we tend to easily believe in the intelligence, beauty, and skills of our children as well as ourselves. Destroying such beliefs requires an avalanche of contrary evidence.

These reasoning errors rarely escape detection under the steely eye of science. When objectivity, empiricism, replication, public scrutiny, and the rigors of the scientific method are applied to "common sense" beliefs, many of our cherished notions quickly explode. ■

ventured down intellectual pathways that have by now become well worn. In fact, its leading light, Auguste Comte, offered an acknowledgement of the impact of important individuals that could serve as his own epitaph: "The dead govern the living."

Auguste Comte (1798–1857)

We begin with Auguste Comte because sociology literally began with him; it was he who coined the term "sociology." Comte's story reveals how a useful intellectual craft began to emerge from the grandiose speculations of the eighteenth century. As a braggart in a uniform can become a warrior under the pressure of combat, so philosophical pronouncements about society became a science under the pressures of a revolutionary era.

The forces that helped to forge both Comte and sociology included two revolutions. The first was the French Revolution which began in 1789, a few years before his birth. This social cataclysm claimed tens of thousands of lives, overturned the existing social order in France, and seemed to prove that the noble ideals of reason, freedom,

An arrogant intellectual who suffered through troughs of despair, twice attempting suicide, August Comte also managed to found a new science of society.

and justice could replace oppressive traditions. The Industrial Revolution soon followed, spawning a ruthlessly competitive marketplace that demanded a new kind of worker, family, and city. The rise of the urban industrial society rendered some religious and philosophical explanations of the world obsolete. A new source of knowledge and guidance surged into the vacuum: science.

Comte carried into this intellectual storm the torch of the eighteenth-century Enlightenment. Philosophers such as Jean Jacques Rousseau and Charles Louis Montesquieu had already set the spark with their revolutionary idea that society was not pressed into a preordained mold but could be reformed or even replaced. Enlightenment intellectuals had begun to hope that, just as uniform laws of physics had explained the motions of the planets, so scholars would discover the laws governing society.

In Auguste Comte we see a confluence of these historical and intellectual currents. Although he did little research himself, he realized the need for precise observations of society, a methodology he called "social physics." And like most early nineteenth-century intellectuals, Comte worked with a broad brush, painting sweeping visions.

He also displayed a considerable ego, practicing at one point what he called "cerebral hygiene," through which he would avoid contaminating his mind with the presumably inferior ideas of others. He attracted something like a cult following and routinely recorded the hour of the day when he began each page of a manuscript describing what he called "the great discovery of the year 1822" (Collins and Makowsky, 1978). This "great discovery" was a typically grand, early nineteenth-century description of the evolution of knowledge in any subject, beginning with the theological stage (in which explanations were based on spirits and gods), followed by the metaphysical stage (with knowledge founded on the philosophical speculations typical of his time). In describing the third stage, Comte foretold—and prompted—the eventual maturation of sociology into a science. He called this third stage "positivism," ruled by scientific explanations based on observation and experimentation.

Thus Comte earned his place as a pivotal figure in the formation of sociology. Shaped by the revolutionary ideas of his time, he built a bridge from "old world" grandiose speculations to the "new world" of a scientific study of society. He served as a prophet for those who would later fulfill his vision.

Herbert Spencer (1820–1903)

Herbert Spencer. Physically weak as a child, using opium to fight insomnia in later years, and heir to a modest sum, he offered comforting notions to the wealthy and powerful.

Evolutionism was one of the great intellectual influences of the nineteenth century. Utopian theorists used it to predict virtually unlimited social progress. Evolutionism's flood tide engulfed leading thinkers of the time, including Herbert Spencer. Building upon the evolutionary theory of Comte, as well as Charles Darwin's discovery that organisms evolve as they adapt to the demands of their surroundings, Spencer formulated what has come to be known as "social Darwinism." This controversial view of society brought him acclaim from the rapidly expanding middle-class reading audience of mid-nineteenth-century England. His theory still fires controversy today, usually in political and intellectual mudslinging.

Spencer argued that societies evolved from simple to complex and that, like animal species, do so through competition and the "survival of the fittest." Those who move up the social ladder clearly prove their superiority to those stuck at the bottom, he claimed. In fact, Spencer saw social inequality as a healthy product of evolution. In his view, charity and government aid only interfered in this sorting-out process and, by hindering society's progress, were counterproductive.

On a superficial level, social Darwinism has an intuitive appeal, especially to opponents of government welfare programs. But its critics point out that individuals can become trapped at the bottom of the social ladder for reasons other than personal inadequacies. The competition for climbing the ladder is rigged in favor of those who begin near the top. Also, barriers such as racial and ethnic discrimination block the way. And even if competition were fair and open, we are left with the moral repugnance at the thought of letting the "unfit" languish in poverty, all in the name of social progress.

Karl Marx (1818–1883)

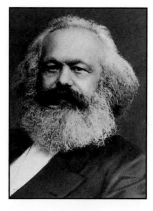

Karl Marx. This son of a liberal lawyer and bureaucrat devoted his life to urging the overthrow of the ruling class.

We are all familiar with the name of Karl Marx because his revolutionary ideas influenced the course of global events for most of the twentieth century. This world shaker began modestly enough. The son of a lawyer and bureaucrat of modest means, Marx attended the University of Berlin, where he spent much of his time in beer gardens, incurring considerable debts, and fighting at least one duel. Yet, in the name of this once disreputable student, entire nations would later be ruled.

Marx's ideas clearly reflect the horrors of early industrialization and capitalism in mid-nineteenth-century Europe. Where others saw mines and factories producing mountains of inexpensive goods for society, Marx saw them devouring the lives of exploited men, women, and children who worked 14 hours a day, six or seven days a week. Where others saw government as a source of guidance and order for the people, he saw an oppressive instrument wielded by the ruling class to protect its advantaged position. He refused to turn a blind eye to the poverty and inequalities of early capitalism's grimy, sooty industrial towns. Marx was one of several socialists of his day who argued that such a society should be replaced, through violent revolution if necessary.

Marx, along with his colleague Friedrich Engels, pointed to the central importance of the economy in society's organization. They contended that the way society allocates the means of production (or capital) determines how all other resources, such as wealth and power, are distributed. In other words, ownership of the means of production, in the form of land, factories, and so on, translates into control of other aspects of society. Marx and Engels called this view "economic determinism."

Marx and Engels saw in the economic structure stress lines along which fractures form in society. These stress lines divide people into various classes with opposing economic interests, such as slaveowner and slave, landowner and peasant, and capitalist and laborer, and the inevitable result is class conflict. "The history of all hitherto existing society," Marx claimed, "is the history of class struggles."

Marx argued that class divisions even permeated people's beliefs and worldviews. Because of what he called "class consciousness," people see the world from the standpoint of their own economic positions. The feudal lords of the Middle Ages, for example, claimed that their station in life, and that of the serfs, was ordained by God. In the present time, Marx argued, the ruling class uses its superior intellectual resources and control of government agencies, mass media, schools and churches to control the flow of information and convince the oppressed classes that their interests coincide with those of their oppressors. In other words, the subordinate classes develop a "false consciousness" that leaves them more easily controlled and exploited. At the root of

Son of a rabbi, Emile Durkheim earned the first chair of sociology in Europe.

this system of exploitation and oppression lies class, the essential tool of analysis according to Marx.

In addition to shaping the world's political landscape, Marx's ideas provided the foundation for a radical dimension of modern sociology called conflict theory, which we will explore later in this chapter. His vision gave birth to a social critique that aims to not simply describe society but to transform it.

Emile Durkheim (1858–1917)

Social disruption and violence wracked Emile Durkheim's world when he came of age over a century ago. The optimistic visions of social evolutionary progress he had assimilated from Comte and Spencer failed to anticipate the swirling intellectual and political crosscurrents of France in the late 1800s. Marxism, the popular alternative intellectual framework that predicted society's inevitable collapse and replacement, did not satisfy his demand for factually based explanations. On the other hand, as a modernist, Durkheim had no sympathy for reactionary appeals for a return to the old order of religion and authority. Caught between the radical and the conservative streams of his turbulent era, Durkheim embarked on his own path to develop a science of modern society.

One aspect of the academic climate in the late 1800s that influenced Durkheim was the philosophical speculation that passed as social "science." Social thinkers usually made pronouncements without offering any verifiable support for their conclusions. Durkheim argued that sociologists should explain society using "social facts," those objective parts of social life external to all individuals and existing independently of people's biases or preferences, such as birth rates, fashion trends, and swings in the labor market.

At least in part due to Durkheim's ideas, sociologists began to search beyond an individual's moral character or biological make-up to explain, for example, criminal behaviors. Moreover, some social facts, such as the equalizing of gender roles, are explained by other social facts, such as the growth of sprawling, interconnected suburbs. These "edge cities" offer employment opportunities close to home for housewives, helping to bring women into the job market and giving them a greater share of social power (Fishman, 1990). Durkheim's insistence that we focus on social facts has helped fulfill Comte's dream that sociology become a science.

Moreover, Durkheim not only urged other sociologists to focus on objective facts, he demonstrated how to do so. In his classic 1897 study, he explained European suicide rates in terms of social facts. Specifically, he showed that the lower suicide rates among Catholics, married people, and parents were understandable in terms of the degree to which a person was integrated into a larger group. Durkheim collected data that linked lower suicide rates to the strong social ties generated in marriage, parenthood, and the community orientation of Catholics (as opposed to Protestants' focus on individualism). Contemporary sociologists have tested and confirmed his basic point about the importance of social integration (Breault, 1986; Pescosolido and Georgianna, 1989).

In fact, the major preoccupation of Durkheim's illustrious career was social integration. This is not surprising in light of the weakening of traditional social bonds in community life at the turn of the twentieth century. As we will see in a later chapter, he emphasized religion's importance as a primary source of social solidarity. Furthermore, he explained that population growth and urban migration were combining to bring more people into more frequent contact with one another, a situation he called "social density." This density led to an increasingly complex division of labor, that is, more specialized job categories. While this could create an interdependence among the members of society, and perhaps a new basis for social solidarity, it also meant people would share fewer experiences in common. As a result, what he called "moral density" would diminish. The society's glue would be weakened. A century later, Durkheim's insights still ring true.

Max Weber (1864–1920)

A man with a brilliant mind and impressive physical bearing, Max Weber became a leading intellectual of Europe. Trained as an economist and lawyer, he also helped established the German Sociological Association.

Durkheim's birth and death coincided closely with that of the German philosopher, economist, and sociologist Max Weber. Like Durkheim, Weber was shaped by the intellectual turmoil characterizing the emergence of modern society. As we will see in subsequent chapters, Weber's explorations touched on several aspects of modernity and are still used by sociologists today. He examined the newly forming bureaucracies which, as he noted, enable modern society to process people as factories process materials. He also identified the several sources of legitimate social power.

Of all the intellectual offerings of his age, the most influential for Weber were the writings of Marx, which dominated German academic and political debate as Weber matured intellectually in the 1880s and 1890s. Much of Weber's work was generated by his need to respond to Marx's economic determinism, which he scorned as simplistic and one-dimensional. For example, he challenged Marx's strictly economic characterization of social class, arguing that an individual's social ranking is determined not only by wealth but by prestige and power as well.

Again like Durkheim, Weber was influenced by the late nineteenth-century admiration for scientific progress. Weber accordingly added a foundation stone to sociology's scientific methodology. He taught that researchers ideally should be "value free," and not let personal biases creep into their interpretations. Moreover, he urged researchers to imaginatively place themselves into the lives of the people they studied; this would lead to an empathetic understanding of the social world, what he called *verstehen*. He also pioneered the use of models or ideal types as tools for making well-founded generalizations about a complex and ever-changing social reality. His models of bureaucracy and class served as abstract building blocks or self-contained modules for constructing an image of the social world.

Sociology Comes to America

Like other human endeavors, sociology was a child of circumstances. After its emergence in Europe in the nineteenth century, various socio-historical pressures combined to bring the science of sociology to the United States. As waves of immigrants crowded into cities already rife with crime, corruption, and other dislocations of a maturing industrial society, sociology was imported as a tool for grappling with such mushrooming social ills. Spurned by tradition-bound eastern universities, the intellectual upstart for decades flourished only in the progressive climate of the University of Chicago. Once firmly established in the academic community of the United States, however, sociology quickly spread throughout the nation's system of higher education, and after mid-century began to develop various theoretical branches, which we will explore next.

SOCIOLOGY'S THREE PERSPECTIVES

In about half the marriages in Bangkok, Thailand, husbands regularly beat their wives. Over three-quarters of lower-class women in Quito, Ecuador, are physically abused. Sudanese girls' genitals are mutilated to prevent premarital sex (Heise, 1989). These facts remind us that in most human societies men enjoy more power than women. They dominate women economically, sexually, and socially. This social fact demands explanation, and it has attracted a great deal of intense and contentious sociological research. In this section, we will explore sociology's three major theoretical perspectives—functionalism, conflict theory, and interactionism—as applied to male dominance.

Functionalism

Functionalism (or structural functionalism): a perspective that assumes society is comprised of interrelated parts which contribute to its stability and maintenance.

Social system: a set of interdependent parts.

In applying the perspective known as **functionalism,** or **structural functionalism,** we split social reality into two levels: the whole (the society itself) and its parts (patterns of activity). The whole can thus be defined as a **social system** comprised of interrelated parts. When using functionalism to understand any element of the system, we ask how that part contributes to the operation of the system as a whole. We will explain male dominance in this way, but first other aspects of this functional approach must be understood.

The functionalist perspective focuses on the system's stability. We can trace its lineage back to Comte, who compared society to a biological organism comprised of interrelated parts. Spencer elaborated on this analogy by comparing society's institutions (for example, education, the family, government, religion, and the economy) to an organism's major parts (organs, muscles, and so on). Such systems are inherently stable in that they tend toward equilibrium, meaning its major parts work together in a balanced, harmonious way. To maintain this equilibrium, the parts must adapt to one another in a kind of balancing act: Changes in one part of the system require compensating changes in others.

Value consensus: an underlying, widespread agreement on a group's goals and the proper means of achieving them.

The society's equilibrium also depends on **value consensus.** Talcott Parsons (1902–1979), an American sociologist who substantially developed functionalism during the middle part of the twentieth century, pointed out that social harmony requires this underlying, widespread agreement about the group's goals and proper means for achieving them.

Obviously, many societies do not function smoothly. Riots, revolutions, and massive migrations shatter social order, but they can be understood in terms of how they upset social equilibrium. Change can be disruptive because one part of the system may change too rapidly or drastically, and the others may not adapt quickly enough. In other words, change threatens stability. A second reason that societies do not always function smoothly is that, especially in a diverse, multicultural society such as ours, the value consensus may be weakened. People of different backgrounds and cultures have different ideas about group goals and how to achieve them. Thus functionalism reveals a dilemma of modern society: The need for consensus clashes with the benefits of healthy diversity.

Robert Merton (b. 1910), another major functionalist theorist in the United States, has pointed to an additional reason for social disharmony: the negative consequences of maladaptive parts, or what he calls **dysfunctions.** Some elements of a society thwart the system's functioning, for example the tradition of large families in overpopulated countries. On the other hand, those large families also contribute a **function,** a positive consequence or effect: retirement security for the parents. By having many children, parents are assured of having someone to take care of them in old age. As Merton notes, social elements can have more than one effect. What is positive for some people or some systems can be dysfunctional for others. Moreover, some consequences will be intended and expected, what Merton calls **manifest functions;** others will be unexpected or unintended, or **latent functions** (Merton, 1968).

Now we are ready to apply functionalism to the topic of male dominance. Recall that, according to the functionalist perspective, society is comprised of interrelated, interdependent parts. Insofar as each part contributes in some way to the system's overall operation, stability and equilibrium are maintained. Thus we must assume that male dominance exists in most societies because it has contributed a positive effect, a function. Parsons and Robert Bales (1955) describe the assertive, dominating traditional male role as naturally complementing the more nurturing and relatively subservient traditional female role. The family efficiency and stability arising from these complementary roles represent positive, manifest functions. Latent functions of male dominance are the social and sexual power men enjoy over women. Dysfunctions come readily to mind: anger and frustration of women, wasted potential, and unsatisfying marriages.

Male dominance was perhaps a useful part of some societies in earlier times, before industrialization ushered in greater flexibility in dividing labor between the sexes. Changes in modern political, economic and educational structures have rendered it increasingly dysfunctional, however, for men as well as women. (We will discuss women's—and men's—liberation in a later chapter.)

Functionalism offers little explanation for these or other changes in social systems; in fact, its critics point to this blindspot as a major shortcoming of the functionalist perspective. Furthermore, it is inherently conservative and supportive of the status quo, perhaps because it matured during the prosperous, stable, and harmonious post–World War II years. The widespread social divisions of the 1960s demanded a more challenging approach.

Conflict Theory

Oppression. Exploitation. Tension. Struggle. These emotionally charged words characterize society as seen through the conflict perspective. Originally formulated by Karl Marx and his colleague Friedrich Engels in the nineteenth century, this theoretical framework began to achieve respectability during the 1960s. It now stands with functionalism as one of the two major **macrosociological** perspectives that consider society as a whole and explore its basic patterns and systems.

The subject of male dominance clearly illustrates the key disagreement between conflict and functionalist theorists in answering the question, "Who benefits from any particular social pattern?" While functionalists argue that male dominance at some time contributed to the social system's functioning, conflict theorists counter that it benefited only the dominant, oppressive elite. Indeed, from this perspective we presume that the people who control most of the wealth and power make the social system work for themselves, not for the majority. In other words, those with the power use it for their own selfish ends.

Dysfunction: the negative consequence or effect a part has for the whole social system.

Function: the positive consequence or effect a part has for the whole social system.

Manifest functions: intended consequences or goals of social elements.

Latent functions: unintended, unrecognized, or unexpected effects or consequences of social elements.

Macrosociological: a perspective that studies society as a whole or its basic patterns or systems.

According to conflict theory, societies experience perpetual struggle due to the unequal distribution of the things people value, such as wealth and power. People clash continuously in an effort to tilt in their own favor the distribution of these always scarce resources. Only when all parties are satisfied with the distribution of resources will society enjoy the harmony perceived by functionalists.

Why does such continuous struggle not tear the system apart? Conflict theorists argue that exploited victims are loyal to the system because of an illusion of consensus. Values such as industry, thrift, and obedience are imposed upon the masses by the ruling elite through their control of the mass media, education, and other transmitters of values and ideas. The people accept these values as their own and dutifully work to maintain the equilibrium of a society that primarily benefits the upper class.

As early as the mid-1800s, however, a few intellectuals in Europe tried to destroy this illusion and expose this "false consciousness." The German philosopher Georg Wilhelm Friedrich Hegel (1770–1831) described history as a series of inevitable conflicts. To this Marx added economic determinism to make class conflict his central theme.

Conflict theorists have identified other dimensions of oppression besides social class. Weber, for example, pointed to conflict among political power groups and between groups with different life styles and interests. Mills (1956) applied Weber's multidimensional view to describe a dominating elite that included big business, the military, and the federal bureaucracy. Ralf Dahrendorf (1973) also diverged from strict Marxian analysis when he focused on power rather than property. He pointed to a division between those who follow orders (workers) and those who give them (managers), neither of whom own the capital. Similarly, Gerhard Lenski (1966) explained that organizational power was pivotal in the distribution of economic surplus.

Another branch of conflict theory, critical feminism, began shortly after Marx's death, when Engels expanded his view beyond class conflict to include oppression of women. He established an analogy between rights to economic property and rights to sex property, or sexual access to the female. Even though nineteenth-century European women enjoyed more freedom than their predecessors in ancient and medieval societies, they nonetheless held a disadvantageous bargaining position, for the same reason factory workers did—lack of economic property. Women needed a husband for economic support, and in exchange gave up their personhood along with sexual favors. Weber, whose wife was involved in the German feminist movement, developed a theory of the family that also included the importance of sexual property, but it was the Engels tradition that served as the springboard for the feminist, sexual-oppression theories of the last several decades (Collins, 1985).

Whatever the particular object of study, conflict theorists presume that coercion, instability, and oppression characterize relations among groups in their continuous struggle over scarce resources. Not all relations among individuals, however, are full of conflict, nor is the occasional conflict always a result of competition, as we see next.

The Interactionist Perspective

The interactionist viewpoint concentrates on daily interaction patterns of individuals, whether it be a husband intimidating his wife, strangers forming a line at a bus stop, or patrons socializing in a bar. With this **microsociological** perspective, we put people under a microscope in trying to understand how they seek to develop appropriate social behaviors. Because of its concrete, person-to-person nature, male dominance fits

Microsociological: a perspective that focuses on interactions among individuals.

nicely under the microscope, as we see in relating to it the several branches of the interactionist perspective.

Symbolic Interactionism   George Herbert Mead (1863–1931), a University of Chicago philosopher, underlined the importance of symbols in human interaction (1934). According to Mead, each individual uses an internal conversation (based on words or symbols) to form a clear picture of the self and to plan how best to interact with others. Moreover, society itself depends on effective symbol-based interaction. After all, our social world is essentially symbolic. The flag is more than colored cloth, a college diploma is much more than a scrap of paper, and displays of masculinity and femininity represent more than mere physiological differences. Our dealings with one another are based on the meanings we derive from such symbols.

Social reality itself emerges from our interactions according to Herbert Blumer (1969), a follower of Mead. Blumer, who developed symbolic interactionism, pictured the social order not as an objective, rigid reality but as a fluid, ever-changing product of continuous negotiations. He built on the theory of American sociologist W. I. Thomas, who said that "if men define situations as real, they are real in their consequences." Thus Blumer saw social reality as whatever people agree it is. The social order is constructed from individuals' definitions of situations. And those individuals are active, creative agents who, having defined themselves, continually redefine the social order.

Male dominance, then, can be interpreted as part of the social reality manufactured in the course of human interaction—for example, in conversational interchanges. Many studies show that men are more likely than women to exercise power in goal-directed conversation, using interruption, different types of questions, and greater speaking time to dominate conversations (Eakins and Eakins, 1976; Fishman, 1980; Argyle, Lalljee, and Cook, 1968). In fact, people of either sex who see themselves as more "male-like" are more likely to employ assertive, challenging statements (Spencer and Drass, 1989). In other words, maleness translates into power. Insofar as people define dominant interaction patterns as appropriately male, these conversations help recreate the reality of male dominance. From the symbolic interactionist perspective, in other words, male dominance emerges partly from negotiations in our interactions with others.

Ethnomethodology   Ethnomethodology, another branch of interactionism, grew from the work of Harold Garfinkel, who attempted to understand the ways people try to make sense of their experiences (1967). He studied the strategies people use to communicate to one another the existence of shared meanings. Rather than assuming these meanings exist, ethnomethodologists explore how people create an awareness of them. Toward this end, Garfinkel tried to perceive reality at the "taken-for-granted" level. He sometimes instructed his students to violate the rules we normally take for granted by acting as strangers in their parents' home. The students would ask permission to use the bathroom, for example, or use formal modes of address. Such exercises showed them that the social order is not something etched in stone but constructed from day-to-day interpretations of situations, always subject to change. From this perspective, male dominance until recently was taken for granted but is now increasingly challenged and interpreted as inappropriate and intolerable.

Goffman's Dramaturgical Approach   Erving Goffman saw social interaction as a series of dramas in which individuals, like actors on a stage, play roles (1959). Each of us tries to manage the impression we make on other people, who evaluate our "performance" as we walk into a classroom, order a meal in a restaurant, "present" ourselves to a new acquaintance, and so on. To make positive impressions, we selectively reveal and conceal information about ourselves, showing only our best side in each situation. Mead had noted that each of us has many "selves," and Goffman described how we display different selves or roles depending on the particular setting or audience. A college student entering her professor's office, for example, may play the role of "serious student," but as she leaves the office and meets her date for the next weekend party, she may adopt the role of "bubbly coed" or "sultry sophisticate."

In a task-oriented setting, people are likely to engage in the negotiation of identities, a game Goffman called "face work" (1967). The object of this game is to successfully define the role one plays and the nature of the relationship, all at the expense of the other player. As we have seen, "male-like" players enjoy an advantage in this game. Moreover, Goffman described how the players usually establish a "working consensus" in which they uphold each others' self-defined roles or "self-definitional claims." Males typically make the more assertive claims, so they enjoy something of a "home field advantage." As our society's consensus regarding male dominance breaks down, though, we can expect these negotiations to become more difficult as women challenge men's claims to greater power.

Exchange Theory   This game also lends itself to interpretation via exchange theory, an interactionist approach formulated primarily by George Homans (1961). According to Homans, society is a huge network of exchanges. At each exchange, individuals interact to maximize rewards (such as prestige, acceptance, and money). Since people tend to repeat whatever action has been rewarding, men can reasonably be expected to continue using dominance strategies as long as such strategies continue to reward them.

All of these approaches focus on the construction of social reality through face-to-face interaction. While interactionism offers insights into daily experience, like the other major perspectives it does not serve us well for all topics. Just as functionalist and conflict theories can be faulted for ignoring everyday reality by concentrating on sweeping, abstract social forces, interactionism tends to ignore the importance of large-scale forces like institutions and social trends. In other words, an exclusive reliance on interactionism invites the danger of not seeing the forest for the trees. We need not choose one theoretical perspective to apply to all topics; we can select the most appropriate one for each.

So far we have considered only one example of how sociologists use the three major theoretical perspectives to explore a topic. In the remaining chapters, we will apply these perspectives to a wide variety of issues. For now, however, we will continue to focus on male dominance as we move from theory to the gathering of evidence.

RESEARCH DESIGN

Before we can collect scientific evidence and form conclusions on male dominance, we must translate this concept into hypotheses and then test them according to the scientific method. Usually the nature of the hypothesis helps the researcher decide which research design would be most appropriate for collecting data for this testing: experiment, survey, observation, or use of secondary sources.

The Experiment

Only the **experiment** enables the scientist to establish a cause–effect relationship between variables, and thus to fulfill some of science's more challenging goals: to explain, predict, and perhaps even control aspects of the social world. It provides the most rigorous test of a hypothesis because it can eliminate alternative explanations of the results. In an experiment, the researcher manipulates all relevant variables in a controlled situation to discover if the suspected cause, or **independent variable,** actually produces—by itself, with no other factor invisibly "helping out"—the observed effect, or **dependent variable.** Although the experiment is the ideal research design, sociologists do not often choose it due to its intimidating demands.

The critical feminist sociological perspective assumes that male domination pervades our society and, more specifically, that the power balance in most marriages favors the husband. Christine Sexton and Daniel Perlman (1989) used an experimental design to test whether wives' careers affect their marital power relations. If so, in dual-career couples the wives, because of their greater contribution of resources, would share marital power more equally with their husbands than would wives in single-earner households.

Selecting participants presented an immediate problem. Of all the couples in the United States, which ones should be studied? Researchers usually want subjects as representative of the general population as possible so that the research conclusion will be applicable or generalizable to a wide audience, such as "all American married couples." For matters of convenience, however, Sexton and Perlman decided to limit their subjects to spouses with professional careers. Accordingly, they sent 465 letters to men and women on membership lists of professional organizations, seeking 50 couples in which both spouses worked in such careers and 50 in which only the husband did. As expected, the researchers encountered difficulties in trying to locate participants. Nearly half of the people receiving letters were ineligible because they did not meet the study's criteria. Over 60 percent of those eligible declined to participate because they were too busy, not interested, and so on. Such uncooperativeness commonly plagues researchers.

An experiment applies the independent variable (in this case, the wife's career) to the **experimental group.** Another group, ideally identical in all relevant characteristics except for the independent variable, is used for comparison: the **control group.** In this case, the couples with only the husband employed served as the control group, while the experimental group was the dual-career couples.

Whenever possible, **random assignment** determines which people will be assigned to the experimental and control groups. Randomness or chance virtually guarantees that, if the population studied is large enough, all pertinent background characteristics will be similar in both groups. Sociologists rarely enjoy this luxury, and in this case Sexton and Perlman could only try to match the couples in both groups according to average age and occupation, and length of marriages. The more evenly matched the two groups, the more confident we can be that any differences in the dependent variable (in this case, the power of the wives) are due to the independent variable (the wife's employment) and not, for example, the different incomes, ages, social classes, or races of the two groups.

Experiment: a research design in which relevant variables are manipulated and controlled in order to test a hypothesis.

Independent variable: in an experiment, the suspected cause.

Dependent variable: in an experiment, the effect or result caused by the independent variable.

Experimental group: the group to which the independent variable is applied in an experiment.

Control group: used for comparison in an experiment, the group that should be similar in all relevant respects to the environmental group except that it does not receive the independent variable.

Random assignment: using chance to sort units of study into experimental and control groups.

Each of the 100 couples in the experiment was asked to visit a university counseling center, where the two spouses were given a brief orientation and then led to separate rooms. After each spouse separately completed a questionnaire on marital conflict, the couple was brought together to discuss their responses and arrive at joint answers. These joint discussions were audiotaped, and an analysis provided measures of wives' marital power, the dependent variable.

Compared to the control group, the dual-career spouses more frequently attempted to influence each other in the joint discussions. These couples exhibited more "give and take," as might be expected between equals. However, contrary to other predictions, when questioned about their everyday interactions the single-career couples reported power balances similar to the dual-career couples. In this study, then, male dominance seemed to play a smaller role in the marital power balances than had been expected. Still, even though the unemployed wives *perceived* little subordination to their husbands, Sexton and Perlman found that career economic resources do seem to affect wives' observed power exchanges with their husbands. And to the extent that these 100 couples represent professionals, this study suggests that male dominance is beginning to diminish for such people.

Surveys

While surveys cannot conclusively identify cause, they have other uses. For one thing, they can discover patterns from which valuable generalizations can be derived. Surveys offer a way of dealing with large bodies of data while demanding relatively little time and energy. They provide a snapshot of a population at one point in time, a quantified picture that can be compared with others by following changes over time. They are especially useful in assessing social facts that cannot be directly observed, such as feelings and beliefs. Surveys also place fewer demands on the participants and raise fewer ethical questions about the rights of the people involved. Whether they take the form of mailed questionnaires, face-to-face interviews, or telephone interviews, surveys can produce results that are precise, statistically manipulable, and comparable to other results. These several benefits make the survey a common device for gathering sociological data.

The question of whom to study is even more critical in the case of surveys than with the experiment. Usually the entire target population (such as all married couples in a nation) cannot be studied, so sampling must be used. The challenge is to ensure that the sample is representative or typical of the target population to which the conclusion will be applied (in this case, all married couples in the nation). A **representative sample** makes us feel confident that whatever is found in the sample will also be found in the target population because it accurately reflects the characteristics of that population.

Representative sample: a subset of the target population that reflects the characteristics of that larger population.

Pat O'Connor (1991) employed the interview technique in a survey studying marital power balances in English couples. Seeking data on the impact of wives' economic dependence, the researcher randomly chose a sample of 71 women from the records of doctor's offices. This simple random sample guaranteed that each member of the population of women attending those medical offices had an equal chance of being selected. This randomness meant that the sample was representative of the target population so that O'Connor could feel confident that the characteristics (such as age, length of marriage, and so on) of the 71 women reflected those of *all* the women attending those medical offices.

We might question, of course, whether the women in these neighborhoods were typical of all women in London, or all women in England, or even all Western women. To generalize the results to such wider populations, O'Connor would have needed to employ more extensive sampling techniques.

To sample all London women, for example, O'Connor could have used cluster sampling, in which the sampling units are not individuals but clusters of individuals such as are found in neighborhoods or city blocks. O'Connor could have taken a simple random sample from all of London's neighborhoods and then interviewed all the women in the neighborhoods chosen.

Multistage sampling would have allowed O'Connor to target all of England. With this technique, the researcher could have divided the country into geographical areas and taken a random sample from each. Each selected area would then in turn be broken into smaller areas, perhaps neighborhoods or square kilometers, and a sample taken from them. Then, in each of these smaller areas, O'Connor could have randomly selected residences.

If O'Connor had been interested in various social classes, stratified sampling would have been appropriate. In this method, a population is broken into categories such as races, ages, or, in this case, income levels. The researcher could have categorized neighborhoods or census tracts as to income level and then randomly chosen several from each level, thereby insuring that the sample was not predominantly from just one income level.

O'Connor was confident that the random sample of 71 women represented the more limited target population. The problem, however, was one common to surveys: Only 60 of the 71 women were actually interviewed. Despite a quite acceptable return of response rate of 84 percent, we must still wonder about the responses the missing 11 women would have given. Did they represent, for example, all the battered wives in the target population? Would their responses have colored the overall results differently?

In any event, O'Connor tape-recorded each interview, which was "semistructured," that is, guided by prepared questions but allowed to wander according to the nature of the responses given by the interviewee. The researcher applied several analytical tools to the interview data to quantify or put into measurable terms the dependent variables (aspects of marital power).

The results showed that, although these wives were financially dependent on their husbands, only about one-third felt powerless within their marriage. O'Connor concludes that "some women create feelings of having power within their marriages by managing their own and their husband's level of emotional dependence—although their ability to do this is limited by . . . financial insecurity" (p. 839).

Questionnaire surveys offer advantages over such interviews. They cost less, offer anonymity to the respondents, and are more easily standardized. On the other hand, respondents can lie more easily or refuse to cooperate altogether, and some of the sample's respondents may not even be able to read the questions with sufficient understanding, assuming they can read at all.

Observation

While we all observe social phenomena, sociologists try to do so objectively, which requires that they not become emotionally involved with the people under observation. They must also take care not to alter the social environment during the observation. To produce data that can be measured and analyzed, the observer must go beyond subjective interpretations and impressions. Toward this end, researchers use a structuring tool such as a checklist or set of observation objectives.

Donna Eder and Stephen Parker (1987) utilized the observation technique to study the adolescent peer culture in a middle school setting, searching for ways that notions about masculinity and femininity are transmitted to teens. Their study was overt, meaning that the subjects were aware of the observing: "We informed students that we were studying adolescent activities and interests. We took notes openly. . . ." (p. 203).

By actually becoming participants in the social setting, observers can gain valuable insight into the motivations and feelings of the subjects. Eder and Parker observed teens' informal activities twice weekly for an entire academic year and "were able to enter the adolescents' world as peers rather than authority figures" (p. 202). The teens, because of their lack of awareness of such matters, were unable to explain how different values applied to the males and females. The observers found, however, that the prevalence of athletic activities in the school helped foster achievement-oriented, competitive values among the boys, while the girls, clearly being directed into subordinate roles, were "reminded of the importance of appearance and emotional management" (p. 200).

Observation also offers insights when those being observed are unable or unwilling to offer information. In some cases, the subjects are uncooperative because their activities are illegal or embarrassing. Such situations sometimes call for covert or unobtrusive observation, in which the subjects are unaware of being observed. This approach can capture the subjects' natural behaviors, but it raises ethical questions regarding privacy.

Using Secondary Sources

Primary data are collected by the researcher through experiments, surveys, or observation. When these techniques are not feasible or adequate for their purposes, researchers may use secondary or archival data: information generated or collected by someone else. For example, scientists commonly use existing census figures or other survey results to explore a hypothesis. Diaries, personal letters, and newspaper accounts can help researchers explore the past. With statistics gathered by the United Nations or World Bank, sociologists can study global issues without leaving their office.

Robert O'Brien (1991) used secondary data to investigate a power-control theory regarding male domination. Based on previous research, O'Brien theorized that men in most societies possess more social and economic power than women, as shown in the paradox regarding rape rates and sex ratios. When men outnumber women (high sex ratios), women gain power in their marital relationships due to their relative scarcity. Paradoxically, they also find themselves confined to the domestic sphere, scarce and precious "commodities" protected and sheltered by their husbands. Thus, men's economic and political power enables them to overcome their wives' statistical advantage. O'Brien hypothesized that the rape rate would be lower when men outnumber women because of the extra "sheltering" imposed on women.

O'Brien employed data from the census to calculate the proportion of men to women, and FBI statistics on rape rates. He used an important tool to analyze these data: **correlation,** a mathematically measurable association between two or more variables. Two variables are positively correlated if they increase or decrease at the same

Correlation: a mathematically measurable association between two or more variables.

"Frankly, Harold, you're beginning to bore everyone with your statistics."

Drawing by Levin; © The New Yorker Magazine, Inc.

time—that is, if one increases, so does the other; if one decreases, the other also decreases. As expected, O'Brien found that rape rates were negatively correlated with the relative number of men per women in the population. In other words, during those time periods when sex ratios were high, rape rates were low.

Such correlations can suggest causative links between variables, but cannot prove that they exist. They may be the result of other factors unmeasured in the study, such as changing patterns in marital relationships, perceptions about the reporting of rape, and so on. Still, correlations can add weight to theories. As O'Brien concludes, "Although more than one explanation is always consistent with any set of findings, (the power-control theory is) supported by the data" (p. 110).

Research Box

Measuring Television Viewership: The Difficulties in Studying Human Behavior

For decades, the television industry has hungered for a more accurate reading of viewership. Interest may have been sparked by the water commissioner of Toledo, Ohio, who noticed a huge drop in the city's water pressure during commercial breaks for the "I Love Lucy Show" and joked about inventing a "flushometer." Millions of advertising dollars hinge on television ratings, but as Erik Larson (1992) explains, these ratings have several flaws due to the difficulties in studying human behavior.

Measuring viewership essentially requires a survey of a sample of viewers. To obtain an ongoing random sample of all American viewers is challenging enough, but to the frustration of researchers participants have been infuriatingly lax in their cooperation. They fail to push buttons; they refuse to keep accurate viewing diaries; they sometimes describe in their diaries what they feel they should have watched.

Researchers have deployed many devices without success to get around human laxity and deceit. A truck that was supposed to roam through the streets with a monitor capturing the tunings of thousands of televisions proved impractical. Something like a "whoopee cushion" was hidden in couches to weigh and identify the viewer, but the cushion could not distinguish between a child viewer and a large dog. Infrared sensors were used to scan rooms for the "hot bodies" of viewers, but they also picked up light bulbs, toasters, pets, and even hot water pipes in walls. Sonar devices and a camera that took pictures of the audience every 15 seconds were used to monitor attention to the television, but technical difficulties and privacy concerns stymied all efforts.

Network demands and pressure from competitors have now forced Nielsen, the dominant ratings research company in the United States, to develop what may be their ultimate weapon—the passive meter, a camera that can identify each household inhabitant's face. But how many Americans will allow such an intruder into their homes? Moreover, Americans are increasingly watching television in bedrooms and bathrooms (not the best places for cameras) and using portable televisions that would be far from the prying eye of a stationary camera. We can expect human behaviors and changing life styles to continue to frustrate researchers trying simply to determine how many people are watching "60 Minutes." □

ETHICS AND THE SPECIAL CASE OF THE FEMINIST RESEARCHER

Scientists' research goals can be driven by vanity, career advancement, or a desire to add to the fund of human knowledge. Such strongly motivated human endeavor carries potential danger, and in the case of sociological research, it involves the rights of the people being studied. Ethics, the concern for proper conduct and moral judgment, demands that the scientist balance effective research strategies with protecting the rights of the subjects. Sociologists must answer the question: What human cost, if any, should be paid for the research results?

This ethical dilemma leads to several other questions. One is the extent of possible damage incurred in the collection of data. Will the costs be borne by a few research subjects or many? We might also ask how deeply the costs will be felt by those under study. Is the danger one of temporary embarrassment or permanent emotional scars? And how large are the expected benefits? Will the research results substantially improve race relations or teaching techniques? Will they help prevent child abuse? In sum, the researcher must decide if the benefits outweigh the costs.

What kinds of costs might be borne by the people being studied? Embarrassment, stress, and anxiety can result from being asked personal questions or observed engaging in compromising behaviors. If promises of confidentiality are violated, the subjects may feel endangered by intimate or insulting information they revealed. Confronted by a diligent interviewer, a subject may squirm with discomfort in dealing with

Scientific research sometimes exacts a price from the people being studied.

especially sensitive topics. Experimental conditions may require the subject to make difficult choices or face threatening or intimidating situations. Participants may experience a residue of guilt or shame if they respond to the experiment in ways they would later consider cowardly or otherwise improper.

Feminist researchers must walk an even narrower ethical tightrope. As Sheila Riddell points out, "the ethical demands of mainstream sociology" are sometimes at variance "with those of feminist sociology" (1989, p. 77). Riddell explains how this conflict confronts the feminist researcher in several ways. For example, she describes the discomfort she experienced concealing her feminist outlook to gain access to interview information. "It would have been catastrophic," she says, "to introduce myself as a feminist" (p. 82).

Power relations can enter into any interview situation, but they are especially complicated for the feminist interviewing women. Should she treat the interviewee as an object and source of data or as another woman with equal status and personhood, perhaps even a friend (thereby endangering objectivity)? Since women are more likely to confide to a female interviewer, she runs the risk of using her gender to exploit her subjects.

Riddell explains that once the data are collected, more ethical questions arise. Do the data belong to the people being interviewed? Should they have some say in how the information will be used? Some feminist researchers feel special qualms in this regard when the subjects are women. Some go so far as to contend that any researcher, especially a feminist dedicated to improving the conditions of women in the world, has an obligation to render results in clear, simple language understandable to women who are not academics. Riddell mentions that some feminist writers even produce two versions of their research findings, one for those in their field and another for women in general. Otherwise, some would argue, female researchers could be accused of advancing their own careers at the expense of their audience.

Overall, feminist researchers feel more obligated than other sociologists to serve the needs of women with the results of their work. Thus they face a tougher dilemma if the results discredit women. Should such information be published or concealed? As with any other research, the ultimate question is, "Do the benefits outweigh the costs?"

SUMMARY

Sociology, the scientific study of human society and social behaviors, offers an enhanced way of perceiving the social world. It enables us to look beneath the surface of "common sense" notions, provides several ways of viewing social phenomena, and, through the *sociological imagination*, explains an individual's situation in terms of broad social and historical events and trends.

Sociology differs from everyday "common sense" in several ways. First, it employs the scientific attitude, which requires *empirical data,* or information that can be observed or experienced by others. It also uses *inference*, or reasoning from the known to the unknown, to build *theories*, or logical, well-supported explanations about relationships among facts. Like other scientists, sociologists try to use *objectivity*, which means perceiving the world clearly and accurately, not allowing one's own emotions or biases to distort perceptions. They also reason from *determinism*, the assumption that every phenomenon is determined or caused by something else. Moreover, researchers have specific goals, including description, explanation, control, and prediction.

Scientists use the scientific method, which begins with a definition of the problem and review of the literature. Next comes the formation of the *hypothesis*, a statement that reaches beyond available knowledge. An hypothesis is an informed guess about the relationship among two or more *variables*, characteristics that vary from one individual group, or time to another. Then the reseacher decides what data to collect and how. After the data are collected, they are analyzed. Finally, the researcher concludes whether the data support the hypothesis or not.

Sociology's nineteenth-century founders were shaped by their historical era, but they also influenced the intellectual currents of their time and later generations. Auguste Comte coined the term "sociology" and encouraged the evolution of knowledge toward the scientific study of society. Herbert Spencer formulated social Darwinism, which promoted the "survival of the fittest." Karl Marx pointed to the exploitation of early capitalism and, with Friedrich Engels, explained it in terms of economic determinism and class conflict. Emile Durkheim studied social integration and showed sociologists how they should use social facts to support their conclusions. Max Weber challenged Marx's ideas and urged sociologists to keep their research value free, to place themselves into the lives of the people they studied. He also pioneered the use of models or ideal types. Sociology was imported to the United States around the turn of the century to deal with swelling social problems. It was first established at the University of Chicago.

Sociologists use three main theoretical perspectives to view any topic. *Functionalism*, or *structural functionalism*, views society as a *social system* comprised of interrelated parts. In this view, we ask how any particular part contributes to the functioning of the whole system. Like a biological organism, society tends toward equilibrium, in which the parts adapt to one another. This requires *value consensus*, an underlying, widespread agreement about the society's goals and proper means for achieving them. Change and diversity threaten this stability. Also, as Robert Merton pointed out, negative consequences of maladaptive parts, or *dysfunctions*, thwart the system's ability to adapt. On the other hand, a social element can also contribute a positive consequence or effect, a *function*. *Manifest functions* are intended and expected; *latent functions* are unexpected or unintended.

Conflict theory, like the functionalist perspective, is *macrosociological* in that it considers society as a whole, exploring its basic patterns and systems. It assumes that a dominant, oppressive elite benefits from most social patterns, and that societies experience perpetual struggle due to the unequal distribution of scarce resources and the class divisions that result. An illusion of consensus holds together the conflict-ridden society, but conflict continues, based not only on class but factors such as gender, power, and other interests. Conflict theorists presume that coercion, instability, and oppression characterize the relations among society's groups.

The interactionist perspective is *microsociological*, exploring people more directly as they try to develop appropriate behaviors. One branch, symbolic interactionism, rests on George Herbert Mead's insight that human interaction is based on symbols. Building on this, Herbert Blumer saw social reality as fluid and subjective, as whatever people agree it is. Ethnomethodology explores the "taken-for-granted" level of reality to understand how people try to make sense of their social experiences. Erving Goffman's dramaturgical approach views interacting people as actors playing roles, carefully managing the impressions they make on others. George Homans noted in exchange theory that individuals try to maximize rewards in their interaction.

Scientists collect data for the testing of hypotheses in four ways. The *experiment* enables researchers to establish a cause–effect relationship. It rigorously tests a hypothesis by manipulating all relevant variables in a controlled situation to eliminate alternative explanations. It aims to find out if the suspected cause, the *independent variable*, actually produces by itself the observed effect, or *dependent variable*. Experimenters try to study a population of subjects that represents the wider population to which they wish to apply their results, but they must often deal with uncooperativeness on the part of the subjects. The *experimental group* receives the independent variable, and the *control group*, used for comparison, does not. Subjects are sorted into these two groups using *random assignment*, in which chance helps guarantee that all relevant background characteristics are similar in both groups, thus providing a fair test of the independent variable's impact.

Surveys cannot conclusively identify cause, but they can discover patterns from which valuable generalizations can be derived. By providing a snapshot of a population at one point in time, they offer a way to deal with large bodies of data, especially those involving social facts that cannot be directly observed. A *representative sample* reflects all the people in the target population. Samples can be simple random, cluster, multistage, or stratified. Low response rates call into question how representative the data are. While questionnaire surveys are cheaper, anonymous, and more easily quantified, interview surveys get higher response rates and do not depend on the respondent's ability to read or write.

Researchers can also use objective observation, often with a structuring tool. This is especially useful when those being studied are unable or unwilling to offer information. It can be overt or covert, and sometimes the observers become participants in the setting.

Scientists sometimes use secondary or archival data, information generated or collected by someone else. Sociologists often use such data in searching for *correlations*, mathematically measurable associations between two or more variables. Correlations can suggest causative links but cannot prove them.

Key Terms

sociological imagination	functionalism (structural functionalism)	microsociological experiment
sociology	social system	independent variable
empirical data	value consensus	dependent variable
inference	dysfunction	experimental group
theories	function	control group
objectivity	manifest functions	random assignment
determinism	latent functions	representative sample
hypothesis	macrosociological	correlation
variables		

2
Chapter

CULTURE AND SOCIETY

WHO IS "CULTURED"?

   CRITICAL THINKING BOX: ARE ONLY HUMANS CULTURED?

IS OUR CULTURE SUPERIOR?

DO NORMS PROVIDE CLEAR DIRECTION?

   RESEARCH BOX: SOCIAL FACTS BEHIND
   FIRST-NAME FASHIONS

WHERE DO A CULTURE'S VALUES LEAD?

HOW DOES LANGUAGE AFFECT CULTURE?

SOCIAL STRUCTURE FOR YANOMAMO INDIANS
AND U.S. COLLEGE STUDENTS

   CRITICAL THINKING BOX: WHICH SOCIAL
   STRUCTURE IS MORE RESTRICTIVE?

TYPES OF SOCIETIES: WHAT'S NEXT
FOR THE YANOMAMO?

In this and later chapters we will explore an issue from a cross-cultural point of view. By traveling to a distant part of the globe, we hope to gain a broader perspective on our own way of life.

WHO IS "CULTURED"?

Deep in the rainforests of South America, several thousand people called the Yanomamo (or Yanoama, one of several tribes of the Yanomama Indians) have established a society, a large, enduring population sharing a territory and adaptations to their surroundings—in this case the dense, malarial jungle. For example, with little sunlight penetrating the forest canopy, surprisingly few foods are available, so the Yanomamo subsist largely on plantains, nuts, and a variety of palm fruits. They supplement this vegetable diet with whatever else they can find, from turtle eggs and honey to insect grubs, caterpillars, spiders, rodents and, when possible, large animals like pigs and monkeys.

Society: a large population, usually enduring at least several generations and sharing a territory and a way of life.

Area inhabited by the Yanomamo

Figure 2-1

A Yanomamo man uses tube to blow a hallucinogenic drug into his friend's nose.

Until recently, the Yanomamo largely escaped the incursions of the outside world. The few anthropologists who have studied them can only guess at their numbers and locations (Chagnon, 1968; Smole, 1976; Early and Peters, 1990; Good, 1991). Still, the modern world has sent a few fingers reaching into this society. Through trade, some aluminum pots and a few steel machetes and axes have made their way from villages on the fringe of Yanomamo territory into the remote interior. Missionary outposts touch the lives of some villagers. And, more recently, goldminers have ventured into inhospitable, thorny, dangerous jungles where the Yanomamo live.

Anthropologist Napoleon Chagnon spent 19 uncomfortable, frustrating months living with the Yanomamo. Although his training had prepared him for virtually any human behaviors, he admits feeling some "culture shock" when, after a two-and-a-half day boat journey with a missionary from the nearest town, he came face to face with his first Yanomamos. "I looked up and gasped when I saw a dozen burly, naked, filthy, hideous men staring at us down the shafts of their drawn arrows! Immense wads of green tobacco were stuck between their lower teeth and lips making them look even more hideous, and strands of dark-green slime dripped or hung from their noses. . . . The stench of decaying vegetation and filth struck me and I almost got sick. I was horrified" (1968, p. 5). His arrival, unfortunately for him, had coincided with their usual afternoon hallucinogenic drug party and signs of an impending raid from their neighbors. Because of the drug's effects (which produced the nasal mucous as well as the wild-eyed look) and their well-founded fear of murderous neighbors, they gave Chagnon a nightmarish welcome. They also give us reason to explore the following question.

Are the Yanomamo Cultured?

In popular usage, we use the term "culture" when referring to classical music, literature, painting and sculpture, and the like. A "cultured" person is thus someone refined and sensitive to the arts, the polar opposite of the image the Yanomamo presented to

Sticks, feathers, and paints adorn this young Yanomamo woman as she awaits a feast. She was given to Kenneth Good, the anthropologist studying her people, and came to the United States with him as his wife.

Chagnon at their first meeting. Social scientists, however, have since early this century used the term more inclusively. They define **culture** in its simplest terms: the way of life of a people. More fully, a culture is a learned, integrated way of life developed through sharing experiences over at least several generations. The Yanomamo way of life has indeed taken form over uncounted generations, a product not of some inner, genetic wellspring but of what they have learned and shared with one another over a long period of time.

Culture: a learned, shared, integrated way of life.

Still, we may find it difficult to call them cultured. After all, they have no written language or cities. Their knowledge of mathematics is limited to counting from one to two to "many." Their villages are made of poles, vines, and leaves and last only a year or two before the roofs begin to leak and the cockroach and spider populations become so bothersome that the entire village is burned to the ground. Their art consists mostly of some body painting and adornment, designs decorating their arrows, and musical chants. Their religion in large part involves casting evil spells on their neighbors and protecting themselves from the same. Such observations, however, smack of the condescending attitude that produced the close-minded, exploitative, often brutal treatment Westerners meted to many such "primitive" peoples. With the help of the anthropologists who studied them, we can look more closely to intricacy and richness of the Yanomamos' learned, shared, and integrated way of life.

For example, the Yanomamo **material culture,** the concrete, physical items they create, helps them make the most of the harsh physical environment, though their tools and possessions are deliberately kept to a minimum due to the people's mobile existence. The simplicity of their technology also means that each village can produce all it needs and thus remain independent of its neighbors—a useful benefit considering the frequent warfare among the Yanomamo villages. Thus they can construct a canoe or erect a temporary bridge over a flooding river in a few hours or build an overnight travel shelter in a half an hour. More sophisticated, long-lasting constructions would be either inappropriate or unnecessary considering the physical environment and the Yanomamos' needs. The people allocate their energy only to those aspects of their

Material culture: concrete, physical, human-made parts of a way of life.

Nonmaterial culture: abstract parts of a way of life, including beliefs, traditions, and customs.

material culture that warrant it, such as their powerful bows and long, specialized arrows with poison tips.

Likewise, the Yanomamo **nonmaterial culture**—the abstractions they create such as beliefs, traditions, and customs—enables them to make sense of their world. Their complex kinship system, for example, specifies that a man may marry only a woman from a precisely defined subpopulation, thereby avoiding incestuous pairings despite a complex history of ever-shifting alliances and fissions among villages. Their intricate, unceasing political machinations make social order possible despite their mistrust of others. And their beliefs about the supernatural origins of their people explain for them the violence and treachery that color much of their social life.

The Yanomamo way of life, then, represents an integrated set of material and nonmaterial elements, each one discovered or created by one generation and shared with subsequent ones. It clearly is just as much a culture as our own way of life, with its urban violence, nuclear weapons, various forms of exploitation, and widespread addiction. Each culture represents an attempt to meet the needs of its people.

Subculture: a distinct way of life shared by a subset of society that has some aspects of the mainstream, dominant culture.

Each culture also exhibits internal diversity; in other words, individuals in each culture live out their lives in somewhat unique ways. This diversity among the Yanomamo takes the form of individual peculiarities. In the U. S. population, it also produces **subcultures,** distinct ways of life within the dominant culture—cultures within a culture. Members of subcultures share their own clusters of values, customs, and beliefs while still participating in the mainstream way of life. In the United States, subcultures are rooted in such social factors as race and ethnicity (African Americans and Hispanics, for example), social class (as seen in the "underclass"), religion (such as Muslims and Jews), sexual orientation, and adolescence. In fact, our extreme diversity also supports **countercultures,** subcultures that in some way stand *in opposition to* the mainstream culture. Among the Yanomamo, those who have not found satisfaction in their social situation simply leave their village to join another or form their own, but they still follow the Yanomamo way of life—unless they leave the territory altogether and merge with the outside, modern culture. In contrast, various countercultures have sprung up in the United States over the years to absorb the disaffected—beatniks, hippies, radical revolutionaries, punkers, progressives, skinheads, and so on. North Americans, but not Yanomamos, have the option of rejecting substantial aspects of the mainstream culture while remaining identifiably part of their own cultural population.

Counterculture: a subculture that in some way(s) stands in opposition to the mainstream culture.

Cultured Means Adaptive but Dependent

The Yanomamo, then, are as cultured as we are, but with this adaptive strength comes the weakness of dependence. Culture is so much a part of being human that the species would not survive without it. To appreciate this point, imagine a global catastrophe: the erasure of all human memory. We would still have our wondrous brains but they would be empty of all the skills, beliefs, and values acquired over the millennia: We would be uncultured. Not knowing how to find food or shelter, most of us would die before we learned how, and many others would perish during the first winter. The survivors would be those who developed a culture soon enough.

The survivors' physical needs would drive them to search for food and drink, but this search would have no guidance except from the experience accumulated since the

	Critical Thinking Box

Are Only Humans Cultured?

Can we safely equate culture with humanness? Exploring this question forces us to examine the vaunted uniqueness of our species and to look further into the concept of culture. We return to the three ingredients of a cultured way of life: learning, sharing, and integration. First, the members of other species live mostly according to their inborn patterns. Some species have developed highly complex social organizations: Different kinds of ants, for example, have labor specialization, warfare, and even slavery. Such sophisticated patterns, however, spring not from learning and discovery but from genetic codes. Second, while they may learn new adaptations, members of other species have a limited capacity for sharing such information. Because they cannot communicate their discovery, the species' ways of life remain unchanged. Third, while the aspects of a species' existence are integrated, the integration of *new* parts apparently depends on modifications in the genetic code rather than social agreements.

Still, some apes have shown the ability to discover, share, and integrate new life style features, especially new foods. Apes in a laboratory cage discovered and shared the idea of pole vaulting (Hoebel, 1966). Do such isolated instances show only a glimmer of culture-building ability, the barest beginnings of what we have defined as culture? Or do they help demolish our cherished notions of uniqueness and superiority?

Ralph Holloway (1969, 1992) offers another line of argument. He has noted that our unrivaled if not unique capacity for tool making and language empowers us—and arguably us alone—to impose arbitrary (we might say cultural) forms upon the environment. Some scientists, however, point to the chimpanzee's manufacture of a termite stick, a rod fashioned from a branch used to extract termites from their mound, as evidence that humans do not stand alone as tool makers. Others claim that several species can use language.

Do we have enough evidence, then, to satisfy the claim that humans are the only cultured beings on the globe? ■

catastrophe. Even if they stumbled into a grocery store they would not be able to take advantage of the packaged, uncooked foods until they learned about can openers, pop tops, cooking, and food poisoning. Unless human nature includes a tendency toward cooperation and trust, the survivors would selfishly fight to satisfy their physical needs. They would have to reinvent language and, after much turmoil and violence, develop rules regarding such matters as sexual restraint, property rights, protection of children, and personal honor. From such notions, some form of social organization would arise. In other words, culture would have to emerge again if humanness were to be restored.

We are left, then, with a paradox. Our ability to invent new adaptations to our environment is at the same time both the ultimate survival tool and the source of our dependence on preceding generations as well as the people around us. Because we are cultured, we, like the Yanomamo, are adaptable, but at the same time, we are dependent on the discoveries of those who came before us and those with whom we coexist.

IS OUR CULTURE SUPERIOR?

The United States boasts the world's largest economy, advanced space technology, and awesome military firepower. The Yanomamo, on the other hand, literally scratch out a living in the bug-infested jungle, leaving no monuments except abandoned garden sites that the overgrowth will quickly reclaim. We dabble with robots using artificial intelligence; the Yanomamo seek magical cures for their snakebites and other maladies. They carry their hammocks and their few tools from one camp to the next; most of us own an extensive list of appliances and conveniences including air conditioners, water heaters, televisions, VCRs, and computers. Isn't our culture clearly superior to theirs?

An Ethnocentric View

Those who too quickly assume their culture to be superior may be blind to what other cultures have to offer. Consider the tourist who brings home a few souvenirs and horror stories about how the crazy foreigners eat, talk, drive, dress, and so on. Rather than enriching their lives, expanding their tastes, or learning from surprises, the tourists perceive differences only as wrong and thus miss opportunities for growth. Their problem is one of **ethnocentrism,** the belief that one's own way of life is superior and properly serves as the standard by which all others are evaluated. With ethnocentrism, culturally "different" becomes "inferior."

By dismissing the Yanomamo culture too readily, we may deny ourselves opportunities to learn from them. Our scientists, for example, now avidly study folk remedies of the kind used by the Yanomamo, searching for medicines in nature that may inform chemists of new research avenues. Some of the Yanomamos' methods of dealing with threatening neighbors might offer insights into interpersonal diplomacy. And who knows, we might find roasted caterpillars as delicious as they are nutritious!

Ethnocentrism: the belief that one's own way of life is superior and properly serves as the standard by which all others are judged.

Ethnocentrism leads us into assuming that technological advances indicate cultural superiority, regardless of the technology's actual consequences.

For those who desire to observe the world without distortions, ethnocentrism poses another danger: a loss of objectivity. Social scientists studying other peoples must be especially on guard. Chagnon, the anthropologist we met earlier, was irritated and angered by the incessant begging, evasive lies, and never-ending thievery of the Yanomamo. Similarly, Colin Turnbull (1972) struggled with feelings of disgust as he studied the starving Ik of Uganda. Their cold-blooded survival tactics, their absence of compassion, sympathy, or sharing, clouded Turnbull's scientific objectivity. For such scientists, ethnocentrism is a professional hazard. But because objectivity has value even to us nonscientists, because we all benefit from seeing things clearly without distortions or bias, ethnocentrism represents an insidious danger for us as well.

The other danger with ethnocentrism lies in the threat it poses for those we evaluate. From assuming they are inferior, it is but a short step to believing them unworthy of humane treatment, especially if they live in ways objectionable to us. History provides many examples of powerful religious groups torturing, enslaving, and massacring nonbelievers. Ethnocentrism has fueled countless wars, goading governments and combatants convinced of the enemy's subhuman status to greater levels of ruthlessness and cruelty.

Perhaps because of our wealth and technology, it is understandably easy for us to slip into ethnocentrism. Surprisingly, however, social scientists find ethnocentrism among all groups. Chagnon reports that when he ignored the Yanomamo's aggressive demands for his food as he ate, they dismissed his behavior as "just a peculiarity of the subhuman foreigner" (p. 8). In Yanomamo legend, foreigners degenerated from the first beings (who, naturally, were Yanomamos) and developed strange ways and language. And Jacques Lizot (1985) reports that they frequently assume strangers in general to be guilty of cannibalism.

We might reason that an attitude so widespread as ethnocentrism must serve some valuable, universal functions. And indeed it does. For one thing, it contributes to a group's cultural stability by maintaining some resistance to outside ideas. The Yanomamo, for example, eagerly accepted steel axes and pots but generally rejected foreigners' values as ridiculous, their ethnocentrism thus maintaining the nonmaterial essentials of their culture.

Second, ethnocentrism increases people's morale, loyalty, and motivation to work and fight for the group to which they belong. Laboratory research suggests that members of weak groups in conflict with stronger ones show high levels of ethnocentrism because they feel so vulnerable. Meanwhile, stronger groups use ethnocentrism to justify their unfair treatment of others to protect the resources they have gained (Grant, 1991). A single-minded acceptance of one's own culture as superior prevents wavering and dispels doubt, strengthening the group's collective resolve.

Ethnocentrism, then, has survival value. Imagine the consequences if a people honestly, objectively—not ethnocentrically—appraised the merits of another group who threatened them with conquest. Their open-mindedness would make them easy prey to future aggression. Just as patriotism reached fever pitch in the United States during the two world wars of this century, each village of the Yanomamo reacts with similar feelings of outrage and indignation when attacked by others. Villages—and cultures—without ethnocentrism do not last long in a hostile environment.

Thus it is understandable, yet still dangerous, when we thoughtlessly declare our own way of life superior to another. While ethnocentrism contributes to cultural solidarity, it also may deprive us of what people like the Yanomamo have to offer us. So how should we judge the culture of the Yanomamo?

As part of the chest-pounding duel between rival villages, one man prepares to deliver a hard blow to the chest of the other. Such rituals serve as substitutes for greater violence.

Using Cultural Relativism

Cultural relativism: the viewpoint through which we judge other cultures relative to how they meet the needs of their people.

Cultural relativism offers a more open-minded, tolerant way of judging other cultures. It requires that we evaluate them on the basis of how well each one meets the needs of its people. Using this perspective means that before condemning a cultural element we are obliged to search for its contribution to the overall system. For example, in the Yanomamos' chest-pounding duel, men of opposing villages take turns striking one another with closed fists as hard as possible on the chest. This formalized ritual serves the purpose of containing intervillage hostilities within innocuous bounds, thus lessening the chance for an outbreak of full-scale war.

Infanticide, the killing of infants, provides a useful illustration of the emotional and moral challenges of cultural relativism. Like numerous other groups, the Yanomamo sometimes kill newborns, especially those that are deformed or sickly. This custom violates the moral standards of many Westerners, but cultural relativism requires us to judge the practice in terms of its consequences for that culture (Foster, 1991). This means that even if a practice is morally repugnant to us, we may not legitimately denounce it if it contributes to the overall well-being of the people. To use cultural relativism, we need not renounce our own responsibility for moral judgment. We must, however, consider the impact of the practice on the larger picture. By maintaining *all* the members born, even those unable to contribute to the group's survival, the level of strength and well-being of the Yanomamo would probably be diminished. In the face of such a danger, infanticide may be the most responsible, even the most moral, practice in this regard. Moreover, infanticide helps control the spread of nonlethal genetic defects in low-energy, inbreeding groups such as the Yanomamo (Harris, 1971).

Critics have charged that over the past few decades cultural relativism has been used to excuse the actions of brutal dictators in nations emerging from their colonial pasts. But, properly used, cultural relativism does not mean we should never criticize others' ways. It does mean we should consider how those ways contribute to the well-being of the population.

Throughout the rest of the chapter, we will use this relativistic perspective in weighing our own culture against that of the Yanomamo. As long as people's needs are being met, we can expect to find both cultures equally worthy of our respect.

DO NORMS PROVIDE CLEAR DIRECTION?

Our evaluation of both cultures begins with a major nonmaterial component: **norms.** These rules or guidelines provide direction for us. They outline those behaviors that are appropriate or permitted in any given situation. They help maintain an orderly flow of social behaviors, guiding our choices with a sense of what is proper and what is not, a sense of "should" and "should not." In the United States, for example, norms inform us that we may have only one spouse at a time, while Yanomamo culture allows a man as many wives as he can support. Here we are taught to use the proper utensils for dining; there they use their fingers and sit in their hammocks during meals.

Norms: behavioral guidelines or rules.

The sense of propriety and morality which norms establish enable us to interact with others in an effective, even enjoyable way. First, norms guide us in choosing behaviors that coincide with the expectations of the people around us, enabling us to work cooperatively with others. For example, a Yanomamo village escaping an attempted massacre knows it can take refuge with another village it once took under its wing. This norm of reciprocity also allows villages to establish insurance of future sanctuary by hosting another village to a feast, thereby indebting it for future requests. In our own culture, we can walk into a college classroom with considerable assurance that the other students will be quiet and polite, allowing the teacher to get to the task at hand. Second, besides providing a basis for social coordination, norms show us how to fit in. Following their guidance, we can relax knowing we are somewhat protected from rejection and ridicule. After all, acceptance is a social reward. Chagnon did not wish to be rejected as timid and unmanly, so he observed Yanomamo norms and used seething anger and ferocity to deny their incessant, aggressive begging. Learning the norms enabled him to fit in. Likewise, most U.S. college students can relax in the knowledge that virtually any form of attire is permitted in class.

If a culture meets the needs of its people, its norms provide enough guidance for people to coordinate their actions easily and enjoy social interaction. But can we expect any discernible difference in how well norms function in two different cultures?

Do Folkways Smooth Social Relations?

As sociologist William Sumner (1906) pointed out long ago, some norms are less important than others. They deal with everyday actions, guiding us through our daily routines. They define what is proper etiquette when we greet people, enter a church, eat in a public place, and so on. These norms also tell us what to wear, how to sit, and what to say. They define what is tasteful or disgusting, and what is appropriate for

Folkways: norms defining proper but not required behaviors.

men, women, and children. These norms are called **folkways.** They require, for example, that we praise the value of a gift we receive, while a visiting Yanomamo man knows to spend several minutes studiously ignoring a gift set before him by his host. They tell us to eat quietly; they tell Yanomamo that loud smacking noises properly show one's enjoyment of the food.

We would surely miss folkways if they disappeared. Without rules of politeness, we would face irritating situations and unpleasant behaviors many times each day. If we simply acted on our own feelings, without folkways, every meeting with a stranger would be an unpredictable adventure full of potential misunderstandings and friction. Strangers we meet might use any form of greeting, from hugging to pinching to wrestling. Folkways clearly help grease the machinery of social interaction. They also help conserve our social energies. We need not spend our time and attention making decisions about routine matters such as how to behave at the dinner table or what to call our instructor. The decisions have been made for us.

Because folkways do not deal with matters of great consequence, they are reinforced by mild punishments and small rewards. Smiles, words of praise, and other signs of approval satisfy most people. Those who violate folkways face scorn and ridicule in the form of frowns, smirks, and gossip.

While every culture needs folkways to guide a variety of social behaviors, this task is especially difficult in a diverse, fast-changing one like ours. A century ago, folkways forbade women to wear trousers; today such attire has become optional. More recently, folkways requiring men to offer their seats to women or allow women to enter doors first seem to be weakening. The use of offensive language in public likewise seems to be moving from the outrageous to the rude category. Such changes suggest that people, especially those from different generations, observe different folkways in any given situation. There is always someone who considers another to be rude or ignorant. Moreover, those of us from different social classes or ethnic groups—that is, different subcultures—may well disagree on whose behavior standard is appropriate. For example, an upper-class person may find a lower-class person's public spitting disgusting. The lower-class individual in turn may find the table etiquette of the well-to-do ridiculous. Such disagreements about folkways do not seem to arise among the Yanomamo, even among the widely scattered and relatively isolated communities. Even the most remote villagers, for example, agree that monkeys should be roasted without removing the fur, that vulture down is appropriate decoration for warriors visiting other villages, and that feasts must be reciprocated.

Along the same lines, social scientists studying the Yanomamo make no mention of the transitory, even cyclical, folkways that we experience in our culture. The Yanomamo, for example, have eaten roast insect grubs for countless generations. In contrast, recently in the United States the hot sales of tequila-flavored lollipops with beetle larvae encased in the middle represented another **fad,** a folkway briefly followed by a small group of people. Fads do not last long because they attract relatively few admirers. Besides, when a fad becomes too popular it loses its "insider" appeal. Fads come out of nowhere, gain a very enthusiastic following, and then quickly disappear, leaving little influence on society. The "streaking" fad of the early 1970s (running nude in public places, such as at half-time during a football game) is an unusually memorable example, though it led to no further folkways—a mere blip on the cultural screen.

Fads: folkways followed briefly by relatively few people.

Cultures such as the Yanomamo likewise display little in the way of **fashions:** longer-lived, yet still transitory, folkways involving life style matters such as appearance or behavior. Unlike fads, fashions usually grow from established trends. For

Fashions: folkways describing some life style matter; longer lasting than fads, they define what is tasteful and respectable.

Hotlix, a tequila-flavored lollipop with an encased, quick-fired beetle larva, sold like hotcakes in 1991. A passing fad?

example, men's ties may grow wider or narrower, but their basic form and function remain the same. These expressions of taste regarding clothing, music, hairstyles, food, architecture, books, art, furniture, and the like are often cyclical, changing yearly or seasonally and often in response to the plans of designers, manufacturers, and retailers. Even intensive organizational planning and advertising campaigns, however, may not create fashions without support from underlying cultural currents, as shown by the expensive but failed campaigns on behalf of dress hats, the maxiskirt, and the Edsel automobile (Schudson, 1984; Tenner, 1989).

Fashions meet the needs of complex cultures faced with an exciting but sometimes confusing array of lifestyle options. They tell us what is—for a while, anyway—respectable and tasteful. They also help us deal with strangers, enabling us to display our social ranking and interests to people who know nothing about us. For example, salespeople take care to choose hairstyles and clothing similar to their clients to show that they are the same kind of folks. Mentioning the last music concert you attended (string quartet or heavy metal?) sends signals about yourself to others at the singles' party. Besides serving as initial indicators of our lifestyles, fashions help us avoid being left behind, culturally speaking. Modern technological societies such as ours usually point to the future as superior to the past or present. Those who do not keep up with today's fast-moving cultural stream may feel sadly old-fashioned and out of touch.

The cultural stream of the Yanomamo moves much more languidly, if at all. The people show a strong attachment to tradition. Their culture offers few life style alternatives: Everyone dresses, speaks, eats, raises children, and grooms essentially the same way. The virtual absence of fashions reflects the fact that the Yanomamo have no need of such transitory guidelines. Their centuries-old isolation and "striking cultural conservatism" (Smole 1976, p. 13) combine to simplify their range of options.

Thus, as we might expect, both cultures' folkways reflect the needs of the two peoples. While our folkways are fairly fleeting, those of the Yanomamo are stable. Our folkways help smooth our more uncertain, impersonal social relations, changing quickly to help us deal with our whirlwind way of life. The Yanomamo folkways contribute to their culture's continuity.

While Yanomamo mores forbid the burying of the dead, they encourage the drinking of the ashes of the deceased as a means of perpetuating in themselves the beloved ancestor.

Do Mores Get Any Respect?

Mores: serious norms defining behaviors considered essential to society's survival.

Mores are norms that are far more important than folkways. They offer guidance about behaviors considered not just polite but essential to society's survival. The mores of any culture give clear clues about what the people believe is necessary for the group's welfare. Our mores forbid murder, theft, rape, and the like. They require parents to care for their children. Yanomamo mores reflect similar concerns, although they permit gang rapes of captured women and allow husbands to beat, maim, and even kill their wives. They permit, indeed encourage, ceremonial eating of the ashes of deceased members' bones, but prohibit the eating of pets. Men must not use one anothers' personal names or the names of animals they are hunting, nor kill animals that carry the man's "mirror soul," because such rash behaviors would compromise relations with the spirit world. Indeed, many Yanomamo mores reflect the people's pervasive concerns with maintaining good relations with the supernatural world.

Violations of mores evoke horror, disgust, outrage, and similarly strong emotions. The resulting punishments are understandably severe. The guilty party likely suffers deep shame as well as banishment, beating, or even death. We favor imprisonment and fines as deterrents; the Yanomamo rely on threats of retaliation from the spirits and possible banishment of the evildoers from the village.

Laws: formalized norms put in writing and publicly decreed by authorities.

Unlike the Yanomamo, so many of us choose to violate mores that our culture requires **laws,** formalized norms put in writing and publicly decreed by the authorities. We have had to establish special authorities ranging from city police departments to the FBI (Federal Bureau of Investigation) to enforce our codes of conduct. Specified punishments are carried out by specified officials according to specified procedures. The Yanomamo have no need for such punishments, authorities, or procedures; apparently, their mores receive greater respect than do ours.

One reason our mores are less effective lies in our cultural diversity and resulting lack of normative consensus. Another is our dizzying pace of cultural change, which hinders the development of tradition and a collective certainty regarding right and wrong. For example, sexual practices that would have warranted severe reprisals a hundred years ago have become for many of us simply a matter of personal preference—a matter of folkways rather than mores.

Overall, we see that the norms of both cultures provide direction but that the accepted path is more clearly illuminated in the slow-changing world of the Yanomamo. Our shifting norms reflect the looser integration of our culture's elements. Like a jigsaw puzzle bouncing in the back of a truck hurrying down a rutted road, the normative pieces of our cultural system never quite settle into a tightly interlocked unit. Our relatively impermanent norms meet our needs for adaptability; the Yanomamo norms provide stability. Does either suggest cultural superiority?

Social Facts Behind First-Name Fashions

Research Box

According to a recent study, the most popular names for white female newborns are Jennifer, Christine, Jessica, Melissa, and Michelle; for African-American female newborns they are Nicole, Tiffany, Ebony, Jennifer, and LaToya. Michael, Christopher, John, David, and Matthew are the leading names for newborn white males. Michael, Jason, Anthony, Christopher, and James head the list for newborn African-American males. What lays behind these first-name fashions? To try to answer this question, Stanley Lieberson and Eleanor Bell (1992) looked beyond individuals' mental notions and perceptions, instead focusing on such objective aspects of social life as educational, racial, and gender differences. Recall from Chapter 1 that Durkheim referred to these as "social facts."

The two sociologists got their data from "a 6.25% random sample of all names given to white or black children born in New York State between 1973 and 1985—a total of 193,142 births" (p. 515). Remember that a random sample gives every member of the population an equal chance of being chosen. This insures that the children in the sample represent, or are typical of, all those born in that state during that period. (See Table 2-1.)

Lieberson and Bell first analyzed the lists of names in terms of gender differences. The results corroborated earlier studies (for example, Rossi, 1965 and Alford 1987) showing boys usually receive more traditional, less fashionable names. In our culture, after all, ancestral names represent the perpetuation of the family through the male heir. Girls, on the other hand, perhaps due to the lesser role assigned to females in our culture, receive more original, less conventional names. Names of French and Latin origin show up much more frequently in the girls' list than in the boys', as do shortened names such as Lisa (from Elizabeth) or Carrie (from Caroline). The same gender differences show up in the most popular African-American names. Overall, Lieberson and Bell found in both whites and blacks the same strong gender difference in first-name fashions: tradition (males) versus innovation (females).

The researchers also found strong associations between the mothers' education and the distribution of various names. Mothers with no more than an elementary school education tended to give their children especially distinctive names (partly because many were ethnic-group members, most notably Hispanic). The names chosen by mothers in the other educational categories showed weaker but significant connections with social class. Some names, for example, showed greater popularity

LEADING NAMES, BY RACE, OF CHILDREN BORN IN NEW YORK STATE, 1973–85

Girls		Boys	
White	Black	White	Black
Jennifer	Nicole	Michael	Michael
Christine	Tifffany	Christopher	Jason
Jessica	Ebony	John	Anthony
Melissa	Jennifer	David	Christopher
Michelle	Latoya	Matthew	James
Nicole	Monique	Joseph	Robert
Sarah	Kimberly	Brian	David
Lisa	Natasha	Jason	Sean
Elizabeth	Christine	Daniel	Kevin
Amy	Michelle	Robert	William
Heather	Crystal	James	John
Stephanie	Melissa	Steven	Joseph
Kimberly	Danielle	Thomas	Steven
Amanda	Erica	Eric	Andre
Kelly	Stephanie	William	Eric
Danielle	Jessica	Anthony	Charles
Catherine	Tamika	Sean	Brian
Rebecca	Lisa	Mark	Richard
Laura	Elizabeth	Jeffrey	Duane
Rachel	Tanya	Richard	Kenneth

Table 2-1

Source: Stanley Lieberson and Eleanor O. Bell. "Children's First Names: An Empirical Study of Social Taste." *American Journal of Sociology* volume 98, number 3 (November 1992): 517. Copyright by the University of Chicago.

in progressively higher-education categories: Allison, Sarah, Lauren, Adam, Andrew, and Daniel. Such associations among blacks were similar but weaker.

Lieberson and Bell next asked, What makes some names more popular among highly educated parents? They discovered that, for girls' names, historical roots and certain ending sounds appealed more to better-educated mothers. For example, well-educated women tend to gravitate toward biblical names and away from novel ones, especially those ending with an *ee, schwa,* or *ell* sound (as in Tammy or Stephanie, Angela or Maria, Crystal or Michelle). The exception is novel names ending with the *n* sound, such as Megan, Erin, and Lauren. The researchers speculate that these names clearly denote femaleness while understating feminine "frilliness" scorned by the upper classes. Indeed, Lieberson and Bell suggest that highly educated mothers choose traditional, no-nonsense names so that their daughters will be taken seriously. For boys, the name's sound had less influence in the class variations. Old Testament origin played the largest role in separating the names of well-educated boys from the others.

Building on previous work on the semantic connotations of various names (that is, the images that names evoke), the two sociologists found in their correlations yet another social-class difference. The better educated a mother, the higher probability she would select a girl's name connoting goodness, strength, activity, sincerity, and intelligence. In contrast, less-educated mothers chose "strong" names for their sons.

Lieberson and Bell also studied the adoption sequences of newly popular names and found that those chosen by highly educated mothers show up in the preferences

A few decades ago such modest attire as this was required by American folkways, perhaps even mores, regarding proper dress.

of slightly less-educated mothers a few years later, and so on down the educational ladder. They found, for example, that Justin appeared among the top name choices of the well-educated mothers in 1977; two years later it showed up in the selections of less-educated mothers, and a year after that it became popular among mothers with only a high school education. Such patterns suggest a class diffusion process: Lower-class mothers choose names that have taken on the patina of the more prestigious classes.

Two more examples show that naming patterns reveal powerful cultural undercurrents influencing name fashions. First, Lieberson and Bell note that the relatively recent trend toward uniqueness in African-American girls' names probably reflects "the major shifts in the position of blacks and the affirmation of a distinctive black subculture in the society" (p. 547). Second, the fact that shortened versions of established boys' names (Rick for Richard or Bill for William, for example) are rarely chosen as formal first names probably indicates that boys' names are taken more seriously than girls' names. And this suggests again that boys themselves are taken more seriously. Name fashions, in other words, tell us a great deal about our cultural values and social attitudes. □

WHERE DO A CULTURE'S VALUES LEAD?

We can continue our comparison of the cultures of the Yanomamo and the United States by asking if each system's **values** point toward a strong future or toward disintegration. Values are shared, persisting standards about what is good, right, moral, or desirable; they point a people in a particular direction by giving them a goal to strive for.

Values: shared, persisting standards about what is good, right, moral, or desirable.

Values provide a foundation for other cultural components such as norms. We might say that values represent the destination of our trip, norms the route marked on our map. And just as several routes can lead to the same destination, so several norms can branch off from one value. The norms that schools should receive equal funding and children equal teacher attention both flow from our culture's value of equal educational opportunity. Likewise, the Yanomamo value of ferocity provides the basis for cultural norms allowing an enraged husband to cut off his wife's ears or a large village to treacherously attack a smaller one.

Pets, Cleanliness, and Other Difficulties

We run into difficulties immediately in trying to compare two cultures' value systems. For one, people take many of their values for granted, rarely taking conscious notice of the standards that guide their important decisions in life. Consider cleanliness, for instance. Many of us take more than seven showers or baths a week, and yet probably think nothing of it until we learn that the Yanomamo "only wash themselves when they are ill, particularly with fever" (Smole, 1976, p. 49). And we must wonder if people in the United States appreciate the importance they attach to their pets until they hear of veterinarians implanting pacemakers, replacement organs, and dental crowns and treating cancer, psoriasis, and cataracts. Our pets have cemeteries, health insurance, and fast-food drive-ins available just for them. This value placed on pets seems

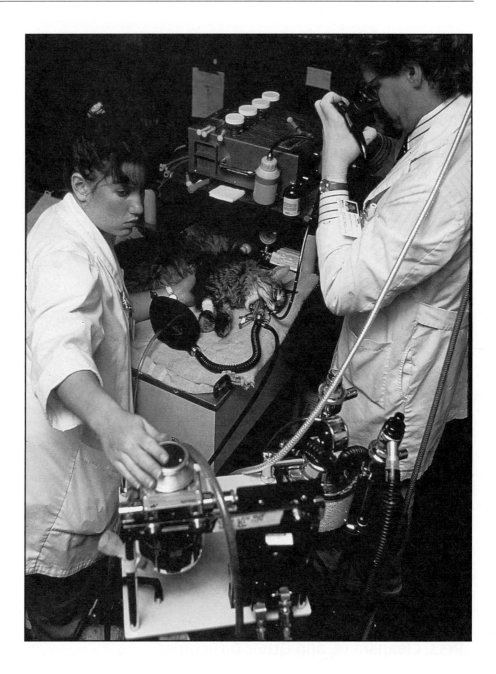

Americans place a relatively high value on their pets' health—about $6 billion worth. Veterinarians offer pets almost all the medical procedures available to humans.

even higher in contrast to the Yanomamo, who usually have little to feed their pets but follow the norm that forbids eating them.

Our society's heterogeneity causes another difficulty. Not surprisingly, such factors as social class, race, religion, age, and gender affect individuals' values. For example, the value we place on work varies with age: Older people in the United States have a stronger commitment to work than younger people (Loscocco and Kalleberg, 1988). And the importance workers attach to job security diminishes as they age. Similarly, working fathers value their jobs more than do working mothers, and single women place more importance on jobs with promotion possibilties than do married women (Braus, 1992). Such variations make it difficult to talk accurately of values in the U.S. in general. We do well to remember that our generalizations mask a great variety among individuals.

Another complication lies in the conflict among various values. For example, our culture is strongly rooted in rugged individualism, but this value is countered by the importance we attach to racial, ethnic, and class groupings (Williams, 1970). And while we generally claim to believe that equality is important, we believe in encouraging personal achievement. Such conflicts sometimes sort themselves out under special circumstances, such as during wartime, when the importance of patriotism outweighs the freedom to criticize the government.

Where Do Values Lead?

Despite such complications regarding the standards of what is good, right, and desirable, sociologists have managed to identify the major values of our culture. And along with help from the observers of the Yanomamo way of life, we can compare the two value systems. We will see some similarities, but in the contrasts perhaps we can discover if one set of values confers on its people more advantages than does the other.

Robin M. Williams (1970) offers the most widely quoted listing of the major values that guide our own society. Like the Yanomamo, we place a high value on equality, freedom, democracy, and nationalism. For example, the Yanomamos' sense of equality leads to norms forbidding the amassing of surpluses, and another requires the destruction of all personal belongings at death to prevent inheritance (Smole, 1976, pp. 193–94). They exhibit the same concerns for freedom as we do, as shown in their vociferous village debates and prideful, autonomous dealings with neighbors. The Yanomamo tolerate dictators no more than we do; their leaders have no formal authority or power, relying instead on their ability to offer sensible suggestions. And the Yanomamos' pride in themselves and in their culture compares to our own patriotic feelings for our nation and its accomplishments. In these ways, then, the two cultures follow similar paths.

As we continue down Williams' listing, however, we can watch U.S. values and those of the Yanomamo diverge. While we believe in progress, for example, they show a strong suspicion of the unfamiliar. While we measure quality of life in terms of material goods and comforts, the Yanomamo keep their personal possessions to a minimum. Our beliefs in achievement and work lead to competition and a mania for activity. The Yanomamo, on the other hand, believe in working no more than necessary. And our beliefs in efficiency and in scientific rationality contrast with the Yanomamos' reliance on sorcery for controlling their world. We do not always behave in accordance with our strong moral judgments of right and wrong, nor do we always help others in need as we recently did the starving Somalis, but the Yanomamo do not even pay lip service to such values of high moral standards and humanitarianism. We see this in their treacherous ambushes, merciless massacres, and relentless kidnappings. However, while we note the Yanomamos' tendency to dominate and exploit their neighbors whenever possible, conflict theorists find great similarities in our own society's domination and exploitation of women and minorities.

Where do such contrasts lead us? If we are still using cultural relativism as our framework, we should ask if these different value systems meet the two cultures' needs. Without suggesting that the Yanomamos' value system is a perfect match for their situation, and without denying the importance of isolation afforded by the surrounding dense forests, we can reasonably point to such values as fierceness and autonomy to

Materialism is one of Americans' most visible values, one not shared by cultures like the Yanomamo.

help explain the Yanomamos' success at maintaining their cultural integrity. While others around them have been swamped by the modern world, their stable value system has kept them relatively self-reliant and uninterested in outside temptations.

What about the United States? Observers of our culture point to some recent, worrisome changes in the values that have served us well for over 300 years. Daniel Bell (1976), for example, describes a growing conflict between two sets of values within our capitalist economic system. He argues that those values most strongly held during the earlier stages of capitalism—such as work, achievement, and thrift—have diminished in relation to other capitalist values focusing on personal pleasure. This has fueled a trend toward what Bell calls hedonism, the seeking of immediate gratification, rather than working, saving, and planning for the future.

This move toward self-gratification resounds in many studies of the United States today. Daniel Yankelovich (1981) found survey evidence of a revolutionary change during the 1960s and 1970s away from the old value of self-denial to a newer concern for self-fulfillment. Rather than working hard to earn material comforts and goods, we increasingly seek time for family involvement, work satisfaction, and personal growth—a shift from possessing things to doing things (Harris and Yankelovich, 1989). Christopher Lasch (1979) writes of our "personal preoccupations" and "self-centeredness." Other surveys indicate that, for many of us, personal freedom now comes before family responsibilities (Yankelovich, 1981; Glenn, 1992). Orlando Patterson (1991) argues that our modern focus on personal freedom has largely overshadowed our concern for the civic freedoms of others. In fact, polls show that our preoccupation with self has gone hand in hand with a declining interest in national security (Rokeach and Ball-Rokeach, 1989).

This rising self-centeredness also accompanies a change regarding a formerly stable part of the value system in the United States: the belief in equal opportunity (Lipset, 1963, 1985). We seem to hold equality of result in very low importance, and even equality of opportunity has lost some support in our culture (Rokeach and Ball-Rokeach, 1989). Our concern with self apparently crowds out our concern for other people's needs or claims.

Such trends in U.S. values may signal an important shift in our cultural base. Perhaps we will have to wait for historians to decide, but for now we might do well to ask, "Does this apparent shrinking of our sphere of concerns point to a future of cultural strength or disintegration?"

HOW DOES LANGUAGE AFFECT CULTURE?

Norms and values make up part of any culture's core, but the linchpin of all cultural components, the part upon which everything else depends, is language. This means of communication is unique to our species because it is based on the use of symbols. Whether language is exclusively oral-based, as with the Yanomamo, or also stored in written form, our dependence on symbols differentiates us from all other creatures. Rather than contrast our own culture with that of the Yanomamo, we here explore how language affects culture in general.

A **symbol** is a stimulus, such as a sound or gesture, that represents something; it has no inherent meaning, so the meaning must be learned. The sounds we make when we speak are incomprehensible to someone who has not learned the meanings we have arbitrarily attached to them. Written marks can be invested with symbolic meaning. So can articles such as a crucifix, a wedding band, an army general's stars, or a flag with a red cross, swastika, or stars and stripes.

A few other species can use symbols in response to situations contrived by humans. Chimpanzees and gorillas can learn a system of symbolic hand gestures to

Symbols: stimuli that represent things or ideas; having no inherent meaning, they must be learned.

carry on a rudimentary conversation with humans. They, along with dolphins and sea lions, can apparently even learn to understand some grammatical rules of word order (Hunt and Agnoli, 1991). They may even be capable of referring to past events, one of the hallmarks of language-using beings. But does their crude, limited use of symbols and grammar constitute language?

This question has for years embroiled scientists in a heated debate. Critics contend that some animals show cleverness in using symbols to make requests but come nowhere near the human ability to communicate abstractions, thoughts, and feelings. Chimps, for example, do not "discuss" much else beyond asking for a banana. In fact, some critics suspect that at least some of the chimpanzees' responses are to unconscious nonverbal cues from their human handlers.

In any case, other species ordinarily depend on communication through signs rather than symbols. Signs or signals carry inherent meaning for the creatures using them. A bird's song or a dog's growl requires no interpretation or learning; the message strikes a chord in other birds and dogs that resounds with inherent meaning. Signs, however, cannot provide the foundation for a learned way of life; they limit their users to communicating only a few messages, such as "danger!" or "this is my territory."

Symbols, however, free humans from this and other limitations. Even prehumans of a million or more years ago may have possessed simple language skills (Bickerton, 1990). Perhaps as early as 200,000 to 400,000 years ago, humans possessed the elongated vocal tract needed to produce the wide range of articulations required for fully developed, spoken language (Finn, 1985; Lieberman, 1991). Whenever the capacity for language began, it has since enabled us to share any new ideas and discoveries that our brains can encompass. In other words, we can create a living, changing way of life: a culture.

Other species use only signals, such as raised hackles, laid-back ears, and bared teeth, to communicate aggression. Humans can also draw upon a huge arsenal of words.

How Does Language Make Culture Possible?

We have noted the necessity for passing on accumulated knowledge from older generations to uninformed younger ones. But without language, adults could not convey their experiences; they could speak only of the present. They could transmit only that information within reach of their senses, only what could be demonstrated in front of the children. They could teach the use of various tools and how to hunt and gather, but not speak of folklore or past dangers. Without the means of encoding experiences and wisdom into symbols, the level of human knowledge would remain relatively flat, nothing comparable to what we recognize today as a human way of life. The Yanomamo would not be able to pass down to their children their rich mixture of legends, lineage information, and village histories. Likewise, we could not tell our children of the heroic accomplishments and tragic wars of our own people. Each generation would make many of the same mistakes as their predecessors.

Moreover, without symbols we could not deal with the distinctively human aspect of our way of life: the abstract. There would be no ideals, morals, norms, or values—nothing beyond the concrete, material world. The etiquette of each situation would have to be worked out through intimidation or force. In fact, it is difficult to imagine social life at all without the communication of norms to establish order for beings lacking instincts to guide their social behaviors.

Without these functions of language, then, humans would live in the present, learning little from the past and unable to plan for the future. Their social relationships would have to be based on either instincts or brute force and coercion. They could not worship together, reason together, or discuss notions of justice or equality. Such hallmarks of humanity would await the development of communication in which meaning could be arbitrarily attached to sounds or gestures. Culture as we know it would await the development of language.

Shaping Our Thinking

The ancient Greek thinker Herodotus believed that because Egyptians wrote from right to left they must have thought differently from Greeks, who wrote from left to right (Fishman, 1980). This curious notion arose again early in this century in the work of an amateur linguist, Benjamin Whorf, and an anthropologist, Edward Sapir. The Sapir–Whorf hypothesis contends that unconscious language habits shape our perception of the world (Sapir, 1929; Whorf, 1956). Just as a house's construction depends on what building materials are used and how they are fitted together, so our mental construction of the world depends on how our language forces us to fit together the available words.

Along this line, Hunt and Agnoli argue that "language differentially favors some thought processes over others" (1991, p. 378). In other words, depending on a language's rules and structures, some thoughts or statements become more manageable or "natural" than others. Such features as vocabulary size and the rules regarding grammar and word order serve to channel or organize our thinking patterns along some paths rather than others. It is a matter of mental cost or efficiency: Our thinking naturally proceeds down those paths that require fewer decisions.

Brian Bloomfield (1989) argues that our view of computers as thinking machines is not only reflected in our language but encouraged by it. He explains that the structure of English-language sentences requires a subject (or agent of action) and a verb (or action). Thus we find ourselves speaking of a computer producing an analysis, making a forecast, or playing chess. In attributing to computers intention or purpose, we regard the machine as an agent of action rather than merely a tool of its human user. For instance, we speak of the computer beating us at chess as though the machine, rather than its human programmer, actually out-thought us. Our language rules make it more "natural" to think of computers as thinking machines.

In the same way, a teenage daughter might find it convenient to refer to the family car which she usually drives as "her" car. By so labeling it, she may come to perceive it as actually hers, even though she uses it only at the pleasure of her parents. Likewise, the Yanomamo have a term ("wanidi") for abnormal (usually deformed or crippled) men or women (Smole, 1976, p. 72). We can easily imagine how, once that term became part of their mental choices, abnormality became institutionalized and children were more readily perceived as candidates for that category. Thus, instead of viewing some Yanomamo as more fit and finely formed than others, their vocabulary encourages them to mentally draw a line separating themselves into different types. It has become "natural" in their culture to categorize people in this way.

Likewise, our language structure makes it "natural" for us to think of women and men as different in ways far beyond their biological natures. Feminists have for several decades criticized the widespread use of masculine generics: "he" and "man" to refer to people in general, both women and men. While this linguistic convention may seem merely convenient and innocent enough, such pervasive masculine pronouns lead to an unconscious assumption that "people" equals "male" (Silveira, 1980). Researchers suggest that exposure to generic male pronouns elicits male imagery (Harrison and Passero, 1975; Hamilton and Henley, 1982) and suppresses female imagery, leading to lower self-esteem in females (Henley, Gruber, and Lerner, 1984). As Mykol Hamilton (1988) notes, this mental channeling creates an unconscious tendency among employers to hire a male when searching for the "best man for the job." Similarly, Fiona Wilson (1992) argues that masculinity metaphors often employed in organizations help alienate, even exclude women. She documents how men, knowingly or not, use expressions like "the bunker," "take no prisoners," "bite the bullet," "lead the charge," and "casualties" when describing their work. Wilson contends that such martial metaphors reinforce the male culture of organizations, creating a gender-based reality.

All of this research takes us beyond the commonplace notion that language reflects the cultural needs of its users. Not only does language provide the basis for building a culture, it also influences the way we think and perceive our world.

SOCIAL STRUCTURE FOR YANOMAMO INDIANS AND U.S. COLLEGE STUDENTS: FREEDOM OF THE WILD VERSUS THE STRAITJACKET OF CIVILIZATION?

Sitting in our car, caught in a traffic jam, our daydreaming may take a sociological turn. We might reflect that cultural values have helped decide our car's use and destination, and norms have dictated the speed limits we obey and the signals we use. It all seems so confining, so limiting. We feel a powerful urge to break out of the traffic and motor freely across lawns and vacant lots to get where we want to go. Instead, we settle for wistfully wondering if somewhere, perhaps in the South American rain forest, people's social worlds offer them soft, leafy forest trails rather than clogged, exhaust-choked highways. In other words, having taken that sociological turn, we yearn for less social structure.

Social structure represents the motorways of our social world: the stable, predictable, patterned relationships among people. This structure organizes our social life and channels our behaviors as the roadways channel the flow of traffic. While it limits our choices and confines our behaviors to certain socially approved alternatives, it also confers on our social life order, routine, and coherence. Daydreams aside, a complex culture such as ours obviously requires such structure to coordinate all its parts so that the system can function.

Social structure: stable, predictable, patterned social relationships.

But what about the Yanomamo culture? Certainly the total absence of any organization of human behavior would invite chaos, but do jungle dwellers enjoy the freedom of substantially less social structure? To shed some light on this question, we compare the social structure surrounding a typical Yanomamo with that faced by a U.S. college student.

Status in the Two Cultures

At the smallest scale and the most personal level, social structure organizes the individual's behaviors through **status,** a person's recognized social position. When we hear that someone holds the title of nurse, son, prisoner, or college student, we recognize those positions as part of the social structure. Likewise, when the Yanomamo refer to someone as father, mother, or child, the meanings of such social positions are understood. Most importantly, people in both cultures know what sorts of behaviors are appropriate for different statuses.

Status: a person's recognized social position.

Here the channeling of people's behaviors comes into play: To each status is connected a **role** or set of behaviors expected of anyone occupying that status. People who hold the status of mother, for example, are expected to care for their children in culturally determined ways. Based on norms regarding what is permissible or expected, roles guide us as we fulfill the responsibilities and enjoy the privileges connected with each of our statuses.

Role: the set of behaviors expected of a person occupying a particular status.

Is Yanomamo social life less structured—we might say, less restrictive—than ours? One answer is that Yanomamo culture offers fewer statuses, which, we will see, means fewer options or paths.

Among the Yanomamo, the most important status for a person is gender; this dominates one's life much more than it does in our culture. From early childhood, the paths of Yanomamo boys and girls diverge into separate worlds. Boys play at hunting and exploring the jungle until they can share in the men's duties. They learn that only men are allowed to cook with clay pots during feasts. They learn how to shove a magical herb up the nose of a reluctant female to make her receptive to sexual advances. All learn to be hunters and warriors; some may choose to become a shaman and commune with the spirit world through drug-induced trances. Girls, in contrast, become assistant workers to their ever-busy mothers at an early age, taking care of their younger siblings, carrying water, and helping with other chores. As women, they haul into camp huge loads of firewood in the late afternoons while the men gather to blow hallucinogenic drugs up one another's noses with bamboo tubes. When they take on

Yanomamo men have the option of becoming a shaman. This new shaman nears the end of his initiation ritual, which includes six days of taking drugs.

the status of wife, they learn not to displease their husbands or they will be beaten with a piece of firewood, slapped with the flat blade of a machete or ax, shot with a barbed arrow, have their ear decorations yanked hard enough to tear open the lobes, or killed. Sex status in their culture imposes much more structure on individuals than in ours. "Sexual liberation" is clearly foreign to the Yanomamo.

The Yanomamo social structure focuses on sex as the **master status,** the status which determines more than any other how people respond to one another. The Yanomamo first think of sex when considering their identity; most of their lives are organized around whether they are male or female. In our culture, sex and race have given way to occupation as the master status for most of us. This is especially true for professionals, whose lives are greatly colored by the income, respect, and power linked with their careers. For U.S. women, "mother" or "wife" may serve as master status even if they are employed, but for most men what they do for a living is more important than their statuses as husband or father.

Although sex overshadows all other Yanomamo statuses, age also matters. Adults have power over children, and the few who reach old age are venerated for their wisdom and experience. Even women in advanced age and with many kin can enjoy considerable influence over village decisions. For the most part, however, a person is either male or female and child or adult; other statuses are of little consequence.

The life of the U.S. college student, in contrast, is organized by a constellation of many statuses beyond sex and age. For example, a student might be an employee, Catholic, member of the track team or computer club, African American, unmarried, and Republican. Who enjoys greater freedom, the student or the Yanomamo? Before deciding, consider more evidence.

In our culture, behaviors are largely organized by **achieved statuses,** those statuses acquired through an individual's actions rather than forced upon her or him by biology or other uncontrollable circumstances. We gain the status of college student, employee, graduate, criminal, spouse, and parent due to our own efforts and choices. Yanomamo have few such options. A male who, along with the proper lineage,

Master status: the status that determines more than any other how people respond to one another.

Achieved status: a social position acquired through a person's actions.

displays superior wisdom and fierceness can become headman. Besides this, however, life offers few alternative paths. A female has no choice about whether she will marry or whom; a man can at least choose to become a shaman.

Instead, the life of the Yanomamö is organized almost entirely by the **ascribed statuses** of sex and age. These statuses are assigned to the individual by biology or the passage of time. Life also thrusts upon them, as it does us, such statuses as brother or sister, aunt or uncle, widow or widower, and so on. In addition to those relational statuses, life in our diverse culture imposes ascribed statuses based on ethnicity, race, and sometimes (in childhood) religious affiliation.

Ascribed status: a social position assigned by factors beyond the individual's control, such as biology or the passage of time.

Our comparison so far reveals that the simpler social structure of the Yanomamö provides fewer options or paths, and less opportunity for individuals to acquire different positions in life. For the most part, biology and time place individuals into channels from which little escape is possible. We might therefore view our many statuses not so much as restrictions but as opportunities, and evidence of greater freedom within our social structure. But complications arise if we look more closely at that structure.

These complications flow from the great number of statuses in our lives. While each status has its expected behaviors, or role, each status also generates several other sets of expectations. For example, a college student behaves differently as she relates to other students in her classes, to teachers, and to the librarian in charge of student workers there. That is, the roles of classmate, sociology major, and librarian aide all center around the status of "student." These several roles related to one status constitute a **role set.** And each set is connected to another. Thus the student's role as library worker links her to other roles as liaison with the duplication department, co-chair of the Christmas party skit, and perhaps union member. Each role leads to another; none stands alone outside a role set. Each of our statuses, then, entangles us in a web of expected behaviors. In contrast, a Yanomamö is subject to fewer entangling expectations because fewer statuses exist.

Role set: several roles related to one status.

This means that the Yanomamö suffer less **role conflict,** the result of incompatible or contradictory expectations between different roles. A U.S. college student, in contrast, may find herself torn between several demands simultaneously—doing her homework, feeding the baby, visiting her ailing mother, and so on. Her many roles make such conflict more likely, although she has some responses available: She can cancel a role (quit school), rank the roles' priorities (baby comes before schoolwork), or compartmentalize the roles (visiting her mother only on weekends).

Role conflict: a clash of two or more roles.

A more specific kind of role conflict occurs when the several demands within a single role clash with another, what is called **role strain.** The role of mother, for example, may require a woman to show both affection and discipline, to encourage the child's explorations yet restrain some of its activities. Likewise, the college teacher may feel an obligation to act both as concerned advisor and objective, impersonal evaluator. Again, the more roles, the more role strain and conflict we face.

Role strain: conflict between several demands within a single role.

Organizers on a Larger Scale: Institutions

Besides statuses, the social structure includes **institutions,** larger building blocks that organize our social relationships on a broader scale. In institutions, cultural norms and values give rise to widely shared, relatively stable, standardized solutions for society's major tasks. These tasks include reproducing the society (family), managing power and preserving social order (politics), producing and distributing goods and services

Institutions: widely shared, relatively stable, standardized solutions for society's major tasks.

(economy), providing and maintaining a sense of purpose and meaning (religion), and providing intellectual stimulation and training (education). The health care, mass media, military, legal, and sports institutions in the United States also help organize our behaviors on a large scale.

In premodern cultures like the Yanomamo, the family dominates the social structure. Beyond its basic tasks of producing well-trained children to replenish society's membership, the Yanomamo family figures large in society's other major tasks, in contrast to the shrinking of the U.S. family's responsibilities. For example, the family in our society has virtually lost its production role to an increasingly distinct economic institution. On the other hand, the Yanomamo economy can be seen largely as an extension of family and kinship arrangements. Both the production and consumption of food operate along household lines; each household head operates his own garden and food is shared among family members.

Similarly, other Yanomamo social needs are so efficiently met by the family that their other institutions have barely developed. Social order flows rather directly from cultural norms and values without requiring much in the way of an intervening political institution. Kinship determines how political struggles split up a village. The headman exerts no institutionalized or formal authority or power; he must persuade rather than command. Decisions evolve from discussions in which the headman and other notably clever or brave, respected individuals have more influence. They have no need of a congress, mayor, police force, or the like. Similarly, the knowledge required of every adult can be learned from informal observation and imitation; they have no need for schools or teaching specialists. Yanomamo religion stands out more clearly from the cultural background: Shamans lead chants to invoke the spirits' aid and protection. Still, they erect no religious monuments, buildings, or shrines.

The Yanomamo social structure thus contains fewer influential institutions than does our society. However, the institution of the family organizes so many of the people's behaviors that to some degree it compensates for the absence of other institutions. Does this translate into more freedom for the individual in Yanomamo society than in ours?

Critical Thinking Box

Which Social Structure Is More Restrictive?

We can expect any culture that functions well to include as much structure as is needed. The complexity of the social structure and the degree of freedom allowed from those patterns depends on the needs of the culture. This means that any individual is granted only as much freedom as the social system can afford. Does our culture require more structuring for individual behaviors than that of the Yanomamo, thereby limiting us to the equivalent of a few clogged highways?

Also, do fewer paths mean more freedom or less? Fewer statuses mean less role conflict and strain. The Yanomamo have few statuses, but those few are ascribed, exerting enormous control over the individual and allowing few alternative paths. Similarly, the organizing power in their culture is concentrated in one institution while the others pale in significance.

Which culture do you think offers the most freedom to plot one's own behavioral course in life? ■

TYPES OF SOCIETIES: WHAT'S NEXT FOR THE YANOMAMO?

Our own society and that of the Yanomamo stand at opposite ends of the sociological spectrum. To see what is in store for the Yanomamo, and perhaps us as well, we will now explore some of the types of societies in between the two.

Hunting and Gathering   As exotically "primitive" as the Yanomamo appear, other peoples are even further removed from the modern world. The oldest and most technologically simple form of society is that based on hunting and gathering. Hunters and gatherers move lightly over the landscape, pausing only briefly in any one place, barely leaving any trace on the earth's surface. They have no need and no means for deeply gouging or scarring the earth. In contrast, the Yanomamo, because they not only gather food but produce it through horticulture, level substantial patches of the forest for their gardens before moving on to the next new site.

Horticulture   The Yanomamo are remarkable in that, as their ancestors moved from hunting and gathering to horticulture, they did not make all the usual accompanying transformations of their way of life. Humans began domesticating plants about 10,000 years ago, and most peoples who have done so eventually produce a food

With the development of horticulture comes eventually a food surplus, which gives rise to leaders who enjoy a superior life-style.

surplus, triggering other developments such as labor specialization and the accumulation of wealth. Along with this surplus, we usually expect to find among horticulturalists distinct social strata such as nobles, highly skilled workers, and servants. But because the rain forest supports only modest food production, and because of their practice of holding feasts to give away extra food, the Yanomamo have no reason to build storehouses or divide labor into specialized tasks to reap fuller harvests. Thus they do not distinguish between specialized craftsman and farmer or rich and poor, as do most societies in this stage, only between male and female and young and old. Moreover, most horticulturalists vest formal powers in special leadership positions such as chiefs and councils of elders. The chiefs in some horticultural societies demand to be carried on litters by their social inferiors and enjoy special housing and clothing. These rulers often own virtually everything and distribute the society's production as they see fit, usually to support their kin and an extensive trade network which supplies the nobility with luxury goods from other regions. But the Yanomamo headman resembles leaders in hunting and gathering bands in that he has no such formal authority. Furthermore, the Yanomamo village units grow to a size only slightly larger than many hunter-gatherer bands.

Farms and Factories

The isolation Yanomamos have enjoyed for centuries has begun to erode in recent decades. Eventually their way of life, unless it completely disintegrates, will probably resemble another society on the sociological spectrum. What does the future hold for them?

Agriculture   Historically, horticulturalists have evolved into an agricultural or agrarian society. They have used irrigation and animal power to increase food production, creating a substantial surplus. From this surplus spring cities and written language, two main characteristics of civilization.

With new agricultural technologies, the Yanomamo could conceivably move into this cultural niche. But if their transformation into large-scale farmers resembles that of others, the Yanomamo will find that they need strong, centralized leadership with formal powers to replace the kinship web's control. They would need a government to coordinate the agricultural system, arbitrate disputes over land ownership, and protect the society's resources. These leaders might claim divine status or at least divine support. In fact, religion would no longer be a means to try to exert control over the spirit world; instead, it would become a powerful tool of the state, an effective means of controlling the people. The Yanomamo would recognize the need for a formal system of education to supply a trained, literate workforce. Tests, credentials, and work schedules would invade their way of life. And families would probably become more formal; husbands, for example, might demand that their wives walk behind them in public.

Industrialization   In another possible scenario, the Yanomamo would move into nearby factory cities, drawn by the allure of industrial jobs and a wide array of modern conveniences. If so, they would begin to look to science rather than sorcery to control their world, and machines rather than human or animal power to help them in their work. Other institutions, such as schools, the military, and health care, would challenge the family's importance. Indeed, the kin system would lose much of its grip on individuals as the opportunities and mobility of industrial society drew young people far from the confines of the extended family's control. Husbands would be less likely to beat their wives, especially if women earned their own paychecks. Families would become smaller as children came to be seen as economic liabilities rather than producers. A complex social system would envelop the Yanomamo, one in which each person's standard of living depended less on kinship than on his or her own productive capacity. In the city's anonymity they would find themselves surrounded by strangers—a far cry from their familiarity with all their neighbors in the rain forest.

Like Us: Postindustrial

Given the incredible speed at which societies change today, we can imagine even the Yanomamo eventually moving along the sociological spectrum to our own postindustrial type of society. This would indeed require considerable imagination, as the two ways of life contrast so starkly. Rather than worry about extracting their next meal from their physical surroundings, the Yanomamo would use the cutting edge of technology to produce goods, services, and information. Instead of clay pots and wooden arrows, they might create robots to operate assembly lines, deliver food trays to hospital patients, and function as security guards. Rather than blow hallucinogenic drugs up one another's nose, they would perhaps take their "trips" via virtual reality machines or high-definition, interactive television. Instead of protecting their children by casting spells, they might dream of gene transplants to choose their next child's characteristics. And rather than hope for steel axes, they might look forward to minirobots that battle disease in the blood system and the manufacture of devices atom by atom.

Anyone moving into a postindustrial society would face, as we do, an occupational market that gives scant attention to people with farming skills, scarcely more to those with assembly-line factory experience. The typical worker is no longer a farmer or factory worker but a clerk or technician. Herein lies one of the painful aspects of "progress." As jobs in industrial production disappear, many skilled workers are forced into lower-paying jobs in the service industry such as janitor and fast food worker, which in turn may soon be dominated by robots that do not demand cost-of-living raises or health coverage. Increasingly, only those workers with high-level skills, especially in dealing with words and numbers in a sophisticated way, will find job security.

Postindustrial society reaches relentlessly into the future.

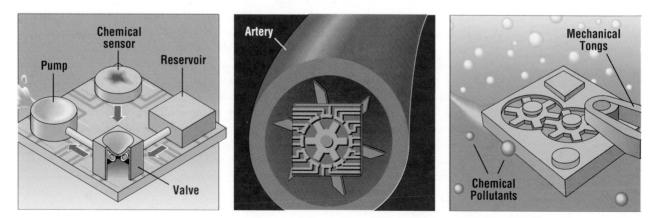

While the postindustrial society offers a cornucopia of comforts and gadgets, it demands ever-higher levels of training and efficiency. Daniel Bell (1973), who first described the postindustrial society, noted the central importance of theoretical knowledge in such service- and information-dominated societies. This explains why the demands of the postindustrial society increasingly sort people into those with intellectual ability and those who become unneeded, in sharp contrast to Yanomamo society, where every adult masters all necessary skills. Pondering the evolution of cultures along the spectrum of complexity, we can understand why social scientists are careful not to regard all change as positive.

SUMMARY

The Yanomamo have established a *society*, a large, enduring population sharing a territory and a *culture*, which is a learned, shared, integrated way of life. Their way of life includes both concrete, physical items *(material culture)* and abstractions such as beliefs and customs *(nonmaterial culture)*. They do not have *subcultures* (distinct ways of life within their dominant culture) or *countercultures* (subcultures that stand in opposition to the mainstream culture). Like us, the Yanomamo are dependent on the culture that serves as their adaptive tool of survival.

Ethnocentrism is the belief that one's own way of life is superior and properly serves as the standard by which all others are evaluated. This attitude, found in all groups, denies us the opportunity to learn from other cultures, distorts our observations, and excuses the maltreatment of other peoples. On the other hand, ethnocentrism contributes to a group's stability, morale, and survival. Using *cultural relativism*, in contrast, requires that we evaluate other cultures on the basis of how well each one meets the needs of its people, even if the practices are repugnant to us.

We can use cultural relativism to judge other ways of life by asking if a culture provides clear direction through its *norms:* rules or guidelines delineating those behaviors that are appropriate or permitted in any given situation. Norms serve to smooth our interaction with others. *Folkways* are the least important norms, dealing with behaviors that others expect but do not require of us. These rules, which vary over time and across social classes, are reinforced only by mild punishments and small rewards. Fast-changing cultures like ours feature folkways followed by very few people for a short time *(fads)*, as well as those that last longer, attract wider followings, and involve some life style matter *(fashions)*. Fashions tell what is tasteful and respectable. Some norms, called *mores,* offer guidance about behaviors considered not just polite but essential to society's survival. Mores are backed up by severe punishments as well as *laws,* which are formalized norms put in writing and publicly decreed by our authorities.

We can also evaluate a culture by seeing where its values lead. *Values* are shared, persisting standards about what is good, right, moral, or desirable. American values are varied and conflicting, but in general show some similarity with those of the Yanomamo. Though some of their values diverge from ours, the Yanomamo seem well served by their overall value system, perhaps better than we are by ours.

Language serves as the basis of any culture, and in turn is based on *symbols,* stimuli that represent things or ideas, and that have no inherent meaning and so must be learned. While other species can use symbols in a very limited way, they depend mostly on signs or signals that carry inherent meaning. Only humans can use language to transmit accumulated knowledge, to deal with the abstract, and to describe the past and future. In fact, according to the Sapir-Whorf hypothesis, our unconscious language habits shape our perceptions of the world. Our language's structure organizes and channels our thinking, making some ideas seem more natural than others.

To some degree, we all follow stable, predictable, patterned relationships with other people, what sociologists call *social structure*. At the most personal level of social structure, our behaviors are organized through *status*, a person's recognized social position. To each status is connected a *role*, or set of behaviors expected of anyone occupying that status. Among the Yanomamo, sex serves as the *master status*, the status that determines more than any other how people respond to others. The Yanomamo have few *achieved statuses*, those acquired through individuals' actions rather than biology or circumstances beyond their control. Instead, most of their statuses are *ascribed statuses* assigned by biology or the passage of time. Several roles related to one status constitute a *role set*. We are more likely than the Yanomamo to suffer from *role conflict*, the result of incompatible or contradictory expectations between different roles, and *role strain*, conflict arising from the several demands within a single role. Social structure also includes *institutions* consisting of widely shared, relatively stable, standardized solutions for society's major tasks. The family is the main institution in cultures such as the Yanomamo.

Sociocultural evolution has produced several types of societies. Hunting and gathering bands leave little trace on their physical landscape. With the development of horticulture come labor specialization and the accumulation of wealth, accompanied by social inequality and special leadership positions. In agricultural societies, irrigation and animal power applied to food production result in large food surpluses and cities, written language, and strong, centralized leadership with formal powers. Industrialized societies use machine power, and their other institutions challenge the dominance of the family. Postindustrial societies focus on services and information, and their reliance on advanced technology creates a new occupational market that requires high levels of training and efficiency.

Key Terms

society	folkways	role
culture	fads	master status
material culture	fashions	achieved status
nonmaterial culture	mores	ascribed status
subculture	laws	role set
counterculture	values	role conflict
ethnocentrism	symbols	role strain
cultural relativism	social structure	institutions
norms	status	

3

Chapter

SOCIAL INTERACTION

Sociologists help explain some of the countless minidramas that make up campus life. For example, a college student straggles into class unshaven, a few ragged bits of clothing carelessly thrown on. Another slips in with no make-up, her hair tied up in a bandana, slippers on her feet. Normally, such a slovenly appearance would signal alienation from the schooling process, a "lack of attachment to the behavioral setting." However, because this is final exam week, the "situational obligations" have temporarily changed (Goffman, 1963) and their display has a different meaning: deep, all-consuming engrossment in their studies.

Elsewhere, a college administrator unnecessarily keeps a faculty member waiting outside his office. Sociologists would explain that the distribution of waiting time reflects the distribution of power: Those higher up in the campus hierarchy deprive others of their time by making them wait (Schwartz, 1974). In the end, this means students spend more time waiting than do others on campus.

Meanwhile, a casual conversation between a male and female student on a campus bench reveals another example of a mini-power struggle. Based on sociological research, we can expect the male to interrupt and talk more (Eakins and Eakins, 1976; Swacker, 1975), and whoever has the more male-like gender identity (regardless of sex) to challenge more (Spencer and Drass, 1989).

Later, a professor chides his students for not offering critical, challenging responses to his comments, for not participating in classroom discussion. Sociologists who have studied the classroom setting would point out that students do not generally view the classroom as an arena for generating ideas but as one in which the teacher, as expert, dispenses knowledge (Karp and Yoels, 1976).

That evening, a squad of cheerleaders exhorts the roaring crowd at a football game to scream a familiar chant. As we will see, sociologists offer explanations for the easy contagion of emotions in the thousands of like-minded fans who have converged on the stadium.

In this chapter, we take a fresh look at such aspects of social life on campus. Like a camera suddenly focusing on one particular aspect of the background, riveting our attention on something we have taken for granted, the sociological perspective reveals the unspoken rules and carefully contrived presentations that underlie everyday interaction.

WHAT HAPPENS IN THE CLASSROOM, SOCIOLOGICALLY SPEAKING?

Social interaction: people responding to one another's interpretations and actions.

We watch the coed's eyes rotate quickly and ever so slightly in the direction of a male as she enters the classroom. We note the increased sparkle, the enlarged pupils. He notices, too, and runs his fingers through his hair and throws his shoulders back slightly. This brief interchange represents an instance of **social interaction**—people responding to one another's actions—which we can put under the illuminating microsociological lens of symbolic interactionism.

This young woman's actions are designed to evoke a specific interpretation in the mind of the observer.

Symbolic Interactionism: Reality in the Mind of the Behaver

Our affected male student does not respond to the subtle *actions* of the young woman in his class. Instead, symbolic interactionists explain, he responds to the interpretation or *meaning* he attaches to her actions (Mead, 1934; Blumer, 1969). Symbolic interactionism has the effect of slowing down human interaction so that we may understand the man's interpretation of her actions. We are able to "watch" as he mentally focuses on her eye behaviors, assesses them, and decides what she meant. Based on the interpretation he assigns to her eye behaviors, he then selects a response he feels is appropriate. All of this in a few seconds.

Social Construction of Reality The students' interaction produces a snippet of social reality. As they fashion meanings around their actions and reactions, they, along with the others in the classroom, construct the social reality of that college classroom at that moment. From the interactionist perspective, the social reality of any given situation equals the total of all the meanings shared by all the participants. The classroom's reality thus lies not in the observer's eye but in the minds of those in this setting.

If this or any other group is to enjoy social order, if the people's interactions are to proceed smoothly and satisfactorily, they must establish shared definitions of their situations. Our cultural training helps us define situations similarly; we learn to interpret most behaviors the same way that others in our culture do. This is necessary because the social structure of a classroom, campus, or society rests upon a foundation of such smooth interaction, in which each participant aligns his or her actions with those of others. This continuous flow of interpretations, assessments, and reactions comes into focus through the lens of symbolic interactionism.

Many of our interpretations of behavior in public places like the college campus are based on what Erving Goffman called the "situational regulations" of behavior

We feel obligated to show "civil inattention" in enclosed public spaces.

(1963). One such regulation involves the right to "civil inattention," which requires, for example, that we avoid staring at others. Similarly, in an enclosed space like an elevator, bystanders must signal that their attention is focused somewhere other than the conversation of the strangers next to them. The conversants, meanwhile, may feel obligated to show their confidence in the bystander's inattention by not whispering or using obvious code words.

Impression Management   Meanwhile, approaching the classroom door, the professor straightens her jacket, smooths her hair, and arranges her facial expression, all in preparation for her entrance. She is, after all, going "on stage," according to Goffman's dramaturgical perspective of human interaction. Recall from Chapter 1 that Goffman saw social life as a form of theater, in which each social setting offers a stage with different roles to be played.

The professor has already "performed" at the breakfast table with her family, in the faculty lounge, and in a committee meeting. Upon each of these "stages," she took cues from others regarding how she might best play her role. In each case, she attempted to evoke positive impressions of her identity.

Her day has been busy and fraught with dangers. Each social setting offers a different audience to please, different threats to various aspects of her identity. At breakfast she might be seen as grumpy and unloving. In the faculty lounge she may be seen as too uptight, uninteresting, or not clever enough. Other members of the committee may perceive her as incompetent or a poor team player. To prevent such harm to her identity, she takes considerable care in each situation to present herself in such a way as to satisfy that particular audience, to elicit in them the desired responses or perceptions. Goffman called such attempts to dictate or control how others see us "impression management."

This impression management becomes obvious as we watch her sweep into the room authoritatively, cheerfully—or however she has decided to play her role in this particular class. In Goffman's terms, she is now "frontstage," like an actor emerging from the curtains into the theater's floodlights. The social script of the classroom, composed of all the roles being played there, is clear, and the audience will alertly notice any behaviors that deviate from that script.

In her office or faculty lounge—"backstage"—she can relax, throwing her feet on her desk with her shoes kicked off, and rail at students' poorly written essays. Of course, even in the lounge, the professor is performing, but she plays for a different audience. She need not fear that the student audience will catch her revealing aspects of her identity that she conceals in the classroom. Just as restaurants and funeral parlors take pains to separate frontstage from backstage areas, so teachers' lounges are off limits to students to give teachers respite from their student audience.

Wordless Interaction: Nonverbal Communication

Well launched into her favorite lecture, our professor begins picking up a message from the students. They don't speak a word, but through their wandering gazes, yawns, slumped postures, and shuffling of books they ask her to finish quickly and painlessly.

Gestures   Such nonverbal communication consists largely of gestures, especially by the face and hands, that can add considerable power to messages. With smirks or stifled yawns, by rolling their eyes at the professor's joke or glancing frequently at the

Without uttering a word, students can transmit powerful messages regarding their interest in classroom activities.

classroom clock, students can communicate strong yet silent messages. These nonverbal messages usually convey the students' feelings more truthfully than do their words, although of course facial expressions can be controlled rather easily. Because we usually have less awareness of what our body posture and hands are saying, the professor would do well to look beyond any artificial smiles to other, less consciously manipulated gestures for a true reflection of the students' feelings.

Returning to the unspoken interaction between the male student and the female as she enters the classroom, we can analyze the nonverbal signals of attraction. Both students have at their disposal an array of gestures—making eye contact, leaning forward, coming close to one another, perhaps touching, and, of course, smiling. Even their voice quality can convey meanings; for example, a babyish voice makes the person seem warm and approachable (Montepare and Zebrowitz-McArthur, 1987).

The female, however, must use more subtle, discreet signals of availability when searching for a serious, long-term relationship. Karl Grammer (1990) suggests that this stems from the woman's need for a committed male to help her raise their children. She may realize the male's fear of committing himself to women who make themselves too easily available (and thus potentially unfaithful partners, a catastrophe for his reproductive strategy to support only children bearing his genes) and that giving blatant, direct signals of availability will probably attract only males interested in short-term relationships. For serious mate searching, she gives a more complex message than does the male (see Figure 3-1). As she takes a seat, having caught his attention, she will probably turn her head and torso away from him (indicating that she does not "come on" to just any male), but at the same time she signals her interest (probably unconsciously) by touching her body (usually between hips and chin) and keeping her arms and legs open. On his part, the male can employ more direct signals because,

NONVERBAL SIGNS OF HIGH INTEREST IN THE OPPOSITE SEX

Figure 3-1

These models are displaying the postures associated with high interest in the opposite sex. She sends a complex message, turning away from him but opening arms and legs to indicate she is available, but not blatantly so. His head, trunk, and limbs gestures all directly, openly indicate his high interest.

reproductively speaking, he benefits even from short-term relationships and thus need not present himself as nonpromiscuous. He will probably lean forward, turn head and trunk toward her, and keep his legs crossed and open. He may also raise his elbows and fold his hands behind his neck, somewhat like a peacock spreading its feathers.

While we may detect a continuous stream of such flirting signals in a college classroom, overall nonverbal communication is less visible on a U.S. campus than, say, in the Middle East. There, hundreds of hand gestures convey well-defined meanings. Extending the "unclean" left hand to a person in Morocco, for example, constitutes a terrible insult. In Lebanon, a man punching his palm with his fist thereby tells a woman he desires her. In our society, hands convey mostly insults, along with "OK," "thumbs up," and the like.

Interpersonal Space   We also give off messages by the way we manage the space between us and others. All over campus people protect their personal space from invasion by strangers. Students choose isolated seats in the classroom or place books around their space at the large library table to protect "their" territory. On the other hand, the student choosing a seat close to another communicates interest in him or her.

Edward T. Hall (1966), who pioneered work in personal space, identified four interpersonal zones used by middle-class adults in the northeastern United States. Each zone is reserved for a different kind of social contact. The intimate zone ranges from touching to 18 inches away. Most of us feel comfortable allowing casual friends, such as classmates, within 4 feet but not closer. In more formal interaction, such as job interviews, others stay 4 to 12 feet from us. The zone beyond 12 feet is used to distinguish a person from the general public, as in someone speaking to a crowd.

These conventions, like other "rules" of social interaction, are not rigid. For example, students in a crowded, noisy hallway tolerate more closeness with casual acquaintances. Also, Hall found that North Americans require more personal space than South Americans. Of course, some personalities use somewhat different distances for their zones, and our mood tends to affect our use of interpersonal space. Thus a student might stand farther from an intimidating professor than from one who elicits no fear.

The Building Blocks of Interaction

Much of the social organization of campus life consists of several basic processes, in somewhat the same way that most matter consists of several kinds of atoms. These processes, in other words, serve as basic building blocks of everyday social interaction.

Exchange Our professor receives an important committee post, but the college administrator granting it expects political loyalty in return. The same administrator habitually asks his secretary to stay past 5:00 P.M. to finish some important typing; in return she receives more power and autonomy in the office setting. Such interaction involving an expectation of repaying is called **exchange.** Like any other slice of social life, the social organization of the campus is held together by exchange. Through this process, the participants continuously maneuver to receive gratitude, goods, favors, and other rewards.

> **Exchange:** a reciprocal transaction involving the giving and repayment of benefits and punishments.

Reciprocity lies at the heart of exchange, so hostilities and punishments are exchanged or repaid. If we send a gift to someone, we expect repayment of some sort: I do for you, you do for me—or else. If the reward is not forthcoming, we may respond with slander or coldness. This works also at the macro level, as when political factions trade dirty tricks or nations repay insults with hostilities.

Exchange provides the foundation for most human interaction; it is part of the glue that holds every group or society together. The exchange of goods and favors helps cement alliances and hold people to their social obligations. The professor is motivated to perform her roles—to do her part in the committee, church volunteer group, and family—because of the security and acceptance she feels when rewarded for her performance and the shame she feels when she does not contribute.

Reciprocal exchange contributes to social solidarity more easily under certain circumstances than others. Within groups like sororities and fraternities, "generalized" exchange—"I do for you but someone else (not necessarily you) will do for me"—leads to generalized obligations to the group, and thus trust and solidarity (Ekeh, 1974; Uehara, 1990). In contrast, exchange works differently when it is "restricted," as in study pairs, where each partner expects repayment from the other. There, the two members spend much of their energies monitoring perceived imbalances in the exchanges. Mistrust flourishes in these brittle, unstable exchange relationships.

Researchers have teased out other principles of the exchange process. Their results help explain, for example, why two people participating in a romantic relationship may not be equally satisfied with the sum of their exchanges (Emerson, 1976; Molm, 1990, 1991). Take a case in which the male controls many more rewards or punishments than she does. She has less to offer and is at a disadvantage, especially in light of the fact that power-advantaged individuals expect greater rewards from their exchanges. If she highly values the resources he can offer (such as prestige on campus), and if she has few alternative sources of those resources, her dependence gives him greater power in the relationship. Moreover, if he controls punishments (such as humiliation), he has even more power, since people generally find it more important to avoid punishment than to seek rewards. Thus rocky relationships can sometimes be explained in terms of unbalanced exchanges.

Cooperation: a form of exchange in which people combine their efforts toward a common goal.

Cooperation   Exchange often takes the form of **cooperation,** in which people combine their efforts toward a common goal. At the classroom level, study groups and group projects serve as examples. In fact, research suggests that reward structures which encourage cooperation produce greater group performance than does competition (Niehoff and Mesch, 1990). Widening our perspective, we can see cooperation linking virtually all elements of the campus. Except possibly for some revolutionary group plotting to destroy the college, all of the organization's parts—the committees, bureaucratic machinery, clubs, and staff—ultimately contribute to the maintenance of the college.

Because so many goals are shared in society, the pervasiveness of cooperation should not be surprising. From the efficient hunting tactics of the wolf pack to the pooled efforts of hunters and gatherers, cooperation clearly shows its importance. Similarly, communist societies strongly promote this process as the most acceptable, proper means of achieving society's goals. And we need not look too far beneath the value of rugged individualism in our own society to find the vast web of cooperation among political factions, economic players, family members, and others. That web holds society together.

Competition: regulated struggle for limited rewards.

Competition   Cooperation makes no sense when rewards are limited, when the prize cannot be shared, or when not everyone can win. In such circumstances, **competition** arises—as, for example, when students struggle with one another for grades

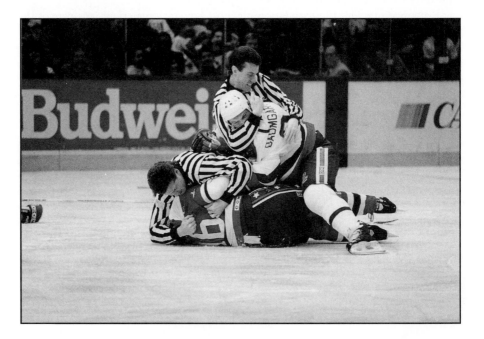

A framework of rules serves to limit the efforts of competitors; otherwise their struggle may quickly become conflict, which is aimed not simply at victory but at harming the others.

(unless all students can win an A). Similarly, as roommates aim for the same scholarship or job, the same track-and-field prize, or the same date, competition displaces their usual cooperation.

In such competitive situations, the struggle is limited in several ways so that the roommates' relationship may endure after all. First, a framework of rules contains the struggle; certain tactics are not allowed, and damage to competitors is minimized. Second, even in the heat of fierce competition the adversaries focus not on destroying or even harming one another but on the struggle itself, and on improving one's own chances. The loser thus survives intact to try again in future competitions. Third, even competitors sometimes find they need one another's help. The roommates may need to pool their resources to afford athletic training equipment, a computer, or transportation. Such mutual aid even in the face of competition helps moderate the hostility.

We have all heard competition characterized as "healthy." Certainly it can push the participants to higher levels of achievement. But such interaction can also spill beyond the limits of pure competition and become conflict.

Conflict   If competitors focus not on the struggle itself but on neutralizing or destroying one another, their interaction has become **conflict.** Conflict arises not only from especially fierce competition for the same prize (as when victory or success is achieved only at the expense of the other) but from clashing values or beliefs, or from real or imagined wrongs (Williams, 1970). Once conflict sets in, each roommate may try to destroy the other's reputation, deplete his or her resources, or otherwise diminish his or her ability to succeed. Unlike competition, conflict is not limited by a clear set of rules, so much damage can be done. In the aftermath, resentment will likely fester, possibly leading to revenge.

On a broader scope, conflict can occur when one group in society comes to believe that the existing rules are not fair, or that the social order is oppressive and must be restructured or destroyed. Here the positive consequences of conflict become apparent: Members of the group are drawn together and society's attention is focused on wrongs that must be addressed. For example, the destructive ghetto riots in Los Angeles in 1992 prompted calls for urban renewal funding. Indeed, Marxists contend that only conflict will purge societies of injustice and inequality.

> **Conflict:** interaction aimed at destroying or neutralizing opponents.

| Research Box |

What Messages Do Touch, Nearness, and Posture Convey?

Reseachers have discovered that some regularly used nonverbal behaviors comprise a shared vocabulary much the same way that words do. For example, we can rely on nonverbal cues to tell us how closely affiliated two people are and whether one dominates the other. Judee Burgoon (1991) of the University of Arizona wanted to discover if different kinds of touch, conversational distance, and posture convey widely recognized meanings.

Based on her review of previous studies, Burgoon decided to extend this line of research in three ways. First, she used a large representative sample in her field experiments, unlike most previous research based on small laboratory samples. Second, Burgoon explored multiple levels of the behaviors: Rather than simply study subjects who were, for example, either touching or not, she studied various kinds of touch. And third, she considered how variables such as gender, physical attractiveness, and status inequality might influence the interpretation of those behaviors.

Because of the complexity of the variables, Burgoon used "the conservative approach . . . of posing research questions rather than advancing hypotheses" (p. 238). Her questions were: (1) What do touch, proximity, and posture say about how people are related to one another? (2) Do different forms or degrees of those three behaviors convey different messages? and (3) How do gender, status, and attractiveness affect interpretation of the messages?

Burgoon used a large sample of 622 adolescents and adults. Nearly half of these subjects were found in a jury roll-call waiting room (a fairly representative sample of registered voters and licensed drivers). The others came from random searches of apartment complexes, motels, malls, and other public places. Burgoon used a common source for her research assistants: students in her classes.

These assistants asked the subjects "to participate in a brief first impressions survey." Each participant was shown one randomly selected photograph of two conversants touching or using distance or posture to various degrees. The participant then indicated on a questionnaire his or her interpretation of the degree of trust, affection, dominance, intimacy, and so on displayed in the behaviors in the photograph.

Analyses of the data revealed surprisingly intricate interpretations of such mundane behaviors as handholding, postural relaxation, and conversational nearness. For example, the handshake conveys trust and receptivity as well as formality, and postural openness (arm and trunk relaxation) conveys intimacy and informality. But attractiveness and status influence how such behaviors are interpreted. For instance, being touched on the face by an attractive person of the opposite sex is interpreted as conveying a high degree of affection. Placing one's arm around the waist of another person of the same sex is seen as an *un*affectionate gesture.

Burgoon's work shows, first, that as social scientists dig more deeply into social reality, they usually find greater complexity rather than simple answers. Second, just as words have nuances and varying meanings depending on the social context, nonverbal messages are not subject to easy interpretation. Such subtleties provide an inexhaustibly rich subject for sociologists to explore. ☐

BOUNDARIES AND DYNAMICS IN THE CLASSROOM

Sociologists remind us that our immediate social surroundings help determine how we act. Our behaviors vary, for example, according to whether we find ourselves in a raging lynch mob, amid raucous soccer fans, or at a somber funeral. When we enter a classroom, we will probably experience the kinds of social boundaries and internal dynamics that characterize what sociologists call a **group:** two or more people who interact recurrently within a structured situation, who share a common purpose or goal and a consciousness of membership.

Group: two or more people who interact recurrently within a structured situation, who share a common purpose or goal and a consciousness of membership.

Is the Classroom a Group Setting?

If we can determine that the typical classroom gathering is indeed a group, we can better anticipate the special influences at work on us. Among those influences are several benefits not found in nongroup settings.

First, a group interacts recurrently, or more than once. Certainly, this applies to the members of the class. Unlike some other groups, which may last for decades, the class comes to an end after final exam week. Still, it exists beyond just one meeting and thus provides opportunities to develop some degree of intimacy with others. The class also differs from other groups' meetings, such as family gatherings, by virtue of its regularly scheduled meetings, each one subject to time limitations. In contrast, a family group may be so widely scattered when the children are grown that they meet only sporadically, perhaps only at holidays or during crises. In any event, during the semester the classroom gathering offers the continuity of a group.

Second, a group has structure; it involves rules, patterns, or behavioral expectations. The typical college classroom displays structure in several ways. The roles of teacher and student are fairly clear, especially after the first few classes. The routine of roll taking, lecture/discussion, and so on quickly becomes established. Students often stake out their own seats. The structure of the classroom affords us the security of knowing what to expect from others and what will be expected of us. We can relax in the assurance that the teacher's powers and demands are limited, as are those of classmates.

Third, group members hold a goal or purpose in common. The members of the college classroom all aim for college credit, perhaps even the same degree. Whatever other goals the members have, they are held together as a group by at least one common aim.

Last, group members enjoy a "we feeling," a consciousness of membership. While some members are more strongly affiliated to a group than others (Granovetter, 1973; Freeman, 1990), they all know who doesn't belong, and are bound together as insiders. Most college classes, if they are not too large, eventually develop this feeling of membership, of boundary, though it is not as strong as in more intimate groups. Still, they share an identity and come to refer to "our class."

Looking at the college class as a group, then, reveals the continuity, structure, commonality, and "we feeling" enjoyed by its members. But, as we will now see, within this context are other groupings that complicate the sociological picture.

What Kinds of Groups Are Most Appropriate in the Classroom?

Most college classes serve as means of transmitting information and skills, and stimulating thought. For such business, *instrumental ties* are most appropriate: Members of a group see the others as ends to means, not to be appreciated for themselves but for what they contribute to the group. Such relationships characterize what Charles H. Cooley (1909) called **secondary groups:** those based on impersonal, goal-oriented relationships. In a class functioning as a secondary group, intimacy and concern for others' needs do not interfere with the business at hand.

Some classes, however, focus on developing *expressive ties*, which are accepting and person-centered. A speech professor, for instance, would probably seek to move

Secondary group: a group based on impersonal, goal-oriented, instrumental relationships.

Primary group: a group based on expressive ties; it tends to be small, cooperative, intimate, and person-centered.

her or his classes toward the "expressive" end of the spectrum of human interaction. Expressive ties figure strongly in Cooley's model of **primary groups,** which describes relatively small, intimate, cooperative groups based on face-to-face interaction. The size and competitiveness of many college classes make this task difficult, but to the extent that such professors succeed, the students reap the emotional benefits of primary groups.

Groups based on primary relationships have irresistible appeal. Our hunger for such relationships helps to hold even poorly functioning families together and leads some of us desperately into marriage. Classrooms that evolve toward the "primary" end of the spectrum have special attraction beyond the "get things done" attitude of those nearer the "secondary" end. What underlies the great appeal of primary relationships?

First, primary groups treat their members as unique individuals, responding to their entire persons in a spontaneous, accepting way—just the thing for a speech class. The members focus less on roles and more on the individuals themselves. In such a class, then, the students may come to enjoy the professor more as an interesting person than simply as someone filling the role of professor. And the feeling may be mutual.

Second, communication within primary groups is deep and extensive. An extreme example of such communication is found in a healthy marriage, in which the partners reveal their innermost feelings using informal language and touch. This requires face-to-face contact. The more intimate the relationship, the broader the range of topics members can deal with. If the speech class develops in this direction, "frontstage behavior" and impression management becomes less important.

Third, primary relationships offer group members greater emotional satisfaction. We see the others as enjoyable unto themselves rather than simply people working toward the same goals and fulfilling their roles. This satisfaction and acceptance are the rewards we seek in marriage and other intimate relationships; to experience them in a classroom setting would be an unexpected bonanza.

Expressive ties, which show acceptance and high valuation of the other person, lie at the foundation of primary groups.

Would primary relationships, however, hinder the business of the typical college classroom? For one thing, such interaction may complicate the setting's contractual obligations. The grading of students is supposed to be decidedly impartial and impersonal, reflecting what Talcott Parsons (1951) referred to as "universalism." Also, Parsons noted that secondary or instrumental settings exhibit highly specific and sharply limited exchanges. This fits the classroom, where students should receive grades based only on their work, not their endearing personal characteristics. Likewise, students owe nothing to the professor beyond the fulfillment of the course requirements.

While most college classrooms function as secondary groups, primary groups may form within such settings. Students may draw together due to their shared values, ethnicity, or hostility toward the professor. Similarly, workers in impersonal bureaucratic settings may form loyalties to one another, as we shall see later in this chapter. The rewards of such relationships appeal to us so strongly that we nurture them wherever they arise.

Another type of group boundary may intervene in the classroom, one that separates "we" from "others." **In-groups** are those we feel part of; we have a sense of membership, and believe that the other members share some of our experiences, values, and interests. They look, dress, and live like us. We can relax with such people and accord them decent treatment. If we include classmates in our in-group, classroom interactions will likely be harmonious. However, when we feel a differentness, a sense of "otherness"—what sociologists call **social distance**—we perceive an **out-group,** consisting of people with whom we do not identify or feel a sense of oneness. Social distance throws up a wall that impedes our interaction with those we perceive as the out-group. The wall may be based on social class, race, ethnicity, gender, or other factors. On a typical college campus, for example, blacks and whites sit at separate lunch tables, their infrequent interaction characterized by an uncomfortable sense of social distance or otherness. Likewise, plenty of graffiti defines homosexuals as an out-group, showing the wall that separates "straights" and "gays."

In-group: those people with whom we identify and have a sense of oneness.

Social distance: the degree to which we feel a differentness or sense of otherness.

Out-group: those people with whom we do not identify or feel part of.

The Classroom as Networking

A sociological eye catches a vast web of lines running across the classroom's social boundary. Each line connects a student in the class with someone outside. Entering into the class group extends the reach of each student's **social network,** the web of social relationships that link individuals or groups directly or indirectly to others. Such linkages may be based on affection, hostility, exchanges of information or resources, or business.

Figure 3-2 offers some appreciation of the nearly incomprehensible complexity of even one person's social network. Imagine the ties to people in other classes through acquaintances just made in a new class, added to links spreading from other classes, clubs, roommates, kin, and so on, and we see that each new social contact opens the individual to far-reaching new linkages. A new class thus establishes another social field in each student's network that, depending on one's age and energies, may include thousands of people.

Social networks represent important social resources. "Dense" networks, those that include a high proportion of close acquaintances, provide a sense of community and protection from the repercussions of loneliness. Before turning to formal agencies, we usually tap into our social networks when looking for a job, seeking advice on financial and interpersonal matters, or choosing a dentist or lawyer. (See Figure 3-3.)

Social network: the web of social relationships that link us directly or indirectly to other people and groups.

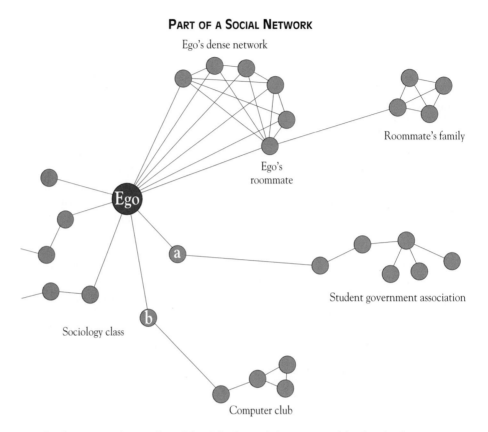

PART OF A SOCIAL NETWORK

Figure 3-2

This diagram represents a portion of the web of acquaintances, or social network, of one person ("ego"). Note how relationships made in the sociology classroom expand ego's direct and indirect ties. Every new group membership broadens a person's range of acquaintances substantially, far beyond the dense network in which the members know one another quite well. Ego's tie with "a" in the sociology class establishes relationships with people in the student government association. Similarly, "b" introduces ego to the computer club. And ego's roommate links ego to the roommate's family.

Just as networks enmesh individuals they link groups, even nations. A sorority or fraternity has ties with others in its national organization. By establishing relations with one Arab country, the United States enters into an international network of nations that, in turn, are connected to others, and so on.

The Class Project: A Study in Group Dynamics

Imagine our professor requiring her class to jointly participate in a project, perhaps running a survey or competing with another class. Such an assignment sets the stage for a study of group dynamics.

Why Contribute?   Some students will immediately raise questions common to all group projects: "What about freeloaders?" and "What will I get out of my work?" First, each student will wonder whether classmates will benefit from others' work without

SOCIOGRAM

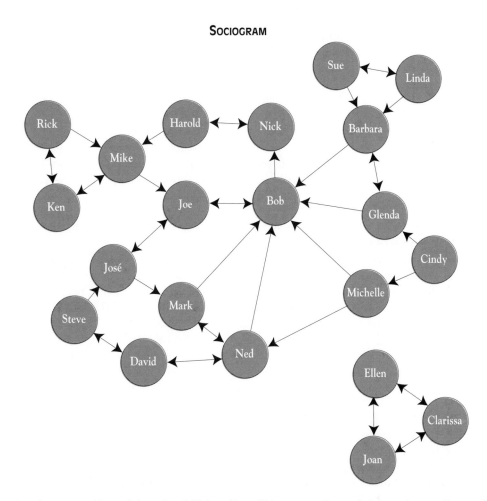

A *sociogram* provides a picture of social interaction within a group. To construct a sociogram, the researcher asks members of the group to choose other members according to some given criterion, such as "With whom would you most like to spend time?" or "Whom do you most admire?" Those choices are then shown symbolically in the sociogram, which can reveal patterns of influence and leadership as well as isolation. In the sociogram above, Bob's central influence becomes obvious, as does the "power behind the throne," Joe, who is chosen by Bob as well as by others. The diagram also reveals Cindy's isolation (she is chosen by no one) and the social segregation of the small group of girls (Ellen, Clarissa, and Joan). Sociograms offer assistance to people wishing to improve or otherwise manipulate the social interaction of groups, as in the case of teachers and supervisors.

Figure 3-3

contributing: the "free rider problem." Second, students may not benefit in proportion to what they do contribute: the "efficacy problem." Indeed, when contributions are pooled, a hard worker will derive a small proportion of the rewards.

Any successful collective action must overcome these two problems. This is difficult when the costs of the group project increase with the number of people who will enjoy the benefits. For instance, according to *rational choice theory* (Olson, 1965), we should expect the few well-to-do members of a congregation to express reluctance to shoulder most of the financial burden for a new church, especially when the sizable number of noncontributing members requires a large building. Similarly, many students who make large contributions to a class project might feel exploited if the work requirements depend on the size of the class. In such situations, "individually rational behavior leads to collective irrationality or poor systems functioning" (Petersen, 1992, p. 470). In other words, the project may founder without skillful management by the professor.

According to *critical mass theory,* such problems are usually avoided when, as is usual in class projects, the costs do not increase with the amount of people who enjoy the results (Oliver and Marwell, 1988). In such circumstances, a small number of the participants—a "critical mass"—make relatively large contributions and get things done. They do not worry about free riders so long as the number of noncontributors does not "cost" the workers anything extra. Thus, once this critical mass is reached, the class project will reach completion as long as the free riders do not add to the work required. Of course, in reality each classroom is complicated by punishments and rewards offered by the professor and by the normative cues generated by classmates (Macy, 1990).

Many students may argue, however, that the free rider problem often plagues class projects. Indeed, researchers have discovered that, contrary to popular beliefs about the heightened motivation wrought by "team spirit" and group morale, people tend to reduce their effort when working in groups, especially large groups. They call this phenomenon "social loafing" (Latane, Williams, and Harkins, 1979). In such settings, each individual tends to work less than she or he would alone. Providing some benchmark for evaluating the group's performance diminishes social loafing (Harkins and Szymanski, 1989). Otherwise, the larger the class size, the less we can expect each student to participate.

Group Size   In assigning a class project, the professor may be trying to foster classroom cohesiveness by making the students work as a unit. The internal dynamics of such task groups do encourage solidarity and the expression of positive emotions (Ridgeway and Johnson, 1990). However, the larger the group the less the cohesion, and overall the quality of the classroom interaction will probably suffer if smaller groupings are not used.

Georg Simmel (1950) identified size as the single most important factor in group interaction. He found that the larger the group, the less intense the interaction. One reason involves the simple lessening of interaction with any other member. The greater the number of other students, the less time available for interacting with each one. Also, dependency relationships become less apparent in large groups. If one student drops out of the class or refuses to participate, the rest of the two dozen or so will pay little notice. In a large group, each student feels—and is—less important to the others. Furthermore, the larger the group the more formal the interaction, and formality hinders intimacy and spontaneity. These reasons help explain why we normally use smaller groups (two or three) for casual work and play (Hare, 1981).

If the professor's intention is to foster more satisfying, primary ties among the students in the class, the sociological literature points clearly to the best tool: the two-person group or *dyad.* Simmel noted that in pairs, simple two-way communication promotes intimacy. At the same time, couples are held together by more fragile, emotional ties: If one member leaves, the group is destroyed. But adding a third member significantly dilutes the intensity of the former pair, as illustrated by an infant's invasion of a married couple's intimacy. In such three-person groups, two members often form a close bond while isolating the third one to some extent, lending some credence to the saying, "Two's company, three's a crowd." Business partnerships, roommates,

While dyads can be intimate, the ties binding the two people can also be fragile and emotional; after all, if one partner leaves, the group disintegrates.

and class subgroups tend to follow the same rule. The professor must consider such rules when attempting to manipulate the interaction in class.

Members of large groups may enjoy their interaction less, but does the task group's effectiveness increase with its size? Research shows that the picture is complicated by several variables, especially the nature of the task. If the task—conducting a survey, for example—is such that every new member's contribution moves the group closer to success, size obviously correlates with group performance. But if the group, say, must solve a puzzle, its size at some point becomes large enough to offer reasonable potential for success, and adding new members contributes virtually nothing more to that potential (Steiner, 1972; Littlepage, 1991). Up to a point, then, group size contributes to effectiveness for certain tasks.

Conformity   If the college class is like other groups, its members will feel pressure to conform to the expectations of their peers. A classic experiment by Solomon Asch (1955) illustrates this point. Asch assembled groups of seven to nine male college students, all but one of whom were told the true nature of the study. The other subject was told that the study dealt with visual judgment—an example of the deception sometimes used in social science research. Each group was shown several pairs of cards. On one card of each pair was a single line. Each student was asked to identify which of three lines on the second card matched the length of the one on the first card. At a predetermined point, the conspirators all chose an obviously wrong answer. More than half the time about one-third of the subjects gave the same wrong answer, thereby yielding to the pressure created by the conspirators' united front. The remarkable lesson from the Asch experiment is that the pressures that affected most of the students came not from a primary group, but simply a collection of strangers. We can wonder how strong pressures must be in a typical college class.

We might also wonder if *groupthink* could arise in the class. Irving Janis (1972) noted that in highly cohesive groups, pressures toward uniformity push the members toward unanimous decisions. These pressures discourage members from thinking critically or questioning the group's line of thought. Rather than searching for the best answer, the group instead aims for agreement. This process can produce disastrous decisions in the corporate boardroom. In fact, Janis described how groupthink in the Oval Office contributed to the failed 1961 Bay of Pigs invasion by U.S.-backed Cuban exiles. Such pressures also explain the silly or poorly founded ideas sometimes produced in class projects and illustrate some of the hidden dynamics underlying group interaction.

Leadership   Sociological principles regarding leadership also come into play as the class works on its project either as one unit or as subgroups. Robert F. Bales (1953) and Philip E. Slater (1955) pointed out long ago that every group needs leadership to satisfy two basic needs: direction and harmony. Instrumental leaders, on the one hand, are directive, persuading the members to stay on task to achieve the group's goals. On the other, expressive or supportive leaders are likeable (Thomas and Tartell, 1991) and focus on the group's general well-being. One style usually eventually overshadows the other, though some leaders can meet both needs.

An instrumental leader who takes charge of a classroom subgroup has several approaches from which to choose. Authoritarian leaders are most effective in emergencies and when they have either very high or very low control (Fiedler, 1967). They tell the group what to do, somewhat like a dictator. Such directive leadership behavior increases with group size (Mullen et al., 1989). Laissez-faire leaders provide little organization or direction, and therefore little help, to task groups. Democratic leaders use persuasion to help the group decide the issue and develop a consensus. This type of leadership generally works best with U. S. groups, probably due to our overall ideological preference, and would be a good strategy for an American college group provided the group's expressive needs are met.

Gender makes a difference in leadership approaches. Women who occupy leadership positions in organizations (unlike those used in laboratory studies of leadership) generally do not use cooperative, supportive styles more than men, but do tend to lead democratically. Men, in contrast, tend to use the autocratic, directive style (Eagly and Johnson, 1990).

Leadership is not simply a matter of gender or personality, but one of putting leadership principles to work. For example, Robert Blake and Jane S. Mouton (1982) identified several aspects of effective leadership that presumably nearly anyone could employ: candor, trust and respect, conflict resolution, consensus, and mutual support. Similarly, Linda Smircich and Gareth Morgan (1982) suggest that leadership success depends partly on controlling the members' definitions of the situation to coincide with the leader's intepretation. Such consensus becomes a firm basis for group action.

If the professor does not choose them, which students are likely to emerge from the classroom groups as leaders? Individuals do not move up in a group's status hierarchy simply by overpowering others; such dominance behavior may be criticized by other members (Ridgeway and Diekema, 1989). Instead, the ambitious would-be leader must capitalize on status characteristics such as physical attractiveness, gender, and educational level. Another requirement is to impress the other group members with his or her apparent influence and ability to get things done for the group. According to *expectation states theory*, the trick is to raise others' expectations of one's performance (Ridgeway, 1987; Balkwell, 1991). Tactics include effective use of voice tone and volume, eye gaze, interrupting, and getting one's ideas accepted by the others (Ridgeway and Berger, 1986; Smith-Lovin and Brody, 1989). In addition, one's position in the group's seating arrangements can help empower an individual: the more central and visible, the better (Bavelas, 1953). Such tactics can serve as leadership skills.

LIVING WITH BUREAUCRACIES—ON CAMPUS AND BEYOND

Formal organization: a social structure purposefully established to efficiently accomplish a specific, large-scale task.

What do Americans do when they face a shared problem? They form a committee. For large problems, they form entire organizations. When we require the coordination of many people's efforts to get something done, we create **formal organizations,** social structures purposefully established to efficiently accomplish a specific, large-scale task. Such organizations abound in any college, from the alumni association to the student government to the faculty union. In fact, the college itself is a formal organization, established for the purpose of teaching and research. Beyond the campus, examples include General Motors, parent-teacher organizations, the Salvation Army, the U. S. Handball Association, and the National Muzzle Loading Rifle Association—all dedicated to meeting some shared need or accomplishing some goal.

The environment of a formal organization imposes certain demands on its members, though naturally the extent of the demands varies with the organization's goals, size, and so on. A student religious organization, for example, may require considerably more emotional commitment and behavioral conformity than a student government organization. Also, the larger the organization, the more structure it usually has. There are more rules and formal procedures at meetings of the faculty union than at get-togethers of the computer club. And virtually all organizations on campus are **voluntary associations,** in which membership is optional and not remunerative. Because the members are not forced or paid to meet, but do so simply out of mutual interest, interaction within voluntary associations tends to lack the tension and power struggles inherent in **coercive organizations** like elementary schools and prisons, where membership is not a matter of personal choice.

Like many sociologists, we will focus on a particular type of formal organization based on hierarchy, division of labor, and rules: the **bureaucracy.** The very word has come to be identified with frustrating, uncaring, impersonal, and inefficient social settings. Still, bureaucracies enable us to accomplish very large-scale tasks, like operating a large university, in a fairly rational and effective way. And whether we appreciate them or not, we cannot easily avoid them. Anyone pursuing higher education must adapt to the bureaucracy's foibles, and most careers are firmly embedded within highly bureaucratic structures. This section offers a survivor's guide, a demystifying look at the internal workings of the bureaucracy.

Voluntary association: an organization in which membership is optional and not remunerative.

Coercive organization: an organization in which membership is not a matter of personal choice.

Bureaucracy: a type of formal organization based on hierarchy, division of labor, and rules.

Anticipating the Bureaucracy: Weber's Model

Whether dealing with the registrar's office to change our schedule or plotting a strategy to get promoted at work, it helps if we know something about the workings of bureaucracies. Max Weber provided an inside look at the "ideal type" of such an organization. His model denotes the essentials of the pure bureaucratic form, which rarely if ever exists in reality. Like other scientific models, however, it enables us to anticipate reality. So, although the model cannot describe the mechanisms of any particular bureaucracy, it can tell us what to expect in, say, a *typical* college.

Division of Labor   To make a bureaucracy, as Weber described it, "superior to any other form in precision, in stability . . . and in its reliability" (1947, p. 337), each worker is assigned a clearly defined and strictly limited part to play in its overall workings. To play that part the worker must possess specialized skills, but those skills are so limited in scope that most individuals can acquire them in a reasonably short time. The aim of this specialization is to maximize efficiency, minimize training and talent requirements, and ensure the competence of all workers. It also makes the low-level bureaucratic worker easy to replace; after all, nearly anyone can acquire the necessary skills. This begins to explain why "bureaucrat" is rarely used as a compliment.

Hierarchy   In a bureaucracy, every worker knows his or her place. Workers at the college, for example, know to whom they report and who reports to them. The hierarchy allots power from the top of the chain of command to the bottom, and this power resides in each office, not the person holding the office. Thus, if the office of assistant dean empowers that person to dictate workloads to the faculty, they must obey, regardless of whether they feel respect or contempt for the person in that office.

Rules   Before the rise of bureaucratic organizations in the Middle Ages, the authority of officials was based on tradition and force of personality. The ruler did what he or she pleased. In today's bureaucracy, at least according to Weber's model, written rules rather than feelings and friendships determine what kind of treatment a worker can expect from the organization. Indeed, impersonality and rationality pervade the model. The rules also limit the ways each worker can distribute the resources of his or her office. For example, they remind the professor to distinguish between her private possessions and those of the bureaucracy, that her office and its property and resources belong to the organization. Also, written guidelines help standardize tasks and work. Thus, while the rules hold each worker to an explicitly stated standard and restrict his or her powers, they also protect that worker from biased treatment.

Hiring Based on Technical Merit   According to Weber's ideal type, workers are hired and promoted according to their technical qualifications, often measured in varying degrees of accuracy by written examinations. We can presume, then, that workers at the college have proved their merit through test scores or other credentials. Likewise, colleges require that most faculty members (professionals in the bureaucratic environment) possess master's or doctoral degrees. Furthermore, people cannot hope to move up in the organization's hierarchy unless they acquire the necessary badges of merit. Thus the clerical aid in the dean's office may need to complete an Associate of Arts degree before reaching the position of administrative assistant. In Weber's model, one's employment and promotion chances in a bureaucracy depend not on *whom* one knows but *what* one knows.

The principles outlined above define the rational, impersonal organizations that arose in response to large-scale production. We need go no farther than the nearest college, however, to find many deviations from Weber's model. Indeed, as we will now see, the model offers only a dim outline of today's formal organization.

Beyond the Model: Other Bureaucratic Realities

For at least two reasons, Weber's model does not fully equip us to deal with bureaucracies. One is the shadow organization existing beyond the hierarchical chart hanging on the boardroom wall. The other is the simple fact that humans' best-laid plans do not always develop as hoped.

Informal Organization   Ask any worker on campus to describe how things get done in his or her department and you may hear precious little about such niceties as rules, rigid hierarchy, and strict specialization. Instead, workers learn to bypass certain individuals in the chain of command as perceived hindrances. They learn of established short-cuts around the infamous "red tape" of bureaucratic rules.

From the interactionist perspective, this organizational culture, this agreed-upon way of getting things done among the workers, is in fact the bureaucracy's reality. This reality changes continuously as workers negotiate new understandings about how much work will be done in their department, how, and by whom. Workers who violate these understandings are considered "rate busters" or "boat rockers."

These unofficial counterparts to the formal bureaucratic plan arise for several reasons. First, the official plan cannot cover every detail in the day-to-day needs of the organization. Thus informal networks develop to rechannel the flow of information and power when the formal chain of command proves too rigid, slow, or unresponsive.

Informal organization within the impersonal bureaucratic setting can provide primary relationships as well as effective networks for working around inadequate rules.

Hampering rules are likewise ignored or loosely interpreted if the organization is to function well. Second, workers can benefit personally from this informal organization. They can use informal contacts to exchange favors or resources captured from the organization (Fung, 1991). They can add a "human touch" to their work environment, a sense of control, and perhaps even primary relationships. Thus the organizational culture accommodates personal sentiments and needs. In doing so it prevents worker alienation, which can occur so easily in environments based on hierarchy, rigid specialization, and impersonal rules. At the same time, it can promote the cohesion and loyalty critical to smooth social functioning.

Sociologists have searched for the keys to such informal liaisons. One seems to be face-to-face communication, which, as we saw earlier in the chapter, plays an important role in our relationships. Lawrence G. Zahn (1991) suggests that such face-to-face communication in an office environment is more likely among people close to one another in the chain of command, of similar status, and whose offices are physically close. Similarly, people in bureaucratic settings tend to ignore or violate rules even to the point of sabotage when faced with pressure from their fellow members to do so, especially if those co-workers function in close physical proximity (Foster, 1990).

Dysfunctions   The second reason Weber's model of bureaucracies is incomplete is that it views them as rational, machine-like organizations—and of course human behavior is riddled with irrational, quirky aspects. In other words, if we look into any department on campus we will probably spot several dysfunctional features not part of the model.

For instance, a clerk behind the registration desk insists that a student follow procedure and acquire an authorizing signature that is actually unnecessary. Robert K. Merton (1940) calls this **ritualism:** rigid conformity to the bureaucracy's rules to the point of forgetting or ignoring the organization's goals. To be fair, the organization's relentless demand for reliable performance calls for methodical adherence to the rules. However, over time the rules can for some workers develop symbolic significance

Ritualism: rigid conformity to an organization's rules to the point of forgetting or ignoring the organization's goals.

When bureaucrats rigidly conform to the rules, the organization's goals can be forgotten, and its clients are not well served.

beyond their original aim. Hence we can find in many departments a worker like that clerk who so unthinkingly conforms to written procedures that he or she loses sight of the department's actual goals, such as helping students with the registration process. The procedural routine, supposedly a means to an end, becomes the end itself.

Ritualism has several causes. According to Victor Thompson (1961), the personally insecure bureaucrat uses extreme conformity to rules to avoid criticism from a threatening boss or to reduce the pressure to make his or her own decisions. Thompson notes that such "organizational pathology" also occurs when workers must make important decisions without objective standards, or when bureaucrats are responsible for decisions for which they have little technical competence. Anthony Downs (1966) adds to the portrait of ritualistic bureaucrats: workers lacking alternatives to their present position who desperately cling to procedures as a means of protecting their job. Unlike professionals who are not trained by the organization or use it to measure their success, "organization men" (or women) cannot easily leave the company for another job with similar status. They depend on the organization to define their personal status and success. Each worker has much invested in its procedural integrity and thus internalizes the rules, earning a reputation as a "real stickler" on company policy. Moreover, organized labor can use ritualism purposefully to slow down production and extract concessions from management.

Michael Crozier (1964) offers still another view of rigid conformity to bureaucratic rules. Each group within a bureaucracy, he argues, sometimes uses rigidity as a tool for protecting its territory and minimizing informal dependence on others. The college bureaucracy could thus be seen as a seething cauldron of infighting and power struggles among various academic departments. By sticking strictly to the rules, each department more firmly controls its own domain.

Ritualism often accompanies what the acerbic social observer Thorstein Veblen (1922) calls **trained incapacity:** an excessive reliance on established procedure that

Trained incapacity: excessive reliance on established procedure to the point that adaptability is impaired.

renders the worker unable to respond effectively to unanticipated demands. In view of today's requirements for creativity and swift adaptability, this incapacity presents an especially dangerous dysfunction in the corporate world. We can likewise envision a college professor who continues to use the same teaching procedures and textbook even when confronted with entirely new student needs.

Northcote C. Parkinson (1957) offers another point of departure from Weber's picture of the efficient organization. **Parkinson's Law,** that "work expands so as to fill the time available for its completion," helps explain the bureaucracy's tendency to grow. Each bureaucrat's importance—and salary—depends on how many tasks, assistants, and funds are in his or her domain. Thus the official will take on more tasks (or create tasks, no matter how unnecessary) to justify an ever larger staff. As work expands, of course, the bureaucrat relentlessly demands more funding and subordinates. As other departments do the same, the organization burgeons. This process added layers of bureaucratic fat to many U. S. corporations, prompting the "downsizing" of the late 1980s and 1990s that eliminated thousands of mid- and upper-level positions.

> **Parkinson's Law:** in a bureaucracy, workers will use all available time to complete a given task.

Another bureaucratic dysfunction involves not just unnecessary workers but incompetent ones. Merit examinations and other screening devices cannot guarantee that only qualified people are hired. Once admitted, the incompetent worker can often find a quiet corner in the organization and dig in. As we saw earlier, punctilious adherence to the rules can protect the worker, and he or she may forever escape notice. Moreover, the organization often consciously ignores such workers to avoid embarrassing publicity. The duties of an incompetent, tenured professor, for example, will be covered by other faculty members as much as possible, and advisors will quietly steer students away from that professor's classes. The organization compensates, and everyone hopes the incompetent worker will remain hidden or simply go away.

One way of getting incompetent workers out of the way is to shift them into positions where they can do little damage. Moved horizontally into a slot of equal position, they may find some task within their abilities. The other ploy is to "promote" the workers to "honorary" or do-nothing jobs. Sometimes these promotions are well-earned, awarded according to the organization's merit criteria, but are still counterproductive. Though not based on rigorous scientific data, this strategy, known as the **Peter Principle,** rings true: "In every hierarchy every employee tends to rise to his level of incompetence" (Peter and Hull, 1969). Thus a professor who shines in the classroom may be rewarded with promotions until she or he eventually becomes a mediocre administrator.

> **Peter Principle:** in a bureaucracy, workers tend to rise to their level of incompetence.

Some sociologists point to a dangerous flaw of bureaucracies: the tendency toward nondemocratic authority structures. Robert Michels (1915) noted long ago the inevitable slide of bureaucracy to **oligarchy,** or rule by the few. As these organizations gain more influence in our society, we may become desensitized to the concentration of so much power in the hands of a few people at the top of the hierarchy, not only in business but in our social institutions as well. Another danger is the formation of a small ruling elite comprised of those who control our largest corporations and government bureaucracies (a possibility discussed in a later chapter).

> **Oligarchy:** rule by the few.

According to Michels's "iron law of oligarchy," a college, for example, will unavoidably become oligarchic. To begin with, the organization's large size requires a bureaucracy to register, instruct, evaluate, and keep track of thousands of students. As flawed as they are, only bureaucracies can accomplish such large-scale tasks. Hierarchy is an essential feature of bureaucracy and, naturally, people who rise into the few top positions for the most part possess superior political and persuasive skills. They can skillfully exploit the resources commanded by their high office, including funds, social contacts, and information. Their power also enables them to ensure that political allies are promoted, thus helping to perpetuate the oligarchy's grip on power. Meanwhile, at the other end of the hierarchy, lower-ranking members usually express no concern with this oligarchic development. They rarely have any desire to accept the responsibilities of power themselves and often admire the leaders.

Michels's view has not gone unchallenged. He spoke of the inevitability of this tendency, but competing factions within organizations can prevent such concentrations of power. Groups have successfully challenged the oligarchy in corporations, labor unions, and politics (Lipset, Trow, and Coleman, 1956; Staggenborg, 1988). Besides, for all its flaws the bureaucracy is usually more efficient than any other organizational framework at dealing with social tasks on a huge scale.

Reality Through the Conflict Perspective   Karl Marx raised some criticisms of bureaucracy that still concern conflict theorists. From this view, even the college bureaucracy, with a few administrators at the top controlling their subordinates, can be seen as a reflection of capitalist society's characteristic class domination and hierarchy. The administrative elite wields the bureaucracy as a tool of oppression, a device for efficiently exploiting workers from the faculty down to the clerical assistants. Specialization and hierarchy help to compartmentalize and isolate the workers so as to head off labor unity. Conflict theorists, then, would agree that the bureaucracy offers production efficiency but would ask, Who benefits and who suffers form this efficiency?

Part of the costs born by workers is alienation, as decried by Marx and some contemporary sociologists. These observers claim that in highly specialized, bureaucratic settings, such as the college data processing center or the accounting department, workers lose a sense of control and self-direction, and feel like cogs in a huge, complex machine they do not understand. They feel so removed from the organization's goals that they have little appreciation of the reason for their work or its worth.

Bureaucracy Forever?

After cataloging the bureaucracy's flaws, it is reasonable to wonder if we will ever develop a better way to accomplish large-scale social tasks. Will there evolve some other organizational form?

Several social trends have generated increasing dissatisfaction with the existing bureaucratic form. For one, our growing demand for intimacy and personal freedom and growth is hardly satisfied by the image of a worker as a cog in a machine. For another, professionals working within bureaucracies (such as college professors) do not easily tolerate the red tape frustrations, rule-imposed restrictions, and orders from "superiors" who know little or nothing about the technical details of their work. Highly trained workers demand treatment that does not fit the classic bureaucratic model, and as organizations increasingly depend on their expert knowledge, pressures mount for change. There is also an increasingly vital need in our postindustrial society for adaptability. Today's fast-moving, highly competitive, global marketplace requires an organizational structure with the same characteristics. Along this line, Alvin Toffler (1970) has predicted a trend toward temporary, task-centered specialist teams that form quickly, accomplish their objective, and dissolve or reconfigure for the next job.

In response to such problems, the *collective* has arisen since the 1960s as an antibureaucratic form. Where bureaucracy stresses specialization, the collective encourages workers to participate in a wide range of tasks. Instead of hierarchical authority, the collective aims for democracy, consensus, and shared decision making. It minimizes rules and status distinctions, trying to create a sense of community among workers. Few observers, however, offer much hope that collectives will supplant the bureaucracy. For one thing, this organizational form works only in small-scale settings; large operations like a college require more predictability, reliability, and order. Also, consensus building takes a great deal of time and emotional energy. Because efficiency can suffer without specialization and hierarchy, collectives cannot easily survive in competitive markets; they are usually found only in small, isolated markets not dominated by larger, more efficient organizations.

The amazing success of Japan since its devastation in World War II has made it a model of organizational success for some observers. While most large Japanese corporations have hierarchy rules, and other classic bureaucratic features, they feature other aspects that may point the way to new organizational forms in our own society.

First, Japanese corporations try to offer permanent employment. Entering the company at an early age, workers expect to stay there until retirement. Indeed, they have little reason to leave: Promotions come from within the organization because it fills high-level positions from its own ranks rather than bring in outsiders. Second, though a chain of command exists, management is "bottom up." Workers' circles make suggestions and decisions that the higher-level officials seriously consider, discuss further, and often approve. Each worker, then, participates in decision making via the small work team. Third, the corporation provides a wide array of benefits, including health care, recreation, and sometimes housing. Like a solicitous parent, the company assumes great responsibility for each worker's welfare. In exchange for this nurturing environment and lifetime job security, workers give the company total loyalty and dedication. They identify with the organization and contribute whatever is needed to ensure its success. As a result, the corporation enjoys a committed, dependable, and hard-working workforce. (It should be noted, however, that recent economic difficulties have begun to change this glowing picture.)

Some of these features, especially the demand for worker obedience and emphasis on the group rather than the individual, simply do not mix easily with American culture, but other aspects of the Japanese corporation may well be incorporated into a new bureaucratic form in our society. For example, the concern for worker welfare, as well as respect for workers' suggestions and decisions, will predictably become competitive requirements.

The bureaucracy will probably endure, but in a more "humanized" form. Besides what we have learned from the Japanese, other reforms such as job rotation, paid leave for parenting and study, and a greater sharing of decision-making will gradually gain widespread acceptance insofar as they help organizations accomplish their objectives in the modern world.

COLLECTIVE BEHAVIOR ON CAMPUS: WHAT ARE THE POSSIBILITIES?

In 1972, on an east coast university campus, some of the 35 female workers at a data processing center complained of a strange-smelling gas, experiencing dizziness, vomiting, nausea, and fainting (Stahl and Lebedun, 1974). Officials checked the air in the building and the victims' blood and urine, but found no toxins. Similarly, in April of

1989, 600 students from several public schools assembled in a California auditorium for an annual concert. Symptoms of headache, dizziness, weakness, abdominal pain and nausea soon swept thrugh the gathering. Eventually these complaints enveloped over a third of the participants, and authorities ordered the largest evacuation effort in the city's history, using eight ambulances and several fire department vehicles. Authorities searched for toxic fumes and other possible causes and found nothing, yet 247 students had become ill (Small et al., 1991).

These cases are just two of many (over 40 reported this century alone) instances of one form of **mass hysteria,** a collective, emotional outburst of behavior stemming from fear and stress. In this form, such physical symptoms as described above occur among people who feel trapped in an inflexible, boring, or stressful situation, such as a boarding school or oppressive workplace. One or two cases of physically based illness typically trigger similar symptoms in others, often through social transmission. We can easily imagine such circumstances occurring on a college campus during final exam week.

Other forms of mass hysteria would perhaps be less likely to invade college life. One involves blaming and persecuting people for some threat or disaster. For example, witches, Jews, and doctors were held accountable for the Black Death during the Middle Ages in Europe. Several hundred women were charged with witchcraft in late seventeenth-century Massachusetts. In the "witch hunts" of the early 1950s, Senator Joe McCarthy searched relentlessly for Communist subversives and ruined the careers of many innocent people. Such mass persecutions have provided a way for people to cope with widespread fear.

Another form of mass behavior is the widespread acceptance of unlikely stories. During World War II, for example, a woman reported being sprayed by an unseen intruder with a mysterious gas, causing temporary paralysis and illness. In the next few days, 27 other people reported similar attacks. Despite an intensive search, no prowler was found. A follow-up study found that the victims were mostly poor, lonely women who, largely due to the war, had been unhappy and under a great deal of stress. A newspaper article explaining mass hysteria ended the reports. The most famous example of this type of mass hysteria occurred in the United States in 1938. Several million people in the New York City area heard and accepted as factual the *War of the Worlds* radio drama describing in realistic detail an invasion from Mars. Many listeners had not heard the announcement at the beginning of the broadcast stating that the drama was fictitious. Some of those people hid in cellars or fled the city. Others tearfully said goodbye to their loved ones and prepared for the end as they listened to the radio description of the Martians' advance through nearby towns.

This widespread belief touched off **panic,** irrational, collective flight from some perceived threat. The college campus is not immune to this: A fire alarm sounding during a stressful period could trigger such a panicked response from students, especially if they had reason to believe that not everyone would escape the danger. A perception of limited means of escape heightens the probability of panic. People need not have any contact with one another to panic. The financial panic accompanying the stock market Crash of 1929 serves as an example which, incidentally, surely involved college students across the country.

Both panic and mass hysteria are types of **mass behavior,** wherein people who have little or no actual contact with one another react to the same stimulus, though in individual ways. Those affected may be scattered over a large geographical area and, even if they are aware of the others' actions, need not know their names. Though they react as individuals, the members respond to the same event or information. Students on campus, for example, react—often in different ways—to some national political

Mass hysteria: a form of collective behavior involving persecutions, widespread acceptance of unlikely stories, or symptoms of physical illness, usually stemming from fear and stress.

Panic: irrational, collective flight from some perceived threat.

Mass behavior: reaction by people with little or no actual contact to the same stimulus, though in individual ways.

event affecting thousands of other students. Or, watching the Olympics on television, some will cheer a victory that viewers in other parts of the world will bemoan.

Clearly, we have moved from the relatively predictable, mundane interaction found in groups and organizations to the sometimes frenzied, irrational behaviors of people who find themselves outside the bounds of everyday social restraints. Without norms, rules, and other structural guides, humans sometimes behave in extraordinary ways, as we have seen in our examples of mass hysteria and panic. Sociologists call such relatively unstructured, unpredictable, spontaneous, and short-lived behaviors **collective behavior.** Ranging from the heroic to the horrible, collective behavior can erupt among people in a far-flung mass or a face-to-face gathering. Some forms occur in everyday interaction. But unlike the structured classroom setting, collective behavior emerges beyond the planned, routine, or normatively controlled setting. What are the chances of collective behavior occurring on a college campus?

Collective behavior: relatively unstructured, unpredictable, spontaneous, and short-lived behaviors shared by people.

Rumor: Why So Pervasive?

In the shipping department, duplicating center, library, and faculty lounge, we can find people informally passing along information to others. Such stories, usually of an unknown source, and therefore of uncertain accuracy, are called **rumors,** and can be found in most any kind of informal human interaction. Why are rumors so pervasive?

We circulate rumors because they help us in several ways. For one, they allow workers to escape a mind-numbing routine. Workers with the most boring jobs embrace rumors most readily. For another, they meet our need for information concerning some disturbing topic. Among college students, stories about changes in the grading system, registration fees, or graduation requirements will immediately become vitally interesting and circulate quickly across campus. Rumors help us cope with fear and anxiety, and they take on more importance and spread more swiftly as we feel more stress.

Rumors: stories of an unknown source passed from one person to another.

Rumors provide information in times of uncertainty and entertainment in the case of boredom.

Rumors can give rise to other forms of collective behavior such as mass hysteria and riots, but, as a dramatic example shows, they also constitute a form of collective behavior themselves. From real or imagined incidents in Detroit following fiery riots in the summer of 1967, monstrous rumors spread quickly. Some envisioned schools being burned, students and teachers being shot, and blacks invading the white suburbs. Others spoke of plans to poison the city water system, or of kidnapping and killing white chidlren. Fear spread that policemen's families would all be killed (Rosenthal, 1971). Clearly, stress and fear fueled these widely circulated, unconfirmed stories that in less anxious circumstances would be ridiculed.

Crowds: From "Hanging out" to Lynchings

Students spend much of their time on campus in temporary gatherings—waiting in line for registration, cheering on the basketball team in the gymnasium, listening to a speaker in the plaza or courtyard, and so on. Such gatherings lack the structure, "we feeling," and endurance of groups, and so come under the domain of collective behavior—more specifically, **crowds.** Members of a crowd share only a common focus for their attention; they have not met before and there are no rules or special expectations, no sense of oneness. On the surface, crowds would seem to be of little sociological interest, but with the help of Herbert Blumer's (1951) categorization of crowds, we find that some approach the extremes of human behavior.

The people stopping to watch some campus construction project would form a *casual crowd*. Such crowds gather simply because a point of interest holds the members together. They have little organization, develop few significant associations among the members, and usually disperse quickly.

In contrast, a *conventional crowd* is not spontaneous or accidental. It assembles for some specific purpose—for example, to listen to a concert or watch a tennis match. As their name implies, these crowds involve conventions or guidelines regarding appropriate behaviors, such as how loudly to talk, when to applaud, and what to wear. Interaction is impersonal and routine. We have all been members of such crowds, and we have rarely found their social interaction to be of unusual interest. They are usually a rather unremarkable part of everyday life.

We can find more excitement in an *expressive crowd*, which forms for the purpose of unleashing emotion and expressing feelings. At some colleges, the campus Spring Festival or Winter Carnival gives rise to such crowds, somewhat like those at the Mardi Gras in New Orleans. At others, the football stadium becomes the scene for unrestrained collective behavior. In these crowds, students dance or gesture wildly, shout rude or obscene remarks, wear odd clothes and accessories, or remove some or all of their clothes.

The *active crowd* generates even more excitement. They form around some specific objective or goal which requires action, usually to right some perceived wrong. These exotic forms of collective behavior are rare on campus or the streets, but are among the most fascinating and fearsome because of their potential for violence, hostility, and destruction.

Active crowds include panic by people in contact with one another, as well as mobs and riots. A **mob** forms because of the belief that something is wrong in the social setting. Its aroused and emotional members usually intend to use violence on a specific target to solve the problem. In recent decades, campus radicals urged mobs to disrupt and destroy various college agencies. Mobs are purposefully aroused and, while

Crowd: a relatively unstructured, short-lived gathering of people who share a common focus for their attention.

Mob: a type of active crowd, aroused and emotional, with a focus or specific target for its violence.

Expressive crowds provide a setting for people to release their emotions in ways that would be inappropriate in other circumstances.

some view them as destructive and hostile, others welcome them as constructive. Most of us, for example, approve of the mobs that participated in the Boston Tea Party in 1773 or those that attacked the Berlin Wall in 1989.

The **riot** also usually involves violence. It arises from a general feeling of social unrest, but, unlike the mob, it has no focus or specific target. Riots, for example, have occurred on U.S. campuses regarding war protests, homosexuals' rights, and racial hostilities. Participants in a riot typically lack agreement as to what person or group is to blame for whatever wrong exists. This may change, however, and a target may be found as the riot develops.

Riot: a type of active crowd, aroused and emotional, with no focus or specific target for its violence.

Explanations of Collective Behavior: Why Do People Do These Things?

Does some sort of collective consciousness or mass mind grip participants in collective behavior? The psychological transformation of normal individuals into a mob or group of rioters lies at the heart of Gustav LeBon's (1895) intuitive theory of collective behavior. LeBon contended that crowd processes somehow seize control of the individual and force that person to act in ways he or she would never normally consider. Sociologists later elaborated upon this notion. For example, Robert E. Park wrote of a "loss of personality by the individual; the individual tends to act impersonally and to feel something less than the ordinary responsibility for his actions" (1930, p. 632). Likewise, Herbert Blumer wrote of a reciprocal restlessness and social contagion that produces collective actions (1939). The problem with these early ideas is that they lacked firm empirical underpinnings. After all, collective behavior is extremely difficult to study due to its ephemeral, unpredictable nature.

Contemporary sociologists have rejected notions of a "mass mind" or robot-like participants so vulnerable to suggestions that they lose control of their behaviors and personalities. While people in stressful or emotional situations may be more susceptible to suggestions, they still seem to retain their individual consciousness, rationality, and control of their behaviors (McPhail, 1989). Instead of some external psychological force hypnotizing crowd members, theories today focus on the interaction among participants that influences their behavioral choices.

Contagion theory attempts to explain how emotions spread from one crowd member to another. After all, if people are to act together, they will likely feel the same motivating emotion. But how do they come to share this emotional state? Moving away from the image of the instinctively stampeding cattle herd, some sociologists have followed up on Leon Festinger's (1954) *social comparison theory*. Evidence suggests that in an emotional social setting people compare their reactions to those of other people who are similar and in the same situation. These comparisons lead to pressures toward conformity and a sharing of emotions (Sullins, 1991). Others (for example, Rosen and Walsh, 1989) find that contagion tends to flow along social network pathways rather than randomly. In other words, emotions flow more readily between friends than strangers.

Convergence theory holds that a crowd of people who have gathered together probably already have similar values and attitudes that make their collective behavior more likely. We might thus expect students on a college campus, because of their similar ages and educational goals, to act more collectively than a representative cross section of society. Similarly, we should not be surprised if a rock concert featuring music that attracts people with antisociety attitudes erupts into a destructive riot.

But not all crowd behaviors result from like-minded individuals converging on the same spot. And not all crowds can be explained by emotional contagion since some act quite deliberately and rationally in pursuing their goals and in choosing their tactics and targets. To explain such cases, we turn to *emergent norm theory*, in which crowd conformity is based on new social agreements that people form as they interact with one another. Imagine a free band concert in the college stadium attended by citizens from the community, people of various ages, races, and social classes. Not a situation for convergence theory. It is time for the concert to begin, but the band is nowhere in sight. The people begin to interact, exploring and testing one another's ideas about what to do: Do we wait politely, complain loudly, riot, or leave? They talk among themselves, eavesdrop on nearby conversations. Some individuals shout suggestions. The crowd members begin to reach a sense of what they should do, and shared notions emerge to guide the crowd, to legitimize some behaviors and discourage others. A few people begin to clap and chant loudly, but they receive only frowns from the rest of the crowd because the norm that has emerged is to politely and quietly leave, and most of the people do so—collectively.

Neil Smelser's (1963) *value-added theory* offers another explanation for collective behavior. He identifies six stages or determinants, all of which must be present before, say, a riot breaks out. As each determinant arises, the next one becomes more likely to occur, and so on.

Imagine the students at a small college sharing worries about a sluggish economy and dismal job prospects for graduates. Smelser would call this *structural conduciveness*, in which general conditions in the community set the scene for some eventual eruption of collective behavior. The second necessary ingredient, *structural strain*, thus becomes more likely. This strain can result from conflict, a lack of trust among parts of the community, or a gap between what people expect and what they deserve. In this case, the latter applies to the students: They hear of recent graduates of their particular college having trouble securing employment and fear they will reap no rewards for their years of studies. This sets the stage for the third requirement, the development of a *generalized belief*. A general agreement forms as to the specific cause of the problem and the solution. The student newspaper persuasively contends that the problem lies in the college president's failure to effectively promote the school's reputation in the local job market. The generally accepted solution becomes: Ditch the president. Next, some dramatic event is needed to trigger collective action in the students. Smelser calls this the *precipitating event*. In this case, it is a speech in which the president scolds the students for their grumblings and suggests they simply are not working hard enough. Students in the audience respond with jeers and a rowdy, angry procession to the campus center. The spark has been provided; the next ingredient is *mobilization* of the rest of the students for action. In this stage, leaders may come to the forefront, making speeches or shouting suggestions. *Social control* factors, the reactions of authorities, help determine the eventual extent of the collective behavior. In our example, the campus police decide to handle the situation without calling in outside forces and fail to control the students. We can easily imagine an active crowd, perhaps even a riot, resulting.

Critical Thinking Box

The Salem Witch Trials: A Case for Women's Liberation?

In the summer of 1692, several hundred people in Salem, Massachusetts, were accused of being in league with the Devil. Most were imprisoned, 19 were hanged, 1 tortured to death. A strong belief in the earthy influences of the Devil and other supernatural spirits helped set the stage for the witch trials. So did the harsh economic conditions of the time. Another cause may have been a fungus that often grew on rye in those days. A person who ate enough of the contaminated bread could show the same strange convulsions, postures, and speech patterns as did eight Salem girls who accused their neighbors of witchcraft (Caporael, 1976). A few hallucinating girls could have set off the mass hysteria that followed.

There may have been another factor at work as well. Perhaps it was only coincidental that only a tiny percentage of those accused and convicted were men. But Carol Karlsen (1987) points out that many of the accused women shared something in common: They had stepped outside the feminine role. Some had engaged in business. Others were over 40 and had neither sons nor brothers, which meant that they would inherit their husband's or father's property. An independently wealthy woman challenged the social order of colonial America. And the social order responded.

Would the trials have been significantly different if the Salem women had enjoyed equal rights? ■

SUMMARY

Sociologists have used symbolic interactionism to offer insights into *social interaction:* people responding to one another's actions. They find that we respond to the meaning we attach to others' actions. Indeed, the reality of a setting is constructed by the participants' interpretations. Also, like actors on a stage, we attempt to manage the impressions others form of our self. Gestures convey messages nonverbally, and more powerfully and truthfully than do words, and, like words, depend on cultural definitions. Similarly, our use of interpersonal space conveys messages according to cultural conventions. The major building block of social interaction is *exchange*, which involves an expectation of repayment. This reciprocity can contribute to solidarity or mistrust and inequality, depending on the circumstances. Exchange often takes the form of *cooperation*, in which people combine their efforts toward a common goal. On the other hand, when rewards are limited, *competition* arises, although the struggle for rewards is limited by rules. Competition can become *conflict* when the participants seek to neutralize or destroy one another.

A *group* is two or more people who interact recurrently within a structured situation, and who share a common purpose or goal and a consciousness of membership. Within *secondary groups* we find more instrumental ties, in which the members see the others as ends to means. Within *primary groups* we find more expressive ties, which are person-centered. The primary relationships in such groups are based on spontaneous, accepting responses to the members, and deep and extensive communication, thereby offering considerable emotional satisfaction. These types of groups serve as *in-groups*, made up of those people with whom we identify or feel a sense of oneness. When we feel a sense of otherness, of *social distance*, we perceive an *out-group* consisting of people with whom we do not identify or feel a sense of oneness. Beyond a group boundary we form a *social network*, a web of social relationships that link us directly or indirectly to other people and groups. These complex webs offer social resources, especially if they are dense.

Successful collective endeavors must overcome two problems. First, according to rational choice theory, many participants may not contribute because they will have to shoulder the burden of others who will benefit but not contribute (the problem of social loafing). However, if the costs of the collective project do not increase with the amount of people who enjoy the benefits, enough people (a critical mass) will contribute their efforts.

Group cohesion and interaction diminish with the size of the group. While the two-person group is based on more fragile, emotional ties, it offers a better chance of intimacy than larger groups. Size can affect the group's effectiveness, depending on the nature of the task. Each group needs leadership to provide harmony and direction, and leaders can choose from several strategies. The democratic approach generally works best in our society, more so than laissez-faire or authoritarian styles. Women generally use more cooperative, supportive leadership styles than do men, but every leader uses principles such as mutual support and control of members' definitions of situations. Leaders arise by capitalizing on status characteristics, impressing the other people in the group, and using various tactics while doing so.

We are pressured into conformity even by strangers. In highly cohesive groups we may not feel comfortable in questioning the group's line of thought, and if everyone aims for agreement, groupthink results.

We create *formal organizations* when we want to efficiently accomplish a specific, large-scale task. Some are *voluntary associations*, in which membership is optional and not remunerative. Membership is not a matter of personal choice in *coercive organizations*. The *bureaucracy* is a type of formal organization based on hierarchy, division of labor, and rules. In Weber's model, the typical bureaucracy is based on a clear division of labor, a hierarchy, rules, and hiring based on technical merit. Beyond this ideal type, informal organization develops as a source of benefits for workers and as a way of getting things done when the official organization proves too hampering. Bureaucracies often suffer from *ritualism*, rigid conformity to rules to the point of inefficiency, and routine can become an end in itself. Also, workers may not respond effectively to unanticipated demands due to *trained incapacity*, the excessive reliance on established procedure. According to *Parkinson's Law*, work expands to fill the available time. Incompetent workers can easily hide within the labyrinth of a bureaucracy, sometimes even rising to their level of incompetence, according to the *Peter Principle*. Bureaucracies often tend toward rule by the few, or *oligarchy*, according to Robert Michels's "iron law of oligarchy." In the Marxist view, bureaucracies serve as a tool of oppression, reflecting capitalistic society's class domination and hierarchy.

Several social trends portend the evolution of bureaucracy into organizational forms that offer more flexibility and satisfaction. For example, collectives feature little specialization of labor, rules, or hierarchy, though these function only on a small scale. And Japanese corporations work well because they offer (until recently) lifetime job security to workers in exchange for their dedication and loyalty. Small work teams send suggestions and decisions up the chain of command.

Beyond the confines of organizations and groups, humans sometimes engage in relatively unstructured, unpredictable, spontaneous, and short-lived behaviors called *collective behavior*. Examples include *mass hysteria* (in which people who feel trapped in an inflexible, boring, or stressful situation engage in a collective, emotional outburst of behavior in the form of exhibited symptoms of physical illness or widespread acceptance of unlikely stories), *panic* (the irrational, collective flight from some perceived threat), and *mass behavior* (people with little or no actual contact reacting to the same stimulus, though in individual ways). People circulate *rumors*, stories of an unknown source passed from one person to another, as a means of dealing with boredom or stress. In *crowds*, people gather together but lack the structure, the "we feeling," and endurance of groups. Crowds range from casual to conventional to expressive to active. Active crowds include *mobs* (aroused and emotional crowds intent on using violence on a specific target to solve a problem) and *riots* (active crowds with no focus or specific target for their violence). Early theorists speculated that crowd processes somehow seize control of individuals and force them into crowds, but most contemporary sociologists use explanations such as contagion theory, which explains crowd behavior in terms of the spread of emotions from one crowd member to another. Also, convergence theory holds that people who gather together already have similar values and attitudes that make their collective behavior more likely. And according to emergent norm theory, the conformity of crowd members is based on new social agreements people form as they interact with one another. Neil Smelser's value-added theory identifies six stages in the development of such collective behavior as a riot, each of which make the next more likely to occur.

Key Terms

social interaction	out-group	oligarchy
exchange	social network	mass hysteria
cooperation	formal organization	panic
competition	voluntary association	mass behavior
conflict	coercive organization	collective behavior
group	bureaucracy	rumors
secondary group	ritualism	crowd
primary group	trained incapacity	mob
in-group	Parkinson's Law	riot
social distance	Peter Principle	

4
Chapter

SOCIALIZATION

Imagine a hunter stalking wearily through a dense, darkening forest. He has had no success after a long day, and he is frustrated. This may be the reason why, at the sound of something moving stealthily behind a thicket, he jerks up his rifle and reflexively fires, even though he is not sure what might be making the rustling noises. His shot seems to hit its mark; he hears a yelp of pain and runs to investigate. Behind the bushes he finds to his horror that he has seriously wounded a boy about eight years old. The boy is filthy, naked, and instead of talking he snarls and tries to bite the hunter. It becomes clear that the boy has been living alone in the woods for most of his life, a sort of "Tarzan," with virtually no human contact.

The boy suddenly dies of his wound, and the hunter is faced with the awful fact that he has killed a fellow human. Or has he? The boy showed no human characteristics beyond the physical—he did not act in any way like a normal boy. The question arises, What is required for the development of humanness?

WHAT IS NEEDED TO ACQUIRE HUMANNESS?

Beyond this hypothetical "Tarzan" are actual cases of children reared in various degrees of social deprivation, in which adequate nutrition, attention, and other elements necessary for normal social development are absent or withheld. These stories illustrate that certain ingredients are essential for acquiring humanness, and that it is not guaranteed for a member of our species.

One of the most famous of these cases was the "Wild Boy" of Aveyron, France, a 12-year-old found inhabiting the woods. It was quite apparent that the child had been deprived of socialization from a very early age. He ran about on all fours and preferred uncooked food. A physician, Jean Itard, worked intensively with the boy, who eventually learned some writing and arithmetic skills but never acquired reading or speaking ability even though he lived more than 40 years. Because of his early social isolation, much of the boy's humanness seemed to have been lost.

Another example of social isolation involved unfortunate "Anna," an illegitimate child kept in an attic room for the first six years of her life. The girl could not talk or walk when she was discovered, and her mental and sensory capacities were seriously stunted. She would lie on the floor for long periods of time, her face devoid of expression, her eyes vacant. With intensive teaching the girl developed some basic human abilities such as walking and brushing her teeth, but clearly much damage had been done by early isolation. Anna never learned to speak, and she died at age 11 (Davis, 1947).

"Genie" was a more recent victim of social deprivation (Curtiss, 1977). She was denied virtually all normal contact except for the beatings she received, especially when she tried to verbalize. When the girl was discovered by authorities at age 13, her development level was similar to that of a one-year-old. In an eight-year therapy program, Genie's progress at learning speech and normal social behavior never brought her beyond the abilities of a four-year-old.

SOCIALIZATION

Socialization: the process by which humans learn the behaviors and beliefs appropriate for their social surroundings.

Cases of social deprivation point to the critical importance of **socialization,** the process by which humans learn the behaviors and beliefs appropriate for their social surroundings. Through the reactions and expectations of the social world we acquire our very humanness: a sense of self, a personal identity—features that help distinguish us from other species. Like a lump of clay, each of us is molded into a being with recognizably human characteristics through socialization. Without this shaping by other people, our human potential remains unfulfilled.

Human Contact Our cases of social deprivation, however, demand further explanation. What are the specific causes of these children's pathetic conditions? In other words, what are the missing ingredients in their social experiences? One answer,

Scientists long ago confirmed what most of us assume: children need loving attention to thrive.

which a great deal of research supports, is simply: attention. Obviously, ethical restraints prevent social scientists from using this element as an independent variable in an experiment. However, several research observations leave no question as to its importance.

A classic study by René Spitz (1945) compared two groups of infants. One group was made up of healthy babies in a nursery. Each baby enjoyed the attentions of his or her own caretaker. The other group was raised in a foundling home, where one nurse cared for eight babies. Little attention could be given to these infants, and this seems to have made an enormous difference. The foundling home infants suffered *hospitalism*, a pattern of deep depression accompanied by weeping and sadness, long periods of immobility or mechanical rocking, and unresponsiveness to other humans. These institutionalized infants suffered a high rate of mortality, and the survivors displayed severely retarded development. They could not speak, walk, dress themselves, or use a spoon.

More recent research links neglect to a constellation of problem behaviors such as aggression, avoidance, fewer prosocial behaviors, and lower self-esteem (Kaufman and Cicchetti, 1989). Corroborating research shows that babies do not thrive without adequate opportunities for imitating appropriate expressions, problem-solving strategies, and other useful behavior patterns (Park et al., 1988; Dodge, 1990; Goodman and Brumley, 1990). In other words, attention or human contact is necessary for the flowering of human potential.

The development of humanness also requires physical contact. Harry Harlow's (1962) famous experiments clearly showed the importance of tactile stimulation or physical touch for monkeys. Harlow raised monkeys in isolated cages and offered them the choice of two surrogate (artificial substitute) "mothers," both with monkey faces. One was a bare wire structure equipped with a feeding apparatus. The other was covered with soft terry cloth, but provided no food. The babies preferred the surrogate with terry cloth to the bare wire surrogate. Although "contact comfort" was important for the baby monkeys, Harlow's experiments say nothing conclusive about human needs. Other findings, however, suggest that humans also benefit from contact comfort. For example, L. Casler (1965) found that just 20 minutes of extra touching a day could improve the rate of development for infants in an institution.

Stimulation   Cognitive or perceptual stimulation also plays a vital role in the development of humanness. The babies studied by Spitz were not deprived physically; they were well fed and clothed. However, kept in bare rooms in cribs with white sheets hung on the sides and only the blank ceiling above, they were deprived of perceptual stimulation. Other studies also show the human need for such stimulation. For instance, Sally Provence and Rose Lipton (1962) found that the longer babies are kept in unstimulating environments the greater the effects of deprivation. By one year of age, deprived babies display the body-rocking behavior characteristic of severely maladjusted humans.

Cognitive stimulation also promotes the development of language, which, as we saw in Chapter 2, serves as one of the distinguishing features of our species. Without language ability, human nature is incomplete. And without contact with other humans, speaking ability does not develop. Humans may possess what Noam Chomsky (1957) calls a "language acquisition device," a prewiring or programing allows us to develop language, but this potential still requires the stimulation of listening and speaking practice.

A human's development depends greatly on how he is treated by the others in his social environment, what sociologists call nurture.

Nurture and Nature

So far we have focused on only one aspect of human development, that commonly referred to as "nurture." Nurture involves influences of the social environment: the praise, ridicule, rules, expectations, and demands of people in one's surroundings. For the full picture of human development, we must also consider "nature," such biological influences as genes, hormone levels, and brain chemistry.

Note, however, that we can become mired in a false dilemma if we try to determine whether a particular personality feature results from either nature or nurture. Rarely if ever are the two influences not intertwined. As we will see next, biology often provides a tendency or potential for some particular behavior pattern to emerge, but the social environment is required to trigger it. And while humans possess the same general biological features, some behavioral aberrations can be partly traced to specific biological deviations.

Critical Thinking Box

What Is "Human?"

Are such stunted individuals as Genie and Anna human? To illustrate the danger in this question, consider that one possible answer is to draw a line between what is human and not-quite-human, using such criteria as mental ability or (to quit social science momentarily) evidence of the soul. What are the logical consequences of this line of reasoning? Humanness may be viewed as a matter of various forms, including a fertilized egg, the robust Olympic athlete, and the terminally ill 90-year-old. What social policies are products of this premise? What, indeed, is "human"? ■

HEINOUS HUMANS: VICTIMS OF BIOLOGY?

On November 24, 1946, a baby boy was born at the Elizabeth Lund Home for Unwed Mothers in Burlington, Vermont. His mother would later call him "the best son in the world"; others would characterize him as warm, polite, sincere, and bright. Indeed, he grew up to be a charmer, as well as a serial killer eventually executed for the vicious murders of three young women and suspected of brutally killing as many as 40 others. Two of his biographers called him a "likeable, lovable homicidal mutant" (Michaud and Aynesworth, 1983, p. 17). His name was Ted Bundy.

Biological Universals

The monstrous acts of people like Ted Bundy and Jeffrey Dahmer serve as motivation for exploring the biological foundations of human nature. It may be that such destructive violence is simply human nature exploding through the walls of social controls. This notion is a logical extension of **biological determinism,** the tendency to reduce the foundations of human behavior to biological explanations. Human violence, in this view, may be simply one of our **biological universals,** the biological features with which all humans are equipped.

The most recent version of biological determinism is **sociobiology,** which posits genetic foundations for many animal and human social behavior patterns, including aggression, territoriality, war, competition, altruism, and male dominance. Sociobiology offers some intriguing explanations for animal behaviors that elude the reach of traditional Darwinian theory. For example, why does the new leader of a lion pride often immediately kill existing and newly born cubs? Sociobiologists answer that it is simply good strategy to eliminate any competition for cubs carrying the dominant lion's genes.

The fundamental premise of sociobiology is that social behaviors enhancing survivability evolve in the same way as physical traits like strength or camouflage. For instance, during evolutionary history aggressive human males would be more likely to win and defend territory and mates. Since they would thus do most of the reproducing, aggressiveness would become firmly encoded into human genes. Similarly, male sexual promiscuity would constitute an effective genetic strategy in the reproductive sweepstakes, as would polygyny (having more than one wife at a time). Sociobiology explains human behavior less in terms of cultural values than in terms of reproductive strategy: Whatever helps the species survive is preserved for future generations.

In animal studies, this line of reasoning has attracted considerable support. Among students of human behavior, however, it is quite controversial for several reasons. For one, acceptance of such reasoning leads too easily to troubling conclusions, such as the innate superiority of males over females or of one race over another. In other words, it suggests that whatever inequities exist must exist naturally, and should therefore be accepted as simply a fact of life. Any attempt to mitigate racism or sexism would necessarily be doomed from the start. A second difficulty with biological reductionism as applied to human behavior is that it ignores the central role played by learning. The evolution of biologically based behavior patterns would presumably take many hundreds of thousands of years, but the human species differentiated itself only

Biological determinism: the tendency to explain human behaviors in terms of genetic or other biological factors; also known as biological reductionism.

Biological universals: the biological features found in all members of the species.

Sociobiology: the study of animal and human behavior patterns that stresses the central importance of evolved, genetic influences.

Sociobiologists contend that some social behaviors, like aggression, are genetically based in some species including humans.

in the last 100,000 years. Male dominance and promiscuity, for example, can be more readily explained by cultural forces such as quickly developed norms and values. Moreover, genetic explanations fail to account for the many monogamous marriages, chaste males, and nonviolent individuals; in other words, the enormous cultural variations found all over the globe weaken the notion of universal, inborn, inevitable behavioral commands. To be fair, some sociobiologists, like E. O. Wilson (1975) do not deny the influence of cultural forces in shaping human behavior; they simply assign more importance to genetic influences than would most sociologists.

Most sociologists would argue that there is nothing inevitable or natural about the violence of people like Bundy. Instead, considering the many nonviolent individuals, it can be said that our biological equipment holds only the *potential* for aggression, just as it holds the potential for cooperation and altruism.

In fact, one of the most important features of humans is our nearly complete autonomy in responding to the environment, the freedom from internal, instinctive commands. While other species are environmentally triggered to build nests, migrate, hibernate, and so on, no human can blame foul deeds on, say, the onset of spring. Some (perhaps superfluous) proof of this was provided by a team of physicians who tested the popular notion that the full moon somehow incites humans to unusually high levels of violence. The doctors found that, contrary to widespread hospital legend, the number of trauma victims did not increase with the onset of a full moon (Coates, Jehle, and Cottington, 1989).

So while Ted Bundy's brutality may reflect a basic human drive for aggression, it is doubtful that the specific acts of violence he committed were biologically driven.

Biological Particulars

While each human may or may not have a compulsion to destroy, some seem to be more susceptible to our violent potential than others. Biological particulars—unique biologically based features—help fashion some of us into charismatic, adventurous dynamos, others into timid, whitebread homebodies, and even a few into vicious serial murderers.

The first and most obvious of these particulars is physical appearance. The way people react to someone's face and form can affect that person's personality. The broadness of the shoulders, hips, and mouth; the length of the nose or legs; the texture and color of skin and hair—all influence the way people treat a person. As unfair as this may seem, such differential responses begin almost immediately in life. "Unattractive" infants are perceived by adults to be less competent than are babies with attractive faces (Ritter, Casey, and Langlois, 1991). Both adults and children generally prefer attractive individuals and attribute positive qualities to them—and vice versa. Our bias against physically unattractive people is so strong that an organization called Uglies Unlimited was formed to help its members cope with problems regarding self-respect and job opportunities (Brooks, 1989). Moreover, good-looking MBA graduates earn an average $2,000 to $3,000 more than less attractive fellow graduates (Frieze, 1990).

Some people clearly are victimized by the particulars of their physical appearance. But in the case of Bundy, his handsome features actually allowed him to gain access to his victims more easily—apparently some went willingly with him because they trusted his boyish good looks. If he was victimized by biology, it was probably in ways not visible: behavioral predispositions.

Physical appearance is one of the biological factors that influence our personality.

Distinctive dispositions are evident in the first weeks of life, presumably prior to any substantial shaping by the social environment (Hubert et al., 1982). Shortly after birth, infants display distinguishing traits regarding activity level, general mood, ability to adapt to changes in the environment, and attention span (Thomas, Chess, and Birch, 1970). For example, some very young babies are irritating and fussy, and their mothers label them as "difficult" (Lounsbury and Bates, 1982). Hormones and brain chemistry seem to influence these and other inherited personality tendencies, such as activity level, adaptability, Type A vs. Type B behavior, and aggressiveness. Intelligence seems to be linked to genes, as are susceptibilities to such mental disorders as depression, hyperactivity, schizophrenia, and probably alcoholism. Herein lies the strongest possibility that biology contributes to a vicious criminal's behaviors.

So was Ted Bundy a victim? Perhaps biological factors may be implicated in brutal crimes, but only—if at all—in an indirect, secondary way by providing unusual predispositions, not commands. Any individual's "victimization" is more likely to be traced to the nurture part of the human equation.

In fact, biological factors only lay the foundation for the construction of a human personality. We saw earlier that socialization breathes into that biological raw material its humanness; now we see how that happens.

Because of biologically-based predispositions, some people seem to be "naturally" pleasant or otherwise.

Research Box

Twins, Genes, and Homosexuality

One way researchers reveal the influence of biological particulars is through the study of identical twins. To the extent that twins exhibit the same personality features, it might seem to be a matter of their sharing the same genes. However, twins usually also share the same social environment, which might easily be the source of the twins' behavioral similarities. Much stronger evidence comes from studies of twins reared in different environments.

For years, researchers at the University of Minnesota studied twins separated early in life and later reunited. The twins displayed striking similarities not only in appearance and voice quality but facial gestures, hand movements, nervous habits (such as nail biting), and talents (in, for example, music or athletics). Intelligence was also highly correlated between the twins. More pervasive personality features such as dominance or extroversion, as well as values and attitudes, were less likely to be identical (Farber, 1981). Biology indeed seems to be implicated in personality.

More recently, twins research has linked genes with male homosexuality (Bailey and Pillard, 1991). Researchers studied three groups of men: 56 pairs of identical twins, 54 pairs of fraternal twins (born simultaneously but from different eggs, and no more similar genetically than other siblings), and 57 pairs of adoptive brothers (with nothing in common genetically). Each pair of brothers was reared together. The researchers reasoned that if homosexuality is caused mostly by the social environment, then the incidence of homosexuality among the brothers in the three groups should be roughly the same. They found, however, that genetic similarity made a difference. When one identical twin was homosexual, the other was nearly three times more likely to also be gay than if the twins were only fraternal.

These results suggest substantial genetic influence regarding sexual orientation, but there are cautions. For one thing, the researchers assigned only about 30 to 70 percent of the cause of homosexuality to genes. This clearly leaves much room for the effects of social experience—an ideal research design would have compared identical twins reared apart. There is also possible influence from other physical factors, such as hormonal levels in the womb. And, finally, the sample included no females.

Still, the results of this relatively large sample corroborate those of earlier, smaller studies. Other research has found shared genetic markers on the genes of 40 pairs of homosexual brothers (Hamer et al., 1993) and evidence of possibly different brain structure in homosexual men as compared with heterosexuals. □

GOOD PARENTING AS EFFECTIVE SOCIALIZATION

Self: the individual's organized set of beliefs, dispositions, values, and interests; one's awareness of what kind of person she or he is.

Socialization not only produces humanness, as we saw earlier, but also renders in each individual a unique manifestation of humanness, a **self.** The self embodies the individual's organized set of beliefs, dispositions, values, and interests—an awareness of what kind of person he or she is. Socialization, then, creates not only a human but a unique human personality.

Socialization agents: the people, groups, and organizations responsible for the molding of individuals.

Various individuals, groups, and organizations, including the family, schools, peers, and mass media, contribute to the shaping of individuals. Of all these **socialization agents,** the most critical are the parents. Equipped with no parenting instincts and only shifting trends in the advice offered by "experts," parents often feel they are groping in the dark. While nothing can make parenting easy, insights on the underlying principles of socialization can shed some light.

Parents today are told to "give the child positive feedback," "help the child build self-esteem," "do not overprotect or hover; instead, help the child work toward independence." Such common admonitions have their roots in the work of Charles Cooley and George Mead.

Cooley's Looking Glass

Self-image: the total perceptions of one's body and personality, capabilities, and other qualities.

The "looking glass" theory of Charles Horton Cooley (1864–1929) explains how a child builds self-esteem. He used the phrase "looking glass self" to describe how we use others as a mirror to construct a **self-image.** According to Cooley, the formation of self-image involves three elements or stages. First, we imagine how we appear to others. Then we imagine how others react to what they see in us. Last, we develop feelings about ourselves based on the judgments we imagine the other people have formed of us. From this process we gain some feelings, either positive or negative, about ourselves.

Imagine first-graders undergoing this looking glass process as they meet their teacher for the first time. First, each child imagines his or her appearance in the eyes of the teacher ("I must look sloppy in these old clothes"). Then the child imagines how the teacher judges that appearance ("The teacher doesn't seem to like the way I look"). Last, the child forms some self-feeling based on the teacher's imagined judgment ("I guess I'm a little slob"). This process is not confined to young children. For

ALBERT TENNER

ALBERT TENNER
(ELECTRONICALLY ENHANCED)

Drawing by Lorenz; © The
New Yorker Magazine, Inc.

example, adolescents who perceive rejection by their parents suffer depression from their lowered self-esteem (Robertson and Simons, 1989). In fact, people of all ages peer into the looking glasses around them.

A complication in this seemingly straightforward process is that the looking glass can reflect distorted images. A first-grader may misinterpret the teacher's enforcement of rules, the teenager may misunderstand his parents' expectations, or the adult may misread a co-worker's grimace upon her entrance. Such misreading of the looking glass is at least partly based on self-esteem. Children with low self-esteem tend to focus on negative responses from their parents; those with high self-esteem pick up more readily on praise (Felson and Zielinski, 1989).

Today, symbolic interactionist theories working after Cooley stress that socialization is not based on the message sent but on the message received. Advice to parents thus becomes: Send clear messages and double-check on how they were interpreted. Parents may well acknowledge that they provide mirrors for their children's self-images, but there is a rather curious, even mysterious element to Cooley's explanation. *How* do children (or adults, for that matter) see themselves as others see them? Perhaps parents could more effectively facilitate the formation of positive self-image if they understood how children perform such mental gymnastics.

Mead's Role Taking

One explanation is provided by George Herbert Mead (1868–1931). Mead explained that self-image arises in part due to our ability to see, refer to, and judge ourselves as objects. In doing so, we are at the same time the person being referred to and the one

Certain people in our lives serve as especially important judges. From the way these "significant others" react to us we learn important lessons about what kind of people we are.

doing the referring; we are simultaneously both object and subject. How do we perform this mental trick?

Mead explained that we must be able to communicate in a complex way, using language to hold a kind of internal conversation. In other words, we "talk" with ourselves about how others see us. Clearly language, or the use of symbols, is central to the formation of self—thus the inclusion of the word "symbolic" in Mead's theory of symbolic interactionism.

Most parents are aware of their special power in shaping their children. Mead explained long ago that parents are among the **significant others** in the socialization process. A child's significant others also include grandparents, teachers, and, especially in adolescence, peers. As adults we are most likely to be interested in the judgments of parents, employers, co-workers, lovers, and our children.

Significant others: persons whose affection, approval, and judgment are especially important in the development of the self.

The child pretending to be a nurse or astronaut is not merely playing, but working to build a self-image. Mead explained that **role taking,** mentally assuming the perspective of another individual, enables us to look at ourselves from the perspective of others. By role taking, the individual becomes aware of his or her self's very existence and can thus build a self-image.

Role taking: mentally assuming the perspective of another person, enabling us to look at ourselves from others' point of view.

According to Mead, this development of self-image involves three different stages of role-taking. In the preparatory stage, the child simply imitates people in her immediate environment, mostly family, sometimes even imaginary playmates. The child spontaneously assumes these roles without comprehending their meaning. In the play stage, around age three or four, the child begins to understand social relationships enough to assume a specific role, and address herself as, for example, a parent or teacher. In the game stage, the school-age child is able to take the roles or attitudes of all the other individuals involved in some game or common activity. The child "becomes" those in a soccer game, for example, so she can successfully play her own part as a midfielder. She is capable of internalizing a set of interdependent roles.

Generalized other: an integrated view of the attitudes and expectations of society as a whole.

Over time the individual becomes able to assume the attitude or role of what Mead called the **generalized other**—that is, members of the community in general.

By our teen years most of us are able to assume the role of members of the community in general, gaining some sense of how others view us.

Promenading through the mall, a young female teenager has some sense of how all the other shoppers see her. She understands their generalized viewpoint and expectations regarding each person's particular status. The attitudes of those subsumed in the generalized other are organized by the individual and taken into one's self, becoming what Mead called the "me." The "me" reflects the social structure surrounding the individual, and is clearly a product of the social environment. The shared meanings of the Alcoholics Anonymous community, for example, are used to construct a new "me" for each member; the new self is purposefully fashioned by the social context (Arminen, 1990). The "me" exists along with the "I," the principle of impulse. It is through the

"I" that the individual can exert some change on the social structure. In sum, the society shapes the individual and creates a self which can in turn change society.

In Mead's view, then, the socialization process involves increasingly sophisticated role taking as a means of building a self-image. Parents may be able to recognize these developments in their children, and presumably should not discourage them.

Freud and Irrational Urges

Repression: the process of forcing unwanted impulses, feelings, or memories to the unconscious level.

Id: the innate, unconscious portion of the personality; it represents selfish desires and drives.

Superego: the portion of the personality dedicated to controlling the id and gaining social approval; it functions as the moral conscience.

Ego: the logical, conscious portion of the personality responsible for balancing the demand of the id with the superego.

While Cooley and Mead investigated the constructive aspects of the interaction between the self and the social world, Sigmund Freud (1856–1939) delved into the *conflict* between them. Freud believed that the most important socialization occurs early in life when our human drives clash with the culture's demands and restrictions. This conflict begins in infancy because we are born with unconscious, irrational, self-centered urges that society cannot tolerate. Parents use their powerful emotional bond with the child to manipulate him or her into conformity with the external world's demands. This control and denial of pleasures creates guilt, fear, and anger in the child, all of which are forced into the unconscious via **repression.** In the Freudian view, then, parents teach the child to hold the lid on a bubbling cauldron of desires.

Every parent realizes that the child must develop an internal guidance system. Freud identified three parts of the mind that must be reconciled for proper socialization. The child is born with the **id,** the unsocialized, selfish desires and drives that must be controlled. This control responsibility falls to the **superego,** the moral codes of society as represented in the surrounding adults, especially the parents. As the socialization proceeds, the norms and values of the adult world become incorporated into the child's superego, which functions as a conscience. A balance between the impulses of the id and the control of the superego is necessary for healthy functioning. This is accomplished through the **ego,** which plays the part of referee, mediating the demands of the id and superego.

Critical Thinking Box

Is Vanity Simply Good Tactics?

Is someone who takes great care of his or her appearance simply vain or a clever social tactician? For at least 8,000 years humans have used face and body paint and other means to convey enhanced images (Payeff, 1989). Wealthy Egyptians of both sexes painted their eyes, usually black above and green below, and wore blue-black lipstick. The women sometimes painted the veins of their breasts blue and the nipples gold. Roman soldiers used make-up, perfume, and hair color. Ladies of tenth-century Japan painted their faces white and, for contrast, their teeth black. And of course in the United States today the enhancement of one's personal image is a multibillion-dollar business. One southern California woman spent about $50,000 a year on a personal trainer, nutritionist, masseuse, suntan parlor, facialist, hairstylist and manicurist—not to mention $10,000 for a face lift (Calistro, 1988).

Before we dismiss such efforts as silly and vain, consider the role of physical appearance on personality development and Cooley's "looking glass" description of the formation of self. Is this age-old human concern justified? ■

Freud's theory thus illuminates an important task of parents in their socializing role: to transmit to children society's values and norms, and help them in their struggle with the id's impulses.

Social Learning

Many parenting authorities inform parents that, whether they know it or not, they serve as role models for their children. According to *social learning theory*, children observe other people (who act as models) and imitate those behaviors. By watching their parents, children establish their own behavior patterns and values. This modeling process obviously saves a great deal of time for the developing child. Rather than originate all behaviors or learn by trial and error, the imitator acquires new behaviors by intelligent observation and copying (Bandura and Walters, 1963).

A picture now emerges of socialization as a giant pair of many-fingered hands kneading, stretching, and molding an unformed lump of potential humanness into a being that will in its turn shape others through the same process. We next consider how socialization works in the specific case of Asian-American families.

FAMILY SOCIALIZATION: THE SECRET OF ASIAN AMERICAN SUCCESS?

Not all families, of course, put the foregoing socialization theories into practice with the same degree of success. Social class, race, ethnicity, and other subcultural variables affect how any particular family raises its children. Asian-American families, for example, have established a reputation for successful socialization; perhaps they can serve as a model for us.

Popular notions regarding Asian Americans tend to focus on two images. First is the disproportionate numbers of valedictorians and PhDs of Asian origin at graduation ceremonies. Several measures of solid educational achievement by the various Asian-origin groups in the United States reinforce this picture. With rare exceptions, the high school and college graduation rates of Chinese, Japanese, Filipino, Korean, and Asian-Indian students are higher than those of whites. In addition, Asian Americans in general earn better grades in high school, higher Scholastic Aptitude Test scores on mathematics, are more likely to attend college and to graduate quickly, and are conspicuously overrepresented in the National Merit Scholarship Program, Presidential Scholars, and the Westinghouse Science Talent Search Program. The second image of Asian Americans is their doting, supercharged home environments. Is the academic success of Asian Americans attributable to something the parents and families do?

If these perceptions are in fact accurate, we might all wonder how the example of Asian-American socialization can uplift American education in general. One of the tasks of sociologists is to examine the accuracy of such important popular beliefs. And after probing into the hidden reaches of this matter, researchers have indeed uncovered some complications.

We start with a useful beginning point for such issues: Are the causes mostly nature or nurture? The genetic avenue was first explored by R. Lynn (1977), who found that at every age level Japanese children outperformed Americans on an intelligence test. Other researchers, however, questioned the legitimacy of those comparisons because of the use of old test norms and inclusion of minorities in the American sample (Flynn, 1987) and the higher social-class levels of the Japanese students (Stevenson and Azuma, 1983). When these methodological flaws were corrected, no overall differences in intelligence were observed between students in Japan, Taiwan, and the United States (Uttal, Lummis, and Stevenson, 1988). But while the genetic superiority of Asians seems to be a myth, the impressive overall academic achievement of Asian-American students remains very real, so perhaps an explanation lies in nurture—more specifically, family socialization.

It is important to first realize that the nurture of the family is entwined with the nature of the child. Just as sculptors must consider the graininess, brittleness, and plasticity of their materials, family members must deal with the child's stubbornness, unresponsiveness, low frustration tolerance, and other particular qualities. In doing so, they themselves are affected by the child. The cranky, bawling, willful infant, for example, can force its parents to acknowledge their own shortcomings as supposedly fully mature adults.

Nevertheless, it is easy to imagine that good students are created to a large extent by the molding hands of parents. Early parent–child interplay fairly sparkles with meaningful nuances as parents give infants their first glimmers of the self. Every nod, smile, and frown seems to be a significant message. In the first few weeks and months, when humans are most malleable, family members have near total influence, providing most of the infant's experiences and stimuli in even rather ordinary moments. Researchers find that mothers teach their infants how to smile, for example, by expressing their own interest and enjoyment (Malatesta and Haviland, 1982). And parents provide infants with their first view of the social world, their first taste of social life. For instance, very young children learn to keep their interaction with mother to a minimum when she is depressed (Breznitz and Sherman, 1987).

Such early lessons seem to reverberate for years to come. A secure child–mother attachment gives the toddler the emotional security needed later to venture away from mother and interact with peers (Jacobson et al., 1986). And part of the reason some children turn out to be popular is that their mothers interacted with them in a special way, such as engaging in turn-taking exchanges with them when they were infants (Vandell and Wilson, 1987) and being reasonable in their demands (Putallaz, 1987).

A list of the effects of family socialization is almost inexhaustible. Table 4-1 offers a sample of research findings. Even this partial picture shows the enormous power of parental influence.

All this evidence of parental power certainly suggests that Asian-American parents do something special to mold their children into superior students. In these families, early socialization is typically guided by strong beliefs that the child is malleable (Chen and Uttal, 1988) and warrants a great deal of nurturance (DeVos, 1983). Furthermore, the emotional restraint for which Asian-American parents are well-known seems to be yielding to more open emotional expression, perhaps as a means of adaptation to the American culture (Lin and Fu, 1990). In fact, one reason Asian-American children tend to succeed is their culture's compatibility with our own demand for diligence, cleanliness, neatness, setting and achieving long-range goals, and politeness

A SAMPLE OF FAMILY INFLUENCES ON CHILD DEVELOPMENT

Family Factors (Leading To)	Child's Characteristics	Researchers
Parental support	Higher self-esteem	Felson and Zielinski, 1989
Parental support	Academic success	Steinberg, Elmen, and Movats, 1989
Parental rejection	Depression	Robertson and Simons, 1989
Less nurturance, inconsistent discipline	Depression, loneliness, and drug use	Lempers, Clark-Lempers, and Simons, 1989
Support	Self-esteem	Hoelter and Harper, 1987; Eskilson and Wiley, 1987
Affection, concern, involvement, and modeling	Drug use	Hundleby and Mercer, 1987
Parental role models	Career preferences	Lavine, 1982
Parents' income and education level	Academic ability	Mercy and Steelman, 1982
Number of siblings	Academic ability	Polit and Falbo, 1987
Parents' attitudes about child's abilities	Academic ability	Parsons, Adler, and Kaczala, 1982

Table 4-1

(DeVos 1973). (It is tempting to comment that they meet these demands better than children whose families have had many generations to become Americanized.) Asian-American families also stress effort, self-improvement, and taking control of one's own fate (Chen and Uttal, 1988). Parents instill the notion that children are obligated to repay their family for the parents' sacrifices, and that the child's failure reflects upon both the family and the entire ethnic community (DeVos, 1983; Lin and Fu, 1990). The well-known Asian-American emphasis on achievement is not exaggerated, and is augmented by values regarding obedience to elders (including teachers) and comparisons to others.

Clearly, the well-focused patterns of Asian-American family socialization partly explain the children's general academic success. Family values, however, are not the whole story. Stanley Sue and Sumie Okazaki (1990) suggest that the superior effort and motivation of Asian-American students are also due to the limited opportunities they perceive in other avenues of social mobility, such as political leadership, entertainment, sports, and politics. After all, when we hear of Asian-American achievement it is almost exclusively in terms of education and business. In short, families put all their eggs in one basket, focusing on education as the only realistic hope to meet success. Another explanation points to the effects of small business ownership on family dynamics (Sanchirico, 1991). For example, the extraordinary academic accomplishments of Chinese Americans since the 1920s is based on the fact that "family businesses often inspire high expectations for the future; these objectives may well be transmitted into high educational aspirations for the next generation" (Hirschman and Wong, 1986, p. 18).

Such evidence reminds us that causes and consequences in the human social world are usually interwoven in a complex web rather than found in a simple one-to-one relationship. So, in answer to our original question, it seems that Asian-American parents do employ a well-focused, achievement-oriented socialization regimen, but that the focus on their children's education is also partly explained by limited opportunities in the social system and values connected to proprietorship. As powerful as parental influence is, it does not tell the whole story.

How College Changes People

Like the family, schools are an agent of socialization, but there are important distinctions between the two. First, while socialization occurs informally in the normal home, schools undertake formal socialization, a process using specially trained adults (teachers), a consciously contrived set of teaching goals (curriculum), and special places (schools). Teachers are often the first non-kin adults to have formal authority over the child. They give the child her or his first taste of society, its demand for performance, its objective criteria for judging that performance, and all the attendant pressures and possibilities of failure.

Certainly the social climate of schools and the expectations of teachers and peers shape young children. But Richard Funk and Fern Willits (1987) describe how even college students are socialized by their experience. Previous research had shown clearly that college attendance usually has a liberalizing effect on students' views on, for example, religion and sex. So many studies reached the same conclusion that there seemed little reason to doubt college's impact. Funk and Willits noted, however, that the research was limited to students only while they were in school. While the college experience might easily be expected to change one's attitudes, Funk and Willits wondered if such changes lasted after students left the college atmosphere. They also wanted to know if the reported changes were due to migration from hometown to a new residential community after college, or perhaps by initially more liberal attitudes in the kind of people who chose to go to college. The two researchers decided to test the liberalizing effects of college attendance itself (aside from other influences such as migration, different initial attitudes, and so on) over time—in other words, to see if college alone liberalized people, and if that effect lasted beyond the college years.

For a longitudinal effect, Funk and Willits used two surveys of the same people conducted 10 years apart. The first, completed in 1970, had 11,000 high school sophomores in Pennsylvania suburbs fill out questionnaires dealing with their attitudes and family backgrounds. In 1981, a random sample of 848 of these former students were mailed questionnaires. Three follow-up mailings resulted in a 64 percent return rate. All were of the same age and nearly all were white, so age and race were controlled. The questions in both surveys dealt with attitudes regarding men's and women's roles and God and religion. Respondents were asked if they agreed with such statements as: "A college education is more important for boys than for girls." "The best place for most women is in the home." "I know there is a God."

The respondents were classified in three ways: migrant status (operationalized as persons having lived in different counties in 1970 and 1981), college attendance (not at all, attended but did not graduate, or graduated from a four-year program), and gender. A sophisticated correlation analysis searched the various variable combinations for statistically significant relationships.

The results confirmed previous studies and added stronger evidence of the liberalizing influence of college. People who had not attended college displayed the least change in attitudes, followed by those who had attended but not graduated. College graduates had changed the most, whether or not they had migrated, whether they were male or female, and whether or not they had expressed liberal attitudes as high school sophomores. In short, the college experience in and of itself seems to liberalize viewpoints.

Clearly, then, schools mold people well beyond the tender elementary school years. We will examine this powerful socialization agent in greater detail in a later chapter. □

MASS MEDIA: ENRICHING OR RUINOUS?

We see in the pervasive influence of the **mass media** perhaps the most humbling example of how susceptible we are to socialization agents. Today more than ever we are continually subjected, often unconsciously, to hints, suggestions, and standards from the mass media that shape our ideas and emotions and how we see ourselves. From the print and the electronic media, we take many of our cues on who we are and what we want to become. Unlike other socialization agents, the mass media affect us not on a person-to-person level but as members of a **public,** a large, dispersed population with some shared interest or purpose—for example, those people across the nation whose parenting strategy is based on a particular author or whose morals are contoured by a situation comedy. Is this influence enriching or ruinous?

From its beginning, mass communication has transformed not only what we think about but *how* we think. The invention of the printing press in the fifteenth century expanded the proportion of the world's population sharing the same ideas. As the storehouse of knowledge became more accessible to more people, scholars could go beyond merely replicating that knowledge and concentrate on reflecting upon and changing it. Culture's knowledge became less fixed, and humans began to search for alternative truths (Eisenstein, 1979).

In this century, books, magazines, and newspapers have been augmented by motion pictures, radio, and television. Of all the mass media, television exerts the most powerful influence and has received the most intense study.

Television has increasingly affected childhood socialization. For better or worse, it introduces the child to the adult world much earlier and more thoroughly than reading and eavesdropping ever did. Social information is no longer acquired gradually with the development of reading skills. Beginning with the first time the child can reach the TV's "on" switch, his or her innocence regarding crime, drugs, and perversions quickly erodes. Insofar as this innocence protects and cushions, television may feed the child more awareness than she or he is able to digest. On the other hand, perhaps this awareness prepares the child for an increasingly harsh and dangerous world.

One major concern is simply the enormous amount of time children spend in front of the TV (more than anything except sleeping), hours which could perhaps be invested more profitably in exercise, reading, and interacting, with real people, especially family members. Television viewing is a relatively passive activity that does not ask children to use any more than their minimal mental powers. They are offered little challenge regarding language skills, vocabulary building, mental concentration, or problem solving. Television entertains children but does little to enhance them. Even

Mass media: means of communication directed at large numbers of people.

Public: a large, dispersed population with some shared interest or purpose.

To learn the secrets of the adult world, children no longer need to go through the bother of eavesdropping on their parents. Television reveals to children far more than most parents would ever let slip.

worse, prolonged TV viewing may alter the brain's structure and functioning, making it a suspect in the increasing number of learning disabilities found in American children (Healy, 1991).

Another criticism is that television provides poor training for citizenship. It may teach children undesirable values and attitudes, such as a lasting sense of mistrust (Dworetz, 1987), and teach them more powerfully than parents do. Television affects us all somewhat like a drug, dulling our minds rather than encouraging us to think through important matters. Television programming also tends to focus our attention on personal, not social problems (Gitlin, 1983).

Furthermore, television may produce negative imitative behavior, in adults as well as children. Researchers have found, for instance, that the suicide rate in the United States rises significantly after heavy TV coverage of suicides on evening news programs (Bollen and Phillips, 1982). Such findings have been disputed (Stack, 1984, for example), but how many parents have seen their children acting out television stories, from flying off roof tops to assaulting other youngsters? For example, eight youngsters in Baltimore claimed they learned how to fashion bottle bombs from a 1990 TV action series. Many laboratory experiments have suggested that violence on television can incite aggressive behavior in children. One study showed that even commercials, with little or no violence, produced aggressive responses in children (Geer et al., 1982).

There is a long list of other concerns. For example, it may be more difficult to produce great leaders due to the ubiquitous television cameras that reveal the backstage behaviors of politicians (Rothman and Lerner, 1988). Moreover, there is evidence that adults who watch TV more than four hours per day acquire a distorted view of the work world, the powers of medicine, and the threat of crime (Waters, 1982). Feminists criticize the negative portrayals of women in the media (Courtney and Whipple, 1983; Cantor, 1987). Other observers claim that the mass culture imposed by television has alienated us from one another, encouraging us to judge ourselves and others according to possessions and appearance (Ewen and Ewen, 1982). In this view, this powerful socialization agent encourages consumerism and fosters social fragmentation.

But once again we are reminded that social reality is not as simple as "television is bad" or "television causes antisocial behaviors." Stephen S. Messner (1986) suggests that people who watch a great deal of TV are *less* likely to engage in violent crimes, perhaps because they are less likely to be on the streets where they might be affected by peers and temptations of the moment. And Cedric Cullingford (1984) argues that children can separate television's make-believe from reality, and thus escape any influence of TV violence. A review of the research literature led D. Anderson and P. Collins (1989) to conclude that children are cognitively active during television viewing, and that it does not displace reading, movie attendance, radio listening, or participation in organized sports. A national survey of American children found that time spent watching TV is not causally linked to lower cognitive abilities (Gortmaker et al., 1990).

Moreover, a child can clearly benefit in some ways from television. The child is shown various morals, manners, and role models that can enlarge his or her range of personal choices, especially with parental guidance of the viewing. Some children's shows promote positive social behaviors ("Mister Rogers' Neighborhood") and preschool academic skills ("Sesame Street"). Such "educational" programs offer lower-class children cultural and academic stimulation they might otherwise miss. Even commercials can be beneficial. Analysis of television advertisements for "Barbie" and "McDonald's" found many examples of sharing and courtesy (Stout and Mouritsen, 1988).

So are the mass media a positive or negative influence? It should now be apparent that this question is too simplistic. To fully consider the issue, we would have to differentiate the print media, which stimulate at least a fair amount of mental effort, from the electronic media, which may require considerably less. Nor are all books or television programs equal in impact on the individual or society. Ranging from comic books to the Bible, from the most mindless situation comedy to the most high-brow television special, the mass media cannot be accurately depicted as a monolithic influence.

Is Cocooning a Problem?

One of the criticisms of mass media is that they are replacing direct, personal, intimate socialization with impersonal and centrally controlled manipulation. From this point of view, an especially worrisome development is "cocooning," the tendency of more Americans to seek whatever diversion they want at home in what used to be called the "TV" room but is now a virtual communications center. As more of us plug ourselves into our television, VCR, computer modem, stereos, and CD players, we have less need to deal with humans in the flesh. This may have already contributed to increasing alienation and diminished social integration, which shows up in the form of rude drivers and vicious muggers.

But is cocooning really a problem? Instead it might be a form of liberation, bestowing upon the individual the freedom to customize his or her life style. Each of us can choose to learn from and be entertained by the best and brightest of society rather than those who happen to live in our house or community. After all, much person-to-person interaction can be troublesome or tedious, and we cannot easily just change channels when a neighbor, spouse, or child becomes too intense or demanding. We can even bare our souls without dealing directly with another human by joining the 200 or so people who daily call Phone Confessions to purge their consciences—to an answering machine. With home shopping networks, we need not venture into the hustle and bustle of stores to deal with harried clerks and impatient customers. With increasingly clear duplication of sound, we need not join the rude, noisy crowds at concerts to hear the pure strains of our favorite music. And with the development of virtual reality technology (which can put us inside a computer-generated, life-like situation), we may someday be able to walk through a Turkish bazaar, an English country garden, or on the moon's surface without leaving our home. Who needs people? Our socialization can be much more sophisticated and efficient in the new world of the cocoon.

Does cocooning create social disintegration or offer the luxury of privacy combined with our choice of mental stimuli? ■

HOW ARE ADULTS MANIPULATED AND SHAPED?

While we all are aware of the socialization in children, it may be less obvious that the process continues long after we reach adulthood. Socialization does not suddenly stop at age 18—rather, the individual's "clay" gradually hardens and he or she becomes less

Through such agents as peer groups, the socialization process continues throughout adulthood.

Reverse socialization: the process in which the supposed targets of socialization influence the supposed socializers.

Peer groups: interacting groups of equals, usually of the same age or sex status.

malleable with maturity. Adulthood socialization is more fine tuning than assembly, modifying a self fundamentally formed in childhood.

Socialization agents continue to shape us, but their array and relative importance change with age. The family remains influential, for example, but spouse and children take on more importance than parents. And as offspring grow into adolescence, they in fact socialize their own parents in matters regarding clothing, food, ideas, and so on (Peters, 1985). This **reverse socialization,** or shaping of those supposed to be doing the shaping, is understandable in a fast-changing culture such as ours where old values and ideas are quickly displaced. The older generation is likely to look to the younger for cues and orientation.

The workplace comes to the forefront as a socialization agent when school recedes. Corporations have been known to dictate to employees the color of their shoes and style of umbrella. And feelings of self-worth are affected by the degree of routinization, autonomy, and complexity workers find in their jobs (Schwalbe and Staples, 1986; Gecas and Seff, 1989).

Peer groups, another agent of influence in childhood and especially adolescence, are less important in adulthood. As in childhood, peer groups naturally form among people of similar age and sex status. And just as children escape adult intervention in their peer groups, adults seek the company of equals to escape the formality imposed by their superiors. The relatively relaxed atmosphere of the peer group affords the opportunity to joke, make mistakes, and express rebellion against authority. This is as evident among office workers sharing a few beers after hours as it is among teenagers acting crazily and criticizing their teachers. But while children use peer groups to learn social skills, adults use them to play out well-developed skills regarding dominance, manipulation, exchange, and cooperation. Older people also use peer groups as they did in childhood to appraise their self-image, but to a lesser degree. The conformity demanded by peer groups regarding values and norms indicates their power over the individual, though that power diminishes considerably as individuals age.

The power of social expectations is illustrated by what sociologists call **anticipatory socialization.** People aspiring to a role such as medical student find themselves, often unconsciously, assuming the sober, judicious attitudes and behaviors that seem appropriate for that role. We can also see such anticipatory socialization in the engaged couple establishing relations with future in-laws, making joint decisions on the purchase of a car or house, and gravitating more toward married couples for company.

Another usually unnoticed influence on adults is **reference groups,** which individuals use as standards to measure their social success and self-worth. Some people are more likely than others to base their self-judgments on the degree to which they share the values and traits of the "successful" adults who drive the right cars, live in the right neighborhoods, and send their children to the right schools.

Reference groups are sometimes forced upon individuals in ways that may not be obvious. An older brother or sister, for example, might be the kind of achiever a person has always aspired to be like. Successful salespeople in a company may be foisted upon other workers as models to emulate. Advertisers certainly attempt to provide admirable reference groups with whom we can associate ourselves by purchasing certain products: the whisky enjoyed by sophisticates, the car for intelligent people, the perfume or cologne used by alluring women and men.

Reference groups induce individuals to try to reduce the gap between who they are and their ideal image of what members of the group are like. In this way, such groups can affect people's actions, goals, and views of themselves. In fact, reference groups have been linked to a wide assortment of behaviors, including sex (Steyn, 1987), date rape (Kanin, 1985), alcohol use (Cochran, Beeghley, and Bock, 1988), and even the choice of foods—specifically, the decision to eat beef (Sapp and Harrod, 1989).

The individual is not necessarily a member of his or her reference groups. Indeed, some are not groups at all, such as those invented and fed to us by advertisers. Even though it is a contrived image, a television family like "the Huxtables" can serve as a reference group, a model or standard to which some people aspire.

Reference groups can also steer the individual away from behaviors and attitudes of people with whom she or he does *not* want to be associated. The clothing styles, slang, and automobile choices embraced by members of a negative reference group become déclassé.

It is easier to appreciate the extent of adult socialization by thinking of it as an onslaught of challenges requiring continuous adaptation to a succession of roles. This involves **desocialization,** unlearning the behavior patterns associated with old roles. Each adaptation is a transition in which the adult unlearns some roles, such as college student, and adds new ones, such as career employee or retiree. In early adulthood, people normally gain more roles than they lose; later in life, they usually lose more roles than they gain.

Another aspect of this flux of adulthood transitions is the different expectations or definitions of roles held over the years. For example, the rights and responsibilities of being a husband may change over time from "Mr. Everything" or "torrid lover" to "best friend" or "helpmate." "Mother" may be self-sacrificing yet all-powerful at age 25, burdensome and superfluous at 85.

Adulthood can be tumultuous when transitions rush upon the individual unexpectedly. Recently, for example, women refugees from Southeast Asia have had to adjust to a very different definition of the wife role. Coming from cultures in which wives were expected to be submissive and to fit into a large web of kinship, these immigrants suffered anxiety and depression in the United States as they suddenly

Anticipatory socialization: the process of learning to perform a particular role with the expectation of assuming that role in the future.

Reference groups: groups or social units a person uses for self-evaluation.

Desocialization: unlearning the behavior patterns associated with old roles.

Advertisers frequently try to associate their products with people we admire; in other words, they try to create reference groups for us.

found themselves expected to perform as co-leaders in small, autonomous, nuclear families (Lovell, Tran, and Nguyen, 1987). Even the expected and normal transition into parenthood can become a crisis if the child's birth coincides with some other, unexpected event, such as the hospitalization of the grandmother or the father's loss of employment.

On the other hand, not all the challenges of adulthood are inherently stressful. Role changes like retirement and even widowhood are easier to manage because they are usually anticipated and considered part of the normal course of adulthood. And even unexpected and difficult changes have less disruptive impact on people who have already been under stress for some time. Negative events such as divorce and job loss are less disturbing when they occur in the context of chronic stress (Wheaton, 1990).

All adulthood role transitions involve to some degree the reshaping that sociologists call **resocialization.** Moving up to supervisor, for example, the employee learns new values and rejects old ones that are no longer appropriate. The professional socialization of graduate school training can also be seen as a reshaping process equipping students with a new sense of self (Egan, 1989).

Resocialization: the process by which the individual learns new values and behaviors in place of older ones.

Some resocialization is part of the ordinary ebb and flow of life, but in its most powerful form it can be aimed at remaking the person entirely. Extreme cases are often called "brainwashing." This radical reconstituting of individuals usually occurs in controlled environments that Erving Goffman (1961) called **"total institutions"** such as mental hospitals and prisons, which regulate all aspects of the inmates' lives. These institutions attempt to stamp out individuality through such strategies as standardized clothing and haircuts. The goal is to create a new self-image for the inmates.

Total institutions: institutions that monitor and regulate all aspects of the inmates' lives.

The most common form of intense resocialization is military training, in which the role of civilian is replaced with the military role. The recruit lives in an isolated, controlled environment, exposed to a limited array of people and ideas. He or she is given a new hairstyle, new clothes, a new label—a new self. Intense resocialization methods are also used in prisons, drug rehabilitation centers, and in some religious organizations. Some corporations specify the acceptable mannerisms and attire for their new employees. From Jim Jones' "People's Temple" cult to prisoner-of-war camps, the aim is the same: the creation of a new identity for the individual.

Resocialization is usually not successful at totally and permanently replacing a person's self, especially if the person resists the change. On the negative side, this means prosocial efforts such as the rehabilitation of criminals often fail. On the positive side, this means the sense of self acquired through early socialization cannot be easily destroyed or replaced, that once people's "clay" hardens they cannot be reshaped against their will.

SUMMARY

Cases of social deprivation show that humanness is not guaranteed for a member of our species, and they point to the critical importance of learning the behaviors and beliefs appropriate for their social surroundings, the process called *socialization*. This process requires human contact and attention, as well as cognitive or perceptual stimulation. Besides this nurture, human development also involves biological influences, often called the "nature" side of the picture.

Indeed, *biological determinism* tends to explain human behaviors in terms of genetic or other biological factors. From this view, some behaviors may flow from biological features found in all humans: *biological universals*. Reasoning along this line, *sociobiology* stresses the central importance of evolved, genetic influences in behavior patterns such as aggression, territoriality, and male dominance. Most sociologists, however, contend that humans are free of such genetic commands, and that biology holds only the potential for behavior patterns. Biological particulars, such as physical appearance and behavioral predispositions, help give humans their unique personalities.

These biological influences, along with socialization, create the individual's organized set of beliefs, dispositions, values, interest, or the *self*. *Socialization agents*, those people, groups, and organizations responsible for molding individuals, contribute to the formation of self. Cooley's "looking glass" theory describes how we use others as a mirror to construct a *self-image*, the total perceptions of our body and personality, capabilities, and other qualities. According to Cooley, we imagine how we appear to others, and how they react to what they see in us, and then we develop feelings about ourselves based on the judgments we imagine they have formed of us. This "looking glass" may reflect distorted images, and the messages sent from others may not be accurately received or interpreted. Mead explains that we build a self-image through a kind of conversational interchange within ourselves about how others see us, especially *significant others*, whose affection, approval, and judgment are especially important in the development of the self. We look back on ourselves using *role taking*, by which we mentally assume the perspective of another person. By moving through increasingly sophisticated stages, we can eventually assume the role of the *generalized other*, in other words, build an integrated view of the attitudes and expectations of society as a whole. In this way we build the "me," which reflects the social structure around us, as well as the "I," the principle of impulse through which we can act on our social surroundings. Freud focused on the conflict between self and the social world. He used the concept of the *id* to explain the unsocialized, selfish desires and drives built into every human. The *superego* represents society's moral code, and functions as the individual's conscience. Between these two is the *ego*, which is responsible for balancing the demands of the id with the expectations of society.

Genetic explanations do not explain Asian-Americans' general academic success, but the vaunted family socialization does not entirely explain it, either. While parents possess tremendous power in molding the child, and while Asian-American parents in general display effective socialization techniques, for a full explanation of their academic success we must also consider broader social influences beyond the family.

The *mass media*, or means of communication like newspapers and radio directed at large numbers of people, affect us as individuals and as members of *publics*: dispersed populations held together by some shared interest or purpose. Mass media have transformed our modes of thought, as well as deeply affecting the socialization process, as we see especially vividly in the case of television. Television introduces children to the adult world, perhaps before they are ready. The enormous amount of time children spend watching television, the poor training for citizenship it offers, and the negative behaviors it seems to promote, give us cause for concern. However, researchers identify possibly positive effects of television watching, complicating our judgment of television's consequences.

Even adults are socialized, sometimes by their children, as we see in *reverse socialization*, where the supposed shapers are themselves shaped. And adults are influenced by *peer groups*, groups of equals, usually of the same age and sex, though children are more strongly affected by such agents. In *anticipatory socialization* we learn to perform a particular role with the expectation of assuming that role in the future. Adults, and children, are also shaped by *reference groups*, which we use for self-evaluation. Reference groups may be forced upon us, and may be contrived, or negative, but they can affect how we act and see ourselves. As we adapt to a succession of roles, we engage in *desocialization*, which is unlearning the behavior patterns associated with old roles. The transitions of adulthood can be especially difficult when unexpected, when they coincide with others, but less difficult when they are anticipated. They also involve *resocialization*, wherein we learn new values and behaviors in the place of older ones, as we see in the extreme case of the "brainwashing" of *total institutions*, such as mental hospitals and prisons, which control all aspects of life for the inmates. Such programs are rarely successful in permanently replacing a person's self.

socialization	role taking	reverse socialization
biological determinism	generalized other	peer groups
biological universals	repression	anticipatory
sociobiology	id	socialization
self	superego	reference groups
socialization agents	ego	desocialization
self-image	mass media	resocialization
significant others	public	total institutions

DEVIANCE

The problem with studying **deviance,** behavior that violates mainstream norms, is that it does not reside inherently in any particular act. There is no list of behaviors universally recognized as lying outside normative boundaries. It is the product of a particular time, place, and social circumstance, an interpretation of conduct that can be either popularly based or imposed by people holding sufficient power.

Deviance: behavior that violates mainstream norms.

Whether an act is labeled deviant or not depends on several social conditions. First, deviance depends on who performs the behavior. Public nudity, for example, is not necessarily deviant for a two-year-old. Second, deviance depends on where the behavior occurs. Many actions that usually take place in a locker room or at the beach would be considered deviant in a church or classroom. Third, definitions of deviance change with time. A woman appearing in public wearing a short skirt and smoking a cigarette would violate norms of the 1890s but not those of the 1990s. Drinking champagne to the point of intoxication might be considered deviant on Easter Sunday morning, but probably not on New Year's Eve. Finally, the subcultural context helps determine whether an act is deviant or not. Behaviors considered normal among juvenile delinquents, homosexuals, or young adolescents might be deviant in other social circles.

The deviant nature of any behavior depends on such things as the statuses of the behaver.

We begin our exploration of deviance by asking whether it is an inevitable part of human social life. We then study its various forms and causes. Finally, we will discuss crime and society's reactions to criminal deviance.

WHY DEVIANCE?

Without knowing humans very well, we might think that rigid laws, backed by traditional or religious authority and harsh punishments, would eventually eradicate deviance. Consider the oil-rich desert kingdom of Saudi Arabia. Unlike Western law, which is derived from notions of human moral nature and rationality, that society's Islamic law (*Shariah*, "the straight path") purports to reflect the very will of God, and theoretically rules every aspect of a Muslim's life. And if the force of this authority were not enough, penalties of the most extreme sort stand behind the law, though these are reserved only for the most heinous crimes. A regicide (killer of a king), for example, was quickly tried, convicted, and beheaded. Stoning, flogging, and mutilation—such as the amputation of a thief's right hand—are sometimes carried out in public to discourage wrongdoers. According to one observer, "In Riyadh, when a thief's right hand is cut off in public by the executioner's sword, a string is tied to the middle finger and it is hung from a high hook on a street light in Justice Square for all to see" (Mackey, 1987, p. 270). Before recent reforms, Saudi Arabian prisons were characterized by crowded and harsh living conditions. A criminal may also face the vengeance of his victim's family, who can legally demand retaliation, either in the form of blood money or exacting the same bodily injury upon the criminal as he inflicted on the victim.

Despite these deterrents, some people in Saudi Arabia still transgress the law. While we can expect high crime rates in highly individualistic, freedom-based societies like our own, why has no society, even the most strict and autocratic, succeeded in erasing deviance from its populace?

Deviance Is Part of the Human Condition

Michael Gottfredson and Travis Hirschi (1990) have revived an old explanation for deviance: Humans tend to seek pleasure and avoid pain, and will step outside normative boundaries to do so unless restrained. The best defense is prevention—that is, effectively socializing the child during the first six or eight years of life to obey societal norms. If individuals do not learn self-control, society can only try to limit their opportunities to seek pleasure at the expense of others.

Expanding on this view, Albert Bandura (1990) argues that even successfully socialized individuals can commit deviant acts under certain social conditions. When swept up in a moral crusade, for example, we can simply redefine the killing of a non-believer, foreigner, or other members of out-groups as justified, even moral and noble. Thus those we consider terrorists may regard themselves as moral crusaders. We can also displace responsibility. Nazi concentration camp officers, for example, committed atrocities that would violate any human's own moral code, but they managed this by shifting responsibility to a higher authority: They were just "following orders." Third, we can disregard or minimize the harmful consequences of our actions. If we cannot or will not see the effects of our antisocial acts, we can commit them more easily. Thus, by distancing themselves from the suffering of their victims, Nazi leaders could perhaps with clear consciences order underlings to commit horrible acts. Finally, we can dehumanize our victims by portraying them as "beasts" or "savages" who deserve vile treatment, thus convincing ourselves that harming them does not violate our moral code. Deviance becomes more understandable when we realize our human tendency for self-gratification is only imperfectly restrained by socialization.

Deviance Is an Inevitable Aspect of Capitalism

Conflict theorists argue that we cannot simply blame human nature for deviance, especially criminal deviance. In their view, society—more specifically, capitalist society—deserves much of the blame for its crime problems.

Elliott Currie (1991) outlines this argument as follows. First, market or capitalist societies focus our efforts on acquiring luxuries beyond our means. Such a society promotes greed and materialism, which drive some people into illegitimate means of acquisition. Second, when the name of the game is private gain, some people inevitably will gain less than others. Instead of settling for less, the persistently poor may use illegal means to even the score. Third, capitalist societies require that many people follow jobs from one community to another, thereby weakening local social cohesion. Fourth, a large pool of unemployable—thus not marriageable—men contributes to family instability, as does the necessity of parents working two or even three jobs.

Following this line of argument a step further, we can also say that capitalist societies have high rates of crime because the dominant elite finds it necessary to define many behaviors as illegal to legitimately bring the full force of the legal system against troublesome or threatening groups (Quinney, 1970). For example, a large population of unemployed workers represents a destabilizing element. Capitalist society deals with this threat by expanding the definition of criminal behaviors to include, say, vagrancy—thus "creating" deviance and triggering more arrests. This explains why incarceration rates rise as unemployment increases in capitalist societies (Chiricos and Delone, 1992; Inverarity and McCarthy, 1988; McCarthy, 1991; Parker and Horwitz, 1986).

From the conflict perspective, then, deviance is an inevitable aspect of capitalist society. We see evidence of this even in China: As that nation adopted more materialist, capitalist values in the 1980s, juvenile delinquency rates rose. While noncapitalist societies have crime, the rates are much lower, presumably because of the greater equality there.

Deviance Is Normal in Any Society

Functionalists counter that deviance is part of any society, regardless of its economic organization. Moreover, noncapitalist societies' crime rates may be much higher than their official statistics indicate, as seems to have been the case in the former Soviet Union (Butler, 1992).

Emile Durkheim helped establish the functionalist explanation of deviance. Initially, he saw deviance only as a negative, dysfunctional social element. Later, however, he pictured social life encompassing both sides of the normative boundary, deviance as well as conformity. In fact, he described deviance as "an integral part of all healthy societies" (1895, p. 67). Following his lead, other sociologists interpret property crimes as strategies used by normal individuals to meet their needs for material goods (Cohen and Machalek, 1988; Vila and Cohen, 1993). Such strategies arise and become common because they work, much as adaptive genetic traits spread through natural selection. This certainly does not suggest that we should work to promote deviance. If individuals are to become fully functioning people, they need the security they enjoy in a well-organized society. We could not be as productive citizens if we constantly worried about our safety. Also, we could not easily coordinate our own prosocial actions with others' unless they were also acting in predictable, conformist ways. But on a manageable scale, deviance has important uses, or *social functions*, and thus a place in any society.

For one thing, deviance clarifies normative boundaries. When we watch an acquaintance push the limits of society's tolerance until he or she is finally punished, we gain a clearer picture of how far we ourselves can go. Our knowledge of this boundary allows us to relax as long as we choose to stay within its confines.

Deviance, oddly enough, also can produce social cohesion. It unites nondeviants in opposition, sometimes even in outrage. The excitement created by antisocial behaviors "quickens the tempo of interaction in the group" (Erickson, 1966, p. 4). In opposing the deviant, members of the moral community, shaking their heads and clucking their tongues, reassert their shared code and thereby reaffirm their solidarity. Without such challenges, a people's moral ideals might grow stale or weak. As walking keeps our leg muscles toned, so coming together against deviance exercises the moral code.

Imagine a small, conservative, Midwestern community undergoing an invasion by a guru of an esoteric religion and his disciples. The town residents would draw together as never before in the face of this perceived threat to their way of life. Their collective fear would overcome the usual petty jealousies and grudges. Their shared indignation would forge powerful feelings of unity. The community's value system would be reaffirmed and strengthened, all because of the deviants.

Deviance also functions as a safety valve. If humans have inherent tendencies toward pleasure seeking, and if some are socialized into risk taking (Hagan, 1989), what happens if they find no release for these drives? Functionalists argue that the resulting tensions can create social upheavals that damage valuable norms. Take the case of a 16-year-old boy who feels a strong need to assert his autonomy, to "walk on the wild side." His drive for rebellion might take the form of sullenness and criticism of his parents' values, thus damaging the family bond. On the other hand, he might rebel by violating society's rules against teenage drinking; this deviance might safely release his inner tension without harming the family bond. Similarly, Japanese can temporarily escape their strict social surveillance through drunkenness, "when quite extraordinary behavior, rudeness, impropriety, or disorder can be tolerated by friend

Deviance sometimes challenges mainstream ideas about what is important.

and stranger alike" (Clifford, 1976, p. 13). In this way, deviance can take the pressure off the social system by channeling antisocial tendencies in less harmful directions.

Deviance can also bring about social reforms by shining a spotlight on aspects of the social order that are in need of change. Workers' marches and strikes in the 1930s and 1940s awakened Americans to the need for labor reforms. Similarly, the sit-in demonstrations and marches of the 1960s civil rights movement forced society to recognize the injustice of racial segregation. In such cases, the spectacle of many people deliberately, sometimes courageously, challenging the social order serves to galvanize society into making long-needed reforms.

Donald Black (1983) takes this functionalist approach still further by arguing that even murder can serve to enforce social control. Most intentional killings, he explains, are responses to personal affronts, domestic squabbles, or property disputes. In such cases, violation of societal norms is punished by individuals taking the laws into their own hands, a kind of privately administered capital punishment. Similarly, robbery "is a form of debt collection" (p. 37). Such "self-help" in the face of an unresponsive legal system constitutes a form of social control.

Given the various functions of deviance, the special problems of capitalist societies, and the human tendency toward self-gratification, it is easy to understand why people routinely violate behavioral norms, even in well-regulated societies. We now turn to the problem of how societies try to control human behavior. In particular, we turn from everyday noncriminal deviance, like crude table manners or wearing a swimsuit to church, to crime: deviance that violates civil or criminal laws.

SOCIAL CONTROL: LESSONS FROM JAPAN, SAUDI ARABIA, AND CHINA

Social control: rules and actions aimed at regulating human behavior.

Society cannot allow individuals to freely choose their actions with no concern for others. The resulting behaviors, predictably selfish, would invite chaos. They would disrupt the necessary coordination of people's actions, and threaten the orderliness and security they need to focus on ends beyond personal survival. The functionalist perspective argues that, because deviance occurs naturally and inevitably, society must counter with a system of **social control:** rules and actions aimed at regulating human behavior.

How do societies manage to control human behavior? To begin with, they exert control both internally and externally. Some societies are much more successful at this than ours, which has among the world's highest crime rates. As examples, we turn to three nations with exceptionally low crime rates: Japan, Saudi Arabia, and China.

The Policeman Within

During its tremendous spurt of industrialization and urbanization after World War II, Japan's crime rate actually decreased. The secret of Japan's success lies in a social structure that fosters internal policing. People in Japanese society each have a "proper place," fitted into a strict hierarchy, from which they derive their self-image. Maintaining one's self-image requires conformity to the social obligations and expectations connected to that place. To commit an act of deviance is to fail to meet these obligations, which brings shame, the primary motivating force for conformity in Japanese society. Deviance thus holds such far-reaching consequences that the Japanese exert great self-control to avoid "losing face." The "internal policeman" largely explains Japan's successful social control (Clifford, 1976).

Internalization: the process by which people make society's norms their own.

As with any other society, Japan's domestic tranquility depends mostly on **internalization,** the process by which people make society's norms their own. This socialization process is more effective than external threats at keeping us within normative boundaries. After all, most of us usually conform to the rules not because we fear arrest and jail but because we choose to respect the rules with which we identify. Through internalization, the individual's conscience becomes aligned with society's norms; guilt and shame gain power in our choice of actions.

Internal controls work most effectively when all the socialization agents point the individual in the same direction. This contrasts sharply with the United States, where a child may hear conflicting moral lessons from his or her mother, father, school teacher, grandparent, movie idol, or neighborhood pal. In Saudi Arabia, virtually all citizens are Muslims, and all the socialization agents promote the same Islamic laws and values. The first words breathed into a Saudi infant's ears are, "There is no God but Allah and Muhammad is His Prophet," a refrain that will probably accompany the Saudi through his or her last dying moments. Islam pervades and dominates Saudi society, providing a monolithic value system. Saudi religious homogeneity gives the society an advantage in social control.

Japan also enjoys this well-focused social control. Its historic isolation and careful restrictions on recent immigration have produced a remarkably unmixed racial population that shares a strong cultural tradition. Part of that tradition stems from

Confucianism, with its strong emphasis on loyalty and fidelity (Westermann and Burfeind, 1991). Racial, cultural, and religious homogeneity help explain how a large society like Japan displays a degree of conformity usually found only in families or villages.

External Social Control

Guilt in the face of God's will and the shame of losing one's place in society's hierarchy are not enough, however. Despite the extremely focused socialization efforts of Saudi Arabia and Japan, deviance occasionally overflows the normative boundaries. To enforce their norms, all societies use **sanctions:** rewards and punishments aimed at regulating behaviors. From commendations and affection to humiliation and beatings, sanctions take up where internal controls leave off.

Sanctions: rewards and punishments aimed at regulating behaviors.

Informal Sanctions   People around us, acting through no special roles or authority, casually apply rewards and punishments to us in what sociologists call **informal sanctions.** In communist China, for example, people take an intense interest in the behavior of their fellow neighbors and employees, diligently and enthusiastically administering such sanctions to wrongdoers. Building upon a tradition of widespread reinforcement of "right thinking," modern Chinese citizens bring a great deal of informal pressure to bear on one another. What we would call intruding busybodies, they would call conscientious citizens (who, by the way, help keep China's prisons undercrowded). Japan likewise has a strong tradition that encourages every citizen to take an interest in neighbors' behaviors and to do his or her part to control actions that might endanger society's well-being. This tradition began in feudal times, when five-family groups, each under a leader, administered law, arbitrated disputes, and kept order. Since then, although these control mechanisms were formally abolished, neighborhood-level organization has helped administer informal controls. Everywhere a Japanese citizen

Informal sanctions: rewards and punishments applied by people with no special authority.

In some societies socialization is especially intense from the first moments of birth until death. Such intensity, consistency, and uniformity can facilitate internalization of society's norms.

In some societies, neighbors take on responsibility for correcting or monitoring the behavior of their fellows. At the cost of little privacy they enjoy low crime rates.

goes, from the crowded neighborhood to school to the workplace, he or she faces continuous scrutiny aimed at ensuring that everyone plays out their allotted roles. Such informal surveillance is explained by a common saying in Japan: "The nail that stands out is hammered down."

Most of the intense scrutiny in Japan and China leads to punishments such as nagging questions, finger-wagging lectures, or social rejection, but sanctions also include rewards. In Saudi society, the person who displays the features of the ideal character—faith, morality, piety—enjoys not only inner pride, an important positive sanction in itself, but also praise and deference from others. We all value these informal rewards very highly. For most of us, conformity is a small price to pay for the sweet taste of respect or affection given by friends and even strangers. Conversely, we have all felt the stinging embarrassment of other people's stares, frowns, or suppressed smirks. Such negative informal sanctions have power to motivate us to toe the line.

Formal Sanctions **Formal sanctions,** official rewards and punishments applied by authorized agents or people playing out specialized social-control roles, stand ready to back up informal sanctions. Formal rewards include military medals of honor, schools' good citizen ribbons, and community "citizen of the year" awards. Punishments include incarceration, fines, enrollment in rehabilitative programs, and public whippings and beheading. Beyond this, Saudis stand liable for arrest on the word of any man. A "citizen's arrest" can send anyone to jail until the charges are examined, but in the meanwhile the arrested person may have to contend with the notoriously rough

Formal sanctions: official rewards and punishments applied by authorized agents or people occupying specialized social-control roles.

treatment of the police, who, with a great deal of informal authority, sometimes cane motorists they have caught speeding or wade through crowds with truncheons flailing (Mackey, 1987).

In China, the communist government has built upon traditional citizen monitoring through residents' committees and "work units." Bureaucratic controls extend into both rural and urban areas, where each residents' committee supervises several hundred families; within this unit, small groups look after 15–40 families grouped in apartment buildings or clusters of houses (Troyer, 1989). These organizations carry out surveillance in the typically crowded Chinese urban neighborhood. Individuals suffer no isolation, but have little privacy either. Because the government assigns citizens to their residences, and permission to move is not readily granted, these small groups represent a stable unit of social control. The production unit at the workplace exerts even greater control. It keeps a personal file on each adult, and any deviance recorded follows the citizen for the rest of her or his life. The work unit's list of sanctions also includes denial of the required approval to purchase certain goods and services, poor housing arrangements, and even denying parents the opportunity to pass their jobs along to their children.

HIGHER CRIME FOR AFRICA: THE PRICE OF MODERNIZATION?

Despite the few social-control success stories of countries like Japan, Saudi Arabia, and China, sociological research tells us that the widespread social dislocations wrought by modernization inevitably bring more criminal deviance. We now turn our attention to such swiftly changing societies and ask: As African nations move toward greater economic development, must they pay a price of higher crime rates? First we explore the theoretical background of this question, then see if it applies to Africa.

Emile Durkheim (1938) first made the connection between social change and crime, observing that as a society grows in size and population density, it develops a more complex division of labor that lessens its cohesion. Family and community ties weaken, diminishing the "social capital" or informal consensus upon which norms are based, thus weakening the effectiveness of social controls (Coleman, 1993). Modernizing society becomes increasingly segmented into a "mosaic" of competing interest groups (Leavitt, 1992, p. 243) rather than a unified population. Such changes deprive the individual of clear-cut guidelines, and result in what Durkheim called **anomie,** a state of confusion or normlessness. The faster the pace of modernization, the higher the level of anomie and the more individuals will choose deviant or criminal behaviors. All of this points to the possibility of higher crime rates in Africa's modernizing nations.

Anomie: a state of confusion or normlessness.

Marshall Clinard and Daniel Abbott (1973) expand on this modernization–crime theme, suggesting that crime levels actually serve as a measure of a nation's economic development. They describe the typical rush of migration found in developing nations like many in Africa: streams of people flowing from the countryside to the cities, where much higher living standards serve as a powerful magnet. However, the cities' limited opportunities for so many undereducated workers result in a large population of alienated people, cast adrift from their religious mooring and extended family controls. The mass media add to these frustrations by raising unrealistically high material expectations. These social pressures find release through high crime rates, especially property crimes. Increases in armed robbery, automobile theft, and government and business corruption easily and inevitably result from rapid modernization and urban overcrowding. As such countries continue to develop, they show more of the types of crime characteristic of developed nations: vandalism, check forgery, and embezzlement.

Clinard and Abbott describe the typical migrant: male, young, unskilled, new to the city, suddenly far from his village ties. Searching for a job that will fulfill his dreams of material success, he quickly learns that he is competing with thousands of other young men like himself. He struggles with problems of identity and economic stress in an urban slum where few people have long-lasting relationships with their neighbors, and where temptations such as prostitution and alcoholism abound. His initial contacts and associations in the city can make all the difference in whether or not he follows a path of crime.

While temptations and stressors abound for migrants in such cities, so do certain opportunities. As a society industrializes, more material goods are unguarded and available for theft as women join the workforce and leave their households during the day (Cohen and Felson, 1979; Kick and LaFree, 1985). The arrest rate of females also increases as a society develops economically, partly because of the greater opportunities for female-based consumer crimes like shoplifting and check forgery (Steffensmeier et al., 1989). These new opportunities, along with the other repercussions of modernization, have led to a surge in many African nations' crime rates.

Can We Measure Increases in Crime?

Any evidence of higher crime rates in developing nations, however, invites some skepticism. Even in the United States, where the gathering of statistics is taken quite seriously, we have an incomplete picture of our own criminal behavior. The FBI regularly collects information about offenses reported to the thousands of law enforcement agencies across the nation. However, those statistics do not reflect the large percentage of crimes that are never reported. The Department of Justice, on the other hand, surveys Americans about their experiences regarding crime and victimization. By combining those two sources, researchers have found that only a little more than a third of all crimes are actually reported to the police, although about half the violent crimes are reported.

Given this serious flaw in the statistical picture of crime in the United States, can we trust measurements of crimes in developing nations? We may question whether such countries possess the bureaucratic discipline and funding required to collect accurate statistics. We can also wonder if their citizens are even more reluctant to report crimes than we are. Like us, they may choose not to report trivial offenses, victimless crimes, or embarrassing victimizations, especially sex offenses, to the police. And they too may lack confidence in their judicial system. Citizens may fear the police, especially if only weak bureaucratic controls stand between them and abuse by civil authorities. In any case, aggrieved citizens have few police stations at which to make their complaint in developing countries. They may decide simply to handle it themselves, perhaps through their kinship system.

Most of these same considerations result in a serious underreporting of crime in any society. To further complicate matters, a developing nation's crime rate may soar simply because of improvements in its reporting system. If modernization brings more efficient recording practices, more effective police practices, and more reliable court-room procedures, the level of reported crimes may rise even if the level of actual crime does not.

As African nations move into the modern world, these complications may have an especially strong impact. Traditional African societies had little reason to report crimes, as most offenses were handled informally by the elders or chief, and off-the-record arbitration, punishment, and restitution probably concealed the true level of crime (Arthur, 1991). Formal law enforcement and judicial agencies are now replacing this informal system. Since these agencies may seek to establish their importance by making many arrests and convictions, Africa's crime rates may appear to mushroom.

These difficulties do not mean that we cannot spot large increases in crime. As Clinard and Abbott point out, "The reported figures, although not reflecting the true extent of crime, indicate a basic minimum figure which, when large or increasing rapidly, is important" (1973, p. 28).

What Is the Future for Africa?

Modernization theory predicts that a developing area like Africa will experience a genuine increase in crime, one that is not simply the result of more accurate reporting. Some theorists also contend that colonialism so completely disrupted traditional social structures that the dislocation associated with modernization has been going on for many generations. Moreover, the built-in inequities of the world economic system ensure that developing nations today have little hope of achieving stability amid such fast-paced change and growth.

Further, nations with swiftly growing populations (like most of those in Africa, even though fertility rates are actually dropping) will predictably show the highest increases in crime rates, in part because such growth weakens the community's acquaintanceship network and diminishes informal social controls (Freudenburg and Jones, 1991). Also, a large influx of newcomers can overload police services. And homicide rates are higher in nations (again, like most of those in Africa) with great income inequality (Krahn, Hartnagel, and Gartrell, 1986). Higher crime seems certain for Africa.

As if this were not enough, the continent's youthful population also seems to promise soaring crime for African societies. Over the past 50 years, researchers have discovered a positive correlation between crime rates and the proportion of young people in a population (Steffensmeier et al., 1989). Though this connection varies somewhat with the type of crime, most criminal offenses rise during adolescence and decline thereafter (Steffensmeier and Harer, 1991). This fact has special significance for most African nations, which on the whole have relatively young populations because of the recent and dramatic reduction of infant death rates.

This drop in infant mortality has sent a huge wave of young people surging through most African societies. So many people born in such a short period of time usually means trouble; those people must compete with one another for legitimate opportunities, and they overload social control institutions, both of which help to raise crime rates (Easterlin, 1978, 1987). Picture a mass of young adults scrambling for jobs and income, unable to afford the stabilizing practices of marriage and childbearing and overwhelming parents, counselors, teachers, ministers, and other agents of control. The inevitable results are feelings of deprivation and alienation, and higher rates of suicide and crime, especially property crime (O'Brien, 1989). At least this has happened in our own society; we hope Africa will escape the same repercussions (Steffensmeier, Streifel, and Shihadeh, 1992).

After applying the sociological perspective in several chapters in this book, we might wonder if the evidence is moving too smoothly toward the conclusion that Africa's crime rates must increase. And indeed—as usual—the more deeply researchers have dug, the more complications they have uncovered. Most importantly, studies have found *declining* crime rates accompanying modernization in some developing nations (J. D. Rogers, 1989). How can this be?

By distinguishing between crimes against persons and those against property, sociologists have discovered that violent crimes usually decrease with modernization while property crimes increase (Bennett and Shelley, 1985; Kick and LaFree, 1985). For example, homicide rates either declined or showed no relationship to the modernization of many European nations during the 1800s (Gurr, 1981; Archer and Gartner, 1984). On the other hand, as peasants migrate to cities that present a tempting array of consumer goods but lack strong normative systems, a nation's property crime rates usually increase (Shelley, 1981; Krohn, 1978).

This distinction seems to clear up the confusion in the connection between modernization and crime. Yet a study of 11 developing African countries with available crime data found that while homicide decreased as expected, major property crimes also decreased—contrary to modernization theory's predictions. Only minor property crimes, such as petty theft and fraud, increased (Arthur, 1991). These nations may not represent all of Africa, but such results clearly suggest that what happened during Europe's development may not precisely predict what will occur in Africa. It also reminds us that modernization is only one of many factors determining a nation's crime rate trends and that making generalizations about social relationships is difficult.

Stephen Earl Bennett (1991) finds more intricacies in the modernization theory that may help us anticipate African crime rates. For example, the rate of theft does tend to increase as countries develop, but only up to a point, perhaps because of the eventual deployment of more effective policing, "target hardening" (better locks, fences, and burglar alarms), and better community surveillance. Such a threshold could account for some of the discrepancies among the various studies. He also finds that development has a greater impact on the homicide rates in some societies than in others. Moreover, each nation's cultural context must be considered (Gartner, 1990). For example, a relatively nonviolent cultural tradition probably explains Egypt's low homicide rate (1.38 per 100,000 inhabitants in 1984), while the Philippines' long experience with antigovernment violence may underlie its very high rate (43.31). The United States' pioneer, "Wild West" tradition may account for its rate of 7.89, in contrast with 1.16 in Great Britain, where firearms are relatively rare.

Modernization theory has not been abandoned, only modified. In applying it, we need to recognize that modernization will not affect all cultures the same way. Louise Shelley (1981) illustrates this by pointing to significant differences among the crime rates of various areas of the developing world. Because they maintain their religious and familial underpinnings, Israel and the Islamic nations of North Africa and the Middle East can more readily absorb the impact of rapid economic development with relatively low crime rates. In the Caribbean nations, a tradition of high rural violence, their location in major drug pathways, and the constant influx of wealthy tourists combine to produce exceptionally high crime rates. Between these two extremes lie South America, Asia, and non-Moslem Africa.

What can we conclude about crime rates in developing African nations? First, though we know to take great care in generalizing about an entire continent, the frequent political and economic upheavals that interrupt or overtake the few studies focusing on individual African nations almost force us to do so. Second, we cannot easily assume that Africa will adapt to modernization in the same way as did Europe, North America, and other areas of the world. Finally, while we cannot see what's in Africa's future, comparing the experience of other societies with those of Africa can sharpen our expectations and alert us to the adaptations any society makes to the various social dislocations that usually accompany modernization. This brings us as close to predicting the future as science allows.

Critical Thinking Box

What Accounts for Different Crime Rates?

Listed below (Table 5-1) are the 10 states with the highest rates of serious crimes and the 10 with the lowest. What factors might help explain the enormous differences? ■

ESTIMATED TOTAL CRIME INDEX, PER 100,000 INHABITANTS, OF OFFENSES KNOWN TO THE POLICE, 1991

Top 10 States	Crime Rate	Bottom 10 States	Crime Rate
Florida	8547	Idaho	4195
Texas	7819	Iowa	4134
Arizona	7405	Vermont	3955
California	6772	Maine	3767
New Mexico	6679	Pennsylvania	3558
Georgia	6493	New Hampshire	3447
Louisiana	6424	Kentucky	3358
Washington	6304	South Dakota	3079
Nevada	6298	North Dakota	2793
New York	6244	West Virginia	2663

Table 5-1

Source: U.S. Department of Justice, Federal Bureau of Investigation, *Crime in the United States, 1991* (Washington, DC: USGPO, 1992), Table 6.

THE MAKINGS OF A CRIMINAL

Here we change our focus from society to the individual. This brings us to the everyday level of crime, where, hearing of the latest assault or swindle, we might wonder, Why do people do things like that? Criminologists have asked the same question, and have identified some of the correlates of crime that help explain why some individuals more readily succumb to the social forces that push people toward criminal behavior.

Biology and Criminality

Researchers have found intriguing hints of a biological link to crime, either through genes or environmental influences like diet and drugs. Though results are preliminary or inconclusive, the biological factors listed on page 136 are among many correlated with criminal behavior.

- Levels of trace minerals in hair (Cromwell et al., 1989)

- Distinctive electroencephalogram (EEG) patterns (Howard, 1984)

- Low levels of the enzyme monoamine oxidase (MAO) (Ellis, 1991)

- Low levels of the neurotransmitter serotonin (Virkkunen et al., 1989; Fishbein, Lozovsk, and Jaffe, 1989)

- High levels of lead (Lester and Fishbein, 1987)

- High levels of testosterone (Schiavi et al., 1984; Booth and Osgood, 1993)

- Premenstrual hormonal changes (Ginsburg and Carter, 1987)

Perhaps the most intriguing question raised by such findings goes beyond biological factors such as drugs and nutrition and asks if criminality is inherited. The evidence suggests a genetic link to crime, but methodological flaws plague the research. For example, studies of families find an impressive array of problem behaviors shared among family members, including temper outbursts (Mattes and Fink, 1987), aggression and violence (Twito and Stewart, 1982), and delinquency (Rowe, 1986). However, such studies leave us wondering whether the behaviors arose from shared genes or shared home environments. Others find that adopted people's criminal histories more closely resemble those of their biological parents than their adoptive parents, but small samples, varying age at adoption, and other important technical difficulties call the results into question. Likewise, studies of identical twins strongly suggest a genetic influence on criminality, but part of that influence may actually result from the twins' social interaction with each other (Carey, 1992). Also, because of such difficulties as similar environments (even when twins are adopted into separate families), results remain inconclusive. All this research suffers from inconsistency and the difficulty of separating biological from environmental effects (Fishbein, 1990; Plomin, Nitz, and Rowe, 1990; Walters and White, 1989). As one researcher concludes, "it seems unlikely that a direct genetic link for crime exists anywhere but in the minds of a handful of investigators" (Walters, 1992, p. 608).

Despite such discouraging complications, while researchers do not expect to find a "criminal gene" or "bad seed" they do hope to identify internal, physical influences that tend to interact with external, social influences to produce antisocial behaviors. In other words, genes may provide the potential, but social forces are needed to activate that potential. For example, a child with inherited impulsivity and high activity level may be something of a loaded gun, needing only parental conflict or at least one abusive parent to produce aggressive, even criminal, behavior patterns (McCord, 1991). Similarly, because of their neurological make-up, perhaps based on genes, psychopaths have such low levels of anxiety, such high pain thresholds, and derive such intense pleasure from thrill-seeking behaviors that few social controls can produce in these individuals enough fear or anxiety to deter them (Blackburn, 1978). As crime researchers probe the link between biology and social forces, they increasingly believe that a full picture of crime causation requires an investigation of biological factors.

A Criminal's Profile

Besides possible biological influences, what else can we guess about the typical criminal's make-up? If one is standing before us in a darkened room, we can say with some assurance and without even turning on the lights that the offender is male and in his teens or early twenties. Young males, after all, have the highest probability of being arrested. Beyond this, we can use a large body of research to make informed guesses about his social background. For instance, our criminal, especially if he is a serious, violent offender, probably grew up in a lower-class home (Weiss, 1986; Rutter and Giller, 1983; Visher, Lattimore, and Linster, 1991). Perhaps poverty could also explain the likelihood that his mother suffered complications during pregnancy and delivery, which correlate with minor difficulties in the formation of the developing child's central nervous system, which in turn correlate with—though may not by themselves cause—delinquency (Mungas, 1983; Nichols, 1987; Kandel and Mednick, 1991).

Looking further into this home, whatever its socioeconomic status, we can expect to find poor parental management skills—inadequate monitoring and discipline, rejection, and little parental involvement (Larzelere and Patterson, 1990; Loeber and Stouthamer-Loeber, 1986). The parents may well have inadvertently rewarded the child's antisocial behaviors or at least failed to consistently punish transgressions or reward desired behaviors (Patterson, 1982; Patterson and Bank, 1989). We should not be surprised to find that our criminal's childhood home also included an incompetent mother, an uninvolved father, low family expectations for their son (McCord, 1991), a delinquent father (Mednick, Baker, and Carothers, 1990), and delinquent siblings (Rowe and Gulley, 1992). We can also confidently expect that our criminal experienced school failure, peer rejection (Dishion et al., 1991), abuse (Kruttschnitt and Dornfeld, 1991), and belonged to a delinquent gang (Curry Spergel, 1992).

We cannot say with certainty that these social experiences *cause* criminal behaviors, and we must remember criminals come from many kinds of social backgrounds. Still, we can predict that as such conditions become more prevalent in our society, the rate of crime will increase.

THE GANG NEIGHBORHOOD: A SETTING FOR CRIME

The juvenile gang conjures up images of vicious, alienated, perhaps hopelessly lost youths. Yet not all such groups engage in criminal acts, and even the delinquent ones do not always fit the brutally violent mass media **stereotype.** Gangs range from informal, largely recreational groups to well-organized enterprises aimed at making as much money as possible in any way possible. Members vary in their commitment from the dedicated to the occasional participant. Keeping in mind the need to avoid stereotypes, we will see that some Los Angeles gangs, though not necessarily representative of others, illustrate how social forces contribute to crime in general, and juvenile delinquency in particular.

Stereotypes: fixed generalizations about all members of a group or category.

As in many large cities, the neighborhoods of L. A., especially those of large ethnic or racial minority populations, contain juvenile delinquent gangs. Every immigrant group is represented, including Vietnamese, Chinese, Filipinos, Samoans, Koreans, and Jamaicans. But the gangs of African Americans and Mexican Americans easily outnumber all others. We will focus on Mexican American, or Chicano, gangs because several writers have provided excellent descriptions of these groups.

Many Chicano gangs have their roots in the 1940s. Since then, some of the ethnically segregated, low-income neighborhoods, or barrios, have periodically experienced waves of gang battles, drive-by shootings, revenge murders, drug busts, and massive police sweeps. While only about 4 to 10 percent of the youths in most barrios belong to delinquent gangs (Morales, 1982), these communities demonstrate what social factors contribute to this particular pattern of crime.

Why Do Gangs Get Started?

There are wide variations among the large number of gangs in Los Angeles, but those typical of the barrios share several background characteristics: poverty, blocked opportunities, and social disorganization. These traits, when combined with the adolescent tendency toward strong peer bonding, help create delinquent gangs.

Poverty In general, people who lack a basic level of material wealth are more likely to engage in criminal behavior (Vold and Bernard, 1986; Patterson, 1991), especially property crimes (Crutchfield, Geerken, and Gove, 1982). Even violent crimes are linked to economic troubles such as widespread unemployment, as seen in the increase in murder, domestic violence, and other offenses that follow the closing of a town's main source of jobs (Koeppel, 1989). Adverse economic forces may leave individuals feeling powerless, and thus less likely or able to take responsibility for their actions, and such irresponsibility may well contribute to criminal activity (Darley and Zanna, 1982; Phillips, 1991). Certainly not all gang members come from poverty-stricken homes, but economic deprivation is a common theme in their self-descriptions.

Another face of poverty, unemployment, also figures strongly in gang members' backgrounds. The link is perhaps understandably stronger for property crimes than violent crimes (Box, 1987; Chiricos, 1987), though simply providing jobs will not necessarily reduce the crime rate in a neighborhood (Crutchfield, 1989). As important as employment is the type of jobs people hold in a neighborhood. When they are mostly unstable, high-turnover jobs such as waitress, domestic servant, and security guard, the resulting weak ties to the workplace and excess idle time contribute to the development of a delinquent gang subculture. Such workers are also less likely to bond strongly to their job or co-workers. They have less to lose in the event of arrest and thus less reason to conform to the norms of the broader society.

This research clearly applies to the typical barrios of L. A. More so than many other cities, Los Angeles lost many high-wage manufacturing jobs in the 1980s. Economic restructuring also eliminated many low-skill slots that barrio youths could reasonably expect to fill. Most of the few remaining jobs paid poorly. As a result, many Mexican-American families suffered from unemployment, or part-time employment with reduced income.

As if poverty were not enough, Mexican Americans have for generations also faced prejudice, and this combination of inequality and injustice produces an even more fertile ground for crime. Many youths from the barrio get their first taste of prejudice in school, where their Anglo peers often dismiss them with a lengthy list of derogatory names. Poverty based on an ascribed status, such as race, will generate a sense of injustice and discontent, and a feeling that such proclaimed values of society as equal opportunity for all are not realized in actual experience (Blau and Blau, 1982; Blau and Schwartz, 1984). The resulting weakening of social bonds can free people from mainstream norms, opening the way to deviance and crime. The documented link between discrimination and violent crime (Balkwell, 1990; Messner, 1989; Messner and Golden, 1992) helps explain why barrio residents lash out at police, teachers, and non-Chicanos.

Well,

maybe there's a way

of being traditional

that's not so... um,

traditional.

If you know what I mean.

Eighty Eight Royale LSS

Torquey 3800 V6. Anti-lock brakes. Front-wheel drive. Four-wheel independent suspension. If it weren't for the full-size comfort and 17.5 cubic-foot trunk, people could get the wrong idea. Call 1-800-242-OLDS.

E I G H T Y   E I G H T

OLDSMOBILE
THE POWER OF INTELLIGENT ENGINEERING.

Lower-class people lack the resources to legally acquire the material symbols of success promoted by society. The resulting social strain can lead some such people to use illegitimate means for achieving their goals.

Social Strain   Of course, poverty by itself does not explain crime; otherwise, crime rates would plummet as living standards rose. However, poverty in the face of others' wealth increases the chances for delinquency, especially if we feel blocked from opportunities to reap some of society's rewards. Robert Merton (1938) describes how anomie arises from the strain between the culture's ideal aspirations and what an individual can realistically expect to achieve. In other words, people feel confused and alienated when they cannot reach the goals set for them by the mainstream culture. This social strain most often reaches lower-class people with few resources to acquire the material symbols of success through the socially approved route of education and high-status employment. Lacking the social and educational tools to legitimately compete, some barrio boys and girls scorn the legitimate path and choose one in which they can find some measure of success—delinquent gangs. Through this adaptation, which Merton calls *innovation*, youths still accept the goal of wealth acquisition, and indeed may work very hard to acquire it, but use illegal means such as petty theft and drug dealing. The barrio experience confirms earlier studies in which lower-class teenagers responded to blocked opportunities by focusing on "toughness" and "troublemaking" rather than academic achievement and conformity to society's laws (Cohen, 1955, Miller, 1958).

Most barrio youths adapt to social strains in other ways. The majority choose what Merton calls *conformity* to mainstream social norms. This involves using legitimate means—hard work in education and legal employment—to reach society's goal of wealth, despite the disadvantages of the neighborhood. A few reject as unobtainable the goal of affluence, and conclude that the hard work holds no promise for them. This path, which Merton labels *retreatism*, involves rejecting society's goals and means, usually through alcoholism and drug addiction. Since the 1950s, the drug of choice in Chicano communities has been heroin. Joan Moore (1991) illustrates one man's retreatism based on this drug: After joining a gang at age 15, he began using heroin at 16, spent his twenties in and out of jail, his thirties doing stints in prison, and his forties kicking his habit and surviving on odd jobs like painting and gardening (Moore, 1991, p. 106). Some barrio youths pursue legitimate means to success, yet satisfy themselves with dead-end jobs that offer no economic future. In other words, they blindly embrace the means while ignoring their professed goal of escaping the barrio, what Merton calls *ritualism*. We find in the barrio, however, little evidence of *rebellion*, in which members of the community aim to replace society's goals and means with new ones, and thus build a new social order.

Social strain theory, with its focus on blocked opportunities, helps us understand some property crime in the barrio, but it says little about violent crime or crime in middle-class neighborhoods. Robert Agnew (1992) expands it, however, to include other kinds of strain, such as the gap between one's *own* expectations and achievements, which can be experienced by *any* social class. This strain can produce anger, resentment, and other negative emotions that can lead to criminality even among people far from the barrio. Other types of strain, more common in the barrio, result from some negative experience or situation, such as the loss of a job, criminal victimization, and overcrowding. Delinquency can also arise from living in the adverse conditions found in many gang neighborhoods (McCarthy and Hagan, 1992), including beatings, shootings, and various forms of intimidation. These extensions of Merton's original theory account for much of the delinquency in the barrio and other neighborhoods.

Breakdown in Social Organization   Several forces can combine to destroy a community's social organization. When this occurs, such communities, like a fruit with its skin pierced, become more vulnerable (Kornhauser, 1978; Sampson and Groves, 1989). As poverty, the most damaging condition, grips a neighborhood, more children receive their socialization in the streets rather than from the family, and few adults participate in community organizations. The gang subculture replaces family, schools, and other approved agents of socialization. Another disorganizing factor, residential mobility, interferes with the development of extensive, local friendship networks. In addition, racial and ethnic heterogeneity breed fear, mistrust, defensiveness, and community segmentation—all barriers to the cohesion required for social controls. Furthermore, high levels of family disruption decrease neighborhood supervision and guardianship of children and of household property (Sampson, 1987; Cohen

Social Disorganization and Crime

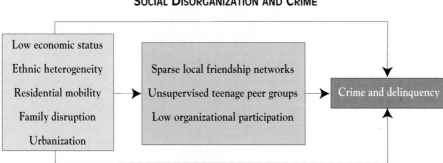

Drawing on Shaw and McKay's original theory of social disorganization, Robert J. Sampson and W. Byron Groves (1989) depict crime and delinquency flowing from various disruptive features in the community. As in most sociological explanations of delinquency, low socioeconomic status plays a central role. Overall, the diagram pictures a neighborhood falling apart and succumbing to criminality.

Figure 5–1

Source: Robert J. Sampson and W. Byron Groves, "Community structure and crime: Testing social-disorganization theory," *American Journal of Sociology* volume 94, number 4 (January 1989), Figure 1, page 783. Copyright by The University of Chicago, 1989.

and Felson, 1979). In such neighborhoods, "The gang has become a 'spontaneous' street social unit that fills a void left by families under stress" (Vigil, 1988, p. 90). (See Figure 5-1 for an illustration of this process.)

We could expect such a disadvantaged neighborhood to have many of the "hot spots" that seem to generate crime (Kennedy and Baron, 1993). In such places, routine activities bring together three elements required of criminal acts: motivated offenders, suitable targets, and the absence of capable guardians (Cohen and Felson, 1979). In many high-crime neighborhoods, bars, taverns, and lounges serve this purpose. In the barrio, most gang members hang out at private houses or the streets to use and deal drugs. The routine activities at such "hot spots" bring together often youthful, drunken people to act as either offenders or easy targets; available cash; and too few parents, relatives, or police to provide informal or formal controls (Roncek and Maier, 1991; Roncek and Pravatiner, 1989).

Social disorganization can also give rise to subcultures of violence. Lower-class, inner-city residents suffering from discrimination and operating in an isolated, aggressive environment more easily take offense and use force to deal with perceived insults and affronts to their personal honor (Bernard, 1990). In some neighborhoods, the slightest jostle or remark may set off a dispute in which aggression is required, and violence is likely. Such violent subcultures are more common among rural, black, urban, and young people, especially males (Doyle and Luckenbill, 1991), but the barrio has its share. As one Chicano gang member explains, "We take pride in our little nation and if any intruders enter, we get panicked because we feel our community is being threatened. The only way is with violence" (Vigil, 1988, p. 131). Youths in such a threatening neighborhood typically join a gang for protection. Another member recalls that he faced two prospects in the barrio, getting beaten every day by the gang, or joining the gang and getting beaten only occasionally by rival gangs (Vigil, 1988, p. 52).

The disorganization of a neighborhood leaves it vulnerable because the forces that normally produce social control do not adequately restrain individuals and bond them to society's norms. According to *social control theory,* people naturally lean toward deviance and will translate that tendency into crime or delinquency unless

Some places generate criminal activities because of their mix of the right kinds of people, temptations, and lack of capable guardians.

social controls prevent them from doing so. The theory's originator, Travis Hirschi (1969), contends that humans need continuous socialization to restrain their inherent criminality and bond them to society's norms. Weak bonds "free" people to engage in delinquency. We see this among college students freed from parental supervision, as well as youths growing up in barrios with high levels of family disruption, poverty, unemployment, and residential mobility. One observer of a barrio reports young children frequently wandering in areas far from home, with no supervision for hours (Vigil, 1988, p. 28). When a social environment exerts little control over individuals, they develop low self-control, the key factor predicting later criminality (Gottfredson and Hirschi, 1990; Hirschi and Gottfredson, 1993). Like water that threatens to spill over a threshold, deviance requires constant containment. People will naturally violate rules unless prevented from doing so—that is, unless they learn self-control.

From this viewpoint, juvenile delinquency becomes understandable, even expected, in a neighborhood torn by poverty and discrimination (although only a small minority of barrio youths turn to serious delinquency). Socialization in such neighborhoods often fails to produce the four elements of bonding needed to hold deviance in check. First, *attachment* to conventional others, such as parents, teachers, and conforming peers, forestalls deviance. In the barrio, however, divorce and desertion hit many homes before children reach adolescence. Moreover, drunken parents, beatings, and incest cause a high percentage of the children to run away from home—hardly evidence of attachment (Moore, 1991, p. 86). Such home environments clearly reduce the level of trust, support, encouragement, love and affection, and positive communication between parents and children that help bond youths to society's norms.

Second, *commitment* to conventional goals and activities, such as school, staves off delinquency and crime. Those who have invested time and energy in acquiring an education or establishing a business may avoid deviance because it could cost them their investment. High school students who have worked hard to maintain a high grade point average are more likely to shy away from illegal pranks than students with nothing invested in their academics. Barrio youngsters, however, justifiably complain of few parks or organized youth activities. As one student explains, "Well, you never carry books with you. If you did, they [the gang members] would make fun of you" (Vigil, 1988, p. 80). For some, in other words, commitment means gang membership.

Third, *involvement* in conventional activities limits the time people have to consider deviant behaviors. The student immersed in studies and work has no time for getting into trouble. Jobs are scarce in the barrio, however, and Mexican-American students often find themselves in the remedial, noncollege "track." One student recalls trying to enroll in a literature class, but being told by the counselor, "I think you'll find our industrial arts subjects more suited to your needs" (Rodriguez, 1993, p. 137).

Finally, the more that individuals believe in the moral validity of society's rules, the less likely they are to violate those rules. Such *belief* in the rules directly reflects a person's bond to morality, and predicts low deviance levels. Those barrio youths who call themselves *cholo,* however, retain some traditional Mexican attitudes and values, and keep a distance from mainstream American culture.

Of course, the typical barrio manages a substantial amount of social control; here we have focused on the deficiencies found in many communities. Moreover, some critics claim that neither self-control nor the four bonding elements entirely explain delinquency (Agnew, 1991; Grasmick et al., 1993; Matsueda, 1989). Thus a large percentage of barrio youths conform to mainstream social norms despite their neighborhood's relatively high level of social disorganization and relatively low level of formal social control.

What Perpetuates the Gang?

As we have seen, the gang subculture arises as a haven for youths who believe they have no other institutions on which they can depend for feelings of identity, security, and success. Fed by waves of new immigrants, and burdened with continued poverty and discrimination, the gang subculture over the past half-century has become well established in many barrios. How have these gangs lasted so long?

Clifford Shaw and Henry McKay (1929) found that in any neighborhood, once delinquent subcultures are established they will probably be transmitted to subsequent generations through local play groups and gangs. Because barrios have generally retained their unusually homogeneous ethnic make-up as well as their social disadvantages, this transmission proceeds easily. But even in communities where one ethnic group moves out to be replaced by another, the delinquency rate remains high. As the new group gradually moves into the area, they learn delinquent behavior by interacting with the remaining members of the other group.

The social force at work here is simply informal socialization. This force works in any segment of society, but Richard Cloward and Lloyd Ohlin (1960) point out that in some neighborhoods the most influential "teachers" are drug pushers and thieves

Some "teachers" in a neighborhood can socialize other youths in the direction of deviance.

rather than parents who value education, good manners, and respectable work. As role models differ from one neighborhood to the next, so do opportunities. Some children learn from older youths in their barrio how to fix their cars, others learn how to steal them. One resident recalls being approached in the third grade by other kids who offered him a cigarette: "I said that I didn't know how to smoke, and the guys that were there just laughed at me when I said that. They said they would show me how." Another says, "At the age of 8 I started smoking weed with my uncle. . . . He also turned me on to reds." And another remembers, "My uncle was a member of a gang and showed me a lot of neat tricks, like how to break in and hot wire a car" (Vigil, 1988, p. 50).

Differential association: the notion that delinquency can be culturally transmitted, depending on the balance of illegitimate and legitimate attitudes a person learns from his or her associations.

Edwin Sutherland and Donald Cressey (1960) use **differential association theory** to explain this cultural transmission process more specifically. They argue that most criminal behavior, like other behavior, is learned in intimate settings from our closest associates. While the learning mechanisms are the same in both delinquent and nondelinquent settings, the balance of illegitimate and legitimate attitudes determines our behavior. This balance depends on the frequency, duration, and intensity of our associations. A teenager associating often and intimately with peers who define schoolwork as useless, vandalism as acceptable recreation, and violence as a sign of personal integrity will predictably display criminal behaviors. To make matters more difficult, delinquent friends tend to be "sticky," not easily lost (Warr, 1993).

The transmission of a delinquent subculture becomes nearly irresistible when gangs monopolize the definitions of situations and the allocation of rewards in a neighborhood. For example, one adolescent was greatly influenced by barrio gang members because "he spent most of the time in the streets where their attitude and behavior dominated the scene. Fearful of being rejected by them or of being outright abused and taunted as 'a sissy,' he conformed to their expectations" and accepted their subculture (Vigil, 1988, p. 69). Once adolescents with little past delinquency join gangs, their rates of criminality rise significantly (Thornberry et al., 1993).

Do Criminals Really Look up to Other Criminals?

Many sociological explanations of crime rest on the assumption that criminals choose a subculture of deviance because it offers an attractive, perhaps glamorous, alternative to the conventional, "straight" life. Some people, in their failure to succeed in the mainstream, may even embrace a counterculture, a way of life that rejects or opposes the mainstream. Such theories assume that criminals accept the values of the criminal world as superior to the mainstream. Several sociologists noted that this assumption has little proof (Matsueda et al., 1992) and decided to test it.

The researchers used data collected in three waves over many months from a random sample of nearly 3,000 male prisoners and drug addicts. The subjects were mostly poor, black, and undereducated—people we might expect to seek success somewhere outside the mainstream, legitimate pathways. These men were asked to rank the respect they gave to people in each of 20 occupations, half of which are illegal. The legal occupations included teacher, factory worker, cleaning person, and car washer. The illegal jobs included gambler, numbers runner, loan shark, counterfeiter, prostitute, drug dealer, pimp, and purse snatcher.

Their rankings resembled those of noncriminals. In other words, these criminals and deviants ranked legal occupations higher than illegal ones, just as conventional people did in other studies. They even used the same criteria in their rankings; for example, they gave more respect to people holding occupations requiring skill, ranking loan sharks higher than purse snatchers, who ranked lowest of all.

The sociologists concluded that these criminals did not reject all the mainstream values and criteria of success. Few belonged to a counterculture, or else they would have ranked the illegal occupations higher than the legal ones. Instead, the data offer support for the *pseudocultural* perpsective, which suggests that deviant cultures are impotent, incomplete, and not very influential—not actually "real," alternative cultures but excuses or rationalizations for the failures of those individuals professing to embrace them. Apparently, many criminals hold the same values that we do. Their deviant actions may not reflect a different set of strongly held values so much as a lack of abilities and opportunities to succeed in conventional society. With better opportunities, many of them might "go straight." □

How Can Arresting a Teen Create a Full-Time Gang Member?

Rather than envision delinquent gang members or other criminals as a breed apart, we should remember that most of us could have arrest records if society had reacted differently to our underage drinking, use of illegal drugs, petty theft, reckless driving, or sexual deviance. *Labeling theory* points out that deviant behaviors are not limited to any one sex, age, ethnic group, or class. People from all categories, including college students, violate some norms, yet not all violators are labeled as deviants—that is, officially designated as troublemakers, criminals, and so on.

The issue here is not the unfairness of such selective labeling but how it can lead to other crimes. Labeling theory focuses on **secondary deviance,** behavior that results from society labeling a person deviant for earlier behavior (Lemert, 1967). It forces us

Secondary deviance: behavior that results from society labeling a person as deviant for earlier behavior.

to face a discouraging notion: Identifying and punishing a wrongdoer can promote, rather than deter, further deviance. This connection does not show up in all cases; it may depend on the offender's criminal experience or previous record of arrests (Smith and Gartin, 1989). Certainly not all people arrested inevitably turn to a life of crime; negative sanctions sometimes do have a dampening effect on subsequent delinquency (Sherman and Berk, 1984). Still, at least in some cases, police and mental health intervention can increase delinquency (Farrington, 1977; Kaplan and Johnson, 1991; Klemke, 1978; Palamara, Cullen, and Gertsen, 1986; Wheeler, 1978). How does this happen?

Consider the example of a barrio teen who sees himself as a peripheral gang member. He adopts the dress style of the gang subculture and enjoys some of the excitement of cruising and partying with the gang, but manages to avoid their thievery and warfare. He maintains passing grades in school and sees himself largely as a dutiful son, not a "real" gang member, and certainly not a delinquent. Like most of us, his occasional deviance, such as drinking, drugs, and spray-painting graffiti, has little impact on his self-concept or social roles. Labeling theorists would call his life style and petty crimes **primary deviance,** behavior that violates social norms but evokes no societal reaction to define the behavior as a deviant. He is simply another teen looking for some excitement on the weekends. One day his partying life style finally earns a criminal label when he is snagged in a massive drug sweep of his neighborhood. He has the misfortune of being caught not simply cruising and smoking marijuana with friends, but doing so with friends who are hard-core gang members with a stash of heroin in the trunk of their car. Rather than treat him as a decent kid getting too rowdy and take him to his parents for discipline, the police react to his dress, marijuana, and friends. He is arrested, subsequently convicted, and labeled as a petty criminal.

Our unfortunate teen soon finds that public labeling is only the beginning of society's response. His gang-member friends slap him on the back and treat him as a comrade, one of them. Other people, however, see him in a new, negative light (Farrell, 1989). From now on, they tend to emphasize his faults and assume other negative aspects of his character, ignoring his many positive points. His past and present behaviors are reinterpreted in view of his exposed deviance. His parents react harshly and bitterly. His other relatives, in their shame, distance themselves from him. His girlfriend's parents prevent him from seeing her again. His schoolteachers, hearing of his arrest, mentally place him in a different category, and he loses his lifeguard job at the city pool. His support system and his ties to respectable society deteriorate.

Moreover, the stigma of arrest and his social rejection cause him to see himself in a different light, and he may embrace the identity of deviant—a fighter or drug dealer. In an effort to salvage his self-worth and to avoid further rejection, he may begin to define illegal activities as having positive value and take pride in being a successful thief, hustler, or fighter. In fact, the deviant status may become a master status, the controlling aspect of his identity (Becker, 1963) and source of self-worth.

Society's reaction to our teen sets him apart, limiting his opportunities for associating with nondeviants. His interaction is channeled toward others who defy the conventional order. Thus he takes the next step toward a deviant career and fully commits himself to a deviant group—the gang. With this circle of friends to offer him emotional support, affirmation, a positive view of deviance, and a new identity, we have less hope now that he will choose Merton's path of conformity. In fact, he may retain his gang-member identity well into his twenties, visiting the old haunts, telling his old "war stories," and using the gang's extensive network for money-making opportunities. If so, the labeling process has produced a career deviant, and not for the first time.

Primary deviance: behavior that violates social norms but evokes no societal reaction to define the behaver as deviant.

The labeling process can result in an individual embracing the identity of a deviant and joining a deviant gang, if other opportunities are closed to him.

Notice that throughout the labeling process, our teenager's fate hinges not only on his behavior choices but society's response. And his lower-class, barrio background influences this response. Whereas a teen from a well-to-do, powerful family stands a better chance of being released into the custody of his parents, the barrio teen was arrested. Thus wealth and power figure into labeling, as in virtually every other social process. Indeed, according to conflict theory, the dominant elite uses all social institutions, including not only the law but mass media, schools, and religion, to label alternative subcultures (even nondelinquent gangs) as deviant. In this view, also called *power control theory*, our system of laws reveals which group enjoys cultural dominance. Over the years, dominant groups in the United States have used their power to enact laws to criminalize drinking, marijuana, gambling, and homosexuality.

Table 5-2

Source: U.S. Department of Justice, Federal Bureau of Investigation, *Crime in the United States, 1991* (Washington, DC: USGPO, 1992), p. 51, Table 2.

ESTIMATED RATE, PER 100,000 INHABITANTS, OF SERIOUS OFFENSES KNOWN TO THE POLICE, 1991

	Total Crime Rate	Violent Crime Rate	Property Crime Rate
Metropolitan area	6,615	885	5,730
Rural area	2,105	217	1,888

Power control theory predicts that punishments will fall more heavily on residents of the barrio and other lower-class communities for two reasons. First, disadvantaged groups lack the power and resources to ensure equal treatment. Thus minority youths receive harsher treatment from the justice system (Frazier, Bishop, and Henretta, 1992). Second, the legal system may hand out harsher punishment to groups whose growing numbers and power threaten the interests of the culturally dominant group (Hawkins, 1987). Either way, according to power control theory, enforcement of laws will reflect the power of one group to control others and label them as criminals. (See Table 5-2.)

Research Box

Are Delinquents Incompetent "Losers"?

Delinquents are often portrayed as victims of unfavorable circumstances that push them into crime. Robert Agnew (1990) reviewed several studies that questioned this image of the delinquent as deprived and passive, and decided to put it to a test.

Previous researchers had cataloged adolescents' resources, including intelligence, automobiles, money, physical size, friends, and skills such as fighting ability. Agnew hypothesized that these resources equip youths with two weapons to overcome barriers to delinquency: autonomy and power. These two factors reduce social controls and provide the means for taking action. Whether these actions will be delinquent or not depends on such variables as a predisposition to delinquency, the costs and rewards of delinquent behavior, and the teen's perception of his ability to carry out his will. Agnew manipulated these variables in testing his hypothesis.

The test used data from two national surveys of adolescents. Some of the teens showed predispositions to delinquency: delinquent associates and values, social strain, low levels of control, and rewards for delinquency. Agnew statistically compared these teens to those tending toward conventional behavior, and measured the impact of the other variables that help determine the direction of a youth's behavior.

Data analysis showed support for the hypothesis. Once predisposed toward delinquency, adolescents with substantial resources become increasingly likely to use them toward delinquent ends. This becomes even more likely if the youths see themselves as "can do" types, and if the costs of delinquency are low and the rewards are high.

A somewhat surprising picture of delinquents begins to emerge from Agnew's study. Rather than powerless "losers," at least some appear to be resourceful youths who have chosen to employ their power and autonomy toward delinquency. Agnew suggests that these results may lead to a more accurate picture of delinquents and help to eventually explain some puzzling discrepancies in other studies. □

DO WHITE-COLLAR CRIMINALS AND OTHER OFFENDERS DESERVE SPECIAL TREATMENT?

Turning from juvenile delinquency to other forms of crime, we immediately encounter a problem: Any stereotype of "the criminal type" dissolves in the face of several distinct types of offenders. The question we consider is whether these different types warrant different treatments from society.

For instance, professional criminals depend on special skills such as safecracking, counterfeiting, forgery, and pickpocketing. They often enjoy considerable status among other criminals. Like other professionals, they devote a great deal of energy to their careers, increasing their skills and improving contacts. Such "professional development" reduces their chance of arrest and imprisonment. When convicted, should they be punished differently than the casual thief?

Similarly, should those who participate in organized crime be given special treatment? Like legitimate businesses, criminal organizations rely on specialized workers and a bureaucratic hierarchy or chain of command to achieve their goals. They differ, however, in their need for secrecy, the illegality of their enterprises, and the means they employ to maximize profits. The enterprises include prostitution, illegal drugs, smuggling, and gambling, along with legitimate businesses; the means include violence, intimidation, and protection from highly paid lawyers and corrupt government officials. In the past, "organized crime" evoked images of a nationwide crime syndicate dominated by Italian-Americans. Increasingly, however, researchers are finding evidence of several, probably autonomous, crime syndicates that include outlaw motorcycle gangs and various ethnic organizations, such as Mexicans, Nigerians, Jamaicans, Vietnamese, and Colombians (Fijnaut, 1990).

It is easy enough to declare that professional criminals and members of organized crimes deserve especially harsh treatment. After all, crime is their business, and light punishments will not persuade them to change their ways. But perhaps a special case can be pleaded for another type of criminal. Edwin Sutherland (1940) coined the term "white-collar crime" over 50 years ago, challenging the widely held assumption that crime was a largely lower-class phenomenon. This category includes fraud, embezzlement, stock manipulation, misrepresentation in advertising, and tax evasion. Most frauds, however, involve credit cards and passing bad checks, and have little to do with a person's occupational status (Steffensmeier, 1989). Moreover, much white-collar "covering up" and "collective embezzlement" resemble organized crime activities (Pontell and Calavita, 1993). Still, "white collar" usually refers to crimes committed by people in relatively high-status occupations and even the collective misdeeds of corporations and businesses (Braithwaite, 1993).

Do these crimes and the people who commit them merit special treatment? Travis Hirschi and Michael Gottfredsom (1989) argue that white-collar criminals are essentially like any other criminal: They lack sufficient control of the innate human drive for short-term pleasure or gratification, and simply take advantage of whatever opportunities they find. Most sociologists, however, contend that these offenders are clearly distinguishable from others (Benson and Moore, 1992). Convicted white-collar criminals have higher-than-average education levels, histories of steady employment, and are typically white males around the age of 40 (Wheeler et al., 1988). They are often

White-collar criminals usually receive different treatment. Ivan Boesky, convicted of inside trading on the stock market, paid $100 million in fines but was allowed to keep much of the rest of his ill-earned fortune.

repeat offenders, though they typically begin their criminal activities later, and commit them less frequently, than do street criminals (Weisburd, Chayet, and Waring, 1990). Moreover, such offenders often do not see themselves as criminal, merely greedy or overly zealous or competitive in their business dealings.

These distinguishing traits may or may not make white-collar criminals deserving of different treatment by the justice system, but they usually get it. White-collar offenders seldom go to jail if convicted; they typically receive probation, sometimes fines, or sometimes must merely promise quietly to cease their illegal activities. In view of the billions of dollars such crimes cost the nation each year, we might understandably wonder why these criminals receive such lenient treatment.

Part of the answer lies in the nature of the criminals themselves. These often otherwise respectable citizens can afford skilled legal defenders, and may face less vigorous prosecution due to their considerable social status and power. Most of the reason for their lenient treatment, however, lies in the nature of their crimes, what Susan Shapiro calls the "social organization of their misdeeds and the policing and punishment problems their crimes pose" (1990, p. 353). To begin with, victims of white-collar crime (such as bank depositors and corporate stockholders) often have no awareness of their victimization. The hierarchies and specialized departments of the corporate world create pockets of privacy to which outsiders have little access. The crimes often remain hidden among thousands of other ordinary, legal business transactions. The evidence of wrongdoing (receipts, memoranda, ledgers, and the like) is easily manipulated and in many cases lies entirely in the possession of the criminals themselves. To crack through this wall of secrecy and fake documentation, investigators often must grant a few of the offenders immunity or leniency. Even for convicted white-collar criminals, Shapiro notes, harsh punishments can end up hurting the victims as much as the wrongdoers. The shareholders, employees, and consumers will feel the impact of large fines or the destruction of the organization. And punishments must be quite severe to overcome the goals and cultures in some corporations that motivate misdeeds (Simpson and Koper, 1992). Besides, jail space must be reserved for violent offenders.

The special treatment typically accorded white-collar criminals, therefore, has less to do with their social status than the larger social context in which their crimes occur. In some cases, leniency saves the organization (often innocent itself) from ruin, and salvages the well-being of many customers and employees. Still, in cases like that involving Silverado Savings & Loan in the early 1990s, white-collar crime brings financial injury to thousands of innocent investors. Though the financial magnitude of such crimes may outrage us, we may still conclude that society should respond differently to these offenders than to, say, armed robbers or murderers.

Should Victimless Crimes be Decriminalized?

Critical Thinking Box

Moralistic or victimless crimes offend the moral standards of the community but involve no direct victim. They include gambling, prostitution, pornography and private sexual acts between consenting adults, and drug use. Decriminalization can range from total legalization (with or without regulation) to partial prohibition (allowing, for example, use and possession, but not sale, of drugs). For decades, there has been a debate over whether some or all of these "crimes" should be decriminalized.

One argument focuses on citizens' rights to engage in behaviors that cause no one harm, except perhaps the participants themselves: personal but not social harm. If a person wishes to seek the services of a prostitute, bet on horses, or smoke marijuana, the government should have no say in the matter. The counterargument is that such activities should be banned because they do in fact produce victims, and thus social harm. The behaviors of the gambler, prostitute client, and recreational drug user often have repercussions for his or her family. And the participants themselves can be victimized in subtle, psychological ways. When many citizens participate in unhealthy or immoral activities, this degrades the emotional or moral health of the entire community.

Other advocates of decriminalization reason that the current system sends prostitutes, drug users, and even compulsive gamblers to jail rather than directs them to the treatment they need. Drug addicts, viewed as criminals rather than sick individuals, resort to desperate crimes to feed their habit rather than seek treatment. Decriminalization would involve applying the medical model to drug addicts as has been done, for example, with alcoholics. On the other hand, critics argue that decriminalization would create even more addicts and open the door to more prostitution, gambling, and pornography.

History shows that people have always engaged in activities that society attempts to banish. For example, alcohol, marijuana, coca derivatives, and other drugs have been used for thousands of years. The human demand for the forbidden seems inevitable and uncontrollable. Moreover, criminalizing such behaviors does more harm than good, burdening police with such frustrating duties as routinely rounding up prostitutes, breaking up harmless poker games, and trying to control the desperation crimes of drug addicts. The enormous profits of the illegal drug trade have enriched organized crime and planted corruption in the law enforcement system. The courts are clogged with people accused of victimless crimes. And law-abiding citizens who desire to engage in these activities are forced into contact with the underworld, and may come to view the entire legal system with contempt.

Opponents of decriminalization contend, however, that we cannot simply be allowed to do whatever we want, that people cannot be trusted to choose behaviors that coincide with the social good. Society must hold the line against human desires that erode the community's well-being.

What do you think? Should we decriminalize "victimless crimes"? ■

WHAT SHOULD THE UNITED STATES DO ABOUT CRIME?

Coming back full circle to the issue of social control, we can now see why crime rates in the United States tower over those in Japan, Saudi Arabia, and China. For one thing, we lack the shared traditions of those societies that encourage citizens to continuously scrutinize and informally impose sanctions on one another. How many Americans would trade their privacy and protection from busybodies for lower crime rates? Second, because of our tremendous cultural diversity, our socialization process cannot impose the same value system on everyone. So, short of trying to entirely reshape American culture, we can only hope to discover formal, external controls that might help us more effectively deal with crime.

Is Deterrence Feasible?

Obviously, deterring criminal behavior is preferable to responding to deeds already done. How can human free will be directed toward socially acceptable behavior? How can costs and rewards be arranged, and society be restructured, to turn people aside from the criminal pathway?

Like the local organizations in China and Japan, citizen-based, community-level crime prevention programs in the United States hope to deter by reducing the opportunities for crime in neighborhoods. Safety precautions and "target hardening" efforts can reduce residents' risks of burglar victimization (Miethe, 1991), though some researchers claim that, since all U. S. communities are not equally well organized, such measures may simply displace crime to more vulnerable residents and neighborhoods (Barr and Pease, 1990).

The "routine activities" or *ecological theory* holds that, because crime does not occur randomly across space, deterrence efforts should be directed at those places that seem to generate crime. Certain types of facilities, such as convenience stores and parks, are more "criminogenic" than most homes (Sherman, Gartin, and Buerger, 1989). Providing more police presence, toughening targets, and reducing the supply of probable offenders in such areas can reduce predatory crimes against strangers (Felson, 1987).

Capital punishment has long been advocated as a possible deterrent to murder. Public opinion polls indicate that Americans generally favor capital punishment (Bohm, 1991), but few social scientists find any deterrent effect in this sanction. Imprisoned offenders claim that capital punishment does not deter, and may even reinforce their violent perspectives (Stevens, 1992). Similarly, William Bowers and Glenn Pierce (1980) suggest that the "brutalizing effect" of execution publicity actually increases homicides. William Bailey (1990) finds no such brutalizing effect, but no deterrence, either. In sum, research offers little support for the belief that capital punishment deters homicide. What, then, works if not threatened execution?

In trying to answer this question, early researchers found that certainty, not severity, of threatened punishment serves to deter. More sophisticated analyses, however, suggest that even a perception of certain punishment has little if any deterrent influence (Meier, Burkett, and Hickman, 1984; Paternoster, 1987). And recall from labeling theory that negative sanctions can actually increase criminal activity.

Perhaps the key to the puzzle lies in the interaction of formal and informal sanctions. Durkheim pointed out that indirect, informal sanctions such as shame lie at the heart of deterrence, and researchers have found support for his insight (Burkett and Ward, 1993; Grasmick and Bursik, 1990; Grasmick et al., 1993). In other words, legal punishment like arrest and jail are most effective when they set off more intimidating informal costs: stigma (embarrassment); attachment costs (loss of relationships); and commitment costs like loss of educational, occupational, and marital opportunities (Williams and Hawkins, 1986). Thus such factors as employment and marital status can help determine whether formal sanctions will deter crime (Berk et al., 1992). Unemployed, unmarried men, for example, rarely face commitment costs—they have few occupational or marital opportunities to lose if they are arrested or jailed (Pate and Hamilton, 1992; Sampson and Laub, 1990). Such people have a low "stake in conformity" (Toby, 1957) and therefore little fear of arrest. Deterrence, then, only works with people who have something to lose in the reverberations of informal sanctions.

Sanctions' effects depend on how the individual's group (such as a delinquent gang) responds to official efforts of norm enforcement. Depending on the strength of the group's grip on its members, society's ability to monitor and punish the group's opposition, and the costs of compliance or opposition, the group can employ its own sanctions to either oppose or reinforce society's wishes (Heckathorn, 1990). Society, in other words, must not simply control individuals but the groups which exert control over individuals. Given the diversity of our society and the high value we place on privacy, deterrence efforts face major obstacles.

Research finds little evidence that capital punishment deters crime.

Punishment or Rehabilitation?

If deterrence fails and people choose criminal behaviors, how should society respond? The two main alternatives are punishment and rehabilitation.

Does Punishment Work?   People have traditionally responded to deviance with punitive sanctions. The earliest societies used ostracism, scourging, mutilation, torture, humiliation, imprisonment, and execution to deal with miscreants. But most societies today use such punishment only as a last resort. For example, even Saudi Arabia depends much more on its well-focused socialization than its no-frills jails and infamous severing of heads and hands. And while punishment serves society's need for vengeance and justice, it has never eradicated criminal deviance. Can punishment make our streets and homes safer?

In the United States, when we think of punishment for criminals we usually think first of incarceration. As crime rates have risen over the last two decades, Americans

With yearly costs of approximately $20,000, who is being punished by imprisonment?

Recidivism: the tendency of released inmates to return to prison.

have demanded that more people be sent to prison. In 1977, 265,000 people were imprisoned; today the number per year surpasses one million. But besides depriving inmates of their freedom, what does imprisonment really accomplish?

For one thing, local jails, as distinguished from state or federal prisons, provide a tool to manage the alienated, marginal underclass—what John Irwin (1985) calls "the rabble." Rather than incapacitating serious offenders, Irwin observes, jails receive and hold persons deemed offensive to mainstream society like prostitutes and vagrants.

Of course, incarceration also removes dangerous offenders from the public domain, but only temporarily: 99 percent will eventually return to society (Rogers, 1989). Moreover, only a small fraction of those who commit crimes ever go to prison: Only about one-third of criminal offenses are reported to police, less than one-quarter of reported crimes result in arrest, and less than one-fifth of the people arrested actually go to prison. This might not seem so futile if those who left prison were not so likely to return. Estimates of **recidivism,** the rate at which released inmates return to prison, range from one-third to two-thirds, with the higher number generally acknowledged as more credible. And presumably, some who do not return to prison are simply not caught. Recidivism serves as a measure of prisons' failure to deal with crime in anything more than a temporary way, and even this carries an increasingly large price tag. The cost of keeping one person in prison for one year now approaches $20,000. This all adds up to an expensive and relatively ineffective means of making society safe (Ekland-Olson, Kelly, and Eisenberg, 1992; Johnson, 1992).

A 1978 study by Rand Corporation intrigued criminologists by showing that a small percentage of inmates account for a large proportion of crimes. Obviously, if high-rate offenders could be identified and given long prison sentences, incarceration would be a more cost-effective sanction. This idea gave birth to the idea of selective incapacitation: reserving prisons mostly for high-rate offenders and using other sanctions for low-rate criminals. This strategy hinges on accurate prediction of individuals' crime careers so as to incapacitate high-rate criminals before they do too much damage (Chaiken and Chaiken, 1982; Greenwood, 1982). However, imprisoning people on the basis of their *predicted* crimes raises obvious ethical questions, and so far predictive instruments have fallen short of the required accuracy (Miranne and Geerken, 1991).

The Chinese prefer to use informal sanctions and mediation committees at the neighborhood level rather than confinement. In the face of prison overcrowding in the United States, we too are seeking alternatives to incarceration. Probation suffers from overloaded caseworkers trying to manage ever higher proportions of dangerous offenders. Still, especially when small caseloads facilitate intense supervision, probation can sometimes offer recidivism rates similar to those of imprisonment but at less cost (Turner, 1992; Cohen, Eden, and Lazar, 1991). Another alternative, financial penalties, reduces the odds of subsequent arrest for some offenders (Gordon and Glaser, 1991). House arrest diverts offenders from prison's "crime college" and into their own homes to serve their sentences and participate in counseling and educational programs. Electronic monitoring and random contacts with supervisors afford surveillance around the clock. Community service provides judges with another non-custody option, often as a way to strengthen the probation sanction. The "boot camp," usually reserved for young, nonviolent, first offenders, uses strict discipline and military-style drills for typically three to six months. So far, evidence shows this "shock incarceration" has failed to fulfill its promise of a quick fix at low cost (Sechrest, 1989; Morash and Rucker, 1990).

These alternatives cost far less than imprisonment and avoid its possible brutalizing effect, but research has yet to offer us a clear comparison in terms of relative effectiveness. Still, the data suggest that although imprisonment certainly has a place in a criminal justice system, the system should not focus too narrowly or depend too strongly on it (Palmer, 1975; Andrews et al., 1990).

On the surface, perhaps the simplest solution for serious crimes is execution. While this carries little deterrent value, it surely punishes. And in some societies, it does so quickly and cheaply. For example, in 1977 a Saudi princess who shamed her family with adultery was publicly shot in the head by a kinsman while another hacked off the head of her lover. No trial was required because this was a matter of tribal law (Mackey, 1987, p. 140). In our society, guarantees of due process and protections against cruel and unusual punishment make execution more problematic. In fact, it punishes society as well as the offender. A death sentence costs taxpayers far more than life imprisonment due to the extraordinary legal processes and maximum security expenses involved. Studies by various states have calculated the costs of each execution at around two or three million dollars (Keve, 1992). Financial cost, of course, is only one consideration; in our society, we must also consider the moral implications of killing a vicious offender as social reparation for the taking of an innocent life.

Has Rehabilitation Failed? Rehabilitation, the other major avenue of societal response to crime, aims to make crime unnecessary and undesirable for the individual. This goal requires augmenting the person's resources and meeting his or her inner needs, usually through resocialization. Toward this end, the Japanese sometimes use a form of mediation or "self-observation" aimed at personality transformation. In some cases, they also prefer to extract formal apologies and restore harmony between feuding citizens (Sanders and Hamilton, 1992). The Chinese use education for "right thinking" in an effort to rectify the wrongdoer's lack of knowledge.

Americans put less faith in rehabilitation. We still see some promise in it, in some forms, for some offenders (Cullen et al., 1990). In general, however, this approach has been attacked as not properly punitive, invasive of inmates' privacy, and ineffective, if not impossible (Durham, 1989; Walker, 1989; Whitehead and Lab, 1989). Other analyses conclude that rehabilitation does work, but only if the criminal's needs are properly targeted with treatment modes appropriate to the individual's needs and learning style (Andrews et al., 1990; Izzo and Ross, 1990; Currie, 1989). Researchers find the most success in therapy administered early in the prison term (Zamble and Porporino, 1990), preferably in non-prison settings (Wexler et al., 1990), or at least when rehabilitation efforts are separated from punishment (DeLuca et al., 1991).

How should society respond to crime? Research indicates greater use of alternatives to imprisonment, plus more clearly focused rehabilitation efforts. These strategies offer costly and relatively ineffective substitutes for widely internalized norms backed up by informal sanctions, but given our fragmented, modern society and America's constitutional guarantees of individual freedom, perhaps they are all we have.

SUMMARY

The classification of an act as *deviance*, behavior that violates mainstream norms, depends on the status of the behaver, the time and place, and the subcultural context. It occurs even in extremely strict societies, perhaps because of an inherent human tendency that social controls cannot always inhibit. From another viewpoint, deviance follows inevitably from the oppressive consequences of capitalism. According to Durkheim, normal social functioning includes deviance as well as conformity because it serves several social needs.

Societies with little deviance and low crime rates are especially effective at *social control*, those rules and actions aimed at regulating human behavior. First, and most important, continuous, well-focused socialization in homogeneous societies encourage *internalization*, in which most of the people make society's norms their own. Beyond this internal control, external controls are imposed through *sanctions*, rewards and punishments aimed at regulating behaviors. These include *informal sanctions*, applied causally by people with no special authority, and *formal sanctions*, applied by authorized agents or people holding specialized roles such as police or teachers.

Crime rates do not necessarily reflect the actual level of crimes, in part because most crimes are never reported. Nevertheless, modernization theory predicts that *anomie*, a state of confusion and normlessness, and other social dislocations produce noticeably higher rates of crime in developing nations. Thus we can expect high rates in fast-growing nations with many people born during the same time period, as in Africa. However, this usually applies only to property crimes; offenses against people typically decrease as nations develop. One study of African countries found that even major property crimes decreased, perhaps due to improved prevention. Africa's unique cultural traditions must also be considered.

On the individual level, researchers have linked crime with several biological factors, and twin studies, although technically flawed, hint at the inheritance of criminal tendencies. While these correlation studies cannot prove a causative link between crime and biology, they do suggest a possible, partial relationship. We can predict with greater certainty that a criminal will be a young male who has experienced problems usually associated with a lower-class social background. However, we must continue to guard against mass media *stereotypes*.

Some neighborhoods contribute to delinquency in several ways. The frustrations and instability associated with poverty, for example, often lead to higher crime rates, as does prejudice. As Robert Merton explains, when social barriers prevent people from using legitimate opportunities to attain widely accepted goals, they may use "innovative" means, or crime. Delinquency also flourishes in communities suffering social disorganization due to not only poverty but residential instability, family disruption, the proliferation of "hot spots," and subcultures of violence. All this contributes to the breakdown of the social controls necessary to inhibit what some theorists see as our inherent criminality.

Informal socialization transmits subcultures of delinquency from one generation to another. According to the theory of *differential association*, the balance of an individual's various associations determines whether he or she will take on delinquent or legitimate attitudes. Labeling theory holds that every individual commits acts that violate social norms but which usually evoke no societal reaction, what is called *primary deviance*. But if society takes note of those acts and labels those individuals as deviants, this labeling process may help push them into further deviance, or *secondary deviance*.

Those involved in professional and organized crime use different methods and generally receive more lenient treatment from society. The same is true for those engaging in white-collar crime (usually people in relatively high-status occupations, often in business settings) because of the nature of the offenders themselves and of their crimes.

Our efforts to deter crime include the control of high-crime locations and capital punishment, but effective deterrence depends on triggering informal sanction costs, such as embarrassment or loss of friendships. Punishment in the form of incarceration removes offenders from the streets but only temporarily, usually at great cost, and with high rates of *recidivism* (the tendency of inmates to return to prison). Less costly alternatives include selective incapacitation, community service, intensive probation, fines, and house arrest. Execution often entails great financial costs. More clearly focused rehabilitation may hold some promise.

Key Terms

deviance	informal sanctions	differential association
social control	formal sanctions	secondary deviance
internalization	anomie	primary deviance
sanctions	stereotypes	recidivism

6

Chapter

SOCIAL STRATIFICATION

IS SOCIAL INEQUALITY NECESSARY?

CRITICAL THINKING BOX: WHAT PRICE EQUALITY?

DETERMINANTS OF SOCIAL RANKINGS: THE UNITED STATES CONTRASTED WITH THE CHEYENNE

RESEARCH BOX: OCCUPATIONS IN CHINA

IDENTIFYING ONE'S CLASS: WHY IT MATTERS

RESEARCH BOX: LOVE AND MARRIAGE, CLASS AND RACE

IS AMERICA A LAND OF OPPORTUNITY?

CRITICAL THINKING BOX: CAREFUL WITH STATISTICS!

MOVING UP: WHAT DETERMINES ONE'S CHANCES

CAN POVERTY BE ELIMINATED?

Humans have always lived with social inequality. History is replete with kings and slaves, chiefs and servants, lords and peasants. Today we speak of the super-rich and the underclass, the "haves" and the "have-nots," the Fortune 500 and the homeless. One observer notes that over the last decade fox hunting has attracted many new enthusiasts, the number of registered polo players has doubled, and lists for country club memberships continue to grow (O'Reilly, 1990). In the meantime, the number and visibility of homeless families has increased dismayingly. To many people, such inequality is a fundamental flaw of society, a hideous aspect of human social life that must be remedied.

IS SOCIAL INEQUALITY NECESSARY?

This is not a new question. Long before sociology came onto the scene in the Western world, intellectuals tried to explain and even rationalize social inequality. Aristotle, for example, asserted that humans were by nature unequal, born with different capacities which suited them to different social rankings.

Few questioned this naturalistic view until the mid-1700s, when the French philosopher Jean-Jacques Rousseau argued that humans are not born unequal. He advanced the shocking notion that social ranks were assigned not by nature or God but by social circumstances. Social inequality, in his view, was not necessary or natural or simply a part of life to be tolerated; it was a problem to be solved.

Rousseau blamed private property. This theme was taken up by a kindred spirit writing in the nineteenth century, Karl Marx. Both men reasoned that when humans established private property rights, inevitably some accumulated more property, or wealth, than others. These people tended to consolidate their socially dominant ranking and transmit it to their children. Followers of Marx and Rousseau saw the resulting system of inequality as unjustified and intolerable—but treatable. The prescription: revolution, or at least reforms banning the accumulation of private property.

But even revolutions did not eradicate social inequality. The ideas of Rousseau are linked with revolutions in France (1789) and North America (1776); Marx is the father of upheavals in Russia (1917) and elsewhere in the twentieth century. But we still have inequality, even in countries founded on Marxist ideas. This perhaps disappointing result brings us back to our question: Is inequality a necessary fact of social life?

Rather than debate the morality of this issue, sociologists have examined the mechanics of the social system to describe the part played by inequality. Functionalists and conflict theorists have clarified the two sides of this ongoing controversy.

Is social inequality necessary?

The Functionalist View

The modern functionalist perspective is derived from the traditional view that inequality is natural, even necessary. This view was brought into sociological focus in the 1940s by Kingsley Davis and Wilbert Moore (1945) who argued that inequality provides the incentive required for the smooth functioning of complex societies. They based their reasoning on the assumption that, first, modern societies require many highly complex tasks, such as designing bridges, managing vast amounts of financial resources, and diagnosing illnesses. Second, not all humans possess the abilities and skills required for those tasks. The most competent people must therefore be fitted into the appropriate slots. But how?

Functionalists answer: unequal rewards. The hope of earning more money (or other social rewards) motivates people to develop and use their talents—to go through apprenticeship programs, for example, or to endure the rigors of medical school. If all occupations paid the same, no matter how difficult, dangerous, stressful, or unpleasant, who would volunteer to be a brain surgeon, police officer, air traffic controller, or proctologist? Anyone who has said, "They would have to pay me an awful lot of money to do that job," has hit upon the functionalist explanation that inequality is necessary for incentive. Moreover, once the job slots are filled, workers must be motivated to perform well. Again, unequal rewards provide incentive: People who work hard and produce are more likely to earn promotions and bigger paychecks. If the incentives are attractive enough, the social system functions smoothly.

The Conflict Perspective

Conflict theorists like C. Wright Mills have argued that inequality does not in fact produce smooth social functioning. For one thing, rewards sometimes go to people who contribute little to society, and who may even harm it. For example, huge salaries are paid to executives of corporations that produce dangerous products such as liquor and cigarettes. Likewise, it is easy to question the social contributions of the highly paid producers of movies, rock songs, and magazines that promote sexual promiscuity, violence, and degradation of women. And while professional athletes do no harm to society, critics wonder if their pay is commensurate with their contribution to social functioning. Meanwhile teachers, police officers, and nurses perform vital functions for the system but are paid relatively little. There are other people who contribute nothing to society but live luxuriously simply because they have inherited wealth, which suggests that our system is not the **meritocracy**—that is, a system in which social rewards flow to people with merit or ability—functionalists describe.

A smoothly functioning, meritocratic society would not erect artificial barriers to thwart potential contributors, but ours does, say conflict theorists. While women and other minorities have gained greater protection of their rights, and attend college at higher rates than ever before, they are still less likely to develop their potential because of prejudice and subcultural disadvantages. By shutting out such people, society wastes their talents. The playing field is not level, and the same people keep racking up the points and gathering in the prizes. Such a system, in the conflict view, is not only unnecessary but a source of resentment and tension. The functionalist explanation merely serves to justify the status quo.

According to functionalist theory, some workers deserve more money because of the importance and demands of their job.

Meritocracy: a system in which merit or ability determines one's place in the social hierarchy.

A Synthesis

Gerhard Lenski (1966) sees merit in both the functionalist and conflict views. He contends that early in a society's evolution, rewards often do indeed go to those individuals able and willing to undergo the training needed to accomplish society's most complex tasks. The functionalists' meritocratic explanation may be valid initially. However, as societies evolve they usually develop more sophisticated technologies and so produce surpluses of highly valued goods. And who gains possession of those goods? The people already in positions of political and economic power, those with leverage. The elite, in other words, use their fairly earned advantages to fortify themselves unfairly with further advantages, whether or not they still contribute to society's well-being. Lenski argues that as societies become more complex the elite's level of control usually rises. Such control and inequality may be far beyond anything needed for smooth social functioning.

Is Social Equality Possible?

From the conflict perspective, an egalitarian society is workable, but only through far-reaching reforms. The most drastic requires an all-powerful government to replace personal greed as a motivation with broad social incentives such as "doing one's duty." A reform more compatible with American values is destruction of the artificial barriers that deny the underprivileged a chance to contribute. This would mean equalizing opportunities for education and employment. Also, the enormous income gap between those at the top and bottom of the economic ladder cannot be justified by needs for incentives, and therefore should be narrowed.

From the functionalist viewpoint, humans in general will not work up to their potential without the promise of personal rewards, and some individuals will inevitably earn more rewards than others. While this creates social inequality, it also ensures the healthy operation of the social system.

Critical Thinking Box

What Price Equality?

Americans have never embraced the notion of equalizing living standards for all citizens. Instead, the goal of reformers has been to alleviate the wretchedness of the poor at the expense of the wealthy—in other words, to reduce but not eliminate social inequality. Americans have also paid lip service to equal opportunity, agreeing that everyone should have a fair chance to climb the ladder of success (although until recently "everyone" included only white males).

Equal opportunity may seem like an unobjectionable goal, but two problems rear their heads. First, it would lead to such policies as increased restrictions on inheritance and even more taxing of the nonpoor to pay for the increased opportunities (preschool, health care, college financial aid, and so on) of the disadvantaged. It is difficult to ask taxpaying voters to give up some of their money for programs that will, if successful, create competitors for their own children as they search for education and job opportunities. Should such equalizing programs be voluntary for taxpayers?

Second, how far should we go in equalizing opportunities? Even if we succeed in providing equal quality schools to all children, we cannot ignore the vital preschool years in which disadvantaged children typically fall farther and farther behind developmentally. Trapped in a stultifying, neglectful environment, such children would be unable to take advantage of even high-quality schools. Should we, in order to guarantee an equal chance to prepare for later academic competition, mandate that all children attend standardized day care, perhaps beginning in infancy? And should we intervene in the homes of disadvantaged families, dictating childrearing strategies and nutritional standards? ■

DETERMINANTS OF SOCIAL RANKINGS: THE UNITED STATES CONTRASTED WITH THE CHEYENNE

Social differentiation: the process of categorizing individuals according to personal attributes.

While egalitarian societies may serve as the ideal for some theorists, we are hard-pressed to find actual examples of any today. To begin with, all societies employ some system of **social differentiation,** which categorizes or distinguishes members by personal attributes. For example, even among the Cheyenne of the American Great Plains in the mid-1800s, members were differentiated by age, family name, gender, courage, generosity, and other personal qualities (Hoebel, 1960). Brave men and exceptionally sensible women stood out, as did homosexuals, who wore women's clothes and served as physicians and matchmakers.

Such categorization almost unavoidably produces differential evaluations or rankings of such characteristics. Individuals are thus perceived not only as socially different but socially unequal. This inequality permeates all societies, but, as we will see here, our own system of inequality is quite complex, especially when contrasted with that of the Cheyenne.

Among the Cheyenne, an individual's social ranking depended on his or her personal qualities and achievements more than advantages gained by family background (as in our culture).

The most important difference between the two societies' ranking systems involves the relationship between personal characteristics and status. A Cheyenne male received a higher ranking than a female. For example, if a sister disobeyed her brother regarding her mate selection, he might commit suicide and she would be disowned. Likewise, women would be hidden away during the climax of the Sacred Arrow Renewal Rite, the most solemn and sacred ceremony of the Cheyenne tribe. This rite also reinforced the authority of the tribe's elders, who played central roles in the four-day ritual, and whose endorsement was required for war parties. Except for sex and age, however, the Cheyenne's social hierarchy was not institutionalized; in other words, no other patterns determined that certain members would automatically receive more social rewards than others. Besides those two factors, an individual's social ranking depended on purely personal attributes such as bravery, beauty, and intelligence. For example, no one automatically became chief; the Cheyenne chose a man who epitomized their ideal personality, which included generosity, energy, wisdom, kindliness, and courage.

In our own system of **social stratification,** on the other hand, most socially significant inequalities are institutionalized, or built into social patterns and based on social norms rather than individuals' personal comparisons. The important hierarchies by which members are ranked in our society include not only age and sex but race, ethnicity, and **social class:** a stratum of individuals sharing similar amounts of social resources.

Social stratification: institutionalized social inequality, in which social patterns determine the allocation of social rewards.

Social class: a stratum of individuals sharing similar amounts of wealth, power, and prestige; according to Marxists, *class* refers to people of similar positions or levels of control in the economy.

Here, by way of contrast with the Cheyenne, we will explore the determinants of social-class rankings in the United States. According to Max Weber, class hierarchies are based on the distribution of three social rewards or benefits. Karl Marx identified only one factor. With the insights of both thinkers, we will gain some appreciation of the criteria by which others rank us.

Weber observed, most obviously, that wealth greatly broadens our life opportunities and makes available more goods and services. But he also noted the importance of **prestige**—honor, respect, and admiration, what he called "status"—and **power,** the ability to impose one's will.

Prestige: honor, respect, and admiration accorded an individual.

Power: the ability to impose one's will.

Wealth

The Cheyenne measured wealth in terms of horses and such equipment as saddlebags and robes. Some families had more than others due to differences in competence and perhaps luck, not because any social patterns or traditions channeled wealth to them.

These disparities were not large, and paled in comparison to those in our society, in which Americans hold vastly unequal amounts of money, real estate, stocks and bonds, and other valued possessions. According to the Census Bureau, the richest fifth of American society holds over three-quarters of the nation's wealth; the poorest fifth holds less than 1 percent.

Chapters 7 and 8 will discuss how sex, age, race, and ethnicity contribute to an unequal distribution of wealth, but here we focus on occupation. Jobs with greater risk of injury or death understandably bring higher incomes (Leigh and Folsom, 1984), as does work requiring scarce skills and education. But researchers point out that such requirements do not fully explain earnings (Berg, 1970; Collins, 1980). One complication is that workers do not compete in a single, perfectly competitive labor market. Earnings are determined in various ways in different segments of the economy (Smith, 1990). Some workers are sheltered from competition because they are trained within the firm, which finds it more cost-effective to pay the workers well than replace them with new workers who must in turn be trained. Discrimination also shelters certain workers from competition with nonwhites and women, keeping some people's earnings unnaturally high and others' low. Similarly, labor organizations can produce internal labor markets that protect members from outside competition (Kalleberg and Sorensen, 1979). When organized workers press their advantage to gain higher wages and job security, however, they often do so by coordinating their interests with those of management, and in the long run give up some of their power (Weakliem, 1990). This tends to mitigate the income differences among various segments of the labor market.

Family background also strongly influences wealth. The education and occupations of one's parents, family size, and one's test scores and healthy personality traits in high school are just some of the factors linked to one's eventual income level (Jencks, 1979).

Generally speaking, the more wealth one possesses the higher one's social class. But access to the very highest class is restricted to those whose fortune has been accumulated so long ago that it seems the family has always been wealthy. This money-aging process, through which one acquires "ancestors" along with affluence, usually requires the passing of about three generations. In the meantime, the family must be content with being merely rich.

Prestige

While some members of Cheyenne society enjoyed more prestige than others, all shared the same life style. However, Weber pointed out that in modern societies such as ours, people of various levels of prestige form somewhat distinct status groups and live differently than others. Members of a status group own, do, and say the same kinds of things. One such group may drive new Mercedes and attend glittering "Las Vegas night" balls. Another, perhaps with a higher level of prestige, may drive ancient Lincolns and attend quiet dedications of privately funded charity hospitals.

More than anything else, personal attributes determined an individual's prestige in Cheyenne society. Bravery in battle brought tremendous respect. In fact, war was a great game in which the Cheyenne kept score through counting "coup," or heroic deeds. The highest scores were earned by touching an enemy without killing him, or by showing military virtuosity within an enemy encampment. Self-torture for the benefit of the tribe also brought great prestige. To obtain supernatural blessings for the

Cheyenne men could earn prestige through heroic deeds or through self-torture endured for the benefit of the tribe. Our prestige system is quite different, often bestowing privileges on people who do nothing themselves to earn such advantages.

tribe, a man would dance suspended by two ropes attached by skewers in his breast just above each nipple. The dance would continue through the night until his exertions tore the skin loose. Or he might have skewers put through his back and attached to buffalo skulls, which he would drag around the camp until they tore out the skewers.

By contrast, in our society the honor we receive from others depends much less on personal deeds than on life style, status symbols, and occupation.

Life Style   Prestige in the United States is not so much determined by wealth as how one spends it. Even winning millions of dollars in a lottery does not guarantee prestige; one must also have the appropriate trappings—the "proper" home, clothes, car, vacation spots, and so on. One's children are expected to attend certain preparatory schools and Ivy League colleges, though since World War II such institutions have become less relevant as indicators of long-established elite status. Leisure time must be spent learning proper manners, gaining appreciation of the arts and the "finer things in life," and gradually establishing the self-assured demeanor of the upper crust. This takes time, usually generations. The prestige-attainment process can be accelerated by hiring a consultant to help one get invited to the "right" parties and charity events, but in general upper-class status is attainable only with considerable effort, time, and "insider" knowledge—and, until recently, mostly by white, Anglo-Saxon Protestants ("WASPs") and a few Catholics. Until the middle of this century, the WASP life style served as the epitome of prestige. However, due to the vast postwar expansion of opportunities and competition from celebrities, WASPs have lost their monopoly over prestige (Aldrich, 1993).

Status Symbols   Prestige also flows from ownership of the appropriate consumer goods, which serve as indicators of one's taste, knowledge, and wealth. These status symbols are more accessible today than earlier this century. Many of us, for example, can finance a prestigious automobile; we can even rent one for special occasions such as high school reunions. Mass merchandisers eagerly provide us with imitations of high-status items. In fact, many advertisements offer prestige rather than simply goods. Liquor and cigarette ads, for example, attempt to associate their products with images of successful, tasteful, attractive people.

Prestige flows not only from owning things, but from doing or being something socially valued. Business ownership, frequent travel, trusteeship of cultural organizations, and occupying powerful positions earn status points (Graf, 1987), as do personal features like beauty, charm, and the ability to speak well in own's own and foreign languages. It also matters if one's children do or become something important, such as qualifying for a gifted-student program or college scholarship.

Occupation   Anyone eager to garner more prestige should focus on occupation. Table 6-1 reveals that, first, the more an occupation pays, generally the higher its prestige. But income is only one of four occupational factors that measure status. This becomes immediately obvious when we note that college professors (with modest salaries) are ranked high as to prestige. The second factor is the job's importance to society, clearly evident in the top-ranked occupations. Third is talent or training required. Most low-ranked jobs require skills that nearly anyone can acquire very easily. While being a garbage collector is socially important, the occupation is given little prestige because the worker can be easily replaced. The garbage collector also ranks low because of the fourth factor: desirability. Low-ranking occupations usually involve serving the personal needs of other people, little social power, and boredom, danger,

THE DIABOLO LOUIS CARTIER WATCH.

THE ART OF BEING UNIQUE.

Cartier

JOAILLIERS SINCE 1847

ADLER'S

Toll Free / 1-800-925-7912
Adler's, 722 Canal Street / New Orleans, LA 70130 / 504-523-5292

Prestige for sale.

or physical discomfort. In contrast, the more prestigious occupations involve making decisions that affect other people's lives, and the workers do not get their hands dirty.

Master Status   It is not difficult to imagine that a nurse or plumber winning $20 million in a lottery would still encounter social rejection from the higher classes. Sociologists explain this as the result of **status inconsistency.** The newly rich person's economic status probably does not fit his or her other statuses. People of one general social level usually have the same possessions, speech patterns, education, and occupation, and are of the same gender and race. In other words, ranking is generally the

Status inconsistency: a condition in which one holds substantially different rankings in various status hierarchies.

same for most of the prestige criteria. This consistency makes it relatively simple to "place" a person, which is often useful in social and business encounters with strangers. Problems arise when some people are ranked high according to one prestige criterion but low according to others. Imagine a $20 million lottery winner who is a divorced, black, elderly woman and former waitress. She may claim a high overall ranking based on her wealth, but many people she encounters may base their treatment of her on her marital status, race, age, sex, and former occupation—and not give her the respect or prestige she feels she deserves. In fact, she may detect contempt rather than admiration from those with far less money but higher rankings in other prestige criteria. What counts in such situations is the weight given to the various criteria. The **master status** is whatever status is given most weight or considered to be most important. In the United States, the master status was race; now it is being supplanted by occupation.

Master status: the status that determines more than any other the individual's overall social ranking.

PRESTIGE RATINGS OF OCCUPATIONS

Occupation	Prestige
Physician	95.8
Mayor	92.2
Lawyer	90.1
College professor	90.1
Architect	88.8
City superintendent of schools	87.8
Owner of a factory employing 2000 people	81.7
Stockbroker	81.7
Advertising executive	80.8
Electrical engineer	79.5
Building construction contractor	78.9
Chiropractor	75.3
Registered nurse	75.0
Sociologist	74.7
Accountant	71.2
High school teacher	70.2
Manager of a factory employing 2000 people	69.2
Office manager	68.3
Administrative assistant	67.8
Grade school teacher	65.4
Powerhouse engineer	64.5
Hotel manager	64.1
Circulation director of a newspaper	63.5
Social worker	63.2
Hospital lab technician	63.1
Artist	62.8
Electrician	62.5
Insurance agent	62.5
Private secretary	60.9

(continued next page)

Table 6-1

As shown here, income is only one of the factors by which Americans rank occupations. The job's importance to society, the talent or education required, and its desirability also determine an occupation's prestige.

Source: Christine E. Bose and Peter H. Rossi, "Gender and Jobs: Prestige Standings of Occupations as Affected by Gender" *American Sociological Review* 48 (June 1983):327–328.

Occupation	Prestige
Floor supervisor in a hospital	60.3
Supervisor of telephone operators	60.3
Plumber	58.7
Police officer	58.3
Manager of a supermarket	57.1
Car dealer	57.1
Practical nurse	56.4
Dental assistant	54.8
Warehouse supervisor	54.2
Assembly-line supervisor in a manufacturing plant	53.8
Carpenter	53.5
Locomotive engineer	52.9
Stenographer	52.6
Office secretary	51.3
Inspector in a manufacturing plant	51.3
Housewife	51.0
Bookkeeper	50.0
Florist	49.7
Tool machinist	48.4
Welder	46.8
Wholesale salesperson	46.2
Telephone operator	46.2
Auto mechanic	44.9
Typist	44.9
Keypunch operator	44.6
Typesetter	42.6
Post office clerk	42.3
Piano tuner	41.0
Landscape gardener	40.5
Truck driver	40.4
House painter	39.7
Hairdresser	49.4
Pastry chef in a restaurant	39.4
Butcher in a shop	38.8
Washing-machine repairman	38.8
Automobile refinisher	36.9
Someone who sells shoes in a store	35.9
Cashier	35.6
File clerk	34.0
Dress cutter	33.6
Cattledriver working for own family	33.0
Cotton farmer	32.4
Metal-container maker	31.4
Hospital aide	29.5

(continued next page)

Occupation	Prestige
Fireman in a boiler room	29.2
Floor finisher	28.8
Assembly-line worker	28.3
Book binder	28.2
Textile-machine operator	27.9
Electric-wire winder	27.6
Vegetable grader	27.4
Delivery truck driver	26.9
Shirtmaker in a manufacturing plant	26.6
Person who repairs shoes	26.0
Fruit harvester, working for own family	26.0
Blacksmith	26.0
Housekeeper	25.3
Flour miller	25.0
Stock clerk	24.4
Coal miner	24.0
Boardinghouse keeper	23.7
Warehouse clerk	22.4
Waitress/waiter	22.1
Short-order cook	21.5
Baby-sitter	18.3
Rubber mixer	18.1
Feed grinder	17.8
Garbage collector	16.3
Box packer	15.1
Laundry worker	14.7
Househusband	14.5
Salad maker in a hotel	13.8
Janitor	12.5
Yarn washer	11.8
Maid (F)/household day worker (M)	11.5
Bellhop	10.6
Hotel chambermaid (F)/hotel bedmaker (M)	10.3
Carhop	8.3
Person living on welfare	8.2
Parking lot attendant	8.0
Rag picker	4.6

Power

Authority: legitimate, formal power based on socially recognized status.

Weber's third dimension of social class is what he called "party," expressed in political parties, voting blocs, or pressure groups. Beyond mere political power, holding a socially recognized position like chairman, school principal, or president confers **authority,** formal power that enables one to legitimately control people and events.

Among the Cheyenne, supreme authority was vested in the 44 members of the tribal council, chosen for their embodiment of the ideal Cheyenne personality. The council exercised ultimate executive, legislative, and judicial power, which flowed from supernatural blessings. These men were expected to maintain empathy with the supernatural forces upon which the Cheyenne depended.

The council's counterpart in our society is a nonreligious entity sociologists call the **power elite** (Mills, 1956). Elite theorists contend that a few hundred people form a unified, dominating stratum in the United States (described more fully in Chapter 10). Leaders of industry, unions, Congress, the mass media, and voluntary associations, federal government appointees, and other influential civil servants comprise this immensely powerful group (Alba and Moore, 1982). Most members of this elite lack the formal authority of the Cheyenne council, and their sphere of influence is not as wide. Still, their power reaches into government, business, and the military.

Pluralist theorists argue that competition insures that power will not become concentrated in the hands of one such elite. Leaders of the oil, banking, and defense industries, for example, must compromise and negotiate with one another and, as a result, offer most people some access to these centers of power.

More mundane than authority, **influence** enables us to pursue our own goals even without holding a special social status. It is a function of personal power and freedom, and can derive from wealth, physical size, intelligence, charm, and other personal traits that help us make our way in the world.

The three determinants of social ranking—wealth, prestige, and power—are intertwined; getting more of one makes it easier to acquire more of the other two. For example, among the Cheyenne, if one acquired more horses or earned greater influence in tribal affairs, one's prestige rose. Similarly, in our society, prestige can give one greater access to power: Both World War II hero General Dwight Eisenhower and actor Ronald Reagan parlayed their celebrity status into winning the highest political office. Likewise, the hero or champion can cash in on his or her prestige through endorsements, speaking fees, and publishing contracts.

Power elite: a unified group of several hundred individuals who exert great control over government, business, and military affairs.

Influence: informal power based on personal attributes.

Marx: Economic Control Is the Key

While Weber focused on three determinants of social class, Marx focused solely on economic control. In his view, the elite in any society are those who own capital, the means of economic production. In contrast to these capitalists, or **bourgeoisie,** are those who own no capital and therefore have no significant social or political power: the exploited workers or **proletariat.**

Contemporary Marxist theorists have extended his ideas. They recognize the importance of other controlling economic factors such as investments, production, and the labor of others (Wright et al., 1982; Kohn et al., 1990). Erik Olin Wright (1985; Wright and Cho, 1992) describes three dimensions of social class. The first he labels property, which is based on ownership of capital. The second is a matter of authority, and involves control of organizational assets—that is, being a manager rather than a worker (although managers are also exploited by the capitalists). Third is expertise, or ownership of skill assets, especially when those assets are scarce or legally recognized as required for certain high-level occupations, as in medicine and law. Control over these dimensions leads to exploitation of others and a higher social ranking.

Bourgeoisie: Marx's term for the class of individuals who own the means of production; the capitalist class.

Proletariat: Marx's term for the exploited working class in a capitalist society.

In Cheyenne society, very little capital existed beyond a few tools and horses. Furthermore, all members of each sex shared essentially the same skills and positions in the economic organization. From the Marxist perspective, the nature of the Cheyenne economy clearly allowed no class exploitation—as ours does.

To summarize: Members of all societies are not only differentiated but ranked unequally. Our system of stratification, in contrast to that of the Cheyennes, focuses on institutionalized hierarchies rather than personality features or admirable deeds. In the next section, we will see how our social ranking influences our life chances and life style.

Research Box

Occupations in China

Probably the biggest factor that determines how much respect or prestige we get from others is what we do for a living. Does this vital variable have universal, or cross-cultural, rankings? In other words, would an occupation earn a person more respect in another country than it does in the United States?

Sociologists have been surveying Americans since the early 1940s on the relative prestige of various occupational categories. Similar studies were begun in other societies a little later. Sociologists expected that any one occupational group would be ranked similarly in other industrial societies, partly because Emile Durkheim had described how a somewhat universal division of labor would develop as part of the modernization process.

Nan Lin (SUNY–Albany) and Wen Xie (Columbia University) wanted to discover whether or not China's unique cultural and political history had produced an equally unique ranking of occupational prestige (1988). They chose 50 occupations common in urban China and familiar to the average person there. A two-stage process was used to draw the sample. First, the households were selected. A subdistrict was randomly chosen from each central district in Beijing. Then one neighborhood was randomly selected from each subdistrict. Half of the households in these neighborhoods were then randomly chosen for the survey. Second, individuals had to be chosen from each household: The researchers wanted one employed or formerly employed adult. If there were more than one such adult in a household, one person was chosen randomly. Out of the 1,800 households in the sample, 1,774 interviews were obtained, resulting in a very strong response rate of 99 percent. The interviews were face-to-face, and were conducted by 15 trained interviewers.

Each respondent gave a rating from 1 to 10 for the prestige of each occupation. The professional occupations got the highest ratings, followed by schoolteachers, officials, accountants, athletes, and artists. Next came such occupations as nurses and police officers, then machinists, plumbers, and sales clerks. Among those ranked lowest were heavy-labor workers and housemaids.

Lin and Xie concluded that, "As a whole . . . the ratings given to occupations by Chinese males and females are very similar in general pattern to ratings in other societies" (p. 823). The universality of the ratings is somewhat startling, given the other differences between our country and China; however, it serves to reinforce the validity of our own ranking system and supports Durkheim's predictions. □

IDENTIFYING ONE'S CLASS: WHY IT MATTERS

We may be reluctant to admit that we rank one another, but without an awareness of class distinctions we would more likely suffer embarrassing social gaffes and humiliating snubs. People often unconsciously use social-class clues to make decisions such as, "Should our daughter marry into that family?" or "Should we invite those people to our party?" In modern society, where we must deal with many people about whom we know so little, we are grateful for any clues about how we stand in relation to others. In other words, we want to know what class we belong to.

Identifying an Individual's Class

Sociologists offer two basic schemes to represent the social classes of the United States. First we explore the economic-determinist approach of Marxists. Then we describe the multi-dimensional class structure based on Weber's theory.

The Marxist Perspective   As we saw earlier, from the Marxist perspective our standing relative to other people is based on the control we have of economic factors. On the simplest level, each of us is in one of just two classes: the owners of the means of production (the capitalists) or the workers. According to one theorist, it should be quite easy to classify ourselves: The upper class is only 0.5 percent of the U. S. population, and it dominates the other 99.5 percent (Dalphin, 1982).

Beyond this classic view, however, Neo-Marxist formulations typically describe three classes in America (Wright et al., 1982; Kohn et al., 1990). The highest class is composed of the bourgeoisie, which controls investments, production, and the labor of others. The middle level includes employed managers and supervisors, as well as employees who can plan and design significant aspects of their work, but do not control others' labor. This level, which includes professionals and other "knowledge workers," is sometimes described as an antibusiness "new class"; its members are politically liberal insofar as their jobs depend on government funding (Brint, 1984; Lamont, 1987). Also usually included in this middle level are the self-employed, a category which has surged in recent years, partly due to the expansion of the postindustrial services sector (Steinmetz and Wright, 1989). At the bottom are those workers with no economic control, including low-status white-collar workers (such as clerks) as well as manual laborers. A diagram of this class structure would be similar to that of earlier stratified societies: a pyramid with a tiny elite of exploiters at the top, the masses on the bottom, and relatively few people in between (see Figure 6-1).

Class Schemes Based on Weber   An alternative social pecking order uses the more familiar non-Marxist categories of Weber's theory. Based on such early community studies as Lloyd Warner and Paul Lunt's exploration of "Yankee City" (1941), these schemes typically offer five or six classes: two lower, two middle, and one or two upper. The larger the community, the more complex its class picture will be; some cities have more highly paid professionals and so will display a larger-than-usual upper-middle class. Depending on local variations, we can expect to have anywhere

THE SHAPE OF AMERICA'S CLASS STRUCTURE

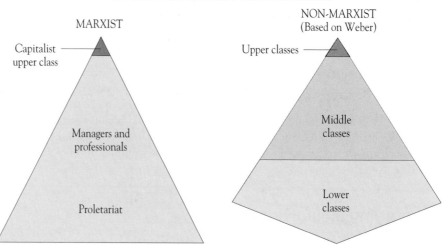

MARXIST

Capitalist
upper class

Managers and
professionals

Proletariat

NON-MARXIST
(Based on Weber)

Upper classes

Middle
classes

Lower
classes

Figure 6–1   Depending on the theoretical perspective used, America's class system bulges at the bottom or just below the middle.

from nearly two-thirds to nine-tenths of the population classified between the very lowest and the top classes. This non-Marxist approach thus produces a diagram of the American class structure with a bulge near the middle, a bottom-heavy diamond shape rather than a large-base pyramid. The difference between the two shapes results from the indicators used by sociologists in the two camps.

Weber's theory focuses on prestige, power, and wealth. The problem, in view of our task here, is that only one of these determinants of social class is easily measured. For more concrete indicators, sociologists look for clues in occupation, income, education, and residence.

Of all these indicators, the most powerful is occupation. When "sizing up" a new acquaintance, for example, one of the first probes we are likely to slip into the conversation is aimed at discovering what he or she does for a living. More than any other indicator, occupation informs us about a person's power, prestige, and wealth. It also hints at the other indicators.

Income can indicate social class in two ways. First, the size of income suggests the kind of life style that is accessible to the individual. Second, the source of a person's income can sometimes cut through questions about varying living costs and inflation over time to more clearly place him or her. If, say, most of a person's income is from dividends or inheritance, one can confidently presume a higher social class as compared with someone whose income mostly comes from public assistance. Similarly, income from salary usually indicates a higher-status occupation than does income from hourly wages. And, of course, "dirty" money, gained from illegal or notorious activities such as crime or wartime profiteering, garners the individual little social prestige.

Educational attainment is another valuable, but not foolproof, indicator of social class. After all, a person can claim four years of college without earning a degree. Looking beyond the sheer number of years spent in school, we might note the degrees awarded, the quality of the college attended (one measure of a college's prestige is its selectivity), and the subject studied (science, for example, is more prestigious than home economics).

A person's address can also reveal social class, but it too must be used with caution. A home with a prestigious address might be the least expensive in the neighborhood, or it may be rented. Still, in most communities some neighborhoods have more status than others.

In searching for one's class identity, then, one may choose from two sociological perspectives. The Marxist view is insightful, but deals perhaps too little with familiar life style matters. The indicators based on Weber's formulation, however, are neither foolproof nor clear-cut. Both approaches, however, provide useful clues to one's place in the social hierarchy. And they both prepare us for the next question: Why does all this matter?

Personal Effects of Social Class

Social class shapes our lives profoundly. It serves as one of the best available predictors of how people will live and raise their children. First, the social-class level of our childhood home substantially influences our probability of living a long and healthy life, what Max Weber termed "life chances." Second, class helps determine our life style, the way we spend our time and money, and our tastes, leisure activities, and consumption patterns. Table 6-2 summarizes the personal effects of social class.

SOME EFFECTS OF SOCIAL CLASS

Lower Classes	Higher Classes
Life Chances	
Higher infant mortality; more obesity and communicable, preventable diseases; use emergency room for medical care; higher rates of mental illness.	Preventative health practices.
Treatment: electroshock and drugs.	Treatment: psychotherapy, private clinic.
Childhood	
Adult-centered home, more siblings. Parents value order and obedience (Bronfenbrenner, 1966).	Parents use guilt, psychological manipulation (Slater, 1976), value self-direction, intellectual flexibility (Kohn et al., 1990), creativity, initiative.
Parents stress luck, fate.	Parents stress achievement, mastery, control, long-range plans.
Greater chance of parental divorce, separation, single-parent family.	Probably higher self-esteem (Coopersmith, 1967) and life satisfaction (Gilbert and Kahl, 1987).
Education	
Less preparation, lower school quality.	More likely to attend college regardless of academic ability (Sewell, 1971; Hout, 1988).

(continued next page)

Table 6-2

Lower Classes	Higher Classes
Marriage	
Less expectation for stable, satisfying marriage or giving birth while married (Farber, 1990).	More restrictive dating, later marriage; more likely to share common interests with spouse, sense of closeness, better communication (Reiss, 1980); more frequent, enjoyable intercourse (Howell, 1973; Rubin, 1983).
Socializing	
Limited largely to kin and neighbors.	More social contacts; memberships in clubs and organizations serve as source of career advancement, status, and information (Hodges, 1964; Lerner, 1982).
Television is major leisure activity.	Concerts, education, lectures, theater.
Politics	
Less likely to vote. Probably Democratic (though not as reliably as before 1980).	More likely to participate in campaigns, parties, interest groups.
Religion	
Fundamentalist sects more typical.	Major denominations: Congregationalist, Episcopalian, Presbyterian.
Fiery, lively religious services.	More subdued services.

To better appreciate the pervasive impact social class has on our lives, imagine a newborn infant put up for adoption. As Table 6-2 shows, the social class of the adopting parents will influence the child's life in virtually every way, from child-rearing techniques used in the home to her or his academic success, sex and marriage relationships, and religious and political activities. For example, the higher the social-class level of the child's home, the better the odds for a long and healthy life, a supportive, enriching, stable home environment, and college graduation. In a middle- or upper-class home, the child will probably be expected to follow internalized principles of right and wrong, a kind of moral gyroscope implanted by the parents. Such parents would also teach the child to defer immediate gratifications for future goals. Even the child's speech patterns will be molded by the social-class level of his or her home environment. The lower the class, the more likely he or she will use double negatives and drop the letter "g" in "-ing," as in "I'm not doin' nothin' for her."

Clearly, then, social class exerts a strong and pervasive influence on our life. The question then becomes, How rooted are we in the social class of our childhood home?

Love and Marriage, Class and Race

The percentage of births to unmarried teenagers has soared since 1960. This trend is worrisome because such mothers and their children are at high risk for long-term poverty. Naomi Farber of the University of Wisconsin, Madison, interviewed unmarried teenage mothers to discover the reasons for their decisions not to marry (1990).

Farber used a qualitative study, which deals with things not easily measured, such as feelings and attitudes. While most sociological research is quantitative, using measurable, numerical data, qualitative studies collect nonnumerical data and are often used to explore new territory and formulate hypotheses that can later be tested with quantitative data and control groups. In Farber's case, she found that previous studies on this subject, mostly quantitative, had not explained the decision-making process behind the teens' singlehood.

Farber conducted interviews with 28 unmarried teenage mothers in the Chicago area. Six groups of blacks and whites of three classes—middle, working, and lower—comprised the sample. The young mothers were found through agencies offering social support services. Most interviews were conducted at the adolescents' homes.

One question probed the young women's value of marriage. Clearly, most of them had not examined this path any more than others their age. Nearly all viewed marriage as the ideal. A typical response: "I wanted to be married, and have a career before I ever had a baby. That's how I wanted it to be. I wish it wasn't like this" (p. 54).

Farber next asked: Why, then, did things turn out as they had? Why did you not get married? A social-class difference emerged from the answers. The middle- and working-class women considered their situation to be temporary; they expected to marry when they found a suitable husband. They explained that they postponed marriage because the fathers were unwilling or not ready for marriage. Also, the mothers themselves were not ready; their families more typically advised them to not rush into an ill-fated marriage. As one says, "I told my boyfriend I didn't want to marry him until after I got out of school . . . that even after we get married, I'm going to stay on the pill for at least a year, if I haven't gotten my career together already" (p. 56).

In contrast, the lower-class women desired marriage, but had little hope of it. The men in their lives were generally unreliable, unfaithful, even brutal. Within this social class, whites were more hopeful of eventually marrying: "We were talking marriage. We still are. I don't see him much. So it's like, I don't know" (p. 61). The black women displayed more cynicism about men in general: "Marriage doesn't make any difference. 'Cause my sister . . . [with] her second child, she was married . . . but it still was like she was on her own" (p. 59). These young women commonly were taught by their mothers to mistrust men: "My ma said if you get married you're a fool. . . . First he's all right. But then he turns into—well, you'll be doing all the giving" (p. 60).

Because of the nature of qualitative research, Farber was not left with factual conclusions supported by numbers. Instead, she deduces from the impressions and descriptions collected that both race and class help explain the rising proportion of pregnant teenagers who do not marry. Poor young women have little hope of realizing the mainstream dream of marriage and family. The poor black women in this study did not even expect childbirth to occur within the framework of marriage, probably due to high joblessness rates among black men as well as changed attitudes toward marriage and family (Wilson, 1991). If these young women are typical, poverty has profoundly affected the relationships between the sexes in urban America. ☐

IS AMERICA A LAND OF OPPORTUNITY?

Americans have always believed that theirs is a land in which anyone can, with enough effort and ability, climb the ladder of success. The over 100 stories written by Horatio Alger after the Civil War were immensely popular tales of poor but honest and hard-working boys who rose in society through pluck and determination. American politicians still vie with one another in attesting to their own humble origins—log cabins, simple farms, and so on. Opportunity and the ability to advance through achievement and skill have attracted millions of ambitious immigrants to our shores. For many generations, America has symbolized **vertical mobility,** movement up or down the social ladder. But is America still a land of opportunity? Does mobility still exist, and is it accessible for everyone?

Vertical mobility: movement up or down the social ladder.

Is America a Caste System?

Compared to many other societies, America is indeed one of rich possibilities. It is a relatively open system, one that allows, even encourages, its citizens to seek higher rungs on the social ladder. In more closed—or **caste**—societies, people are bound to the same social level as their ancestors. Their castes are inherited, ascribed statuses. The wall between the caste levels are rigid, preventing what sociologists call **intragenerational mobility,** or social mobility within one's lifetime.

Caste: a stratum in a closed system of stratification in which social mobility is not allowed.

Intragenerational mobility: social mobility within one's own lifetime.

Several rules govern the smooth functioning of a caste system. For one, an individual may not marry outside his or her caste. This prevents questions regarding the status of children resulting from a mixed-caste marriage. Another rule is that individual qualities and performance have no effect on a person's caste designation. Because of this, no one can work his or her way into a higher caste. The caste system also requires, or at least expects, people to accept their social rankings. Religion has been an important source of support for such systems, most notably in India, where Hinduism has held that one's social ranking in this life is the direct result of one's spiritual progress (or lack of it) in previous lives.

Clearly, a caste society is no land of opportunity. But is not the United States at least in some respects caste-like? How else can we explain why nonwhites have been for so long clustered near the bottom? Has there not been a caste line based on race? Furthermore, conflict theorists forcefully argue that an individual's class position in the United States is virtually inherited, preordained by one's own parents' status as well as various structural barriers (Rytina, 1992). Children born in loftier niches have enormous advantages; their families enhance the children's cognitive skills and motivations so much that a college diploma is almost assured at birth. Because of this, America's new meritocracy, based on a high-powered educational background rather than "old money," may soon resemble a caste as much as the WASP elite once did

(Glastris, 1993). Still, even though our class system is based on unequal opportunities, it is much more open than a caste system such as India's. But are America's class boundaries more open than those in other class societies?

No industrialized or postindustrialized society can afford a caste system because it would deny too many of its members an opportunity to contribute. A nation's prosperity today depends on legions of skilled, educated workers; societies with masses of peasants trapped in ignorance and illiteracy cannot compete in the global economy. It is not surprising, then, that rates of movement upward or downward in social class between generations—**intergenerational mobility**—are not significantly higher in the United States than they are in other developed nations (Lipset, 1982; Winfield et al., 1989).

Intergenerational mobility: social mobility between generations, usually measured by comparing one's own class level with that of one's parents.

Still, America's self-image as a land of opportunity has been justified. Upward intergenerational mobility has always been more probable than downward movement. A small but steady rise in social mobility has been evident since the turn of the century (Hodge and Lagerfeld, 1987; Guest, Landale, McCann, 1989). This trend was also discerned in the several studies of "Middletown" (Muncie, Indiana), a typical American city. Robert and Helen Lynd first studied the city in the late 1920s, then again in 1937. Howard Bahr followed up more recently and found "fewer social barriers between the classes and more social contacts across class lines than there were during the Lynds' time" (1987, p. 129). Furthermore, in their survey sample of 20,700 men, Peter Blau and Otis Duncan (1967) found that nearly 10 percent of men from working-class homes climbed into high-prestige occupations. Maybe half of Americans were not socially mobile in the sixties, but those who moved were more likely to move up than down. Lower-status jobs were being replaced with higher-status ones. Also, differences in birth rates among social classes (the higher classes did not replace themselves to the degree lower classes did) helped create an upward draft.

Diminishing Opportunities

Since the 1970s, however, the promise of a better life than one's parents has no longer been assured. The odds have shifted so that, as Frank Levy and Richard Michel note, "a 30-year-old man is earning about 10 percent less than his father earned when the young man left home" (1986, p. 36). Even though Americans enjoy more comforts and conveniences than ever before, they have "lost the psychology of plenty" (Samuelson, 1992). Relative income has declined from that of previous generations as costs have climbed (most notably health care benefits), and many workers compete for scarce jobs: Almost 3 million out of 21 million manufacturing jobs disappeared during the 1980s (Dentzer, 1991). Higher worker productivity has come to mean keeping the company competitive, not bigger paychecks. When family incomes have increased it has often been because the wife works and brings home a substantial paycheck (Bradbury, 1990). One study found that "the probability of falling from middle-income to lower-income status increased significantly after 1980" (Duncan, Smeeding, and Rodgers, 1992, p. 38). Another figured that of the 8 percent of those who left the middle class between 1978 and 1986, 2.8 percent rose to the top income group and 5.2 percent fell (Rose, 1986).

Opportunity in the United States has been eroded by two emerging trends: the increasing distance between the two ends of the income spectrum, and the rise of a new kind of wall between those who are well-off and everyone else.

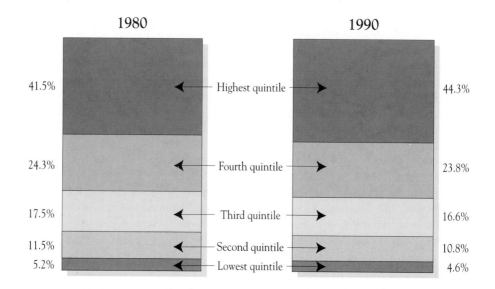

FAMILY INCOME DISTRIBUTION BY QUINTILES

	1980	1990	
41.5%	Highest quintile		44.3%
24.3%	Fourth quintile		23.8%
17.5%	Third quintile		16.6%
11.5%	Second quintile		10.8%
5.2%	Lowest quintile		4.6%

Figure 6–2

This figure divides American families into quintiles, each of which contains one-fifth of the total number of all the nation's families. The top quintile contains the 20 percent of all families with the highest incomes, the lowest quintile the poorest 20 percent of all families. Comparing 1980 and 1990, we see the rich (the top 20 percent of families) getting an even larger proportion of aggregate income, while the poorest 20 percent of families received a smaller share.

Source: U.S. Bureau of the Census, *Statistical Abstract, 1992,* 112th ed., p. 450.

The Richer Rich and Poorer Poor   For evidence of increasing inequality we return to 1968, when the richest 20 percent of households in the United States claimed about 44 percent of aggregate household income—roughly double what their share would be if income were distributed equally throughout society. During the 1980s, their share climbed significantly while the poor got an even smaller slice of the pie, as we see in Figure 6-2. While so many other families saw their earnings stagnate, those who prospered were typically college-educated spouses, both working. These top households seem to be pulling away from the rest as we near the end of the century. According to one observer, very few members of the generation coming of age now will rise to this top group. Most will settle for a scaled-down version of the American Dream, and some will fall into a large class of alienated, disillusioned Americans with few prospects (Dychtwald, 1989).

The increasing inequality of the last decade may just be a return to economic normalcy after the aberration of widespread prosperity after World War II, but some social scientists detect a more ominous trend. In the past, there have always been income gaps between men and women, whites and nonwhites, well-educated and undereducated workers. Now there is increasing inequality even within each of these categories: among full-time, year-round male workers; among full-time, year-round black workers; and so on. Moreover, within each industry (except for agriculture), earnings inequality also has been increasing: within the service sector, the blue-collar production sector, for example. (Ryscavage and Henle, 1990).

The New Dividing Wall   The drift toward greater inequality is accompanied by a rising new wall in America's class structure, one based not only on familiar cultural and racial factors but increasingly on educational status. The resulting picture is not simply the rich getting richer and the poor getting poorer, but the educated getting richer and everyone else either stagnating or being left behind.

This separation is due to the growing link between pay and knowledge (Kaus, 1990). In the earlier industrial age, workers were all paid roughly the same wage because there were modest differences in workers' skills: Either a worker could operate a stamping machine or he couldn't. But political economist Robert Reich (1991) observes that in today's postindustrial society much higher income will go to those workers with superior ability to analyze complex data, solve problems, and manipulate information. Reich calls such well-educated people "symbolic analysis" workers, and explains that they are earning vastly greater salaries and are seceding from the rest of society, joining instead the global community of similarly educated people.

The income gap may thus continue to widen, perhaps inexorably, because the emerging global economy has less use for workers on the wrong side of the wall, those who are not well-educated. Opportunities are shrinking for those who are unable to jump through the hoops of the education system. One demographer predicts that as educational requirements more rigorously sort out workers, "whites and Asians could increasingly dominate high-income high-status occupations, leaving blacks and Hispanics with low-income low-status occupations" (Riche, 1991, p. 32).

The separating wall seems to be rising in the middle of the class spectrum, heaving the middle class into either affluence on one side or financial vulnerability and insecurity on the other. In other words, there are fewer middle-class occupations. The manufacturing jobs that offered solid, respectable incomes for families in the decades after World War II have been disappearing, shrinking from one-third of all jobs in 1947 to one-fifth by 1985. Meanwhile, the service sector (including restaurant workers and salespeople) grew during that same time period from one-tenth to one-fifth of the labor force.

This shift to relatively low-paying service jobs increases income inequality. It is as though a large group of passengers on a ship moved from the middle (manufacturing) to the rear (services), thereby lifting the ship's nose higher out of the water. This expansion of the service sector, combined with more high-tech employment, account for about two-thirds of the overall increase in income inequality in recent decades (Grubb and Wilson, 1989).

The statistics reveal opportunity for only a small portion of the population. This polarization is disturbing to those who favor the status quo. After all, one requirement of democracy is a strong, stable middle class. Citizens demand a share of the power and desire a steady course. If a population becomes proportionally too poor, calls will grow louder for quick fixes, radical change, and more powerful leaders. The future of America may see the development of precisely the conditions desired by a would-be dictator: widespread suffering and resentment and a growing consensus that the existing government is incapable of restoring the country's former glory. Many radical observers would see such a scenario as confirmation of Karl Marx's predictions of capitalism's ultimate self-destruction.

America, then, is not the land of opportunity it once was. Still, while the rungs of the ladder seem to have been greased, and moved further apart, some Americans are climbing upward—for the most part, those who can think in sophisticated ways and have a quality education. Of course there are other determinants of mobility, as we see next.

Critical Thinking Box

Careful with Statistics!

Caution should always be the byword when using statistics, but even greater care must be exercised when dealing with politically tinged numbers such as those describing wealth inequities. Danger lurks in the selective presentation of quantitative facts, which can result in a distorted picture. For example, as Paul Krugman (1992) points out, it is perfectly accurate to say that per capita income rose about 23 percent during the 1980s. However, if we note that the proportion of children and dependents decreased during that time, real family income rose only about 8 percent. Moreover, while the 1980s was a period of overall economic growth for the United States, the real income of families in the middle range actually fell by about 5 percent, and poorer families saw theirs drop twice as much. In the meantime, the average family income rose by nearly $3,000. How can this be? Krugman explains that the upper 5 percent of families gained about 95 percent of the overall increase in family income, while the wealthiest 0.2 percent enjoyed over 40 percent of the increase in family income! ■

MOVING UP: WHAT DETERMINES ONE'S CHANCES?

What improves one's chances for upward social mobility? Luck can make a difference, as can personal resources such as industry and ambition. While sociologists acknowledge these factors, they have focused on the external forces that help shape our inner selves as well as our opportunities. Society, they have found, exerts much influence on both structural and individual mobility.

Structural Mobility

Social changes often reshuffle the opportunities for advancement. The Industrial Revolution, for example, introduced new machinery that eliminated large numbers of farm jobs. While 90 percent of all occupations in the United States were once agriculture-related, the number today is only 10 percent. In the recent past, America saw the elimination of millions of unskilled occupations through automation, and the expansion of government and corporate bureaucracies. Such structural changes produced many higher-income jobs, pulling many Americans up the social ladder. Today, as we saw earlier in this chapter, the generation now coming of age has the hard luck to face economic conditions that make upward mobility more difficult than in earlier decades. For one thing, the fastest growing occupations (mostly in the service sector) do not pay well, and foreign competition and automation combine to eliminate ever more industrial jobs. Second, the top jobs are clogged with a huge cohort of baby-boomers. Third, it is mostly the few very well-educated workers who enjoy exceptionally favorable prospects.

Structural mobility: widespread changes in class status caused by changes in society, especially the economy.

These conditions illustrate **structural mobility,** widespread changes in class status caused by changes in society, especially the economy. Another source of structural mobility is the **birth rate differential,** the tendency of upper-class people to have fewer children than lower-class people. A smaller number of higher-status children to fill top-level positions creates more opportunities for those less privileged.

Birth rate differential: the tendency for upper-class people to have fewer children than lower-class people.

Individual Mobility

Of course, social mobility is not completely determined by forces beyond one's control. Individual choices and characteristics play an important role. For example, those intent on social advancement can make geographical moves to wherever opportunites are available. Accordingly, millions of Americans have fled the northern "Rust Belt" and "Frost Belt" to seek jobs in the "Sun Belt." Also, people can, within limits, improve their appearance, which tends to open doors for job-seekers. For example, slimming down might make a difference: In one study, young obese women earned about 12 percent less than comparable nonobese women (Register and Williams, 1990). Another strategy is to marry someone with good income potential. This is increasingly possible for people of modest backgrounds because one's own educational level is becoming more important than parents' social class regarding mate selection (Kalmijn, 1991a).

For the most part, however, important personal characteristics are determined by one's family background (Eggebeen and Lichter, 1991). In fact, Christopher Jencks and his colleagues (1979) analyzed all major mobility studies up to 1978 and conclude that more than any other variable, family background profoundly affects one's chances for later social success. Chances for moving up the ladder are much smaller if a man's parents break up during his childhood (Biblarz and Raftery, 1993). And in mother-only households, individuals are likely to face more stress and receive less parental attention. In such cases, low mobility chances would be directly linked to economic deprivation, which in turn is linked to poorer school quality, fewer extracurricular activities, and unfavorable neighborhood conditions (McLanahan and Booth, 1989).

The personal constellations within the childhood home also make a difference. For example, the fewer siblings, the greater are one's chances for upward mobility (Blake, 1985), partly because of the greater attention and financial support children receive in small families (Steelman and Powell, 1989). Similarly, the first-born son, the youngest son in a small family, and only children have better opportunities than other children to move up the social ladder. Moreover, because parents often see sons as better long-term financial investments, several brothers are more serious obstacles to an individual's mobility chances than are sisters (Powell and Steelman, 1989).

Considerable research has focused on parents' influence on their offsprings' mobility. Fathers coming home from occupations in which they exert control over the work of others convey a sense of self-direction to their children (Kohn et al., 1990). Sons born to older fathers have an advantage because such fathers tend to have higher educational, employment, and economic statuses, and weaker competing role demands (Mare and Tzeng, 1989). And mothers serve as models for their daughters regarding work behaviors (Tickamyer and Blee, 1990).

The Status Attainment Model

Clearly, chances for upward mobility are to some extent determined well before the time the individual leaves home for school. It is in this bubbling stewpot of the home environment that sociologists discern the forces that eventually determine one's

SOME FACTORS AFFECTING SOCIAL MOBILITY

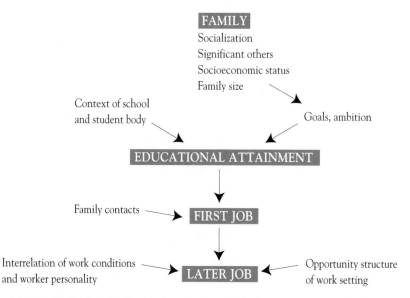

Figure 6–3

This arrangement of factors involved in the status attainment process focuses on occupation as a measure of social mobility.

Source: Based on Alan C. Kerckhoff, "On the Social Psychology of Social Mobility Processes," *Social Forces*, volume 68, September 1989, pp. 17–25.

social-class ranking. These forces are best pictured by the status attainment model formulated by Peter Blau and Otis Duncan (1967) and expanded by others (such as Sewell, Haller, and Portes, 1969). The model centers on (1) the parents' socioeconomic status and its impact on (2) educational attainment, which in turns helps determine (3) the first job, which influences (4) the eventual occupational niche and social class position in life (see Figure 6-3).

We saw earlier in the chapter that middle-class homes are more likely to emphasize high achievement goals, deferring immediate gratifications, self-direction, independence, creativity, and intellectual flexibility. Well-educated parents are more likely to pressure their children toward academic achievement, monitor their progress, and help with homework. Such parents display proper grammar and "standard" English, and tastes and behaviors appropriate for high-level occupations. They also possess the financial resources that lessen any need for their children to hold jobs throughout their high school and college years. For all these reasons, it is not surprising that parental socioeconomic status makes as much or more difference in the next crucial step along the pathway to upward mobility, educational attainment, than does the child's intelligence. Compared with bright children from poor homes, children who come from advantaged homes are more likely to earn a four-year college degree regardless of their intelligence (Sewell, 1971).

Most Americans acknowledge that college education can open doors. In many occupations, there are two career ladders. The one for non–college graduates starts with low pay and power, and usually can take the individual at best to only a moderate standard of living. Moreover, high school dropouts today face an increasing stigma of incompetence (Olneck and Kim, 1989). The ladder for college graduates starts higher and leads to greater heights. The four-year college degree is a requirement for most high-status jobs, and is a key variable in intergenerational mobility (Hauser and Logan, 1992). However, because college graduates are not as rare as decades ago, the four-year degree is no longer a virtual guarantee of success.

Family background and educational attainment point to the next step on the status attainment path: one's first job. The family not only helps an individual get through college, but provides valuable contacts afterward: fraternity brothers, sorority sisters, and business associates who can pave the way for an old friend's son or daughter. Entering the labor market at a high level clearly puts a high-status occupation within easier reach.

Researchers elaborating on the classic status attainment model have fleshed out some details of this "first job" stage. A picture emerges detailing the significantly different "opportunity structures" of various work settings (Kerckhoff, 1989). Some corporations, for example, allow more mobility than others. And some occupations offer more security, niches, and open employer–worker relationships. Such jobs are found mostly in the "core" sector of the labor market, according to **dual labor market theory.** Huge, dominating corporations generally offer more chances for advancement, higher income levels, and better benefits, especially for women (Villemez and Bridges, 1988). In the past, African Americans and immigrants have been channeled into the "periphery" sector, which offers less security, fewer benefits, and lower pay.

Furthermore, the labor market at any one time rewards certain skills more than others. A person's mobility chances depend on the match between individual abilities and the demands of the market. One's **human capital,** or potential to contribute to society, is a strong predictor of mobility (Jacobs, 1985). Thus, those who have amassed educational credentials, appropriate work experience, and relevant job skills are best fitted to move up the social ladder.

Once the individual enters the labor market, job promotions depend to some extent on education, but it is not simply a matter of more being better (Spilerman and Lunde, 1991). Workers tend to rise according to how well they appraise and anticipate job opportunities and match them with appropriate educational accomplishments (Halaby, 1988), including years of schooling, earned degrees, quality of college (partly measured by its selectivity), and college major. The climb up the job ladder also depends on social networks and ties: the old story of "it's who you know." One researcher finds that, indeed, better jobs can be found by contacting people within one's own network who have superior knowledge and influence (Wegener, 1991).

Chances for upward mobility are not so simple as predicted in the status attainment model. Ascribed statuses of sex, race, and class background complicate and second-guess the model. Women, nonwhites, and people from lower-class backgrounds are still less likely to attain high-status occupational positions. And while occupational inequality of women and racial minorities diminished during the 1960s and 1970s, the 1980s saw much less bridging of those gaps (Carlson, 1992).

Clearly, the status attainment process does not work for women as it does for men. Although their college graduation rates are comparable to those of men, only 3 percent of women earn incomes of $50,000 or more, compared to 15 percent of men. One researcher estimates that gender discrimination accounts for at least one-quarter of the male–female income gap (Hagan, 1990). Another complication is that a married woman usually considers her husband's ranking (his occupation, education, and income level) along with her own when ranking herself, whereas husbands pay little attention to their wives' status when ranking themselves. Since the 1970s and 1980s, however, married women have begun to give their own accomplishments equal weighting with their husbands' (Davis and Robinson, 1988).

Dual labor market theory: the theory that there is an advantageous "core" job sector with superior worker benefits as contrasted with a "periphery" sector with lower pay, less security, poorer benefits, and fewer opportunities for advancement.

Human capital: the potential to contribute to society, usually measured in terms of educational level, skills, and work experience.

African Americans remain greatly disadvantaged in the competition for social status. They are still overly represented in the lower income and occupation categories. Part of the explanation lies in discriminatory barriers. Beyond this, the status attainment model points also to many blacks' family background factors, such as typically larger families, a higher proportion of female-headed households, and parental modeling of lower-status occupational attainment and work behaviors (Tickamyer and Blee, 1990).

The status attainment model, however, does help explain two features of the American social landscape. First, while many people will experience some mobility, most will not end up far from their own parents' ranking. This is due to the central influence of family background: More than anything else, parental nurturing and modeling fashion goals and personal resources. Second, because so many of one's opportunities to climb the social ladder depend on ascribed factors, it is easier to understand why America cannot quickly transform itself into a true meritocracy.

CAN POVERTY BE ELIMINATED?

Only as recently as the 1960s did poverty become a social problem rather than merely a fact of life in the United States. Added to long-standing religious mandates to help the needy was the innovative idea that the poor are victims of an uncaring, unfair society. Moreover, ferocious riots of mostly inner-city blacks frightened taxpayers into accepting the need for governmental policies that would at least mollify the poor. Poverty became a worry as well as an embarrassment.

Poverty line: an official line designating the minimum income needed to feed, house, and clothe a family.

Absolute poverty: lack of an income adequate to provide necessary food, clothing, and shelter.

Thus emerged the welfare system. A **poverty line** was established to identify those families living in **absolute poverty**—that is, those with incomes inadequate to purchase food, clothing, and shelter. It was based on the U. S. Department of Agriculture's food plan for emergency or temporary use—a bare bones diet—and from this the remaining income needs were calculated. (The "poverty line" is actually made up of over 100 different lines to cover such variations as family size, sex of the head of the family, and farm versus nonfarm residence.) Liberals contend that the poverty line is too low, that the base income level is inadequate for today's standard of living. Conservatives argue that if the calculations included noncash benefits, such as food stamps, Medicaid, and housing subsidies, the percentage of Americans classified as poor would shrink.

Nevertheless, to the frustration of social reformers and politicians the percentage of Americans officially living below the poverty line has not consistently diminished since the welfare system was instituted. After an initial drop in the 1960s, the poverty rate has hovered stubbornly between 11 percent and a little over 15 percent over the past few decades (see Figure 6-4).

Relative deprivation: insufficient income to afford what others have; discontent that occurs when people perceive their living standards as lower than others' or their own in the past.

America's problem with poverty is complicated by **relative deprivation,** an insufficient income to afford what others have. Because people tend to compare their plight to others', they can feel deprived even if their income level is well above the line of absolute poverty so long as they lack the luxuries possessed by those around them. Eliminating relative poverty would require equalizing living standards.

All of which leaves Americans in a social policy quandary. After acknowledging poverty as a problem, and pouring billions of tax dollars into welfare policies, society

THE NUMBER OF POOR AND THE POVERTY RATE, 1959–1991

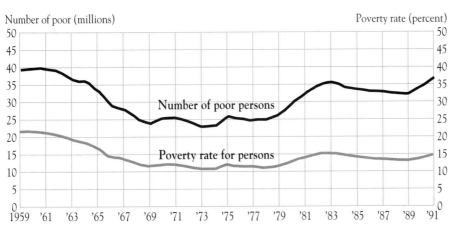

Note: The data points represent the midpoints of the respective years. The latest recessionary period began in July of 1990.

Source: U.S. Department of Commerce, Economics and Statistics Administration, Bureau of the Census, *Current Population Reports*, Consumer Income Series P-60, No. 181, "Poverty in the United States: 1991," page ix.

Figure 6–4

still has a sizable percentage of poor. Answers to two questions may help us decide if efforts to fight poverty are hopeless: Who are the poor? and Why are people poor?

Who Are the Poor?

Certainly the poverty population is not monolithic. Most poor people in the United States are white, but minority groups have disproportionately high rates, as Table 6-3 shows. While the poverty rate for whites is around 10 percent, the rate for Hispanics and African Americans is triple that. Furthermore, poverty has a predominantly Southern face. Table 6-4 indicates that poverty rates and income vary among regions in the United States, and that it hits hardest in inner cities and rural areas.

Another aspect of poverty is revealed by the telling phrase "feminization of poverty." About half of all poor families are female-headed. In fact, most of the poor are female. This should come as no surprise; after all, women have for generations

POVERTY AND RACE/ETHNICITY

Persons	Percent Below Poverty Level, 1991
Total	14.2
White, not of Hispanic origin	9.4
Black	32.7
Hispanic origin (may be of any race)	28.7
Other races	17.6

Table 6-3

Source: U.S. Department of Commerce, Economics and Statistics Administration, Bureau of the Census, *Current Population Reports*, Consumer Income Series P-60, No. 181, "Poverty in the United States: 1991," Table A, page x.

POVERTY AND GEOGRAPHY

Urban vs. Rural Poverty Rates

Residence	Poverty Rate, 1991
In metropolitan areas	13.7%
Central cities	20.2%
Outside central cities	9.6%
Outside metropolitan areas	16.1%

Personal Income by Region and State

Region	Disposable Personal Income per Capita, 1991
United States	$16,318
Northeast	$18,782
West	$16,711
Midwest	$15,913
South	$14,910
Top Five States	
Connecticut	$21,967
New Jersey	$21,884
Massachusetts	$19,385
Alaska	$19,320
New Hampshire	$18,710
Bottom Five States	
Oklahoma	$12,951
Arkansas	$12,917
Utah	$12,492
West Virginia	$12,381
Mississippi	$11,528

Table 6-4

Source: U.S. Department of Commerce, Economics and Statistics Administration, Bureau of the Census, *Current Population Reports*, Consumer Income Series P-60, No. 181, "Poverty in the United States: 1991."

Source: U.S. Bureau of the Census, *Statistical Abstract, 1992*, 112th ed., p. 437.

been subordinate and largely unwelcome in all but the lowest levels of the labor market. Moreover, many women, divorced or deserted by their husbands, are unable to compete successfully in the job force because of child care responsibilities and lack of job skills. Sharing the poverty in those female-headed households are millions of children, who comprise a third of all poor people in the country today (see Table 6-5 and Figure 6-5). In fact, children have comprised the largest age group among the poor since the mid-1970s.

Poverty confronts us most visibly in the homeless, especially in the fastest-growing segment of those living in shelters and the streets: families, usually headed by women. As anyone who has visited a large city center knows, this population has grown in recent years; estimates range from several hundred thousand to several million people.

POVERTY AND HOUSEHOLD TYPE

Type of Household	Poverty Rate of Families, 1991
All families	11.5%
Married couple families	6.0%
Male householder, no wife present	13.0%
Female householder, no husband present	35.6%

Table 6-5

Source: U.S. Department of Commerce, Economics and Statistics Administration, Bureau of the Census, *Current Population Reports*, Consumer Income Series P-60, No. 181, "Poverty in the United States: 1991."

Calling these people "homeless" leaves them without a face. They typically lack such resources as child care, social skills, work experience, and savings. They don't have the social support of friends or family on whom they could depend. Many of the homeless have backgrounds of mental hospitalization, abuse as children and adults, and problems with drugs and alcohol. These deprived backgrounds produce a host of physical and mental illnesses that leave them weakened and vulnerable to losing their homes. Once homeless, they suffer new psychological traumas in the form of street

DISTRIBUTION OF THE POPULATION ABOVE AND BELOW THE POVERTY LEVEL, BY AGE, 1991

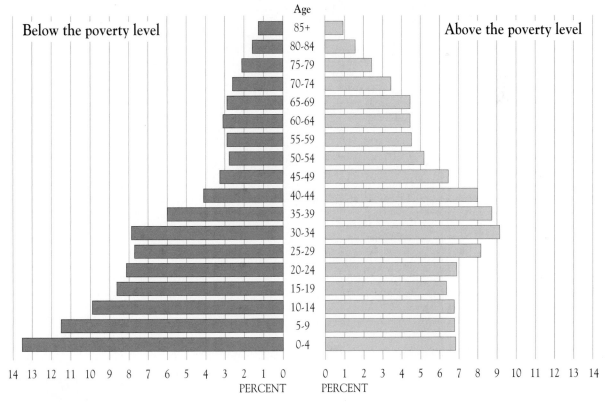

Since the mid-1970s, children have been more likely to be poor than any other age category.

Figure 6–5

Source: U.S. Department of Commerce, Economics and Statistics Administration, Bureau of the Census, *Current Population Reports*, Consumer Income Series P-60, No. 181, "Poverty in the United States: 1991."

Though this population is difficult to count, the increase in the number of homeless families was clearly visible last decade. According to the Interagency Council on the Homeless, the median age of homeless persons is 36, about 80% are unemployed, about one-third have problems with alcoholism or other substance abuse, and about one-third suffer from severe mental illness.

violence and abuse as well as the harshness of shelter life. Communal sleeping arrangements, overcrowding, lack of privacy, exposure to the weather, and dangers in the streets all contribute to poor mental and physical health. Children face malnutrition, depression, increased risk for HIV and other infections, stunted development, and academic underachievement (Molnar, Rath, and Klein, 1990; Rafferty and Shinn, 1991; Rotheram-Borus, Koopman, and Ehrhardt, 1991).

Why Are People Poor?

What puts people into such pathetic situations? This question is simplistic, and holds the danger of suggesting that poverty is a matter easily explained—which it is not. Still, from the tangled, complex explanations emerge two fundamental solutions to the poverty problem: Change individuals or change society.

"Blaming the Victim"   It is easy to blame the poor themselves. The drifter or homeless wino evokes little sympathy. Descriptions of lower-class life are replete with examples of laziness and irresponsibility. The images that come into focus reveal recalcitrant school children disrupting schools, women bearing children casually and indiscriminantly, men eschewing family responsibility for the cheap thrills of the street. Thus, employed inner-city blacks strongly censure the unemployed residents of the ghetto, citing the hostility between the sexes that makes stable family life virtually impossible and the reluctance of the men to accept anything but "easy" jobs (Wilson, 1987, 1991).

Such disdain for the poor is widespread. Many Americans, who may have never been in a truly poor neighborhood or known a poverty-stricken person, see poverty as a symptom of a lack of motivation and skill. While the homeless may get more sympathy (Lee, Lewis, and Jones, 1992), opinion polls routinely report the well-entrenched American conviction that the poor in general need to be put to work rather than given "government handouts." These attitudes rest on a particularly strong American **ideology:** each individual is responsible for his or her own achievement and failure. Supporting this ideology are beliefs regarding the value of work, equal opportunity, and individualism. Viewed through this prism, the poor deserve little pity or help: They are responsible for their failure. Nationwide surveys demonstrate this ideology (Feagin, 1975; Kluegel, 1987). When asked to explain poverty, Americans primarily identify characteristics of the poor themselves: lack of thrift, effort, ability, and morals.

This ideology of achievement and individualism logically leads to what William Ryan (1971) calls "blaming the victim." The crushing social forces that create the apathy, fatalism, and hopelessness often found among the poor are largely ignored. The problem with this ideology is that it is founded largely on myths about poverty and opportunity in America. For example, studies unanimously indicate that most poor people do not, as popularly believed, prefer to live off welfare rather than work (Warren and Berkowitz, 1969; Schiller, 1973; O'Hare, 1986, among others). The absence of job opportunities and the exorbitant costs of child care and health care cause some mothers to turn to welfare as a means of simple survival (Edin, 1991). Another myth is that the poor remain on welfare indefinitely and that they constitute an enormous drain on America's wealth. In fact, most families receiving Aid to Families with Dependent Children (AFDC) are on the welfare rolls for no more than five

Ideology: a set of ideas or beliefs that explains and justifies social arrangements.

In trying to explain the plight of such people, do we blame their personal traits or the social forces that produced them?

years, and federal spending on social welfare programs is only about 11 percent of total GNP (U. S. Bureau of the Census, 1991).

In light of such research, many sociologists have turned from a search for "character flaws" to an examination of the social forces that contribute to such self-defeating personality traits.

Social Causes   Several decades ago, the anthropologist Oscar Lewis (1966) gathered evidence of immensely powerful social forces that cause poverty. Lewis traveled through the United States studying families that had been poor for generations. He concludes that these people's values and norms handicapped them, virtually excluding them from effective participation in the dominant culture and economy. Lewis describes a **culture of poverty** that includes fatalism, little if any planning for the future, a goal of immediate gratification, acting on impulse, and a dislike of authority. This way of life may have begun as an adaptation to poverty, but once established it can become self-perpetuating, trapping families in poverty for generations and helping to form an **underclass,** a persistently poor, economically and socially isolated social stratum.

Members of the underclass are typically concentrated in areas with very high poverty rates, and remain mired in poverty for years (O'Hare and Curry-White, 1992). We find such concentration of people even in rural areas, where they are more likely

Culture of poverty: a way of life embodying fatalism, apathy, and other attitudes that perpetuate social and economic disadvantages.

Underclass: a persistently poor, economically and socially isolated stratum.

to be older, male, Southern, and white. All together, members of the underclass include an estimated three million adults who display most of the problems associated with the culture of poverty: unemployment, welfare dependency, illegitimacy, and high crime rates.

This self-perpetuating and self-defeating way of life causes some poverty. In other cases, the source is more clearly external: discrimination. Racial and ethnic minorities and women face system-wide barriers to employment and educational opportunity. Any effective poverty-fighting program would have to abolish both formal and informal discrimination. As we will see in Chapter 7, most of the legislative work has already been done, but animosities in our interpersonal interactions remain deeply rooted.

The **structural theory of poverty** points to other social factors beyond the control of the poor: low minimum wages, lack of security and health care insurance, and persistent patterns of unemployment. In other words, the economy is structured in such a way that at any one time there are millions of "losers," people who have at least temporarily fallen below the poverty line. Part of this structuring lies in government taxing and spending policies that funnel tax dollars from many families of modest means to a smaller number of wealthier families through hidden subsidies and tax deductions. Well-to-do farmers clearly benefit from agricultural price supports, and people earning six-figure incomes enjoy huge mortgage deductions and tax shelters. Another part of the structuring of poverty lies in the free-wheeling, boom-and-bust nature of capitalist economies. Workers are hired when market demands drive production; they are laid off during slumps. Such intermittent hard times—and rises in poverty rates—are virtually guaranteed. And when high unemployment rates combine with a declining stock of low-cost housing, many poor families find themselves homeless.

Economic restructuring also contributes to poverty, especially the formation of the underclass. Over the last few decades, most major cities in the United States have shifted from manufacturing to information-processing centers. This means bad news to those inner-city residents who lack the skills required in such new occupations (Kasarda, 1989). Increasingly, new jobs requiring little education have moved to the suburbs, out of the reach of a largely immobilized and isolated urban population (Blackley, 1990; Osterman, 1991a). This labor mismatch leaves many black men unemployed, and thus unable to assume the husband–father role, contributing to the high percentage of female-headed households in the African-American population. It also sets off a devastating exodus of the black middle class, the social backbone of black urban neighborhoods (Wilson, 1987, 1989). Similarly, a decline of manufacturing and farming jobs in rural areas has helped create a less noticeable rural underclass.

These social explanations of poverty all point to the same conclusion: Rather than blame individuals, a more effective strategy would be to deal with the social forces that shape people's behaviors. Of course, such a strategy would face political impediments at every turn. For example, solutions along this line would include creating an economy that guarantees employment at livable wages, provides health care for all, and has tax policies that transfer wealth to the poor instead of the well-to-do. Various incentives would have to be employed to lure low-skill jobs into areas of poorly educated residents. Eliminating the culture of poverty would also involve imposing taxpayers' values on the persistently poor while providing them with more resources.

The current welfare system includes Medicaid (medical care for the poor); food stamps; Supplemental Security Income for the blind, disabled, and elderly; and Aid to Families with Dependent Children, to provide income to poor women with children.

Structural theory of poverty: the theory that poverty is largely built into the patterns and policies of society and the economy.

Few people admire this system, but researchers do not provide clear direction for reform. Charles Murray (1984) and others contend that it provides food and shelter to the poor, but also creates dependency and robs its recipients of their dignity and incentive. Other research finds little support for this view (Sanders, 1991), arguing, for example, that welfare pays too little to entice single mothers into welfare dependence (Edin, 1991).

Most recent political responses to the poverty problem have taken either of two approaches. One advocates changing the opportunity structure by providing more low-cost housing, subsidized child care, education and training, better wages, and, most importantly, more jobs. Otherwise, supporters claim, the poor cannot cope with the strained economy and harsh job market. Critics reply that many of the poor have no interest in taking advantage of an invigorated economy or new job slots, and that they need motivation rather than merely opportunity.

The second tack focuses on building incentives into the current welfare system. Proponents of this view argue that government welfare policies today do not reward people for holding down jobs and maintaining families. Instead, they say, the present system produces dependency. Cutting public assistance spending, especially popular in states strapped for cash, offers one way to get poor people back into the labor market. Various "workfare" proposals also flow from this line of reasoning. Such programs require people who receive public assistance to make some effort to achieve self-sufficiency by participating in job training, counseling, or educational programs, and eventually getting established in a job. In the meantime, such programs usually provide medical care, child care, and housing assistance. In this view, those receiving welfare have an obligation to the taxpayers, and also owe it to themselves and their children to become independent. The work requirements in workfare programs, however, often have huge loopholes, exempting large numbers of people. Besides, critics contend, few jobs materialize even for those who go through the training programs. And we must wonder if government-based incentives will convince poor people to change their life styles.

Clearly, poverty is not caused only by the personal inadequacies of the poor or external conditions beyond one's control. It results from a complex interaction between the individual and social forces. Society cannot be changed without influencing the individuals who comprise it, and changing individuals requires that we alter the social environment that shapes them. Eliminating poverty will require a comprehensive, perhaps even a revolutionary, approach.

SUMMARY

Since the 1700s, Europeans have asked whether social inequality is necessary. Sociologists have joined the debate, with functionalists arguing that inequality provides the incentives required for the smooth functioning of complex societies. Unequal rewards help fill difficult and demanding occupations and motivate workers to do their best. Conflict theorists point out that social rewards do not always go to the workers with merit or ability, as in a *meritocracy*. Besides, they say, artificial barriers prevent some people with merit from earning their due rewards. As Gerhard Lenski points out, both views may be true. Meritocracy may reign early in a society's development, but eventually the elite erect barriers to consolidate their position. A truly egalitarian society would require far-reaching reforms.

All societies show some *social differentiation*, by which members are categorized or distinguished by personal attributes such as age, gender, and so on. The ranking system of the Cheyenne, which depended mostly on personal characteristics such as strength or beauty, contrasts sharply with our own. In our system of *social stratification*, or institutionalized social inequality, rankings are built into social patterns largely beyond the individual's control, such as sex, race, and *social class*, a stratum of individuals sharing similar amounts of social resources.

Max Weber explained that social-class rankings are determined by three factors, the first of which is wealth. The Cheyenne had relatively little disparity regarding wealth; our own society's considerable inequality is based on such factors as occupation, which is subject to labor market forces. Family background, especially if it traces a long history of privilege, also predicts one's level of affluence.

Weber's second factor determining one's social ranking is *prestige*, the honor, respect, and admiration accorded an individual. Cheyenne with different levels of prestige shared essentially the same life style, but in our society such people form distinct status groups and live differently than others. We generally garner prestige not from personal deeds, like the Cheyenne, but from life style, possession of status symbols, and occupation. Prestige is most influenced by our *master status*, which helps alleviate *status inconsistency*, a condition in which one holds substantially different rankings in various status hierarchies.

The third determinant of social-class ranking according to Weber is *power*, the ability to impose one's will. We get legitimate, formal power, or *authority*, by holding a socially recognized status such as school principal. The Cheyenne vested authority in a tribal council. The counterpart in our society may be a *power elite*, a unified group of several hundred individuals who exert great control over government, business, and military affairs. Pluralist theorists argue that, instead, competing elites share power. On an everyday level, we pursue our goals through *influence*, informal power based on personal attributes. Wealth, prestige, and power are intertwined; getting more of one makes it easier to acquire more of the others.

In contrast to Weber, Marx argued that only one factor determines a person's social-class ranking: economic control. The capitalist class, or *bourgeoisie*, owns the means of production and thus sits at the top of the social-class structure. Below them are those who own no capital, the exploited workers, or *proletariat*. Other Marxist theorists note that property, authortiy, and expertise also figure into the formula.

Using Marxist theory to identify our own social class, we fit ourselves into one of just two categories: capitalists and workers. Neo-Marxists see an in-between class of employed managers, supervisors, professionals, and the self-employed. Using Weber's scheme, sociologists discern one or two upper classes, two middle classes, and two lower classes. Our own position is indicated by occupation, income, education, and residence. Social-class level greatly influences our life chances and life style.

The United States has long symbolized *vertical mobility*, movement up or down the social ladder. This picture contrasts with *caste* societies, which allow no *intragenerational mobility*, social mobility within one's own lifetime. Still, some point to structural barriers that limit movement from one class to another in America. In fact, the rate of *intergenerational mobility*, or social mobility between generations, is not much higher in the United States than in other modern societies. Although upward mobility was more common than downward mobility in America for most of this century, opportunities have diminished since the 1970s. The middle-class dream has become more elusive, while the richest Americans have been accumulating a larger share of the nation's wealth and the poor have lost ground. Inequality has increased even within categories. More than ever before, education is separating the successful from the rest in our society. Many well-paying manufacturing jobs are disappearing, with new jobs appearing mostly in the service sector. Many of these new positions do not pay well, contributing to a polarizing trend like that predicted by Marx.

Part of our chances to climb the social ladder are a matter of *structural mobility*, widespread changes in class status caused by changes in society, especially the economy. These changes include shifts in the labor market and the *birth rate differential*, the tendency of upper-class people to have smaller families than lower-class people, thus creating an upward draft. Of course, individual choices and characteristics also determine our mobility chances. We can control some of the changes in our residence and appearance, for example. Still, most personal features depend on our family background, which includes such factors as the number of parents and siblings we have and our parents' occupation.

The status attainment model highlights the importance of parental socioeconomic status, educational attainment, one's first job, and one's eventual occupation. Also, according to *dual labor market theory*, we can end up either in an advantageous "core" job sector or the "periphery" sector with lower pay, less security, poorer benefits, and fewer opportunities for advancement. Our *human capital*, or potential to contribute to society, also helps determine our chances to move up, as do gender and race.

In our efforts to reduce poverty in the United States, an official *poverty line* was established designating the minimum income needed to feed, house, and clothe a family. This helps identify families living in *absolute poverty*, those who lack adequate income for necessities. Others experience *relative deprivation*, a feeling of lacking what others have. While most poor people are white, minority groups have disproportionately high rates, as do Southerners, rural and inner-city residents, and female-headed families. The poverty of the homeless is often associated with mental illness, abuse, problems with alcohol and other drugs, and lack of resources and social support.

We can explain poverty in terms of the characteristics of the poor themselves, and many Americans do so because of an *ideology* (a set of ideas or beliefs that explains and justifies social arrangements) that centers on individuals' responsibility. "Blaming the victim," however, ignores the social forces that produce the irresponsible behavior of many poor people. We might instead search for solutions to the poverty problem in social causes. A *culture of poverty*, for example, a way of life embodying such attitudes as fatalism and apathy, perpetuates social and economic disadvantages, which in turn has produced an *underclass* of persistently poor, economically and socially isolated people. Discrimination also helps explain poverty, as does the *structural theory of poverty*, which points to the patterns and policies of society and the economy that contribute to poverty, including government schemes and economic restructuring. One strategy aimed at solving America's poverty problem would provide help in the form of housing, training, and so on, to help the poor cope with oppressive structural features. Another would require that welfare recipients make an effort to contribute to society, usually through some type of "workfare" program. Perhaps both strategies are needed.

meritocracy
social differentiation
social stratification
social class
prestige
power
status inconsistency
master status
authority
power elite
influence

bourgeoisie
proletariat
vertical mobility
caste
intragenerational
 mobility
intergenerational
 mobility
structural mobility
birth rate
 differential

dual labor market
 theory
human capital
poverty line
absolute poverty
relative deprivation
ideology
culture of poverty
underclass
structural theory
 of poverty

7

Chapter

RACIAL AND ETHNIC MINORITIES

WHY MINORITIES?

CAN WE PUT AN END TO RACIAL AND ETHNIC
HOSTILITIES IN THE UNITED STATES?

WHAT HAPPENS TO IMMIGRANTS
IN THE UNITED STATES?

AFRICAN AMERICANS: FREE FROM THE PAST?

   CRITICAL THINKING BOX: A GLIMMER OF HOPE?

   RESEARCH BOX: DISCRIMINATION IN EVERYDAY LIFE

HISPANICS: THE NEXT "MODEL MINORITY"?

ASIAN AMERICANS: STILL A MINORITY?

MUST NATIVE AMERICANS RELINQUISH
THEIR CULTURAL HERITAGE?

   *CRITICAL THINKING BOX: AFFIRMATIVE ACTION:
PRO AND CON*

Most societies in the world make claims of equality for their citizens, yet deny some groups the benefits of full membership. West Indians living in Britain are the first to be fired in economic downturns, pay more for housing, and obtain few mortgages. Koreans face invisible barriers to housing, bank loans, and jobs in Japan. In East Pakistan, the Hindus are generally the landowners, the Moslems the farmworkers. These cases illustrate the features of a **minority group,** a culturally or physically distinct population subset whose members are assigned subordinate status and given little access to social resources. Why do such minorities arise?

Minority group: a culturally or physically distinct population subset whose members are assigned subordinate status and given less access to social resources than the dominant majority group.

WHY MINORITIES?

Minority status is not always the result of small population size. Certainly most minorities account for considerably less than half of the nation's population; for example, disadvantaged Koreans comprise less than 1 percent of those living in Japan. Exceptions occur, however, as seen most dramatically in the Republic of South Africa. There the **majority group,** which controls access to cultural, political, and economic resources, is the dominant whites, who comprise only about 20 percent of the population. For decades, the enormous numerical superiority of South Africa's nonwhites made little difference in their subordinate status. Similarly, in the United States and most other countries, women suffer subordination though they outnumber men.

Majority group: that part of a population that controls access to cultural, political, and economic resources; the dominant group.

Minority status is determined not by smallness of numbers but by lack of power. The majority, regardless of its size, holds the important cards such as control of the political system and access to jobs and education. Without power, minorities remain victims in their own society, targets for hostility and mistreatment.

Why do humans tend to oppress other groups? Sociologists have looked for answers in four main social patterns—group differences, ethnocentrism, competition, and unequal power.

Group Differences

If people could not be so easily divided into distinct categories like Gypsy, Jew, Moslem, Turk, or Bantu, it is doubtful that any groups would be considered minorities. But natural boundary lines emerge along groups' physical and cultural differences. These boundaries provide bases for conflict and hostility throughout the world.

Racial and ethnic minorities will increase from one-quarter to nearly one-half of the U.S. population by the middle of next century.

Race: a population with a common genetic heritage and distinctive physical features.

Race   While **race** exists because of biological processes, it carries social implications regarding various groups' supposedly inferior abilities and worth. If racial differences did not exist, a powerful base for minority oppression would be removed from the world. As far as can be determined, races formed as isolated populations struggled to adapt to different environments, long before the advent of thermal underwear, sunscreen, and other aids. As the unique demands of their physical surroundings eliminated those individuals lacking advantageous genetic features, the survivors took on a collective genetic profile—and physical appearance—distinct from other humans adapting to different environments. Races proliferated after the several initial groupings broke their isolation and began migrating and mixing. Today, anthropologists faced with the daunting task of making some sense of the resulting chaos cannot even agree on how many racial categories exist—from 3 or 5 to over 100.

Not surprisingly, this racial proliferation has created imprecise, unclear boundaries. Few scientists, who require precision in their terminology, care to use such labels as "Negroid" or "Caucasoid" when categorizing individuals. Such racial labels necessarily involve constellations of physical features of which many in a population possess only some. An individual may have, for example, the hair texture typical of one race and the body proportions typical of another. To confuse matters even more, the distributions of two races' features usually show substantial overlapping. Thus a person considered "white" may have darker skin than some "black" people. Similar overlapping is manifested in eye color, hair color and type, and other physical characteristics.

Clearly, then, race is not a precisely demarcated category. In fact, in some South American societies, it is not even fixed. There, race is at least partially a function of one's social class: Richer people are considered to be "whiter." We might also note that race is neither a matter of language nor nationality, as in the "English" or "Chinese" race. Moreover, race should not be confused with religion or subculture, as in the "Jewish race."

RACE AND ETHNIC CATEGORIES USED IN SELECTED CENSUSES

Census	1860	1890	1900	1970	1990
Race	White	White	White	White	White
	Black	Black	Black (Negro descent)	Negro or Black	Black or Negro
	Mulatto[1]	Mulatto[1]	Chinese	Japanese	American Indian
		Quadroon[2]	Japanese	Chinese	Eskimo
		Octoroon[3]	Indian	Filipino	Aleut
		Chinese		Hawaiian	Chinese
		Japanese		Korean	Filipino
		Indian		Indian [Amer.]	Hawaiian
				Other	Korean
					Vietnamese
					Japanese
					Asian Indian
					Samoan
					Guamanian
					Other API[4]
					Other race
Hispanic Origin				Mexican	Mexican or Chicano or Mexican-Am.
				Puerto Rican	
				Cuban	Puerto Rican
				Central/So. American	Cuban
				Other Spanish	Other Spanish/ Hispanic

Table 7-1

The U. S. Census Bureau has had to adjust its categories to fit the nation's changing racial and ethnic profile as well as new notions of racial and ethnic consciousness.

[1]Three-eighths to five-eighths black.
[2]One-quarter black.
[3]One-eighth black.
[4]Asian and Pacific Islander.

Note: Prior to 1970, census enumerators wrote in the race of individuals using the groups cited above. In the 1970 and subsequent censuses, respondents and enumerators filled in circles corresponding to the category with which the respondent most closely identified. Persons choosing other race or Indian were asked to write in the race or Indian tribe.

Source: William P. O'Hare, "America's Minorities—The Demographics of Diversity," *Population Bulletin* 47, no. 4 (Washington, DC: Population Reference Bureau, Inc., 1992).

Humans generally refuse to allow such ambiguity to deter their efforts to racially classify one another. Ignoring the hopelessly unclear biological boundary lines, societies commonly identify categories with social considerations, such as one's racial community. For example, in 1970 the U.S. Justice Department officially defined "Negro" as a person "considered by himself, the school, or the community to be of African or Negroid origin." Such definitions are typically employed when biological considerations are too confusing, which is usually the case. (See Table 7-1.)

Thus, racial categories continue to serve as a basis for minority oppression. And while the United States is notorious for racial divisions, race matters elsewhere, too. The Japanese, for instance, have always valued "white" skin as beautiful (they do not consider themselves to be "yellow") and regarded dark skin as pitiable. Ex-colonial societies throughout the world esteem white skin. Lighter-skinned people enjoy feelings of superiority—and usually political control—in such far-flung places as the Philippines, Algeria, Egypt, Trinidad, Fiji, Sierra Leone, and Gambia.

Ethnicity   Like race, **ethnic group** differences provide a basis for ascribed hierarchical statuses and in-group and out-group memberships. Also like race, ethnic boundaries are often vaguely defined. Still, it is clear that members of an ethnic group share a distinctive subculture. They identify with their common culture and are bound

Ethnic group: a socially defined group distinguished by its nationality or distinctive way of life.

together by it, perhaps using it as a master status. Membership is inherited and can be based on race (African Americans), nationality (Greek Americans), religion (the Amish), language (Hispanics), and traditions (Jews).

Ethnicity sometimes serves as a basis for minority status, but not necessarily. In fact, over the last several decades it has become fashionable in the United States to make awareness of one's ethnicity a matter of pride. Genealogy exerts a strong appeal, and ethnic clubs have proliferated, as have bumper stickers proclaiming PROUD TO BE POLISH or HAPPINESS IS BEING IRISH. Despite America's famous "melting pot" image, researchers find a rising number of people of mixed ethnic ancestry who identify themselves in terms of one group (Alba and Chamlin, 1983). In addition, non–English-speaking Americans show a strong preference for spouses of the same ancestry (Stevens and Swicegood, 1987).

Ethnicity undoubtedly can help individuals feel special and proud. But it can also bring the curse of minority status. A culturally distinct population runs the risk of being singled out and targeted. After all, "different" often translates into "inferior." In fact, wherever ethnic groups come into contact, minority persecution becomes a strong possibility. Witness the bloody friction between Protestants and Catholics in Northern Ireland, and the violent conflict between the Kurds and both Iraqis and Turks. As thousands of African and Asian immigrants stream into Italy looking for jobs, "A week rarely goes by without some disturbing episode of racist violence, *xenophobia*, or conflict between immigrants and Italians" (Stille, 1992, p. 28).

American history clearly illustrates the power of ethnic differences in creating minorities. In the 1840s, waves of Irish immigrants faced hatred and mistreatment because of their cultural distinctiveness, especially their Catholicism and Gaelic language. As they congregated in large northeastern cities, the Irish suffered more discrimination than any other European immigrants. The classified ads of Boston newspapers, for example, used the code "I.N.N.A." (Irish Need Not Apply) to exclude members of that minority from employment opportunities.

A flood of immigrants from Asia and southern and eastern Europe beginning in the 1890s sparked a frenzy of fear and hatred. Because many of these newcomers were of more swarthy appearance, non–English-speaking, and non-Protestant or non-Christian, ethnicity became a lightning rod for persecution and minority status. In 1888, a New York newspaper had this to say about Irish and Italian immigrants: "The flood gates are open. The bars are down . . . the sewer unchoked. Europe is vomiting. In other words, the scum of immigration is viscerating upon our shores. The horde of . . . steerage slime is being syphoned upon us from continental mud tanks" (quoted in Adamic, 1944, p. 27).

The influx of ethnic immigrants today is producing another backlash, though a much milder one so far. A 1993 Newsweek poll found that most Americans view current levels of immigration with disfavor, worrying that immigrants take jobs from native-born citizens and contribute to the welfare burden. For years, researchers could counter such fears by pointing to the beneficial impact such incoming groups had on our economy. Thomas Muller (1984), for example, showed that the steady flow of Mexican immigrants into California actually contributed to the state's prosperity in the 1970s. Such benefits can still accrue—the impact varies from one locale to another—but recently the overall welfare dependency of new immigrants has risen while their skill level has declined, thereby raising the net cost of immigration in the short run. Thus a panel of researchers recently concluded that while the picture is complex, immigrants may well produce a small negative impact on the national economy (Riche, 1993). This may be only a temporary downturn, but it is bound to add fuel to intergroup hostilities.

Ethnocentrism

The relentless, ancient drumbeat of ethnocentrism continues today. North African workers are attacked in Italy. In France, an Arab mosque is bulldozed, Jewish cemeteries are desecrated, and swastikas and Stars of David are painted on Jewish stores. Hutu and Tutsi tribes in Africa continue to massacre each other. Gypsies are hounded in the former Czechoslovakia, Turks in Bulgaria, Hungarians in Romania. Non-British peoples find Australian citizenship virtually out of reach. Muslims have suffered starvation, deportation, and military attacks under an "ethnic cleansing" program in Bosnia. Wherever one looks, minority oppression is driven by the sense that "our" group is superior to all others.

Usually at any one time some form of ethnic conflict rages somewhere in the world. The breakup of the Soviet Union spawned several ethnic struggles in the 1990s, and as Yugoslavia disintegrated, Serbs, Croatians, and Muslims clashed.

Competition

Even without ethnocentrism, competition fosters intergroup hostilities. In the late nineteenth century, when Irish dockworkers in New York City were being displaced by blacks, resentment predictably festered. When the catches of Vietnamese-American shrimpers threatened the livelihood of other local fishermen in Texas in the 1980s, violence erupted across minority–majority boundary lines. Formidable competitors can elicit fear and antagonism that, like water seeking the lowest level, tend to settle on racial and ethnic differences.

Middleman minorities: minority groups limited to serving society's needs at mid-level occupations.

Researchers have found that ethnic competition leads to intergroup conflict when the competition is perceived as unfair and when the groups do not depend on one another (Belanger and Pinard, 1991). For example, by the early 1990s, Japanese imports had captured a large segment of the U. S. automobile market through trading practices widely regarded in this country as unfair. As this competition resulted in painful factory closings, "Japan bashing" became a fashionable political pastime.

Because of their competitiveness, **middleman minorities** are magnets for racial or ethnic abuse. The Jews in feudal Europe, the Chinese and Indians in Africa, and Arabs in West Africa are all examples of minorities limited to mid-level roles such as small business and trading. Strong ethnic solidarity and pooled family labor typically make such groups formidable competitors, attracting the ire of the majority group and the hatred and jealousy of other minorities. Like the bottom-rung minority, the middleman minority's position is tenuous: While playing an important role in the local economy, it cannot be too successful lest it draw hostility from the rest of society.

Unequal Power

Fair head-to-head competition between equals may fuel resentment, but does not by itself create a minority–majority dichotomy. If one group achieves an advantage, however, it is likely to exploit it fully. The Spanish Conquistadors made the best use of their superior firepower, horses, and organization to enslave peoples of the New World. South African blacks have for decades felt the crunch of the nation's well-equipped and disciplined police force, Kurds have been battered by Iraqi tanks, and the Bosnians decimated by Serbian artillery.

Sociologists thus offer a clear scenario of how minority status arises in society. Once the balance of power is tipped between distinct ethnic groups, competition and ethnocentrism quickly sort the various groups into a majority and multiple minorities. We now turn to how this process has operated in the United States.

CAN WE PUT AN END TO RACIAL AND ETHNIC HOSTILITIES IN THE UNITED STATES?

Racial and ethnic conflict is a consistent theme throughout U. S. history, at once intense and seemingly irremediable. In the 1690s, the enslavement of blacks expanded and became legitimized. A century later, the relentless westward thrust of settlers began to push Native Americans off their lands. The 1890s witnessed a wave of hysteria against the threat of a "Catholic invasion," "wild Slavic huns," and the impure blood of other immigrating foreigners; meanwhile, Jewish businessmen were stoned and their stores burned, and African Americans were subjected to lynchings and legal segregation.

In comparison, intergroup hostilities in the 1990s mostly play out in court battles, petty rudeness, and other relatively subtle ways, but violent incidents recur with dismaying frequency. The complete eradication of America's racial and ethnic animosities would require removing their main underpinnings: discrimination and prejudice. Can it be done?

Discrimination

Discrimination against a person can take many forms—refusal of service in a restaurant, a room at a hotel, a bank loan for a home mortgage, or a chance to work. It is differential, unequal treatment of people based solely on their group membership. Technically, discrimination can take the form of favoritism—saving the best seats in an auditorium for members of a particular ethnic group, for example. In its more important, negative form, however, it involves the denial of social rewards and opportunities to people not because they lack personal merit but because of their group membership.

Many Americans today contend that the government can and should redress this persistent injustice. However, antidiscrimination laws like the civil rights legislation of the 1960s, even when enforced, have failed to eliminate the evil of discrimination. Court orders have opened public facilities and schools to minorities, but many quickly become resegregated. Affirmative action programs, as we will see later in this chapter, have opened some doors but are now roundly attacked as counterproductive. The high hopes of the 1960s have given way to weary disappointment and the sobering realization that legal measures can impact only overt injustices. Like an iceberg, the bulk of the problem lies beneath the surface of our social relations, untouched by most government efforts.

Institutionalized Discrimination   Sociologists have identified part of the underlying problem as **institutionalized discrimination.** This is a particularly subtle, sometimes unintentional form of unequal treatment of minority group members, often involving entrenched, customary barriers and restrictions. Nonetheless, it produces the same outcomes as overt, intentional discrimination.

Even in the absence of malice, traditions and policies can handicap minorities. For example, officials in the criminal justice system may unconsciously assume guilt in a black suspect more so than in a white one. School policies may rely strictly on (possibly biased) intelligence tests that inadvertently place disadvantaged groups disproportionately in dead end programs and classes. Standards for university admissions may be set so high that they unintentionally screen out certain groups. Hiring officers may simply choose those applicants they are most comfortable with, thereby giving little consideration to minorities. Blacks face double the probability of being fired, even those working in the federal government (Zwerling and Silver, 1992). The segregation of neighborhoods may continue simply due to the momentum of tradition, or it may be maintained through **redlining,** the practice in which banks and other lending institutions refuse to qualify low-income groups, especially minorities, for home mortgages. The intent to discriminate may lay behind such practices, but is nearly impossible to prove. The elusive nature of institutionalized discrimination makes it more difficult to eradicate than legal discrimination.

Clearly, legislation cannot single-handedly erase discrimination, especially in its more subtle forms. Is there some other way? Perhaps solutions can begin with an understanding of why the problem exists.

Explanations of Discrimination   First, functionalists point out that despite its injustice and waste of human potential, discrimination has benefits, even for the oppressed. Intergroup conflict sharpens group boundaries, which clarify one's identity in an otherwise confusing jumble of "others." Also, such conflict promotes solidarity within those groups. Oppression creates strong bonds among its victims, and indeed some majority members may envy minorities' stronger sense of community and oneness.

Discrimination: differential, unequal treatment of people based solely on their group membership.

Institutionalized discrimination: unequal treatment of minority group members based on entrenched social policies and customs; may be unintentional.

Redlining: the practice in which banks and other lending institutions refuse to qualify low-income groups, often minorities, for home mortgages, thereby excluding those groups from certain neighborhoods.

The suffering of 1960s civil rights demonstrators helped end legal discrimination, but barriers remain.

For the majority group, discrimination offers more obvious benefits. Cheap labor boosts any economy. For decades, blacks in South Africa received about one-seventh the wages paid whites for the same work. The country's economy, for the dominant group, enjoyed prolonged prosperity. Over the years, the American economy has taken advantage of indentured servants, native and African slaves, desperate immigrants, nonwhite and foreign-born workers excluded from the protections of labor unions, and frightened illegal aliens. Research has recently documented how South and East European immigration resulted in occupational gains for men of North and West European heritage (Landale and Guest, 1990). Similarly, Jewish workers in Israel benefit from the minority status of Arab workers (Semyonov and Cohen, 1990).

Discrimination also provides a tool to protect the majority group's political power. Immigrants and alien workers are commonly denied voting privileges in their host countries. In the United States, even after the federal government mandated equal voting rights for African Americans, local policies of charging a poll tax or requiring literacy tests as a prerequisite to voting effectively circumvented the Constitution.

Second, besides its benefits, discrimination exists because of fear. High concentrations of minorities generate this fear and its attendant discrimination (Corzine, Creech, and Corzine, 1983). The most severe restrictions on slaves in the United States were generally found in those colonies with the highest concentrations of blacks. By the 1800s, three-quarters of the slaves in New England had been freed, but the institution continued in the South, where the number of blacks was much higher and whites feared for their physical safety and jobs if blacks were freed. At the turn of the century, the frequency of black lynchings correlated with perceptions by the white majority that blacks' numbers posed an economic and political threat. The flood of immigrants at that same time triggered exclusionary immigration policies and political and social movements aimed against the foreign-born and nonwhite. More recently, economic recession and affirmative action programs have combined to generate a backlash of resentment toward minorities. Still today, as the size of an area's black population increases in proportion to whites, whites perceive greater threat from blacks and offer less support for racial integration (Fossett and Kiecolt, 1989).

Finally, even minorities, with their limited social power, can discriminate against one another. Conspicuous success by one group can attract resentment by others. Physical beatings, boycotts, destruction of stores, and murders poison relations between both Jews and Asian Americans and their other minorities.

Where do these explanations lead us? Certainly, the emotions of fear and resentment cannot be legislated out of existence. But unless the attitudes underlying discrimination are weakened or destroyed, people will find ways around laws as long as discrimination benefits the dominant group.

Prejudice

Discrimination is usually fueled by **prejudice,** the belief that members of another group are inferior. Removing prejudice would undermine discrimination, but not eliminate it. As Robert Merton (1976) explains, prejudice and discrimination do not always go hand in hand. Prejudiced people may not discriminate if they are surrounded by members of the minority group, or if legal sanctions effectively dissuade them, but unprejudiced individuals can still mistreat minorities due to social pressures. For example, a white restaurant owner may bear no ill feelings toward African Americans, but discourage their patronage for fear of losing his white customers. Still, eliminating prejudice would remove the most effective justifications of such mistreatment. Majority members would be forced to admit that the unequal treatment meted out to minorities is not warranted by any inherent inferiority or unworthiness. Instead, discrimination would be revealed as an instrument protecting the majority's advantaged economic and political position.

One difficulty in rooting out prejudice lies in its irrational, rigid nature. The tendency to prejudge people based solely on their group memberships does not simply melt in the face of contrary facts. Positive information about a minority member is usually ignored, treated as exceptional, or simply denied as inaccurate. Prejudice thus involves not only prejudging but misjudging individuals.

Sources of Prejudice   The persistence of prejudice even in the face of contradictory information attests to the power of **stereotypes,** fixed generalizations about all members of a group or category. In dealing with the immensely complex social world, we all use generalizations based on our limited contact with members of other groups. If the few Vietnamese Americans we have seen are hard-working, or if we have heard that "most" British people are exceedingly polite, we tend, not unreasonably, to expect all others in those groups to fit the stereotypes—until future experiences force us to modify our expectations. Prejudicial thinking, in contrast, ignores such new facts. The stereotype provides a firm foundation for prejudging all members of a targeted group as fundamentally alike, usually inferior. These assumed characteristics usually include greed, laziness, stupidity, and tendencies to be happy-go-lucky, passionate, quick-tempered, or devious.

Stereotyping certainly simplifies judgments for the prejudiced individual, but it's a two-edged sword. If the majority group is exposed to enough minority members who

Prejudice: an emotional, rigid attitude that prejudges people on the basis of their group membership.

Stereotypes: fixed generalizations about all members of a group or category.

Scapegoating: placing the blame for one's own misfortune on someone else.

Racism: belief in the innate inequality of races; the notion that differences in individual and cultural achievements are determined by race.

Prejudice allows us to view other people as unworthy of humane treatment. Here we see a child of Pakistan whose family, along with many others in the world, is virtually enslaved by an indebtedness passed down through generations.

obviously do not fit the derogatory stereotype, the scaffolding of prejudice can eventually weaken and even collapse. Therein lies some of the strategy behind school desegregation and affirmative action.

Another source of prejudice is **scapegoating.** In ancient Jewish tradition, the high priest symbolically placed all the people's sins on a goat, which was sent to its death in the desert. The scapegoat's sacrifice served as absolution for their own wrongdoings. Similarly, today prejudiced people place the blame for their own troubles on some other less powerful individual or group. Scapegoating allows a person to feel superior to someone else, a safe and convenient target on which to vent one's anger and frustration. An unskilled white male, then, can blame his employment woes on minorities who were "given jobs through affirmative action" or "those hordes of cheap immigrant workers."

Belief in the inferiority of whole categories of people serves as an excellent justification for the mistreatment of minorities who might otherwise be competitors. Colonizing nations have always exploited, enslaved, and massacred members of other societies deemed subhuman or otherwise unworthy of humane treatment. As historian Kenneth Stampp describes, "Some masters used the lash as a form of incentive by flogging the last slave out of his cabin in the morning. Many used it to 'break in' a young slave and to 'break the spirit' of an insubordinate older one" (1989, p. 177). Such abuse persists today. How else could labor agents in India, for example, trap landless peasants into debt, then use torture and beatings to hold them in bondage for sometimes eight generations? How else could sugar-cane plantation foremen use routine whippings, deny food, and pay workers 20 pesos a day while charging them 21 pesos for rent, food, and tools (Masland et al., 1992)? How else could such profiteering on human suffering be justified but by viewing the victims as less than human?

Where does one learn the proper targets for scapegoating, or how to appropriately prejudge individuals? Prejudice comes from socialization, a fact which raises hopes that if it is learned, it can also be unlearned. However, the roots of prejudice are often firm and deep, and reinforced by primary relationships and peer-group pressures. Community norms usually provide a protective web of support for prejudicial notions. The difficulty is modifying a subculture's norms, or disentangling the beliefs of one generation from the teachings of the older one.

Racism   Any effort to reduce intergroup hostilities must take into account **racism,** a widespread variant of prejudice built on the belief that individual and cultural achievements are explained in terms of racial abilities and that races are innately unequal. As shown by the nineteenth-century saying, "There is no such thing as a full-blooded, civilized Indian," racism affirms that no member of a supposedly inferior race has the genetic capability for advancement and thus little can be expected of the race's culture.

This emphasis on group membership rather than individual ability reveals the prejudicial nature of racism. The racist assumes that one's biological categorization (which, as we saw earlier, is actually built upon largely social definitions) predicts certain personality features, and thus serves as an adequate basis for evaluating an individual. With this mindset, one can ignore past exploitation, differing cultural needs and values, and accidents of geography and history in explaining one group's "inferiority"—however that term is defined. In other words, if a population of humans has not developed a written language or a railroad system, it must be due to an innate lack of ability.

Haitians who claimed they were escaping political persecution in their homeland have been routinely arrested and detained when they reached the United States. Authorities argued these illegal aliens did not deserve entry because the immigrants' motives were economic rather than political. Others suspected racism lay behind the policy, but as always, racism is difficult to prove.

Racism has provided a useful justification over the centuries to exploit others. Just as early European explorers were excused from the inhumane treatment of non-Christian "savages," so colonists could later justify enslavement and exploitation on the basis on their victims' inherent inferiority.

Today racism is widely and loudly condemned as reprehensible and a thing of the past. Researchers find it is not increasing in the United States (Steeh and Schuman, 1992), and may even be waning, especially in the South (Firebaugh and Davis, 1988). But racism's appeal and usefulness are so strong that it has not disappeared, merely become less blatant. Instead of proclaiming or admitting racism, a white who hates blacks may say, "I have nothing against blacks, but . . . they don't want to work for what they get" or "they are too pushy, never satisfied." This espousal of racial equality in principle but blaming other races' lack of success on their supposed innate inferiority is "modern" or **symbolic racism** (Kluegel, 1990), also described as "the behavioral bedrock under a recent superficial deposit of tolerance" (McClelland and Hunter, 1992).

Clearly, eliminating discrimination and prejudice requires something akin to excising a deeply rooted tumor. Until American society acknowledges the need for major surgery, the ills will persist.

Symbolic racism: espousing racial equality but blaming other races' lack of success on their supposed innate inferiority.

WHAT HAPPENS TO IMMIGRANTS IN THE UNITED STATES?

Millions of people chose to emigrate to the United States even after a dominant group established itself sufficiently to treat newcomers as unwanted foreigners. At best, if they were familiar enough and their numbers too small to be threatening, they could expect indifference. Usually, however, immigrants were rejected, at least at first. For some groups, this rebuff was in time replaced by acceptance, and they in their turn could complain about invaders from other lands.

Before identifying the patterns of rejection and acceptance newcomers to this country have faced, we must note that even the worst treatment meted out to Europeans and Asians did not begin to match that inflicted on Native Americans. In that case, the dominant group exercised two of the most extreme options of rejection: expulsion and **genocide.** Native Americans were forcibly removed from their territories and banished to western lands considered undesirable. Genocide, extermination or annihilation of a racial or ethnic group, was behind such measures as forced marches, the deliberate introduction of contagious germs, and outright massacres.

The only group forcibly brought to North America, black Africans, endured the other extreme form of rejection by the dominant group: slavery. This pattern of ownership and control grew out of the initial condition of servitude. Slavery offered tobacco farmers greater profits, and black slaves proved more profitable than Native Americans or European immigrants.

Except for these instances, immigrants to the United States have confronted a less drastic form of rejection: separation or isolation from the dominant group.

Segregation

Segregation involves not only physically isolating a minority group but relegating them to living conditions almost always inferior to those of the majority. (The sometimes up-scale Jewish ghettos in medieval Europe are an exception to the usual deprivations of minorities' segregated communities.) Some isolation is self-imposed, as is the case with the Amish and Hasidic Jews, but as an expression of the dominant group's hostility, segregation into inferior neighborhoods, schools, and public accommodations effectively transforms immigrants into a minority. The Irish immigrants encountered such segregation in the mid-1800s, as did other groups after them. Today Puerto Ricans, Southeast Asians, and Haitians face similar patterns of rejection in the United States.

Groups forcibly segregated from the mainstream can salvage some benefits from their rejection, including cohesion and unity. Christopher Ellison (1991) found, for example, that the distinctive African-American churches that emerged from centuries of enforced segregation have strengthened solidarity among blacks. According to Ellison, religious participation in their traditional denominations contributed to **ethnic identification,** or feelings of closeness and shared interests. Belonging to nontraditional faiths such as Islam provides another source of unity among African Americans, **separatism,** the desire for cultural distance from the dominant group. Other research has demonstrated that African-American men enjoy greater employment opportunities as managers and professionals in black neighborhoods, where their "blackness"

Genocide: extermination or annihilation of a racial or ethnic group.

Segregation: physical isolation and social exclusion of a minority group from the dominant group.

Ethnic identification: feelings of closeness and shared interests among members of an ethnic group.

Separatism: the desire for cultural distance from the dominant group.

gives them a competitive edge (Stearns and Coleman, 1990). Their separateness has also contributed to blacks' participation in political activities at rates higher than whites (Ellison and Gay, 1989).

The dominant group's rejection shows most clearly in the case of **de jure segregation,** when the separation is sanctioned by law. No immigrants have suffered this type of isolation as completely as African Americans. Beginning in the late 1800s, the infamous Jim Crow laws dictated the separation of blacks from whites in public transportation, schools, and other facilities. U. S. laws and policies also supported the separation and isolation of Native Americans on reservations.

De jure segregation: legally sanctioned separation and exclusion of a minority group.

Perhaps the best example of de jure segregation was the Republic of South Africa's system of apartheid (apartness), written into the nation's constitution "for the divine purpose of Christianizing the heathens." Blacks in South Africa were denied full voting and employment privileges, forced to carry "passes" and avoid white neighborhoods during certain hours, and banned from whites-only parks, public benches, beaches, and even stores. Apartheid began to crumble in the 1980s, and was finally abolished in the early 1990s. Few examples of de jure segregation remain in the world today.

Still, examples of unofficial, informal, **de facto segregation** abound. Most immigrants face this type of exclusion due to the dominant group's traditions or customs, and the ethnocentric tendency of individuals to avoid people who are different. In the United States, immigrants and more established minorities often find themselves effectively shut out of many jobs and restricted to certain schools and neighborhoods. Such separation confers upon them second-class citizenship.

De facto segregation: separation and exclusion of a minority group based on custom, tradition, and personal choice.

Immigrants have also been the victims of **split labor markets,** wherein members of some groups are paid less than other workers for the same work. Business interests profit by pitting newcomers against more established minority workers to depress wages. In the nineteenth century, Chinese were imported into the United States to build western railroads, Irish to work in mines and on eastern railroads, and blacks to man plantations. The British likewise encouraged ethnic segregation among Muslims, Chinese Buddhists, and Indian Hindus in their Malaysian colony because "a divided country is always easier to rule" and exploit (Parmer, 1987, p 62). More recently, Mexicans have been brought into the United States as cheap labor. Other workers can hardly compete with commonly desperate immigrants. Marxists argue that employers deliberately foment separateness and hatred among various ethnic and racial groups to prevent formation of a liberating working-class consciousness. Immigrants, they claim, serve as tools in this oppressive strategy.

Split labor markets: the condition in which members of some groups are paid less than other workers for the same work; a means of driving down wage levels.

Cultural Pluralism

Not all immigrant groups face rejection. Culturally distinct groups sometimes coexist with the dominant group in some degree of mutual respect and tolerance. This arrangement, called **cultural pluralism,** serves as the goal for many immigrant groups. Such distinct ethnic communities do not interact to any great extent with the broader society. The parties involved understand the boundaries and are comfortable with them.

Both the majority and minorities profit from a pluralistic arrangement. Ethnic communities enjoy the unity and cohesiveness provided by their language and religious and folklore traditions. Mainstream society also usually gains from the immigrant groups' cultural contributions. "Little Italy," "Chinatown," and other ethnic

Cultural pluralism: the coexistence of ethnic groups with some degree of mutual respect and tolerance for one another's cultures.

enclaves in many American cities attest to the pluralistic tendencies of many immigrants and the benefits of such cultural diversity.

Pluralism is well illustrated by the "salad bowl" metaphor. A pluralistic society, like a salad, grows in richness as new peoples, or ingredients, are added. Each ethnic group retains its own distinctive "flavor" while enhancing the "taste" of the whole. A truly pluralistic society values diversity and offeres a "win–win" situation for the majority and minority groups, but such cases are rare.

In Switzerland, pluralism comes closest to fulfilling its ideal of "separate but equal" cultures successfully coexisting for generations. That country is a peaceful mixture of German, Italian, and French peoples, each maintaining its own language and way of life.

More typically, conflict underlies pluralism, as in Canada. There, the Catholic, French-speaking population in Quebec province demands with growing militancy either sovereignty or special protections for their distinct culture in the predominantly Protestant, English-speaking nation. Antagonism often lurks just under the surface, ready to erupt into violence when immigrants become too successful or too numerous.

In our own nation, as in most pluralistic societies, immigrants often are, at best, tolerated so long as they keep to themselves. While the ethnic enclave often attracts some resentment and suspicion from outsiders, it can offer economic advantages for its members. Besides meeting the unique material needs of the immigrant community, businesses in such enclaves offer workers a viable alternative to competing in the mainstream economy (Wilson and Portes, 1980; Portes and Bach, 1985; Model, 1992). While some researchers suggest that only the business owners benefit (Sanders and Nee, 1987), others point to the informal training systems in the enclave that can help the immigrant gain an economic foothold in America (Bailey and Waldinger, 1991).

Assimilation

Accommodation: the process by which a minority group lives side by side with the majority and adapts to the mainstream culture without embracing it.

Assimilation: integration or absorption of a minority culture into the dominant culture.

Acculturation: the process by which a minority group accepts the culture of the dominant group.

Pluralism requires a balancing act between an ethnic group's desire to maintain its distinct way of life on one hand and the need for acceptance and greater opportunities from society on the other. This requires **accommodation,** in which a minority group lives side by side with the majority and adapts to the mainstream culture without embracing it. Often this balance is tipped in favor of **assimilation,** the process by which a minority culture is absorbed into the mainstream culture, thus losing its distinctiveness.

In the past, newly arrived immigrants to America used accommodation as a strategy for adapting to life in the new land while maintaining some degree of cultural identity. However, their children (the "second generation") usually chose another course: **acculturation,** accepting the culture of the dominant group. Because of the pressures they faced in school and on the street, the second generation sought to hide or abandon their ethnicity to escape ridicule, hatred, exclusion, and other disadvantages of being different. They preferred the safer label of "American" to one such as "Italian American." This tension between accommodation and acculturation has created interfamily conflict among immigrants for generations.

Like other social processes, assimilation does not proceed uniformly for all groups or individuals. Milton Gordon (1964) identifies up to seven different types of assimilation. More recently, Allen Williams and Suzanne Ortega (1990) narrowed Gordon's list to three essential categories: (1) cultural or behavioral, as shown in taking on the language or cultural practices and traditions of the dominant group; (2) structural, characterized by entry into cliques, clubs, and primary groups of the majority; and (3) attitude and behavior reception—not facing prejudice or discrimination. Not surprisingly, ethnic groups assimilate in different patterns. Williams and Ortega found, for example, that Mexican Americans are more assimilated structurally than they are culturally, and the Swiss more structurally than the Swedes. Racially distinct groups like African Americans, Asians, and Puerto Ricans seem to face additional, reception-type assimilation barriers beyond their control (Hwang and Murdock, 1991). Clearly, saying that immigrant groups in America tend to become assimilated is to simplify a very complex process.

Researchers have identified other structural factors affecting immigrants. One study found, for example, that female immigrants' incomes depend on male labor force participation: The fewer men in the workforce, the more money the newly arrived women make (Hughey, 1990). Also, structural assimilation becomes more likely with increased contact between groups. According to Peter Blau (1977), such contact depends on structural features like the size of the minority group and the number of different groups represented in the population. Research has confirmed that contact increases as the minority group grows and as more such groups are represented (Fitzpatrick and Hwang, 1992). Furthermore, if group contact takes place in a framework of income equality, intermarriage increases (Blum, 1985), providing a strong indication of assimilation. If the minority group increases in size but is residentially segregated, intergroup crime will likely result (South and Messner, 1986), thus impeding assimilation.

Amalgamation

Amalgamation signifies the strongest indication of a host society's acceptance of immigrants. While assimilation demands that newcomers abandon their own culture and be absorbed into the mainstream, amalgamation combines various subcultures to produce a new culture and, through intermarriage, usually a new population. Instead of transforming immigrants into "people like us," amalgamation accepts their contributions as new ingredients to the "melting pot."

America's self-image as a melting pot is not completely accurate. Certainly intermarriage among European groups has risen dramatically since World War II, especially among small groups with few available mates (Alba and Golden, 1986). On this limited scale, amalgamation has produced a slightly different dominant culture, though it remains essentially European in character. Other racial and ethnic groups, however, have not been asked to contribute to the shaping of American culture. Instead, the alternatives for nonwhites and non-Europeans have been either exclusion or abandonment of their cultural distinctiveness through assimilation.

Amalgamation: the blending of subcultures to produce a new culture and, through intermarriage, usually a new population.

AFRICAN AMERICANS: FREE FROM THE PAST?

To understand African Americans' status today requires an appreciation of the oppression they have faced over the past several centuries.

America's Legal Immigrants: Who They Are and Where They Go

The United States accepts more immigrants than all other industrialized nations combined. In fiscal 1991 the United States government granted 1,827,167 people legal permanent residence. Seventy-nine percent of these legal immigrants, looking for everything from freedom to financial opportunity, chose the seven states below as their new homes.

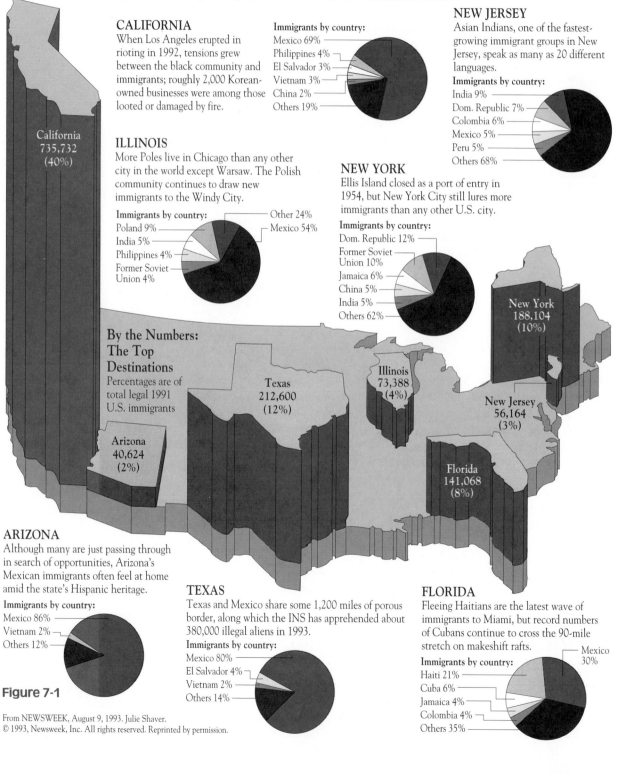

CALIFORNIA
When Los Angeles erupted in rioting in 1992, tensions grew between the black community and immigrants; roughly 2,000 Korean-owned businesses were among those looted or damaged by fire.

Immigrants by country:
Mexico 69%
Philippines 4%
El Salvador 3%
Vietnam 3%
China 2%
Others 19%

ILLINOIS
More Poles live in Chicago than any other city in the world except Warsaw. The Polish community continues to draw new immigrants to the Windy City.

Immigrants by country:
Other 24%
Mexico 54%
Poland 9%
India 5%
Philippines 4%
Former Soviet Union 4%

NEW JERSEY
Asian Indians, one of the fastest-growing immigrant groups in New Jersey, speak as many as 20 different languages.

Immigrants by country:
India 9%
Dom. Republic 7%
Colombia 6%
Mexico 5%
Peru 5%
Others 68%

NEW YORK
Ellis Island closed as a port of entry in 1954, but New York City still lures more immigrants than any other U.S. city.

Immigrants by country:
Dom. Republic 12%
Former Soviet Union 10%
Jamaica 6%
China 5%
India 5%
Others 62%

California 735,732 (40%)

By the Numbers: The Top Destinations
Percentages are of total legal 1991 U.S. immigrants

Texas 212,600 (12%)

Illinois 73,388 (4%)

New York 188,104 (10%)

New Jersey 56,164 (3%)

Arizona 40,624 (2%)

Florida 141,068 (8%)

ARIZONA
Although many are just passing through in search of opportunities, Arizona's Mexican immigrants often feel at home amid the state's Hispanic heritage.

Immigrants by country:
Mexico 86%
Vietnam 2%
Others 12%

TEXAS
Texas and Mexico share some 1,200 miles of porous border, along which the INS has apprehended about 380,000 illegal aliens in 1993.

Immigrants by country:
Mexico 80%
El Salvador 4%
Vietnam 2%
Others 14%

FLORIDA
Fleeing Haitians are the latest wave of immigrants to Miami, but record numbers of Cubans continue to cross the 90-mile stretch on makeshift rafts.

Immigrants by country:
Mexico 30%
Haiti 21%
Cuba 6%
Jamaica 4%
Colombia 4%
Others 35%

Figure 7-1

Past Oppression

Beginning in the early 1500s, black Africans were hunted, trapped, and enslaved. Portuguese, Dutch, and English slavers crammed them into squalid holds on ships bound for the Americas. In the New World, Africans were subjected to further physical and psychological brutality—their families broken up, their cultures suppressed, their identity as a people threatened with extinction. In 1712, for example, South Carolina law decreed that slaves convicted of petty larceny were to be "publicly and severely whipped"; for a second offense, the slave "shall either have one of his ears cut off, or be branded in the forehead with a hot iron." A third offense meant he "shall have his nose slit," and a fourth offense could bring death. An 1831 North Carolina law prohibited teaching slaves to read.

Even after the Thirteenth Amendment to the United States abolished slavery (1865), and the Fourteenth (1868), and Fifteenth (1870) Amendments granted blacks citizenship and voting privileges, suppression continued in America. After the Civil War, Southern states passed the Black Codes or Jim Crow laws reinstituting most of the restrictions of slavery. The laws mandated segregation in public facilities, such as schools, hotels, restaurants, and trains. Black freedmen in Opelousas, Louisiana, were not allowed on the streets after 10:00 P.M. without a written pass from their employers. Blacks wandering in search of work could be charged with vagrancy, whipped, and "hired out." Children of destitute parents could be "apprenticed." In the face of such penalties, many blacks entered into labor contracts that stipulated long work days and forbade them to leave their place of employment. Black servants could receive visitors only with the consent of their masters. While any white was authorized to arrest any black, blacks usually could not even sue or testify against a white.

Violence backed up the Jim Crow laws. Besides everyday intimidation and threats, blacks were often tortured and hanged by white mobs incensed by real or

During the late 1800s and early 1900s, Jim Crow laws mandated separation of the races in many public facilities.

alleged violations of the Black Codes. Over 3,000 lynchings occurred between 1880 and World War I. Predictably, the frequency of such attacks rose with economic difficulties and fell with black out-migration (Beck and Tolnay, 1990; Tolnay and Beck, 1992).

Such violence and persecution combined with greater industrial employment in the North to create a vast northward migration of African Americans, an exodus that reached an astonishing five million between 1940 and 1970. Before this migration leveled off by 1980, it distributed nearly half of all blacks in regions outside the South and made race no longer a peculiar Southern problem. It also coincided with new opportunities for African Americans.

Opportunities

The post–World War II period held promise for African Americans escaping the ghosts of the past. President Truman ordered the desegregation of the armed forces in 1948. The 1954 Supreme Court decision in *Brown* v. *Board of Education of Topeka* resulted in the desegregation of all public schools. The Civil Rights Act of 1964, the Voting Rights Act of 1965, and the Fair Housing Act of 1968 were among several legislative victories confirming the constitutional rights of all citizens regardless of race, and forbidding discrimination in employment and public facilities. In the 1970s, the federal government ordered preferential hiring and admissions practices for blacks and other minorities.

Recovery?

Have African Americans been able to shake off the effects of a history of cultural and physical oppression? Some evidence gives little reason for optimism. African Americans still suffer high poverty rates, low representation in professional occupations and politics, low education attainment levels, and shorter life spans. Even college education does not erase the disadvantages of being black: College-educated black men make about one-third less than whites with similar backgrounds. (See Table 7-2.)

But signs of progress cannot be ignored. Over the past three decades, employment and educational opportunities have expanded for blacks in America. More blacks than

MINORITY STATUS IN BLACK AND WHITE

	Blacks	Whites
Median household income, 1990	$18,676	$31,231
Average weekly hours of multiple jobholders	57	51.6
Percent of persons 25 years old and over who have completed 4 years or more of college, 1991	11.5%	22.2%
Percent of civilians 16 years and over who are unemployed, 1991	7.8%	4.0%
Families below poverty level, 1991	29.3%	8.1%

Table 7-2

These selected comparisons show that African Americans still feel the effects of their past oppression.

Source: U.S. Bureau of the Census and U.S. Bureau of Labor Statistics.

ever entered into the upper-middle class during the 1980s, quadrupling the proportion of affluent African Americans in 1967 (O'Hare et al., 1991). By and large, these are the people whose education, attitudes, and skills enabled them to take advantage of the doors opened by civil rights legislation and affirmative action.

In troubling contrast to this flourishing black middle class, perhaps one-third of African Americans are locked into a process of "hyperghettoization" beyond their control (Wacquant and Wilson, 1989). These underclass neighborhoods, the most spatially isolated in our society (Massey and Eggers, 1990), show the continuing impact of racial discrimination and the power of local social environmental forces to overshadow residents' personal characteristics (Osterman, 1991b). With few family-sustaining jobs available, many young black males in these neighborhoods seek proof of manhood in the image of sexual prowess promoted by the peer group, not through familial responsibility (Anderson, 1989). "Social capital" is scarce in these ghettoes, and alienation is rife: One study found that few members have kin or friends who might provide aid; half have no one they are living with; and few belong to community organizations, attend church, or know their neighbors (Wacquant and Wilson, 1989). Unlike immigrant ethnics, the underclass has virtually no business class (Boyd, 1990), and has limited ethnic solidarity, few self-help business associations, and many fragmented families (Kasarda, 1989). As these neighborhoods increasingly became repositories for those without the means to escape, welfare and the underground economy became the only apparent means of survival. Such environments become traps that hold their residents captive.

While the ghetto culture may be a major obstacle for the African-American underclass (Harrison, 1992), there is no escaping the fact that black skin color itself is a disadvantage. The darkness of one's skin is still strongly correlated with one's income and occupational and educational attainment (Keith and Herring, 1991). Skin tone predicts these measures even more strongly than does the social class of one's parents. Moreover, researchers find that "blacks were only half as likely as others to move into high-income status, even after adjusting for differences in schooling, household composition, age, and income" (Duncan, Smeeding, and Rodgers, 1992, p. 38). Even though discrimination cannot be directly measured, some researchers claim it lays at the root of "large unexplained differences in the wages of black and white males and females" (Cotton, 1989). Others document that employers avoid recruiting inner-city blacks. Even when given job opportunities, these blacks typically are weeded out in job interviews because "A spotty work record will have to be justified; misunderstanding and suspicion may undermine rapport and hamper communication" (Neckerman and Kirschenman, 1991, p. 445).

Race also figures strongly in another cause of high poverty rates among African Americans: segregation (Massey and Eggers, 1990). Blacks remain nearly twice as residentially segregated as Hispanics or Asians, even when escaping the inner city (Massey and Denton, 1988). And school segregation depresses the academic success of black children almost as much as poverty (Entwisle and Alexander, 1992). African Americans likewise face segregation in nursing homes and hospitals (Wallace, 1990).

African Americans, then, have yet to escape completely the disadvantages of slavery and Jim Crow. Signs of progress are everywhere swamped by evidence that blackness remains a burden in America. Claude Steele (1992) observes that African Americans learn in countless ways, from mass media images to invitation lists for junior-high school birthday parties, that society devalues them, expecting only the worst. They face a "daunting and everlasting struggle" to prove themselves worthy of respect.

A large number of African Americans swept into the middle class during the 1980s, but one third of all blacks remain in deprived straits.

A Glimmer of Hope?

Steven Cohn, Steven Barkan, and William Halteman (1991) found that blacks and whites share similarly punitive attitudes toward criminals. Does this not offer a glimmer of hope regarding American race relations? Unfortunately, the researchers also discovered that whites' belief that society should deal more harshly with criminals was tinged with racial prejudice. "Those criminals" were perceived largely as black. African Americans also wanted to "get tough" with criminals, but their attitude was more typically based on fear of being victimized. It is easy to see a continuing racial divide between the haves and have-nots. ■

Discrimination in Everyday Life

According to the 1964 Civil Rights Act, anyone, regardless of race, religion or ethnicity, "shall be entitled to the full and equal enjoyment" of public places such as restaurants, stores, and hotels. While much concern has shifted to the problems of the underclass, University of Florida sociologist Joe Feagin (1991) wondered if middle-class African Americans still face discrimination in everyday public encounters.

In several cities across the country, Feagin located individuals known to "knowledgeable consultants" as members of the black middle class. These respondents in turn identified other members, and eventually Feagin and his (black) research associates were able to conduct 135 interviews between 1988 and 1990. For more in-depth interviewing, he chose a subsample of 37 respondents who had mentioned public discrimination while discussing barriers to employment, education, and housing. These people were clearly middle-class citizens: 90 percent had been to college; half earned incomes between $36,000 and $55,000, and the rest made more; and occupations ranged from sales workers to corporate managers. What forms of mistreatment did these people face?

A little more than half the discrimination incidents occurred in public accommodations, the rest in the streets. Of the first type, most took the form of rejection or poor service. A typical annoyance described was being kept standing at a restaurant entrance without being seated. In another variation, a utility company executive and her husband stopped at a little neighborhood store to buy their son a snowball. The white proprietor told the black couple he could serve them at the outside window but not inside, even though several white people had just been served inside the store. Other blacks, including a school board member, described excessive surveillance by store personnel, and clerks who "won't put change in your hand, touch your skin." A physician recalled that while staying at an expensive hotel, "people think that we work in housekeeping." The respondents painted a picture of lifelong slights, racial slurs, always getting the worst tables in restaurants and the worst rooms in hotels, and having to "sound white" over the phone to facilitate such transactions as reserving car rentals.

The street offers fewer protections. There, discrimination is likely to take a more severe, even violent turn. Feagin's respondents recalled incidents ranging from "hate stares" to physical attacks. In one typical incident, a carful of white teenagers hurled racial epithets at a professor in her car while she stopped at an intersection. Whites frequently cross the street to avoid passing by a black male of obviously middle-class status, or else they "tighten their grip on their women. I've seen people turn around and seem like they're going to take blows from me. The police constantly make circles around me as a I walk home . . ." (p. 111). Young black males are frequently stopped by police because their color seems to warrant suspicion of criminality. And so are black women: A professor reports being pulled over in her old car six or seven times in two years for suspicion of robbery.

This research shows plainly that despite civil rights legislation and the economic progress of many African Americans, antiblack discrimination persists. These few examples represent the kinds of incidents that accumulate into a burden of fears and concerns that whites do not have to worry about. As one respondent explained, a black person "uses twenty-five percent (of his energy) fighting being black, with all the problems being black and what it means" (p. 115). Feagin concludes that "these microlevel events of public accommodations and public streets are not just rare and isolated encounters by individuals; they are recurring events reflecting an invasion of the microworld by the macroworld of historical racial subordination" (p. 115). □

HISPANICS: THE NEXT "MODEL MINORITY"?

The U. S. government declared the 1980s during which the Hispanic population increased by 30 percent, four times the rate of the general population, to be the "Decade of the Hispanics." Members of this minority now make up 9 percent of the U. S. population, but the Census Bureau predicts their proportion will rise to 23 percent by the year 2050, while African Americans will be only 16 percent. In fact, Hispanics will outnumber blacks by the year 2010. This burgeoning, increasingly visible segment of our society may be moving to the forefront among ethnically distinct groups in the United States.

Diversity

The "Hispanic" label is convenient but misleading. For one, it points too much to Spain at the expense of other Spanish-speaking cultures to accurately characterize its members. This is a major reason for the increasing popularity of the term "Latino." Second, the term masks the heterogeneity of the category. Although Hispanic peoples generally speak Spanish (of different dialects) and practice Catholicism (though Protestant fundamentalism has been making inroads), various subgroups display different racial and cultural features.

A long history of racial intermarriage greatly contributes to the diversity among Latinos. In many parts of South and Central America, miscegenation resulted from several factors. First, many European immigrants were men without families. Second, the Roman Catholic Church's stand against slavery and inhumane treatment of nonwhites helped prevent the formation of caste barriers such as those in North America.

HISPANIC DIFFERENCES

	Poverty Rates, 1991	Female-Headed Families, 1991	Percent of Total Hispanic Population
Mexican	28%	19%	63
Central and South American	25%	26%	14
Puerto Rican	41%	43%	11
Cuban	17%	19%	7
United States	14%	17%	

Table 7-3

Source: U. S. Census Bureau.

Also, some countries like Brazil encouraged interracial mixing to "whiten" the population in hopes of improving the nation's international image (Telles, 1992). The result was a considerable mélange of native, European, and African racial features in those populations.

When Hispanic immigrants encounter our relatively high level of race consciousness and low level of interracial contact, they find themselves sorted by race. For example, research shows that among Mexican-American males, those with negroid or "Indian-looking" features receive significantly lower incomes than those with lighter skin and more European appearance (Telles and Murguia, 1990, 1992). Hispanics are also fragmented by substantial subcultural differences. Before we can consider Latino prospects to become another "model minority," therefore, we must understand that the chances for success depend greatly on one's country of origin. Table 7-3 indicates some of the differences among Hispanic populations.

Mexican Americans, the largest Hispanic subgroup, reside mostly in the Southwest. Some families, called Hispanos, populated this region before it became part of the United States, and have retained a higher social standing than later immigrants who now comprise the vast majority of Mexican Americans. Despite the cultural subordination Mexican immigrants have faced, economic and demographic pressures at home, combined with better job opportunities in the United States, have sustained a steady flow of migrants across the border. This continuous immigration, mostly of young and poorly educated people, hinders the upward social mobility of Mexican Americans as a whole.

The living conditions of this group do not yet approximate those of an up-and-coming minority. A generation ago, most Mexican Americans could be accurately depicted as rural manual-laborers. Today, many have moved horizontally to take unskilled jobs in the urban industrial sector, often filling the same economic and occupational niche as African Americans. This is especially true of recent immigrants, many of whom must work at minimum-wage jobs because they lack legal status. Unionization efforts to secure better wages and extraseasonal employment have made little headway. Poorer Mexican Americans remain largely confined to segregated neighborhoods called "barrios," and migrant farm workers in particular have little access to adequate medical care or educational facilities.

Compared to Mexican Americans, upward mobility may come somewhat faster for those of Central and South American origin. Because of the greater distances involved, these immigrants are more likely to enter the United States through legal immigration channels for people with special job skills and professional training. Many also qualify as political refugees. As a result, a relatively high proportion of this group occupies upper occupational statuses.

Like Mexican Americans, many Puerto Ricans are foreign-born and lack language proficiency, which contributes to high dropout rates and low educational levels. Yet, of the two groups, the living conditions of Puerto Ricans are far worse, largely due to high unemployment. Family instability is also a factor in their poverty rate: 43 percent of Puerto Rican families are headed by single females. These factors, along with racial prejudice and discrimination based on language and culture, help explain why this is the only Hispanic group sometimes included with blacks in the underclass (Lemann, 1991).

Recent trends may improve the overall prospects for Puerto Ricans in this country. First, many have returned to Puerto Rico, possibly due to the economic straits in which they found themselves. Second, economic recession has driven a higher proportion of highly skilled workers and professionals from Puerto Rico to the mainland. Still, this group remains the least promising Hispanic model of success.

The overall status of Cuban Americans is complicated by two distinct waves of immigration. The rise of Fidel Castro in the late 1950s set off an exodus to the United States of largely well-educated, white-collar professionals. Their educational and occupational strengths enabled them to establish well-organized, financially stable communities, most notably Miami's "Little Havana." The second wave of Cuban immigrants, in the 1980s, consisted of younger, less-educated, and less-skilled people.

Their emphasis on work, marriage, and patronizing Hispanic businesses has enfused many Latino neighborhoods, especially in Southern California, with vitality and stability.

This group has encountered hostility both within the Cuban-American community and from society at large.

All told, however, Cuban Americans represent an Hispanic success story. They have the highest educational levels of all Latinos. Their strong rate of female labor-force participation contributes to relatively comfortable income levels (Perez, 1986). Cuban Americans' home ownership rate, exceeding those of other Hispanics, is another indication of their socioeconomic success. Also typical of higher status communities, Cuban Americans have smaller families than other Latinos, which helps make them the oldest subgroup.

A Success Story in the Making?

Will the various Hispanic groups build on their numbers and, like the Irish, Scandinavians, Italians, and other immigrant groups before them, ascend the American social ladder together? One discouraging sign is a decline in the economic well-being of Latinos in general (Santiago and Wilder, 1991). The continuing flow of newcomers tends to depress occupational and income figures for Hispanics as a whole, contributing to negative stereotypes. Also, the residential segregation of poor Hispanics has been increasing. Moreover, of all major minorities in the United States, Latinos have the highest school dropout rates: Only about half of 18- and 19-year-olds graduate from high school (Velez, 1989). Racial distinctiveness remains a disadvantage for many.

On the other hand, the swelling Hispanic populations have reasons for a growing pride and hope for a brighter future. Voting rates are rising among Mexican Americans (Longoria, Wrinkle, and Polinard, 1990), and Latinos' increasing numbers are winning political power at the local level (Bullock and MacManus, 1990). They await a national leader who can galvanize the groups into a potent national political force. Another encouraging consideration, except for Puerto Ricans, is the lack of a developing underclass among Hispanics. Latino communities suffer no exodus of middle-class people, and still retain viable families, churches, and businesses (Moore, 1989).

Some of the main barriers to economic prosperity for Hispanics may soon weaken. First, a slackening of immigration would facilitate established Hispanics' entry into

EDUCATION LEVELS OF HISPANICS AND OTHERS, 1991

			Percent Distribution				
	White	Blacks	Hispanics (Total)	Mexican	Puerto Rican	Cuban	Central and South American
Years of school completed, persons 25 years old and over							
Elementary School, 0 to 8 years	9.9	15.2	33.6	40.0	24.3	28.4	27.5
High School, 4 years	39.1	37.7	29.3	26.8	33.0	28.1	32.1
College, 4 years or more	22.2	11.5	9.7	6.2	10.1	18.5	15.1

Table 7-4

Source: U. S. Bureau of the Census, *Current Population Reports*.

the labor market and speed up structural assimilation. Second, according to one study, Hispanic men with at least 12 years of education and who speak English "very well" can expect occupational success close to that of white non-Hispanic men (Stolzenberg, 1990). Finally, by casting Latinos as victims of racial discrimination, some leaders hope to attract more political attention and government support (Skerry, 1992).

Will Hispanic groups eventually mirror the accomplishments of Asian Americans? Like that similarly diverse "model minority," race is a factor, and education and language facility are key elements. Without the benefits of good schooling, Hispanics may become another large but poor minority. (See Table 7-4.) With it, they may yet become a model of success.

ASIAN AMERICANS: STILL A MINORITY?

Although they have been the fastest-growing minority in the United States since 1980, Asian Americans still make up less than 3 percent of the U. S. population. However, their well-publicized occupational and educational achievements have left their minority-group status in doubt. Concentrated largely in California and a few metropolitan areas elsewhere, this category of Americans is as diverse as any. It includes people from over 20 countries, including Japan, China, Korea, the Philippines, Taiwan, Vietnam, Cambodia, India, Laos, and Iran. In assessing the minority status of Asian Americans, then, we must keep in mind that the picture is not uniformly bright.

Chinese Americans, for example, have probably had to endure the fiercest hostility of all Asian groups since they began arriving in the 1850s. Originally welcomed in this country as cheap laborers to help build the transcontinential railroad, Chinese workers soon came to be seen as competitors for other kinds of work. They were taxed, excluded from many occupations, and prohibited from owning land, attending school, or giving testimony in court. The 1882 Chinese Exclusion Act forbade further Chinese immigration until 1943, when, during World War II, they were viewed with less disfavor than the Japanese enemy.

Similarly, Japanese immigrants were welcomed as a source of cheap labor in the late 1800s until they too became rivals for better jobs. In some parts of Western states, Japanese were prohibited from attending schools with whites, owning or leasing land, and even from becoming U. S. citizens. During World War II, the federal government ordered all those of Japanese ancestry, most of whom were American citizens, into "relocation centers," or concentration camps, lest they aid Japan through sabotage or espionage. The racist implications were evident in the fact that people of German ancestry were not similarly confined. Forced by circumstances to sell their homes and other assets, families lost thousands of dollars. The Supreme Court condoned these actions as necessary wartime security measures. Not until 1988 did the U. S. government offer an official apology and $20,000 to each Japanese American imprisoned during the war.

Like other racially distinct immigrants, Asians have suffered harassment and violence, but in many ways they hardly fit the profile of a disadvantaged minority. As a group, they are justifiably called "America's . . . most affluent minority" (Bodovitz and Edmondson, 1991). This prosperity is clearly depicted in Census figures that rank their 1989 median household income ($36,102) well above that of non-Hispanic whites ($30,406), Hispanics ($21,921), and blacks ($18,083).

In fact, Asian immigrants often "leapfrog" lower-class positions to middle-class status in our society. Newcomers from China, Japan, and India have higher business ownership rates than Americans in general, and Korean Americans have the highest of anyone—88.9 per 1,000 people compared to 64 for Americans overall (Manning and O'Hare, 1988). One key to the success of Asian Americans is their typically high level of education, especially among those of Japanese, Filipino, and Korean ancestry. Their strong basic skills performance and reputation for good citizenship (see Figure 7-2) combine to help them generally excel in school (Farkas et al., 1990). Asian Americans' high school and college graduation rates exceed those of the general U. S. population. They also earn more doctoral degrees and are more likely to hold professional occupations than members of the majority group.

In light of their impressive overall success, small wonder that Asians have been called a "model minority." Beneath the surface, however, lies evidence of the same kind of restrictions and subordinate status that characterize other minority groups.

Many Korean Americans, for example, have reason to feel deprived of their just rewards. Their average incomes are lower than those of whites and some other Asian Americans despite their high rate of business ownership, and they earn less than people with similar levels of education. It was Korean-American businesses that Los Angeles rioters targeted in May of 1992. For these reasons, many Korean Americans resent the label "model minority"—the American dream does not seem to include them (MacFarquhar, 1992).

There are other signs that Asian Americans receive unequal access to social resources. This is not only the case among recent, uprooted immigrants from Vietnam and Cambodia. Despite their admirable scholastic achievements, Asian college graduates find that good jobs, promotions, and high salaries elude them. Evidence suggests that their incomes are not commensurate with their academic success (Barringer, Takeuchi, and Xenos, 1990), and that Asian-American women, with extraordinarily high education levels, are still concentrated in less prestigious professions (Woo, 1989). Doubts persist in corporate America about the Asian worker's ability to manage people assertively or to perform in any role other than specialist in a narrow technical field, so they remain underrepresented in top business leadership positions. And while their successes often disqualify them from affirmative action programs, they lack

Figure 7-2

The ways in which young people spend their time gives some insight into the different futures that various racial and ethnic groups typically face.

Source: William P. O'Hare, "America's Minorities—The Demographics of Diversity," *Population Bulletin* 47, no. 4 (Washington, DC: Population Reference Bureau, Inc., 1992).

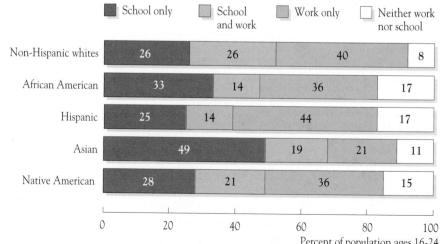

MAJOR ACTIVITIES OF YOUNG MINORITIES, 1991

■ School only ■ School and work ■ Work only □ Neither work nor school

	School only	School and work	Work only	Neither work nor school
Non-Hispanic whites	26	26	40	8
African American	33	14	36	17
Hispanic	25	14	44	17
Asian	49	19	21	11
Native American	28	21	36	15

0   20   40   60   80   100

Percent of population ages 16-24

Despite their educational and occupational successes, Asian Americans still have reason to feel frustrated in trying to fulfill the American Dream.

the power of a dominant group, as is seen in the beatings and harassment incidents they suffer every year.

Asian Americans, then, offer a paradox: a well-educated, high-income minority with a "continuous sense of ethnic otherness" (Ueda, 1989, p. 16), successful in some ways but still subordinate in others.

MUST NATIVE AMERICANS RELINQUISH THEIR CULTURAL HERITAGE?

Native Americans stand out from other minorities in several ways. Rather than start out as displaced and destitute outsiders, they were originally masters of this continent. Instead of moving up the social ladder, they eventually lost most of their land and power, so that today they are the poorest, most disadvantaged group in the United States. Unlike other minorities that gained a foothold and then flourished, the Native American population has shrunk to almost nothing. Instead of seeking assimilation, Native Americans have generally sought cultural separateness. While this has allowed them to salvage something of their heritage, it has also helped depress their standard of living. Can Native Americans afford continued cultural isolation?

If the U. S. government had had its way, Native American societies would have disappeared long ago, either through extermination or assimilation. The natives were assumed to be racially inferior, and thus unworthy of respect or humane treatment. Even the dubiously positive image of the American Indian as a "noble savage" quickly gave way to simply being a "savage." The decimation of the original population by between 50 percent and 90 percent (Roberts, 1989) occurred in part as a result of

U. S. military action and the disruption of food supplies and subsistence patterns, but mostly it was due to the (sometimes intentional) introduction of European diseases such as smallpox, typhus, measles, and scarlet fever.

According to the ethnocentric reasoning of the white invaders, if the native people were inferior, then so was their way of life. If the "savages" would not submit to Christianization, they should be treated as subhumans. The settlers' racism and contempt showed in bounties offered for Indian scalps, attempts to use natives as slaves, and outright massacres. On top of such atrocities, whites usurped the natives' lands.

The land grab was accomplished through treaties if possible, force if necessary. Treaties signed by Indians who often did not represent their tribes gave legal sanction to the relentless, westward expulsion of native peoples. Even if they were actually valid, settlers and miners violated the treaties at their convenience. After all, "manifest destiny" dictated that white Christians were preordained to push aside the heathens and civilize the land. The Removal Act of 1830 accordingly supplied money to move Eastern tribes to inhospitable lands west of the Mississippi. The forced migration of Cherokees, Seminoles, and other Southeastern tribes to Oklahoma through a bitter winter chillingly illustrated the federal government's disdain for Indian's rights. Thousands died from disease and mistreatment along the infamous "Trail of Tears."

Once corralled on reservations, Native Americans became wards of the government: fed, protected, and controlled by representatives of the victorious white culture. Tribal powers were restricted, although at first federal policy respected to some extent the sovereign powers of these independent nations. Soon, however, the government's Indian policy began its decades-long vacillation from forced assimilation to separateness. In the process, American Indian cultures were shattered.

Pressure to assimilate began in earnest in the late 1800s. The practice of native religion was suppressed, in some cases considered a criminal offense. Native American children were compelled to attend federal schools. Policymakers decided that the most thorough indoctrination could be accomplished in boarding schools, where children would be isolated from tribal influences and skills training and strict discipline would produce useful workers. Teachers cut the students' hair, burned their clothes, and gave them new, English names. Use of their native language or clothing brought punishment. A federal land policy established in the late 1800s allotted land parcels to individual Native Americans. This especially potent assimilation tool struck at the heart of tribal life, the collective ownership of land.

By the 1930s, federal authorities shifted from forced assimilation to greater respect for Native American rights and heritage. This change coincided with warnings from anthropologists that "primitive" cultures were disappearing throughout the world and should be protected. The 1950s saw a return to an assimilationist Indian policy, only to be reversed again in the 1970s.

Today the U. S. government encourages and supports Native American political sovereignty, economic development, and cultural preservation. But however well-meaning its current intentions, past federal policies are largely to blame for the current wretched conditions of so many American Indians.

The diversity of the over 300 tribes, comprising nearly two million people, cautions against general descriptions. However, the few individual and tribal success stories are eclipsed by an overall dismal picture. Concentrated in the Southwest, and about evenly distributed between reservations and cities, Native Americans are the poorest minority group in the country. Their populations usually display high percentages of female-headed households and low rates of educational attainment. Unemployment typically remains at three to four times that of the U. S. average. Health

A resurgence of pride—and business enterprise—among American Indians has provided some hope for economic improvements for the long-beleaguered peoples.

statistics reflect this poverty. Alcoholism and violent death are common. Native American adolescents use cigarettes, alcohol, marijuana, and cocaine at higher rates than whites or Hispanics, who use such drugs more than blacks or Asians (Wallace and Bachman, 1991). Suicide rates exceed those of all other ethnic groups (Grossman, Milligan, and Deyo, 1991). One study of Northwestern American Indians found many at high risk levels for AIDS (Hall et al., 1990). The increase in Native American–owned businesses and the discovery of valuable mineral deposits on some tribal lands may indirectly alleviate a few of these social problems, but outside economic forces are still beyond the control of local tribal leaders.

What is the best hope now for Native Americans? For the past century, the choice has been difficult. On the one hand, tribal life offered pride and a certain amount of security. On the other, mainstream society beckoned with much higher living standards. Today it may be possible to have it both ways. A strong ethnic pride movement has generated renewed interest in Native American heritage and cross-tribal solidarity. Approximately 1 in 35 U. S. citizens claim at least some American Indian ancestry, and the growing tendency among people to identify themselves to census-takers as Native Americans has resulted in a 38 percent increase in the population over the last decade (Fost, 1991). At the same time, some tribal members have managed to ascend the mainstream economic and occupational ladder, and a college-educated middle class has emerged. Cultural pluralism may thus represent a viable alternative to isolation in poverty or work at the price of rootlessness. But standing in the way of this ideal are the same barriers faced by other pluralistically minded ethnic groups in America: racism, ethnocentrism, and the demands of a relentlessly competitive economy.

Affirmative Action: Pro and Con

Should affirmative action programs be terminated? For over 20 years, the federal government has extended preferential treatment to designated minorities regarding hiring and admissions decisions. The goal is to enable all segments of our society to eventually compete on an equal footing. The controversy regarding this policy revolves around three questions, each of which has valid opposing arguments. Does your opinion take each of these points into consideration?

Is Affirmative Action Fair?

Yes. Prejudice persists, and thus the leveling influence of affirmative action is still required. Any consideration of fairness cannot ignore the continuing consequences of past discrimination. Many members of minority groups still suffer disadvantages in socialization patterns, education success, and self-esteem that stem from previous injustices. Until these effects have been eradicated, true equity cannot be achieved. Furthermore, for many reasons the white male monopoly is unlikely to even consider extending opportunities to minorities unless forced to do so.

Reverse discrimination: preferential treatment given to minorities at the expense of the majority group.

No. Discrimination against anyone is unfair. Preferential treatment given to minorities at the expense of the majority group, or **reverse discrimination,** treats individuals as members of a group rather than recognize their personal qualities; it assumes that all white males have enjoyed advantages and all members of minorities have suffered discrimination. Affirmative action punishes a generation for the sins of their ancestors. Moreover, such programs only benefit women, African Americans, Hispanics, Native Americans, Hasidic Jews, Appalachian whites, and Innuits, but not smaller, less organized groups who may have also suffered.

Can Affirmative Action Work?

Yes. The policy has already enabled minorities to create their own "buddy systems" and gain a foothold on the "inside." Role models now inspire the youth of formerly demoralized neighborhoods.

No. These unjust programs simply fan the fires of racial hatred, accentuating our intergroup boundaries instead of healing our divisiveness. Minorities unfairly taking jobs away from others become targets of resentment and doubts about their competence.

Will Affirmative Action Hurt Society?

No. Numerical goals force employers to consider workers from the entire spectrum of the labor force, more effectively tapping our nation's potential talent. Besides, we do not have objective or foolproof means to determine which applicant will perform best once hired. Allowing minorities a few points on entrance exams and civil service tests, for example, does not mean we are not getting the best person for the job.

Yes. The quotas imposed by affirmative action force gatekeepers to lower their standards, to accept the most qualified minority members rather than simply the best applicants society can offer. Employee morale often suffers.

Considering these arguments, should affirmative action be discontinued? ■

SUMMARY

A subset of people within a population becomes a *minority group*, with a subordinate status and restricted access to social resources, not because of its numerical size but because it lacks the power enjoyed by the dominant *majority group* which controls access to cultural, political, and economic resources. Minorities form around cultural or physical differences. *Race,* for one, refers to populations with a common genetic heritage and distinctive physical features. Races formed as isolated populations that adapted to different environmental demands, but scientists cannot agree on their numbers and their boundaries are unclear and imprecise. Second, *ethnic groups* are distinguished by their nationality or distinctive way of life, which can be a source of both pride and persecution. Ethnic immigration is causing growing concern on the part of many Americans today. Ethnocentrism and competition lead to the creation of successful *middleman minorities,* which serve society's needs at mid-level occupations such as small business and trading. Minorities also form when one group gains more power than another.

Eliminating America's racial and ethnic hostilities would require removal of discrimination and prejudice. *Discrimination* is differential, unequal, and usually negative treatment of people based solely on their group membership. (Critics of affirmative action claim that it produces *reverse discrimination,* which gives preferential treatment to minorities at the expense of the majority group.) While legislation has removed most overt injustices, informal and sometimes unintentional barriers remain. For example, customs and entrenched social policies can lead to *institutionalized discrimination.* In some cases, racial segregation is maintained through *redlining,* in which banks and other lending institutions effectively exclude minority groups from certain neighborhoods by refusing to qualify them for home mortgages. Discrimination persists because it benefits the majority group economically and politically, and even enhances the minority's solidarity. It also endures because of the fear generated in the majority group by high numbers of minority members. Minority groups discriminate against one another as well.

The other underpinning of intergroup hostilities is *prejudice,* the emotional, rigid belief that members of certain other groups are inferior. Prejudice does not always go hand in hand with discrimination, but eliminating the former would reduce the latter. Prejudice is based on *stereotypes,* fixed generalizations about all members of a group or category, and *scapegoating,* in which the blame for one's own misfortune is placed on someone else. Prejudicial thinking is used to justify the mistreatment of minorities; it has deep roots and is reinforced in primary relationships and peer group ties.

Intergroup hostilities also often involve *racism,* belief in the innate inequality of races. Thus individuals are judged on the basis of the group they belong to rather than on their own merits; inferiority is presumed. *Symbolic racism* espouses racial equality but blames other races' lack of success on their supposedly innate inferiority.

Most immigrants have faced mistreatment in the United States, ranging from *genocide*, the extermination or annihilation of a racial or ethnic group, to slavery, to *segregation*, (physical isolation and social exclusion). Segregation can produce in the minority group *ethnic identification*, feelings of closeness and shared interests, and *separatism*, a desire for cultural distance from the dominant group. Society's rejection of a minority is most evident in *de jure segregation*, wherein separation is sanctioned by law. Today unofficial, informal *de facto segregation* persists. This shows in the existence of *split labor markets*, which pay different groups different wages for the same work. In a few cases, culturally distinct groups coexist with the dominant group in some degree of mutual respect and tolerance that benefits both majority and minority, an arrangement called *cultural pluralism*. This "separate but equal" condition can function smoothly, as in Switzerland, but more typically conflict underlies pluralism, as is the case in Canada. In pluralistic societies, ethnic groups benefit from enclaves. In *accommodation*, a minority lives side by side with the majority and adapts to the mainstream culture without embracing it. Often, however, the minority culture is absorbed and loses its distinctiveness, a process called *assimilation*. While first-generation immigrants have usually followed the strategy of accommodation in the United States, their children have often aimed for *acculturation*, or accepting the dominant culture. There are several types of assimilation—cultural, structural, and attitudinal—and various groups assimilate differently along these lines. Other factors, such as gender, the immigrant population's size, and its income inequality also affect the assimilation process. In a "melting pot" scenario of *amalgamation*, the majority culture merges with that of immigrants, producing a new culture and usually, through intermarriage, a new population.

African Americans, who make up 12 percent of the U. S. population today, suffered horrendous oppression in the past, even after Constitutional amendments nominally guaranteed them civil rights. Violence and Jim Crow restrictions, combined with expanding employment in industrial cities, led to a great northward migration in the middle of this century. Opportunities for blacks improved after World War II, but as a group they continue to lag behind in many measures of social success. A large black middle class has flourished, but an underclass remains locked in poverty. African Americans still face disadvantages on the basis of their skin color, and are segregated in several subtle ways, suggesting there are obstacles yet to overcome.

Hispanics, or Latinos, comprise 9 percent of the U. S. population, and their numbers are expected to grow significantly in the next few decades. This broad category is very diverse racially and subculturally. The largest Hispanic group, Mexican Americans, is continually augmented by young, poorly educated immigrants who depress the statistical profile of this group as a whole. Those from Central and South America, generally have high occupational statuses, while Puerto Ricans on the whole display high poverty rates. The status of Cuban Americans depends largely on which wave of immigration they joined, but overall this group represents a success story. The continuous flow of immigrants, and their residential segregation, have presented barriers for Latinos in general, but their growing population and signs of lowering economic barriers give reason for optimism that they may become a model minority.

Although Asian Americans have been the fastest-growing minority in the United States since 1980, they still comprise only 3 percent of the overall population. While Chinese Americans endured fierce hostility in the past, as did Japanese Americans, many of whom were packed into relocation centers during World War II, Asians generally move quickly up the ladder of success, largely on the basis of solid educational achievement. Despite their overall prosperity, however, these diverse groups have reason to feel subordinated. Korean Americans, for example, have relatively low incomes despite a high rate of business ownership. Well-educated Asian Americans are also underrepresented among top business leadership positions.

Native Americans have generally sought separateness to preserve their cultural heritage. Their population has been greatly reduced by a combination of European diseases, U. S. government policies, and disruption of food supplies. While Native Americans lost their lands to forcibly imposed (and usually broken) treaties and military force, racism and ethnocentrism nearly destroyed their cultures. On the whole, this diverse minority group shows distressing poverty and other social ills, but the emergence of Native American–owned enterprises and a resurgence of ethnic pride and tribal solidarity offer some bright spots. There is reason to hope that Native Americans will be able to take the path of cultural pluralism.

Key Terms

minority group	prejudice	de jure segregation
majority group	stereotypes	de facto segregation
race	scapegoating	split labor markets
ethnic group	racism	cultural pluralism
middleman minorities	symbolic racism	accommodation
discrimination	genocide	assimilation
institutionalized	segregation	acculturation
discrimination	ethnic identification	amalgamation
redlining	separatism	reverse discrimination

GENDER AND AGE

Not all societies differentiate as to social class, race, or ethnicity, but all distinguish between male and female, old and young. The men's clubs of New Guinea, for example, once provided males with a social segregation that enhanced their solidarity and dominance. The age-based groupings of earlier East African and North American societies, where young men served as warriors and police, illustrate the usefulness of age differentiation. Of course, such differentiations invariably involve inequalities regarding rights, respect, and power. In this chapter, we explore the social repercussions of age and **gender,** status based on culturally determined distinctions of men and women.

Gender: social status based on culturally determined distinctions of men and women; a set of personality traits associated with being female or male.

MUST GENDER ROLES BE DIFFERENT?

Why should girls and boys receive different kinds of toys and punishments? Why do women face more obstacles in higher education and the job market than men? Why must husbands and wives deal differently with sex, grief, and fear, watching their marriages founder upon missed communication? Are biological differences responsible? Is it *natural* for women to be treated differently than men?

If **gender roles,** the behavior patterns considered appropriate for each sex, are based on vital biological sex differences (nature), we may not want to change those roles. If they are fundamentally the products of cultural shaping (nurture), however, we might wish to consider reshaping those roles.

Gender roles: behavior patterns considered appropriate for each sex.

But why stop there? Why not erase gender roles and their effects altogether? The result would be **androgyny:** the absence of cultural restrictions on personality, and thus freedom from gender expectations. In an androgynous society, each person would freely choose the personality features with which he or she is comfortable. People would not be restricted to either "masculine" or "feminine" characteristics but could select the best of both. The individual would be free to grow, to branch out in any direction.

Androgyny: the absence of cultural definitions of femininity or masculinity; including characteristics of both genders.

Short of androgyny, perhaps cultural forces could modify gender roles so that neither sex suffers inferior treatment. As we now see, this is feasible only if those roles do not flow naturally from relevant biological differences.

How Much Are Gender Role Differences Based on Biology?

A Natural Division of Labor?   The most obvious and important way most cultures treat women and men differently is in the **sexual division of labor,** separating work

Sexual division of labor: the separation of work into distinct specializations deemed appropriate for males and females.

into distinct specializations deemed appropriate for males and females. Is this assignment of chores based on biological differences—that is, is it natural?

The answer is simple: In the past, yes; today, no. For thousands of years, most cultures assigned men, with their greater strength and without the burden of pregnancy, tasks such as hunting and herding. This also made sense for reproductive reasons: Because only a few men are necessary to impregnate any number of women, males could be assigned the more dangerous tasks. Women were usually expected to stay near camp to gather, prepare and preserve food, and carry water—activities that, although possibly exhausting, can be performed by people who lack physical power and who may be pregnant or nursing. While there were certain exceptions to this pattern, biological differences with respect to strength and reproduction originally played an influential part in establishing gender work roles. In today's labor market, however, physical strength is less important and gender work roles are increasingly interchangeable.

Are Men Naturally More Powerful?   Another common role difference is that most cultures allot men more social power than women. We would expect men to be naturally dominant if they possessed greater innate aggressiveness, superior physical strength, or higher intelligence. But do they?

First, we could understand male dominance in nearly every culture if men possess an inborn tendency toward aggressiveness. Males in virtually all societies, from very early ages, engage in more belligerent behavior than women. Hormones may play a crucial role. Both sexes produce "male" and "female" hormones, though in differing proportions. In animals of both sexes, injections of male hormones lead to more aggressiveness. The impact of these hormones in humans is not so clear, but girls whose mothers took synthetic male hormones during pregnancy sometimes seem to be more tomboyish and physically aggressive than their siblings (Brody, 1981). This and

Are men naturally more powerful? If social power is allocated according to strength, perhaps we should consider not only physical power but other measures of strength, such as survivability.

other evidence suggest that while hormones do not in themselves produce behaviors, they may create behavioral *tendencies*. Perhaps these tendencies have provided the foundation for the assignment of gender roles in most cultures. It would surely be easier to expect males to play a more aggressive role if they naturally lean that way anyway, as they seem to do.

Second, it is clear that men are typically larger than women and have superior upper-body strength, lung capacity, and muscle bulk. But strength can be measured in other ways, too, such as survivability. Women have greater resistance to disease, and in the United States generally live an average of about seven years longer than men. Males show greater vulnerability before birth as well: About 140 males are conceived for every 100 females, but only about 105 males are born for every 100 females.

A study of the infamous Donner Party lends more weight to the argument that women enjoy more survivability than men (Grayson, 1990). This unfortunate group of 87 pioneers, stranded by heavy snows on the eastern side of the Sierra Nevada mountains in 1846, was forced to resort to cannibalism. Among the survivors was a higher proportion of women than men, suggesting that females are better able to endure famine and extreme cold. Who, indeed, is the weaker sex?

Finally, there might be some justification for granting males more social power if they are more intelligent. While neither sex can clearly claim overall intellectual superiority, mental differences exist. At least some of these differences are biological. The male sex hormone testosterone causes the male brain to develop differently. One result is that in women's brains, mental skills, such as language, are more evenly balanced between the right and left hemispheres; another is that men seem to lose their verbal abilities faster than women as they age (Gur, 1991).

Perhaps more importantly, males and females score somewhat differently on tests of various mental abilities. However, the disparities are not as great as in the past, which suggests cultural rather than purely biological influence. Nearly two decades ago, Eleanor Maccoby and Carol Jacklin (1974) surveyed many studies of sex differences and concluded that boys displayed better mathematical and visual-spatial skills than girls, while girls were generally superior in verbal abilities. More recent research, however, reveals that these variations have diminished substantially (Friedman, 1989; Hyde, Fennema, and Lamon, 1990; Feingold, 1992). Males and females show greater similarities than differences in mental abilities, except at the extreme high end of math and spatial-skill scores, where men outnumber women (Hyde, 1981; Benbow, 1988). The justification for unequal gender expectations has weakened as girls and women receive more encouragement to develop intellectually.

The evidence, then, points to the conclusion that traditional gender roles were originally rooted in real biological differences that are much less significant for our culture's needs. Personality tendencies regarding aggression are just that: tendencies. Disparities in physical strength are not all clearly in favor of males, and are becoming increasingly irrelevant in today's society anyway. Differences in mental ability are important, but they are not substantial.

How Much Does Culture Shape Gender Roles?

If gender roles are no longer biologically determined, they must be based on culture. The extent of this influence is revealed by studying the pervasive process by which males and females are taught behaviors and attitudes considered appropriate to their sex, a process called **gender role socialization.**

Gender role socialization: the process by which males and females are taught behavior and attitudes considered appropriate to their sex.

Gender Role Socialization   Beginning with pink and blue name tags and blankets in the nursery, girls and boys are socialized in different ways. Parents, probably because of the way they have been socialized themselves, treat their sons and daughters according to separate social scripts. Michael Lewis (1992) notes that parents tend to denigrate a daughter's whole self when she has done something wrong: "You are not smart." For a son, they are more likely to focus on that specific misdeed. Girls, therefore, are more likely than boys to feel shame and embarrassment when they violate rules or norms. Moreover, mothers respond with a wider range of emotions to their infant daughters than to their sons, and show greater disapproval to their daughters' anger (Malatesta and Haviland, 1982). In one study, mothers discussing past experiences with their 2- and 3-year-old children tended to use more affirmative emotion words with their daughters, attribute more positive feelings to them, and talk more about sadness with their daughters than with their sons (Fivush, 1989). While fathers do not usually spend as much time socializing their children, they tend to treat sons and daughters even more distinctly, being gentle with their daughters but rough-and-tumble with their sons (Jacklin, DiPietro, and Maccoby, 1984). Other examples of gender role socialization include boys being punished more than girls, girls being taught more care-giving behavior, girls being interrupted more by parents, and the sexes receiving different language cues (Shapiro, 1990).

Of course, this differential shaping extends well beyond the family. Boys often receive more encouragement, attention, help, and praise in the classroom. Even our everyday speech reflects the "inferiority" of females. Language continuously reinforces the secondary status of females, as we see, for example, in the U. S. Constitution's use of only masculine pronouns and the habit of referring to "men and women" rather than "women and men." In advertising, another pervasive shaper of gender consciousness, "women are shown almost exclusively as housewives . . . either pathologically obsessed by cleanliness and lemon-fresh scents" or as sex-object mannequins, "thin, generally tall and long-legged, and, above all, . . . young" (Kilbourne, 1992, p. 349).

Perhaps for these reasons, children show a strong inclination to distinguish themselves as either masculine or feminine, usually in their third year (Maccoby, 1990). Preschoolers acquire **gender identity,** self-conception as a female or male, in part through imitation: Boys do what men do and girls what women do. In this way, children socialize themselves, observing and experimenting with clothing, hairstyles, and role-playing games (Cahill, 1989). Children are also socialized by rewards and punishment from adults. When a child behaves in a manner the parents consider inappropriate for a child's gender, he or she receives discouragement, perhaps a frown or negative word. The child likewise receives praise for behavior seen as appropriate. Even if parents attempt to foster "unisex" notions, at age 3 and 4 boys still tend to play with boys' toys and girls with girls' toys (Lloyd, Duveen, and Smith, 1988).

These differences do not fade as we get older, of course. For example, both sexes use different strategies to reason about moral dilemmas during their elementary and high school years (Donenberg and Hoffman, 1988). Studies in the United States and New Zealand show that female college students are more intimate and emotional with same-sex friends than are males: Women emphasize talking, emotional sharing, and discussing personal problems; men emphasize simply sharing activities (Aukett, Ritchie, and Mill, 1988). Gender differences show their strength as far up the educational ladder as medical school. Women rarely enter training as surgeons; instead they choose primary care—where they earn lower salaries (Martin, Arnold, and Parker, 1988). Female medical students also display a greater number of illness symptoms than their male counterparts (Grossman et al., 1987).

Gender identity: self-conception as a female or male.

NORDSTROM

CHANEL

"Perfume is a part of you; no elegance is possible without it."
Coco Chanel

Advertising often depicts women as housewives or sex objects, thus reinforcing other gender role socializing.

Sources of Socialization Patterns   Why, after decades of "women's liberation," do we still socialize girls differently than boys? Are these socialization patterns so deeply entrenched that they can't be changed?

Conflict theorists claim that gender roles, especially the tradition of male domi-nance, were created in the earliest human societies by the most physically powerful members: men. In early agricultural communities, men captured brides and treated

Capitalist patriarchy: the interaction of capitalism with male supremacy that results in the occupational subordination of women.

wives as property to be exploited. Dominance over females was useful not only to ensure productivity but to guarantee paternity of the children. The behavior of women thus had to be controlled. Industrialization saw the development of **capitalist patriarchy:** the interaction of capitalism with male supremacy to keep women in subordinate occupational roles. Women had become useful in work outside the home, but to maintain control over them men enacted laws and enforced traditions restricting the kinds of jobs they could hold, the number of hours they could work, and the property they could own. According to this view, our continuing differential treatment of the sexes today is part of a long tradition of male dominance.

Functionalists point not to exploitation but a natural division of labor based on physical differences between the sexes. From this viewpoint, as we have already seen, practical considerations traditionally assigned men the task of hunting and women the domestic chores. Hunting demands more size and strength than housekeeping and cannot be interrupted by pregnancy. Furthermore, Talcott Parsons and Robert Bales (1955) contend that a woman best contributes to a family's functioning when she plays an **expressive role,** minimizing group tension and maximizing solidarity to provide emotional support and social integration. **Instrumental roles** which focus on goal achievement and economic security for the family, are natural and proper for men. When the husband and wife play such complementary roles, each spouse has ways to achieve respect and satisfaction without competing with the other. In this way, gender role differences have—at least in the past—efficiently fulfilled the family's needs.

Expressive role: usually associated with femininity, this set of expectations focuses on providing emotional support and social integration.

Instrumental role: usually associated with masculinity, this set of expectations focuses on performing tasks and achieving goals.

What about today? Conflict theorists argue that the customary roles of man as provider and woman as domestic helpmate must change because they continue a tradition of oppression. Functionalists simply observe that such roles have become dysfunctional in today's society.

How Much Room for Change?   Clearly, changes have occurred. The opportunities, rights, and responsibilities accorded males and females have become less disparate. Women have gained more access to the labor market. Men are freer to express their tenderness and affection. But many differences remain. How much farther can we lessen gender differences?

A lot farther, according to research done several decades ago by Margaret Mead (1935). In studying three cultures located within a 100-mile area in New Guinea, she found extreme contrasts in ideas about gender. In the Arapesh culture, for example, males and females were both expected to be gentle, mild, and maternal—what would be considered "feminine" in the United States. Arapesh beliefs contrasted sharply with those of the Mundugumor, in which both sexes were expected to be fierce, competitive, and aggressive. A traditionally feminine American woman would not fit in there; nor would she in the third culture Mead studied, the Tchambuli. Among these people, gender roles were the reverse of North American customs. Tchambuli females were the leaders, clearly dominating the men in their society. They were responsible, no-nonsense breadwinners, acting in ways we traditionally expect of a "real man" in our culture. Tchambuli males wore curls and much adornment, spent most of their time on gossip and art, and tried to please and earn praise from the women, on whom they were emotionally dependent.

The female-dominated Tharu tribe of India likewise illustrates the power of culture in determining sex roles. Tharu women so thoroughly control their men that neighboring tribes assume they use strong spells and magic. Men may not touch the drinking pots or enter the kitchen, and must ask their wives' permission to sell their own personal property. They supply the raw materials from which women fashion marketable items such as baskets and mats. Also, through their gardening and fishing, women provide most of the food for the family, and require that men do most of the heavy labor and sleep in the fields to guard the crops. Observers conclude that "Tharu men do not seem to have learned to think independently. They have great reliance on their womenfolk" (Singhal and Mrinal, 1991, p. 172).

Despite the biological differences between the sexes, then, culture can shape gender roles into nearly any conceivable form. So long as society's subsistence needs do not require, say, a strong hunter to literally "bring home the bacon," socialization patterns can be altered dramatically. The progress of the last two decades in the United States may only be the beginning of a process of even more substantial change in gender roles.

Are Women Taught to "Neighbor"?

Research Box

Do women "neighbor" more than men? If so, is it the product of biological predispositions or gender socialization?

Observation would enable researchers to discover whether women neighbor more than men, but the tremendous amount of time needed to capture the routines of many people is prohibitive. Plus, identifying the causes behind those behaviors would require information that cannot be observed, such as the need for intimacy. Therefore, Karen Campbell and Barrett Lee (1990) decided to conduct a survey including a questionnaire and an hour-long interview. They could then subject the survey results to statistical analysis in search of meaningful patterns.

Campbell and Lee surveyed a portion of Nashville, Tennessee, with a variety of neighborhoods, ranging from near the inner city to some with one-acre lots. Fully 88 percent of the eligible persons in these neighborhoods cooperated in the survey. The participants were asked about their neighborhood intimates and frequency of neighbor contacts.

The results showed clearly that women neighbor more than men. Furthermore, analysis of the survey data suggested that this difference is not due to such possible causes as having more available time, being in the neighborhood more often, being married, or having children. Unless some genetic influence is discovered, the deciding factor for women's greater neighborliness seems to be the cultural expectation that women be more sociable, more involved with other people. In other words, America's gender roles shape women into more neighborly people. □

ARE WOMEN A MINORITY GROUP IN THE UNITED STATES?

Minorities suffer. We saw in Chapter 7 that members of minority groups must deal with segregation, restricted access to social resources, and other forms of discrimination. Does this picture apply to women?

In cultures around the world, women bear all the hallmarks of a minority. For example, many Muslim, Hindu, and Sikh women in Pakistan, Bangladesh, and northern India uphold their personal honor and that of their families by covering their faces in the presence of most men and secluding themselves at home. These practices, collectively known as "purdah" (curtain), serve to protect women from men outside the home and to preserve the family's internal solidarity (Mandelbaum, 1988). The rules command a woman to cover her head at the approach of, say, an older male of her husband's family. She can venture out of her home only when necessary, and must hurry back without tarrying. She must also avoid loud speech and direct eye contact with men, and if she speaks in the presence of men, she is required to cover her mouth with her hand or a cloth to show respect. Violating these strictures invites vicious village gossip and harassment by her mother-in-law. For disobedience, her husband may beat her, divorce her, deny her permission to visit her family, or send her to her family and refuse to take her back.

Purdah rules vary by region, class, and ethnic group, but the devaluation of females pervades these cultures. Even in well-educated, urban Hindu circles, for example, the birth of a daughter can evoke deep disappointment. In fact, mothers may not even mention daughters when asked about the size of their family. Daughters face lower chances of survival, largely due to neglect that borders on infanticide. Male babies enjoy lavish attention and the best food and care the family can provide, while female infants often receive little nurturance or medical care. "A little girl very quickly learns to leave a bigger and better share of food for her brother because she learns about her secondary position from the way her mother behaves" (Kumar, 1991, p. 146). Such early-life experiences teach women to accept their secondary, minority-group status as a consequence of the destiny *(karma)* determined by their previous lives.

Do American women today also face minority status? Perhaps not. After all, women generally live with the male "majority group" and share their husbands' resources. The women's liberation movement that began in the 1960s has produced laws banning sexual discrimination. Even though the proposed Equal Rights Amendment in the U. S. Constitution failed to win ratification in enough states during the 1970s, polls show that a majority of Americans support its guarantee of equality for women, and Congress has passed other legislation aimed at protection of women's rights. Title IX of the Education Amendments of 1972, for example, addresses discrimination that females face in school: single-sex classes (such as boys-only shop), underfunding of girls' athletics programs, unfair hiring and promotion practices, and admissions and financial aid policies that give preferential treatment to males. Despite such exclusionary treatment, schools generally seem to offer an amenable atmosphere to female students: Girls are more likely than boys to graduate from high school, attend college, and graduate with a bachelor's or master's degree.

There are other signs of growing advantages for women on the political front. The voting age population consists of more women than men, and women are now more likely to register and vote. Polls indicate that more people than ever before say they would vote for a female candidate for president. The number of women in state legislatures increased 100 percent from 1974 to 1984, largely due to recruitment through such organizations as the National Organization for Women, founded in 1966 (Rule, 1990). Women candidates enjoy greater voter trust, especially on such issues as child care, the environment, and ethics. Moreover, two women have been appointed to the U. S. Supreme Court since 1981, President Clinton appointed several women to high-ranking cabinet positions, including attorney general, and his wife has maintained a high profile in his administration. Since the 1960s, women in the United States have gained greater freedom to enter virtually any field of work or study. The number of women in science and engineering has jumped—more than doubling, for example, in chemical and mechanical engineering—and affirmative action programs have opened a number of occupational and educational doors.

Given these facts, we may legitimately question whether women are still oppressed, still denied equal access to social resources, still a minority group. As we will now see, the evidence is not all positive.

Actual Economic Discrimination?

We would expect some income gap between the sexes since a higher proportion of women work part-time. Even comparing full-time workers, however, women's incomes lag substantially behind men's, regardless of educational level (see Table 8-1). While there are signs of improvement—gender affected earnings in 1980 less than it did in 1970 (Parcel and Mueller, 1989), and the gap narrowed throughout the decade—the pace of equalization has since slowed (DiPrete and Grusky, 1990), and the returns on experience and education have increased for men but not for women (Grusky and DiPrete, 1990).

The child-care responsibility of motherhood explains some of this income gap. A woman who has children at home finds working and going to school more difficult (Floge, 1989). Combining family and career is even tougher in male-dominated, white-collar professions (Olson, Frieze, and Detlefsen, 1990). Large corporations (with better opportunities for higher pay and promotions) especially prefer to employ single and childless female workers, who presumably have lower turnover rates than workers with children (Peterson, 1989). Moreover, seniority suffers from child-related interruptions such as maternity leave. In short, children can be career liabilities for their mothers, but not usually for their fathers.

Perceptions of wifely duties also depress women's earnings. When one spouse is offered a career opportunity that requires geographical relocation, the husband's job usually takes precedence. William and Denise Bielby (1992) found that a husband's potential loss from a move appears to deter his wife from taking a new job, but her potential loss does not deter her husband.

The millions of women willing to shoulder both child-care and spousal responsibilities also face a restricted labor market. Although occupational segregation has diminished since 1970, many fields still tend to be dominated by one or the other sex (Jacobs, 1989a). For example, though it is true that more women are becoming scientists and engineers, males continue to dominate high-paying occupations while such

THE GENDER INCOME GAP: MEAN INCOME OF YEAR-ROUND FULL-TIME WORKERS, AGE 25 AND OVER, 1990

	Total	4 Years High School	4 Years College	5 or More Years College
Men	$34,886	$28,043	$44,554	$55,831
Women	$22,768	$18,954	$28,911	$35,827

Table 8-1

Source: U. S. Bureau of the Census, *Statistical Abstract of the United States: 1992.* 112th edition.

LABOR MARKET SEGREGATION: MEN'S AND WOMEN'S WORK, 1991

Occupation	Percentage of Female Workers
Dental hygienists	99.8
Secretaries	99.0
Receptionists	97.1
Cleaners and servants	95.8
Physicians	20.1
Dentists	10.1
Aerospace engineers	8.7
Civil engineers	5.6
Mechanical engineers	4.9
Airline pilots and navigators	3.4

Table 8-2

Source: U.S. Bueau of Labor Statistics, *Employment and Earnings*.

low-paying jobs as secretary and servant are almost exclusively filled by females (see Table 8-2). Career women also have to contend with a "glass ceiling" barring their entry into corporate ranks above the middle-management level. This barrier has channeled many women into smaller firms or self-employment. Even there, however, they often face skeptical bankers and unequal access to government contracts (Miller, Springen, and Tsiantar, 1992).

Do Women Have Less to Offer?   Some theorists point to "nonmasculine" traits that handicap women in the job market. Traditionally masculine (or instrumental) personality traits are required in most prestigious, well-paying jobs—what might be termed "masculine chauvinism" (Glick, 1991). In this "supply side" viewpoint, women generally lack the highly valued, productive traits that men usually possess. Such acquired capabilities for contributing to the economy are called **human capital.**

Human capital: acquired capabilities for contributing to the economy.

According to this theory, most women do not invest their energies as intensely into acquiring the valued skills, education, and experience as do men. Moreover, most women lack the strong attachment to their careers that men typically display. Robert Fiorentine (1987), for example, found that though many females enter premedicine college programs, they are much less likely than males to actually apply for medical school later on, perhaps because women in our society have the alternative of not having a strong career commitment. Women may thus handicap themselves by selecting jobs that accommodate their household and maternal responsibilities, that is, jobs with flexible hours and small penalties for interruptions due to pregnancy and child-care emergencies. They also seek jobs requiring less effort (Becker, 1985), and show more concern with comfort, flexible hours, and a pleasant work environment than career progress (Daymont and Andrisani, 1988; Filer, 1985). A recent survey of college business school seniors revealed that females planned to work fewer years than the men did (Blau and Ferber, 1991). Randall Filer (1989) points out that this tendency leads to an oversupply of workers and depresses wages.

Sex Discrimination   Women's lower human capital or job choices do not fully explain their inferior pay or occupational segregation. Differences in human capital only account for between one-third and one-half the gender income gap (Corcoran and Duncan, 1985; Stoper, 1991). Women who enter "male" fields still earn on average less than men (Crispell, 1991). In fact, the income gap is worst in managerial occupations, where women earn only 61 percent as much as men. Even female applicants who display "masculine" personality traits are less likely to be hired than males with perceived identical traits (Glick, Zion, and Nelson, 1988). Furthermore, researchers have found that employed mothers do not voluntarily trade higher pay for easier jobs: Most of the jobs women hold do not accommodate their child-care and household responsibilities (Glass and Camarigg, 1992). Moreover, those in predominantly "female" jobs are not especially likely to quit work when their children are born (Desai and Waite, 1991), and do not find their jobs easy or flexible (Glass, 1990).

Clearly, then, to fully explain the gender income gap we must turn to sex discrimination. Simply being a female seems to be a disadvantage in the workplace—and this certainly indicates minority-group status.

One such sex-based obstacle is the "statistical discrimination" practiced by risk-aversive employers (Olson, 1990). Employers wish to hire only the most dependable, productive workers, and they tend to believe that, all things being equal, men as a group are more productive than women. Women are thus more likely to be excluded from competitive, high-paying occupational paths. For example, those who hire college faculty are inclined to perceive male professors as more academically productive than females (though there is little if any empirical support for this assumption), thereby giving men a significant career edge in higher education (Tolbert and Oberfield, 1991), especially at the more prestigious colleges and universities. Women who teach in college earn less than similarly qualified men, and are more likely to hold lower-level positions (Bellas, 1993).

Men and women are routinely sorted into occupations dominated by their respective sexes. Once a job becomes "feminized" within an organization, a sort of inertia tends to maintain this stigma (Baron and Newman, 1990). As Peter Glick explains it, "if men dominate a profession, then the image of a successful incumbent that comes most quickly to mind is a man and, in turn, male applicants may be seen as a better match for the job" (1991, p. 353).

Occupational segregation is in some cases rather obvious. All-male labor unions and "protective" legislation have simply barred women from some occupations. In other cases, the barriers are more subtle. A job's prestige and working conditions may change as its proportion of female workers increases, making promotion more difficult and hierarchies more rigid. For example, bank tellers and clerical workers were exclusively male management-trainees until World War I, when large numbers of women began filling these job slots. Thereafter, such positions were no longer the bottom rungs of a prestigious career ladder, but lowly "women's" jobs on a very short ladder.

Men entering predominantly female professions enjoy advantages—a "glass escalator" rather than a "glass ceiling" (C. Williams, 1992). In contrast, when women manage to break into well-paid, traditionally male occupations they often encounter adverse working conditions, notably sexual harrassment and sex discrimination. Despite the higher pay, female workers in "men's" jobs report significantly lower job satisfaction and more stress (Mansfield et al., 1991). One reason is that some men perceive female co-workers first as women and second as workers, which can lead easily to sexual harassment (Gutek and Morasch, 1982). Women working in steel plants, for example, complained that male co-workers would not teach them jobs taught to other men and assigned the women menial tasks (Deaux and Ullman, 1982). Part of the animosity toward the women was the result of their seldom being assigned physically demanding jobs. Similarly, men working with women in a large government agency admitted treating them less favorably (Palmer and Lee, 1990). Such experiences with male hostility discourage women's entry into male-dominated blue-collar jobs, despite their generally better pay, fringe benefits, security, and training and promotional opportunities.

A large employee class (as opposed to self-employed business owners) and an expanding service sector contribute to women's disadvantaged economic status. In a survey of 25 industrial economies, Maria Charles (1992) found that as the service sector grows, women usually end up in subordinate, caretaking, domestic-type jobs reflecting traditional feminine roles. As a smaller percentage of workers are self-employed, bureaucratic organizations dominate the work world and create more routinized, low-skill jobs that men abandon to women in favor of managerial and professional careers.

Overall, segregating patterns in the labor market tend to channel women workers into lower-paying occupations (Rytina, 1981; Roos, 1981) and even into low-paying organizations within the same field (Bielby and Baron, 1984). In other words, where women workers go, income levels drop (Tienda, Smith, and Ortiz, 1987), as does the field's prestige.

Capitalist Patriarchy Conflict theory offers a simpler explanation for the gender income gap: Working women are exploited by capitalist patriarchy (Dawson, 1988; Heath and Ciscel, 1988). As we saw earlier, this Marxist argument holds that male supremacy is a capitalist tool to keep women in subordinate, poorly paid work roles. Ideology helps maintain this patriarchy: One of the barriers women face in the corporate world is the belief among men in positions of authority that, because of their primary devotion to their children, women do not desire top jobs that require travel, training programs, and long hours. Besides, according to this reasoning, the capitalist system tries to confine women to the domestic sphere because it needs them to produce new workers and provide support—without wages—to males in the form of child-care services, house-cleaning labor, and sexual access.

Do Schools Devalue Females?

As we have seen, female students graduate from high school and college at higher rates, but males do better on college entrance tests and are more likely to choose majors in high-paying, high-prestige fields. Men also earn more doctoral and professional degrees. While women are making progress on the educational front, the road at the very top remains especially steep for them.

Many obstacles for girls begin early in life. Researchers found, for example, that parents of daughters have different perceptions of their children's mathematical ability than do parents of sons (Parsons, Adler, and Kaczala, 1982). Even when elementary school boys and girls perform equally well, girls' parents believe that their daughters have to work harder than boys and that advanced math courses are not very important. Apparently, the cultural stereotype of the "math dumb" girl is communicated at least partially through parents.

Penelope Peterson and Elizabeth Fennema (1985) observe that teachers spend more time in class helping boys than girls, and in subtle ways structure activities so that boys have a learning advantage. The American Association of University Women issued a 1992 report summarizing over 1,000 studies that describes widespread classroom bias in elementary and secondary schools. Boys, for example, receive more latitude and attention while girls lose self-confidence and intellectual competitiveness. Though critics contend that some of the older studies cited in the report ignore recent progress (such as women's superior graduation rates), the overall impact is troubling. Beyond this study, the research literature abounds with evidence of advantages enjoyed by male students, from boys being assigned to high-ability math groups (Hallinan and Sorensen, 1987) to a pro-male bias in SATs (Altenhof, 1984; Becker, 1990).

Women continue to face discrimination at the college level. They encounter a "chilly climate," while male students enjoy a "friendlier" classroom environment (Hall and Sandler, 1982; Crawford and MacLeod, 1990). Linda Rubin and Sherry Borgers (1990) found sexual harassment pervasive in all types of universities throughout the 1980s.

Politics: Women as Outsiders

Women's greater voting strength has translated into more elected female officials at the local and state levels, but, with women making up less than 20 percent of state legislatures, they still do not begin to approach the level of political participation enjoyed by men. In 1993, the 103rd U. S. Congress included only 7 women in the Senate and 48 in the House. Why?

Discrimination in the political process is a chief suspect, but research has revealed other explanations as well. For example, Edward Costantini (1990) found a consistently lower level of political ambition among female political activists. Women are less motivated by a desire for power, profit, and prestige, the rewards that usually drive successful politicians.

The exclusion of females from the public sphere dates back many generations. A few women from elite families and the wives of powerful men wielded considerable informal power in advancing or hindering the careers of male politicians, but formal participation was not allowed until women won the right to vote in 1920. Still, they remain marginal players for two reasons (Colley, 1992). First, largely because of historical necessity, women stress the importance of collective action through voluntary associations rather than participation as individual candidates. Political institutions are still seen largely as alien territory. Second, women have chosen to concentrate mostly on "women's issues" such as abortion, education, and child care, leaving such broad matters as foreign policy and economics mostly to men.

Still a Minority?

Regardless of her accomplishments or potential, a woman in the United States faces obstacles and limitations her male counterpart does not. The root of this discrimination is **sexism,** the prejudiced belief that males are innately superior to females. Sexism provides the foundation for male dominance in the labor market, education, politics, and elsewhere.

Sexism: the prejudiced belief that males are innately superior to females.

Sexism touches virtually every aspect of life. For example, Nancy Kutner and Donna Brogan (1991) found that physicians appear to favor males in offering optimal treatment for kidney failure, apparently believing it is more important to get men back to work. Diana Dull and Candice West (1991) also criticize doctors for assuming women to be more likely candidates for cosmetic surgery due to their "essential nature." Another study concluded that American courts typically respect the euthanasia preferences (turning off life support systems) of male patients but reject women's wishes because they are considered more immature and in need of protection (Miles and August, 1990).

Society's interpretation of a woman's physical appearance reflects some of this underlying bias. A telling study by R. E. Rainville and J. G. Gallagher (1990) found that male college students rate vulnerable-looking women more attractive than dominant women. On the other hand, the hiring process for high-status, leadership jobs favors males and those who are "maturefaced" rather than "babyfaced" (Zebrowitz, Tanenbaum, and Goldstein, 1991). Another study revealed that obese women earn over 12 percent less than nonobese women, while obesity has no effect on men's earnings (Register and Williams, 1990).

This pervasive sexism lies behind the "undeclared war against American women" described by Susan Faludi (1991). She contends that the progress of the women's movement over the last few decades has aroused an antifeminist backlash. Equal pay still remains out of reach, and sex discrimination complaints have soared. According to a 1991 *Newsweek* poll, most men believe women have been making gains unfairly at the expense of men, while women for the most part do not think men really understand women's concerns. The chasm between the sexes remains, and women retain their minority status.

WHAT WILL WOMEN'S AND MEN'S LIBERATION BRING?

The women's liberation movement, now in its third decade, has yet to fulfill its goals of social and economic equality. Still, this continuing revolution has generated changes that will reverberate for years to come in the lives of both women and men.

The steady rise in the number of female elected officials foretells not only more women with political power, but an accompanying change in their political "voice" (Kelly, Saint-Germain, and Horn, 1991). In the past few decades, a woman's public role generally corresponded with her domestic and social one: superintendent of schools rather than sheriff, for example, or serving on a committee dealing with health services rather than technical issues. As women's political representation increases and gender stereotypes diminish, the differences in the kinds of offices women and men hold may likewise decrease as women confront a wider variety of policy goals than they have previously. So, while Hillary Rodham Clinton was entrusted to manage the Clinton administration's health care plan (a "woman's issue"), the president appointed Janet Reno as attorney general, a traditionally male domain.

The most dramatic repercussions of gender role liberation will continue to occur in the economic sector. A falling birth rate and longer life expectancy mean proportionately fewer workers in the future and thus a greater dependence on women to meet our economy's hunger for skilled workers. We can thus expect to see more women in the labor force.

By 1990, polls began to detect a swelling wave of dissatisfaction among working women. Many complained of too much strain between vocational and domestic roles. Women in a 1990 Gallup poll reported increasing difficulty combining childrearing and a career, and a sense of unfulfilled expectations. Another survey the same year showed a huge leap in the number of women who want to opt out of the labor force permanently (Piirto, 1991). They reported bringing less work home from the office and spending more time with their children. Their approval of careers for mothers decreased for the first time in 20 years. Meanwhile, as polls were revealing these changes, the percentage of women aged 20 to 44 in the work force dropped, and fertility rates rose.

Does all this indicate a trend of women withdrawing from the labor force? Surely financial need will keep many women working, but pressure is building for progress on two fronts: more help at home from husbands and a new workplace.

First, increasing numbers of working women demand bigger changes in the domestic division of labor. One poll reports that after income inequality, the biggest complaint of employed women is "how much my mate helps around the house" (Townsend and O'Neil, 1990). Resentment and impatience have grown over husbands' failure to live up to their professed belief in equal sharing of domestic chores.

Second, as women have altered the profile of the labor force, they have begun to agitate for improvements in the work environment. While earlier feminists demanded more occupational access for women, neofeminists now call for a remodeling of the workplace to accommodate those who do not want to sacrifice their mothering role. They contend that the economy needs women's talents, and to keep them employed the workplace must offer a more congenial, supportive atmosphere, including more on-site day care, job sharing, and parental leave.

Most of all, women—and increasingly, men—demand flexibility to help them balance career and home responsibilities. A 1991 DuPont poll found more men placing a higher value on flexible work schedules that offer them more time with their families. Thus the future may bring additional "parent track" opportunities: more flexible and less demanding jobs with less pressure but fewer raises and promotions. For many parents, especially mothers, high-quality, part-time work (with job security and benefits such as health care) meets their needs.

Besides greater flexibility, the workplace of the future may show more positive "feminine" characteristics, especially in management: openness, sharing, collaboration rather

Perhaps the growing numbers of female supervisors and managers will bring a more effective, open, collaborative management style to U.S. business.

than competition, and participation instead of domination. Some neofeminists argue that such an approach will enhance a business environment now burdened with a hierarchical male culture that invests too much energy and time in the assertion of power and control. Others worry that distinguishing "feminine" and "masculine" styles will only reinforce stereotypes that lock women out of the top echelons of management.

On a more personal level, gender role liberation could lead to better physical and emotional health for both sexes, according to the *androgyny model*. An extensive body of research points to numerous benefits from the freedom to develop both expressive and instrumental personality features. In other words, androgyny would relieve women and men from the health problems associated with exclusively "feminine" and "masculine" modes of expression (Buss, 1990). Extreme masculinity, for example, has been linked with higher risk of coronary heart disease (Helgeson, 1990), stress (Saurer and Eisler, 1990), and lack of intimacy (Stark, 1991), among other things. Countless marital breakups have been blamed on the notoriously inexpressive "macho" male. And the limitations of the traditional feminine role have been linked with poor self-image, depression, ineffective coping styles, and eating disorders (Boggiano and Barrett, 1991; Frank, McLaughlin, and Crusco, 1984; Brems and Johnson, 1989; Barnett, 1986; Thornton, Leo, and Alberg, 1991). The androgyny model points to the best of both traditional gender roles as the prescription for better physical and psychological well-being.

The androgyny model has its critics. Proponents of the *traditional model* assert that gender role liberation would deprive women and men of the gender typing that provides their anchor for emotional health. They worry that androgynous tendencies lead women and men astray from the best road to contentment: the self-efficacy of the stereotypical masculine role (Bassoff and Glass, 1982; Whitley, 1984).

Critical Thinking Box

Possible Problems with Liberation

An attempt to predict the consequences of gender role liberation raises several questions. First, will women force changes in the generally male-dominated upper levels of the business world or will they have to adapt to the workplace if they are to compete beyond the middle-management level? Second, any "feminization" of the American work environment would involve more use of people skills and intuition rather than domination and control tactics. Would such an addition enhance or weaken American management, especially in light of growing global competition? Finally, will any continued blurring of gender roles usher in an era of better marital communication and generally healthier personalities, or will women's and men's liberation founder on biologically determined behavioral differences? ■

AGING AS A SOCIAL PROCESS: HOW DO SOCIAL FORCES AFFECT OUR LIFE PATH?

Age, like sex, serves as a basis of social differentiation. The Incas distinguished 10 age grades for males, the Andaman Islanders 23, each one according different rights and obligations (Linton, 1942; Tomashevich, 1981). And also like sex, age is largely determined by biological forces. Yet, as we shall see, the aging process is not entirely beyond our power of control.

Certainly biological factors cause hormones to rage and later subside, breasts to blossom and then sag, beards to sprout and later turn gray. But a complex web of social attitudes and expectations overlays the biological and chronological aspects of aging. In fact, aging may legitimately be seen as a social process, one in which we are classified and ranked according to how old we are. Thus, how we manage our lives through the years is greatly influenced by society's perceptions and expectations about people our age. For example, most cultures permit females to marry earlier and retire earlier than males (Cowgill, 1985). In Samoa, the aged enjoy considerable freedom from the usual rules of decorum; they may deliver long and rambling speeches at village meetings or perform lewd songs and dances at parties while the younger members of the community smile indulgently. Age, then, like sex, social class, and race, acts as a pervasive influence in our lives.

Shifting Social Perceptions of Aging

As we age, we become different people in the eyes of society. Each new age status carries with it a corresponding role, a constellation of expectations and rights. Most societies perceive children, for instance, as requiring control and protection. Once they take on adult status, however, they are expected to contribute to the economy, maintain economic independence, marry, and reproduce.

Social attitudes toward any particular age status change over time. For example, during the Middle Ages in Europe, children were seen simply as small adults, with no particularly special nature that distinguished them from grown-ups (Aries, 1962). As soon as they discarded swaddling clothes, children assumed the dress of men or women of their social class. And after infancy, they played the same games as adults: hide-and-seek, cards, dice, blind-man's bluff, and so on. Only by the 1600s and 1700s did Europeans begin to view children as a special social group with specific needs, including protection from sexual and economic exploitation. Beginning in upper-class families, children became objects of amusement for adults, who coddled them and gave them distinctive clothes and toys. Soon reformers and moralists argued that, because of their vulnerability, children required not simply free-flowing affection but constant tending. A concern for proper nurturing replaced a centuries-old indifference toward children, who gradually acquired a central place in the family. In recent years, children have gained more legal rights, accusing parents of abuse and choosing which parent—if any—with whom they will live after the parents divorce.

The status of elderly people likewise has changed with historical currents. In colonial America, age brought honor and respect. The aged were seen as founts of wisdom. Advanced age lost its luster between the Revolutionary War and the 1820s, when youth became regarded as more desirable (Fischer, 1978). Afterwards, especially with the rapid changes wrought by industrialization, the aged were increasingly seen as those who had lost energy, beauty, and the capacity to contribute to society.

Indeed, modernization generally brings a loss of status for the elderly (Cowgill, 1985). Industrialization and urbanization combine to weaken the integrity of the kin network in which the aged so often play a central role. Such developments also loosen parents' firm control over land, the source of power in preindustrial societies. Also, modernization's focus on new knowledge devalues the experiences of the aged, whose wisdom may be seen as obsolete. In classical Chinese society, the aged represented the most immediate ancestors and were thus revered; obedience to one's parents was a

Until a few hundred years ago in Western cultures, children were dressed essentially like small adults. Are we witnessing today a reversal, as many adults seem to take on the dress of the young?

sacred duty. The elderly in Thailand still receive many favors large and small because religious precepts encourage sons and daughters to accumulate spiritual assets by honoring the aged. Modernization substitutes such traditional views with a cult of youth and progress, so that in industrialized societies many elderly live in institutions permeated by boredom and purposeless behavior.

The negative modern image of old age reported by social workers, psychiatrists, and others who deal with the needy segment of the elderly faces challenge by a new image less well-defined but in some ways more positive. The population of seniors today includes a diverse group, both the "young–old" and the "old–old," the lively and the rocking-chair bound (Neugarten, 1973). Moreover, researchers are racing against the clock, seeking ways to make the later years of aging baby boomers more healthy—and less financially burdensome to society (Schmidt, 1993). Stereotypes will become increasingly inadequate in capturing the essense of old age.

Moving Through the "Life Course": Cultural Influences

Individuals do not enjoy full control over the social aging process any more than they do over the biological aging process. Cultural forces largely dictate when we become adults or seniors. For example, when do Americans make the transition to old age? Age 65? Full Medicare and Social Security payments have for years begun at this age, and statisticians routinely use this as the dividing line between middle age and old age, but this may change. As Peter Uhlenberg (1987) explains, government planners rather arbitrarily selected 65 during the 1930s, and recent government decisions indicate that the boundary for old age will probably shift upward. Congress decided in 1983 that full Social Security payments will eventually begin at age 67, and the mandatory retirement age for most jobs has moved to 70. And as Americans live longer and healthier lives, economic considerations will probably extend the old age boundary even further.

The sociological picture of aging includes much more than individuals simply moving through different age stages. Any person's "life course" can be viewed as a pattern of trajectories and transitions (Elder, 1985), largely socially determined. We trace such pathways along lines of employment, marriage, parenthood, self-esteem, and so on, each interwoven with the others and marked by transitions. The work-life trajectory, for example, can be marked by entry into the labor force, promotion, job loss, reentry into the labor force, and retirement.

Sociologists have identified some of the factors affecting life transitions, which brings us back to the notion that aging is not simply a biological or chronological process. The timing and sequence of life transitions, and our reactions to them, result from the interplay of such social forces.

Personal Background Affects Life Transitions   First, social background helps determine one's reaction to transitions such as job loss or parenthood. For example, people's social class largely influenced their adaptations and responses to the Great Depression (Elder, 1974). Family size influences whether one attends college or enters the labor force earlier. The timing of marriage depends in part on whether a person lived with one or two parents during adolescence: Growing up with a single parent is linked with early marriage (Goldscheider and Waite, 1986). Biological and psychological factors (such as cancer and depression) enter into the equation, as do the various social roles that compete for the individual's time and energy. Blair Wheaton (1990) finds, for example, that the stress of a life transition depends on one's gender and previous level of role stress.

Society Changes the Rules and the Schedule   Second, each individual's life course occurs within the context of broad social and historical events and trends. A woman's entry into the labor force, for example, can be greatly influenced by society's attitude toward employed women. Certainly the liberation movement of the 1970s sent many women's trajectories into new directions, as did the concomitant rise of the service economy (Wandersee, 1988). Similarly, the size of one's age cohort can affect the intensity of competition for jobs and mates, and thus work-life and marriage pathways.

Historical and social forces likewise change the normative schedule for transitions. For example, the dropping birth rate in recent decades has accelerated women's movement out of the parenthood stage. The Great Depression and World War II delayed the transition to full adulthood for men in both Japan and the United States (Hareven and Masaoka, 1988). In fact, during the first half of the twentieth century, Americans entered full adult status later in life because of industrialization, rising family incomes, compulsory schooling, and required military service (Hogan and Mochizuki, 1988). Americans now generally show less variation in the schedules of their life courses (for example, at what age they marry or retire) because of new school attendance rules, labor market changes, welfare policies, and retirement systems (Cooney and Hogan, 1991; Meyer, 1986; Mayer and Schoepflin, 1989).

The confluence of these factors helps explain an individual's life path and illustrates the social nature of aging. We now turn to an overall view of life stages in our society.

LIFE STAGES: WHAT CAN WE EXPECT?

Despite the broad social forces that shape our life transitions, each person follows a unique course. In fact, the longer we live, the more opportunities we have to become different from one another. Besides our particular social backgrounds and personal experiences, special events such as a debilitating accident or disease, winning the lottery, or losing a spouse unexpectedly contribute to our individuality. Not surprisingly, then, a study of high school graduates found that over half had "disorderly" life sequences, such as going back to school after entering the work world (Rindfuss, Swicegood, and Rosenfeld, 1987). And many "incompletely launched young adults" return to their parents' home after failing to establish a career (Schnaiberg and Goldenberg, 1986, 1989).

Notwithstanding such variations in life patterns, Daniel Levinson (1978), Gail Sheehy (1982), David Karp (1988), and many other researchers have discerned some broad outlines. Keeping in mind the inherent diversity in humans' genetic make-up and social experiences, their efforts help each of us to better anticipate the various trajectories of our own life course.

Adolescence

Those readers still in their teens, for example, may be surprised to learn that until the 1980s adolescence was viewed as a period of "storm and stress" (Hall, 1904). Erik Erikson (1959) characterized the teenage years as a time of identity crisis. Sociologists generally attributed the difficulties of adolescence to the clash of social changes in industrial societies with normal physical and psychological development (Gecas and Seff, 1990).

Researchers now find little evidence of the "generation gap" so widely described in the 1960s and 1970s.

By the 1980s, however, researchers found no particular turbulence or stress in the teen years (O'Malley and Bachman, 1983; Steinberg and Silverberg, 1986). In fact, in one study adolescents in 10 countries generally reported favorable attitudes toward their parents, themselves, and their futures (Offer et al., 1988). Parent–teen conflict typically arose in matters of appearance and taste, but with respect to educational goals, career plans, and other major issues, teenagers saw little "generation gap" (Bachman, Johnston, and O'Malley, 1987; Montemayor, 1984).

Even though adolescents' values often did not actually coincide with those of their parents, they *perceived* congruence, probably due to the general conservative climate of the 1980s (Gecas and Schwalbe, 1986; Whitbeck and Gecas, 1988), as opposed to the more adversarial one of the 1970s (Acock and Bengtson, 1980). Perceptions of any gap between two generations may depend more on the overall cultural climate than on the identification of their values.

Young and Middle Adulthood

Events such as completing school, entering the labor force, and establishing an independent household mark our transition into adulthood. The normative schedule for this transition is now less flexible or erratic than it was earlier in this century. This is because people increasingly have formed their own families and begun their careers more in response to the dictates of their own age norms rather than the needs of their original family (Modell, Furstenberg, and Hershberg, 1976; Hogan and Mochizuki, 1988). In the nineteenth century, for example, a man might delay schooling or marriage until he had fulfilled his obligations to his parents or orphaned siblings. A woman might not marry as long as a mother or sister required her care. While our own life schedule is not in lockstep with that of others the same age, it is likely to proceed in a somewhat more orderly, predictable way than was true a hundred years ago.

Young adulthood demands that we direct our personal resources toward career and family. Child care and job promotions engage our energies and time. Rather than stability, this stage simply brings more change and an array of hectic demands.

During the more thoroughly studied middle years (beginning in the mid-thirties), we can expect to take stock of our careers and other goals, launch our children on their own paths, and adjust to the beginnings of physical decline (Tamir, 1982). Indeed, this period rivals adolescence in terms of the biological, psychological, and social changes we will probably face (Stevens-Long, 1984).

For the middle-aged man, family becomes increasingly more important to life satisfaction than career (Rosenberg and Farrell, 1981; Levinson, 1977). He reevaluates his work role, looking more for intrinsic rewards and satisfying interpersonal relationships than for external measures of success (McKenry et al., 1987; Tamir, 1982). No longer feeling pressured to fulfill the "good provider" role, many middle-aged men begin to develop some of their inherent "feminine" personality traits, such as affiliation and expressiveness. Researchers generally see this androgynous tendency, this reappraisal of traditional masculine values and traits, as healthy and adaptive (Rosenberg and Farrell, 1981; Gutmann, 1987).

While the midlife transition likewise offers women the benefits of androgyny, it also involves menopause and new work-role decisions. The decrease in the female hormones estrogen and progesterone can bring on a number of physical and cognitive changes, including hot flashes, sleeplessness, irritability, migraine headaches, and short-term memory loss. Though many women suffer few if any such difficulties, for

After concentrating on breadwinning for many years, middle-aged men often shift their focus to family and other expressive ties.

"What is it, Leonard? What happened to your lust for life?"

Drawing by Saxon; © 1983 The New Yorker Magazine, Inc.

some the symptoms can be severe. And unlike men, women in middle age have fewer employment opportunities if they are married or have children (Sorensen, 1983; Waite, 1980).

Middle age also usually brings a reorganization of marriage and family relationships. The problems associated with parenting adolescents contribute to marital discord (Pasley and Gecas, 1984; Umberson, 1989). As children leave home and the family contracts, the remaining members must make adjustments to a smaller household and establish new relationships with the independent offspring. When adult offspring remain financially dependent or chronically unemployed, parent–child conflict easily arises (Aquilino and Supple, 1991).

The plethora of changes confronting people in middle age may trigger what has been popularized as a "midlife crisis." While some researchers have found evidence of increased personal disorganization in middle-aged men and women, others find that this stage is characterized by satisfying adaptation (Julian, McKenry, and Arnold, 1990). The contradictions in the research suggest that a midlife crisis is not universally experienced. Our chances of going through such a crisis depend on how successfully we deal with the challenges of this life stage.

By late middle age, the children have left home and we face the "empty nest." According to the popular image, we should expect loneliness and a sense of abandonment. Indeed, social scientists once described this "empty nest syndrome" as one of role loss, accompanied by alienation and dissatisfaction (Phillips, 1957) and depression (Curlee, 1969; Bart, 1972). More recently, however, cross-national data indicate that release from the stressful parent role brings relief and increased life and marital satisfaction (Glenn and McLanahan, 1982; Menaghan, 1983; McLanahan and Sorensen, 1985). In fact, marital happiness increases when the offspring leave home, but parents still benefit from frequent contact with those children (White and Edwards, 1990). Overall, studies show a U-shaped pattern of marital satisfaction: high levels during the early (prechildren) stage, low during the years of parenting adolescents, and higher when the children are older or independent (Rollins and Cannon, 1974; Anderson, Russell, and Schumm, 1983). Empty-nesters still in their first marriage are generally the happiest pairs of all, having weathered storms together and come to a deeper understanding of each other (Sheehy, 1982).

Due to the greater longevity of today's population, late middle age has come to include more responsibility for elderly parents. Typically, adult siblings weigh one another's resources and competing responsibilities to arrive at some agreement regarding care for the parents; both the elderly parents and the offspring usually try as much as possible to avoid institutional care (Doty, Liu, and Wiener, 1985).

Care for frail elderly parents falls disproportionately on female offspring. For every son that takes on the main responsibilities, there are four daughters who do so (Brody, 1990). A survey found that 72 percent of the primary, informal caregivers of incapacitated elderly persons were female (Stone, Cafferata, and Sangl, 1987), a pattern that holds true whether or not the parent lives in a nursing home or the daughter is employed (Brody, Dempsey, and Pruchno, 1990; Matthews and Rosner, 1988). This caregiving interferes with daughters' daily schedules, vacations, and other personal matters, and is especially stressful for those who aren't married (Brody et al., 1992; Kleban et al., 1989). For the many middle-aged divorced women in today's population, with its growing number of elderly parents, this paints a somber picture of late middle age.

Old Age

If we reach old age, our probable life course traces an even more complex pattern. Despite the heterogeneity of the elderly population, we may find in researchers' descriptions some portent of our own old-age experience, at least with respect to material needs and socioemotional health.

Meeting Material Needs   In hunting and gathering societies, such as the Bushmen of the Kalihari Desert in southern Africa, elderly women retain their status as experts in finding berries and tubers in the desolate landscape, and old men still assume decision-making power regarding distribution of meat and selection of new hunting areas (Thomas, 1959). Also, in agrarian societies the aged can participate in the economy for many years. An Ibo man in Nigeria, for example, accumulates land and wives so that in old age he may be able to live off the toil of his descendants, spending his time visiting friends and engaging in leadership functions. In traditional Corsica, the elder male, as owner of all animals and land, enjoyed complete economic power in his household (Cool, 1980). Similarly, a Sidamo girl in Ethiopia hopes to work her way up the hierarchy as she ages. If she gives birth to many sons, they will bring many daughters-in-law under her control, and she may even demand that a grandchild be given to her to serve her (Hamer, 1972).

In the United States, our economic power in old age is less predictable. Although sociologists in the past routinely listed the elderly among the high-poverty categories, today's older generation enjoys more wealth than any in recent history. Over the past several years, the poverty rate for the aged has consistently been lower than that for the general population. Rising Social Security benefits, indexed to inflation, along with private pensions account for the elderly's improved standard of living. Mark Hayward (1990) reports that one man in three returns to work within a few years after retirement. This is especially likely among those who retired early and those with general rather than highly specialized skills. White-collar workers usually go back to work for the satisfaction of the job rather than out of financial need.

In contrast to the comfortably retired, the aged poor are especially vulnerable to illness, isolation, homelessness, and other difficulties. Barriers such as lack of transportation or information and feelings of humiliation prevent many from utilizing various health and social services (Yeatts, Crow, and Folts, 1992). Services for the elderly do not easily reach the homeless (Cohen et al., 1988; Cohen, Onserud, and Monaco, 1992) who, perhaps, are consequently more likely to suffer from isolation and mental disorganization (Keigher and Greenblatt, 1992). For the aged who are poor and alone, housing alternatives usually range from substandard, unsafe homes to the streets or emergency shelters, and nursing homes if they are infirm. Not surprisingly, most hold on to the typically inadequate arrangements with which they are familiar.

Which scenario awaits us? Personal efforts aside, our own financial fate depends on several factors beyond our control, such as economic inflation (which diminishes the value of our savings), the changing profile of the labor market, our evolving health care system, and the baby boom generation, which threatens to overwhelm the Social Security system.

Poor or not, we will probably not live in a nursing home. The elderly, like others, prefer to live independently, either alone or with their spouse. Over half of all unmarried people in old age manage to maintain their own household, and the rate has risen in recent years. Such an arrangement affords privacy and a feeling of autonomy, but is available only for those with sufficient economic resources (Mutchler and Burr, 1989, 1991). Approximately 30 percent of the elderly are on their own, most of them women whose survival rates are not negatively affected by living alone, as are men's (Davis et al., 1992).

If independent living is not possible, usually the next choice is to reside with offspring or other family members. Depending on their resources and needs, older people can either contribute significantly to the household or impose burdensome demands. Those family members who take on this responsibility sometimes become overwhelmed by the associated claims on their time, money, and energy. The result can be "elder abandonments," or "granny dumping" (Beck and Gordon, 1991). Hospital emergency rooms report a growing number of old persons being dropped off by family members who give fake addresses or simply need to get away for the weekend and have no place to put granny in the meantime.

Nursing homes represent for most people the least desirable living arrangement. Financial resources play a relatively small role in this decision. When family care becomes inadequate, placement into a nursing home is usually determined by poor health (Mutchler and Burr, 1991), not poverty or abandonment. A 1987 federal law required nursing homes to establish a plan to improve or at least maintain each resident's health and abilities. The legislation also specified certain rights for patients, so that nursing home procedures would increasingly be based on their comforts rather than the staff's convenience.

Along with residential arrangements, transportation will predict life satisfaction in our old age. It provides independence, a wide range of options for social participation, and access to services. Stephen Cutler and Raymond Coward (1992) found, however, that personal transportation becomes less available with age. Inner-city residents and women are especially likely to lack access to private vehicles.

Socioemotional Well-Being   The losses and difficulties of old age—including physical dysfunction, low personal control, and losses in marriage, employment, and finances—seem to preclude happiness in this last life stage. Depression reaches its highest level in adults past their seventies, especially women (Mirowsky and Ross, 1992; Berry, Storandt, and Coyne, 1984). Widowhood, for example, leads to difficulties with household management for men and financial strains for women (Umberson, Wortman, Kessler, 1992). Suicide, especially among those in nursing homes, not uncommonly follows major losses such as that of a spouse or child (Osgood, Brant, and Lipman, 1990). The elderly may also suffer physical and psychological abuse as well as financial exploitation (Shapiro, 1992).

Such sad ends, however, do not necessarily await all those in this last life stage. For example, worrying does not necessarily beset the elderly to any greater degree than younger people (Powers, Wisocki, and Whitbourne, 1992). Even the generally dreaded entry into a nursing home does not necessarily lead to unhappiness; adjustment depends greatly on the individual's control over the decision (Reinardy, 1992). In any event, coping efficiency tends to increase with advancing age, and morale does not generally diminish until health fails (Gove, Ortega, and Style, 1989; Meeks et al., 1989).

Another determinant of adjustment in old age is sex-role orientation. We have long known that males are socialized to use more effective, problem-focused coping strategies. More recently, the research focus has shifted from sex to gender role. Women and men with more instrumental personality traits use more externalized coping strategies while those with "feminine" personalities use more "turning-against-self" coping defenses (Long, 1989; Lobel and Winch, 1986; Blanchard-Fields, Sulsky, and Robinson-Whelen, 1991).

Despite the influence of such personal variables, old age does not free us from the effects of the social environment. On a large scale, when many people reach old age at the same time, they enjoy the benefits of bigger voting constituencies and larger, more powerful lobbying groups (South and Tolnay, 1992). Lower suicide and mortality rates result. On a smaller, more personal scale, elderly who participate in a rich social context of volunteer work, clubs, and multiple roles usually enjoy better health than those with few social contacts (Moen, Dempster-McClain, and Williams, 1992). While a sister can often be an important helpmate (O'Bryant, 1988), "the most important resource a frail elder can have is responsible and caring children" (Matthews and Rosner, 1988, p. 185). Indeed, children link the elderly to not only grandchildren but other relatives as well (Johnson and Troll, 1992).

A SOCIOLOGICAL GUIDE TO GROWING OLD AND DYING IN AMERICA

Most of us consciously intend to live well. What does sociology have to tell us about successfully growing old and, in life's last challenge, dying well?

As we enter old age, we will probably acquire a new minority group status because of **ageism,** social attitudes and stereotypes that devalue old age and the elderly (Butler, 1987). Such prejudice is mixed with other elements; this mushrooming segment of the population attracts both pity and jealousy, sympathy and rejection. Robert Binstock (1985), for example, describes "compassionate ageism," by which the elderly are seen as helpless and deserving of special care. On the other hand, television portrayals of elderly people as extremely healthy and active, along with the greatly improved

Drawing by Anthony; © 1983 The New Yorker Magazine, Inc.

Ageism: social attitudes and stereotypes that devalue old age and the elderly.

financial status of the aged as a group, have produced what Erdmore Palmore (1990) labels "positive ageism."

Society's apparently confused perceptions of old age rest partly on the lack of a clear role for the elderly. Society assigns few responsibilities or obligations to the old. The role carries few directions, goals, or links with other roles. We therefore have few criteria with which to judge the appropriateness of an old person's behaviors or demands. As we age, we may interpret this rolelessness as either freedom or confusion.

The Importance of Roles

Throughout our lives, roles give meaning and guidance to our existence, provide us with a sense of self, and relate us to society. The more roles we have, the greater our well-being. According to *role theory*, the lifelong aging process initially involves acquiring roles, then making role transitions and, finally, losing roles. Irving Rosow (1973), who applied role theory to aging, argues that the role loss of old age brings a corresponding social isolation and decline in self-esteem. Leaving school, establishing a family, and entering the labor force all lead to social growth early in life, earning one increasingly more responsibility, authority, and prestige. In old age, we not only stop gaining such social rewards, we begin losing them. As Rosow explains, the sting is worse because the losses beset old people not due to any failure on their part but simply because they have survived.

Role loss at any time usually carries stress, but in old age we face irreversible losses due to forces beyond our control in a very short period of time and without clear guidelines as to how to handle the strains. Anxiety, boredom, and reduced self-esteem can easily ensue. Diminished contact with society makes us feel depreciated, marginal, and alienated.

Combining role theory with *activity theory*, gerontologists recommend that we hold onto social relationships as we age. They note that old people's self-evaluation depends mostly on social interaction, which provides an "inoculation" against isolation attending role loss (Pilisuk, 1982). The biggest losses accrue at three points: retirement, death of one's spouse, and the onset of poor health. All of these events tend to cut one off from the wider world of social interaction. By savoring, nurturing, and maintaining our social relationships, then, we can to some extent protect ourselves as we lose roles and loved ones.

Disengagement Is Not Inevitable

According to *disengagement theory*, the elderly voluntarily withdraw from society, most significantly from work and child-rearing roles (Cummings et al., 1960). As they seek fewer social contacts, interaction becomes more expressive and less norm-directed. Older people thus gain freedom from new roles and responsibilities, but at the expense of becoming increasingly isolated, caught in a cycle of disengagement.

Unfortunately, by describing the aging process for *some* people, disengagement theory may have negatively shaped the experience for many more by influencing those who have entered this supposedly irreversible process. Taking the theory's "hint," many old people may see themselves as sliding into what seems an inevitable decline once they lose a spouse or some physical capabilities: a self-fulfillment prophecy. Though we can guard against this psychological trap, the onset of ill health often initiates disengagement (Palmore, 1981), and social forces may conspire to force the elderly to withdraw.

Perhaps society makes the elderly an offer they can't refuse. From the functionalist viewpoint, society has a stake in moving the elderly off the stage. A fully functioning system requires the most able players to fill important roles, and must assure the next generation that rigorous preparation and training will be rewarded with prestigious and satisfying social positions. To prevent a social bottleneck, therefore, incentives such as pensions and release from responsibilities are provided to the elderly to disengage and relinquish their roles.

But do the elderly reap compensating benefits from their "voluntary" retirement? Some are given a "golden handshake" and shoved aside with inadequate pensions; others receive a one-way ticket to the nursing home. All too often, disengagement theory is used to simply justify abandonment of the old.

Anticipating Challenges

Various theories suggest that we all face certain stages of psychological development. For example, Erik Erikson's eight "ages of man" (1963, 1968, 1982) point to inherent predispositions toward specific changes. In each of Erikson's stages, the individual faces a challenge or crisis in social relationships. Failure to cope with these challenges can warp or arrest further psychological development. Successful coping produces

An intergenerational clash arises when the elderly are percieved as non-contributing but demanding ever-more entitlements.

ERIKSON'S LIFE STAGES

LIFE STAGE	PSYCHOSOCIAL CRISIS
Infancy	**Trust versus mistrust.** During the first year of life, the infant learns whether or not the world will dependably provide for her or his needs.
Early childhood	**Autonomy versus shame, doubt.** During the second and third years, the child develops a sense of control, especially over his or her body.
Play age	**Initiative versus guilt.** The development of language and imagination predominate during the next three years.
School age	**Industry versus inferiority.** A feeling of competence develops as the child learns culture's rules and how to accomplish tasks successfully.
Adolescence	**Identity versus identity, confusion.** The individual must grapple with important physical and emotional changes in an effort to build a stable sense of self.
Young adulthood	**Intimacy versus isolation.** The major task is to develop intimate relationships.
Adulthood	**Generativity versus stagnation.** Middle age takes one beyond personal needs to a concern for society and future generations.
Old age	**Integrity versus despair.** Success in past stages makes it easier for the individual to contemplate his or her past with satisfaction.

Figure 8-1

According to Erikson, individuals go through psychosocial crises during specific periods of their lives. Each crisis can either be resolved satisfactorily or create potential difficulties for future stages. Successful completion of each stage produces a more positive conception of self as well as increased ability to cope with challenges in the next stage.

Source: Adapted from *The Life Cycle Completed, a Review,* by Erik H. Erikson, by permission of W.W. Norton and Company, Inc. Copyright © 1982 by Rikan Enterprises, Ltd.

greater maturity and a healthier self. By recognizing these crises, we can increase our chances for dealing with them and aging successfully.

As Figure 8-1 shows, old age represents our last challenge, the last chance to effectively cope with society's demands. This stage revolves around the issue of "ego integrity versus despair." Integrity consists of acceptance of one's life experience as appropriate and meaningful. If we negotiate old age well, our final years bring a sense of wisdom and self-fulfillment; we face death without regret or fear. Otherwise, old age brings despair and dissatisfaction with what we have done with our lives.

Carl Jung (1958) and Daniel Levinson and his colleagues (1978), among others, have followed Erikson's lead, describing a drive for accomplishments during adulthood and more reflection and contemplation in old age. More recently, Carol Ryff (1985) and Walter Gove, Suzanne Ortega, and Carolyn Style (1989) have found evidence that the social environment provides the sequential challenges through which the individual must pass while constructing a self.

Preparing for Conflict

Conflict theorists argue that, like other groups, the elderly are victims of oppression. Compulsory retirement represents a way to reduce the costs of labor by replacing older, usually more highly paid workers with younger ones. It enables the managers of the capitalist economy to reject anyone perceived as increasingly unproductive or expensive. Critics point out that noncapitalist societies have stigmatized older workers as less productive, and that socialist nations often share the same negative stereotypes and assumptions about the elderly. Still, whenever advancing age forces people out of the work force, the power of society to shape our late years is unmistakably revealed.

The conflict viewpoint also highlights the hostility fostered by society between the old and the non-old. Bryan Turner (1989) uses *exchange theory* to explain the foundation for this intergenerational conflict. He notes that exchange, a reciprocal giving and taking, characterizes all social interaction. Those who are dependent, who do not fully support themselves financially, attract the scorn and resentment of those supporting them. Thus "the aged become stigmatized as parasitic recipients of social benefits" (p. 600). Because Social Security and private pensions do not cover the needs of most retired people, especially if they retire early and live a long time, they are perceived as taking much more than they ever gave.

Although the elderly are generally seen as nonproductive, their numbers and political power are growing, and their expanding claims on entitlements put them in competition with other citizens. The Census Bureau reported three million people over age 85 in 1990. But in 2031, the first of the baby boom cohort will turn 85, and the number in that age category will swell to 17.8 million by 2040. The mushrooming costs of old-age pensions and health care will be born largely by the non-old. We can expect the clashes arising from such competition for resources to intensify during periods of economic stagnation or slow growth.

This intergenerational conflict is perhaps most dramatically portrayed in the work of Daniel Callahan (1987, 1990), who opposes expensive, life-prolonging care for terminally ill old people. He argues for a health care policy that focuses less on end-of-life treatment and cures than on preventive medicine and care for the young. As debate flares around proposals for age-based rationing of health services, attitudes toward the elderly may become more negative.

"Dying Well"

Cultural forces affect how we die as much as how we live. While our ability to accept or even welcome impending death certainly depends on previous personal experiences, it also is influenced by our culture's conceptions of dying and life after death. If, like people in preindustrial societies, we want to die honorably, suffer as little as possible, and face good prospects for a desirable afterlife (Simmons, 1960), we might profit by comparing death in those societies with our own.

First, in cultures that envision a joyful afterlife, the anticipation of death holds less fear. Traditional Samoans, for example, were so certain of a beautiful life beyond death that if an aged man could not die gloriously in battle, he might ask for the honor of a live burial to hasten things along. Normal funeral services included eulogies and the exchange of property, usually pigs, but in these special cases the honored one was still alive to enjoy the proceedings. After thus showering honors upon him, his children and friends lowered him into a round, deep pit, covered him with mats, and filled his grave with dirt, suffocating him at what might well be the high point of his life in this world, sending him to what he fully believed would be an even better one.

Second, premodern societies forthrightly accept the reality of death. Most people become familiar with death as they watch their loved ones die, prepare their corpses, and bury them. In fact, the elderly sometimes actually ask their offspring to help them die. In traditional Eskimo culture, for instance, a man no longer able to hunt and provide for himself might ask his oldest son or favorite daughter to put a rope around his neck and hang him. A woman might ask for a dagger in the heart. These honors would usually be administered at the climax of a party honoring the person about to die.

In contrast, few of us become familiar with death because it is regarded as taboo, usually taking place in a segregated, bureaucratized setting. We rarely nurse dying family members, and do not touch the corpse, leaving these duties instead to strangers—nurses, physicians, and morticians. In fact, the only dead people many of us see are made to appear as if they are only asleep. The dying are set apart, almost as though death is contagious or an embarrassment for the rest of us. Such experiences socialize us to approach our own death alone, quietly, without bothering others with our fears or misgivings. Beyond encouraging us to anticipate an afterlife, our culture offers little help in accepting the reality of our own approaching death. Perhaps by normalizing death, by not denying its reality, we too can learn to "die well" in the United States.

Critical Thinking Box

A "Duty to Die"?

Do the elderly ill have "a duty to die" to make way for the young? Due to the rapidly growing number of such people and the skyrocketing medical costs to maintain them, this deeply troubling question will confront us with increasing urgency as we enter the twenty-first century. Some argue that the enormous resources required, for example, to provide organ transplants to those in their eighties effectively usurps medical treatment from those who have not yet lived one decade. The costs of preventive care for children and infants comes nowhere close to those needed to prolong the lives of persons of advanced years. Financial considerations may force us to consider age in rationing medical care. Would such age discrimination be justified? ■

SUMMARY

Social rankings are based on such factors as age and *gender*, culturally determined distinctions of men and women. If our culture were based on *androgyny*—that is, if there were no sex-related cultural restrictions on an individual's personality—we would have no *gender roles*, behavior patterns considered appropriate for each sex. To some extent, gender differentiation seems biologically rooted, as suggested by the widespread *sexual division of labor*, the separation of work into distinct specializations deemed appropriate for males and females. The bases for this division of labor, however, are relatively weak. Instead, many gender differences seem to result from *gender role socialization*, the process by which females and males are taught behaviors and attitudes considered appropriate to their sex. Through this process, individuals develop a *gender identity*, a sense of being male or female. Conflict theorists contend that this socialization supports a *capitalist patriarchy*, in which notions of male supremacy and capitalism combine to exclude women from prestigious occupations. Functionalists argue that, at least in the past, families functioned most effectively when men played *instrumental roles* focusing on goal achievement and economic security and women played *expressive roles* by providing an emotionally satisfying atmosphere for the family. The variations found among cultures attests to the influence of social forces on gender roles.

Despite some improvements in their social condition in the United States, women still suffer economic discrimination. One explanation is that they accumulate less *human capital:* productive, highly valued personality traits. Other studies find strong evidence of sex discrimination, perhaps based on capitalist patriarchy, the economic subordination of women. Females also face barriers in school and in politics, where they function largely as outsiders. Women's minority status is rooted in *sexism,* the prejudiced belief that males are innately superior to females. As women's liberation brings more political power and employment opportunities, pressure is building for changes in the domestic division of labor and in the nature of the workplace.

Social forces strongly influence the aging process. First, social perceptions of age roles change over time. Second, both our personal backgrounds and society's changing rules and schedules affect the transitions of our life trajectories or pathways.

Each life stage holds certain general expectations. Adolescence is no longer fraught with serious stress or feelings of a "generation gap." Our entry into young adulthood is increasingly orderly, and brings an array of hectic demands. The middle years are characterized by tremendous changes regarding work and family roles, and possible problems related to menopause for women. A midlife crisis is not inevitable; in fact, the empty nest phase can bring relief and happiness, although more of us will be burdened with demands to care for aged parents. Economic security for the elderly has improved in recent years, but great inequalities remain. Residential arrangements for the elderly usually do not include nursing homes. Such factors as strong social support can help protect socioemotional well-being in old age.

Entering old age brings us a new minority status based on *ageism,* social attitudes and stereotypes that devalue old age and the elderly. To age successfully, the sociological literature suggests that we maintain our social roles, beware the self-fulfilling prophecy of disengagement theory, anticipate the developmental challenges that confront most of us, and prepare for the conflict of either economic abandonment by the capitalist system or of clashing generations. Other cultures show us that dying well depends on belief in a joyful afterlife and familiarity with and acceptance of death's reality.

Key Terms

gender	gender role	instrumental role
gender roles	socialization	human capital
androgyny	gender identity	sexism
sexual division of	capitalist patriarchy	ageism
labor	expressive role	

9

Chapter

FAMILY

"Family" figures prominently in most people's life plans. As we will see, however, the word increasingly holds varying connotations for us. We will also explore the deterioration of the American family, the determinants of marital satisfaction, the impact of divorce, and the special problems of stepfamilies.

WHAT DOES "FAMILY" MEAN?

Overarching social changes have stretched our conceptions of what "family" means. A century and a half ago, Americans were likely to include not only parents and children but grandparents, cousins, and others related by blood: the **extended family.** Only a couple of decades ago, the notion of family had narrowed to refer to one or two parents and any unmarried offspring: the **nuclear family.**

As we have narrowed our definition of the size of the family, however, we have simultaneously broadened our image of the forms that fit into that category. The Census Bureau defines **family** as "two or more persons related by birth, marriage, or adoption and residing together in a household" (U. S. Bureau of the Census, 1991, p. 5). Sociologists would add that these people form an economic unit. And court rulings and government policies have helped extend the meaning of "family" to cover single parents and cohabiting couples who are unmarried.

Extended family: those related by blood.

Nuclear family: one or two parents and their unmarried offspring.

Family: group of people related by blood, marriage, or adoption who form an economic and household unit.

The Tiwi: Polygyny and Zero Illegitimacy

Anthropologist C. W. M. Hart's description of the Tiwi in the late 1920s (Hart and Pilling, 1960) reminds us how notions of family vary through time and space. Like other isolated peoples, the Tiwi had long envisioned themselves as the only humans in the world, one consisting simply of their own islands and the northern coast of Australia 25 miles away. Another of their beliefs, that human conception occurs through a spirit entering the woman's body, led to some unique living arrangements.

Since a spirit might plant a baby in a woman at any time, the Tiwis determined that every female, no matter what her age, must be married. By providing a husband for every female, from ancient crones to newborn girls, the Tiwis attained

The Tiwi, like most societies, permit a man to have more than one wife. Indeed, polygyny is the most widely preferred form of marriage in the world, although most men can afford only one wife.

Polygamy: marriage form involving several spouses for either the husband or the wife.

Polygyny: form of polygamy in which the husband has more than one wife.

Polyandry: form of polygamy in which the wife has more than one husband.

Patriarchy: family system placing authority in the hands of the husband or, in the case of the extended family, the eldest male of the household.

Matriarchy: family system placing authority in the hands of women.

Patrilineal: tracing ancestry through the father.

Matrilineal: tracing ancestry through the mother.

zero illegitimacy. They also created huge households, dramatic examples of **polygamy** (several spouses per person), or more precisely, **polygyny** (multiple wives per husband), the world's most popular marital form. (The other option, **polyandry,** or multiple husbands per wife, occurs rarely.)

A few Tiwi males accumulated over 20 wives; many had a dozen. These arrangements resulted from the mechanisms of infant betrothal and widow remarriage played out in a complex game of status competition among males. A father could betroth his infant daughter to another man as part of a swap, or to curry the other man's favor and indebt him. Or the infant might be promised to an up-and-coming young man, who might later be in a position to help the father-in-law in his old age. After being so marked as a young man with a future, other infants would soon come his way. Widows, useful for food production and housekeeping, would be married off by their sons or brothers in other strategies involving exchange and alliance.

Clearly, the Tiwi family system was based on **patriarchy,** wherein authority is vested in the husband or the eldest male of the household. Women had little say in their marriage partner. Instead, they served as pawns and prizes in the men's competition to accumulate wives and thus earn distinction as a "big man." Unlike some so-called patriarchal societies, where domestic realities actually suggest a **matriarchy,** Hart reported no instances of women wielding power behind the scenes. Male power and importance was also seen in their **patrilineal** social structure; the men, and of course their wives and children, traced their ancestry through their fathers. A **matrilineal** system, in which ancestry is traced through mothers, was impossible because a Tiwi woman gained a new name every time she was widowed, and this might easily happen five or six times.

Can we travel through time and space to the Tiwi society over 60 years ago and acknowledge their household arrangements as "families"? Such a mental feat requires cultural relativism. Immersed as we are in a culture of **monogamy** (one spouse per person), **bilateral descent** rules (ancestry traced through both parents), and a tendency toward **egalitarianism** (equal sharing of power between spouses), can we define the Tiwi system as a valid form of family? Perhaps this is easy; after all, this was a different time and place, and thus we can be more tolerant. But what about exotically different family forms today, in our own society?

How Far Can We Stretch the Definition of "Family"?

A woman in her late thirties has established a career, but has found no acceptable choice for a husband. Her strong desire to become a mother prompts her to use donor insemination to bear a child. Alternatively, like many other single parents, she could adopt a child, probably one with special needs. Either way, she joins a growing number of older, financially stable women who help account for the 60 percent surge in single mothers over the last decade. Eventually, she will explain to her child that theirs is one of many family forms outside the traditional definition of family.

Homosexuals can use the same methods to acquire a child. In very rare instances, adoption agencies have allowed "joint adoption," awarding same-sex partners equal legal rights regarding the child. A lesbian couple can also use donor insemination to become parents. Are these valid family forms?

Since 1970, the rates of cohabitation (unmarried couples living together) have risen so dramatically that today about half of all recently married couples have already lived together (Bumpass and Sweet, 1989). Some of these unions last for years, and may include children. Do they constitute families?

Clearly, some Americans view such diverse domestic arrangements as families. One recent survey by a life insurance company found a large majority of Americans agree that a family is "a group of people who love and care for each other" (Ames et

Monogamy: one spouse per person at any one time.

Bilateral descent: tracing ancestry through both parents.

Egalitarianism: when applied to the family, the equal sharing of power between spouses.

Our image of the American family may require stretching to include gay parents with their children.

al., 1992). Is defining what family means simply a matter of eliminating unnecessary or outmoded criteria? Can we go as far as to say that family means for people whatever they say it means?

Who Should Get Marital Rights?

The recent explosion in cohabitation rates has forced the question: Should unmarried couples residing together receive all the benefits accorded married couples? Supporters argue that "domestic partnerships" fulfill all the functions of marriages and thus deserve legal recognition to end discrimination against such people. Some companies and local governments have agreed to extend to domestic partners the same health insurance, sick leave, bereavement leave, and other benefits available to married employees. Critics, however, fear such official endorsement threatens the institution of marriage. Why make an official commitment as spouse and potentially as parent if one can enjoy the benefits of marriage without the legal responsibilities? Moreover, such inclusive policies would open the door for possible fraud. An employee could agree to allow a friend to claim "domestic partner" status simply to grant that friend health insurance coverage.

The gay liberation movement has also brought this issue to the forefront, as a sizeable minority of cohabiting couples are homosexual. Some gay couples share their lives as fully as do heterosexual married couples, but because they cannot obtain marriage licenses they do not enjoy the legal benefits of marriage. Since most Americans still view homosexuality as an unacceptable alternative life style (Hugick, 1992), homosexual demands for legal marital status have found little support among the general public.

Should domestic partnerships be granted legal status? Do they undermine the social order or can they simply be viewed as part of the new family diversity, which has no room for intolerance? ■

HAS THE AMERICAN FAMILY DETERIORATED IN RECENT DECADES?

Many of us yearn for the "good old days" when families seemed to provide stability and security. Actually, they also featured dictatorial fathers and husbands, tremendous pressure to marry, limited choices in a marital partner or in the framework of the relationship, and little opportunity to escape an unhappy or violent marriage. While some bemoan the state of the family today and see only disaster for the next generation, others welcome modern freedoms as a measure of progress. Still the American family appears to be sinking beneath waves of tumultuous change, breaking into fragments inadequate for meeting many people's personal and social needs. The statistics usually offered as evidence of the family's decline are indeed alarming, but we can put them in perspective by comparing American family trends with those of Sweden, a country famous for pushing the boundary of what "family" means.

Rate per 1,000 population

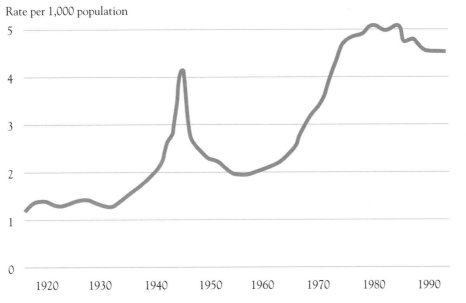

Figure 9-1

DIVORCE IN THE UNITED STATES, 1920–1990

Source: Based on U. S. Bureau of the Census *Historical Statistics of the United States, Colonial Times to 1970, Bicentennial Edition, Part 2*, Washington, DC, 1975, and *Statistical Abstract: 1992* (112th edition), Washington, DC, 1992.

Disruption and Violence

Rising divorce rates seem to offer the clearest and most dramatic evidence of the American family's disintegration. As Figure 9-1 shows, the divorce rate in the United States increased slightly after World War I, shot up after World War II, and rose sharply again after the creation of no-fault divorce laws in the 1970s. Other modern societies have experienced similar trends, though our divorce rates still top others. To illustrate, about 36 percent of Swedes born in 1945 are expected to divorce. This fairly substantial rate (matched by similar ones in Denmark, England, and Wales) does not measure up to the 42 percent rate of Americans that age. According to one estimate, about two-thirds of recent marriages in the United States will not last (Martin and Bumpass, 1989). Even though our divorce rates have stabilized, as have those of Sweden, they may still suggest an overall decline of the family. Likewise, news accounts of family violence seem to indicate a breakdown of our domestic order. Do these two disturbing indicators prove that the American family is deteriorating?

Divorce as Today's Way of Terminating Marriage   Throughout the history of Western civilization, there have been ways to end marriages. For example, divorce in ancient Greece and Rome was common. A man could end his marital responsibilities simply by returning his wife to her parents along with the property she brought into the marriage. Wealthy Roman men typically married several times, freely exercising divorce as a male prerogative.

The advent of Christianity removed the divorce option. The Catholic Church regarded (and still regards) marriage as a sacred union that should not be broken. People still required some means of escaping unhappy marriages, however, and the Church offered two ways. In limited divorce, which today we would call legal separation, the couple could live apart but not remarry. Annulment, which declared that the marriage never existed, freed the individuals to remarry. The Catholic Church still grants annulments, as do civil courts, but until new criteria went into effect in 1977, annulments through the Church were difficult to obtain. Beginning in the sixteenth century, the new Protestant churches viewed marriage as a civil contract which could be broken for very serious reasons, such as adultery, cruelty, or desertion.

Many couples avoided such difficulties through informal wedding ceremonies without the Church's blessing, sometimes consisting of simple spoken vows and an exchange of gifts or the snapping of a silver coin in two. Such nonlegal unions, or common law marriages, have for centuries served as a popular means to avoid legal entanglements, especially for the poor. Leaving such a "marriage" was often accomplished by simply walking out. Alternatively, in Medieval England, the husband could sell his wife in the village marketplace, usually to her lover, and thus free himself from responsibility (Stone, 1990).

From the historical perspective, then, recent increases in divorce rates do not seem so alarming. The desertion rates of generations past, had they been tabulated, would probably have elicited far louder cries about the decline of marriage. Also, death at a relatively early age once effectively broke up marriages just as divorce does today. One could thus view the record-breaking divorce rates of the last two decades as the replacement of desertion and death with a more common means of terminating a marriage. For convincing proof of the deterioration of America's family, we must look elsewhere.

Is Increased Violence Tearing the Family's Fabric?   With dismaying regularity, headlines in the United States today report violence among family members. Looking beyond those dramatic cases, sociologists estimate that wives are occasionally beaten in 16 percent of families, regularly battered in 3.4 percent (Straus and Gelles, 1988). From 2 percent to 5 percent of children also suffer abuse (Straus and Gelles, 1986; Kaufman and Zigler, 1987). Sexual abuse in the form of parent–child incest is, not surprisingly, underreported, but it is estimated to affect 3 percent of female children and 2 percent of males. This is about one-fifth the rate of sibling incest, reported by 15 percent of female and 10 percent of male college students in one study (Finkelhor, 1980). Abuse occurs in every conceivable form among family members, from wives beating their husbands to children beating their parents or grandparents. It is more likely to occur in association with alcohol and other drugs, inequality and privacy in the home (Williams, 1992), young marriage partners, and large families (Straus and Sweet, 1992). While comparable Swedish statistics are difficult to come by, we can wonder if abuse levels are lower in the first nation to legally forbid parents to hit their children.

However they compare to other countries, family abuse and violence surely act as a destructive force in our society. They produce consequences that sometimes reverberate throughout the victims' lives and even in future families. Victims of incest suffer alienation and other emotional difficulties into adulthood (Carson et al., 1991; Canavan, Meyer, and Higgs, 1992). Abused and neglected children are more likely to become violent, criminal adults (Alexander, Moore, and Alexander, 1991; Widom, 1989). In general, abused children show a variety of difficulties, including aggressiveness, problems relating to peers, lack of empathy, depression, and trouble in school (Emery, 1989; Salzinger et al., 1993; Starr, 1988; Youngblade and Belsky, 1989).

Children need not be physically victimized to suffer from it. Simply being around marital discord and violence can produce emotional, social, and academic problems (Emery, 1989; Groves et al., 1993; Jouriles, Murphy, and O'Leary, 1989). Those who see their parents hitting each another are more likely to inflict aggression on their own spouses in the future (Kalmuss, 1984). Furthermore, distressed mothers who punish their children in anger can become emotionally unavailable to their children

Even if the child is not the direct target of violence or abuse, discord in the family environment, somewhat like second-hand cigarette smoke, can have negative effects on the child.

(Dunn, 1988), and often administer inconsistent discipline, an important cause of children's behavior problems (Holden and Ritchie, 1991).

This destructiveness sometimes reproduces itself: About one-third to nearly one-half of abused children will transmit the problem to their families as adults (Herrenkohl, Herrenkohl, and Toedler, 1983; Kaufman and Zigler, 1987). Whatever the number, we cannot assume that abused people will automatically abuse their own children. Those who succeed in breaking the cycle have emotional support from a nonabusive adult during childhood, receive therapy, or enjoy a good marriage themselves (Egeland, Jacobvitz, and Sroufe, 1988).

Violence clearly tears at the family's fabric, but it is hardly a recent development. In early civilizations, children were viewed as wild animals to be tamed, and parents believed their duty was to literally "beat the devil" out of them. An ancient Egyptian schoolteacher left the advice that "the ears of the student are on his back; he hears best when beaten." Women, too, have long suffered abuse. During the Middle Ages, they were sometimes burned at the stake for threatening or nagging their husbands (Davis, 1971). Husbands in the United States as late as the 1860s were allowed to beat their wives so long as they used a stick no thicker than their thumb (hence the "rule of thumb"). Violence has long been part of family life—only recently has it become widely viewed as a "problem."

Despite the alarming publicity surrounding family violence, it may actually be diminishing. Murray Straus and Richard Gelles (1986) note a substantial drop in the national rates of child and spouse abuse between 1975 and 1985, perhaps due to more egalitarian marriages, shelters for battered women, and innovative treatment programs. Part of the explanation may also lie in an increased reluctance to report or admit behavior now regarded as morally wrong and criminal. Even if violence among family members is actually decreasing, however, the reported levels remain unacceptably high.

Shrinking to Insignificance?

If divorce and violence statistics do not directly account for the deterioration of the American family, perhaps its shrinking size does. Since 1850, the size of the average household in the United States has slowly declined from an average of 5.5 members to just over 2.6. This compares to an average size of 2.2 in Sweden, but, as typical Swedish households have never been large, this lower number does not reflect a great decline from the past. Similarly, the number of Americans living alone climbed from 11 million in 1970 to 23 million in 1990, though again this does not match the rate in Sweden, where 20 percent of adults live alone.

Looking more closely at census data, however, sociologists note that the 140-year trend of shrinking family household size has leveled out. In fact, the severe economic recession of the late 1980s and early 1990s has forced more single and married young adults to live with relatives in an extended family arrangement, at least until they can afford to establish their own households (Rawlings, 1992). Another factor holding family members together under one roof is the increasing number of elderly parents who need care and reside with their adult offspring, usually daughters. So, for the time being, these compensating trends have apparently stabilized the size of the American household.

Figure 9-2 shows another possible sign of the family's decline: The married-couple family that seemed so firmly entrenched during the 1950s has faded to barely half of all households. At least part of the reason is that fewer couples today view children as more desirable than other satisfactions such as money to spend and invest, neat and orderly households, hobbies, and time to spend with each other (Neal, Groat, and Wicks, 1989). One demographer predicts that as baby boomers enter their "empty nest" stage, the fastest-growing household type in the 1990s will be married couples with no children, followed by women living alone (Ambry, 1992). As in Sweden, the American family seems to have fragmented into small clusters and individuals.

It should also be noted that the lower fertility registered in the United States since the 1950s is simply a continuation of a long-established shift toward a smaller family. The post-war decade represented an aberration, an interruption of a trend that began with industrialization and urbanization. Beginning in the mid-1800s, fertility

Figure 9-2

MARRIED-COUPLE FAMILIES IN THE UNITED STATES, 1950–1992

Source: Steve W. Rawlings, *Household and Family Characteristics: March, 1992,* U. S. Bureau of the Census, Current Population Reports, P20-467, U. S. Government Printing Office, Washington, DC, 1993, Table A-2.

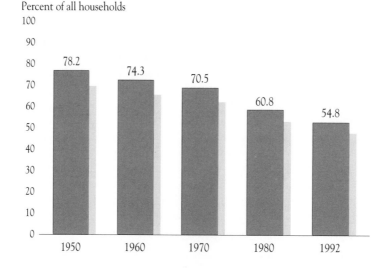

slowly declined; from 1945 to about 1964, it soared to produce the "baby boom." The recent incidence of lower fertility, then, is not evidence of "family decline."

The Decline of Marriage: For Better or Worse?   If shrinking household and family size are not as troublesome as they might appear, perhaps we should worry instead about the declining importance of marriage. Marriage rates in the United States have dropped in recent years, although not as far as those in Sweden, which are the lowest among all industrialized countries. According to the Census Bureau, 72 percent of American adults were married in 1970; in 1991, the number was down to 61 percent. Among blacks the slide is even more pronounced, down from 64 percent in 1970 to just under 44 percent in 1991. Even remarriage rates declined after the late 1970s (Glick and Lin, 1986). Although 90 percent to 95 percent of Americans still eventually marry, they wait longer to do so: Over half of women aged 20 to 24 have never married, compared to only one-quarter of such women a generation ago. Most Americans now delay marriage until their mid-twenties—over 26 for men and 24 for women, a century high. Thus at any one time a significantly larger proportion of our population, like Sweden's, lives outside the bounds of matrimony.

Some conflict theorists contend, however, that the demise of marriage and the family as we know it should bring no regrets, especially from women. Marriage, they argue, decreases women's autonomy and sense of control, with few corresponding losses for men (Ross, 1991). In fact, from the Marxist perspective (largely formulated by Friedrich Engels), marriage functions as a tool for the exploitation of women. The housewife provides children (and future workers), house-cleaning labor, child care services, and sexual access—all for no wages. Even today, despite the unstoppable surge of women into the labor market, patriarchal capitalism has managed to block most females from positions of power. Moreover, women who insist on a place in the labor market typically face a " 'double day' of wage work and housework" (Hartmann, 1981, p. 386). Unlike men, employed women are burdened by child care and housework demands in addition to their paid job. From the socialist–feminist approach, men still control and benefit from women's labor (Calasanti and Bailey, 1991), not only in the economy but within marriage itself. In this view, the decline of the traditional institution of marriage is long overdue and not to be mourned.

On the other hand, the decline of marriage may well have produced problems for individuals and society. Unmarried women and men, at all age levels, both whites and nonwhites, show higher rates of mental and physical disease and disability than their married counterparts. Middle-aged males living alone, for example, exhibit a higher mortality rate than those living with a spouse (Davis et al., 1992). Such research does not prove that marriage in and of itself produces better health; perhaps individuals with such difficulties are less likely to marry (Mastekaasa, 1992). Marriage, however, may provide a sense of purpose and meaning to one's life and a source of physical and social support that promotes good health. In any case, according to Bryce Christensen, "The decline of the family in recent decades has contributed both to serious health problems and to rising health care expenditures, especially by government" (1992, p. 70). Barbara Whitehead (1993) argues that the decline of family stability is a major cause of the most serious social problems of our day: poverty, crime, and poor educational performance.

Single-Parent Households   Critics who declare the sky is falling on the American family point also to the fact that 29.7 percent of households with children have only one parent, surpassing even Sweden's high figure of just under one in five households.

Strikingly, the number of American households headed by women without husbands doubled from 1970 to 1990. Also, more and more fathers, divorced or separated, are struggling to learn how to iron clothes and shop for children's shoes. In fact, such fathers account for about 15 percent of single parents. However, critics worry less about those single parents than they do about their children. An estimated 60 percent of all children born today will live at some point with only one parent, and about one-quarter of all children now do so—twice the proportion in 1970. Does this trend have any detrimental effect on society?

Certainly some single parents, especially those with a strong commitment to meaningful values (Weisner and Garnier, 1992), manage as well as those with part-ners in raising socially and emotionally healthy children. Usually, however, children with only one parent experience more difficulties than do those with two. They show greater risks for repeating a grade in school and being expelled, requiring treatment of behavioral or emotional problems, and suffering physical injury and illness (see Daw-son, 1991, for review). Adolescents in one-parent homes show higher levels of depres-sion (Gore, Aseltine, and Colton, 1992). Many single mothers and their children move frequently in search of jobs and affordable housing, trying to stay one step ahead of poverty that is usually neither brief nor mild (McLanahan and Garfinkel, 1986). In sum, it would appear that single-parent households are not usually as healthy for chil-dren as two-parent families.

Before we rush to judge the current state of the American family, then, we need to keep in mind that many recent changes reflect long-established trends. We may also take some small comfort from knowing that Sweden and other societies face simi-lar changes in their families. Still, Americans today are uneasy. According to one recent *Newsweek* poll, the stay-at-home-parent ideal remains strong, 49 percent of the respondents believe the American family is worse off than it was 10 years ago, and 42 percent believe it will continue to worsen (*Newsweek*, 1990). It seems that many of us believe the family has indeed deteriorated recently.

Choosing Cohabitation

As marriage has become less popular in the United States, rates of cohabitation have soared since 1970, accounting for about two-thirds of the drop in marriage rates (Bumpass, Sweet, and Cherlin, 1991). In other words, although a smaller percent of our population is now married, a larger proportion of the unmarried are living with someone. Does this trend represent disintegration of the American family?

We might first acknowledge that other modern nations, such as France, Australia, and Canada, have experienced rising cohabitation rates. And once again, Sweden leads the way. There, cohabitation has become a common alternative, rather than merely a prelude, to marriage. About 25 percent of all Swedish couples cohabit at any one time, compared with approximately 4 percent in the United States, but about one-quarter of Americans have done so at some time (Bumpass and Sweet, 1989). Will we follow Sweden and, if so, will the consequences be harmful?

We seem to be well on the road traveled by Sweden. Despite the popular image of cohabiting college students, researchers have found this arrangement more commonly among the least educated and those who grew up in single-parent and welfare families (Bumpass and Sweet, 1989). Moreover, 40 percent of cohabiting households include children, making it "very much a family status" (Bumpass, Sweet, and Cherlin, 1991, p. 926). People of more recent generations show a greater likelihood to cohabit:

Although cohabitation rates in the United States have increased greatly since 1970, our rates still lag far behind those in Sweden, where we could most safely guess that this couple has chosen not to marry.

Nearly half of those in their early thirties and half of the recently married have done so. For many people, especially the young, cohabitation is replacing marriage as a family form in the United States as it has already in Sweden.

Whether this trend threatens the strength of the family may depend on how the needs of those who cohabit, which vary considerably, are met. People choose this arrangement for economic reasons, as when they lack a stable job or adequate income. They live together while waiting for one partner to obtain a divorce or finish school, as part of the courtship process, or even as a permanent alternative to marriage. Cohabitation surely works for people in some of these situations, but it generally provides a poor substitute or preparation for marriage. Cohabiting couples are more likely than married couples to experience violence in their relationship (Stets, 1991), and to have an unsatisfying marriage or to divorce if they eventually marry, in Sweden as well as the United States (Bennett, Blanc, and Bloom, 1988; DeMaris and Rao, 1992; Schoen, 1992; Thomson and Colella, 1992). Perhaps the unconventional nature of those who choose this arrangement, the economic difficulties many of them experience, and their weak commitment to marriage explains the sobering reports on cohabitation's effects. These generalizations mask the fact that many cohabiting couples are happier than many married couples; still, we must wonder if this increasingly common "family status" indicates deterioration of the American family or simply an adaptation to other social changes.

The Family's Loss of Functions

Not only has the American family fragmented, shrunk in size, and increasingly done without a legal marital basis, but many of its functions—crucial for a society's well-being—have been assumed by other institutions.

Biological Reproduction   The successful reproduction of the species depends on a relatively structured family environment. Without nurture and protection, the dangerously dependent human offspring may not survive in sufficient numbers. Since the 1960s, however, marriage has become increasingly separated from sexual intercourse and childbearing (Cherlin, 1990). The proportion of out-of-wedlock births has risen substantially: About 40 percent of babies are conceived by unmarried women, and increasing numbers of these women do not marry before their baby is born. The link between marriage and reproduction has weakened in our society, although not as much as in Sweden, where half of all children are born out of wedlock.

Furthermore, an array of biological and social innovations are poised to transform the family and perhaps strip it of its reproductive function. New technologies, now limited to a small segment of society such as infertile couples, offer far-reaching options that can render the family superfluous regarding childbearing. The list includes *in vitro* fertilization (which can produce "test tube" babies), artificial insemination, cryopreservation (freezing of embryos), ovum transfers (one woman donates an embryo to a recipient who carries it to term), genetic engineering, and eventually, cloning (the reproduction of identical individuals). Exploring the possible repercussions for the family, John Edwards (1991) speculates that these new scientific advances will allow individuals to select their offspring's sex, even appearance and intellectual potential—all without the requirement of a spouse. Singles, gays, and lesbians also gain easier access to biological parenthood. Such trends will spell a decline in the family's importance.

Socialization   The human infant lacks the skills and knowledge necessary to survive and transmit culture. All societies rely on the family to provide the child with cultural fundamentals, but in America today, other socialization agents increasingly compete with the family. In part because the family's performance has been judged inadequate, schools now often take responsibility for, among other things, reading readiness skills, sex education, and values clarification. Day care centers, children's television programs, and organizations like Boys Clubs and the Girl Scouts step into the void left by harried or dysfunctional families—or, of course, simply to augment fully functioning ones.

Social Order   Insofar as the family socializes each generation, society enjoys tranquility and orderliness. Born with few internal promptings, humans depend on some social agency to provide direction and the motivation to conform to social norms. The recent proliferation of random violence, senseless brutality, and antisocial attitudes in the United States suggests that many families have failed to provide social controls, leaving formal agencies such as the courts and police to fill the vacuum.

Economic Support   For most of human history, individuals have depended on the family for physical survival. In modern societies like ours, however, government welfare policies and increasing personal economic security have made family ties less necessary. This trend has moved farthest in Sweden, where the state insures the individual the economic safeguards once provided by family membership (Popenoe, 1991). As more women in the United States find financial independence without husbands, more choose to divorce or never marry. As fewer people need marriage for economic reasons, its importance declines.

Although the family has lost many of its other functions, it remains our primary source of emotional security.

Physical and Emotional Care   For centuries, individuals have turned to the bosom of the family for protection from harm, the nursing of ills, and emotional support. Today, families risk litigation if they protect themselves instead of call the police. They rely on the expanding health care system for most medical treatment. Where else can we turn, though, for an emotional haven? As we have seen, people integrated into families enjoy healthier lives. In our increasingly impersonal society, the family remains the primary source of physical and emotional well-being.

Stripped of so many traditional functions, has the American family deteriorated? From the functionalist perspective, we can view the family as one of several major institutions, all of which are evolving and adapting to changes in the others, each one striving to maintain equilibrium. Furthermore, many of these changes are occurring in other industrialized nations, sometimes at higher levels. They also represent long-standing evolutionary trends rather than an abrupt breakdown. And we would be hard pressed to discover a period in history when the unsteady course of the family gave no one cause to worry about its decline. On the other hand, perhaps we can justifiably label the deep-rooted changes over the past century as deterioration, making the imminent decline of the family seem both inevitable and worrisome.

Critical Thinking Box

Can We Blame Women's Liberation for Our Broken Families?

Barbara Whitehead (1993) argues that the family in the United States has deteriorated because of women's demands for more power and freedom at home and in the workplace. In fact, since the 1970s, Americans have decided that women's rights rank above children's welfare. Has women's liberation hurt the family? ■

HAPPY MARRIAGES AND CHILDREN: CAN WORKING WIVES HAVE IT ALL?

Married women, of course, have always worked. Long before industrialization, wives labored on farms or traded alongside their husbands, in or near their homes. As men went off to factories, white middle-class women became the families' domestic specialists, and the homemaker role became the ideal. However, from the late 1800s, financial realities began to push more women into jobs outside the home. As Figure 9-3 shows, American women's participation in the labor force has slowly increased over the last century. The percentage of married women working outside the home went from about 14 percent in 1890 to over half today; in fact, even 50 percent of mothers with infants are now employed outside the home. Other industrialized nations have experienced similar increases in the number of working mothers, but there is considerable variation. In Great Britain, only about a quarter of women with very young children work, mostly part-time. The percentages are somewhat higher in France and Germany, but still lower than in the United States. Nordic countries show the highest rates of employment of mothers, and again Sweden sets the pace, with 80 percent of women with preschool-age children employed.

Figure 9-3

WOMEN IN THE WORK FORCE, 1890–1990

Over the past 100 years, the percentage of women in the work force has increased steadily, as has the percentage of married women employed outside the home.

Source: U. S. Bureau of the Census.

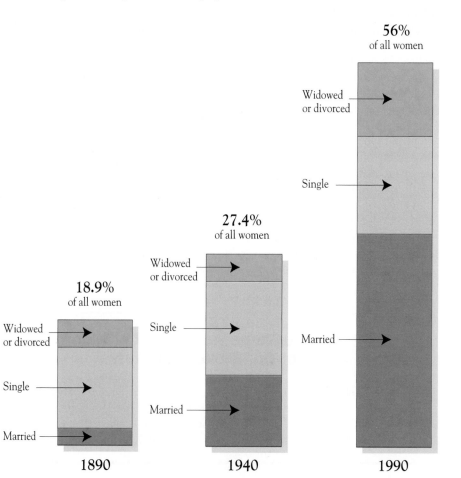

The American experience with the rising employment of mothers, then, reflects similar trends in other modern nations. While we may regard this development simply as an inevitable consequence of modernization, we might also question whether its often harmful impact on marriages and children is inevitable. In other words, can working mothers have happy marriages and be good parents?

Combining Work and a Happy Marriage

Research indicates that women generally benefit from employment. Most obviously, it offers a higher material standard of living, although taking into account work-related costs such as babysitting and child care, the dual-earner family's economic advantages (largely higher income and home ownership) can decrease by as much as 68 percent (Hanson and Ooms, 1991). Employment also seems to promise better mental health, as women who work full-time generally report greater work satisfaction than full-time homemakers (Weaver and Matthews, 1990). Women in general suffer more psychological distress than men, but employment can narrow that gender gap if their income is great enough to give them more decision-making power in the family and if household demands decrease (Rosenfield, 1992).

On the downside, as women's participation in the labor force has increased, so has divorce in the United States and other nations (Cherlin and Furstenberg, 1988; South, 1985; Trent and South, 1989), suggesting that work does not always mix easily with marriage. We now explore two possible explanations for this phenomenon, and how married women may enjoy satisfaction both at home and on the job.

Household Division of Labor   At least some of the difficulties associated with wives' employment lie in the extra costs women must bear, and the resentment and anger they feel as a result. After observing and interviewing 50 dual-career couples, Arlie Hochschild (1989) calculated that the wives worked about 15 hours more per week than their husbands, adding up to an extra month of household labor per year. Hochschild calls this extra burden a "second shift" for women, and describes how husbands repeatedly botched household chores, burned food, forgot grocery lists, and generally made their wives regret asking for help around the house. In some cases, the husbands contributed in small ways, perhaps walking the dog or grilling fish, but the wife typically did almost all the cooking, laundry, and child care duties. Only when a wife's work schedule places extreme demands on her husband does he take more responsibility for child care (Peterson and Gerson, 1992). Despite past decades of women's "liberation," husbands still contribute precious little to the domestic workload (Shelton, 1990; Bielby and Bielby, 1989; Coverman, 1985).

Why do most wives get such a bad bargain in the household division of labor? According to *cultural resource theory*, as wife and husband negotiate domestic responsibilities, the man enjoys considerable cultural advantages. Income and job prestige figure prominently in such negotiations, and the existing social structure grants men privileged access to high-paying, prestigious jobs that buy the husband a lighter workload at home (Scanzoni, 1972). Even when the wife brings home considerable income, she gains leverage only when the accompanying professional demands do not interfere with her roles as wife and mother. In other words, a married woman's success on the job may undermine what society considers to be her central, domestic duties. Another cultural disadvantage of working wives is the greater importance attached to the husband's career (Gilbert, 1985; Steil, 1983; Steil and Weltman, 1991). Wives

Most husbands contribute, if anything, largely symbolic household labor in support of their working wives.

offered a job opportunity will typically refuse it if it requires geographical relocation and disruption of the husband's career (Bielby and Bielby, 1992). A long list of research studies reveals that working wives have less power and more work in their households than their husbands (see, for example, Pleck, 1983; Spitze, 1988).

Such an imbalance helps explain not only the anger many women feel, but higher divorce rates among working wives. As Patricia Voydanoff notes, "women are sharing the provider role to a greater extent than men are sharing family work" (1988, p. 277). Many wives may look more favorably on divorce if they conclude, as Heidi Hartmann suggests, that "husbands may require more housework than they contribute" (1981, p. 383).

Role Conflict   Besides an equitable sharing of household work, marital happiness among working couples depends on resolving the clashing demands of several roles. Such conflict naturally increases when both wife and husband work outside the home, and it detracts from marriage satisfaction, especially for women (Greenglass, Pantony, and Burke, 1988; Yogev, 1986), marital adjustment (Greenhaus, Bedeian, and Moss-holder, 1987), and family cohesion (Mertensmeyer and Coleman, 1987).

Role conflict tends to arise in dual-career marriages in response to such factors as "role overload" and inadequate family support (Wiersma and van den Berg, 1991). First, when too little time is available to perform household tasks (especially important for the wife) or career responsibilities (more important for the husband), a spouse can experience role conflict and predictably bring tension into the family climate. Second, the less emotional support (respect, appreciation, offers of help, and so on) each spouse receives from other family members, the more likely he or she is to experience role conflict, and the more likely divorce will eventually result due to the pressures of a dual-career household. Also, and not surprisingly, the chances for divorce increase when the wife makes little money, works long hours, and has several young children to care for (Greenstein, 1990; Guelzow, Bird, and Koball, 1991).

Flexibility seems to be the key in dealing with role conflict in dual-career marriages. Adjusting traditional expectations of the husband and wife roles would represent a huge step toward reducing role conflict (Vannoy and Philliber, 1992). Because inequitable relationships produce emotional distress (Rachlin and Hansen, 1985), working out a division of labor that both spouses perceive as fair can help prevent competing role demands from threatening the marriage's stability. Other coping responses include lowering standards for housework, avoiding additional career responsibilities, and reappraising the importance of various problems.

Do Working Mothers Shortchange Their Children?

Worry and guilt about their children's development add to the strains of working mothers. The research literature also gives us some reason to be concerned, but it suggests some solutions as well. On the negative side, day care children of working mothers in America face higher risk of emotional and behavioral problems (Belsky, 1990; Vandell and Corasaniti, 1990). Boys seem more vulnerable than girls to adverse effects of maternal employment (Crockenberg and Litman, 1991; Vandell, 1989), as are children in their first year of life (Baydar and Brooks-Gunn, 1991; Howes, 1990). Other studies, however, find no adverse effects of day care (Henggeler and Borduin, 1981; Clarke-Stewart, 1989; Mills and Stevens, 1985; Scarr, Lande, and McCartney, 1989). Such contradictory results suggest the need to dig more deeply into such a complex issue to identify the variables involved. When we investigate Sweden's day care system, for example, we find no indications of harmful effects on children, and, in fact, real benefits (Andersson, 1989, 1992). Indeed, the Swedish example shows that mothers can enjoy the full benefits of employment without worrying about their children's development. Why?

Parental Strain   A worried mother can pass her distress along to her children, and American parents have few social supports to relieve such strain. Working mothers tend to show rejecting and punitive parenting behavior when they dislike their job or when they lack social support for their work role (Crockenberg and Litman, 1991; MacEwen and Barling, 1991). Lower-income women can usually afford fewer labor-saving devices and services and must usually work longer hours, all of which can produce greater stress and negative, power-assertive parenting (Crockenberg and Litman, 1990). Stuck with a demanding, full-time job, unreliable child care, and little help from her husband at home, the American working mother may find it difficult to put forth her best parenting effort.

High levels of parental strain are not inevitable, however. Swedish parents benefit from social policies aimed at alleviating such stress. First, they enjoy paid parental leave at nearly full salary for months after the child's birth; in fact, parents can split up to a year of such leave between them. Second, many part-time employment opportunities are made available to reduce stress on mothers (Moen and Forest, 1990). These policies reflect the Swedish belief that worry-free parents make more productive workers. Third, volunteer "contact families" provide support for troubled families, especially single mothers with small children and low income, who may need, say, someone to call in times of loneliness or frustration or to provide child care during weekends to give them a break. Fourth, as we see next, Swedes believe that good child care is essential to a healthy society, so parents have no doubts about the quality of their day care centers.

Quality Child Care   After some early studies in the United States showed contradictory effects of child care, researchers began to ask about the type and quality of nonparental day care. Jay Belsky (1990) notes that during the 1970s no negative outcomes were found in child care largely because the day care centers studied were high-quality, university-based ones. Although those results were somewhat misleading about the harmlessness of day care in general, they did reveal that small group size, low adult-to-child ratios, and specialized training of care-givers provide important measures of day care quality and are linked to healthy child development (Clarke-Stewart, 1987; Phillips, 1987). While such high-quality child care may be difficult to find (and afford) in the United States, Swedish children enjoy uniformly well-equipped, well-staffed day care. Parents can choose specially trained "child-minders" who come to the child's home or municipal day-care centers that offer part-time and before-school and after-school care. Parents pay only 10 to 15 percent of the costs directly, while local and national governments subsidize the rest.

The Swedish system, however, tells us only that new American social policies could offer more help to working parents and their children. Until such a system becomes available in this nation, parents can take comfort in knowing that (1) high-quality child care poses no threat to the child's development, and (2) parents themselves can make a difference; that is, parental nurturing can compensate for mediocre nonparental day care (Belsky, 1990). Even mothers employed full-time can provide the responsive care that produces securely attached infants (Benn, 1986; Moorehouse, 1991), as can fathers (Belsky, 1988).

Because of their own offsprings' addictions and divorces, millions of grandparents have assumed important child-care responsibilities. In fact, the Census Bureau reports that in 1991, of the 3.3 million children who live in a household with grandparents, 28% reside with only a grandparent but neither parent present.

Should the Government Do More for Our Children?

Looking beyond our own borders, we see a number of alternative policies designed to help families with children. Government programs, of course, cost money, and other nations' programs may not be as successful here because of cultural differences, but Sheila Kamerman and Alfred Kahn (1989) offer an embarrassing reason to reassess our approach to the problem: The United States, one of the richest nations in the world, has among the highest child-poverty rates of industrialized countries. The percentage of poor children in our nation, for example, is more than *twice* that of Sweden, Switzerland, Germany, and Norway. Why?

Most European countries have established income-transfer systems to specifically meet the needs of children. Cash payments are provided to all families with children (usually tax free and offered as long as the child is of school age), by which society shares with the family the cost of raising children. Also, in most developed countries the government gives supplemental housing allowances to families, guaranteed parental leave (with full job protection and often full pay) ranging from three months to three years, and free child care for preschool children beginning at about age two and a half.

In contrast, the United States offers a hodgepodge of poorly coordinated programs that vary in scope and effectiveness from state to state. While we await the Clinton administration's health care plan, America remains the only industrialized nation without guaranteed health services for children and their families. In effect, poor children have no assurance of standardized benefits, only a "safety net" with gaping holes. As a result, about one child in five lives in poverty, while child poverty elsewhere in the industrialized world is unusual.

Why has the United States not adopted such policies? Should we? ■

FINDING MARITAL SATISFACTION: A SOCIOLOGICAL ANALYSIS

Despite the dizzying changes of the last few decades, most Americans still seek a satisfying marital relationship. No wonder: Marital happiness contributes more than anything else to a general sense of happiness (Glenn and Weaver, 1981). Sociological research offers guidelines on how to build a satisfying marriage.

Mate Selection

Choosing an appropriate partner provides the foundation of a happy marriage, and this means finding someone with those general characteristics that contribute to a stable and satisfying relationship. Obviously, for example, affiliative, nurturing, and succoring individuals have happier unions than those who are anxious, neurotic, or hostile (Mehrabian, 1989). We can also search for someone with either of two personality types that contribute to marital happiness: (1) "feminine," which includes being emotionally attuned to and interested in intimacy, or (2) androgynous, which draws

The traditional masculine personality is not linked to marital happiness.

upon the strength of both gender types (Kurdek and Schmitt, 1986; Peterson et al., 1989). One study suggests that a man with liberal views who strongly desires to marry has a good chance of being content in marriage (Shachar, 1991). We can also improve our luck by finding a mate with a sense of humor (Ziv and Gadish, 1989; Lauer, Lauer, and Kerr, 1990). Having a healthy personality, we might say, contributes to a happy marriage.

On the other hand, some have a low probability of marriage success. Such people show such traits as irritability and impatience, characteristics of the Type A behavior pattern (Barling, Bluen, and Moss, 1990). Lower-income people are at higher risk for divorce (South and Spitze, 1986), as are those who have already experienced divorce, either through their parents or their own previous marriage. Perhaps prior experience reduces the fear and uncertainty that might otherwise inhibit divorce (McLanahan and Bumpass, 1988). In some cases, people carry into second marriages the same characteristics that helped destroy their first marriage, or the cause may lie partly in the special difficulties faced by stepfamilies (White and Booth, 1985). Clearly, we improve our chances for marital satisfaction by not choosing mates who have certain traits and experiences.

Sociobiology suggests that inherent sexual preferences guide our selection of mates (Allman, 1993). In this view, the evolutionary process has built into males a concern for finding a mate whose youthful and healthy appearance indicates fertility, the better to pass along his genes. Women, on the other hand, look primarily for mates with enough social resources, including money and power, to help raise the offspring in a protected, secure, and advantaged environment.

Despite such findings about mating preferences, most researchers would not advise using a checklist of desirable characteristics to shop for a partner. Marriage success requires not just a partner with the "right" traits but an appropriate matching of both people's personalities. Several theories offer guidance.

First, finding someone of a similar age, race, social-class level, and educational and occupational status enhances the probability of marital happiness (Bumpass and Sweet, 1972; White and Hatcher, 1984; Mehrabian, 1989). This tendency of people to pair off with others of similar social backgrounds, called **homogamy,** shows that marriage does not occur randomly in a population. Most Americans manage to make homogamous matches, especially with respect to religious faith (Bumpass and Sweet, 1972; Heaton, 1984; Heaton, Albrecht, and Martin, 1985), but the tendency is weakening for the country as a whole. Instead, education is replacing religion as a major factor in homogamous mate selection (Kalmijn, 1991a, 1991b).

Homogamy: the tendency of people to select marriage partners of similar social backgrounds.

Although people usually prefer to marry others like them, the marriage market does not always allow it. For example, women who delay marriage until after age 30 face a shrinking supply of eligible males of a similar background, and often forgo homogamy by marrying men of different age, race, or educational status (Lichter, 1990). Similarly, educated black women typically face a shortage of equally educated mates, and they respond by either remaining single or by being less selective.

According to the *matching hypothesis*, people usually date and end up marrying others of approximately the same level of attractiveness as themselves. This similarity may even contribute to a marriage's survival chances: studies find significant physical matching in couples married many years (Schafer and Keith, 1990; White, 1980).

A related theory suggests that we search for a mate the same way we shop for a major appliance. The *exchange model* holds that we seek a spouse who offers the greatest benefits at the lowest cost. Marital satisfaction rests on both partners' belief that, like good shoppers, they have found the best bargain available. Rewards include the valued behaviors, services, and resources the other partner contributes, costs the inconvenient and otherwise unpleasant aspects of the relationship (curfew, glowering parents, nagging, and so on). Scott South (1991) found that men typically feel they have a good exchange if they are paired with a youthful, attractive wife, while most women seek a partner with stable employment and good earnings.

As when shopping for a big-ticket item, however, we do not always get what we want. In the mate selection game, those with few resources to exchange may have to settle for less than they would like. They may make less homogamous matches, thereby lessening their chances of marital satisfaction. Such people are also likely to have less control in their marriage. As Willard Waller and Reuben Hill (1951) pointed out long ago in their "principle of least interest," the person who has the least interest in maintaining the relationship can control it. The partner with the most rewards to offer clearly has more leverage, but such an unequal power balance may contribute to strains in the marriage.

The research also indicates that one should not select a mate too soon. Marrying before the age of 20 is consistently associated with higher marriage failure rates (Booth and White, 1980; Martin and Bumpass, 1989). In fact, the negative effect of wedding early resounds long into the marriage (Heaton, Albrecht, and Martin, 1985) and even into subsequent generations, possibly due to poor role modeling (Martin and Bumpass, 1989; Booth and Edwards, 1985). However, waiting too late reduces the pool of eligible mates, forcing one to search more widely in the marriage market. The optimal time for settling on a mate choice seems to be during one's twenties, when the supply of similar partners is greatest and when age-graded institutions such as colleges bring together people of similar backgrounds (Blau, Blum, and Schwartz, 1982).

He gets a young, attractive wife; she gets financial security. Both feel they have made a good exchange, but what special problems may arise from such a match-up?

Wife–Husband Interaction

Making a good match, of course, is only one key to marital satisfaction. A major, ongoing task is maintaining fairness between spouses. *Equity theory* holds that partners who share resources, labor, and power equitably feel relatively contented (Houlihan, Jackson, and Rogers, 1990; Aida and Falbo, 1991). Fairness is especially important for wives, who often have less decision-making power than their husbands (Peterson, 1990; Fowers, 1991). Wives, for example, expect their husbands to contribute to "female" tasks and show appreciation of the wives' household labor (Blair and Johnson, 1992). Other factors include husbands' expressiveness, which tends to enhance marital adjustment for both spouses (Lamke, 1989), and wives' giving style of loving (Martin et al., 1990). In general, marital happiness partly depends on emotionally healthy individuals making reasonable, equitable decisions.

Even finding a partner with appropriate traits and then making adjustments as needed in the relationship, however, cannot guarantee success. Structural factors beyond the spouses' control, especially economic trends, can take a toll on the marriage. For example, Scott South and Stewart Tolnay (1992) estimate that approximately 10,000 divorces occur for every 1 percent rise in the unemployment rate. Of course, some couples cannot afford to split into separate households. Still, economic hardship erodes marital quality by producing hostility, primarily in the husband, and by decreasing supportive behaviors of both spouses (Conger et al., 1990; Lorenz et al., 1991). Financial difficulties also disturb the "exchange" balance or role reciprocity in some marriages, especially in low-income families. If the primary breadwinner, usually the husband, fails to provide for the family, his wife may express her dissatisfaction by contributing less affection and companionship to the marriage (Clark-Nicolas and Gray-Little, 1991). Shift work also detracts from marital quality, resulting in more disagreements, sexual tension, and child-related problems (White and Keith, 1990).

Life Stage Effects

The passage of time complicates the search for a happy marriage. Although marital quality remains remarkably stable over time (Johnson, Amoloza, and Booth, 1992), historical events, social trends, and physiological aging can still impinge on the spouses' relationship (Heaton, 1991). The women's liberation movement, swings in the economy, sexual impotence, and other changes can unbalance a marriage as years pass. The arrival and departure of children in the family play an especially prominent role in this scenario. Despite the recent rise in childlessness, over 80 percent of married couples still make the important transition into parenthood, and this affects husband–wife interaction in complex ways.

On the one hand, children can enhance marital stability and commitment, especially during infancy, and if they are sons (Morgan, Lye, and Condran, 1988). On the other hand, the stresses of parenthood demand considerable adjustment between the spouses. In general, the addition of a third member to the household tends to disrupt the intimacy and communication of the marriage dyad. Studies find that for many couples marital satisfaction begins to fall after the first (relatively happy) month of parenthood, bringing a decline in feelings of love for the spouse, less open communication, and more conflict (Belsky and Rovine, 1990; Wallace and Gotlib, 1990).

Other variables, however, complicate the picture. Many new parents maintain the quality of their marriage (Belsky and Rovine, 1990); others may share less companionship but experience no greater decline in general marital satisfaction than nonparents during the same early years of their marriages (MacDermid, Huston, and McHale, 1990). Researchers also find that couples who make adjustments during pregnancy and feel little parenting stress are more likely to make the transition to parenthood with their marriage still strong (Wallace and Gotlib, 1990). Such stress, by the way, depends to some extent on the importance the mother or father puts on the parental identity: The more important the role, the more vulnerable the parent (Simon, 1992). Also, the infant's temperament can affect parents' stress level (Belsky and Rovine, 1990). Some couples manage to successfully adapt to the strains and changes parenthood brings to their relationship; for those who do not, marital quality typically declines during childbearing years and rises only when the children begin to leave the nest (Stattin and Klackenberg, 1992). In sum, marital happiness can survive parenthood if the partners remain flexible and ready to make adjustments.

One of the most important adjustments required of new parents involves renegotiating responsibilities. A typical stumbling block is a lack of congruence between spouses' sex role attitudes and their division of household labor (MacDermid, Huston, and McHale, 1990; McHale and Crouter, 1992). Also, many wives are dissatisfied with the child-care assistance offered by their husbands (Kalmuss, Davidson, and Cushman, 1992). In fact, a general resentment over the division of work around the home increases over the life cycle until the children leave (Suitor, 1991). Exchange theorists explain this U-shaped curve as mothers' feelings that they are making disproportionate contributions during the childrearing years, that the marital exchange is not equitable.

If a couple keep their marriage intact by making the necessary adjustments throughout the parenting stage, they can expect their reward when the children leave home but still maintain contact (White and Edwards, 1990). The "empty nest" stage typically brings relief from parenting strains and other role demands, a lessening of household chores, and a rise in marital satisfaction (Glenn and McLanahan, 1982; Menaghan, 1983; McLanahan and Sorensen, 1985). Furthermore, incomes often peak

Having held their marriage together through the storms of crises and parenting, the empty nest couple typically enjoys marital satisfaction comparable to the newlywed stage.

at this stage since household spending drops about 30 percent when the children leave (Ambry, 1993). Empty nesters still in their first marriage are generally the happiest of all couples, having jointly weathered storms and come to a deeper understanding of each other (Sheehy, 1982).

Can we expect retirement to enhance marital satisfaction? Early research discerned a "honeymoon stage" in the early years of retirement (Gilford, 1984). This would be expected: Spouses usually experience less role conflict and overload, have more time and energy to devote to each other, and initially enjoy economic security and good health. However, this honeymoon does not last, and difficulties can arise when wives continue to work after their husbands retire (Lee and Shehan, 1989). Apparently, the retirement years do not necessarily produce any lasting, positive impact on marriage.

We conclude with two discouraging notes. First, sociological research cannot provide a clear road map to marital happiness; it can only identify some of the errors to avoid, show what works for some couples, and point to adjustments that must be made throughout the life cycle. Second, because of greater economic pressures, the romanticization of marriage (or growing disillusion with it), an increased emphasis on individual gratification, a longer life span, and a number of other social forces, marital satisfaction seems to have become more elusive in recent years (Glenn, 1991).

Research Box

Is a Less Satisfying Marriage the Price of Parenthood?

Early research supported the popular belief that the arrival of the first baby brings a decline in marital quality which persists until the last child leaves the home. A less satisfying marriage, in other words, seemed to be the price a couple pays for the joys of parenthood. Later studies, however, challenged this notion, finding that the romantic glow of early marriage dims somewhat even without the arrival of a baby. Also, the couples' happiness depends on what aspects of the marriage are measured. Marital activities (recreation versus child care, for example) are affected by the transition to parenthood, but the amount of conflict and the spouses' subjective evaluations of their marriage do not always change with parenthood.

Shelley MacDermid, Ted Huston, and Susan McHale (1990) set out to untangle these loose ends of the research picture. They compared two groups of couples during the first two and one-half years of marriage. Fifty-two of the ninety-eight couples became parents during that time. The sociologists hypothesized that both groups of couples would show some decline in marital quality, but that in some ways the marriages of those who become parents would show greater declines. They included other variables in an attempt to identify what aspects of parenthood actually diminish marital satisfaction.

The data indicated that even after a year into parenthood, the parents showed no more decline in their evaluations of their relationship than did the nonparents, whose feelings had cooled to about the same degree. As expected, however, the parents spent less of their interaction time in companionate activities and more in instrumental activities (such as child care and household work) compared to the nonparents. Moreover, the couples with a baby did not all respond to the parenthood transition the same way. The differences in their responses were explained by how well their sex-role attitudes fit their division of household labor. The parents whose marriages suffered the most were those with traditional attitudes who divided the labor in nontraditional (egalitarian) ways.

MacDermid, Huston, and McHale concluded that young couples who successfully renegotiate their marital roles can adjust to parenthood with little damage to their marriage. Babies do not necessarily lower marital satisfaction. ☐

WHAT IS THE IMPACT OF DIVORCE?

During the 1970s, divorce swept through the United States like a storm, blowing apart over one million families a year by the early 1980s. The rate of divorces per 1,000 population rose from 2.5 in 1965 to a high of 5.3 in 1981 before leveling off at just under 5.0, where it has hovered in recent years.

Sociologists trying to predict America's marital future offer divided opinions (Darnton and Wingert, 1992). Most optimistically, the present generation of adults, the first to grow up in an era of high divorce rates, may learn from the pain and mistakes of their parents—thus, the divorce rate may hold steady, even diminish. On the other hand, this generation's scars may hinder their ability to maintain long-lasting unions. Also, increasing numbers of young adults may avoid marriage altogether in favor of cohabitation, thus contributing to a drop in both divorce and marriage rates.

Beyond such predictions, we know that divorce will probably touch many of us, either in the breakup of our own marriage or those of people we know. What impact can we expect from divorce?

Is There Any Good News for Adults?

Millions of unhappy couples have decided that anything would be better than continuing their marriages. While divorce offers freedom from unhappy and destructive marriages, and another chance at marital bliss, that freedom is seldom free from its own heavy costs.

Economic Consequences   Financially, divorce can sometimes be good news—for men. Most recently divorced men enjoy higher standards of living because they maintain their income level while jettisoning most family responsibilities and expenses (Duncan and Hoffman, 1985; Weitzman, 1985; Hoffman and Duncan, 1988). On the other hand, evidence abounds regarding the economic losses of divorced women. Not only do most women lack men's career resources, but after divorce they usually shoulder the burden of child-care responsibilities and must therefore either enter the labor market or work harder and longer hours (Peterson, 1989). For many such women, remarriage offers the best path to economic improvement (Johnson and Minton, 1982; Duncan and Hoffman, 1985).

Legal reforms in recent decades have contributed to the economic burdens of divorce to women. Courts usually divide the spouses' wealth equally, ignoring the health insurance, retirement benefits, earning capacity, and other advantages commonly enjoyed by the husband (Weitzman, 1988). Few settlements award the wife alimony, and in those that do it is usually for only several years; even then, few divorcées actually receive anything near the full payments ordered. A divorced mother's chances of receiving child-support payments depend not so much on the degree of her economic suffering as they do upon the father's financial circumstances (Teachman, 1991).

Educated women and those already in the labor force before the divorce enjoy a stronger economic position. Age also makes a difference: Younger women have a better chance for remarriage and its financial rewards. For middle-aged and elderly women, however, remarriage is a remote option, and divorce can leave them financially devastated (Uhlenberg, Cooney, and Boyd, 1990).

Health Consequences   Those who divorce are also more susceptible to a wide array of psychological difficulties: They are 6 to 10 times more likely to use inpatient psychiatric facilities (Seagraves, 1980), are at greater risk to commit suicide (Stack, 1990), and suffer higher rates of anxiety, depression, phobias, and general unhappiness (Gove and Shin, 1989; Kurdek, 1990, 1991). Worse, divorce can act as a chronic stressor, causing long-term mental problems (McCubbin and Patterson, 1982; Wallerstein and Blakeslee, 1989).

The correlation between divorce and psychological distress, although strong and well documented, does not clearly indicate a cause-and-effect relationship. It is possible that people with emotional difficulties are simply more likely to divorce. Some researchers suggest that, at least in the case of women who divorce several times, dysfunctional personalities make some wives more "divorce prone" than others (Brody, Neubaum, and Forehand, 1988). However, longitudinal studies that monitor spouses' depression over time find that depression typically appears at the time of divorce and its related stress (Aseltine and Kessler, 1993). Likewise, Alan Booth and Paul Amato (1991) analyzed three waves of data collected from married people, some of whom divorced during the study, and discovered no signs of continuously high levels of psychological stress in those who eventually divorced. Only just before the divorce did stress levels rise, eventually declining afterward, suggesting that the distress of many recently divorced people results not from a general psychological unfitness but from the crisis itself. In some cases, then, divorce causes mental depression.

Women are especially vulnerable to the strain of divorce. Because of their socialization, women assume more of the responsibility for the marriage's success or failure, and thus suffer considerable distress during and after divorce (Kurdek, 1990). Similarly, women's self-esteem may depend more than men's on the quality of their relationships and interactions (Haffey and Cohen, 1992). Therefore, women in troubled marriages are more likely to become depressed rather than angry, confused rather than assertive, and to assume the peace-keeping role rather than protect their own interests. It bears mention, however, that gender differences may be smaller than studies have indicated. Most research has simply asked divorced people to report on their emotional well-being, and men typically are much less willing to admit such problems (Kitson and Morgan, 1990).

We can also expect a higher incidence of physical illness among divorced and separated couples than those who are happily married (Gove, Style, and Hughes, 1990). The explanation may lie in the suppressed immunological functioning found in people who are divorced, separated, or in unhappy marriages (Ader, Cohen, and Felton, 1990; Kielcolt-Glaser et al., 1987). Whatever the reason, divorced people, especially women (Kurdek, 1991), are at higher risk of physical as well as psychological maladies.

The divorce research offers some good news. While the adjustment to divorce may last the rest of a person's life, the worst of the distress, an "aftermath state," typically ends after a year or two (Dreman, Orr, and Aldor, 1990). By that time, self-esteem and feelings of competence begin to reemerge. Also, the adjustment is not equally painful for all; those with high levels of education, income, social support, and of younger age find the aftermath easier to navigate (Booth and Amato, 1991). "Career directed" divorced women likewise adjust more easily to the new single-parent identity (Wijnberg and Holmes, 1992).

The research also offers some advice for adjusting to divorce. Cultivating social networks, for example, can make a big difference (Gerstel, 1988; Milardo, 1987). Preoccupation with a former spouse depresses well-being, so making a clean, final break can facilitate long-term adjustment (Masheter, 1991; Tschann et al., 1989; Wallerstein and Kelly, 1980). Joint physical custody of the children has at least one benefit: Arranging for children to live alternately with both parents often contributes to higher levels of cooperation and financial support between former spouses (Pearson and Thoennes, 1990).

Nevertheless, beyond freedom from a dysfunctional marriage, there is little sociological evidence to recommend divorce, especially for women. While some individuals possess the resources to rebound quickly, for most people divorce requires painful financial adjustments and coping with either long-standing or crisis-related health problems.

What Happens to the Children?

We can also expect the children of divorced parents to suffer in some ways. These children typically show higher levels of depression and a sense of loss (Johnston, Campbell, and Mayes, 1985; Wallerstein and Kelly, 1980). They also exhibit lower self-concept scores (Beer, 1989), suffer more injuries (Dawson, 1991), and experience more anxiety, behavior problems, and academic trouble (Furstenberg, Morgan, and Allison, 1987; Hoyt et al., 1990). They often carry their difficulties into adulthood, showing higher-than-average levels of psychological maladjustment, educational failure, and violent behavior (Amato and Keith, 1991; Billingham and Gilbert, 1990).

We cannot predict, however, that all children will suffer similarly from the impact of divorce. In fact, some are better off than children in intact but discordant families (Emery, 1982). Divorce may actually bring relief from the constant bickering and frequent violent eruptions in some marriages. In any event, boys react differently than girls. For one thing, girls usually adjust somewhat better than boys, who often respond with uncontrollable behaviors (Hodges, 1986). Also, family troubles begin to take a toll on girls before the divorce, while boys usually do not show the effects until afterwards (Doherty and Needle, 1991). Age also matters: At least in the short term, younger children have more difficulty adjusting (Tschann et al., 1989). Children around age 7 or 8 tend to show sadness and grief when the marriage breaks up; by the time they reach 9 or 10, anger and embarrassment are more likely responses (Kelly and Wallerstein, 1976).

The Mechanics of Pain   How does the divorce experience translate into depression and other problems so common in people whose parents have divorced? Paul Amato and Bruce Keith (1991) offer a three-fold explanation. First, the drop in children's living standards that usually accompanies divorce brings the disadvantages of lower-income homes and neighborhoods, social handicaps that increase the probability of low educational and occupational attainment, poverty in adulthood, and the attendant marital and psychological stresses.

Second, some postdivorce difficulties stem from living in a single-parent household. The children, for instance, usually have less contact with their fathers (Amato, 1987). Also, many divorced mothers have too little time and energy to devote to their children and, compared to married mothers, use more critical statements, questions, and commands when interacting with them (Webster-Stratton, 1989). We need to recognize, however, that many of these mothers manage to offer consistent support to their children, even though they have little time to spend with them (Demo, 1992).

Third, some of the pain of postdivorce adjustment results not simply from the family's breakup but the discord that led to the divorce (Cowan, Cowan, and Heming, 1989; Doherty and Needle, 1991). Sometimes it occurs indirectly, through changes in the parent–child relationship (Kline, Johnston, and Tschann, 1991). Predictably, parents undergoing marital distress offer less warmth, consistency, and structure, and more rejection to their children. Exhausted, self-absorbed parents have a temporarily "diminished capacity to parent" (Wallerstein and Kelly, 1980). More directly, conflict between parents can cause depression and withdrawal, aggression, delinquency, and other behavior problems in the children, whether or not the parents eventually divorce (Shaw and Emery, 1987; Emery and O'Leary, 1984; Hershorn and Rosenbaum, 1985). The children may model the aggression of their disputing parents or learn to withdraw to avoid conflict (Kalter, 1987; Shaw and Emery, 1987).

Manageable Aspects Divorcing parents can take some steps to soften the impact on their children. Most importantly, they should maintain a civil relationship with each other if at all possible. Continued parental hostility after divorce hinders the children's adjustment (Peterson and Zill, 1986; Johnston, Gonzalez, and Campbell, 1987; Kline, Johnston, and Tschann, 1991). As happens in intact households, conflict between parents spills over into the parent–child relationship, contributing to children's adjustment difficulties (Forehand et al., 1991; Donnelly and Finkelhor, 1992). If the divorced parents can control their mutual hostility, arranging access to the non-resident parent (usually the father) can help the child better manage the transition (Bisnaire, Firestone, and Rynard, 1990).

To summarize, we can expect divorce to bring difficulties to any children involved as well as the adults. Only in limited circumstances will the impact be anything but painful and lingering.

Critical Thinking Box

Should We End Easy Divorce?

Seeing a link between divorce and crime, poverty, and other social woes, "profamily" groups are seeking to make divorce far more difficult to obtain in the United States (Schrof, 1992).

The battle has several fronts. One strategy is to modify no-fault divorce laws, which have made it convenient for spouses to abandon their families. In some states, legislators suggest a two-tier marriage system: a marriage of convenience or compatibility and a marriage of commitment that allows few grounds for divorce. Another promotes the use of court-appointed lawyers to represent society in arguing against divorce in every case involving a family with children. Also, new laws could hinder divorcing couples' efforts to sell their jointly owned home. The most direct strategy is simply to ban divorce for parents with young children.

Opponents of this movement argue instead for increased assistance for divorced families and other family forms that have proliferated in response to today's social changes. They point out that people have always found ways to terminate marriages, and blocking the divorce route would only produce new escape paths. Rather than try to preserve some outdated version of the traditional family, they argue, resources should be spent to help individuals adjust to whatever family forms they create.

Should we make it harder to divorce? ■

WHAT SPECIAL DIFFICULTIES CONFRONT STEPFAMILIES?

As we know from fairy tales, stepfamilies are nothing new; for centuries, death in early adulthood sent many men and women with children in search of a second marriage. Since the 1970s, however, stepfamilies—perhaps more accurately known as *blended* or *reconstituted* families—have been forming not so much after the death of a spouse as after divorce. This change, along with predictions that over one-half of today's young will become stepchildren (Glick, 1989), generated a surge of research studies beginning in 1980.

Imagine a newly remarried couple bringing together children from previous marriages. The couple starts with unrealistically high expectations that love and understanding will overcome the children's guilt and anger, that earnest intentions will make everything right this time around, and that the stepfamily will replace the original, biological family. As reality sets in, their dreams will quickly fade. The parents must reconcile the differences in their child-rearing approaches, and each will be cast as an intruder as the other's children realize that any reunion between their biological parents is now impossible. Despite their initial intentions, both parents will probably show less effective problem-solving skills and communication, and enjoy less cohesion than original families (Bray, 1988; Peek et al., 1988).

Even if this new family can make all the necessary adjustments, they will find that society still lags behind. Schools may not allow stepparents to take a child to a doctor appointment. Emergency rooms may not accept the stepparent's permission for medical treatment. In short, the stepparents will probably find they have no legal rights yet all the moral responsibilities of biological parents.

The greatest obstacle to the success of this remarriage, however, is the presence of children not biologically related to both parents (Pasley and Ihinger-Tallman, 1984). If he is typical, the stepfather will take the role of a disengaged, polite stranger, reluctant to take control or show disapproval (Hetherington, 1989; Thomson, McLanahan, and Braun-Curtis, 1992). As we will see, he can expect special difficulties with his stepdaughters. As a complex blended family (with children from both parents) this newly remarried couple will have high risks of parent–child conflict (Schultz, Schultz, and Olson, 1991).

Our hypothetical parents will thus find that trying to build a strong stepfamily is like treading through a mine field, that there are dangers besides the typical adjustment problems required in first marriages. Founded upon loss (either through death or divorce), stepfamilies face somewhat greater probabilities of divorce, abuse, and emotional difficulties for the children.

Searching for Satisfaction in Remarriage

Still, contrary to popular images, remarried people experience only slightly less marital satisfaction and overall well-being than those married for the first time (Guisinger, Cowan, and Schuldberg, 1989; Vemer et al., 1989). If our couple are miserable in this second marriage, they were probably so in their first one, too. Nevertheless, the disenchantment, discouragement, and related stress that they may have brought into this remarriage make their probability of divorce about 10 percent higher than that in their first marriages.

Several factors threaten our couple's chances for marital success. They face special role strains in melding two sets of family traditions, routines, and philosophies, especially if they bring school-age children into the new marriage (Whitsett and Land, 1992; Wineberg, 1992). They will have to struggle with ambiguous family boundaries, to redefine the family roster to include or exclude nonresident children, any number of grandparents, and so on. This, along with poorly defined role expectations, creates stressful situations. Society offers few guidelines for boundaries and roles; the stepfamily must work out its own solutions.

The Special Difficulties of Stepchildren

Now we can put ourselves in the place of the children of this blended family. After the trauma of parental divorce or death, they face another round of emotional trials. As a result, they will show slightly higher rates of problem behaviors such as fighting, poor academic performance, depression, and anxiety—essentially what children in single-parent families experience (Bray, 1988; Ferri, 1984; Zill, 1988).

There are a number of reasons for the special difficulties faced by stepchildren (Coleman and Ganong, 1990). First, family reorganization deprives them of stable role models. As a result, they may receive inadequate socialization. Second, neither children nor stepparents have a clear script for their relationship. The stepparents may be uncertain whether they should offer friendship or authority, support or control, a replacement for the nonresident parent or only a second-best substitute. The blended family must write its own scripts, and tensions may easily develop. Third, sociobiologists (who point to genetic foundations for our social behaviors) claim that the higher rates of abuse and neglect from stepparents should come as no surprise: Such parents have no inherent motivation to care for children who are not carrying their own genes, and the children thus lack any normally innate protection (Giles-Sims and Finkelhor, 1984).

An important potential trouble spot in blended or reconstituted families is the often strained relationship between daughter and stepfather, who may be seen as an intruder or even a sexual threat.

As with divorce, boys tend to react differently to reconstituted families than girls. While the girls probably adapted relatively well to our hypothetical parents' divorce, they will likely show a more intense and longer-lasting negative reaction to their mother's remarriage (Bray, 1988; Hetherington, 1989). The daughters' relationship with their stepfather is almost sure to be strained. He stands a fair chance of establishing himself as a strong role model and companion with his new sons, but less so with the daughters, who see him as an intruder threatening the mother–daughter ties formed before the remarriage. Also, they may be uncomfortable with the presence of a non-related male in the household, a potential sexual aggressor, especially in their early adolescence. Whatever the reason, relations between the girls and their stepfather are likely to remain strained (Vuchinich et al., 1991).

Despite these trouble spots, our reconstituted family will not inevitably become a cauldron of pathology and conflict. For one thing, problems visually flow not from the stepfamily itself but from processes, such as parenting strategies, typically found within such families (Fine and Kurdek, 1992) and within their control. Moreover, we must remember that any family situation contains areas of potential discontent and anger. While they do face more complications, stepfamilies are not much more likely than members of other two-parent families to be overwhelmed by their problems.

SUMMARY

Families in our culture are based on *monogamy* (one spouse per person), but others like the Tiwi allow a husband to have several wives *(polygyny)*, which is the world's most common form of *polygamy* (several spouses per person). (Few societies allow a woman to have several husbands, an arrangement known as *polyandry*.) As our system is based on rules of *bilateral descent* (tracing ancestry through both parents) and the ideal of *egalitarianism* (equal sharing of power between spouses), we must use cultural relativism to imagine how other societies can function smoothly with a *matrilineal* system (in which ancestry is traced only through mothers) or a *patrilineal* system (ancestry traced only through fathers); power can also be vested in the women *(matriarchy)* or, more familiarly, in the men *(patriarchy)*. Even in our own society, we must remember to include not only *nuclear families* (one or two parents and their unmarried offspring) but *extended families*, which include all those related by blood. And we are increasingly being challenged to stretch our definition of "family" to include unmarried women with their children and cohabiting heterosexual and homosexual couples (some with children). A sociological definition that covers all these forms must be quite inclusive: a *family* includes people related by blood, marriage, or adoption who form an economic and household unit.

We often hear that the American family has declined during the past several decades, but our alarming divorce rate, highest in the world, has leveled off, and probably represents, along with death and desertion, simply another way of terminating marriage. A disturbing level of family violence has also been uncovered, and while it often produces long-lasting consequences in children (even if they merely witness it), and tends to reproduce itself in subsequent generations, it is no recent development. Another statistic offered as evidence of the family's recent deterioration is shrinking household size, but this too has leveled off. Similarly, fewer families take the form of married couples with children, though the trend toward smaller families began over a century ago. Marriage rates have also dropped, though this may signal release from an oppressive institution as well as portend problems for society and individuals. The growing number of single-parent households likewise worries some critics of recent family changes, and indeed the children of such households typically experience more problems than those in intact families. Similarly, soaring rates of cohabitation, increasingly common among more strata of the population, may represent an unhealthy alternative to marriage (because of the higher rates of violence and eventual divorce among such couples), or simply an adaptation to other social changes. The family's decline may also be evident in its increasing loss of functions, including biological reproduction, socialization, social order, economic support, and physical and emotional care. It is important to remember, however, that the same trends occur in other industrialized nations and that many of the changes are a long time coming.

The great increase in working mothers (in the United States and other industrialized nations) raises questions about its impact on marital satisfaction and children's development. An employed wife typically feels angry because her husband, with his superior cultural resources, contributes little to the domestic division of labor. Role conflict also often arises as a result of role overload and inadequate family support for stressed spouses. Such marriages require flexibility to make them work. The children of working mothers are more likely to be exposed to negative treatment from parents under strain, or sent to poor-quality child care, especially in the United States, where the government provides little help along those lines.

Choosing an appropriate partner for a successful marriage means paying attention to several personality features as well as matching one's own social background (*homogamy*) and level of physical attractiveness. According to the *exchange model*, in successful marriages both partners feel they receive the greatest rewards at the lowest cost. Avoiding early marriage also increases chances of success. Once married, *equity theory* suggests sharing resources, labor, and power fairly, although such outside factors as economic trends complicate such negotiations. Parenthood, the most important life stage effect, can detract from marital happiness unless the partners remain flexible in making necessary adjustments in matters like the household division of labor. The empty nest stage can bring relief from parenting strains; retirement can bring satisfaction as long as health and finances last.

The high but stabilized divorce rate in the United States may discourage some adults from marrying, emotionally damage others, or may offer lessons about what mistakes to avoid in building a stable marriage. When divorce does intervene, men can find their financial situation improved, while most women suffer. And divorced people, especially women, generally show higher levels of psychological and physical illnesses, although these difficulties often subside eventually and have a lower effect on those who employ coping strategies and have more social and emotional resources. The effect divorce has on children depends on their sex and age and various manageable aspects. Their pain may be caused by the drop in income, the difficulties of living in a single-parent household, and conflict between parents before the divorce.

Divorce, more than death, now accounts for the formation of most stepfamilies (or blended or reconstituted families). The remarrying couple with children confront an extra layer of required adjustments, including lagging social policies, but tensions between parents and their stepchildren present the greatest challenge. Newly remarried parents also face somewhat higher probabilities of divorce because of special role strains, ambiguous boundaries, and few social guidelines. Stepchildren often exhibit the same difficulties as those in single-parent families because they are without stable role models, have no clear script for their relationship with their new parents, and lack innate protection from their nonbiological relatives. Daughters' difficulties may last longer and be more intense. Like other families, however, blended families are capable of managing the processes of their complex situation.

extended family	polyandry	monogamy
nuclear family	patriarchy	bilateral descent
family	matriarchy	egalitarianism
polygamy	patrilineal	homogamy
polygyny	matrilineal	

10
Chapter

ECONOMIC AND POLITICAL INSTITUTIONS

WHY ARE AFRICA'S ECONOMIES UNDEVELOPED?

SOCIALISM OR CAPITALISM: WHICH IS BEST FOR AFRICA?

GETTING AHEAD IN THE U.S. ECONOMY

POLITICS IN AFRICA

RESEARCH BOX: WHY SO MANY MILITARY COUPS IN AFRICA?

IS DEMOCRACY BEST FOR AFRICAN NATIONS?

CRITICAL THINKING BOX: DEMOCRACY FOR NIGERIA?

WHAT STANDS BETWEEN U.S. VOTERS AND POLITICAL POWER?

Many of the ideas of Karl Marx, such as his prediction of capitalism's demise, now lay in ruins. Others, like his vision of the ideal society, were distorted into schemes that legitimized oppressive states. His insight into the central importance of the economy in society, however, is generally acknowledged across the political spectrum. Using Africa as a setting, we will examine the role of the economy in conjunction with a closely related institution: government.

Undeveloped countries, like most of those in Africa, feature destitute masses in stark contrast to a very small elite.

WHY ARE AFRICA'S ECONOMIES UNDEVELOPED?

Technically, "undeveloped" societies are those lacking the organization and technology for industrial mass production. In real terms, though, it means hundreds of millions of destitute, illiterate, starving people subsisting on the equivalent of a few hundred dollars *a year*. It means modern conveniences and luxury goods for a small elite, bare subsistence for the masses. It means minimal health care, and epidemics sweeping through weakened populations.

Until recently, such nonindustrialized societies fit one of two categories. The Second World included all communist countries, even those not industrialized, like Vietnam. The Third World encompassed noncommunist, nonindustrialized societies, largely in southern Asia, South America, and Africa. (All the noncommunist, industrialized nations, such as those in western Europe, the United States, and Japan made up the First World.) The "Third World" category unfortunately lumped together countries with vastly different governments and living standards, ranging from the economic dynamos of Singapore and Taiwan to the troubled regimes in sub-Saharan Africa. And since the abrupt disintegration of the Second World at the end of the 1980s, this three-fold classification has become even less useful.

An alternative system distinguishes between "developed," "less developed," and "undeveloped," but there are still some nations that simply do not fit any of the three categories— some would more accurately be labeled "developing" or "underdeveloped." As we explore Africa's economies, we must also remember that we are covering a huge territory, from the highly developed economy of South Africa to torn and tattered Somalia. Despite its inherent shortcomings, however, we will use this more descriptive system.

Excepting South Africa, most of Africa's economies fit all too easily into the undeveloped category. Most struggle to build a few factories, create some jobs, and feed their exploding populations. For the past few decades, adverse global economic forces, droughts, overgrazing, intertribal slaughter, and inept governing have produced one pitiable situation after another. For example, war and hunger have haunted Angola since the fall of colonialism; the government has used much of the nation's wealth to fight rebels—and to build a presidential palace. Likewise, Sudan has endured a decade of civil war between Islamic fundamentalists in the north trying to impose their rule on the south, home to Christianity and various tribal religions. Some cases attract the world's attention, as did Ethiopia in the 1980s and Somalia in the early 1990s. The International Red Cross reported, for example, that one-fourth of Somalia's children under the age of five died in 1992. Hundreds of thousands of Somalian refugees fled to neighboring countries to escape the paralyzing warfare between rival clans.

The United Nations took the extraordinary step in 1986 of establishing an economic development program for just this one region of the world. Four years later, the U.N. reported that economic conditions in Africa had actually declined, going from bad to worse. Gross national product per person shrank in most countries on the continent. Domestic and foreign investment remained low, savings stagnated. Africa as a whole lost $50 billion due to falling commodity prices. The flow of resources into the continent decreased despite U.N. efforts.

What has retarded Africa's economies while so many others have surged? News stories tell one side of Africa's difficulties: civil strife, political instability, overpopulation, a staggering burden of foreign debt, and poor soil and weather conditions. Encroaching masses of desperate populations strip forests and abuse the land, turning it into desert. But sociologists tell another side of the story, one focusing on external forces that, like a heavy hand, weigh down upon the continent.

According to **world systems theory** (Wallerstein, 1974), modern industrial societies (the "core" of the world system) exploit less developed nations like those in Africa (the "periphery"). The periphery provides raw materials, cheap labor, and new markets by which the core enriches itself further. In this view, a nation's position in the world system determines its chances for economic development. Those on the periphery find themselves in a hole, with small chance of getting out. Indeed, African nations encounter a "zero sum game" when they enter the global economy. With a fixed amount of wealth in the world and some players enjoying far greater skills and resources than others, core nations usually gain wealth at the expense of those on the periphery.

> **World systems theory**: the theory that developed societies (the "core") exploit the less developed nations (the "periphery") for their resources, labor, and markets.

Much as the capitalist elite in any one country uses its advantages to maintain its superordinate position over the laboring classes, core nations use unequal exchanges with other nations to preserve the global capitalist system. The major instrument in this process is **multinational corporations** (also called transnationals), or **MNCs**. As their label implies, MNCs transcend national boundaries, with branches and facilities in many countries (see Figure 10-1). Their reach extends over the globe, enabling them to buy and sell from an advantageous position. Multinationals enjoy control over production technology, marketing tools, and finance capital. With such leverage, the core nations can continually strengthen their own political and economic position without threat from the periphery. (See Table 10-1.)

> **Multinational corporations (MNCs)**: business organizations that transcend national boundaries, with branches and facilities in many countries.

In some ways, MNCs benefit their host countries. In fact, *modernization theory* assumes that private foreign investment boosts the economic fortunes of developing countries. MNCs have broadened their strategy from merely extracting raw materials for home-based manufacturing to building manufacturing facilities in host nations. The products of these factories are either exported or offered in poorer nations' domestic markets. This investment strategy brings into the undeveloped world not only jobs, especially for women (Clark, 1992), and a flood of consumer goods, but beneficial technology and other resources (Clausen, 1987). From this viewpoint, the host countries are indeed fortunate to be "exploited" by MNCs. These corporations, however, tend to invest in countries that show some development already, economic growth, a high level of government consumption, and a growing, educated population (Crenshaw, 1991). Because of their high poverty rates and weak consumer demand, most African nations have little hope to enter the global economy let alone emulate recent successes such as Hong Kong and South Korea.

Dependency theory, however, reveals a more insidious side of the influence of MNCs. From this perspective, a less overt form of neocolonialism has replaced the old colonial exploitation. Like a large and aggressive parasite enfeebling its host, the penetration of foreign capital eventually undermines the fragile domestic economies of

> **Dependency theory**: the theory that the penetration of foreign capital undermines the economies of developing countries.

Industry	Company Global 500 Rank	Country	Company sales (in millions)
AEROSPACE	Boeing 35	U.S.	$30,414
APPAREL	Levi Strauss Associates 274	U.S.	$5,570
BEVERAGES	PepsiCo 51	U.S.	$22,084
BUILDING MATERIALS, GLASS	Saint-Gobain 91	France	$14,297
CHEMICALS	E.I. Du Pont de Nemours 26	U.S.	$37,386
COMPUTERS, OFFICE EQUIPMENT	IBM 7	U.S.	$65,096
ELECTRONICS, ELECTRICAL EQUIPMENT	General Electric 9	U.S.	$62,202
FOOD	Philip Morris 17	U.S.	$50,157
FOREST AND PAPER PRODUCTS	International Paper 100	U.S.	$13,600
INDUSTRIAL AND FARM EQUIPMENT	Mitsubishi Heavy Industries 49	Japan	$23,011
JEWELRY, WATCHES	Citizen Watch 428	Japan	$3,328
METAL PRODUCTS	Pechiney 111	France	$12,344
METALS	IRI 6	Italy	$67,547
MINING, CRUDE-OIL PRODUCTION	Ruhrkohle 81	Germany	$15,712
MOTOR VEHICLES AND PARTS	General Motors 1	U.S.	$132,775
PETROLEUM REFINING	Exxon 2	U.S.	$103,547
PHARMACEUTICALS	Johnson & Johnson 97	U.S.	$13,846
PUBLISHING, PRINTING	Matra-Hachette 133	France	$10,416
RUBBER AND PLASTIC PRODUCTS	Bridgestone 96	Japan	$13,860
SCIENTIFIC, PHOTO, CONTROL EQUIP.	Eastman Kodak 61	U.S.	$20,577
SOAPS, COSMETICS	Procter & Gamble 36	U.S.	$29,890
TEXTILES	Toray Industries 192	Japan	$7,862
TOBACCO	RJR Nabisco Holdings 79	U.S.	$15,734
TOYS, SPORTING GOODS	Nintendo 289	Japan	$5,213
TRANSPORTATION EQUIPMENT	Hyundai Heavy Industries 232	S. Korea	$6,518

Figure 10-1

BIGGEST COMPANIES IN THE WORLD BY INDUSTRY

Developing nations face a huge disadvantage competing in the world economy against giants like these.

Source: *Fortune*, vol. 128, no. 2, page 190, July 26, 1993. Used with permission. © 1993 Time Inc. All rights reserved.

developing countries (Bornschier and Chase-Dunn, 1985). The economic dependency on outside investment leads to a number of social problems, including a lag in the decline of fertility (London, 1988), urban bias (London and Smith, 1988), lower prosperity for the masses (London and Williams, 1990; Stokes and Anderson, 1990), repression and collective political violence (Boswell and Dixon, 1990; London and Robinson, 1989), and the exclusion of the lower classes from the political process (Timberlake and Williams, 1984). Research also exposes how MNCs increase income inequality within the host country (Bornschier and Chase-Dunn, 1985). Transnational corporations discourage unionization and government policies that redistribute wealth, and try to use as little labor as possible while simultaneously paying high salaries to the managers and technicians they employ. All this tends to polarize

MULTINATIONAL CORPORATIONS BASED IN THE UNITED STATES, 1992

Company	Total Revenue (Millions of Dollars)	Foreign Revenue as Percentage of Total
Exxon	103,160	76.8
General Motors	132,429	32.0
IBM	64,523	61.8
Mobil	57,389[1]	68.1
Ford Motor	100,132	35.7
Texaco[2]	50,041	52.6
Chevron[2]	46,612	44.1
Citicorp	31,948	60.3
E.I. du Pont de Nemours	37,208	46.9
Procter & Gamble	29,362	49.7

Table 10-1

[1] Includes other income.
[2] Includes proportionate interest in unconsolidated subsidiaries or affiliates.

Source: Reprinted by permission of *FORBES* magazine. © Forbes, Inc. 1992

incomes. Furthermore, Dale Wimberly (1991) reports a correlation between MNC penetration and hunger as measured by a decline in the host nation's consumption of calories and protein. Economic stagnation, however, heads the list of negative consequences of MNC involvement. But how can foreign investment, which brings in huge sums of badly needed capital, harm a host nation's economy?

Foreign investment does less for the host economy than would domestic investment (Firebaugh, 1992). For one thing, the MNC typically invests in only one type of product without forming links with other industries in the host nation. Without such linkages, the rest of the economy receives little if any stimulation. For another, multinational corporations often manage to avoid taxes, and thus may provide little in the way of public revenues. MNCs also funnel much of their profits back to their home-base nations rather than reinvest in the host economy.

Sociologists find several harmful consequences of foreign corporations reaching into undeveloped areas like Africa.

According to dependency theory, MNCs actually *retard* local economic growth. "Decapitalization," a long-term decline in investment, results from the MNC destroying fledgling domestic businesses that simply cannot compete with the muscular outsider. Also, the MNC soaks up much of the local resources and talent. It uses its marketing savvy to stimulate among the populace a hunger for expensive goods available only through the MNC's local industry. The consumer's funds are thus diverted away from domestic businesses. The transnational's dominance of the economy enables it to raise prices in the host market, including prices of its own cheaply imported goods. The profits thus reaped mostly find their way back to the home country rather than the host nation. As the domestic market reaches saturation, the MNC invests less and less in the host nation, and stagnation ensues. What looked like a looming wave of prosperity often recedes before it ever reaches shore.

As developing nations, including many in Africa, move into a new type of dependence arrangement, the scenario becomes more complex. In "classical dependence," the core nation simply exploits the host's raw materials and inhibits economic development (Frank, 1972). More recently, however, peripheral countries have enjoyed substantial economic growth through "dependent development" (Evans, 1979). When the core's interest changes from merely extracting resources to manufacturing, MNCs acquire land and materials in the host nation. Such foreign investment triggers growth, but only in the "modern" (mostly industrial) sectors of the host's economy. This arrangement, which requires a triple alliance of multinational corporations, local businesses, and the host government, enables the core to not only use the low-wage workers of developing nations but to access their consumer markets. Local businesses contribute their well-developed commercial networks, while the government uses import tariffs, tax laws, and other policies to protect the MNC's investment. A small elite of bureaucrats and managers then share in the wealth created by foreign capital.

Kenya offers a clear example of an African nation making the transition from classical dependence to dependent development (Bradshaw, 1988). Most of its foreign investment, coming from dozens of companies including Firestone, Singer, Esso, and Pepsico, goes into manufacturing concerns. The government has lured this capital by promising not to nationalize foreign assets, allowing MNCs to ship most of their profits back home, protecting the investors with import tariffs, and limiting the number of products competitors can produce in or import to Kenya. For example, in the 1960s it levied an import tariff of 15 to 50 percent on goods that competed with those already manufactured by transnationals in Kenya (Eglin, 1978). In 1969, the government banned all tire imports into Kenya not permitted by Firestone (Langdon, 1978). At the same time, it protected domestic industry by banning noncitizens (mostly Asians) from trade and requiring foreign manufacturers to use local distributors. The Kenyan government has set up several cooperative ventures between the state treasury, local firms, and MNCs. In these cases, it gains not only tax revenues but direct profits. Although Kenya's business elite does not usually enjoy equal footing with the multinational corporations, they still reap handsome benefits.

According to Glenn Firebaugh's analysis of foreign capital penetration (1992), Kenya's economic growth should come as no surprise. By "adding appropriate measures of investment," most less-developed nations (including those in Africa) benefit from foreign investment *over the long run*. In fact, his data indicate that accumulated foreign investment boosts total, long-term investment rather than decapitalization.

Kenya's story, however, reveals a darker side to this MNC-inspired economic growth. Certainly millions of investment dollars have entered the country since the early 1960s, but perhaps even more wealth, in the form of MNC profits, has flowed out

(Bradshaw, 1988). Of the generated capital that stays in Kenya, most of it remains in the hands of politicos and business leaders allied with the transnationals. As in other cases, dependency creates uneven economic development—that is, growth only in certain sectors of the economy to the benefit of a select few.

In sum, then, while African economic development is in part hindered by civil strife and government ineptness, two major external factors are also at work. First, the consequences of foreign investment offer at best mixed blessings. Second, Africa's undeveloped nations must deal with a global system in which weak and inexperienced nations face enormous disadvantages.

SOCIALISM OR CAPITALISM: WHICH IS BEST FOR AFRICA?

In the quiet villages of traditional societies still found in Africa and other undeveloped areas, the two main tasks of the economic system, production and distribution, flow naturally from the people's traditions. Son follows father's occupational footsteps, daughters perform the same tasks as their great grandmothers, and few technological changes intrude. The people produce what they always have, taking whatever the land and local opportunities offer. They share the resulting goods and services according to ancient kinship patterns. This traditional economic arrangement leaves no room for worries about unemployment or career choices, but it results in a relatively low material standard of living.

As such societies begin to move toward modernity and industrialization, tradition can no longer adequately direct production and distribution. Their economies change in one of two directions (see Table 10-2). The path of **socialism** leads toward collective ownership of the means of production (or capital, which includes land, factories, mines, and so on), and central control of the distribution of goods and services. Socialist governments effectively decide what will be produced and who gets what. Equality guides distribution policies: Ideally, no one prospers or suffers more than anyone else. Work is motivated by concern for the common good rather than personal advancement. In contrast, **capitalism** is based upon private ownership of the means of production and the pursuit of personal profit. Citizens may own, say, a factory, farm, or railroad, and keep any profits gained. Ideally, together these profits increase national wealth, enlarging society's economic "pie." Market forces (supply and demand) determine production and distribution: Capitalists provide whatever goods and services

Socialism: economic system in which the means of production are collectively owned; the state directs production and distribution.

Capitalism: economic system in which the means of production are privately owned; market forces determine production and distribution.

SOCIALISM VERSUS CAPITALISM

	Capitalism	Socialism
Ownership of means of production	Private	Public, collective
Control of production and distribution	Self-adjusting market mechanisms	Centralized government planning
Motivating factor	Individual initiative, profit motive	Collectivism: work for the people
Goal	Increased wealth	Economic equality

Table 10-2

consumers demand, and they are distributed to whomever can afford them. The individual is allowed to prosper or suffer privation, depending on her or his initiative and performance.

The descriptions above clearly refer only to model economic systems. Neither occurs in its pure form in reality. Any economy includes features of both models; that is, all economies are mixed. Socialist-oriented economies—China, for example—allow some degree of profit taking, and the United States economy exhibits socialist features in the government's manipulation of the money supply, its intervention in investment patterns through taxing and spending policies, Social Security, business regulations, and Medicare. Thus, when we categorize an economy as "capitalist" or "socialist," we mean it more closely resembles one or the other system. Our question here is, Which route should developing African nations take?

Many African countries that gained independence from capitalist European colonial powers after World War II turned to socialist economic strategies. Leaders sought to marshall their nation's resources to ensure that each individual enjoyed a decent standard of living, free from want and exploitation. Food, education, health care, and housing were to be free or within the reach of any family. Postcolonial nations wanted to avoid the horrid flaws of their former "masters": cutthroat competition, the disgraceful gap between rich and poor, hedonistic materialism, and exploitation of workers by powerful and greedy capitalists. Newly independent Ghana and Guinea, for example, created huge state-run steel and cement corporations. Tanzania forced 85 percent of its population into experimental communes. Many governments assumed control of agriculture and commerce and offered subsidies for food, housing, and transportation. State employment mushroomed (along with corruption and inefficiency). Socialist programs enjoyed the support of foreign financing and temporarily high prices for the cocoa, coffee, sugar, and oil produced by many African countries.

These nations found, however, as did the former Soviet Union and many other socialist governments, that inequality often persists—an elite of bureaucrats and black-market profiteers enjoy a decidedly better-than-equal standard of living due to endemic corruption. Also, in the absence of profit motivation, productivity often falters. In most African countries, these problems were complicated by heavy borrowing, incompetent administration, ambitious state enterprises that ran up enormous debts, and, by the early 1980s, dropping prices and soaring interest rates around the globe. Many African economies crashed. The interest on some nations' debts ate up nearly half their export earnings. Bankrupt African countries turned desperately to the International Monetary Fund and the World Bank.

These two agencies agreed to come to the rescue of those nations that would move toward the capitalist end of the economic spectrum. Most have done so with an enthusiasm born of desperate hopes. For many African countries, capitalism holds the promise of economic salvation, and they have sought to get the fumbling, corrupt hands of government out of their economies and to attract investors through tax breaks and free-trade zones. Several organizations are aimed at creating regional markets and spreading technology throughout the continent to become more competitive in the global market.

Other nations' experiences show the dangers that lurk in this headlong rush toward capitalism. America's "robber barons" of the late 1800s—John D. Rockefeller, Cornelius Vanderbilt, Andrew Carnegie and others—showed that unrestrained, or "pure" capitalism creates a fabulously wealthy elite who use their power to consolidate their own position and lock out the poor. In Africa, this would simply continue the

economic inequality introduced by the ruling class of the colonial era and the post-colonial dictators. Michael Burawoy and Pavel Krotov (1992) note that in the former Soviet Union's transition to capitalism, the old state-run enterprises retain their stranglehold and transactions are based on back-door bartering rather than free-market forces.

The experience of newly developing economies may be different. Researchers note that the recent shift from socialism to capitalism in China, for example, redistributes economic power from bureaucratic officials to the masses (Nee, 1991). But as we saw earlier, neocolonialist MNCs complicate the course of capitalism in developing economies today, often exploiting the host nation.

Recent developments in U.S. commerce highlight another unpleasant aspect of capitalism: unfair competition that holds consumer prices unnecessarily high. While the free market and fierce competition supposedly guarantee top-notch products and low prices, some businesses have used ingenious ways to eliminate rivals and dominate markets (Hage, Boroughs, and Black, 1992). Farm lobbies, for example, fight for government subsidies that maintain high prices for milk, sugar, and peanut butter. Physicians refer patients to high-priced laboratories in which the doctors hold financial interests. Cable television companies use barriers to lock out competitors while raising their rates three times the pace of inflation. And a consumer buying an airline ticket will probably be steered to one of the giant companies that control the special computerized reservation system used by most travel agents. Will not African capitalists use similar tactics to exploit their own economic opportunities?

Those African economies that move into the advanced stages of capitalism may feature **corporatism,** in which top labor and business leaders negotiate wage and price

One of the dangers of unrestrained capitalism lies in the rise of fabulously wealthy and powerful individuals, like John D. Rockefeller, who exerted enormous influence in the late 1800s. Africa, unfortunately, has experienced its share of powerful leaders in the past few decades, but without the fruits of capitalist development. Zaire's leader Mobutu typified Africa's "Big Men," presiding over his country's economic collapse during three decades of dictatorial rule.

Corporatism: form of advanced capitalism in which top labor and business leaders negotiate wage and price agreements at the national level.

agreements at the national level. Such high-level collaboration usually contributes to economic growth and generous welfare policies (Hicks and Patterson, 1989; Wilensky and Turner, 1987), but it also tends to stifle labor militancy (Panitch, 1986). Small African nations with social democratic governments that face great financial uncertainty and have little clout in the global economy are the most likely candidates for corporatist development (Western, 1991).

Will capitalism serve Africa's needs better than socialism? The question involves more than a choice between social equality and economic vigor. Like socialism, capitalism has a number of inherent flaws when applied to real-world scenarios. Also, emerging nations face a number of capitalist forms. Many developing nations in East Asia, such as Singapore and Malaysia, follow the Japanese model of capitalism. That is, rather than rely on wide-open competition and consumer demand to drive their economies (as in the United States), they exercise more government control and show more concern for workers. Perhaps African nations would be advised to shelter chosen industries from foreign competition until they can effectively compete in the global marketplace. Or they might rely on a new, "African" brand of capitalism, one based on traditional peasant methods of production and exchange and home-grown enterprises such as dye and textiles (Hydan, 1983; Iliffe, 1983). For now, in any case, Africa's economic future seems to hang on the success or failure of various capitalist models.

GETTING AHEAD IN THE U.S. ECONOMY

We now shift our focus from the global economy to more immediate concerns, such as finding a good job or succeeding in business here in the United States. We saw in Chapter 6 that social mobility depends on several personal factors, such as family background and education, which largely determine one's eventual occupation. But once in the marketplace, many Americans feel like they are groping for the stairs in a dark building. As we will see, sociologists have discovered some of the stairways and dead-end passages of the labor market's structure. They can also identify some of the factors that cause a business venture to succeed or fail. Together these insights provide some guidance in getting ahead in the U.S. economy. (See Figure 10-2.)

Labor Unions

For decades, labor unions have secured rights and concessions that benefit all American workers but to appreciate current trends it is important to understand the rocky road labor has traveled. From its emergence in the late 1880s, the movement faced fierce, even violent opposition from management and sometimes the government. Part of the hostility directed against labor organizations stemmed from the widely reported involvement of socialist radicals. The movement was also weakened by internal conflict between the American Federation of Labor, which represented skilled craft workers, and the wider constituency represented by the Congress of Industrial Organizations. Critics claim that highly skilled, white males benefited most from unions and by ignoring their fellow workers, abandoned the movement's original goals of worker solidarity and equality. Prejudice against nonwhites, women, and immigrants prevented the emergence of a united laboring class waging war against capitalists.

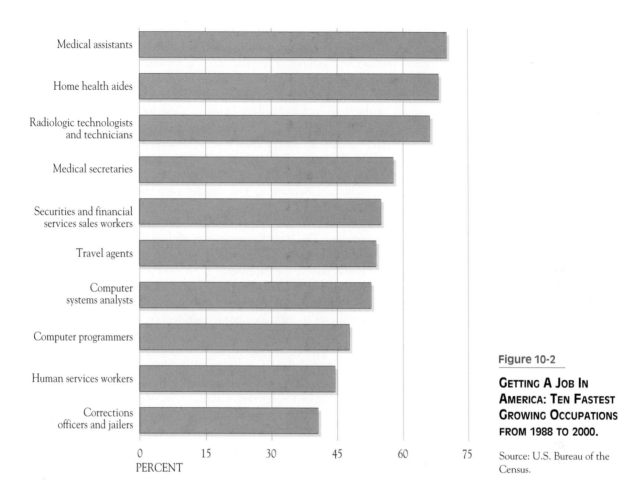

Figure 10-2

GETTING A JOB IN AMERICA: TEN FASTEST GROWING OCCUPATIONS FROM 1988 TO 2000.

Source: U.S. Bureau of the Census.

Organized labor finally achieved some respectability and a firm legal footing in the 1930s. By then it had largely lost its identification with bomb-throwing anarchists. The Great Depression had created national sympathy for workers, and Congress granted unions empowering rights regarding collective bargaining and union membership. According to Judith Stepan-Norris and Maurice Zeitlin (1991), Communist Party labor leaders led the way in gaining prolabor provisions in contracts with management. However, factions within the labor movement effectively stripped Communists of their power after World War II, opening the door for a new era of labor–capital cooperation. Employers offered higher wages and job security to organized labor in return for a relatively docile, reliable work force. Unionized workers gained a greater share in the growing prosperity of the postwar economy, and capitalists enjoyed a sharp decrease in the number of disruptive strikes.

The labor movement clearly enhanced workers' bargaining leverage through the 1950s and 1960s, creating job slots with higher pay, shorter working hours, and greater safety, benefits, and security than would have existed otherwise. In fact, labor organizations still exert indirect influence: Even the threat of unionization can prompt employers to raise the wages of nonunionized workers under certain circumstances (Leicht, 1989). While the United States, unlike most major industrialized nations, does not protect all workers from arbitrary dismissal, union members cannot be fired except for "good" or "just" cause (Grenig, 1991). By using their collective strength, unions have created enormous "support groups" for all workers in the labor force.

Since the 1970s, however, unions have lost much of their power to shape opportunities in the labor market. Union membership has declined from 34 percent of the labor force in the 1950s to around 16 percent today. With fewer members, unions cannot mount strikes as effectively, and can gain fewer concessions from employers. The loss of blue-collar, manufacturing jobs, where unions drew most of their strength, explains much of the drop in membership. Many of these jobs were lost to overseas competition: The tight job market allowed employers to more easily replace striking workers with "scabs" willing to accept lower wages. Unions were also slow to recruit women, minorities, and white-collar workers, who have displaced many blue-collar workers over the past few decades. Those union workers who did enjoy higher wages often lost their anticapital orientation. The unions' own success contributed to a weakening of labor solidarity.

With the arrival of the 1980s, its strength slipping, labor increasingly had to make concessions to management. President Reagan's shattering of the air traffic controllers' strike in 1981 signaled the start of a new era, one in which corporate management utilized the strength it had gained at the expense of labor. Ever since World War II, management had used the strategy of tying workers' interests to the corporation, thus weakening labor organizations' capacity to confront management. This surrender of power also allowed capitalists to introduce production technologies that reduced skill requirements. From this position of strength in the 1970s and 1980s, management successfully demanded wage reductions and other concessions from organized labor (Burawoy, 1985). From the conflict perspective, this labor-control strategy offered workers short-term gains but weakened workers' collective strength in the long run.

Workers entering the labor force today will find that unions play a smaller role than decades ago. However, they show no signs of declining into insignificance. Adjusting to new realities in the work force, labor organizations have been recruiting more women than ever before; in fact, women are joining at a higher rate than men. Also, unions have found increasing success organizing teachers and government and clerical workers. Even professionals have been forming professional associations. Unions' goals have also shifted with economic changes. Instead of seeking higher wages from employers caught in fierce competition with foreign firms, unions now generally seek to maintain or improve working conditions and benefits. They measure success more in terms of better child care, less job stress, more comprehensive medical care, and career development and job training. Clearly, labor unions still have an impact on work in the United States.

Spatial Considerations

Looking at the labor market geographically, we see that some places offer better opportunities than others. The transformation of the United States to a postindustrial economy has caused a spatial redistribution of jobs. There is a greater need for administrative, professional, and technical workers, but these information-based service jobs are generally found in cities rather than the suburbs, where personal service (waitress, for example) and clerical work are more in demand.

Not all of us, however, have the high level of education required for these desirable jobs. Ironically, a large proportion of the people living close to them have the educational credentials more suited to the typical low-skill jobs commonly found in the suburbs. In fact according to the **spatial mismatch hypothesis,** this shift of low-skill job growth to the suburbs helps account for the high unemployment rates of minority groups, who are concentrated in the inner cities.

Spatial mismatch hypothesis: that the shift of low-skill jobs to the suburbs accounts for the high unemployment rates of minorities in the inner cities.

J. F. Kain (1968) first noted that residential segregation patterns, based on housing market discrimination, isolate minorities, especially African Americans, from employment opportunities. D. T. Ellwood (1986) points out that businesses view minority neighborhoods as poor risks for opening up production facilities, so this supply of labor goes untapped locally. Instead, these potential workers, with few resources, are forced to locate jobs in faraway suburbs and then pay commuting costs. Other researchers, however, argue that discrimination in the labor market, more than residential segregation and spatial changes in the job market, cause the generally lower wage levels of blacks (Blackley, 1990). Either way, inner-city minorities face extra disadvantages in getting ahead in the U.S. economy.

Women present a special case. As professional opportunities opened up for women in the 1970s, the spatial distribution of female employment changed. Once clustered in very large cities, highly paid women professionals have diffused across the nation's urban network (Kodras and Padavic, 1993). The changing structure of the labor market has thus freed this class of workers geographically.

Labor Market Segmentation

Another part of a sociological guide to the labor market involves the market's fragmentation or segmentation. The entering worker would do well to note the advantages offered in some segments or sectors of the market.

This segmentation perspective contrasts with the neoclassical model, which assumes workers operate in a competitive labor market where wages tend toward equilibrium over the long run, employers must eventually pay the "going rate" or "equilibrium wage" to attract and retain qualified workers. Paying below the equilibrium wage loses employees to higher wage offers elsewhere. Paying above the going rate drives costs so high as to diminish the firm's competitiveness. Most sociologists, however, would advise job seekers to work under a different assumption.

Most researchers today find a **dual labor market** comprised of a primary sector, in which workers enjoy strong bargaining powers, and a secondary one, in which workers face lower wages and less stability. For example, the pay and fringe benefits enjoyed by employees in the oil industry is generally about 50 percent above average; the tobacco industry and public utilities offer a total compensation package 40 percent and 30 percent higher, respectively, than the norm. On the other hand, retailing pays about 15 percent below the average, and restaurants roughly 30 percent below average (Katz and Summers, 1989).

These disparities stem from the fact that workers' leverage in wage negotiations depends on such factors as skill requirements, turnover costs, and firm-specific skills. Employers in the primary sector need highly skilled workers to maximize productivity, and so must pay higher wages. Furthermore, companies that rely on senior workers to teach job skills usually pay their workers better than the going rate because they are expensive to replace. Such workers also enjoy insulation from competition from most other workers; instead, they operate within a small internal labor market, vying for vacancies in the established hierarchy of promotion slots in their company. Many jobs in the primary sector are covered by union contracts, which offer workers not only higher wages but better security and working conditions, including more safety protections and less harsh, autocratic employer control (Brown, 1980; Edwards, 1979). These workers tend to stay with their company and move up its authority hierarchy (Hachen, 1992). Workers in the secondary sector, in contrast, are more replaceable and usually face competition from outside their companies, forcing them to accept

Dual labor market: a segregated labor market in which workers in the primary sector enjoy advantages that those in the secondary sector do not.

lower wages and poorer working conditions. Such disadvantages characterize the wholesaling, textiles, apparel, lumber, and furniture industries, while mining, chemicals, oil, rubber, and machinery generally offer more advantages to workers (Hodson, 1978; Weakliem, 1990).

Workers would also be well advised to seek jobs in "core" firms that dominate their sector of the national economy, or even the local one (South and Xu, 1990). Such corporations wield considerable political and financial power and enjoy relatively constant demand for their products. They can thus use capital-intensive production techniques (that is, a high degree of mechanization and automation rather than human labor) to achieve high profit margins. Because companies in such favorable circumstances grow faster than others, core firms tend to be large (Villemez and Bridges, 1988). They have the financial resources to pay skilled workers high wages.

In contrast, workers in "periphery" firms, or the "competitive fringe," face more layoffs and plant shut-downs. Periphery firms confront relatively unpredictable demand, and thus must use more elastic production techniques to meet sudden swings in the market. This translates into labor-intensive methods rather than expensive technology that may stand idle for days. Worker costs must also be kept low and flexible, which means hiring many part-time workers with few benefits and getting rid of workers when demand drops.

Dual labor market theory thus suggests that workers will increase their chances of success in the U.S. economy by entering professional, managerial, and other high-skill occupations or those depending on firm-specific expertise, in core industries, in large firms, and in jobs covered by collective bargaining (union) contracts (Sakamoto and Chen, 1991). This model, however, may be less applicable today. The segmentation of the labor market began after World War II, when unionized employees won highly favorable concessions, and core workers pulled away from those in the periphery. But these differences began to diminish after the mid-1970s (Gordon, Edwards, and Reich, 1982). Since then, the wages and working conditions of the core have stagnated, perhaps as a result of previously described labor-control strategies used by management (Weakliem, 1990). This decline of union power may have weakened the differences between primary and secondary sectors in the U.S. economy (Mills, 1985; Pfeffer and Baron, 1988). As the market changes, the dual labor market theory may eventually give way to another model.

Sociologists trying to understand the repercussions of the new postindustrial society have identified another development in the structure of the labor market. Daniel Bell (1973), Larry Hirschhorn (1984) and others contend that market competition and new technologies continuously create new skilled occupations or lead to the upgrading, or "reskilling," of existing ones. Automation eliminates low-skill manual jobs, and those that remain involve more autonomy, skill, and decision-making responsibilities.

On the other hand, conflict theorists like Braverman (1974) argue that capitalists maximize their exploitation of labor by minimizing the number of scientifically and technologically advanced (and expensive) workers while "deskilling" as many jobs as possible. This tendency polarizes the labor force by creating more low-skilled workers and fewer high-skilled ones. Management, for example, makes use of "floating" workers who move from one poorly paid job to another, older workers, and new workers, many of whom are women displaced from agricultural and household labor by child care, food processing, and clothes-making professionals. Such semiskilled and unskilled service workers, along with the underemployed (those working at jobs below their ability), make up the "industrial reserve army" or "labor reserve" capitalists use to

As Watanabe (1991) explains, the Japanese quality control circle helped Japanese industries shift from low cost to excellent quality in the last several decades. Just after World War II. . . .

minimize labor costs. According to Thomas Steiger and Mark Wardell (1992), while postindustrial changes do create some new, highly skilled occupations, the labor market tends to be flooded with many more low-end jobs. In fact, they predict that as companies create more "flexible" (largely part-time) jobs, "the workforce increasingly will contain a minority of aristocratic workers compared to a disproportionate number of marginalized workers" (p. 428). This pessimistic forecast promises attractive opportunities for very few new workers.

Another view offers a more complex picture: The economic environment and the decisions managers make about organizing their companies and choosing technologies will determine what kinds of jobs arise in each firm (Form et al., 1988). For example, a company in the core sector or one that operates in a market demanding high quality, specialized products or services will foster job-skill upgrading (Kelley, 1990). Whatever the outcome of current trends in labor market segmentation, it is probably safe to say that some parts of the economy will offer workers more opportunities for long-term success than others.

Succeeding in Business

An increasing number of Americans today are opening new businesses to get ahead (Steinmetz and Wright, 1989). Those seeking to become entrepeneurs, however, should be aware that a high proportion of new businesses fail soon after they begin (Bruderl and Schussler, 1990). A look at the demands of today's economy explains this high rate of failure. As Anthony Carnevale (1991) explains, success requires using new technologies to deliver exactly what the consumer wants. This means customized, high-quality goods and convenient services delivered in a timely manner. Instead of producing huge quantities of low-quality goods using cheap labor, as American corporations have done so successfully for many generations, new manufacturers rely on

Most successful founders are middle aged and often have had previous experience in leadership or in the industry. Bill Gates, founder of industry-leader Microsoft, the most successful business of the Information Age, is a college drop-out who became the nation's richest man (worth about $6.3 billion) at age 37.

loosely knit, flexible networks of more autonomous workers, somewhat like teams of old-time artisans. Rising companies today are replacing the traditional autocratic climate with a democratic one (Solomon, 1993). They are also striving to keep their employees informed about the company's goals and involved in making decisions. Communication no longer travels merely from top to bottom, it now tends to embrace more employees in a vast, fluid web of respectful interchange.

Beyond these general observations, sociologists have identified several factors that can help make or break a company. Most have focused on personal qualities of the business's founder. One study, for example, found that those who start their business in middle age achieve higher rates of success than those who are young or in advanced years (Preisendorfer and Voss, 1990). The founder's "human capital" (educational, family, and occupational background) serves to attract more customers and investors, increase productivity, and earn higher profits (Bates, 1985). Other predictors of business success include the founder's prior self-employment, leadership experience, and time in the industry (Scase and Goffee, 1982; Young and Francis, 1991), and self-employment of her or his parents, who presumably serve as role models (Bates, 1990).

Research also suggests how to better structure one's budding business. First, consider an employee ownership plan, which increases employee commitment when the workers feel they derive real influence and financial rewards from the arrangement (Buchko, 1992). Second, study the industry and discover the minimum start-up size for that particular field; remember, small new businesses have a higher failure rate (Bruderl, Preisendorfer, and Ziegler, 1992). Third, consider a form of organization known as "virtual corporation." This type of business is run.like a family, with no hierarchy. Finally, it may be beneficial to create a network of partners, other businesses with which you can work closely and cooperatively, sharing capital and markets. Trust and loyalty reign among such partners; deals are arranged on the basis of handshakes rather than complex contracts crafted by lawyers.

Features in the organization's external environment or ecology also predict its success or failure. For example, when a new field opens up in the economy, such as personal computer software, many businesses fail because they have little legitimacy and cannot easily attract customers, investors, or other resources. As more companies enter the field, however, their legitimacy increases and resources become more accessible until the "carrying capacity" is reached. At that point, more organizations mean overcrowding, and a shake-out ensues, raising the failure rate in the field. This research suggests that timing, as in other things, is important: One should ideally enter a field after it has become established, but before it is saturated (Hannan, 1989).

POLITICS IN AFRICA

Moving from economic to political institutions, we enter the domain of power, wherein people exert their control over others. More specifically, here we begin to explore **politics,** the process through which people gain and use power. Africa's rich history offers an exceptionally broad panorama of political forms, as well as boasting some of the world's earliest political institutions. Here we see why societies develop governments, and how those institutions work.

Politics: the process through which people gain and use power.

Why Government?

Max Weber defined a **state** as an institution that claims a monopoly on the use of physical force within its territory. Those who occupy positions of power in the state, and the institutions they form, constitute the **government.** Thus, government officials, as representatives of the state, can force citizens to serve on juries and pay taxes, and can even enter a private home and drag its residents to prison. Why have people created such restraining and intrusive institutions?

State: an institution that claims a monopoly on the use of physical force within its territory.

Government: those who occupy positions of power in the state, and the institutions they form.

The earliest human groupings required no political institutions. Control and punishment flowed from the elders and along kinship lines. Among the !Kung of Namibia's Kalahari Desert, for example, the headman leads the collection of interrelated nuclear families that comprise the hunting and gathering band.

The need for government arose along with the surplus produced by agricultural societies. Some circumstantial evidence suggests that food production may have begun quite early in the forest zone of Africa, but more concrete evidence points to the domestication of barley and wheat, as well as cattle, sheep, and goats, in the Lower Nile region of Egypt by 5000 B.C. Those kin groups that gained control of the surplus wealth rose to prominence to meet the growing societies' needs for greater coordination and control. Some of these early African rulers, like the pharaohs in Egypt and the kings of Ghana, Mali, and Songhai of the vast Sudan region, held nearly absolute power. Observers centuries ago reported kings surrounded by gold, silver, and silk, ruling over domains that took four months to travel across. The ruler of a state of the

Mali empire was said to command 10,000 horsemen and 100,000 foot soldiers (Davidson, 1969, p. 232). The Egyptian rulers commanded the people to build palaces and monumental burial tombs. Ancient Ghanan emperors ruled over "the land of gold."

All these states developed, from the functionalist perspective, in response to the evolving needs of societies. First, any society requires some structure to maintain order and enforce its norms so that some people's irresponsible behaviors will not harm the common good. The seventeenth-century English philosopher Thomas Hobbes argued that human nature's tendencies toward selfishness, brutality, and violence made a state necessary to protect people from their neighbors. As societies began to produce surpluses, they were increasingly differentiated into social strata with various value systems. Because of this differentiation, they could no longer count on elders and kinship structures to spontaneously enforce folkways and mores. They found they needed a centralized, coordinating body to fill the void and maintain order.

Second, states provide planning and policymaking. When many people coordinate their work with others', as in the early, specialized agricultural societies of the Nile Valley, they require, for example, water-rights policies and work regulations. Today, private citizens would probably not anticipate needs for new roads, sewer lines, or schools. Nor would they dependably accumulate the necessary funding for such public projects. Grandiose public works like Africa's new airports and dams required the prodding and strong-arm tactics of the continent's "big men," or postcolonial dictators. Likewise, African government officials must establish policies regarding such common concerns as the use of natural resources, national economic development, and the regulation of multinational corporations. Because of such needs, few African countries tried to revert to traditional tribal governing after gaining independence from their colonial rulers.

Third, when neighboring peoples create large nation-states, others must counter with their own to defend themselves against incursions from huge armies. Individual citizens with their own personal weapons offer ineffective resistance to such organized, well-equipped foes, but government can mobilize huge resources for defense—or conquest. Government representatives can also coordinate diplomatic maneuverings more effectively than the mass of citizenry. Whether conducting war or peace, government manages a people's relationship with other societies.

Conflict theorists see the state as a tool of oppression rather than an institution that serves the people. The eighteenth-century French philosopher Jean-Jacques Rousseau offered one of the earliest critical views of the state. He contended that the establishment of private property made government necessary to protect people's possessions. Protection easily leads to oppression. Following this line of reasoning, Marxists argue that groups which seize control of the means of production gain control of other aspects of society, and use their institutionalized power to subjugate the masses. The state is thus an organization for the violent suppression of the working class. Africa's ancient kings, colonial overlords, and present-day dictators all illustrate how government forcibly extracts labor and wealth from the people for the benefit of a dominating elite.

How Do States Govern?

How does the state rule? How do a small group of people direct and control millions? A state ultimately depends on force. It must possess the power to inflict pain on people, deprive them of freedom, or withhold from them money and other rewards. To

Government representatives can carry out the directives of the state without using force if the government enjoys authority or legitimacy in the eyes of its people.

rule effectively, however, a state must also wield **authority:** power regarded as legitimate or appropriate. Authority confers on the state the right to rule, direct, regulate, and restrain its citizens, all without resorting to demoralizing and disruptive force. In turn, those who believe their government rules legitimately enjoy a sense of unity, loyalty, and civic membership—the opposite of alienation (Weatherford, 1991).

Authority: power regarded as legitimate or appropriate.

The legitimate ruler can also embody the hopes of the people. In many African kingdoms, the monarch was considered mystically united with the kingdom's fate. Among the Margi of northeastern Nigeria, for example, the king's performance foretold the success or failure of the year's harvest, which he was believed to personify. This cut both ways: Well into the twentieth century, the Margi killed rulers who were ill, weak, or presided over deteriorating social conditions (Vaughan, 1964).

Legitimate political systems can also offer people a sense of identity and cohesion. For example, the ancient Yoruba of western Nigeria conceived the state as a projection of the family. Each family was headed by a spiritual leader who in turn was subject to a hierarchy of spirits, all under the protection of a supreme being. Likewise, each town's headman fit into a web of increasingly strong spiritual leaders, all ultimately under one man who derived his power from the mythical founder of Yoruba society. The state's authority structure thus paralleled that of the family, with each person enjoying a place in a vast family-like hierarchy (Davidson, 1969, p. 227).

Regardless of its specific form, every government must have a basis for its authority. Max Weber (1921) identified three such sources of legitimacy.

Traditional Authority   First, many leaders derive their power from long-standing customs. Across the Sudan region of Africa, all along the southern edge of the Sahara, dynasties ruled for centuries without any written laws. Instead, the kings claimed ownership of all the state's lands and livestock, demanded taxes, and presided over a royal court with numerous attendants and ministers, all because such ways had been observed for as long as anyone could remember. As is often the case, traditional authority in these ancient states was based on religion: The rulers were considered to have divine status, much as European kings later ruled by divine right.

Legal-Rational Authority   In the face of encroaching European influences, a few nineteenth-century Sudanese rulers broke with tradition and based their governments on what Weber called legal-rational authority. Samori, a West African leader, formed a political system based on an appointive bureaucracy rather than hereditary chiefs; policies and decisions were based on reason rather than ancestral customs. His innovation foreshadowed the legal-rational governments imposed by the conquering European colonial powers.

Such systems, like our own, govern by laws rather than tradition or force of personality; authority is derived from the office, not the merits of the individual holding that office. Laws, usually written in the form of a constitution, limit the powers of government officials so that, at least in theory, leaders cannot act arbitrarily as did the rulers of ages past.

Charismatic Authority   Charisma, or extraordinary persuasiveness, magnetism, and charm, can also serve as a basis of authority, especially in religious movements where the leader has personal contact with his or her followers. Jesus is the most striking example, but such sect and cult leaders as Jim Jones (of the People's Temple in Guyana) and David Koresh (of the Branch Davidians in Waco, Texas) also held their adherents by force of personality.

The role of charisma in political legitimacy is less clear (Spinrad, 1991). Inspirational oratory and an exciting personality do not in themselves guarantee the obedience and political loyalty of the masses. As Weber explained, charismatic leaders must still "deliver the goods," that is, earn their followers' respect through political efficacy.

Traditional rulers govern on the basis of customs while in legal-rational systems government rulers operate by written rules limiting the powers of their offices.

Actually, few political leaders lead simply on the basis of personal aura. Many supposedly charismatic leaders, such as Fidel Castro, the Ayatollah Khomeini, Mao Zedong, and Ho Chi Minh, gained power through legal or otherwise well-structured channels, military prowess, or other accomplishments having little to do with charisma. Similarly, Lenin acquired legitimacy more through fanaticism, deception, and opportunism than personal magnetism. In Africa, the authority of postcolonial leaders like Kwame Nkrumah, Julius Nyerere, and Gamal Abdul Nasser, was based on their role in anti-colonial uprisings, not simply charm. In such cases, a "cult of personality" or mythology of charisma is constructed by fervent followers only after the leader's political and military accomplishments have fired the people's loyalties and imaginations.

Research Box

Why So Many Military Coups in Africa?

New African nations have the world's highest rates of military coups (defined as irregular changes in government by internal armed forces). Why?

Sociologists Craig Jenkins and Augustine Kposowa (1990) searched for an explanation by testing several theories generated by recent research. One theory points to the power, resources, and coherence of the military that make such coups more likely. Another focuses on ethnic awareness and antagonisms arising out of competition for jobs, political power, and housing. In other words, ethnic clashes can disrupt the entire political structure, potentially fueling violent takeovers. Such tribalism has caused recent troubles not only in Africa but in the Middle East, the former Yugoslavia, the former Soviet Union, and Somalia. Third, *modernization theory* contends that rapid economic development produces social dislocations, causing many people to search for answers and security in ethnic loyalties that may collide violently with others. Fourth, the economic dependency model (discussed earlier) describes how MNCs create a distorted economy, inequality, and stagnation, all possibly leading to social unrest. And finally, *ethnic dominance theory* holds that one group's monopoly over economic resources raises political tension and resentments.

Jenkins and Kposowa used methods of statistical analysis to look for relationships among several variables, essentially plugging the variables into a formula and letting the computer perform the necessary calculations. The difficulty lay in quantifying factors such as foreign investment and economic development. The researchers measured the dependent variable (propensity for military coups) in terms of reported plots, attempted coups, and successful ones. The independent variables (the suspected causative factors) required more ingenious operationalization. For example, they measured rate of economic development in terms of change in the proportion of people in the industrial labor force. In measuring ethnic dominance, Jenkins and Kposowa combined data on population percentages of the various groups, the percentage of the population speaking the largest group's language, and the representation of the largest group in the nation's cabinet.

Data on all the variables for 33 Black African nations were entered into the formula. The results supported the first four theories: Military coups are associated with military centrality, ethnic competition, rapid economic development, and economic dependency. The fifth theory appeared to work in reverse: Dominance by one group actually contributed to political stability. These results remind us that one explanation rarely explains social conditions completely.

Like other researchers, Jenkins and Kposowa discuss remaining questions in their conclusion. They wonder, for example, if these explanations for Black African political instability apply to other locales. And they identify other avenues that need further exploration if we are to understand why "the military is clearly on the march across Black Africa" (p. 873). ☐

IS DEMOCRACY BEST FOR AFRICAN NATIONS?

Democracy: form of government in which power rests in the hands of the governed.

Is **democracy,** in which power rests in the hands of the governed, the best form of government for African nations? It definitely has an appealing aura. Most governments, from the United States to the People's Republic of China, claim to be democratic in some ways. But can we safely assume that it is best for *all* peoples? On the one hand, it seems to be the most just system, as the American theologian Reinhold Niebuhr noted: "Man's capacity for justice makes democracy possible, but man's inclination to injustice makes democracy necessary." But on the other, Plato argued, "tyranny naturally arises out of democracy," characterizing it as "a charming form of government, full of variety and disorder, and dispensing a sort of equality to equals and unequals alike."

Perhaps, before recommending it to the peoples of Africa, we should thoroughly evaluate the democratic model. Here we study it as one end of a political spectrum that, at the other extreme, includes the autocratic model. As is the case with the economic models of socialism and capitalism, these political models do not describe actual governments; they only help us anticipate reality, which lies somewhere between the two.

The Democratic Model

In the ideal democracy, each individual has a meaningful vote, and rule is by majority vote. Ultimate power is thus in the hands of a large proportion of the people. Of course, "the people" usually does not include children or others considered unable (or for some reason unqualified) to wield decision-making power. Still, the less exclusive its voting restrictions, the closer a government is to the democratic model.

For practical reasons, citizens in a democracy usually do not make government decisions themselves— what is known as *direct democracy*. Rather, they delegate that responsibility to officials whom they directly or indirectly choose, in what is called *representative democracy*. In either case, power rests ultimately in the hands of "the people."

Between 1974 and 1990, a "global democratic revolution" swept southern Europe, Latin America, East Asia, and Eastern Europe; in all, over 30 nations shifted to the democratic end of the political spectrum (Huntington, 1992). In the 1990s, the wave reached Africa. The World Bank and International Monetary Fund have contributed to this development by requiring African governments to carry out democratic reforms before extending financial aid. Having lost the support of either of the two Cold War superpowers, Africa's "big men" began to allow freedom of the press and more than one political party. In fact, by the early 1990s, over three-quarters of Africa's 47 sub-Saharan states were at least allowing multiparty elections, though few came anywhere near to the democratic model. Still, human-rights, religious, and other prodemocracy organizations have sprouted across the continent (Ransdell, 1992). This wave of liberalization follows upon the heels of the collapse of most of Latin America's military dictatorships during the 1980s.

This democraticizing trend may represent only a swing of the political pendulum, soon to be followed by more dictatorships as happened in many countries after World War I. Calls for undemocratic rule have been raised in South America and Russia in the 1990s amid seemingly continuous revelations of governmental corruption. Also, if newly democratic governments falter economically, people may embrace dictators who promise quick fixes and reject democracy as a luxury they cannot afford. More vulnerable than most, Africa's fledgling democracies perch precariously atop artificial national boundaries and a patchwork of tribal identities.

The depth to which Africa's democracies will plant their roots depends partly on economic conditions. Unlike wealthy nations, which have the resources to weather economic storms like the global recession of the late 1980s and early 1990s, the democracies of developing countries in Africa lack a secure foundation. Seymour Lipset (1959) identifies a direct relationship between economic development and

Democracy means "power to the people," but rarely does this mean direct decision-making by ordinary citizens.

democracy, but the nature of this relationship remains something of a puzzle. Development can create the impetus toward democracy because it produces modern, urban, educated middle-class people who tend to demand political power. But sometimes, as in several communist and socialist nations, economic failures can result in popular calls for democratic reforms. In any case, in Africa's special situation, foreign aid is often required to help struggling democracies meet the peoples' material needs, and the international community of lenders has made it clear that they have no intention of funding repressive, corrupt, wasteful regimes. This policy imposes Western-style democracy on African nations.

Other requirements for democracy apply more universally. Political power must be diffused among various competing interests. Too much authority concentrated in the hands of one religious group, tribe, or ethnic group can eventually undermine democratic institutions. Citizens must likewise feel financially stable and secure. Also, they must have free access to information. Censorship of ideas and government actions carried out in secret prevents voters from making informed choices and fully exercising their political power. Similarly, citizens must be allowed to speak out, to dissent, to criticize government policies. Another important feature is a written set of rules limiting powers of state officials. Moreover, the people must generally agree that the democratic form of government is desirable. A tradition of civil rights and popular participation helps form such a consensus, which can sustain the people as they deal with democracy's shortcomings, including frustratingly slow responses, endless arguments and discussions, and disappointing compromises.

Beyond this, sociologists have tried to find the key to democratic stability. John Higley and Michael Burton (1989) argue that it results from elite consensus—that is, the usual conflict among powerful interest groups is somehow overcome. Others contend that the key to stability lies in compromises between capitalists and workers (Neuhouser, 1992). At least in some countries, workers will realize that their economic well-being depends on the success of the capitalists, who in turn realize that keeping the workers satisfied means fewer strikes and more consistent consumer demand. Perhaps in African societies as elsewhere, both types of compromise can contribute to democratic stability.

To the extent that these socioeconomic conditions are met, Africa can develop and sustain democracies. But these requirements present formidable obstacles. As we will now see, there is an alternative governmental form that may better serve the needs of these struggling nations.

The Autocratic Model

The world had few democracies until the twentieth century. **Autocracy** was the basis of rule in most states—power rested in the hands of one person or a few people who imposed their will on the masses.

Africa has had its share of autocratic rulers, from the earliest kings to today's dictators. More recently, however, another form of autocracy has appeared: **totalitarianism,** in which the state uses its concentrated political power to totally shape the lives of its citizens. Totalitarian governments control all aspects of society, from the mass media to the economy, presenting themselves as the only legitimate power. A secret police helps control communication among citizens, smothering dissent. Such governments also allow only one political party; citizens have no real choice in so-called "democratic" elections, in which they may vote "yes" or "no." Angola, Ethiopia, and other African nations aligned themselves with the Soviet bloc during the Cold War, but never developed fully totalitarian governments.

Since the breakdown of colonial rule, African autocracies have instead taken the form of **authoritarian** governments, which control only the political system, not all aspects of society. They give the people little say in important political decisions, but allow more freedom regarding religion, education, family, and other social matters.

Is autocracy the best model for some of Africa's governments? Consider first that desperately poor nations need rapid reforms, and democracies operate with notorious slowness. Expediency may seem short-sighted, but those African nations writhing under famine, economic stagnation, and social disorder may not have the luxury for open, popular debate or long-term plans. Autocracies, in contrast, get things done quickly.

Autocracy: form of government in which power rests in the hands of one person or a few people.

Totalitarianism: form of autocracy in which the state uses its concentrated political power to totally shape the lives of its citizens.

Authoritarian: form of government in which the state controls only the political system.

Indeed, while economic development often leads to calls for more democracy, more democracy does not necessarily lead to economic development. Most Western countries became prosperous under thoroughly undemocratic regimes at home and colonial exploitation overseas. Political liberalization came later. Some relatively well-developed African nations, such as Kenya, Togo, Nigeria, and Ghana, have sometimes benefited from strong rulers who imposed effective economic programs on their people.

One African leader recently described how the government in Equatorial Guinea had used its authoritarian powers to force people to construct an airport runway extension: "Boom, boom, boom, they worked and worked 'til late at night . . . and when the big jets came into the airport . . . the people were proud of themselves. That is what we have to do when everyone is poor . . . we need strong leadership, we need to launch work like hospitals, roads . . . [so the people] can see the results and feel proud" (quoted in Klitgaard, 1991, p. 43). The Polish government's strong hand similarly benefited the people when, after the downfall of communism in the late 1980s, democratic freedoms impeded economic reform. Moreover, Chile, Singapore, Taiwan, and South Korea have shown how authoritarian governments can effect desirable economic changes in developing countries.

It should be remembered that Africa suffers from soaring population growth, civil wars, the world's largest refugee problem, and per-capita income that is lower today than 30 years ago. While democracy promises freedom *of* speech, worship, dissent, and so on, autocracy freedom *from* want, malnutrition, illiteracy, and other ills. Of course, autocracies do not always deliver on such promises, but starving people understandably value speedy material improvement to civil rights. Considering all these aspects, is the premise that democracy best serves all peoples an ethnocentric trap?

Critical Thinking Box

Democracy for Nigeria?

Consider Nigeria: sunken in debt, burdened with an exploding population, and suffering seven coups in the last 32 years. What kind of government would best serve this country's needs? Autocracies offer rapid, forced change, but not always what the people want or require. Furthermore, such governments sometimes collapse quickly due to the death of a leader, the loss of a war, or other catastrophes that might simply wash over a solid democracy. Democracies also provide more effective guarantees of civil rights. But in the short run, for a struggling country like Nigeria, how important are rights and freedom? What is best for Nigeria *now?* ■

WHAT STANDS BETWEEN U.S. VOTERS AND POLITICAL POWER?

Democracy promises "power to the people," but does it deliver in the United States? According to the model of representative democracy, elected officials carry out the wishes of the voters. In reality, however, we see an interruption in the flow of power from the people to their representatives. What stands in the way?

For one thing, many citizens do not vote. Political alienation rose appreciably during the 1960s, despite TV news images of widespread activism. Lack of political trust and efficacy lies behind this increase in alienation (Easton, 1965; Gamson, 1968; Herring, House, and Mero, 1991). First, people do not trust government when they believe its policies show no responsiveness to the people's needs. And second, people feel efficacious only when they feel able to influence the direction of policies and events. Historical events are another contributing factor. The tide of discontent in the 1960s and 1970s rose against the backdrop of the Vietnam War, the Watergate scandal, and a combination of inflation and economic stagnation. Such large-scale changes produced a wave of alienation that touched virtually all parts of society (Etzioni and DiPrete, 1979). Such voter apathy clearly disrupts the line of power extending from people to their government.

Also, the great leveling principle of democracy—"one citizen, one vote"— breaks down because some citizens tend to vote less than others. As Table 10-3 shows, young people, minorities, and the poor—those who potentially have the most to gain from government programs—vote the least. While women have closed the gender voting gap, African Americans and Latinos still lag behind. Formal education predicts voting frequency more than any other variable: the better one's education, the more likely one is to vote. Noncollege youths now vote at even lower rates than in the 1960s because of their weaker economic position, declining interest and trust in the political process, and reduced efforts by political parties to mobilize them (Bennett, 1991). We might say, then, that the U.S. government reflects choices made mostly by advantaged citizens, not "all the people."

PERCENT OF U.S. VOTING-AGE POPULATION REPORTING THEY VOTED

Category	In 1988 Presidential Election	In 1990 Congressional Election
18–20 years old	33.2	18.4
21–24 years old	38.3	22.0
25–34 years old	48.0	33.8
35–44 years old	61.3	48.4
45–64 years old	67.9	55.8
65 years old and over	68.8	60.3
Male	56.4	44.6
Female	58.3	45.4
White	59.1	46.7
Black	51.5	39.2
Hispanic	28.8	21.0
School years completed:		
8 years or less	36.7	27.7
High school:		
1–3 years	41.3	30.9
4 years	54.7	42.2
College:		
1–3 years	64.5	50.0
4 years or more	77.6	62.5
Employed	58.4	45.1
Unemployed	38.6	27.9

Table 10-3

Source: U.S. Bureau of the Census, *Current Population Reports*.

Besides these departures from the democratic model, several major factors limit voters' and political power.

Political Parties

While not specifically mentioned in the U.S. Constitution, parties play a dominant role in our political process. In seeking to gain control of government offices, parties perform several functions, such as recruiting candidates, sponsoring campaigns, formulating policies, and organizing the structure of Congress (as in deciding who chairs the various Senate and House committees). While these activities can help draw citizens into the political process, the two-party system lies behind some of the apathy that increasingly afflicts voters.

Many other democracies are based on *proportional representation*, in which several parties share power in proportion to the votes they win. Since a party winning, say, only twenty percent of the vote gets twenty percent of the legislative seats, people enjoy a wide array of choices, including fringe candidates. Thus voters may be satisfied because their political views, no matter how narrow, are represented. However, proportional representation is inherently unstable because the government rests on often tenuous coalitions of many parties. In contrast, the U.S. system is very stable because it promotes compromise rather than radical posturing. The candidate winning the most votes in a given district receives all the district's votes. This "winner take all" rule leads parties to offer broad-based platforms that appeal to as many potential voters as possible. Candidates with narrow, well-defined agendas usually end up with no power. Each party's candidates thus make vague promises that neither offend nor satisfy most of the public. On the other hand, while they enjoy an impressively stable form of government, American voters complain that the candidates and platforms of the two major parties offer no real choice. Why bother voting, many ask, when all the candidates are alike?

The Mass Media and Campaign Consultants

Before it reaches the citizen, political information filters through the mass media and campaign consultants. This involves a good deal of distortion and manipulation. Some of this distortion results from the compression of campaign messages on television news programs. The size of the average "sound bite" allowed important candidates shrank from 48.9 seconds in 1968 to a mere 8.9 seconds in 1988 (Hallin, 1992). Newspapers and newsmagazines show the same trend (Stempel and Windhauser, 1991). Voters thus have little time to investigate a candidate's character or values. Knowing this, and to some extent responsible for it, office-seekers simplify and distort their promises and beliefs into a few memorable one-liners.

Manipulation comes partly from journalists, who arrange and analyze political news, thus mediating between candidates and voters (Hallin, 1992). This packaging sometimes devotes more air time or newsprint to experts, political insiders, and the campaign itself than to the actual candidates. Of course, this is partly due to the fact that experienced campaign managers limit candidates to sound bites rather than a clear presentation of their views.

Christopher Hitchens (1992) describes how public opinion polls, an increasingly important manipulative tool, help drive campaigns. Rather than simply attempt to take the pulse of the public, pollsters often try to shape voters' opinions. By carefully wording questions, they can often create deceptive images of the campaign that portray their candidate as the front runner and sway voters to join in his or her apparent momentum. When poll data do not agree with the desired results, the public may not hear about it. Likewise, pollsters tell candidates what words to mouth, what issues to raise that day. The new "smoke-filled backrooms" of today's campaigns contain rows of computers, fax machines, and cellular phones by which polling experts cultivate and manipulate the political reality.

As a result of the manipulations of the candidates' "handlers" and political commentators, we rarely get more than a glimpse of the "real" candidate. This smoke-and-mirrors approach to campaign coverage may have dulled the ability of American voters to distinguish between mediocre candidates and great ones (Cornfield, 1992), though they may also have become more adept at seeing through the media hype and campaign "spin control" (Popkin, 1991).

Money

One major obstacle to voters exercising power is the enormous amount of money now required to wage political campaigns. Of course, as Frank Sorauf (1992) points out, influence also comes from nonmonetary sources, like the ability to mobilize large numbers of letter-writers and voters (as in the case of the National Rifle Association). And such special-interest groups as feminists, homosexuals, and environmentalists enjoy or lack power to the extent that they can incite the public with their ideologies. For the most part, however, power in our democracy flows along decidedly financial lines. Because of this fact, and because campaign dollars today achieve lower electoral returns than in years past, very high levels of funding are required to unseat incumbents in the U.S. House of Representatives (Abramowitz, 1991). Increasingly, money is a prerequisite for political success.

Without money, candidates cannot hire expert pollsters, speechwriters, and consultants. In fact, candidates must first spend "seed" money to hire professional campaign organizers just to gain the appearance of a high-quality operation; without this, they can expect few contributions from individuals or organizations (Herrnson, 1992). Presidential candidates need vast sums of money to buy the all-important television advertising that has become vital since TV coverage in the 1950s established the importance of state primaries over national conventions (Donovan and Scherer, 1992). Ross Perot's 1992 presidential bid illustrates the enormous impact of television in establishing a campaign. Likewise, citizens wishing to put before the electorate an initiative or referendum, such as a ballot on balancing the state budget or lowering insurance rates, must be able to pay for direct-mail petitioning, fund-raising drives, and TV and radio ads (Hadwiger, 1992). Otherwise, such grass-roots movements usually wither into oblivion. Corporations need money to help elect more probusiness legislators to Congress or simply to support incumbents who protect their particular interests (Clawson and Neustadtl, 1989). Unions use their political funds to influence those lawmakers serving on committees with jurisdiction over labor matters (Endersby and Munger, 1992). Without money, the democratic process simply cannot move.

Events in recent decades have to some extent weakened the barrier between voters and the political process. Ferdinand Lundberg described in 1937 how 60 wealthy American families dominated politics through huge campaign contributions. Other researchers similarly found that a few large-scale contributors exercised enormous

TOP 10 PAC SPENDERS, 1991–1992

Political Action Committees	Contribution
Teamsters	$11,825,340
American Medical Association	$ 6,263,921
National Education Association	$ 5,817,975
National Rifle Association	$ 5,700,114
National Association of Realtors	$ 4,939,014
Association of Trial Lawyers of America	$ 4,392,462
American Federation of State, County, and Municipal Employees	$ 4,281,395
United Auto Workers	$ 4,257,165
National Congressional Club	$ 3,864,389
National Abortion Rights Action League	$ 3,831,321

Table 10-4

Source: Federal Election Commission.

political influence. But the 1971 Federal Election Campaign Act, and its subsequent amendments, set limits on the amounts that individuals or groups could contribute to national political campaigns. Individuals could contribute no more than $1,000 to both primary and general election campaigns, but could give up to $5,000 to any political action committee (PAC) or national party organization, the total of which could not exceed $25,000 to all campaigns in any federal election cycle. Thus, the influence of wealthy individuals declined, and PACs became the primary vehicle through which people could translate money into political power (Allen and Broyles, 1989, 1991).

In the 1970s, federal campaign finance reform, coupled with an increase in business regulations, encouraged the formation of PACs, especially by large corporations heavily unionized and in heavily regulated industries (Andres, 1985; Humphries, 1991; Masters and Keim, 1985). In fact, the number of corporate PACs increased by 1,780 percent between 1974 and 1984 (Conway, 1986). Though it travels through different channels today, money still talks in American politics, and those individuals and businesses without huge financial resources find themselves left at a serious disadvantage. (See Table 10-4.)

Interest Groups

Interest groups: voluntary associations that attempt to influence political policies for the benefit of their members.

U.S. presidents and other elected officials often criticize special interests as wielding extraordinary, behind-the-scenes power. However, **interest groups,** which are simply voluntary associations that attempt to influence political policies for the benefit of their members, can actually open opportunities for ordinary people to participate in the political process. Any group of citizens can work to accumulate the necessary membership size, funds, and organizational resources to push their own agenda.

Interest groups range from the powerful American Medical Association and the highly visible Parent Teachers Association to less familiar organizations like the National Tire Dealers and Retreaders Association. Whether well-known or obscure, small or large in membership, working openly or secretively, they employ the same narrowly focused tactics: funneling campaign funds to key committee members, seeking to influence appointments to regulatory boards, and so on.

Paul Peterson (1990–91) notes that, after gaining power in the 1960s and 1970s, interest groups have lost much of their clout in the last decade. Many have struggled just to maintain the size of their ranks. As V. O. Key (1964) observes, interest groups lose leverage when political parties exert strong control over the political landscape. Backed by powerful party organizations, politicians can resist the demands of special interests (Dahl, 1961). Also, as the nation's political power becomes concentrated in the hands of relatively few decision makers, interest groups typically lose influence because there are fewer points of access.

Do interest groups subvert the democratic process? Peterson characterizes them today as ants busily exploring the cracks and crevices of the political structure rather than aggressive hogs greedily feeding at the government trough. In his view, special interests simply represent groups of citizens in relatively open competition. From a functionalist perspective, they supply energy and impetus to the democratic process. On the other hand, conflict theorists point out that most interest groups promote the agendas of advantaged members of society, particularly professionals and business people. In either case, special interests still exert substantial influence on the political process, circumventing the democratic model's ideal of one person, one vote.

Elites

Sociologists have seen behind all the aforementioned barriers to the democratic diffusion of political power a huge hand (possibly several hands) quietly moving the mass media, campaigns, and interest groups like pieces on a chess board.

The Elite Model   According to *elite theory*, the national elite includes "persons who are able, by virtue of their authoritative positions in powerful organizations and movements of whatever kind, to affect national political outcomes regularly and substantially" (Burton and Higley, 1987, p. 18). C. Wright Mills (1956) describes a unified elite of powerful leaders in the military, big business, and government who strive to harmonize their sometimes clashing interests in order to maintain a firm grip on the nation. Researchers following Mills's lead describe an upper class, united through intermarriage and shared experiences (in, for example, exclusive boarding schools, Ivy League colleges, and private clubs) that controls the United States (Useem, 1984).

Conflict theorists contend that the elite consists essentially of business interests, and that both government and military leaders largely follow the line put down by capitalists (Domhoff, 1990, 1992). "Instrumentalist" Marxists envision the state as a direct tool of the capitalist elite, like a puppet on a string. Patrick Akard (1992), for example, describes how a well-organized business lobby forced on the government a class-conscious, probusiness economic policy during the late 1970s to counter the enervating stagnation of the early part of the decade. "Structuralist" Marxists, however, posit a relatively autonomous state that sees beyond the sometimes short-sighted vision of the business lobby and works for the long-range vitality of the capitalist economy. In either case, ordinary citizens serve only as spectators as powerful unseen forces determine the nation's political future.

The truism that "things aren't like they used to be" applies to America's elite. E. Digby Baltzell (1964) explains that by the 1880s, the U.S. economy had grown beyond the scope of local, family-owned businesses and landed gentry into one requiring coordination on a national scale. A select group of talented WASP men gradually formed an exclusive fraternity to direct U.S. foreign policy. Beginning in the 1920s,

America replenishes its ruling class from the ranks of families that share experiences in exclusive surroundings, such as elite preparatory schools.

for example, about 100 members of this elite class regularly convened in a Council on Foreign Relations. While few held elected office, this national "Establishment" assumed command of high-level government positions, "think tanks," and financial institutions to lead America through World War II and into international prominence during the postwar period (Holland, 1991). However, divided over the Vietnam War and how to respond to the economic stagflation that followed, the elite consensus began to weaken in the 1970s (Judis, 1991). New groups such as the Trilateral Commission, the Heritage Foundation, and the American Enterprise Institute rose to fill the foreign policy vacuum, but none gained the dominance of the postwar Establishment. John Judis explains that contentious interest groups have replaced the unified elite, and that "American foreign policy, once the realm of the gods, has become the domain of mere influence peddlers" (1991, p. 55). This same fragmentation of power has also occurred in the health care field (Imershein, Rond, and Mathis, 1992).

The Pluralist Model   *Pluralist theory* sees a constellation of competing power centers, including unions, corporations, trade associations, professional organizations, and government bodies, rather than a unified elite. Their conflicting interests have insured their disunity. While oil interests seek offshore drilling rights, the environmental lobby fights it. While bankers push for free international trade, labor unions and many domestic manufacturers desperately oppose it. David Knoke and Franz Urban Pappi (1991) argue that policies emerge from a battle among tightly knit interest group coalitions, especially labor unions and central business associations. Indeed, Richard Lachmann (1990) contends that a single elite can rule only under strict conditions, such as a command economy that can take resources from the masses, a lack of rival elites, and the inability of any part of the elite to withdraw their support.

Whether America's political power lies in the hands of one unified elite or is shared among competing interests, the resulting picture does not match the democratic model. Instead, we face the fact that "Governments have invariably relied on informal networks of private citizens, organized through pressure groups, lobbies, political organizations, and elite groupings . . . to fill the interstices between individual will and public power" (Judis, 1991, p. 55).

SUMMARY

Rather than refer to Africa as the "Third World," it is perhaps more useful to describe it as undeveloped, meaning it lacks the organization and technology for industrial mass production. Economies across the continent have been retarded by civil strife, political instability, overpopulation, foreign debt, and poor weather and soil. But according to *world systems theory*, "core" nations exploit the resources, labor, and markets of less developed "periphery" countries like those in Africa. They accomplish this mainly through *multinational corporations* (MNCs), business organizations that transcend national boundaries. In some ways, MNCs benefit their host nations by bringing in jobs and goods. But *dependency theory* points out that foreign capital penetration undermines the economies of developing countries and produces a long list of undesirable consequences because MNCs typically stimulate only one part of the host economy, pay few taxes, and funnel much of their profits back home. The theory also describes how the activities of transnationals cause eventual economic stagnation through decapitalization. As MNCs move from "classical dependence" (exploiting the host nation's raw materials) to "dependent development" (manufacturing in the host nation), they sometimes stimulate economic growth in the long run, at least in the industrial sectors. This development depends on cooperation with the host government and local businesses, and largely benefits the domestic elite.

Africa's traditional economies no longer adequately direct production and distribution, the two main tasks of an economy. They must change in one of two directions. *Socialism* aims for equality through collective ownership of the means of production and central control of the distribution of goods and services. *Capitalism* encourages the pursuit of personal profit by allowing private ownership of the means of production and letting market forces determine the distribution of goods and services. Socialism holds out the promise of a decent standard of living for all citizens, and less privation, exploitation, and inequality. The failures of socialism have driven African nations, among others, toward the capitalist end of the economic spectrum, raising the dangers of increased class divisions, unnecessarily high prices, and other ills. Advanced capitalist economies in Africa may move toward *corporatism*, in which top labor and business leaders negotiate wage and price agreements at the national level. The choice between socialism and capitalism is more than a choice between social equality and economic vigor.

Our chances of getting ahead in the U.S. economy are influenced by several factors. For decades, labor unions have won rights and concessions for all American workers, especially since gaining respectability and a firm legal footing in the 1930s. After World War II, organized labor made deals with employers, trading worker cooperation for job security and higher wages. However, since the 1970s, union strength has declined, and workers have lost some bargaining leverage. Shifting their goals and strategy, unions continue to help shape capital-labor relations in the United States. Our opportunities for success also depend partly on where the jobs are to be found. The *spatial mismatch hypothesis* suggests that the shift of low-skill job growth to the suburbs helps account for the high unemployment rates of the inner cities. This has put minorities at a disadvantage, but has freed women geographically in their search for careers.

Because of varying skill requirements, turnover costs, firm-specific proficiency, and other factors, the *dual labor market* offers higher wages, more stability, and other advantages in the primary sector than it does in the secondary sector. Also, powerful "core" firms that use capital-intensive production techniques offer better pay and benefits than ones on the "periphery." The labor market may not be as segmented as before. Some sociologists argue that in the new postindustrial society automation tends to eliminate low-skill manual jobs and upgrade, or "reskill," existing ones. Others contend that the trend is toward "deskilling" jobs, using a few technologically advanced workers and drawing upon a "labor reserve" of less-skilled, marginalized ones.

Succeeding in one's own business now requires using new technologies to offer exactly what the consumer wants and relying on flexible networks of more autonomous workers. We can often predict the prospects of a new business by looking at the founder's characteristics, the organization of the company, and the external environment.

Politics is the process through which people gain and use power. Those who occupy positions of power, and the institutions they form, constitute the *government*. Political institutions become necessary with the production of surplus in agricultural societies. The *state*, which claims a monopoly on the use of physical force within a territory, fulfills several functions: maintaining order, enforcing norms, planning and policy-making, and defense. Conflict theorists, however, describe the state as a tool of oppression. Governments rule through *authority*, power seen by the people as legitimate or appropriate. Authority can be based on tradition, rationally produced legal frameworks, and personal charisma.

African nations must choose from a spectrum of governmental forms. *Democracy* puts power in the hands of the governed, either directly or through representatives. Africa has experienced a democratizing trend in recent years, but the promised rewards have often proved elusive. Part of the reason lies in the lack of economic development, political stability, citizens' access to information, civil rights, elite consensus, and other prerequisites of democratic rule. *Autocracy* puts power in the hands of one person or a few people. One form of autocracy, *totalitarianism*, uses the concentrated political power of the state to totally shape the lives of its citizens through control of all aspects of society. African autocracies have instead taken the form of *authoritarian* governments, which control only the political system. These deny the people some civil freedoms, but they can force desirable changes and provide for people's material needs with greater speed than can democratic processes.

In the United States, democracy does not completely deliver "power to the people," in part because of political alienation and differences in voter participation.

Political parties perform some positive functions, but the two-party system also contributes to voter apathy. Furthermore, democratic processes are distorted and manipulated by the mass media and campaign consultants. And power in our democracy is closely linked to money. Today, rather than wealthy individuals, political action committees (PACs) wield considerable power through their financial contributions. *Interest groups*, voluntary associations that attempt to influence political policies for the benefit of their members, offer opportunities for ordinary citizens to influence government policies; they have lost some of their clout over the past decade. According to C. Wright Mills a unified power elite of leaders in the military, big business, and the government controls the United States. Some conflict theorists argue that the capitalist elite manipulates the government like a string puppet. Others contend that the state works toward a strong capitalist economy but does not always accede to the short-term wishes of business lobbies. This elite arose as a kind of exclusive, national fraternity during the 1880s, weakened during the 1970s, and is being replaced by various interest groups today. Pluralist theorists maintain that power is shared not by one elite but by a constellation of competing power centers.

Key Terms

world systems theory	spatial mismatch	democracy
multinational	hypothesis	autocracy
corporations (MNCs)	dual labor market	totalitarianism
dependency theory	politics	authoritarian
socialism	state	interest groups
capitalism	government	
corporatism	authority	

11

Chapter

RELIGION AND MEDICINE

WHY RELIGION?

WHY HAVE DENOMINATIONS LOST GROUND
IN AMERICA?

HAVE AMERICANS BECOME MORE
RELIGIOUS, OR LESS?

*CRITICAL THINKING BOX: HAS AMERICA BECOME
LESS RELIGIOUS?*

DOES RELIGION REALLY MAKE A DIFFERENCE?

*RESEARCH BOX: BODY AND SOUL: A DIRECT LINK
BETWEEN HEALTH AND RELIGION?*

WHO GETS SICK, AND WHY
THE SOCIAL DIFFERENCES?

HOW CAN HEALTH CARE BE A TOOL
OF OPPRESSION?

FREE, UNIVERSAL HEALTH CARE IN AMERICA?

*CRITICAL THINKING BOX: DO AMERICANS HAVE A RIGHT
TO MEDICAL CARE?*

WHO'S WHO IN THE HOSPITAL:
DOMINANCE AND HIERARCHY IN HEALTH CARE

Uncertainty and the unknown have always been with us. For most of human existence, religion and magic have been used to deal with a threatening, unreliable world. Over the last several centuries, we have also called on science in an effort to know and confront life's mysteries and dangers. In this chapter, we cast a critical eye on religion and medical science as two ways we try today to know and deal with the unknown, and for both institutions we find sociological undercurrents beyond the obvious.

WHY RELIGION?

Several hundred thousand years ago in China, human skulls were broken in a careful, methodical way that suggests to anthropologists the brains had been removed, probably to be eaten to gain power from the deceased's spirits. Less than 100,000 years ago in Europe and the Middle East, Neanderthals sometimes buried their dead with ritual effects. In one case, a ring of goat horns surrounded a child's grave; in others, flowers, tools, and weapons accompanied the corpses, presumably for use in some existence beyond the natural world. A more recent grave (about 22,000 years old) in eastern Russia included decorations of ivory beads requiring thousands of hours of labor. Some 17,000 years ago, generations of Cro-Magnon artists in southern France decorated cave walls with powerful images possibly depicting hallucinations and magical hunting ceremonies. About 3,000 years later in northern Spain, humans fashioned two mounds of animal parts and colored clay in a small cave. On one mound they erected a stone head, half human and half beast; on the other they placed a large stone slab. The circumstances all point to one explanation: a shrine for religious rituals. More recent cultures have left evidence—figurines, altars, and other relics—of our ancient and universal interest in the supernatural, a world beyond the reach of human senses, a place where we long to find answers, security, and certainty.

What Do People Find in Religion?

When the first nomadic tribes reached North America thousands of years ago, they brought with them the same questions and fears that all humans have. They also brought their **religion,** a system of beliefs and practices shared by a people as they relate themselves to the supernatural. Why this worldwide, seemingly eternal human interest in religion?

Religion: a system of beliefs and practices shared by a people as they relate themselves to the supernatural.

For one thing, religion fills in gaps between what people know about their surroundings and what they don't understand. For example, the traditional religion of the Eskimos, the first people of the New World, helped them make sense of life in an inhospitable physical environment that offered at best an unreliable food supply. Explanations of their natural world partly involved **animism,** the belief in spiritual forces and souls. Poor hunting luck could be explained by evil spirits driving away game, or someone breaking a taboo. Similarly, the loss of one's soul, either through its careless wandering during sleep or theft by a malevolent shaman, could account for illness.

In our own culture, science provides many explanations of the world around us, but those answers that lie beyond the reach of our senses also lie beyond the reach of science. To understand the meaning of life, the existence of God, and the reality of death, most of us turn to religion.

Religion provides a related personal function: emotional security or comfort. The aboriginal religion of the Eskimos, for example, securely fitted them into their physical surroundings. Each part of the environment, from rocks and animals to food and even sleep, was considered alive and "owned" by someone (Birket-Smith, 1971, p. 182). Each Eskimo was thus integrated into the frigid, harsh natural world as owner. For all cultures, the promise of an afterlife helps humans face their own death and that of loved ones with less anxiety (Bohannon, 1991). Religion can also replace worrisome uncertainty with reassuring certainty about the meaning of life and death. And it has always provided a long-view timekeeping function, orienting the individual with weekly and seasonal ritual observances, and connecting him or her with the generations that have shared those rituals for ages (Zerubavel, 1981).

Also, by turning to the supernatural, humans can achieve a sense of control over powerful and threatening forces. In their traditional spring whale ceremony, the Eskimos hoped to insure future hunting success by placating the spirits of those whales killed during the season just ended. The use of hunting charms and amulets hung on the masts of their boats for good luck illustrates their belief in **mana,** a supernatural force existing within certain beings and objects. Besides such charms, acquired through purchase or inheritance, the Eskimos used ritual songs and the observance of taboos to try to control the weather, hunting, and sickness. The shaman, or religious practitioner, enjoyed special intimacy with the spirits, and employed trances to cure illnesses, speak with the dead, search for lost souls, and battle evil spirits. Such efforts involve **magic,** a set of beliefs and practices intended to control natural and supernatural forces.

In our own culture, many of us appeal to the supernatural to overcome fears and face threats. Sometimes we use religious means such as prayers. We may also use magic in the form of lucky charms, extra charitable contributions, and superstitions. Those who desire to manipulate their fate may turn to astrology and mind-readers.

Religion also gives the individual a sense of identity. When the superior hunting and medical technology of the modern, Christian world proved more powerful than their own animistic beliefs, many Eskimos became Presbyterians, Episcopalians, or members of the Assembly of God. They sought, as people do everywhere, a feeling of belonging, of being socially connected—what Emile Durkheim called a "community

Animism: the belief in spiritual forces and souls.

Mana: a supernatural force thought to exist within certain beings or objects.

Magic: a set of beliefs and practices intended to control natural and supernatural forces.

Religion provides a sense of
identity, of belonging to a
community of believers.

of believers." This is especially important in a pluralistic, heterogeneous society like
our own, where many of us may feel cast adrift in a sea of strangers.

As we saw in Chapter 1, Durkheim (1897) recognized long ago that religion helps
bridge the gap between the individual and anonymous mass society. As the modern
world invaded traditional Eskimo society, the extended family declined in importance
and villagers lost a sense of community. The Christian churches established by missionaries thereafter became the focal point of most villages because they offered a new
source of social support.

In any society, the more extensive this web of commonly held beliefs and rituals,
the more protection religion offers against alienation and, ultimately, suicide.
Durkheim, for example, argued that European Protestants exhibited higher rates of
suicide than Catholics because of their lower degree of community integration. By the

1970s, however, researchers found little connection between religious category and suicide rates in the United States (Breault, 1988; Girard, 1988; Stack, 1982). They also pointed out that Durkheim studied Western European societies with well-defined Protestant or Catholic regions, while in America Protestant diversity has increased so much that few generalizations can now be made about the effects of Protestantism.

Religion may still inhibit suicide, but not in terms of simple religious affiliation. The key seems to be the support of network ties. So, while Catholics (and, to a lesser degree, Jews) have low suicide rates, members of generally cohesive, evangelical Protestant congregations show a suicide rate almost as low as that of Catholics, and considerably lower than mainstream Protestants (Pescosolido and Georgianna, 1989).

Today in the United States, the extent to which religion integrates the individual into the community is partly due to geography (Pescosolido, 1990). For one thing, religious groups are not distributed evenly across the country. The small number of Jews in the South, as compared to the high concentration in the Northeast, makes it difficult to build an integrated, supportive community based on religious faith. The same is true for Catholics in most parts of the South. On the other hand, long-established Protestant groups like Episcopalians and Presbyterians have deep historical roots in New England and some areas of the Midwest. The newer evangelical churches have relatively weak networks in the Northeast. And in any region, large urban populations offer greater opportunities for the individual to find a supportive community of co-religionists.

Religious practice also enhances one's stock of human capital—that is, the potential to contribute to society (Iannaccone, 1990). That capital, in the form of friendships and familiarity with doctrines, rituals, and traditions, in turn contributes to a person's religious satisfaction.

Besides such practical ends, religion also produces transcendent experiences that are rewarding in themselves (Luckmann, 1990). Participation in religious ceremonies can result in what Mihaly Csikszentmihalyi (1975) calls "flow," a "peculiar state of experience" also attainable through chess, rock climbing, art, and other engrossing activities. Rituals provide a situation in which we can overcome our feelings of isolation, concentrate our thoughts to the exclusion of extraneous stimuli, feel challenged to our limits by the discipline of the spiritual path, and confront the uncertainty of the supernatural. Such moments of total involvement—of merging self and environment and past, present, and future—bring intense satisfaction. Among the Eskimos, the traditional shaman's writhing, ecstatic trance may have involved such flow, just as the charismatic, "letting go," Christian services do today.

From the conflict perspective, these supposed benefits of religion act as an unwelcome, numbing narcotic. Karl Marx called for subjugated peoples to rise up against their oppressors, to throw off their chains and claim the rewards of power and wealth withheld by the capitalist class, but religion would only forestall revolution. People would instead peacefully and meekly accept their earthly troubles as spiritual trials. For Marx, the "opium of the people" was only an obstacle to social progress.

Why Do All Cultures Include Religion?

While not every individual embraces religion, all cultures do to some extent (see Table 11-1). In trying to explain that fact, Durkheim described it as a sort of social glue that holds together the milling, clamorous mass of individuals we call society. In

ESTIMATED SIZES OF WORLD RELIGIONS BY THE YEAR 2000

Religion	Number of Adherents	Percentage
Christians	2,019,921,366	32.3
Muslims	1,200,653,040	19.2
Hindus	859,252,260	13.7
Buddhists	359,092,100	5.7
Chinese folk religionists	158,470,664	2.5
New religionists	138,263,800	2.2
Tribal religionists	100,535,850	1.6
Sikhs	23,831,700	0.4
Jews	20,173,560	0.3
Shamanists	9,946,530	0.3
Baha'is	7,649,150	0.1
Afro-American spiritists	7,132,900	0.1
Spiritists	5,605,700	0.1
Confucians	5,356,000	0.1
Jains	4,303,800	0.1
Parsis	218,700	0.0
Other religionists	2,191,960	0.0
Non-religious and atheists	1,334,335,920	21.3

Table 11-1

Source: David Barrett, editor, *World Christian Encyclopedia,* Nairobi: Oxford University Press, 1982, Global Table 4.

the early 1900s, Christian churches in Alaska agreed to divide the region into territories, each to be monopolized by one denomination (Chance, 1966). Thus, the typical Eskimo village had one established church. The villagers shared the same religious beliefs, attended the same services, and participated in the same church-dominated social activities. This fostered a strong sense of shared community identity. Later, when the evangelical and sect missionaries moved onto the scene and established second churches in villages, the people were often divided along denominational lines. This weakened the village's cohesion, but still provided shared identity within each church community.

Religion also contributes to social harmony. The basic commandments of most major faiths stress love of God and love of one's neighbor. This sometimes extends to loving even those of other faiths. We might say that religion teaches good citizenship—but not always. Clearly, the unifying function of religion cuts both ways.

Just as the members of a congregation are bonded to one another through their shared faith and rituals, they find themselves pitted against members of other faiths. The Eskimos of the older, mainsteam denominations ridiculed the long lists of rules imposed by the newer missionary churches, and the evangelicals criticized them for their lack of strict morals. Such views have a familiar ring for us today in the United States, as ardent proselytizers knock on doors across the nation and evoke fear and resentment in churches losing members to such groups. But perhaps the worst interfaith conflicts in our society's history arose in response to the tidal wave of non-Protestant immigrants at the turn of the century. Catholics were suspected of plotting, under direction of the Pope, to subvert American culture. Jews became lightning rods, not for the first time, for the fears and frustrations of a society undergoing massive transformation. Ethnocentric hostility and suspicion is still common today, and certainly not only in our culture. The 1990s have seen massive, murderous clashes between Hindus and Moslems in India. The Russian Orthodox Church battles for influence against aggressive Protestant missionaries and a resurgence of Roman Catholicism. Violence between Arabs and Jews continues in Jerusalem and on the West Bank. Protestant and Catholic terrorism still plagues Northern Ireland. And most recently, Serbian and Bosnian Christians in former Yugoslavia mounted a large-scale military campaign to "cleanse" their region of Moslems.

When one religion holds sway in a society, it contributes to the legitimacy of the status quo. Durkheim pointed out that religion's power to maintain social order flows from its immersion in the **sacred,** out-of-the-ordinary beliefs and practices that inspire awe and reverence. Like the Eskimos' many food and hunting taboos, any rules, customs, and laws backed by religion enjoy special respect; after all, they are believed to be divinely inspired. If the society's entire power structure rests upon such a sacred foundation, it can function smoothly.

> **Sacred:** out-of-the-ordinary beliefs and practices that inspire awe and reverence.

We see this among the Eskimos, where, until encroaching modern civilization undermined it, traditional religion provided cultural stability and cohesion. As animistic beliefs lost their hold in the face of the greater power and efficiency of modern technology, social order deteriorated. Youths ignored the curfews and other restrictions of the elders, sexual promiscuity and drug use arose. The Christian churches now provide a source of authority for some Eskimos, but it is not all-encompassing like the aboriginal religion.

At the same time, religion's power for social control can lead to oppression, exploitation, and brutality. The ancient god-kings of Mesopotamia and Egypt imposed forced labor on a massive scale and subjugated whole peoples. Countless wars, persecution, and torture have been perpetrated over the centuries in the name of various faiths. In the United States today, money-making schemes, sexual abuse, and frauds are sometimes based on religious appeals and authority.

Throughout the twentieth century, totalitarian communist governments have performed many of the same personal and social functions as organized religion. Indeed, after the collapse of the Soviet state, many citizens protested against the new government—some even taking up arms—presumably because they missed not only subsidized food prices and guaranteed employment, but also the sense of security and identity provided by an all-powerful, and thus god-like, government.

Religion also provides its usefulness by generating social change, for good or ill. Religion has supported social movements dedicated to the end of slavery and abortion, the spread of civil rights and literacy throughout the world, and prison and urban reform. Muslim fundamentalism, a radical departure from mainstream Islam, instructs its followers to use any means, including terrorism, to bring other peoples under its power. The Spanish conquistadores carried out their subjugation of the natives of South and Central America under the banner of religion, just as the North American pioneers marched westward under the banner of "Manifest Destiny" ("God gave this land to us Christians").

In one of the most important examples of religion's power of social transformation, Max Weber described how Protestantism provided fertile ground for the rise of capitalism in Europe. Catholicism had long emphasized prayer more than industry, spiritual progress over financial gain. In contrast, Protestantism promoted the values of work and thrift, and argued that worldly success was not necessarily a sign of moral bankruptcy. Thus after the Reformation, Protestantism encouraged Europeans, and the Puritan colonists of North America, to engage in tireless toil and profit-seeking.

Clearly, religion deserves its status as one of society's major institutions. It speaks to some basic human needs, and plays an important role in both the stability and reform of society.

WHY HAVE DENOMINATIONS LOST GROUND IN AMERICA?

Traditional Eskimo culture, undistracted by the temptations and revelations of modern technology and scientific progress, may seem a likely setting for a pervasive, intense religious influence. But it has been our own postindustrial society, surprisingly, that has resounded with a rising chorus of "hallelujahs!" Over the last two decades, there has been an explosion of **evangelism,** a revivalistic, "old-time," Bible-based type of Christianity that seeks to establish a personal relationship with Christ through conversion, ardent worship, and an appeal to the primary authority of the Bible. A small

Evangelism: a revivalistic, "old-time," Bible-based type of Christianity that seeks to establish a personal relationship with Christ through conversion, ardent worship, and an appeal to the primary authority of the Bible.

In recent decades, emotional forms of Christianity have been the success stories in American religious organizations.

Fundamentalism: an antimodern, antisecular approach to religion based on a literal interpretation of scripture and a return to "original truth."

but significant part of this evangelistic movement involves **fundamentalism,** an antimodern, antisecular approach to religion based on a literal interpretation of scripture and a return to "original truth."

Evangelism has made inroads not only among the Eskimos and in contemporary American society, but throughout the world. In the United States, it has shrugged off its former aversion to politics, generating well-financed, grass-roots campaigns promoting conservative causes. By 1980, the New Christian Right had become a formidable part of the political scene, and evangelism now offers serious competition to denominations.

John Egerton (1974) and Mark Shibley (1991) have traced this nationwide movement to what they call the "Southernization" of American religion. This "born again" approach to Christianity spread largely through the migration of Southerners to other regions of the United States, and has had its impact not only in humble inner-city storefronts and exotic tent meetings on the outskirts of town but within long-established, widely respected churches including Roman Catholics, Southern Baptists, Methodists, and Lutherans. Evangelism is most common, however, among Pentecostal-holiness groups, Assemblies of God, Mormons, Seventh-Day Adventists, and similar organizations, which have enjoyed increasing memberships since 1950 and mushrooming expansion since the 1970s.

Much of this evangelistic growth has come at the expense of the formerly dominant Protestant denominations, such as Presbyterians and Episcopalians. The United Church of Christ, United Methodists, Disciples of Christ, and other robust churches have also suffered declines in influence and membership. In searching for answers to this somewhat surprising trend, we will explore the reasons why people in the United States leave one religious organization and join another in what has become a cafeteria-style array of choices. Then we examine the nature of the several competing denominations.

Who Switches, and Why?

As the insightful French writer Alexis de Tocqueville observed in the 1830s, Americans have long been considered a nation of joiners, engaging in a multitude of voluntary associations. We might also call ourselves a nation of switchers, as we have taken full advantage of our society's openness and opportunities, moving geographically as well as changing from one social commitment to another. This fluidity has included a great deal of interfaith conversion, "with something like a third of Americans changing their religious affiliation at least once during their lifetime" (Sandomirsky and Wilson, 1990, p. 1212). Much of this religious mobility has recently involved people abandoning mainstream churches, but any kind of switching can disrupt relationships with family and friends as well as members of the old congregation. What kinds of people make such difficult changes?

As we might expect, younger people change their religious preferences more than do their elders (Newport, 1979; Sherkat, 1991). After all, they have had less time to sink deep roots, and are more change-oriented anyway. Women show a greater tendency than men to "stay home" regarding their affiliation. They are also generally more religious and stable in their church memberships (DeVaus and McAllister, 1987; McPherson, 1981; Sandomirsky and Wilson, 1990; Thompson, 1991). This probably results from the different socialization daughters and sons receive. Parents exert more extensive controls on their daughters (Hagan, 1989), and women are usually less willing to take the risky step of abandoning their childhood faith.

Social networks figure large in a person's switching probability. People usually drop one religion for another when their church offers too little social support (Bainbridge, 1990; Stark and Bainbridge, 1980). We are more likely to leave a church to join others of a similar socioeconomic status and to solidify a marriage with someone of a different faith (Newport, 1979). Also, we can more easily change our affiliation if our religious ties are not extensively interwoven with other social relationships (Sandomirsky and Wilson, 1990). This explains why Catholics and Mormons, for example, have lower switching rates: Since family rules and practices are closely tied to religious beliefs, leaving such churches requires the breaking of kinship associations and family traditions as well as friendships within the congregation. Researchers also find that people living in areas dominated by homogeneous ethnic traditions, language, and customs have stronger commitment to their religion (Land, Deane, and Blau, 1991). We can expect people in ethnic enclaves to be less likely to abandon their religious ties because their social–religious roots are deeper. Conversely, those not linked to such social networks are more likely to switch faiths.

All this tells us something about why people change religious affiliation, but it doesn't account for the general drift in the United States from mainstream churches. The answer may lie in the nature of the various options available on America's religious menu, which we turn to next.

> Switching is most likely between denominations similar in the formality of their services, geographical distribution of members, ethnic affiliations, and degree of urban concentration. Thus, movement between Lutherans and Episcopalians is more probable than between Catholics and Baptists, which are much farther apart on a scale of similarities (Babchuk and Whitt, 1990).

Why Have Denominations Lost So Many Members?

Among church groups in the United States, **denominations** have been the big losers in membership over the last several decades. These large, wealthy, widely respected organizations, tolerant of other belief systems, have struggled to compete with newer, more aggressive and usually less tolerant groups. Is all this the result of disaffection with the mainstream churches, or do their competitors offer something better?

> **Denomination:** a large, widely respected, wealthy, tolerant religious organization.

CHURCH MEMBERSHIP IN THE UNITED STATES, 1989–1990

Religious Body	Percentage
Catholic	26.2
Baptist	19.4
Methodist	8.0
Lutheran	5.2
Presbyterian	1.8
Pentecostal	1.8
Jewish	1.8
Episcopalian	1.7
Mormon	1.4
Other	24.2
None	7.5

Table 11-2

Source: Barry A. Kosmin, *The National Survey of Religious Identification, 1989–90*, Graduate Center, City University of New York, March 1991.

Loss of Denominational Appeal　Denominations in their varied forms offer many attractive features. Despite their recent setbacks, Methodists, Lutherans, Catholics, Episcopalians, Presbyterians, Baptists, and other organizations still account for a large proportion of church members in the United States (see Table 11-2.) They have met the spiritual and social needs of millions of Americans for generations. And they still enjoy considerable respect and influence. Certainly they lack the power of a state church or *ecclesia*, which holds a monopoly on religious authority and dominates society, like the Roman Catholic Church of Medieval Europe or the eighteenth-century Church of England. (Of course, the Constitution's First Amendment prohibits the establishment of such a state church in the United States.) But denominations as a whole, at least in the past, have come close to such dominance. The typical member is still likely to be middle class, and most if not all members of the power elite, including a majority of U.S. presidents, have belonged to such organizations.

Part of the denominational church's appeal lies in its accommodating approach to modern life. It imposes relatively few controls over its members regarding dress, recreation, or other life style matters. Formally trained, full-time ministers offer their congregations relatively unemotional, somewhat intellectualized religious services and themes. Membership is largely socially determined, as children pass through formal rituals toward adult membership.

Millions of Americans, however, have decided that mainstream churches have made too many doctrinal compromises, that instead of promoting traditional values and beliefs they are pursuing an activist political agenda. Robert Wuthnow (1989) explains that this liberal–conservative split among American Protestants began over a century ago, when there emerged the social-gospel view that churches should actively engage society's problems and adapt to a changing world. Fundamentalists argued against such a course. Recently, this split has widened as increasing numbers of Americans feel that denominations have traveled too far down the liberal path. Those churches which have advocated a global, internationalist view of foreign relations (as opposed to a promilitary nationalism), restrictions on free enterprise (via strong government policies redistributing wealth), and a modern, relativistic morality that sanctions abortion, women's rights, and homosexuals' rights have generally lost members, suffered a decline in participation, or both. If denominations have done something "wrong," it is to have followed a road that many in our society have not taken.

In response to this groundswell of conservatism in America, some denominations, from Catholics to Presbyterians, have grown evangelical offshoots to meet the needs of those who seek a more emotional and personal religious experience. "Charismatic" groups, which typically deal in such beliefs as faith healing and speaking in tongues, have also sprung up within various mainstream churches.

Still, for many people, denominations cannot change far or fast enough. For example, a new religious movement, a feminist brand of Neo-Paganism, attracts some who believe that dominant religious systems support women's oppression. The movement's members have abandoned Christianity and Judaism altogether because, they believe, these faiths have been too conservative and contain too many patriarchal images that stand in the way of women's equality (Goldenberg, 1979). Perhaps mainstream faiths cannot hope to retrieve such thoroughly disaffected people.

Sect Attraction **Sects,** usually small religious organizations at odds with larger society that claim sole legitimacy, have offered refuge for disaffected people in many societies, including our own. They typically form as a protest against mainstream churches, and often against society in general. Sect members usually see the present world as evil; they look for hope in the next world. They accuse traditional religions of envisioning God as too remote, and often claim to have discovered the "true" path. In contrast to the denomination's "softness," sects offer their members a sense of certainty and doctrinal purity.

Sect: a usually small religious organization that claims sole legitimacy and is at odds with larger society.

The Mission for the Coming Days illustrates the degree to which some will go for truth and certainty. This organization arose in the rapidly changing, politically tenuous, economically troubled society of South Korea in the early 1990s. An estimated 20,000 South Koreans eagerly awaited the Rapture, when they would be lifted to heaven at the end of the world at a time prophesied by the sect's leader. Many of the believers burned their furniture, sold their homes, left their jobs, abandoned their families, and had abortions in preparation for the heavenly ascent. The appointed time passed without incident, and the leader was arrested for bilking hundreds of thousands of dollars from his followers.

Still, sects do provide a sense of certainty in several ways. First, many are fundamentalist, interpreting the Bible as word-for-word, literal truth, leaving little room for doubt among believers. Second, sects usually impose a great deal of control over members' lives through strict rules and prohibitions regarding such matters as diet and dress. Conforming to a clear set of guidelines can impart a sense of certainty. Also, the often intensely emotional rituals of sects can help alleviate doubts. For example, new members typically must enter the congregation through emotional public conversion as proof of their firm faith.

The success of some sects can also be explained in terms of their effective marketing techniques, which can produce churches somewhat different than the model. Most sect members (along with some Methodists, Catholics, Lutherans, and Southern Baptists) are "evangelical" or "born again" Christians, meaning they have not only rededicated their lives to Christ but feel an obligation to spread the faith. To reach out to the unchurched, in some cases they conduct marketing surveys and then offer people what they want to hear. This strategy thus includes a more consumer-friendly "soft sell" rather than the "hell-fire" preaching typical of some sects. Moreover, while sects are usually much smaller than denominations, these new Evangelical churches can grow to sizes that dwarf long-established organizations. Their well-targeted messages, effective marketing techniques, talented preachers, and huge auditoriums can draw upwards of 20,000 weekly participants. As Deidre Sullivan (1991) observes, the booming Evangelical churches have been especially effective at presenting themselves to baby boomers as the guardian of the American family. With sixty percent of such households containing children, their profamily image gives these organizations a bright future.

The adept, finely honed recruitment techniques of many sects likewise accounts for their large membership gains. Mormons, for example, through careful study have evolved an effective recruitment strategy based on creating social networks (Stark and Bainbridge, 1980). Mormon missionaries going from door to door without introduction have a success rate of only 0.1 percent. They are successful half of the time, however, when contact occurs through a Mormon friend or relative. Thus, members of the Church of Jesus Christ of Latter-Day Saints cultivate intimate ties with nonmembers, linking them into a Mormon social network. Recruitment instructions offer pointers on establishing interpersonal bonds as a prelude to introduction to the faith. The Mormons' phenomenal growth speaks for the effectiveness of such techniques, which are rarely employed by most well-established—and declining—denominations.

The Lord's House

A partial lineage of the major Christian churches of the 20th century.

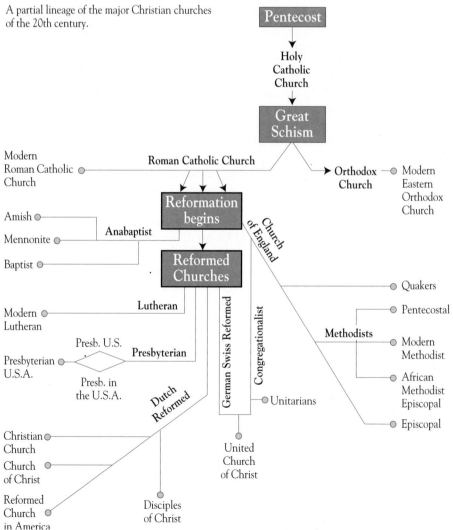

Figure 11-1

Source: Adapted from *U.S. News & World Report*, March 4, 1991; drawing by David Merrill.

Most sects never get past the stage of borrowing homes for meeting places and trying to patch up rifts among a small, unstable congregation. Those that manage to grow in size, however, typically evolve in the direction of denominations, gradually decreasing the tension between their organization and mainstream society. In other words, as they gain large numbers they usually gain the respect and stability that come with cultural assimilation. Along the way, however, elements within the sect may accuse the leadership of straying too far from the authentic truth. Eventually they may even produce splinter groups that establish their own sects, continuing the cycle of organizational maturity and fragmentation (see Figure 11-1). Some groups, however, retain their sect-like characteristics in spite of their large size. A few, like the Mormons, even reverse the sect-to-denomination trend after a period of assimilation (Mauss and Barlow, 1991).

It is difficult to describe the typical sect member because sects range from a few dozen people following a barely literate preacher to the new Evangelical "megachurch" featuring a well-polished leader, a fleet of buses, and its own television program. Historically, sects have attracted the poor or others suffering from some type of deprivation, people with a grievance, or those dismayed by what they see as the immorality of modern society. Since the 1970s, they have attracted more middle-class people as well. Still, "born again" Christians, usually sect members, are more likely to be low income, over 50 years old, southern, and African American (Sullivan, 1991).

Why Do Cults Still Attract Members?
By the end of the 1960s, many Americans felt so disoriented by the upheavals in their society that they searched even further afield than sects for answers and comfort. Many turned to **cults,** usually small religious groups headed by a charismatic leader offering an innovative belief system outside the cultural mainstream. While most cults last only a short while, some have successfully established themselves as alternatives to denominations and sects.

On the surface, we might wonder why anyone would join a cult. After all, these fringe organizations exist in a state of constant tension or conflict with the broader society. And rather than offer the security of "old truths" as do sects, cults espouse a "new word" imported from another culture. In many cases, cults offer not so much a closer relationship with God as a new social network or a Utopian vision of a new society. Moreover, most of us would probably object to following the commands of a dictatorial leader. Most cults are held together by a charismatic figure who can inspire great loyalty, but may also demand complete obedience. Jim Jones' hold over the nearly 1,000 members of his People's Temple was strong enough to order their mass suicide in 1979.

In some ways, cults compete with denominations for members. Like any religion, they offer explanations (through the leader's confident pronouncements) and emotional security (in the form of an intense social network). Some researchers describe typical cult joiners as young people from comfortable, sheltering homes that helped them form dependent personalities (Schwartz, 1979). However, while there is great variety among cults, they generally attract followers from different segments of the population than do mainstream religious organizations. For example, Marc Galanter (1990) found psychological distress and alienation in many of those joining the cult-like Unification Church. Others report that cult members have weak emotional ties with their parents (Marciano, 1987), and are especially likely to join during a transitional life stage or in a period of "seekership," during which they search for meaning in life (Martin, 1982; Thomas, 1979). Cults have their greatest success among those living in areas of high residential mobility rates and weak ties to traditional Christianity

Cult: a usually small religious group headed by a charismatic leader offering an innovative belief system outside the cultural mainstream.

(Stark and Bainbridge, 1985). In his study of a satanic cult, William Sims Bainbridge (1978) notes that the prime market for members consisted of young social isolates, often students far from home and hungry for social attachments. And as with other groups, cults reach recruits first through interpersonal bonds, which then lead to acceptance of the group's beliefs (Stark and Bainbridge, 1980). People join cults, in other words, for some of the same reasons others join denominations and sects, but they focus more strongly on social and emotional needs than spiritual ones.

Those who stay in cults for any length of time usually derive some benefits. Galanter (1990) found that the altered consciousness, social cohesiveness, and shared beliefs of cults, like that of est, Recovery, Alcoholics Anonymous, and other zealous self-help groups, can offer relief from psychological problems. As long as members accept the cult's belief system and conform to its behavioral guidelines, such as verbal expressions of support and demonstrations of affection, they enjoy the therapeutic rewards.

While some observers claim cults employ coercive brainwashing techniques that destroy ego, decision-making capacity, and free will, sociologists find little actual evidence of this (Robbins, 1988; Snow and Machalek, 1984). The typical cult does not depend on force to recruit or retain members, but binds followers through the same techniques of social control used by other, more conventional groups, such as monasteries and the military. Cult members typically stay with the group because they do not want to lose its emotional and social security. Stuart Wright (1991) likens the difficulty in breaking from a cult to that of going through a divorce. Like a marriage, commitment to a cult initially brings high hopes and a sense of well-being. Gradually, it gains a hold on the individual. But the emotional bonds may weaken; the individual feels disillusioned, angry, or confused; and he or she finally makes a difficult, but still voluntary, decision to abandon the commitment.

Abuses occur, such as at the People's Temple, where Jones had his followers practice mass suicide many times to test their dedication and to maintain a clear boundary between the cult and what he depicted as a threatening, oppressive world. Cults often pressure new members to sever ties with the outside and subject themselves to invasive scrutiny of their private lives; still, force is rarely used. A few survivalist cults, like the Church Universal and Triumphant, prepare themselves in the far reaches of the American West for the world's end, reportedly amassing considerable arsenals. As in the case of the branch Davidians in Waco, Texas, such groups may well receive extensive media attention, especially if they defy civil authority.

In sum, sociologists have found little evidence of the "evil cult" envisioned by the mass media. Instead, most offer alienated, lonely people living on society's fringe an opportunity for emotional and social satisfaction. From a sociological view, these groups represent yet another offering in the American marketplace of religion, one that, to the disadvantage of denominations, has opened up considerably in recent decades.

HAVE AMERICANS BECOME MORE RELIGIOUS, OR LESS?

We hear a lot in the popular media about the Protestant evangelical revival in the United States. But is this just an anomaly, a side show to the overall creeping secularism of modern life? Can a postindustrial society sustain an institution as nonscientific and otherworldly as religion? And if not, will our culture find other sources of cohesion and harmony to replace religion?

Secularization Theory: Religion is Headed for Extinction

According to *secularization theory*, as societies modernize, they discard the pervasive, protective umbrella of religion, and people find they must look elsewhere for explanations and security. The modern mind subjects the tenets of faith to individual, intellectual scrutiny, leaving religion unable to guide or unify society. In this view, because of its incompatibility with a modern world's need for technological solutions and empirical answers, religion recedes into the cultural background, eventually becoming extinct.

Peter Berger (1979) argues that secularism tends to undermine religious traditions by fostering religious pluralism. In such a competitive atmosphere, with claims and counterclaims bandied about, belief in a religion is no longer taken for granted. Each religion's "plausibility structure" is laid on the line as simply one more product on the market. This makes it difficult for any faith to present itself as the "one truth," and to demand loyalty and obedience.

Steve Bruce (1990) claims that the schismatic nature of Protestantism will ultimately bring about the faith's own demise. Protestantism relies on subjective Biblical interpretation rather than a central church authority. Consequently, different groups follow their own interpretations into different spiritual directions. This process of fission contributes to gradual secularization as each group's claim to legitimacy undermines the claims of the others. Bruce predicts a downward spiral of religious faith marked by increasingly smaller waves of revival.

Along with pluralism, modernization results in geographical mobility and urbanism, two more trends incompatible with religion. As it becomes easier and cheaper to travel, fewer people tend to remain in any one locality, disrupting communities held together by shared opinions and faith. Many move to cities, where they may lose touch with the intimate social networks upon which religious commitment thrives. As they become more cosmopolitan, sampling from a numbing array of competing belief systems, their religious faith erodes (Roof, 1978).

We might also expect religion to lose appeal as a population grows younger and more comfortable. According to some researchers, as modernization produces a higher level of education and wealth, religion becomes less important to people (Albrecht and Heaton, 1984; Stark and Bainbridge, 1987). Also, young people tend to abandon religion, at least temporarily. Thus, as the huge baby boom generation entered their teens and early adulthood in the 1960s and 1970s, their youthful questioning of authority, combined with the general social upheaval of the Vietnam War era, created a crisis among America's churches. About one-third have since returned to the religious fold as they assumed parental responsibilities, but most have not, especially highly educated and childless married couples (Roof, 1992).

While baby boomers as a group have abandoned formal religious institutions, many believe in astrology and reincarnation, practice meditation, and generally contribute to what one observer calls the "privatization of faith" (Roof, 1982). Like many others today, they focus inwardly toward personal growth rather than membership in a congregation, or they shop around for an organization that does not interfere with their individualized faith. Will the decline in religion that began with the baby boom generation establish a momentum predicted by secularization theory, or is it a lull produced by unique historical circumstances?

Another View: Religion Is Holding Its Own

Once widely accepted, secularization theory has been shaken by recent events. Some empirical studies indicate that religion is alive and well in America, at least in some parts of society. The evidence comes from several quarters.

First, historically there is no "golden age" of faith from which we have supposedly declined. Puritan Boston in the 1600s had far lower church attendance and membership rates than today's Las Vegas or San Francisco (Finke and Stark, 1986). Attendance nearly doubled between 1924 and 1978 in the much-studied town of Muncie, Indiana (Caplow, Bahr, and Chadwick, 1983), and membership, even in the less religious American West, has risen steadily this century (Finke and Stark, 1986). Meanwhile, churches have proliferated, especially conservative and evangelical types, infusing Protestantism with a new vigor. At the same time, a new type of "communal" Catholic has arisen, loyal to tradition and ethnic/immigrant heritage (Greeley, 1977). Jewish associations promoting local welfare, education, and cultural projects have likewise added another dimension to contemporary Judaism. None of these facts indicate that America has become less religious.

Spiritual programs in the mass media provide a very visible sign of religion's strength in America. Evangelicals began using radio in the 1920s, and today over 1,000 stations offer religious formats. But television has a far greater reach and influence. The pioneers of television preaching, Billy Graham and Oral Roberts, have recently been joined by several other widely popular "televangelists." Jerry Falwell has attracted millions of viewers on both cable and commercial networks. Pat Robertson attempted to translate his large religious following into political power in the 1988 presidential campaign. Nearly 13 million households tuned in to Jim and Tammy Bakker until his involvement in a sex scandal in 1987. Jimmy Swaggart's successful televangelical career likewise took a turn a year later for the same reason. A general slump in donations to such organizations followed these embarrassments (Mason and Ticer, 1988), but television preaching still commands large audiences in America.

Survey data suggest for the most part that American religiousness has remained steady for decades. Andrew Greeley (1989a) marshals a variety of data to describe an American society that over the past 50 years has lost none of its religiousness: The levels of belief and attendance today are about the same as in 1940. Attendance dropped among Catholics after the progressive changes stemming from the Second Vatican Council of the 1960s and the Pope's 1969 decree forbidding artificial birth control, but rates stabilized by 1975. And Protestants, as we have seen, shifted in large numbers away from mainstream denominations. Overall church membership has remained remarkably stable (see Table 11-3).

Results of other studies, however, question Americans' religious intensity. Research by Hadaway, Marler, and Chaves (1993) suggests that attendance rates may be about one-half what is generally believed because many people who claim in surveys that they go to church do not actually attend. Moreover, a survey by Kellstedt, Green, Guth, and Smidt (1993) reveals that only about nineteen percent of American adults are seriously committed to the practice of their faith. Still, the overall picture hardly looks like religion's last gasp in American society.

America's famed "civil religion" has also survived, though in a more shadowy form. Robert Bellah (1967) uses this term to refer to a nonsectarian, national faith founded on Protestantism, with sacred symbols embedded in the people's consciousness and the country's history. In this view, Americans have believed they are a Godly people who enjoy His special protection. Evidence of this infiltration of religion into

CHURCH MEMBERSHIP AND CHURCH ATTENDANCE
IN THE UNITED STATES, 1940–1993

Percentage of People Who Say They Are Members of a Church/Synagogue		Percentage Reporting Recent Church/Synagogue Attendance	
Year	Percentage	Year	Percentage
1940	72	1940	37
1944	75	1950	39
1947	76	1954	46
1952	73	1955	49
1965	73	1957	47
1976	71	1958	49
1979	68	1962	46
1982	67	1967	43
1983	69	1969	42
1985	71	1972	40
1987	69	1979	40
1988	65	1981	41
1989	68	1982	41
1990	69	1983	40
1991	69	1985	42
1992	71	1987	40
1993	71	1988	42
		1989	43
		1990	40
		1991	41
		1992	41
		1993	41

Table 11-3

Source: Adapted from *Gallup Poll Monthly*, April 1992, p. 41.

civic affairs abounds, from the "In God We Trust" on our money to the Pledge of Allegiance's pronouncement of our "nation under God" to the religious invocations we use to open and close various political and social occasions. While this fabric of shared values and national consciousness has diminished under the force of pluralism and secularism, its forms remain, largely as "a tool for legitimating social movements and interest-group politics" (Williams and Demerath, 1991, p. 418).

What happened to the predictions of secularization theory? Roger Finke and Rodney Stark (1988) find that religious pluralism, contrary to most predictions, has actually been associated with an increase in religious participation. Populations in urban areas, with their great diversity and religious competition, show *higher* rates of participation than rural ones. The researchers persuasively argue that rivalry stimulates religious growth. Faiths proliferate, and in a market full of options, fewer searchers will go hungry. At the same time, competing organizations must vigorously attract and retain members, thereby creating a more intense religious society. We might also speculate that religion has held its own because humans still need the comfort, social integration, and identity that it offers.

Critical Thinking Box

Has America Become Less Religious?

Large-scale trends like religiousness are difficult to measure. Surveys regarding church attendance, membership, even beliefs, may not tap exactly what we mean by so broad a concept. Certainly, some people may claim religious membership for social or even business reasons. Likewise, the increase in religious television programs and evangelical revivals are countered by high rates of drug use, sexual abuse and promiscuity, and crime.

Still, a student of society should hold an informed opinion about the course of such an important institution. So offer your opinion: Has America over the past several decades become less religious, more religious, or remained at about the same level but with changed forms? Be ready to explain your reasoning. ∎

DOES RELIGION REALLY MAKE A DIFFERENCE?

We have seen that religion attracts people because they seek social and emotional rewards; whether they are members of a denomination, sect, or cult, they want to transform their lives. Here we search for signs of such change as we ask whether religion really makes a measurable difference in people's attitudes and behavior and, if so, how.

Does Denomination Matter?

A century ago, American Protestants and Catholics lived in separate spheres. One group dominated the social and political landscape in terms of numbers and power; the other largely contained poor, non-English-speaking, widely despised immigrants. Today, if we lump together all Protestant denominations (65 percent of the U.S. population), we find that, excepting Hispanics, Catholics (about 25 percent) have pulled ahead in levels of education and income, and have more liberal attitudes on social and sexual matters (Greeley, 1989a). Moreover, some evidence now suggests that Catholics' fertility rates are lower than those of Protestants (Mosher, Williams, and Johnson, 1992). Researchers also find that traditional Protestant–Catholic differences in social and political attitudes matter less, so that liberal Protestants are more similar to Jews (about 2 percent of the population) and Catholics than they are to conservative Protestants (Pescosolido and Georgianna, 1989). To distinguish Catholics from Protestants, therefore, we must contrast the former with fundamentalist and evangelical Protestants. At that level, we see that denomination does make a difference.

Fundamentalist and evangelical Protestants stand out in several ways. They generally prefer punishment of criminals to deterrence or rehabilitation (Grasmick et al., 1992), advocate the use of physical punishment for children (Ellison and Sherkat, 1993), and actively support the pro-life movement (Luker, 1984). They generally oppose the Equal Rights Amendment (Brady and Tedin, 1976) as well as female participation in politics (Peek and Brown, 1980). Except for those in the South, evangelicals have become steadily more Republican over the past two decades (Kiecolt and Nelsen, 1991). Fundamentalists tend to hold more sexist beliefs (Peek, Lowe, and Williams, 1991), are less likely to engage in premarital sex (Beck, Cole, and Hammond, 1991), and prefer patriarchal family forms (Grasmick, Wilcox, and Bird, 1990).

Emile Durkheim and Max Weber both noted long ago that Catholics hold a different view of the world than Protestants. Weber (1904) described Catholics as more "communitarian," in contrast to the "inner-worldly asceticism" of Protestantism. Perhaps this community-mindedness explains why predominantly Catholic countries today show not only lower suicide rates but lower rates of heart-disease mortality than similarly developed Protestant nations (Watson, 1991). And after many decades of urbanism and secularism, Catholics still see God, their fellow humans, and the social world in a different light than Protestants (Greeley, 1989b).

We must exercise caution, however, in concluding that these denominational differences are *caused* by denominational experiences. It might largely be a matter of self-selection: For example, people who are already conservative are attracted to conservative organizations. But when we study the effects of religion of *any* type on its adherents, as we see next, the evidence suggests more strongly that the religious experience can, in and of itself, cause changes in individuals.

Does Religion Change People?

Perhaps people who are already satisfied with their lives tend to join religious organizations (because they still long for a transcendent experience). Maybe such self-selection accounts for the high rates of life satisfaction researchers find in religious populations (Gee and Veevers, 1990). And maybe this also explains why levels of happiness, family contentment, and life excitement are generally higher among people with strong religious affiliation (Reed, 1991); why strongly religious people in general suffer less psychological distress (Ross, 1990); and why belief in a "helping God" is correlated with lower levels of loneliness (Schwab and Petersen, 1990). In fact, dozens of studies find a positive relationship between religious commitment and psychological well-being. More specifically, they find a link between positive mental health and ceremony, social support, prayer, and relationship with God (Larson et al., 1992).

Religion also correlates with the way people relate to others. Those engaging in frequent devotional activities are more open, less suspicious, and friendlier than less-religious people (Ellison, 1992). People with strong religious commitment tend to engage in more volunteer work (Forst and Healy, 1991), participate in political activities (Finley, 1991; Stone, 1981; Tipton, 1982), put more emphasis on family than career (Jones and McNamara, 1991), violate fewer laws and rules (Grasmick, Bursik, and Cochran, 1991; Grasmick, Kinsey, and Cochran, 1991; Tittle and Welch, 1983; Welch, Tittle, and Petee, 1991), and are less likely to cohabit (Thornton, Axinn, and Hill, 1992), or have premarital sex (Jensen, Newell, and Holman, 1990).

Religious participation thus appears to strongly impact people. But these studies do not establish that it actually *causes* these changes. Other evidence, however, suggests that such correlations do describe consequences of church attendance and membership, that religion does in fact produce emotional and social changes in people, and even promotes better physical health.

How might this happen? For one thing, joining a religious congregation gives one support in the form of friendship, social networks, material assistance, and helpful information in time of need (Maton, 1989; Taylor and Chatters, 1988). Some religions promote healthy life style norms (Levin and Vanderpool, 1987). Prohibitions against caffeine, tobacco, and alcohol, for example, help explain the greater longevity and lower rates of cancer and circulatory diseases among Mormons and Seventh-Day Adventists (Oleckno and Blacconiere, 1991). We can easily see how religion can enhance emotional and psychological well-being by offering a firm sense of order, meaning, and understanding (Antonovsky, 1987; Pollner, 1989). Better mental health also seems to flow from collective ritual events (Petersen and Roy, 1985) and prayer (Ellison, Gay, and Glass, 1989). Prayer provides solace and guidance as the individual establishes an intimate connection with a divine power that can take control, support, and forgive (Pollner, 1989). In fact, Melvin Pollner concludes that "relationships with divine others" predict well-being more strongly than race, sex, income, age, marital status, and church attendance. And finally, Ellen Idler (1987) suggests that religion protects health by providing a special meaning system that gives people hope during times of physical suffering.

Prayer apparently can produce psychological comfort and perhaps even enhance physical well-being.

Research Box

Body and Soul: A Direct Link Between Health and Religion?

In his famous study of suicide, Emile Durkheim (1897) saw the religious community's supportive social network as one of many possible factors inhibiting suicide. Researchers Ellen Idler and Stanislav Kasl (1992), however, detected in Durkheim's line of thought some hint of a more direct link between health and religion. Perhaps something in the individual experience of sacred rituals *directly* gives churchgoers a protective advantage against death and disability. If so, they reasoned, those periods of more intense religious worship (Easter and Christmas for Christians; Yom Kippur, Rosh Hashanah, and Passover for Jews) should offer greater health benefits to the faithful. Specifically, they hypothesized that: (1) Christians and Jews would show lower rates of death, functional disability, and depression during their respective special ritual seasons; and (2) the impact of religious holidays would be greater for more religious individuals, those who describe themselves as deeply religious, and people who attend rituals frequently.

Idler and Kasl drew a random sample of people aged 65 and over who lived independently (that is, not in nursing homes) in a New England city. The sample represented people from various levels of housing quality, from public projects to private homes. The researchers achieved a response rate (the precentage of those in the sample who agreed to participate) of 82 percent. Follow-up interviews, which assessed the respondents' health over the several years of the study, showed even higher response rates—around 95 percent. During the interviews, Idler and Kasl obtained measures of the independent variables regarding religiousness and the dependent variables regarding depression, ability to perform activities of daily living, and physical health. Mortality was monitored throughout.

Analysis of the statistical measures showed a strong link between health and religion, especially public religiousness. First, Idler and Kasl found a significant correlation between public religious involvement and functional ability; in other words, the more participation in ritual observances, the more people maintained their ability to perform self-care and other physical activities. The researchers tested for any effects of such variables as gender, age, educational level, exercise, optimism, and social contacts. Without the effect of religion, none of these variables fully explained the level of physical ability. As the authors conclude, "the findings suggest that it is not behaviors, networks, or attitudes alone, but some other element of the religious experience felt by those who attend services frequently that makes the difference" (p. 1074).

On the other hand, private religiousness presented a more complex picture. As expected, deep religious feelings were associated with less depression, but only for men with worsening disability. Surprisingly, most of those reporting such feelings were more likely to be disabled. To account for this finding, the researchers speculate that those who say they receive the most comfort and strength from their faith may be those whose poor health status requires extra emotional aid. Also, people who have turned inward, or shifted their focus from physical health and survival to the spiritual world, may "let themselves go" physically. In any case, Idler and Kasl note that public and private religiousness deserve separate study.

As expected, death was significantly less likely during the 30 days before religious holidays, but it was much more unlikely for those who frequently participated in ceremonies, especially Catholics and, to a lesser extent, Jews. Again, health behaviors, social contacts, and optimism explain some of this connection but not all of it.

The researchers conclude that "the ritualistic enactment of belief" somehow affects physical well-being. At least for elderly people, they detect an even stronger, more direct link than did Durkheim between the physical realm and the awe-inspiring world of the sacred. □

WHO GETS SICK, AND WHY THE SOCIAL DIFFERENCES?

All cultures provide ways to deal with the mysterious uncertainties of death and disease. Because many people consult the supernatural world for explanations and remedies, magic and religion figure prominently in most systems devoted to controlling health and death. The Yanomamo, for example, sprinkled magic powders on a woman's head to prevent conception, and employed sorcery to inflict illness and death on their enemies (Smole, 1976). They also felt the need to put some of their faith in health aids more firmly rooted in the natural world, such as various medicinal plants, and certain insects used to clean out ear wax.

Like the Yanomamo, most societies contend with the uncertainties of death and disease with methods both sacred—forbidden, reverent, otherworldly—and **profane**—ordinary, commonplace, secular. In prescientific societies, hit-or-miss attempts to find medical cures have little success, so magic holds relatively high importance. In our own society, medical science has largely displaced magical cures. However, because it has not eliminated uncertainty from death and illness, we still reserve a place for "alternative" medicine, faith healing, and charms.

Profane: dealing with the ordinary, commonplace, and secular.

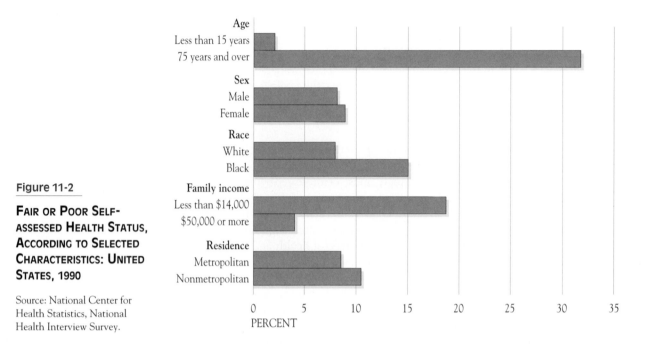

Figure 11-2

FAIR OR POOR SELF-ASSESSED HEALTH STATUS, ACCORDING TO SELECTED CHARACTERISTICS: UNITED STATES, 1990

Source: National Center for Health Statistics, National Health Interview Survey.

As we begin our sociological approach to health and sickness, we note that, like most important elements of social life, illness is not distributed equally in the United States (see Figure 11-2). Researchers find links between sickness and various social statuses; in other words, some types of people suffer more medical problems than do others, for reasons beyond simple physical constitution. For example, married people show lower mortality rates, have fewer mental and physical health problems, and rely less on health services than those who are unmarried (Berkman and Syme, 1979; Morgan, 1980; Ross and Mirowsky, 1989; Schoenborn and Wilson, 1988). Much of these differences can be explained in terms of married people's social support (Sherbourne and Hays, 1990). Other statuses, such as age, race, and sex, evoke different behaviors and pressures that directly or indirectly affect the individual's health. Here we examine what kinds of people get sick more frequently, and why.

Why Do the Poor Suffer More Health Problems?

Numerous studies have shown that poor people have higher-than-average rates of heart disease, high blood pressure, kidney failure, lung disease, psychiatric disorders, obesity, and diabetes. They die sooner and live with more injuries and mental and physical illness (Kaplan, 1989). While the poor's greater health problems are not surprising, we might wonder if, short of making them no longer poor, society can somehow decrease their level of suffering? Is it simply a matter of more access to health care, or are higher rates of disease and illness simply an inherent part of indigence?

Clearly, most poor people lack access to high-quality primary care. Many rely on crowded public clinics or emergency rooms. They often find that even not-for-profit hospitals, beleaguered by cutthroat competition, avoid serving the uninsured poor (Relman, 1992). The uninsured suffer more than twice the number of negligent medical injuries than do insured patients (Burstin, Lipsitz, and Brennan, 1992), and uninsured women receive inferior prenatal care (Haas et al., 1993). Figure 11-3 shows the

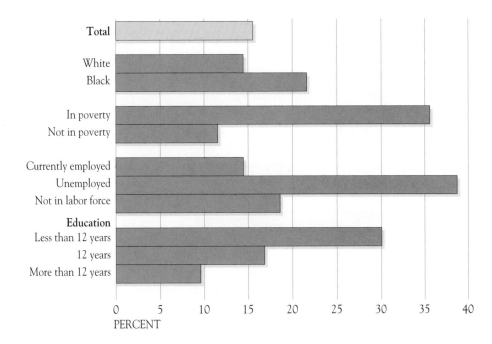

Figure 11-3

PERSONS UNDER 65 YEARS OF AGE WITHOUT HEALTH CARE COVERAGE, ACCORDING TO SELECTED CHARACTERISTICS: UNITED STATES, 1989

Source: National Center for Health Statistics, National Health Interview Survey.

low level of medical coverage received by the poor, unemployed, and poorly educated. At least part of the health care gap, then, can be narrowed by increasing access to services and insurance coverage.

But beyond the lack of adequate and affordable health care, the poor's own life style exposes them to more stress and fewer coping resources (Kessler, 1979). Financial setbacks such as job losses, mortgage foreclosures, and evictions may directly explain their greater vulnerability to illness (Liem and Liem, 1978). Poverty may also act more indirectly by, for example, weakening social integration and producing greater feelings of powerlessness (Mirowsky and Ross, 1986). Also, their lower educational level and lower control they have over their jobs can contribute to lower self-esteem and less problem-solving ability, making it more difficult to cope with personal crises (Menaghan, 1983). In short, the undesirable life events of lower-class life render people less emotionally hardy and more vulnerable than those more privileged (McLeod and Kessler, 1990).

The life style typical of the poor also includes some behavior patterns that contribute to bad health. Lower-class people are more likely to drink, smoke, and delay seeking medical attention. Also, nutritional deficiencies partly stem from food choices and cooking habits. For example, a study of rural poor in New York State found high rates of smoking and obesity, frequent salt use, high levels of cholesterol, and social isolation (Gold and Franks, 1990). Clearly, any attempt to improve the health of indigent people must go beyond providing better access to medical care.

Why Does Race Matter?

Figures 11-4 and 11-5 show that race and ethnicity are strongly correlated with an individual's health. Note that because the two figures show *rates* of death, they enable us to compare the relative threats to each group. Figure 11-4 points dramatically to homicide rates for blacks and suicides among American Indians and Alaskan Natives.

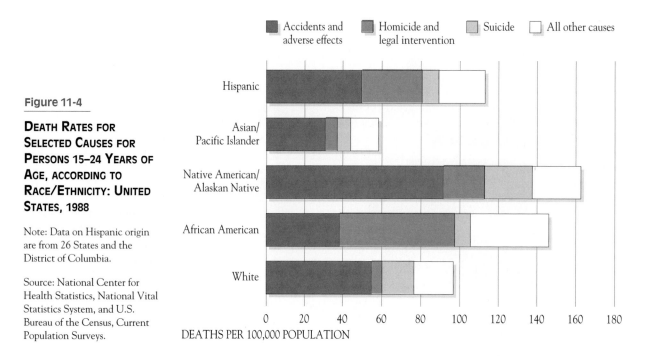

Figure 11-4

DEATH RATES FOR SELECTED CAUSES FOR PERSONS 15–24 YEARS OF AGE, ACCORDING TO RACE/ETHNICITY: UNITED STATES, 1988

Note: Data on Hispanic origin are from 26 States and the District of Columbia.

Source: National Center for Health Statistics, National Vital Statistics System, and U.S. Bureau of the Census, Current Population Surveys.

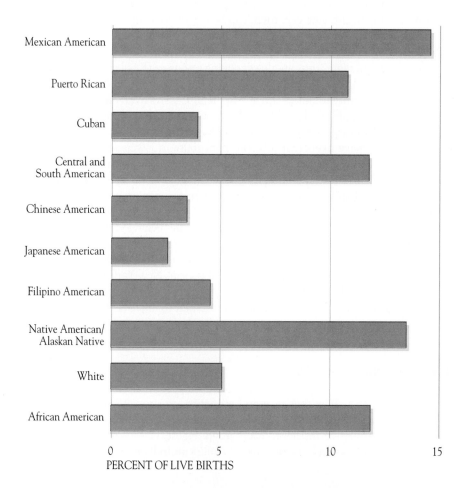

Figure 11-5

PROPORTION OF MOTHERS WITH LATE OR NO PRENATAL CARE, ACCORDING TO RACE AND ETHNICITY OF MOTHER: UNITED STATES, 1989

Note: Early prenatal care is defined as care beginning in the first trimester of pregnancy. Late prenatal care is defined as care beginning in the third trimester. Data on Hispanic origin of mother are from 30 States and the District of Columbia.

Source: National Center for Health Statistics, National Vital Statistics System.

Figure 11-5 suggests that because of their mothers' poor medical care, infants in some groups receive less protection against possible health problems. Death rates from AIDS among Hispanics are more than double that of whites; rates among African Americans are 3.6 times the white rate. Asian Americans have the lowest death rates of any group at any age. Clearly, the social environments of some minority groups in our society pose greater health dangers than do others.

Poverty-related illnesses and deaths strike the African-American population especially hard, and we use this group to understand how minority status translates into poorer health. Blacks show especially high rates of disease and mortality at any age (Farley and Allen, 1987; Ford et al., 1990). But is this a problem of socioeconomic status or racial/ethnic subculture and discrimination—that is, class or race? This question arises from the fact that even when social class is controlled, racial differences in health remain.

For example, one study found that blacks were less healthy than whites of the same educational level (Ferraro, 1989). We also know that blacks report poorer health than whites with similar financial strain (Krause, 1987) or similar income (Dowd and Bengston, 1978; Mutchler and Burr, 1991). And in veterans hospitals, blacks are less likely than whites to receive bypass operations and other sophisticated treatments for heart problems. The explanations lie in a web of complex factors, including possible bias among physicians and a greater tendency among blacks than among whites to avoid surgery (Whittle et al., 1993). These studies suggest that something about being a member of a minority group, and not necessarily poor, detracts from an individual's health. In other words, other forms of inequality besides education and income may help to explain African Americans' relative vulnerability to illness and disease (Wilson, 1978).

In search of such subtle influences, some researchers point to political empowerment. For example, the risk of dying during infancy for blacks is almost double that of whites. This seems to reflect blacks' social inequality, as seen in their residential segregation, poorer health services, and higher poverty rates (LaVeist, 1989, 1990). Perhaps surprisingly, political inequality may also help explain this health indicator (McKnight, 1985). Political empowerment—whether in the form of black politicians funneling more government funding to minority neighborhoods or greater community-level activism on behalf of better services and grants (LaVeist, 1992)—does in fact appear to reduce infant mortality among African Americans. This suggests that not just more equal incomes but greater sharing of political power may be required to close the racial health gap.

This gap may also reflect differences in coping strategies. Researchers find that lower-class blacks suffer more from depression and psychological distress than lower-class whites (Neff, 1984). This may stem from some greater vulnerability to the impact of undesirable life events (Ulbrich, Warheit, and Zimmerman, 1989). This does not hold true, however, for economic troubles. Apparently, chronic economic disadvantages have forced African Americans to develop coping strategies for on-going difficulties that trigger depression more easily in others, including resignation, prayer, and heavy reliance on informal social support (Neighbors et al., 1983; Veroff, Douvan, and Kulka, 1981).

Why Do Women Get Sick More?

Like the poor and African Americans, women as a group are more at risk for health problems. Compared to men, women in the United States have higher rates of physical illness in terms of both daily symptoms and chronic conditions such as arthritis.

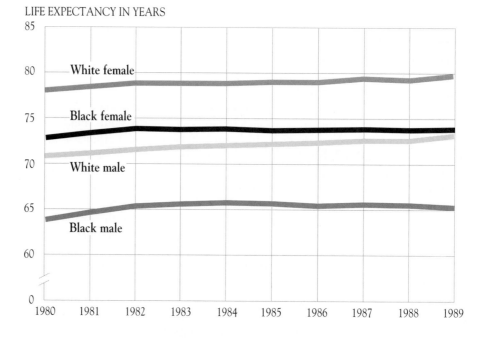

LIFE EXPECTANCY IN YEARS

Figure 11-6

LIFE EXPECTANCY AT BIRTH, ACCORDING TO RACE AND SEX: UNITED STATES, 1980–1989

Source: National Center for Health Statistics, National Health Interview Survey.

They also have higher rates of psychological disorders such as anxiety and depression. Consequently, women take off more time from work for medical reasons and use health services more frequently. Is this a matter of genetic weaknesses or social influences?

Actually, evidence suggests that women have a biological health advantage over men, but social factors overwhelm it. As Figure 11-6 shows, men have higher mortality rates, probably due to genetic or hormonal disadvantages and to their more reluctant use of health care. But women still show higher rates of illness, in part because they are more likely to report their symptoms to interviewers, but mostly because of the "acquired risks" they pick up from their social environment (Fuller et al., 1993; Verbrugge, 1989). While men indulge in smoking and suffer more job hazards, women are subject to greater psychological pressures generated by their social milieu.

The social stigma associated with alcohol and drug abuse by women illustrates one aspect of this mental stress. When men abuse such substances, they suffer less dissonance with their social roles. Male sex-role norms encourage physical stamina, risk taking, and defiance of social convention, all of which makes drunkenness or drug highs relatively less shameful for men. In most societies throughout history, such deviance has brought far more disgrace to women. One reason is that a drunken woman's neglect of her child has greater negative social consequences than an incapacitated man's inability, say, to tend his fields. (Child, Barry, and Bacon, 1965). Such behavior could also render the woman more sexually vulnerable or promiscuous. Thus, in an effort to protect her femininity, a woman is under greater strain to conceal this type of deviance. Still, she will feel more shame and guilt than will a man (Knupfer, 1982), who abuses drugs and alcohol with less concern about his masculinity. The alcoholic or drug-dependent male may suffer social consequences, such as loss of job and friends, but the female's distress is also turned inward, resulting in more mental health problems (Robbins, 1989).

Besides this need for sobriety, females are pressured by role overload (Bird and Fremont, 1991). Women generally hold less rewarding roles; they have less paid work and lower wages when they do work. They spend more hours on housework, child care, and helping others, and consequently have less time for leisure and sleep. Such social factors, rather than biological ones, seem to largely account for the discrepancy between men's and women's illness rates.

Another line of research suggests that women, especially if they are married, suffer poorer health because of their low sense of personal control. Because she has few resources and little prestige, the housewife lacks decision-making power, without which she is more susceptible to anxiety and depression (Burger, 1984; Mirowsky and Ross, 1984). Working outside the home can give a married woman some sense of personal control, which should contribute to her emotional health, but the overlapping demands of housework, child care, and employment ultimately render her more vulnerable to illness (Rosenfield, 1989). If women were relieved of such burdens of their gender role, they would not only outlive men (as they do now), but show lower rates of illness (Bird and Fremont, 1991; Verbrugge, 1989).

Clearly, certain categories of people—the poor, blacks, and women—get sick more frequently than others, and the reasons lie in the circumstances attending their social statuses. The resulting behavior patterns, deprivations, and pressures create physical and mental vulnerabilities that affect the health of such socially disadvantaged groups.

HOW CAN HEALTH CARE BE A TOOL OF OPPRESSION?

Like the other institutions that have arisen in response to society's evolving needs, health care forms a vital part of any culture. We need only imagine what would result from its breakdown: Chronic disabilities and ravaging epidemics would produce a demoralized, sluggish, and vulnerable population. As functionalists point out, we depend on the health care system to maintain a strong workforce and thus help ensure society's smooth operation. Other theorists, however, see beneath this manifest function latent consequences that involve oppression and control. How can this happen in an institution supposedly devoted to healing?

Is Health Care a Capitalist Tool?

Conflict theorists argue that, when capitalism tightened its grip on European nations during the mid-1800s, medical science changed to serve its new master (White, 1991). In line with capitalist ideology, the blame for many common working-class ailments shifted from the environment, befouled by the industrialists, to the individual. The capitalist class thus absolved itself of the health problems of the masses. According to Friedrich Engels (1845) and his successors, however, many illnesses were directly the outcome of social processes. The capitalists' unbridled pursuit of profit created foul air and water, wretched housing, and an unwholesome food supply. The poverty and unhealthy working conditions of the lower classes contributed to accidents, alcoholism and communicable diseases such as tuberculosis and typhoid. Capitalists called this a matter of personal responsibility; Engels called it "social murder."

Medicalization: a trend in which the medical establishment increases its control over even more parts of society.

Looking at today's health care system, conflict theorists discern a trend called **medicalization,** in which the medical establishment increases its control over even more parts of society (Conrad and Schneider, 1980). What were formerly regarded as moral matters or simply personal quirks are now defined as diseases requiring medical attention. Alcoholics, drug addicts, sexual perverts, and other deviants are now widely viewed as "sick" rather than "bad." By gradually imposing its definitions and analyses on a wider range of behaviors, the medical institution has increased its power greatly.

From the conflict perspective, physicians play a central role, however unintentionally, in another hidden capitalist agenda (Waitzkin, 1989). The medical practitioner focuses attention on patients' responsibilities for their health problems rather than what are often the underlying social causes. After all, the doctor cannot solve poverty and alienation; she or he can only encourage the patient to cope and adjust to society as it is. So, "despite the best conscious intentions, the practitioner thus helps reproduce the same institutional structures that form the roots of personal anguish" (Waitzkin, 1989, p. 227). By depoliticizing and individualizing social problems, doctors unconsciously but effectively act as agents of capitalist ideology.

We might expect physicians to maintain a system that gives them a licensed monopoly over medical care, heavily subsidizes their professional education and supportive research, and gives them considerable autonomy over their professional domain. Moreover, doctors act not only as advisors but purveyors of the services that their patients, or their insurance companies, will purchase. We are left to assume—or hope—that physicians will not take financial advantage of their position of trust (Relman, 1992).

Critics observe that the capitalist system (intentionally or not) creates health problems, escapes blame, and profits handsomely from it (White, 1991). By subjecting workers to harmful living conditions, the system causes poverty-related illness but blames workers for poor health habits and self-destructive life styles. Then, having displaced folk medicine with factory-like hospitals, a high-tech focus on symptoms rather than causes, and consumption of expensive drugs, the ever-expanding health care industry rakes in huge profits. The federal government has lent support to this approach by encouraging construction of technology-intensive hospitals after World War II (Starr, 1982) and supporting research studying illness instead of prevention (Peck and Bezold, 1992). And until the 1980s, the federal government maintained a hands-off, free-market attitude toward the health care industry (Ruggie, 1992).

Those opposed to "capitalist medicine" offer alternatives, such as more government intervention and greater public education. Jonathan Peck and Clement Bezold (1992) suggest an entirely new health care model that shifts the emphasis from disease, hospitalization, and physician dominance to a holistic, consumer-oriented focus on health. Rather than fight disease, the aim would be to maximize people's performance through treatment of the spirit and mind as well as body. Health care workers would consider social causes as well as personal life style influences on the patient's problems and craft a customized medical response that relies less on drugs and hospitalization than behavioral changes and outpatient treatment.

How Does the Health Care System Subordinate Women?

From the conflict perspective, we would expect any social institution to serve the interests of the elite, which, as feminists quickly point out, has always been exclusively male. Thus, it is not surprising that women generally occupy those occupations near the bottom of the health care hierarchy: orderlies, aides, and nurses. Physicians and administrators are predominantly male. But this is nothing unusual; males enjoy superior status in any field. For further signs of sexism in the medical field, we must dig a little deeper.

The evidence unearthed by researchers covers almost all aspects of medicine. Critics point to the destruction of women's health care networks, most notably midwifery and female healers (Donegan, 1978; Litoff, 1986; Sharp, 1986), and sexist attitudes in medical textbooks and journals (Lennane and Lennane, 1973; Koutroulis, 1990; Scully and Bart, 1973). J. Barker-Benfield (1979) and others contend that by diagnosing a multitude of problems as results of incomplete feminization or simply being female, gynecologists have helped subordinate women and counter early feminism (Ehrenreich and English, 1978; Holmes et al., 1980; Leeson and Gray, 1978). Critics detect a medical patriarchy in the ready prescription of tranquilizers to women and the medicalization of childbirth, which has moved a relatively natural, women-centered process into the high-tech domain of male doctors (Cooperstock and Lennard, 1979; Donley, 1986; Pihl et al., 1982). They even accuse physicians of blaming mothers' psychological disorders for some of their children's problems, including asthma, colic, and eczema (Contratto, 1984; Friedan, 1963; Matthews, 1984). Certainly the growing assertiveness and confidence of women has challenged this picture, and we cannot assume that all male physicians exhibit this patriarchal attitude, but feminists argue that, in general, the medical establishment imposes a generally male authority on women and enforces their passivity, dependence, and submission (Broverman, 1979).

FREE, UNIVERSAL HEALTH CARE IN AMERICA?

Unlike other postwar industrialized countries, the United States has moved very slowly toward comprehensive health care for all citizens. In 1965, Congress established the Medicare program to serve the elderly and disabled, and Medicaid to help the poor and institutionalized. For the most part, however, our system has depended on nongovernmental programs: People have had to find their own, private source of health care. While this system fit our free-market economic model and has provided the world's finest medical treatment to insured patients, it has also meant that a large number of Americans have had poor access to health care.

Several trends combined over the last few decades to create greater health care inequities. Both Medicaid and Medicare, for example, contributed to sharply rising medical costs because they required state governments to reimburse hospitals and physicians at "reasonable" levels determined by health care providers. Predictably, reimbursement was very generous, and expenses grew quickly. Such skyrocketing medical costs, combined with the general sluggishness of the economy in the late 1980s and early 1990s, put health care out of reach for many Americans. The loss of over two million jobs during the last two decades added to the growing number of people without medical insurance. The remaining jobs—increasingly nonunion, part-time positions in the services sector—offered few, if any, health benefits (Renner and Navarro, 1989).

The Acquired Immune Deficiency Syndrome (AIDS) epidemic put an added burden on the U.S. health care system. The disease claimed over 80,000 lives up to 1990, with the number expected to swell quickly to several hundred thousand as the latency period ends for those already infected but not yet showing symptoms. Many of these patients are unemployed, and lack medical insurance, and have unmet needs beyond health care, including counseling services, housing, and transportation (Piette et al., 1993). So far, AIDS has mostly hit male homosexuals, but in its second decade the epidemic has begun making inroads into the heterosexual population, primarily through intravenous drug users and their sexual partners, disproportionately impacting minority and poor populations. As the disease spreads, the costs of research, treatment, and lost productivity add up to billions of dollars each year.

For all these reasons, pressures grew throughout the 1980s and early 1990s for health care reform in the United States. In response, in 1993 the Clinton administration began formulating plans for a national health care system that, like those of other major industrialized nations (except for South Africa), offers universal medical care. The plan features "managed competition" and cost-containment measures to extend basic health care coverage to even the unemployed.

These reforms will move the United States down the road already traveled by such countries as Sweden, Great Britain, and China. From their example, we can perhaps catch a glimpse of our own future. Sweden, for example, uses a government-run, command-and-control system (rather than a free-market approach) to provide maximum quality care to all citizens. Britain likewise instituted a popular system of "socialized medicine" that has largely remained intact even after more than a decade of Conservative rule. China has vastly improved its people's health status, doubling life expectancy since the 1930s.

Despite these achievements, however, each of these nations is now attempting to reform its system. All three face similar problems. Sweden and Great Britain are experiencing growing inequities between the health care offered to their social classes; in China, rural and urban residents are increasingly receiving unequal care. Another common dilemma is aging populations, which place a heavy burden on medical facilities and government budgets. And of course AIDS threatens all areas of the world. Also, costs rise because of new technologies and rising demands by an increasingly sophisticated public. Patients in each of these countries complain about the quality of care. Some British patients choose to pay their own medical bills or use private insurance to avoid the long waits typical in the public system. Researchers in Sweden describe inefficient, alienated, demoralized health care workers providing dehumanized care (Gustafsson, 1989; Saltman, 1991). Patients also have little choice of physicians and restricted access to primary care and certain types of surgery (Diderichsen, 1993). In all three nations, many of these problems are simply the result of too many people demanding too many services at a time of severe economic recession.

To meet this growing consumer demand, these and other countries have retreated somewhat from socialized medicine. Sweden is encouraging a "planned market" or "mixed market" approach that features private care centers and competition among health care providers (Saltman, 1991). China has instigated decidedly nonsocialist financial incentives to improve productivity levels and encouraged the development of private practitioners to augment overcrowded public facilities (Yang, Lin, and Lawson, 1991). Britain has established cost-containment measures.

As the United States moves into the future regarding health care, it may meet others returning. Those pioneers have probed the boundaries we may discover as we explore the possibilities of free, universal health care.

Do Americans Have a Right to Medical Care?

Most political discussions involving health care reform in the United States eventually touch on the topic of rights. The Constitution makes no mention of medical care, but its Fourteenth Amendment guarantee of "equal protection under the laws" has been interpreted to include, for example, equal educational opportunity. Do citizens also have a right to decent medical care?

Of course, equal access to medical services requires transferring wealth from some to cover the needs of others. This can be justified by pointing to the overall benefits to society: a more productive workforce, with less waste of human capital. But another question arises: What level of care would be guaranteed?

Oregon has spent several years identifying what medical care government can and should fund. For example, the state pays for prenatal care (a relatively low-cost/high-payoff investment), but not for infants born so prematurely that their treatment costs over $200,000 or their probability of survival is under ten percent. Similarly, the system funds bone marrow transplants for some cancers, but not expensive and risky types. And the system pays for liver transplants unless the patient has a history of alcoholism.

By guaranteeing health care to all Americans, we would soon confront the fact that we cannot afford to give everyone every medical treatment they want, or even need. Health care must be rationed, and such a system requires subjective quality-of-life judgments that invite enraged criticism and create deep resentment.

But still another question arises: What kinds of treatment are legitimate? In an effort to cut costs, the federal government has been evaluating so-called "alternative" medicine, which usually costs far less than the usual high-technology approach. Will taxpayers end up paying for distilled floral potions, herbal medicine, crystal healing, or psychic surgery?

Returning to our initial question, we see it has led to yet another: If all citizens have a right to medical care, what should be universal? What guidelines would you recommend to those officials charged with making the list? For example, should the patient's age be taken into account (the 90-year-old who needs a new kidney)? The patient's life style (smokers, heavy drinkers, drug users, and others with self-inflicted problems)? The patient's contribution to society (unemployed habitual criminal versus medical researcher, or long-time taxpayer versus chronic welfare recipient)? ■

WHO'S WHO IN THE HOSPITAL: DOMINANCE AND HIERARCHY IN HEALTH CARE

People in group settings usually establish some form of hierarchy. Looking at the hospital as an intricate web of social relationships, we see that the top of the health care hierarchy is dominated by highly educated males with a great deal of political power (Aguirre et al., 1989). Uniforms, for example, identify the players' distinct roles. The physicians' expensive shoes and watches show around the edges of their lab coats and, along with the stethoscope, function as badges of authority and prestige. On the other hand, patients are put in their place with humbling gowns. Nurses' distinctive uniforms separate them visibly from medical technicians, whose clothing distinguishes them from the janitorial staff, and so on. In fact, the importance of such markers as uniform colors was revealed when the medical technicians in one hospital were told to begin wearing yellow uniforms. These workers loudly objected because the hospital maids also wore yellow. The technicians felt their status would be diminished by the "identifying tag" of yellow uniforms (French, 1968, p. 49).

Doctors: Too Powerful or Too Pressured?

Some observers perceive physicians as the villains of the hospital setting, egotistical dictators playing God not only with their patients but with co-workers. The doctors themselves point to the huge medical liability insurance costs they must bear on top of the awesome life-and-death decisions their job demands. Here we explore both the power and pressures of the physician's role.

Holding on to Power   Hierarchy permeates the physician's world. Even among doctors, status varies according to such factors as medical specialty (neurosurgeons, for example, enjoy relatively high prestige among their fellows), and place of medical training (graduates of foreign medical schools rank relatively low). Moreover, health care reforms may be dividing physicians into an administrative, speciality elite and rank-and-file doctors subject to more surveillance and evaluation (Annandale, 1989). Beyond these internal differences, doctors' dominance of the hospital setting rests largely on the technical expertise that clearly sets them apart. Physicians theoretically follow policies set by the hospital bureaucracy, but in reality they wield considerable power in the delivery of services. All these hierarchical advantages are reinforced by the doctors' typically upper-middle class backgrounds.

Still, doctors face increasingly stiff competition. Hospital administrators have gained power relative to doctors over the last decade largely as a result of efforts to control medical costs. Chiropractic and osteopathic physicians (D.O.s) have gained licensing boards in most states and offer diagnostic and therapeutic services increasingly similar to those of M.D.s (Krause, 1977). Though they have yet to gain full acceptance and integration into the health care field, midwives are challenging obstetricians and gynecologists: They attended more than 40 times the births in the 1980s than they did in the 1970s (Baldwin, Hutchinson, and Rosenblatt, 1992). Dentists, podiatrists, opticians, and other independent specialists indirectly compete with general practitioners. Clearly below these players stand medical technicians and other hospital personnel. Not so clear is the position of nurses, as we will see, and of "physician extenders," specifically nurse practitioners and physician assistants (Ferraro and Southerland, 1989). These workers help provide front-line primary care and help fill the void left by physicians going into specialized fields. They provide a quality of care that is in some ways equal to that of doctors, and they see themselves more as colleagues than subordinates.

This male-dominated profession faces challenge from still another quarter: women, who now make up 39 percent of first-year medical students (almost five times the percentage 35 years ago). Around 30 percent of all practicing physicians will be female by the year 2010, compared to 17 percent today. Some professionals hope that the "feminization" of health care at the top may produce more doctors who carefully and respectfully listen to the patient, a greater emphasis on nurturing, and less reliance on "masculine" technology. It may also expand medical research on women. For example, the National Institutes of Health has only recently begun to fund gynecological research (Cotton, 1993). Still, women face many obstacles in the field, from entrenched sexist attitudes to a grueling career track that forces women to choose between their career and motherhood, or at least a less prestigious specialty with a less demanding training program (Brownlee and Pezzullo, 1992).

Still Dominating Patients?   Talcott Parsons (1951) argues that, because they have access to valued goods and services, doctors dominate their relationships with patients. Perhaps this degree of control is necessary if the physician is to put to full use her or his technical expertise. The patient may likewise want to put complete trust in the healing powers of the practitioner. Illness can sometimes foster in the patient a child-like dependence, which in turn leads to a child–parent relationship between patient and doctor.

Nevertheless, researchers have documented how physicians undermine patients' power by ignoring their opinions and perspectives and imposing the authority of the medical model. In other words, doctors use their cultural prestige to control their encounters with patients (Starr, 1982). Patients usually submit because of the doctor's gatekeeping monopoly over surgery, therapy, prescriptions, and sick leave (Freidson, 1970).

Besides this professional authority, most physicians also use communication tactics to dominate patients. The "voice of medicine" (Mishler, 1984) imposes a purely scientific attitude, insists on only technical terms, and deflects or suppresses patients' real-world concerns and unique circumstances. Physicians also exert control by withholding critical information about diagnosis and treatment. They decide when patients may take a turn in the conversation and may ignore the life contexts surrounding their

Although patients have gained some power relative to their physicians, doctors usually hold the advantage.

symptoms. Doctors ask more questions than do patients, interrupt more frequently, and control topic selection (Beckman and Frankel, 1984; West, 1984). This wall of impersonal, scientific objectivity intimidates most patients into submission.

The physician's relationship with patients depends on several factors. For one, the nature of illness helps determine if the patient will be passive (as in cases of acute delirium and coma), cooperate (as in cases of acute infections), or participate as a partner (most typical in cases of chronic illness) (Szasz and Hollender, 1956). Also, increasing numbers of patients enter the relationship with a consumerist attitude, shopping around for physicians and second opinions and demanding full information on their cases. Still, a large body of research describes doctors' continuing control relative to their patients (Maynard, 1991).

Moving from the micro- to the macrosociological perspective, conflict theorists contend that this physician dominance reproduces and reflects the class oppression in society as a whole. In this view, physicians are agents of social control acting to maintain the capitalist system. They frame the patient's illness solely as an individual matter and ignore (perhaps necessarily) the social roots of the problem.

This state of affairs may become a thing of the past as new generations of physicians filter into the profession's ranks. Most medical schools now cover such topics as the doctor–patient relationship, cultural differences, interpersonal skills, and empathy (Novack et al., 1993). Along with the "feminization" of the profession and the growing consumerist attitude among patients, the doctor–patient relationship may change significantly.

Coping with Pressures   Focusing only on the physician's power however, gives a one-sided picture of the practitioner's role. Another part involves coping with tremendous pressures. Consider the extensive training regimen medical students must endure. Not only must they understand and retain mountains of information, students must grapple with a growing cynicism in the course of their long and expensive education (Becker and Geer, 1958). They find that they spend most of their time studying in the first few years, and rarely see real patients. Their professors seem to know little about the actual practice of medicine, and many of their courses appear to be irrelevant. They later find themselves so overloaded by their studies that they cannot find the time to "care" for patients beyond technical details. Add to this disillusionment the realization that they must eventually make life-and-death decisions for their patients, and we can begin to appreciate the pressures felt by medical students.

Once fully licensed, the physician faces heavy everyday role demands. Having learned generalizations about various treatments and usually provided with inadequate information about each case, the doctor must recommend specific treatments for a dizzying array of patients, each of whom demands his or her full attention and a confident diagnosis.

The physician often grapples with uncertainty in making momentous decisions. Medical science offers incomplete knowledge of disease and physical functioning, a fact recently magnified by the complexities and mysteries of AIDS (Yedidia, Barr, and Berry, 1993). And this uncertainty increases because it "borders the edges of knowledge, so that the larger the territory known, the more extensive are the settings in which uncertainty is experienced" (Gerrity, Earp, and DeVellis, 1992, p. 1022). Also, the doctor cannot master the entire body of medical knowledge. Rather than searching for the one, absolute truth regarding a patient's situation, he or she must deal with probabilities and then render a professional judgment that carries legal liabilities.

This uncertainty adds considerably to the physician's role demands. One survey revealed that most doctors feel guilty about missed diagnoses, feel troubled when patients suffer because of physician's mistakes, and were not aware when they chose their career of the high degree of uncertainty it involved (Gerrity, Earp, and DeVellis, 1992). Their socialization produces coping mechanisms such as limiting the information patients have regarding diagnosis and therapy options (Waitzkin and Waterman, 1974). They also receive "training for certainty," in which they learn to look for "established facts" to search for solutions to the medical "puzzle" (Atkinson, 1984). Other tools include gallows humor and calling in others for consultations (Bosk, 1980).

Patients' differing perceptions of the physician's role add more pressure. Some may expect the doctor to patch them up so they can get back to work, others may seek immediate cures or confirmation of their self-diagnosis, and still others may be looking for solutions to psychological troubles (Greengard, 1990). Also, while patients may not heed the advice provided by their doctor, they will still hold her or him accountable for the progress of their illness. And the practitioner is rewarded for accuracy rather than speed, but still must face an average of at least four patients per hour to ensure a reliable cash flow (Phillips and Jones, 1991).

Finally, it should be mentioned that the doctor's famous high income cannot be taken for granted. Physicians are perhaps defined in this regard as "typically small business people who sell their advice and abilities at specialized procedures to patients for a specified fee" (Phillips and Jones, 1991, p. 756). And increasingly, like others in business, physicians must compete for paying patients (Relman, 1992). Doctors are no longer in short supply, except in urban slums and remote rural areas, and find themselves in a buyers' market. Also, they often enter practice with medical school debts of hundreds of thousands of dollars. All this pressure conflicts with the physician's professional ethics to recommend medical services to patients without seeking to maximize fees. Arrangements with manufacturers of medical products and drugs may reward physicians for prescribing or recommending products that are more expensive. And doctors might direct patients to health care facilities, such as laboratories and convalescent homes, in which they own financial interest.

How Do Nurses Fit In?

While physicians have long enjoyed a place firmly atop the health care hierarchy, nurses have struggled to rise from what was once a lowly position. Beginning with the first hospitals in medieval Europe, nurses (usually members of religious orders) provided the day-to-day, personal care for patients. Because they had few specialized skills, nurses functioned as charity workers rather than professionals. Lay workers began to replace nuns in the middle 1800s; for example, few of the approximately 20,000 nurses who served during the Civil War were members of religious orders, though most still acted as volunteers (Schultz, 1992). During the late 1800s, largely due to the work of Florence Nightingale, nursing began to establish professional standards, organizations, and training requirements. Nightingale, however, saw the nurse's place as clearly subordinate to that of the physician; she refused to allow nurses to render any service without a doctor's orders. Even though nurses received increased training early in the twentieth century, the profession followed her model and remained firmly situated beneath the dominant physician.

Nurses have been fighting to escape the subordinate role they have traditionally held relative to doctors.

During the past few decades, nurses have moved from the position of physician's assistant toward that of professional colleague. This transition involves greater autonomy, responsibility, and expertise, but it is by no means complete. Because of their higher social class, greater knowledge, and (usually) maleness, doctors still dominate their working relationship with nurses.

One sign of progress is changes in the "doctor–nurse game," first described by Leonard Stein in 1967. Until recently, nurses, entirely subservient, were expected to make recommendations to doctors, but without appearing to do so. Since then, doctors have lost their image of omniscience and are increasingly likely to be females working with male nurses. The nursing shortage and experiments in collaborative roles for nurses have also challenged the doctor's dominance. The women's liberation movement has certainly been a factor in these changes, as has the shift in the focus of nursing training from subservience to equal partnership with other health care workers. Nurses are thus acting with more authority and independence (Stein, Watts, and Howell, 1990).

What Happens to Patients?

Even if we do not enter a hospital, when we become ill we define ourselves as unable to fully perform our normal roles. We thus take on the sick role (Parsons, 1958), which involves special privileges along with obligations. First, sick people are not held responsible for their incapacity. Second, illness exempts them from normal role obligations. Third, patients are expected to view illness as undesirable and to want to get well as soon as possible. Finally, sick people are expected to seek competent help and cooperate with health care experts in order that they may quickly resume normal social obligations.

Upon entering the hospital, patients assume a position of subservience and become virtual captives. They retain their rights to a competent diagnosis, recommended treatment, and access to their medical records (Phillips and Jones, 1991), but other aspects of the hospital's social organization lead to submissiveness and conformity to rules and procedures (Tagliacozzo and Mauksch, 1979). The sick role demands that patients do all they can to regain their health, but from the moment they receive the hospital bracelet they find themselves dependent on the care-givers. Hospital staff hold the power to heal and cure. They control access to information as well as food, medication, and other bodily needs and comforts, from extra blankets to help getting to the toilet. Most patients are unfamiliar with the hospital's norms and so hesitate to judge the treatment they receive. They cannot easily form an information network with other patients to find out what demands or expectations are considered appropriate, but they see enough to know that others are much worse off than they are. The hospital's environment also reminds them that the staff are overworked, rushed, and not expected to render special "personal" care. Overall, because of patients' uncertainty and dependence, the social structure encourages conformity as the best way to fulfill the sick role and receive the best treatment from care-givers.

The sociological perspective has revealed for us here the undercurrents of science-based attempts to cope with the uncertainties of death and disease. Complex patterns of authority and economics have formed around medical science just as they have around religion. In our need to cope with matters beyond our control, we have built these two powerful and complex institutions.

SUMMARY

Humans have always sought help in dealing with the unknown through *religion*, a system of beliefs and practices shared by a people as they relate themselves to the supernatural. As shown by *animism*, the belief in spiritual forces and souls, religion offers explanations, emotional security, and comfort. It also gives people a sense of control over the world through such forms as *mana*, a supernatural force thought to exist within certain beings or residing in objects, and *magic*, a set of beliefs and practices intended to control natural and supernatural forces. Religion also provides a sense of identity and protection against alienation, as Emile Durkheim's study showed. Durkheim also noted that religion deals with out-of-the-ordinary beliefs and practices that inspire awe and reverence, the realm of the *sacred*. Religion enhances one's human capital and offers transcendent experiences but, according to Marx, it actually functions as a numbing narcotic for the exploited masses. While it fuels ethnocentrism and serves as a tool of oppression, religion also produces social cohesion, harmony, change, and order.

In recent decades the United States has seen the rise of *evangelism*, a revivalistic, "old-time," Bible-based type of Christianity that seeks to establish a personal relationship with Christ through conversion, ardent worship, and an appeal to the primary authority of the Bible, and *fundamentalism*, an antimodern, antisecular approach to religion based on a literal interpretation of scripture and a return to "original truth." Americans have a history of changing religious affiliation, a tendency most common along the young, men, and those without deep roots in social networks. Much of this switching has recently been away from large, wealthy, respected, tolerant *denominations*. While these organizations have traditionally provided an accommodation to modern life, imposed relatively few controls regarding life style matters, and offered relatively unemotional worship services and themes through full-time, formally trained clergy, the fundamentalist element has broken ranks. Many disaffected members join *sects*, usually small religious organizations at odds with larger society that claim sole legitimacy. Sects have grown dramatically, thanks in part to their use of well-targeted messages and effective marketing and recruitment techniques. Larger ones tend to resemble denominations, from which other sects may eventually split. Most members are poor, but sects are increasingly attracting middle-class people as well. Others, especially those suffering from alienation or isolation, join *cults*, usually small religious groups headed by charismatic leaders offering an innovative belief system outside the cultural mainstream. Cults offer some of the same attractions as do denominations, but they focus more on social than spiritual goals. Emotional and social benefits, rather than coercion, hold members to most cults.

According to secularization theory, modernizing societies devalue religion. The nature of Protestantism encourages religious pluralism, which undermines the credibility of competing faiths. Religion is also weakened by increased geographical mobility, urbanism, and higher levels of education and wealth. Contrary to the predictions of secularization theory, however, religion has not lost ground in modern America. Its strength is evident in television preaching, relatively stable attendance and beliefs, and the survival of America's "civil religion." Religious pluralism has actually been associated with *higher* religious participation.

People in the United States sort themselves into different denominations. Fundamentalists and evangelicals stand out from other Protestant groups; Catholics are distinct from Protestants. Religious people differ from nonreligious people in many attitudes and behaviors, although religion may not actually cause these differences. Still, religion's social support, the solace of prayer, and ritual events all seem to produce personal benefits, including good physical and mental health.

People cope with life's uncertainties, especially mortality and disease, using medicine. Unlike religion, medical science uses not a sacred but a *profane* approach dealing with the ordinary, commonplace, and secular. The poor suffer more health problems than the rest of society as a result of low-quality health care, more life stresses, and fewer coping resources. Most racial and ethnic groups likewise experience greater risk of illness and disease because of unequal political power, different coping strategies, and other factors. Similarly, women report higher rates of psychological and physical problems. Despite their biological health advantages, women apparently suffer from greater social and psychological pressures, including guilt, role overload, and low levels of personal control.

Functionalists claim that the health care institution helps maintain a strong workforce, but conflict theorists argue that it has historically shifted the blame for ill health from the environment to the oppressed poor and through *medicalization* has extended its control over ever more parts of society. Even today, medical science focuses on the individual's responsibility for sickness rather than social causes. The capitalist system causes health problems, but uses the medical institution to escape blame and even profit from them. Suggested alternatives include more government intervention and greater consumer education. Conflict theorists also point out that the health care system helps subordinate women by relegating them to the lower rungs of the occupational ladder and imposing patriarchal authority.

The American health care system provides excellent treatment for insured patients, but many people have poor access to the system, and inequities have recently increased due to AIDS and other factors. This has prompted calls for reforms, including free, universal health care, which most other modern nations offer to their citizens. Many of these countries, however, have retreated from socialized medicine because of rising costs and increasing consumer demands.

Sociologists find in the hospital a hierarchy of power and influence, with physicians firmly at the top. Status varies even among doctors, who face increasing competition from other health care workers and women. Still, because of their professional authority and communication tactics, doctors dominate their relationships with patients. According to conflict theorists, physicians as a class represent the interests of capitalism. Despite their power, however, doctors face tremendous stress in the enormous amount of information they are expected to master, their everyday role demands, the uncertainties they face in making diagnoses and recommending treatments, varying patient attitudes, and financial pressures. Nurses have struggled to rise from the status of unskilled worker to doctor's professional colleague. Patients accept certain obligations as well as privileges, but the sick role mostly involves submissiveness and conformity to hospital rules and norms.

Key Terms

religion	sacred	sect
animism	evangelism	cult
mana	fundamentalism	profane
magic	denomination	medicalization

EDUCATION

EDUCATION IN TWO SOCIETIES: THE MANUS AND THE VIETNAMESE

Five thousand years ago in Mesopotamia, children as young as 4 bent over flattened clay, etching it with styluses and struggling from dawn to dusk to learn the myriad hieroglyphics of the newly invented writing system. A select few worked similarly in ancient China and Egypt. Nearly all these early schoolchildren came from families of the elite. Today, not only do most students learn streamlined systems of writing featuring alphabets, they come from homes of modest means. Societies now largely depend on mass education; few can rely on everyday socialization to prepare upcoming generations for adult roles. By contrasting a schoolless society with one in which formal education has arisen in response to gradually perceived needs, we can see the functions of education.

Education among the Manus of New Guinea

Some cultures require no formal education. Children learn all they need to know by watching adults.

In the late 1920s, anthropologist Margaret Mead studied the culture of the Manus, a preliterate people living along the coast of an island off New Guinea (Mead, 1930). Their thatched huts perched on stilts in a lagoon lying between the coast and the reef. No schoolhouse stood among the huts. No schoolteacher admonished laggard children. No formal lessons were offered or required. For the Manus, life simply did not require formal education.

Yet Manu children had to learn many things. They first had to learn how to negotiate the slatted floors or climb the notched post that served as a ladder in the house. Next, growing children had to master the canoe, which meant developing the ability to balance on the rim of the boat while guiding it accurately along an islet or through a throng of other vessels. They also had to learn to swim and dive. Such skills were usually acquired by age 5 or 6, and all without a classroom or someone designated as a teacher.

In preliterate societies like the Manus, anyone possessing the needed skills can serve as instructor, often unintentionally. Some knowledge, like grasping the mother's neck while riding on her back, was purposefully taught. For the most part, however, Manu children learned informally, through play and imitation of adults and older children. Swimming and boating skills were acquired through hours of play. Dancing, drumming, war skills, and fishing techniques were all learned through casual imitation of the surrounding adults, without threats or whippings. There were no formal tests or schedules of instruction. The children were nevertheless highly motivated; they intensely wished to be able to do what everyone else in the village could.

So long as a society requires of all adults the same skills and the cultural storehouse of knowledge is relatively small, informal education suffices. When some new and complex skill like writing is introduced, the need for formal instruction arises, ushering in schools, teachers, and curricula. This happened to the Manus.

The enticements of the outside world had already been seeping into Manu society when Mead studied them. During the next two decades, civilization flooded their lagoon culture: Missionaries brought reading and writing, World War II brought the gadgets and technological wonders of the combatants. Education quickly became an integral part of the Manu way of life, as it has for nearly every other society in the world today.

Education in Vietnam

In contrast to the Manus, the development of an educational system among the people of Vietnam spanned thousands of years and occurred as a response to emerging social needs. Since the invasion and occupation of their country by the Chinese in the second century B.C., the Vietnamese have shown a high respect for scholarship. Though it is poor, undeveloped, and ravaged by centuries of warfare, the country has an impressive overall literacy rate of 78 percent. The functions of formal instruction in Vietnam well illustrate the social needs of virtually any culture today.

Transmission of Knowledge and Skills   Two cultural elements inherited from their Chinese overlords—Confucian scholarly tradition and strong central government—both required that the Vietnamese maintain a system of formal education to transmit that tradition and supply qualified government officials. Moreover, schools became necessary because families could not reliably pass on the classical Chinese writing and literature. Beginning in 1075, even minor officials had to pass civil service examinations. A training institute was established to inculcate the necessary knowledge and skills in the ruling class of scholar-officials.

In Vietnam today, the knowledge transmitted by schools is scientific and technical rather than classical. This formal process constitutes a thread in Vietnam's 4,000-year-old history. Like nearly every other civilization, Vietnam has relied on its schools primarily to pass on to each succeeding generation the skills and knowledge required by society. This invaluable function makes formal education a virtually universal institution.

Transmission of the Dominant Culture   Formal education can also serve as a powerful tool for imposing one society's values on another. By requiring Confucian scholarship for entry into Vietnam's ruling elite, the Chinese conquerers exerted a cultural influence far greater than their invading armies ever could. In fact, China continued to culturally dominate Vietnam for centuries after they ended their 1,000-year occupation of the country.

A question arises in this context: Who receives this cultural instruction? In most societies, schooling is too expensive to offer to everyone. A selection process must determine which citizens will be offered the empowering values, norms, and special knowledge of the dominant group. Unless educational opportunities are based exclusively on merit, countries generally exclude or discriminate against the masses. In Vietnam, an examination system was open to all, but for the most part only children from aristocratic families successfully advanced. As we will see later in this chapter, critics claim that the selection process in the United States screens out most members of the lower classes.

A related question is, Which culture will be transmitted? Of course, power decides the answer. For centuries, the Vietnamese elite was able to mandate that classical Confucianism would dominate the educational system. Christian missionaries in the 1800s offered a more indigenous, non-Confucian curriculum in their schools but were forced underground when it threatened the hold of the ruling class. When communists took control of North Vietnam after the country's division by the Geneva Agreements of 1954, they imposed socialist ideology on the schools. The regime in the South ordered that Vietnamese history and literature dominate the curriculum.

Over the last decade, feminists and various minorities have challenged the curriculum of U.S. schools as limited to the white, European cultural traditions and to the contributions of men. They have managed to influence course content and textbooks at all levels of education. The resulting power struggle highlights one latent function of schools: the transmission of selected aspects of the culture.

Social Integration   Critics of multicultural and "cultural diversity" advocacy groups worry that the splintering of the U.S. curriculum threatens the integrative function of education. If various schools focus on the cultural traditions of their particular ethnic populations, they argue, the schools will not be as effective a unifying force. Similar arguments are offered against bilingual education, which is sometimes provided to children whose primary language is not English. Bilingual instruction is intended to ease immigrant children into the U.S. cultural mainstream, but critics contend an English-language curriculum is vital for social integration.

Critical Thinking Box

Is Bilingual Education an Individual Right or a Threat to National Unity?

Several million schoolchildren in the United States have little if any proficiency in English. Should they be taught social studies and science exclusively in the dominant language of our country or should part of their education be in their native tongue?

Since immigration reforms in 1965 opened doors for many more Asian and Latin American newcomers and the Supreme Court's ruling in 1974 that immigrant children have a right to special help in schools, the demand for bilingual education has increased. The growing clamor for these expensive programs, however, has met with a backlash of criticism.

Opponents claim that language diversity threatens national unity. They argue that bilingual programs divert energies and funds from the pursuit of academic excellence. Even some members of language-minority groups contend that all students should receive instruction in English as a means of progressing academically and eventually entering the American mainstream (Rodriquez, 1982; Porter, 1990). In this view, encouraging students to retain their native language only exacerbates social and political tensions. Accordingly, over a dozen states have passed legislation establishing English as the official state language.

Proponents of bilingual education claim children need to develop an academic foundation in their own language before they can learn in English. Such instruction also legitimizes the culture of language-minority students, thus boosting their self-esteem and enhancing their chances for academic achievement. Without it, supporters claim, they are likely to drop out of school. (Unfortunately, the research findings on these points are so diverse as to give little guidance—Cziko, 1992.) Moreover, the U.S. Constitution's guarantee of free speech implies the freedom to choose one's language. Not only is it an individual right, but it is a necessary means of achieving one's social goals. Forcing children to learn in a foreign language (English) puts them at a tremendous disadvantage.

Which is more important, encouraging national unity or preserving individual rights and opportunity? ■

Certainly the government of Vietnam today appreciates this integrating function of education. After reunification of the North and South in 1975, the socialist government of the victorious North took over all public and private schools in the South. Teachers from the North were sent into the South to ensure that all students in the nation were indoctrinated in the same socialist-ideology curriculum. The schools were seen as a primary vehicle for achieving the integration of North and South.

The power to impose cultural traditions on schools' curriculum also implies power to shape individual students. Students are molded, trained, and prepared to embrace the values and behavior patterns dictated by the educational system. By mandating schools to promote Confucian values for centuries, the Vietnamese aristocracy shaped the demeanor and philosophy of generations of individuals as well as the society's intellectual and moral tone.

In the United States, schools typically attempt to inculcate in their students such values as industry, punctuality, responsibility, obedience, and orderliness. While most parents presumably would applaud this latent function of the schools, conflict theorists point to the sinister aspects of this social control. They refer to a **hidden curriculum,** the largely middle-class values and standards of behavior implicitly and explicitly taught in school but not part of the formal curriculum. These latent social objectives prepare students to accept adult roles but may also communicate, without much examination, racism, mindless conformity, ethnocentrism, and other undesirable values.

Innovation   Another manifest function of education is to create as well as transmit knowledge. While for centuries its essential task was the preservation of classical knowledge, Vietnam's schools increasingly emphasize innovation to meet the challenges of the fast-paced modern world. This requires a two-pronged approach. First, universities provide research laboratories and other facilities for the generation of new theories and technological applications. Since 1987, Vietnam has expanded research and development at its higher institutions (Can, 1991). Second, schools must produce individuals with the academic ability to perform research. Research has demonstrated

Hidden curriculum: the unofficial program of studies or agenda of schools in which students are taught largely middle-class values and standards of behavior; not part of the formal curriculum.

Schools impose a "hidden curriculum" of largely middle-class values and behavioral standards. This is an unannounced agenda showing education's latent social control function.

that formal education leads to a general rise in a nation's "intellectual capital" (Husen and Tuijnman, 1991).

Research has long been an important function of universities in the United States. Students at the graduate level are required to add to the fund of knowledge in masters theses and doctoral dissertations. Professors are evaluated largely on their academic output under an incentive system commonly known as "publish or perish." Private corporations, "think tanks," and government agencies also carry out research, so much so that university laboratories are increasingly being called upon to participate in business and public-policy studies.

Other Latent Functions   As the role of education expands in a society, as in Vietnam, we can expect its latent functions to multiply. Functionalists point out that other institutions must adjust to the growing social importance of schools. This is most apparent in the family. As children begin their education earlier and study for more years, the family loses some of its socialization responsibilities and powers. At the same time, the child care function of schools frees more mothers to participate in the labor market, which further changes the dynamics of the family. The economy in turn must adapt to the greater human resources available.

The labor force is also affected because students stay in school longer before entering the labor market. Adolescence becomes more clearly differentiated as a life

One latent function of education in the United States is the support of an adolescent subculture via the enforced interaction of masses of teenagers on a regular basis.

stage by the nurturing of a teenage subculture in high school. This concentration of teens helps forge a shared identity and common value system that is sometimes at odds with the mainstream culture. Schools thus unintentionally help to create a potent social force.

In the next section, we explore one more important latent function of schools in most societies today: providing opportunity for social mobility.

OPPORTUNITY OR OBSTACLE?

Horace Mann, an important proponent of public education in the United States in the 19th century, believed that the nation's schools should act as "the great equalizer" through which any able citizen can realize the American dream and rise in the social hierarchy. Education serves this latent function, however, only if opportunities are open to all students and if merit rather than social background determines how far one can climb. During the past two decades, a number of sociological studies have focused on whether schools in fact contribute to social mobility or instead serve as a barrier against the lower classes to protect the position of the privileged elite.

The Functionalist View:
Education as the Means to Success

Certainly education provides a ladder to climb toward a greater share of society's rewards. As we saw in Chapter 6, it is increasingly the determining factor in success or failure in the emerging global, postindustrial economy (Reich, 1991). We also saw that educational attainment holds a central place in the status attainment process. The payoff of schooling in terms of income rose slightly during the 1960s, declined during the 1970s, and rose dramatically in the last decade. The "human capital" gap continues to widen between high school graduates and dropouts, who suffer intensifying economic disadvantages (Olneck and Kim, 1989). As one observer notes, the benefits of college graduation "have increased to levels that make it an extraordinarily attractive investment" (Kosters, 1990, p. 65).

This avenue for social success, moreover, is open to virtually anyone in the country. The number of years of free public schooling available to U.S. citizens expanded significantly in the last century. Furthermore, students often have a menu of alternative schools and programs from which to choose including those specializing in the arts, college preparation, and science. And college study is within reach of most people, through financial aid as well as relatively inexpensive "open door" community colleges.

Education, then, pays off for the individual and is increasingly accessible (although rising college costs and admissions standards have effectively blocked out more minorities recently). But to function as a true catalyst for social mobility, education must provide complete equality of opportunity. Conflict theorists contend that, like many other elements of our society, education works only for the advantaged elite. Next we explore the various dimensions of this argument, noting how schools and home environments together confer advantages on some individuals and erect barriers to others.

Conflict Theory:
School Failure or Success Begins in the Home

One of the most powerful predictors of academic success or failure is socioeconomic status. Simply put, the higher the social-class level of a child's home, the more likely he or she will succeed in school. The mother's level of education has a particularly strong correlation with a child's academic performance (Ensminger and Slusarcick, 1992; Snow et al., 1991). Of course, it is not parental income or level of education per se that is responsible for a child's success in school. Sociologists point instead to such factors as the "cultural capital" that affluent parents transmit to their children (Bourdieu, 1977, 1989). Students from the upper classes not only learn reading skills and numbers during their preschool years, they also read appropriate books, visit museums, attend symphonic concerts, and in other ways acquire through their family socialization all the experiences, values, and personality traits that schools require for academic excellence. One study found, for example, that students' work habits and citizenship figure strongly in the way teachers award grades (Farkas et al., 1990).

Disadvantaged homes, on the other hand, can be identified by several markers: minority racial or ethnic identity, low income, single-parent head of household (especially if poorly educated), and non-English-speaking background (Pallas, Natriello,

Middle-class parents transmit their "cultural capital" to their children through enriching activities and experiences. This gives their children significant advantages in school.

and McDill, 1989). (See Figure 12-1.) How do these social characteristics stand between a child and school success?

Having a single-parent head of household is an especially strong predictor of dropping out of school (Fitzpatrick and Yoels, 1992; McLanahan, 1985). Students from such homes earn lower grades and test scores, partly because single parents are likely to be minority members and to have low levels of education. Also, single parents (and stepparents) tend to give their children less encouragement and help with schoolwork (Astone and McLanahan, 1991). The rest of the explanation lies less in

Risk factor, by race/ethnicity

PERCENT

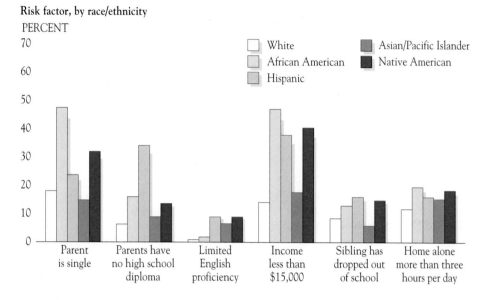

Number of factors, by race/ethnicity

PERCENT

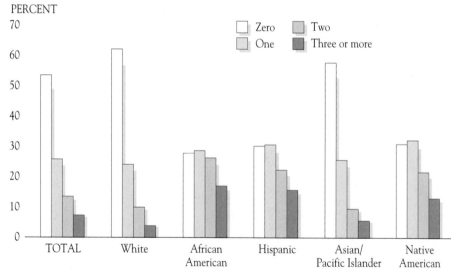

Figure 12-1

EIGHTH-GRADERS WITH RISK FACTORS, BY RACE/ETHNICITY AND NUMBER, 1988

Source: U.S. Department of Education, National Center for Education Statistics, National Education Longitudinal Study of 1988, base year survey: *A Profile of the American Eighth Grader*.

such families' economic circumstances than in the students' own misbehavior, including absenteeism, lateness, and not doing homework (Mulkey, Crain, and Harrington, 1992). The research does not explain such misbehaviors, but anger, frustration, and inadequate parental supervision are cited as possibilities. While students from single-parent homes certainly can do well in school, this background factor is generally viewed as a disadvantage.

Racial or ethnic minority students also face a number of social obstacles to school success. African Americans and Hispanics often view the payoff of schoolwork as so remote that they do not persevere in their efforts (Fine, 1991; Ogbu, 1978). Even though many students hold positive abstract views about the value of education as a social stepping stone, they tend to base their actual school behaviors on the frustrations and failures of their parents (Mickelson, 1990). As a result, as William Velez (1989) found in his study of various Hispanic groups, often students cut classes, get suspended, and eventually drop out. Even if minority students manage to overcome the discouraging signals in their environments, financial difficulties typically lengthen their odds of attending college. One study documents that black parents (who are more likely to be single mothers, poorly educated, and financially strapped), simply have fewer resources to support children who want to go to college (Goldscheider and Goldscheider, 1991).

Obviously, children who do not speak English, or speak it only as their secondary language, will encounter difficulties in U.S. schools. Even mathematics achievement can be adversely affected by speaking a language other than English in the home (Rosenthal, Baker, and Ginsburg, 1983). However, language barriers can be more subtle. English-speaking students from minority and low-income backgrounds can face language discontinuities in school. In other words, the way their parents question and talk to them does not correspond to that used by most teachers (Delgado-Gaiton, 1987; Heath, 1982; Mehan, 1992). This mismatch between language used in the home and that demanded in the classroom can cause serious difficulties for some children.

Researchers have identified another disadvantage students can bring with them to school: large family size. Generally speaking, family size correlates negatively with academic success—the larger the family, the lower achievement tends to be (Hauser and Sewell, 1985; Blake, 1989; Alwin, 1991)—though race, the mother's age, the presence of other adults in the household, and other factors complicate this picture (Thompson et al., 1992). The difference may result from children in small families receiving more attention and intellectual stimulation from their parents (Steelman and Doby, 1983).

Sociologists have tried to identify specific parental behaviors that create either opportunities or obstacles for children in school. White-collar families typically serve as models through their own educational accomplishments (Cohen, 1987). Also, the home's learning environment varies with social class (Majoribanks, 1991). Middle-class parents provide intellectual and academic stimulation: speaking and reading to children, asking them questions about a story, and so on. Beyond this, parental participation in school life promotes a child's academic success (Seeley, 1984). In fact, one study found that declining parental involvement as children near high school plays a critical role in student underachievement (Snow et al., 1991). Middle-class parents are more likely to show interest in their children's studies, monitor and challenge the instructors and the school, attend parent–teacher conferences, and use outside experts (tutoring, testing, and so on) if necessary (Laureau, 1987). Such parents serve as sophisticated, confident, and effective advocates and guides throughout their children's education. Parental expectations are positively correlated to students' achievement (Carpenter and Fleishman, 1987) and college attendance (Hossler and Stage, 1992). Clearly, some homes offer advantages that others do not.

The Schools' Differential Treatment of Students

For those students who find school to be a friendly and familiar environment, social mobility may well prove to be relatively accessible. For others, school is a maze of strange rules and expectations that invites only frustration and failure. Although much of this inequality originates in the home, it can be magnified in the schools by teachers' expectations.

Teachers' Expectations   Teachers are generally quite accurate in predicting which students will succeed in school (Hoge and Coladarci, 1989; Kenealy, Frude, and Shaw, 1991), but are such prophecies self-fulfilling?

An ingenious study by Robert Rosenthal and Lenore Jacobsen (1968) revealed the power of teacher expectations. The researchers tricked a group of elementary school teachers into expecting a great deal from an ordinary group of students. At the beginning of the school year, Rosenthal and Jacobsen administered a standard intelligence test to the students but told the teachers it was a special test designed to identify those students who would blossom intellectually that year. The "special" children identified by the test were in fact simply chosen randomly from the student body. There was no reason to expect these children to "bloom" that year more than anyone else but for the fact that the instructors had been informed they could expect a "spurt" from them. Apparently, however, those teacher expectations made all the difference for the chosen group. All students were tested at the end of the school year, and those randomly chosen as "bloomers" did in fact show more improvement in their IQ scores than the rest of the student body. The gains were biggest among children in the early grades, but the impact for the older students carried over more strongly the following year.

This study has been criticized on several points, including the researchers' methodology and their claim that intellectual ability as well as achievement is affected by teacher expectations (Jensen, 1980; Weinberg, 1987). Still, the power of teacher expectations on students' achievement is widely accepted. Instructors are likely to invest more time, attention, and patience in students expected to transform those investments into success.

What determines which students will enjoy the powerful effect of high teacher expectations? The answer, according to many school critics, is the child's home environment. Instead of acting like the "great equalizer," schools actually magnify the advantages or disadvantages children bring into the classroom from home. Teachers award grades not only on the basis of mastery of coursework but such factors as diligence, submissiveness and "teacher-pleasing" behavior, and their own prejudice (Farkas, Sheehan, and Grobe, 1990). Many of these factors flow from differences in social background. Also, the child who upon entering school has undeveloped reading or math skills may be unfairly categorized, formally or informally, as unable. Moreover,

Can we expect teachers to give every student the benefit of their powerful attention and support?

much categorizing is based on tests that are themselves regarded by many as biased against children from disadvantaged backgrounds. Intelligence and achievement tests can help block social mobility for some students by dooming them to placement in low-ability groups, low teacher expectations, and poor academic performance.

Ability Grouping and Tracking   Most schools group students according to ability, either within or between classes. The rationale for this strategy is that student needs vary, and that those needs can be identified and appropriately met when students are grouped with others like themselves. Moreover, the argument goes, those of superior intellectual ability should not be held to the slower pace of others, while lower-ability students should not be required to compete with high achievers. In this view, ability grouping allows more appropriate and effective instruction.

The practice is very common in elementary and secondary schools, despite the fact that over 50 years of research has found ability grouping generally ineffective in enhancing student achievement and perhaps even damaging (Slavin, 1987; Oakes, 1992). The low achievers lose the benefits of the role modeling and stimulation of high-ability students. The pace of low-ability classes can slow to a crawl due to low expectations. Furthermore, low-ability groups tend to contain a disproportionate number of lower-class and racial or ethnic minority group members, thus contributing to social division. Perhaps the most troubling criticism of ability grouping is that the categorization of students is based on test-taking skills—and thus perhaps socioeconomic background—rather than individual effort or abilities not measured by specific tests.

The one bright spot in the practice of tracking—grouping students in different classes according to ability, usually in high school—is that it usually enhances the intellectual ability of students in college-preparatory tracks (Shavit and Featherman, 1988). Those students receive a high level of encouragement, resources, and attention (Alexander, Cook, and McDill, 1978). They are also exposed to more academic coursework and to "high-status knowledge," the critical-thinking skills, expository writing, and literature demanded by colleges (Lee and Byrk, 1988; Oakes, 1985). And college-track students receive superior instruction and learning opportunities (Gamoran and Berends, 1987; Gamoran, 1987). Despite these beneficial effects, however, tracking widens the gap in achievement and probability of graduation between students of high and low socioeconomic backgrounds (Gamoran and Mare, 1989; Natriello, Pallas, and Alexander, 1989).

Critics argue that students from disadvantaged families are likely to be locked out of the college track regardless of their abilities. One study concludes that a very good student from a lower-class background has only about a 52 percent chance of ending up in the academic track, while a comparable student from a higher-class background has around an 80 percent chance (Vanfossen, Jones, and Spade, 1987). Other researchers, however, have found no conclusive evidence that students are tracked by socioeconomic status (Rehberg and Rosenthal, 1978; Garet and DeLany, 1988).

One reason for such mixed findings may lie in the differing organizational contexts of high schools. Sally Kilgore (1991) found that tracking policies range from arbitrary, in which many students are placed in tracks above or below their abilities, to meritocratic, in which few are inappropriately placed. For example, she discovered that the latter type is more likely to develop when tracking decisions are delegated to members of the school organization who know most about students' abilities and interests: the teachers. Kilgore also notes that students allowed to choose their own tracks often select a lower track than their potential warrants to minimize their efforts. When student demand for the college-preparatory track is high, as is typical in schools with high proportions of students with high socioeconomic backgrounds, there are pressures to make the tracking process more exclusive, shutting out many able students. The array of such school organization variables makes it difficult to generalize about the fairness of tracking policies.

Along the same line, students are not placed into special classes for the mentally retarded or educationally handicapped entirely according to their scores on intelligence tests (Mehan, Hetweck, and Meihls, 1985; Mercer, 1974). Gender, ethnicity, and socioeconomic background play a role in categorization but are played out within the organizational context of the school, a puzzle of practical circumstances, philosophical leanings, and legal constraints. The "differential educational opportunity is, sometimes at least, an unintended consequence of bureaucratic organization," (Mehan, 1992, p. 13), rather than simply discrimination or student ability. Even though such far-reaching decisions about students' educational futures are complex and often not intentionally discriminatory, they nevertheless constitute barriers for some.

Different Types of Schools as Tracks   Another form of tracking is seen in the differences in opportunities offered in private and public schools. An important report by sociologist James Coleman, Thomas Hoffer, and Sally Kilgore (1981) contends that private schools are more conducive to academic achievement than public ones, even when the students' family backgrounds are the same. Other research indicates that Catholic high schools promote academics more effectively and are less likely to amplify initial scholastic difficulties among students (Lee and Byrk, 1988). These institutions owe their success partly to the smaller ability gaps and the greater ease with which students can move from one track to another (Gamoran, 1992). Moreover, graduates of private high schools are more likely to attend college—again, for reasons having to do with the schools themselves rather than the socioeconomic backgrounds of the students (Falsey and Heyns, 1984). Selective schools likewise produce better academic results than do others (Kreft, 1993).

Critics have subjected these results to close scrutiny. The Coleman report may actually have measured differences in preceding elementary schools and junior high schools instead of the high schools. Lee Wolfe (1987) argues that the study examined only short-term effects. Others contend that the perceived advantages of private schools are distorted by the fact that public schools must accept nearly any student who wants to enroll (Alexander and Pallas, 1983). William Morgan (1983) found that the quality of student life is higher in private schools but that the actual amount of learning is no greater. Clearly, it is too simplistic to conclude that private schools are "better" than public ones.

The tracking system extends beyond high school in that the type of college attended affects adult occupational status. Some universities obviously confer degrees that carry far more weight than others in the career world. During the last decade, costs have soared for the most prestigious universities, effectively excluding many bright middle-class students who simply cannot afford over $20,000 per year in costs. These able students then turn to the less expensive but still highly regarded state universities, bumping others down to less prestigious schools, and so on (Toch and Slafsky, 1991). Also, compared with students at four-year colleges, those who begin their studies at a community college are less likely to realize their goal of a four-year degree or receive full occupational return for each year in college (Dougherty, 1992; Monk-Turner, 1983, 1990; Lee and Frank, 1990). The disproportionate number of women, minorities, and students from lower socioeconomic backgrounds who attend community colleges may thus face a greater barrier to upward social mobility.

Private schools seem to confer educational advantages on their students.

Education as Reproduction of the Socioeconomic Status Quo

As we saw earlier, students from lower- or working-class homes and minority groups tend not to perform as well in school (as measured in test scores and grades) as socioeconomically advantaged students. Samuel Bowles and Herbert Gintis (1976) use the Marxist perspective to explain that schools serve to reproduce the social-class system of the haves and have-nots. According to their **correspondence principle,** the organization of the schools mirrors that of the workplace. Working-class students are placed in tracks that teach them docility, compliance, and conformity to authority, along with manual work skills. In contrast, students from the homes of the capitalist elite end up in tracks

Correspondence principle: theory that the organization of the schools mirrors that of the workplace.

that foster independence and leadership. Other researchers, however, contend that this principle exaggerates the degree to which the upper classes control the structure and function of schools (MacLaren, 1980; MacLeod, 1987) and that it reduces students and teachers to passive role-players in the capitalist system (Mehan, 1992).

Whether or not the higher failure rates of the working class are the result of a capitalist strategem, the argument remains that the school experience tends to legitimate social-class inequalities. Not realizing that the system works against them, those from disadvantaged backgrounds typically learn one overriding lesson in school: They are not as able or competent as students from the middle class. For these students, schools are a source of discouragement rather than social mobility.

Credentialism   The educational requirements for many jobs have been increasing in recent years. The demand for ever-higher educational levels that are irrelevant to or unnecessary for actual job performance is called **credentialism.** Critics decry it for reinforcing existing inequalities, since few people from lower-class or minority backgrounds have the resources to acquire the necessary credentials. Those who do obtain them often find that requirements have been simply changed or raised another notch. Conflict theorists see credentialism as yet another barrier to equal opportunity in the labor market.

> **Credentialism:** the demand for ever-higher educational levels that are irrelevant to or unnecessary for actual job performance; a means of restricting job competition to only those from advantaged backgrounds.

Of course, a rationale undergirds credentialism. Employers cite the increasing complexity of jobs in the postindustrial economy. Also, if all applicants are qualified, an employer is likely to choose those with qualifications beyond the minimum, thereby establishing a higher level of requirements. After all, hiring better educated or trained workers raises the importance and prestige level (and thus the income demands) of those doing the hiring. Also, even though many credentials do not relate directly to job performance, they do indicate that the holder has undergone a particular socialization process and demonstrated desired traits that are otherwise difficult to measure: self-discipline, responsibility, ability to learn and think, and willingness to "play by the rules."

Overall, a clear conclusion emerges from the research literature: Intentionally or not, schools reflect the broader inequalities of our society. For students from already advantaged backgrounds, education serves as the road to social success. For others, it presents barriers that only a few overcome. Our next logical step is to explore the possibilities of equalizing educational opportunities.

Who Gets into Harvard?

Research Box

"Gatekeepers" hold the keys for admission to organizations such as corporations and colleges. These powerful individuals often decide which requirements will be used to screen applicants, and then apply those criteria. Gatekeepers do not perform these functions in a vacuum; they are influenced by various interest groups around and within the organization, what Paul DiMaggio and Walter Powell (1983) collectively call the "organizational field."

David Karen (1990) of Bryn Mawr College aimed to develop a theory of gatekeeping that considered this organizational field of elite colleges. From his review of the research literature, Karen suspected that neither of the two major macrosociological perspectives fully explained elite-college gatekeeping processes. While functionalists assume that the selection process is basically meritocratic, offering those from

Who gets into Harvard? Some types of applicants stand a considerably better chance of acceptance: exceptionally bright students, especially from elite prep schools; minorities; children of alumni; and athletes.

disadvantaged backgrounds an opportunity for upward social mobility, conflict theorists regard gatekeeping as exclusionary. One such theorist argues that since the breakup of family capitalism in the early twentieth century, the upper class increasingly relies on organizations like highly selective colleges to transmit elite status to the next generation (Karabel, 1984). But do such schools still perform this function?

Karen decided to study the microprocesses of the selection process to discover the degree to which either macroperspective fit reality. He hypothesized that neither would be sufficient to fully explain "what has been going on inside the black box of schooling" (p. 227). To test his hypothesis, Karen analyzed secondary data through the *case study method*. This technique provides an in-depth analysis of one situation (or a very few situations), often lighting the way for other, more broadly based research methods. He searched for patterns among data on all applicants to Harvard from the class of a particular year.

The data revealed several admissions criteria at work, some meritocratic (in other words, based on individual ability), some class-based (and thus excluding those from disadvantaged backgrounds). First, because of pressure from the faculty, the graduate schools, and employers, the gatekeepers tend to select exceptionally bright students. However, other forces undermine this meritocratic tendency. The gatekeepers are more likely to accept bright students who have also attended elite prep schools, largely because such schools have for many years successfully trained students to display the personality characteristics most appreciated at Harvard. The prep schools, therefore, constitute a significant element in the organizational field. So does the pressure to admit minorities, which originated in the civil rights movement and manifests itself in affirmative action guidelines and an overall sensitivity in the gatekeeping process. As a result, blacks, Hispanics, and Native Americans have a higher probability of being accepted than do whites of equal ability. The tremendous financial support Harvard enjoys from its alumni also plays an important part in the organizational field: Children of alumni are admitted at a rate more than double that of other applicants. The benefits of fielding strong athletic teams also influences gatekeeping processes. Successful teams (especially football) produce television revenues and tend to increase alumni contributions. Athletic applicants therefore enjoy considerably higher rates of admission.

Karen concludes that his hypothesis was born out by the data: Both meritocratic and class-based factors play a role in the gatekeeping process in this elite college, but neither completely accounts for admissions outcomes. A full understanding would require an exploration of the organizational context within which the gatekeepers develop and apply admissions criteria. He recommends further study of his proposed theory to "test the breadth of its applicability and adapt it accordingly (p. 239)." ❑

EQUAL EDUCATIONAL OPPORTUNITY: AN IMPOSSIBLE DREAM?

An infant lies in a crib, staring at a blank white ceiling most of the day. A stuffed bunny holds her bottle; her mother rarely holds the infant or speaks to her. By the time she enters the third-rate school in her neighborhood, her body and brain will be smaller than they should be, and she will probably never catch up with children from less-deprived households. Any potential for social contribution she held at birth will be wasted. Can we hope to change our educational system so that such children's potential will not go unfulfilled?

Equalizing School Quality

One obvious approach to make sure all children are offered a decent—perhaps even an equal—opportunity to use education as a springboard to social success is to equalize the quality of all schools. Researchers, however, have found that school quality is difficult to define or produce.

Funding   State-by-state comparisons of funding levels indicate a need for equal funding policies, as Table 12-1 shows. Some states spend over $8,000 per pupil, while others spend less than $4,000. Moreover, since local property taxes usually provide the

STATE SPENDING PER PUPIL IN AVERAGE DAILY ATTENDANCE IN PUBLIC ELEMENTARY AND SECONDARY SCHOOLS, 1989–1990

Top 10 States		Bottom 10 States	
District of Columbia	$8,904	South Dakota	$3,732
Alaska	$8,374	Kentucky	$3,675
New York	$8,062	Tennessee	$3,664
New Jersey	$7,991	New Mexico	$3,518
Connecticut	$7,604	Oklahoma	$3,512
Rhode Island	$6,249	Arkansas	$3,485
Massachusetts	$6,237	Alabama	$3,327
Vermont	$6,227	Mississippi	$3,096
Maryland	$6,196	Idaho	$3,078
Pennsylvania	$6,061	Utah	$2,730

Table 12-1

Although funding level does not clearly reflect educational quality, students living in some states receive much less taxpayer support than do others.

Source: U.S. Department of Education, National Center for Educational Statistics, *Digest of Educational Statistics, 1992.*

base for each school district's funding, great spending discrepancies exist within states as well. The richest districts typically offer a computer for every few students, well-equipped science labs, varied foreign language and art courses, and extensive athletic facilities. The poorest districts have little room in their budgets for such amenities.

Courts have ordered states to narrow such discrepancies since the 1970s, but lagging enforcement and the particularly keen effects of recession on poor districts have actually broadened inequities in many states. More recently, several state funding systems have been ruled unconstitutional. Perhaps the most radical ruling, in 1990, directed New Jersey to guarantee funding in poor districts to be at least equal to that of affluent ones. It remains to be seen, however, if these recent court decisions will be more effective than previous ones in equalizing school funding levels.

Even within school districts, budgets can vary significantly. Many districts pursuing quality over equality have recently created "magnet" schools to lavish the finest facilities and faculty on their brightest students. The invigorating sense of commitment and the intense intellectual stimulation in these institutions often pay off dramatically in terms of college scholarships and other academic awards. The resources contributing to such success, however, are usually skimmed off the other schools in the district. The best students, teachers, and equipment typically are diverted to the magnet schools. Quality education for the few comes at the cost of mediocrity for the many (Toch, Linnon, and Cooper, 1991).

Financial inequities, however, may have less impact on school quality than is commonly assumed. Over 20 years of research has consistently demonstrated that school spending is not systematically related to student performance (Jencks et al., 1972; Hanushek, 1989). Evidence is weak or mixed regarding the impact of such budgetary concerns as class size, teacher education and experience, administration, and facilities. While money may be a prerequisite for quality education, increasing or redistributing school funding will probably do little to equalize school quality unless researchers can discover how to target financing more effectively.

Staffing   Probably the most effective way to equalize school quality would be to redistribute what is arguably the most powerful resource in the school environment: teaching quality. Researchers, however, have yet to be able to identify confidently or measure those traits or qualities that make some instructors so much better than others. What makes excellent teachers has in fact long been a Holy Grail of educational research. But even if that dream is accomplished, the practical problem of equalizing the distribution of teachers throughout the school system would remain. Staffing would become a political, administrative, and ethical nightmare.

Compensatory Programs

Americans have believed that poor children should be offered special programs to compensate for their disadvantaged backgrounds since the 1800s. Charity schools, Sunday Schools, and infant schools provided some help, and until the end of the nineteenth century, such children received roughly the same classroom instruction as more advantaged students (Vinovskis, 1992). Renewed concerns for educational equality in the 1960s spawned new compensatory programs. With federal funding of Head Start in 1965, designed to help culturally deprived children of preschool age prepare for school, early intervention became an established strategy.

Early research on Head Start's effectiveness, however, indicated that most disadvantaged children require more than a six- or eight-week summer program before first grade; many need at least a year or two of Head Start. Even then, however, the benefits are likely to diminish or disappear during the first year or so of school. To produce more enduring gains, Head Start funding would have to be doubled.

One solution for sustaining the progress made by Head Start is to extend compensatory programs into the elementary school years. Several such programs offer extra help in reading, special teacher training for working with disadvantaged children, and involvement of the family (Kantrowitz and McCormick, 1992). The major federally funded program of this type, Chapter 1, has yielded mixed results. For example, benefits, especially reading, are more likely to accrue for students in lower grades (Palmer, 1991). However, children in such classes too often face a great deal of seatwork, little chance of exiting the program, and low expectations from teachers (Anderson and Pellicer, 1990).

Another solution focuses on earlier preschool intervention. Obviously, waiting until the child is five or six years old only allows that much time for a stunting home environment to put him or her at greater risk. Cognitive readiness in kindergarten, for example, significantly affects a child's early school success or failure (Reynolds, 1991). And students who do not participate in the classrooms of their earliest grades often do poorly later on (Finn and Cox, 1992). To prevent such unequal starts, early intervention programs sometimes go into homes to teach disadvantaged parents how to provide heightened intellectual stimulation for their children, problem-solving strategies, and information about child development. Programs that provide such family support along with educational day care centers, beginning in infancy, generate significant cognitive gains for children (Wasik et al., 1990).

Even such intensive compensatory programs, however, cannot overcome all the disadvantages faced by "at risk" children. The home's cultural capital can be augmented but not easily raised to the level of sophistication found in most middle-class homes, where parents are more able to help their children work on schoolwork, perform science projects, and prepare for college-entrance exams as well as provide a powerful incentive of hope through their own successful use of education.

Gender

When formal educational opportunities began to expand in the Colonial period, few families sent their daughters to school. The traditional female role did not require literacy skills, and cultural values discouraged the development of women's intellectual abilities. While women in this country made literacy gains beginning in the 1700s (Main, 1991), their educational needs were considered secondary to men's until only a few decades ago. Few early American schools accepted female students, and "women's" courses of study consisted mostly of "decorative" education, such as embroidery and the arts. As late as the early twentieth century, small-town elementary school teachers (overwhelmingly women) were often forbidden to smoke, drink, leave town without permission, or marry. They were generally barred from administration and college teaching. Intense criticism of sex discrimination in education during the 1960s and the early 1970s finally produced legislation in 1972 outlawing sex-segregated classes, unequal funding of women's athletics programs, and discriminatory hiring and promotion policies.

Although women in college have outnumbered men since 1979, and have increased their presence in previously male-dominated majors, inequalities persist. A 1992 report by the American Association of University Women concluded that women still receive less attention in classrooms, face biased tests and textbooks, and

Women outnumber men in America's colleges, but they still face a "chilly" climate due to cultural patterns and sexism.

are channeled away from math and science. Rosemary Sutton (1991) found that boys have more access to computers at school. R. M. Hall and B. R. Sandler (1982) observe that women face a "chilly" climate in college classrooms, are ignored, and lose confidence in their abilities. A follow-up by Mary Crawford and Margo MacLeod (1990) similarly found that male college students participate more and are more assertive (mirroring studies of earlier grades), although teacher discrimination is not the cause.

The research suggests the need for continued scrutiny of textbooks and curricula for negative stereotypes of females, more aggressive enforcement of civil rights laws, more encouragement of girls to study mathematics and science, and further screening of achievement tests to eliminate gender biases.

Race and Ethnicity

In 1954, the U.S. Supreme Court reversed an earlier ruling in 1896 (*Plessy* vs. *Ferguson*) that had legitimized separate but equal schools for blacks and whites. The *Brown* vs. *Board of Education of Topeka* decision held that separate schools are inherently unequal in quality and that they denied African Americans equal protection under the law as guaranteed by the Constitution. Following this landmark case, hundreds of court-ordered desegregation plans were enacted across the country.

Sociologists played a part in the desegregation effort. The conclusions of a 1966 report by James Coleman and his colleagues lent support to the idea of mixing children of different races in schools. The report claimed, among other things, that desegregation would boost the school achievement of minority students and have no ill effect on whites. Coleman and his colleagues acknowledged that other factors, such as acceptance of desegregation by teachers and white students, were required for equalizing educational opportunities, but the report raised hopes.

To some extent, those hopes have been fulfilled by court-ordered busing plans in over 500 school districts. A 1992 survey by the National School Boards Association found that fewer than 20 percent of students in the South attended schools with more than 95 percent minorities, a significant improvement over the 1960s. (Ironically, this progress in the public schools contrasts with the increasing racial segregation and tensions on America's college campuses.) As well, a 1994 report by the Harvard Project on School Desegregation detected evidence of resegregation in the South, where much progress had been made. School segregation is still higher outside the South and is increasing for Hispanics, but overall the mixing of the races in schools has had positive results (Whitman and Friedman, 1992). Acceptance of busing has increased among Americans, friendships have formed across racial lines (Shrum, Cheek, and Hunter, 1988) and, more to the point, desegregation has narrowed the black–white academic achievement gap (Crain and Mahard, 1983).

A discouraging development, however, has been the link of school desegregation to "white flight" from many city centers. This exodus has been most noticeable in large Northern and Western metropolitan areas, where inner-city schools are dominated by minority students, and whites reside mostly in outer suburban school districts as well as attending private schools. Indeed, the boundaries between central-city and suburban districts play a major role in demarcating areas of largely minority and largely white schools (James, 1989). High district-wide percentages of minorities sometimes coincide with dropping white enrollment even in schools not directly involved in desegregation (Smock and Wilson, 1991). Some of the white flight is apparently motivated less by racism than urban ills such as crime, higher taxes, and pollution, as well as dropping birth rates among whites. In fact, the exodus to the suburbs is largely a middle-class phenomenon, including blacks and other minorities. Nonetheless, all these social changes have combined with other factors to produce resegregated school systems that rarely fully recover white enrollments (Welch, 1987). Desegregation plans stall with too few white students to achieve racial balance.

In the early 1990s, the U.S. Supreme Court eased the rules by which school districts can end mandatory desegregation programs. An increasingly popular alternative to "forced busing" uses incentives to encourage voluntary racial integration. Through extra funding, a special theme or focus, and wide publicity, magnet schools attract students of different races from all over the district. Parents then choose, as they would in any free marketplace, the best school value for their children. Magnet schools, however, are no cure-all substitute for mandatory busing programs. In one study of a Maryland school district, for example, white families generally chose magnet schools with low minority enrollments while minority families gravitated toward schools in lower-income neighborhoods with a concentration of minorities (Henig, 1990). Still, some research suggests that voluntary programs produce greater long-term interracial mixing, largely because of the white flight typically generated by mandatory desegregation (Rossell, 1990).

What happens when whites are mixed with racial and ethnic minorities in schools? First, minority students are not as easily victimized by inferior staffing and materials. Second, such students often find the academic standards and teacher expectations higher in predominantly white schools. If these expectations are high enough to challenge but not so high as to frustrate or threaten, student achievement can be enhanced. But merely placing minority pupils in predominantly white schools will not necessarily equalize their educational opportunity.

A growing body of research indicates that culturally different students need special teaching sensitivities and strategies. The relationship between white teacher and minority student is often fraught with tension and misunderstanding. One experiment found, for example, that black students perceived white teachers' evaluations to be unfair, underestimating the students' abilities and performance (Coleman, Jussim, and Isaac, 1991). Another revealed consistently negative teacher expectations for African-American male students, probably due to fear of their perceived nonsubmissive, independent attitudes (Ross and Jackson, 1991). Other evidence suggests that blacks' unique perceptual style, categorization strategies, and emphasis on interpersonal relationships require special teaching approaches (Shade, 1982). Similarly, Jay MacLeod (1987) observes that black students respond differently to their environment than do whites. Michelle Foster (1989) describes how readily inner-city African-American students respond to familiar language structure and deliberate body motions. Finally, the success of black students at predominantly white colleges hinges significantly on their beliefs about how they are viewed by faculty and other students (Kraft, 1991).

Other culturally different students also require special teaching approaches to equalize their educational opportunities. Particular turn-allocation practices (conversation turn-taking practice) are effective with Puerto Rican students (McCullum, 1989), cooperative learning helps linguistic minority children (Kagan, 1986), cooperative contexts are more familiar for Native American students (Philips, 1982), and native Hawaiian children respond best to small groups and bilingual discussions (Tharp and Gallimore, 1988).

Equalizing the educational opportunities of racial and ethnic minorities paradoxically demands integrating students in schools while simultaneously employing different teaching strategies to accommodate those of different cultural backgrounds. In doing so, of course, schools may be criticized for placing minority students in separate classes or tracks. The problem is that special treatment means separation, which, as the Supreme Court decided in 1954, often translates into "unequal." As long as culturally distinct groups populate U.S. schools, equalizing opportunities will remain problematic.

EDUCATION AS A REFLECTION OF CULTURAL VALUES AND ATTITUDES

Parents and students in the United States today are continually reminded by some study, commissioned report, or poll that their schools are deteriorating. When compared to what they once were, or to what other nations' schools are now, ours appear riddled with problems: declining academic performance, endemic apathy, and growing violence. Here we compare U.S. schools with Japan's to explore the connection between the flaws of an educational system and the values and attitudes of the culture that supports it.

Problems in U.S. Schools

Declining averages on U.S. college entrance exams probably cause more handwringing among school critics than any other indicator of academic performance. Average scores on the Scholastic Aptitude Test are significantly lower than they were in the mid-1960s. (We should note, however, that the SAT is designed to measure reasoning ability rather than achievement.) Also, the higher percentage of test-takers from disadvantaged backgrounds may have helped pull average scores down (Murray and

Herrnstein, 1992). The poor results cannot be explained away, however, without considering that too few American students attempt the math and science courses that would prepare them for the SAT and college. Moreover, schools have no control over the 91 percent of students' time spent outside the classroom. And peer culture and mass media often counteract and overwhelm the school's influence.

Most achievement tests administered by elementary and secondary schools in the United States produce reassuring but inflated measures. They are so infrequently revised and "re-normed"—that is, updated to reflect the average performance of those who take the test—that virtually all school districts can proudly report above-average scores. More accurate assessments, such as those by the National Assessment of Educational Progress, reveal a disturbingly high percentage of students performing below grade level. International comparisons are similarly discouraging and embarrassing.

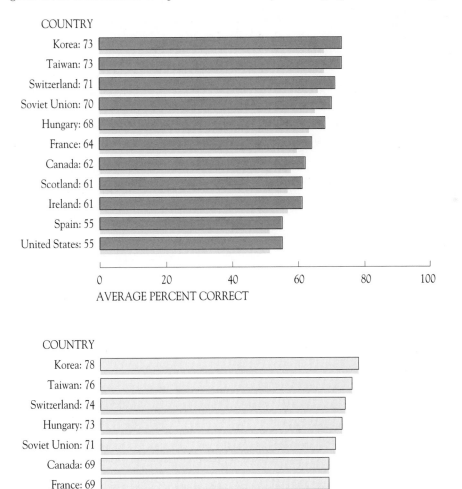

Figure 12-2

INTERNATIONAL COMPARISONS OF ACADEMIC ACHIEVEMENT

Source: U.S. Department of Education, National Center for Education Statistics, International Assessment of Educational Progress, *Learning Mathematics*, by Educational Testing Service.

Source: U.S. Department of Education, National Center for Education Statistics, International Assessment of Educational Progress, *Learning Science*, by Educational Testing Service.

PERCENTAGE OF PUBLIC ELEMENTARY AND SECONDARY SCHOOL TEACHERS AND PRINCIPALS REPORTING DRUG AND DISCIPLINE PROBLEMS[1] IN THEIR SCHOOL, BY INSTRUCTIONAL LEVEL AND LOCATION OF SCHOOL: 1990–1991

Problem	Total		Instructional Level			
			Elementary		Secondary	
	Teachers	Principals	Teachers	Principals	Teachers	Principals
1	2	3	4	5	6	7
Student alcohol use	23	11	4	2	54	33
Student drug use	17	6	5	1	38	16
Student tobacco use	24	13	6	3	53	40
Sale of drugs on school grounds	6	1	2	(2)	12	2
Physical conflicts among students	28	22	32	23	23	21
Racial tensions	14	5	12	4	19	6
Robbery or theft of items over $10	12	7	8	5	19	13
Student absenteeism/ class cutting	37	25	25	19	57	39
Student possession of weapons	5	3	3	2	7	4
Student tardiness	39	34	31	28	53	51
Trespassing	9	7	9	6	9	8
Vandalism of school property	22	12	17	11	30	14
Physical abuse of teachers	3	1	3	1	4	1
Teacher absenteeism	—	14	—	12	—	19
Teacher alcohol or drug use	—	1	—	1	—	1
Verbal abuse of teachers	29	11	26	9	35	14

Table 12-2

[1]Teachers and principals rated the problem as serious or moderate.
[2]Less than .5%.
—Data not collected.

Source: U.S. Department of Education, National Center for Educational Statistics, *Digest of Educational Statistics,* 1992, Table 141.

Behind the slipping test scores lies a depressing picture of widespread student apathy. John Bishop (1989) observes that U.S. students actively engage in learning less than half the time they are in school, spend 3 or 4 hours a week on homework, and about 24 hours a week watching television. One student relates a typical after-school schedule: "When I get home from my after-school job around five, I go to my room and start watching my regular programs." After dinner, she returns to her nighttime TV shows until about 9:30 P.M., and "then comes the best part. I turn on the VCR and get caught up on my soaps" until about midnight (quoted in Welsh, 1991, p. 81). Bishop describes high school classrooms of "tranquil and bland" atmosphere in which the teacher does not push the students and they do not push the teacher, an agree-

Location of School							
Urban		Suburban		Town		Rural	
Teachers	Principals	Teachers	Principals	Teachers	Principals	Teachers	Principals
8	9	10	11	12	13	14	15
16	9	22	7	28	9	29	16
17	7	18	4	18	6	17	6
21	12	22	10	30	13	25	17
8	1	6	2	5	0	4	1
37	29	27	26	25	22	18	14
20	8	18	5	10	4	6	3
15	9	14	6	10	4	8	9
44	36	36	24	38	23	28	20
10	7	3	1	3	2	1	1
47	48	41	33	34	30	28	27
16	13	7	7	5	3	4	5
30	18	20	10	21	7	16	11
6	5	4	(2)	2	1	(2)	(2)
—	20	—	14	—	11	—	12
—	2	—	2	—	(2)	—	2
41	17	28	10	22	10	21	7

ment that reduces teacher and student effort to a bare minimum. He attributes the students' lassitude to three factors: (1) High school grades have little bearing on later job opportunities or promotions; (2) peer groups discourage academic effort; and (3) the college admission process requires only good grades in comparison to other students, not a high level of learning.

The dropout rate—about one-quarter of U.S. students do not graduate from high school—offers perhaps the most dramatic evidence of the failure of American education. The more commonly cited reasons for dropping out include lack of interest and motivation, problems functioning in school, and pregnancy and marriage plans (Toby and Armor, 1992).

Ironically, American parents are among the world's most satisfied regarding the academic quality of their children's schools, instead focusing their concern on the rising level of school violence. Thirty years ago, discipline matters revolved around students talking too much in class or chewing gum. As Table 12-2 shows, discipline problems in American schools have changed dramatically since then. One researcher notes that in 1950 there were 18,000 assaults on teachers in American schools, but by 1979 the number had risen to 110,000 (Goldstein, 1992). News stories cite distressingly frequent instances of violence in our schools. In 1991, for example, a 13-year-old girl killed the varsity football captain in a Texas school cafeteria. The following year, a student in a Brooklyn high school killed two classmates, and a 13-year-old boy used a rifle to take his teacher hostage in a Georgia middle school. Students must also endure sexual harassment. According to a 1993 survey by the American Association of University Women, 85 percent of girls and 76 percent of boys in grades 8 to 11 reported that they had been sexually harassed, mostly verbally, at school.

Japanese Schools: Test Score Success

The success of Japan's schools in producing high test scores is as well-established as the generally poor academic performance of U.S. students. Japanese students score near or at the top on international comparisons (in part because the tests they take more closely match the curriculum of Japan than that of the United States—Westbury, 1992). Rather than apathy, Japanese worry about students studying too much. Most high school students do not date, help out around the house, or hold part-time jobs—they study in preparation for "examination hell." Children's playgrounds are often devoid of junior high students in the afternoons: Most are attending *juku*, or "cram school." Japan achieves a higher graduation rate than the United States (about 90 percent), largely because high school grades strongly affect job opportunities even for vocational school graduates (Kariya and Rosenbaum, 1987a). Moreover, Japanese students generally face more rigorous curricula, especially in foreign languages, science, and math. Finally, although the level of violence in Japan's schools has risen recently, it does not approach the scale of the problem in America.

Cultural Explanations

Any suggestion to simply reproduce the Japanese system in the United States, however, ignores two hard facts. First, schools in Japan are not without their flaws, as we will see. Second, their current system is the product of century-old reforms essentially based on European and American models, from school uniforms to the elementary–junior high–senior high formula. In other words, Japan's educational successes result neither from a novel approach nor greater funding but from cultural values and attitudes conducive to academic achievement. The nation's homogeneity is an advantage, too. The United States must deal not only with incredible diversity (a school in Brooklyn, for example, resounds with 26 different languages) but also with cultural dispositions that impede educational success.

These cultural differences show up early. According to Robert Hess and Hiroshi Azuma (1991), Japanese children can freely act out their impulses at home but are expected to be diligent, patient, and compliant at school (Peak, 1991). The Japanese preschool emphasizes social skills and character rather than academics. It expects children to pay close attention to instructions and to display patience and persistence in solving tasks. At this age, American children are generally more impulsive and less attentive. U.S. parents primarily stress independence for their children, an admirable characteristic but not one contributing to orderliness and obedience in a bureaucratic school environment. An especially telling contrast is that Japanese parents and children tend to assume that poor academic performance is due to internal factors; usually, "lack of effort" is cited as the explanation. Students are thus responsible for their success or failure. In the United States, parents and students are much more likely to attribute failure to factors beyond the student's control: conditions in society or the school, or the student's "lack of ability." In other words, one culture extols hard work; the other tells its children that unless they have advantages or inborn ability, there is not much use in trying hard. It is therefore not surprising that, unlike Japanese parents, American parents rarely stress homework, tutoring, or after-school classes (Stevenson and Lee, 1990). Hess and Azuma also note that in Japan children are expected to adapt to the school's demands while in the United States schools are expected to alter their climate and requirements to fit the needs of the student. The researchers refer to this differentiating factor as "cultural support" for education.

On the surface, Japan's schools enjoy cultural support in the form of cooperative, motivated students and highly paid and well-respected teachers. Their students generally stay in school and perform well on tests, although the dropout rate is increasing, as are other manifestations of student dissatisfaction such as violence (Amano, 1989) and school phobia (Wataru, 1990). A small but growing number of elementary and junior high school students rebel against attending school, hiding in their rooms and ignoring pleas, cajoling, and threats from their distressed parents. Part of the reason may lie in the increase over the last decade of bullying, which contributes to violence and suicide (Murakami, 1989). Japanese reformers complain that the excessively competitive examination system denies students the chance to enjoy childhood or to

Japanese schools mix periods of academic applications with substantial time for rest, social interaction, and extracurricular activities. Their teachers spend a great deal of time preparing lessons, learning new techniques, and sharing teaching ideas with their colleagues. The result is a longer day but a more enjoyable and effective learning atmosphere for students.

develop their personalities fully. They worry that Japanese students lack what characterizes many U.S. students: the ability to think independently and creatively. This represents the next goal for Japanese education.

The news regarding another facet of education, students attaining their educational goals, is similarly not all good for Japanese schools and bad for ours. Both societies value meritocracy, but other cultural ideals create different outcomes (Kariya and Rosenbaum, 1987b). For the United States, the difference entails the troublesome fact that many students hold unrealistic educational goals and are unsure about college preparation plans. Because college admissions are based on many factors, including interviews, recommendations, and extracurricular activities, many American students exist in a kind of limbo until they receive their acceptance or rejection letters from colleges. Critics claim that high schools and community colleges consequently serve as sites for the "cooling out" process necessitated by such an ambiguous system. Instead of straightforwardly recommending some students to prepare for a noncollege track, the system allows them to wander through courses aimlessly, uncertainly, and unsuccessfully until they finally drop out with feelings of failure and with no vocational preparation. These problems flow from the value Americans place on maintaining equal educational opportunities for students as long as possible.

Japanese college admissions, in contrast, are rigidly based on grades and test scores as accurate measures of student merit. Children therefore know by the 10th grade if they are going to college, and choose their career majors early in high school. This clarity of purpose enables students to prepare appropriately, but it also demoralizes many who might be late bloomers, and has been linked to increasing student rebelliousness in Japan (Mochizuki, 1989). It also ignores all other student characteristics beyond grades and test scores. The Japanese value of rigid meritocracy produces a different, not necessarily superior, educational form.

America's educational system has its strong points—for example, it offers many opportunities and fosters creativity—but clearly there are grounds for concern that our deteriorating schools will undermine our economic future. One cultural factor in this decline in school quality may be our aversion to elitism. Jacques Barzun (1991) contends that while Americans call for educational excellence, we share an unconscious prejudice against those blessed with "brains" (that is, genetic or socioeconomic advantages). Superior athletes, on the other hand, are showered with praise and admiration rather than resentment or jealousy regarding their advantages. Though we might not admit it, we often express more interest in the qualifications and achievements of the high school football coach than that of the superintendent.

Perhaps, as Barzun says, the quality of our schools reflects the values we hold most dear rather than those to which we give lip service. In fact, the educational system of any nation offers a clear picture of that culture's underlying values and attitudes.

WHAT WORKS: HOW TO REFORM U.S. SCHOOLS

It seems that nearly everyone considers himself or herself qualified to offer suggestions on how to improve our schools. Increasing concern that mediocre schools are imperiling America's global position have strengthened the chorus of criticisms and recommendations from parents, journalists, and politicians as well as researchers. Here we explore some of the educational reforms that have actually been tried and found useful.

Teacher Improvement

In part because so much depends on them, teachers catch most of the criticism directed at U.S. schools. After the home environment, the teacher's relationship with students is probably the most powerful influence on children in school. However, teachers today must deal with increasing violence, student apathy, and bureaucratic constraints, much of which is beyond their control.

One reform strategy to emerge recently is to improve the school's organizational climate to enable teachers to perform more effectively. For example, researchers have identified several factors that reduce teacher alienation: orderly student behavior, encouragement of teacher innovation, teacher knowledge of other teachers' courses, administration responsiveness, mutual aid among teachers (Newmann, Rutter, and Smith, 1989), and high-track, motivated students (Raudenbush, Rowan, and Cheong, 1992). Another study identifies influences on teacher commitment: the sense that what one does matters, feedback on the positive results of one's efforts, autonomy and discretion, school management of discipline problems, support from principals, and the socioeconomic status of the student body (Rosenholtz and Simpson, 1990). Some of these factors can be controlled, suggesting ways to lower or remove organizational barriers between teachers and teaching.

By 1990, most states had followed the popular suggestion that teacher competency tests be used to weed out ill-prepared novices—and sometimes even measure the ability of experienced instructors, although this has typically produced political fireworks. Questions inevitably arise about how well paper-and-pencil exams or scheduled observations measure teaching quality. Judging from continuing concern about teacher quality, such tests have not solved the perceived problem. One researcher concludes that competency tests force teachers to focus their energies on avoiding failure, thus substantially *reducing* their teaching quality (Smith, 1991).

Critics sometimes deride teachers even before they get to the classroom. One observer of teacher-training colleges describes the students as either bureaucrats in waiting or inarticulate and uninformed (Kramer, 1991). In this view, such colleges emphasize equality and students' feelings rather than student responsibility and achievement. Couple this indictment (and many others) with the fact that most education majors are overrepresented near the bottom of college entrance exam scores, and a number of reforms suggest themselves: recruit brighter teacher-trainees, and either eliminate teacher colleges or upgrade them with more practical theory and instruction, more liberal arts courses, and fewer education courses. Indeed, the focus is now shifting from effective teaching tactics to a strong academic background for the teacher.

Toward this end, nearly two dozen states are modifying accreditation laws to make it easier for noneducation majors to become teachers. Teach For America, for example, tries to entice bright college graduates into teaching through a tough, reality-based eight-week training course. More than 40 similar programs attempt to inject fresh energy into the nation's schools by means of graduate school work and grueling schedules of summer and night classes. The efficacy of such reforms is difficult to gauge, largely because teaching quality is so difficult to measure. However, certification-test scores for alternative-path teachers are high, and observers report encouraging early returns in terms of enthusiasm, interest from established teachers, and floods of inquiries (McCormick, 1991; Saltzman, 1991; Mabry et al., 1990).

Would not higher teacher pay attract more competent people into the profession and raise the commitment of teachers already in the classroom? Again, the difficulty of measuring teaching quality makes such claims dubious, and researchers find no link between teacher effectiveness and pay (Hanushek, 1989). Political pressures usually prevent school boards from firing incompetent teachers, and taxpayers balk at raising the pay level of teachers in general. But merit pay programs, in which especially competent teachers are paid bonuses, usually founder on the measurement of teachers' merit. The result is that poor teachers are paid on the same scale as excellent teachers: a poor environment for generating dedication and commitment.

Empowering Parents

Parents today demand, and are attaining, more say-so in how schools are managed and which ones their children will attend. Community participation has generally proven effective in enhancing students' school-related behaviors and academic achievement (Nettles, 1991). Yet, while such heightened interest on the part of parents is heartening to some observers, it worries others.

The controversy of parent empowerment revolves mostly around voucher plans or open enrollment, in which parents choose their children's schools from any in their district, sometimes including private ones. Proponents argue that choice will not only increase parental involvement in education but spur competition among schools for pupils in the same way that businesses compete for customers. Schools would be forced to improve or else close their doors. Like many other reforms, however, the reality tends to be more complicated than the measures proposed to deal with it. Squabbles arise over whether vouchers should permit parents to choose private schools that may promote religious or ethnocentric programs or that lie outside the administrative jurisdiction of elected school officials. Transportation costs to support parental choice can soak up huge amounts of the system's resources. Critics fear that schools will market gimmicks and frills rather than actually improve academic offerings. Most troubling is the impact of "bright flight." As the most able students are freed to attend any school of their choice, they often become more concentrated in the few elite schools in the district, thus increasing the mediocrity or deterioration of the other schools. As we saw earlier, parental choice in the form of magnet schools is not always successful in promoting racial desegregation because parents often choose schools with students predominantly of their own race. Still, parental choice enjoys political support and has produced some positive results.

The logical extension of parent empowerment is home schooling. Several states permit parents to withdraw their children from school and educate them at home. Support for this alternative began in the late 1960s and gathered strength in the 1980s, fueled largely by dissatisfaction with the educational system and the desire to instill in children the family's own religious beliefs and values while avoiding the peer subculture and violence of the schools. Students taught at home generally do as well as or better than their classroom counterparts on standardized achievement tests (Tompkins, 1991; Rakestraw and Rakestraw, 1990).

Higher Expectations for Students

The ultimate goal of school reform is higher student achievement, and this is perhaps most directly accomplished by demanding more from students themselves. Toward this end, most states adopted minimum competency examinations in the 1970s. Many have also boosted their graduation requirements and require students to show scholastic progress before moving to the next grade. Some districts have established minimum academic requirements for participation in extracurricular activities, including team sports.

The major difficulty with these increased demands on students lies in the tests used to measure academic performance. In some cases, "minimum skills" tests tend to "dumb down" the curriculum as teachers focus too narrowly on the bare essentials targeted by such exams. Also, test norms, which determine students' relative achievement, are often outdated and thus produce artificially high scores. Another concern, however, is with the testing process itself (Haladyna, Nolen, and Haas, 1991). Teachers and principals, under tremendous pressure to produce high test scores, may actually supply students with solutions, tamper with answer sheets, spend inordinate classroom time coaching students on specific test items, or dismiss low-achieving pupils on testing day. Researchers also find that low achievers tend to become anxious about tests and cheat or try half-heartedly, thus undermining the validity of the results (Paris et al., 1991). The rage for testing that swept the nation during the 1980s apparently produced some unintended, negative effects.

New forms of testing are now filtering into classrooms across the United States. Rather than depend on the less expensive multiple-choice format, performance-assessment exams typically include written essays, lab experiments, and portfolios. The new tests often reflect the demand for mastery of knowledge rather than mere familiarity with many topics. Their problem-solving slant requires teachers as well as students to work at higher intellectual levels.

A national examination may serve to upgrade academic standards in all states. Such a test would probably require the development of a nationwide curriculum that clarifies what competence means in each academic area. Of course, concerns will arise regarding the unequal preparation of students from disadvantaged backgrounds.

We cannot simply demand more from students without changing the ways they are treated in the classroom. Successful schools exhibit several features, some of which could conceivably be incorporated into others: a strong academic curriculum, an orderly environment, commitment and interest from teachers, and a sense of community (Lee and Byrk, 1989). Another suggested reform is "authentic work" that involves students producing socially useful, personally meaningful knowledge rather than merely reproducing facts (Wehlage, Smith, and Lipman, 1992). The traditional nongraded elementary school organization, which produces higher student achievement in conjunction with cross-age grouping, is making a comeback (Gutierrez and Slavin, 1992). Smaller class sizes promote a more effective learning environment, especially in early grades and for minority children (Finn and Achilles, 1990). Similarly, while a longer school day and year may not automatically elevate student achievement, it does give teachers more time with children.

Concerns about our shrinking pool of skilled workers has attracted some reformers to the notion of youth apprenticeship. Learning from successful European models, American apprenticeship programs shift some of the formal instruction from the high school to the workplace. To be successful, such efforts need strong linkages between schools and employers as well as high-quality training on the job (Bailey, 1993). Such programs offer an alternative to college for many students.

American's search for educational 'excellence will be frustrated unless our schools can overcome the worsening alienation and apathy of teachers and students, shift their emphasis away from superficial, testable knowledge, and put competent, committed teachers in front of all students. Parents must likewise do their part to prepare children intellectually and socially and inculcate in them a strong work ethic and sense of personal responsibility.

Summary

The example of the Manus shows that some cultures require no formal tests, teachers, or schedules of instruction to educate their children. The experience of Vietnam showcases the functions of formal education. Schools transmit a society's knowledge and skills. They also transmit the culture of the dominant group, which decides what is taught and to whom. In the United States, this integrative function is served through a *hidden curriculum*, the largely middle-class values and standards of behavior implicitly and explicitly taught in school but not part of the formal curriculum. Modern nations also need schools to innovate, to offer laboratories for research and train people to use them. As the role of education expands in modern societies, other institutions must adjust. The school's impact is also seen in its latent functions.

A closely studied function of American schools is to provide opportunity for upward social mobility. This critical factor in the status attainment process is universally accessible in our society and pays ever higher dividends for individuals, but conflict theorists contend that schools actually serve the interests of the elite and represent barriers for the poor. Students from lower-class homes do not typically use the schools as a stepping stone to success because they lack the background advantages of middle-class students. The same generally holds true for students from single-parent, minority, and non-English-speaking backgrounds and those from large families. In contrast, middle-class parents usually behave in ways that confer real academic advantages on their children.

Another explanation for the inequalities in American education lies in the schools' differential treatment of students. Teachers, for example, have higher expectations for children with the skills and behaviors instilled by a good home environment. The common practice of grouping students according to ability likewise directs more attention and resources to those who are already advantaged. In high school, tracking offers more challenging and stimulating instruction to students preparing for college, while lower-class pupils may be locked out. The organizational context of the school plays a large role in how tracking policies are implemented.

Private schools may in some ways provide higher-quality education than public schools, although the complexity of this issue engenders much controversy. There is little disagreement, however, that some universities offer more valuable diplomas than do others, and that their high costs and academic requirements compel many able students to attend less prestigious institutions or community colleges.

According to the *correspondence principle*, the schools reproduce the social-class system of haves and have-nots because the organization of the schools mirrors that of the workplace. In this view, the educational system legitimates social-class inequalities and discourage students from disadvantaged backgrounds.

An instance of such a barrier to social mobility is *credentialism*, the demand by employers for ever-higher educational credentials that are irrelevant to or unnecessary for actual job performance. Such requirements simply serve to restrict competition in the labor market to only those from advantaged backgrounds. On the other hand, while educational credentials may not be directly relevant to job performance, they can still indicate other valuable traits.

In an effort to equalize educational opportunities in the United States, courts have ordered states to narrow discrepancies in funding among school districts. This has had a limited impact so far, and in any case financial inequities remain even within districts. But funding probably has little impact on school quality. A more effective strategy would be to redistribute the most powerful resource in the school:

teaching quality. Unfortunately, this factor is not easily measured. Another approach to equalization is special compensatory programs for children of disadvantaged backgrounds like Head Start. The variable quality and short duration of Head Start limits its long-range impact. Earlier preschool intervention tries to reach the child before he or she falls too far behind. Such programs, however, cannot easily counter the negative effects stemming from a bad home environment.

Educational opportunity also depends on gender. Traditional gender roles fostered sexual discrimination in the past. Legislation has demolished some barriers for females, but they still face special problems in schools.

Similarly, racial and ethnic minorities have benefited from laws eliminating formal discriminatory practices in American education. Court-ordered busing has had limited success in desegregating U.S. schools, but this and other social forces have produced "white flight" and resegregation. The magnet school approach has achieved some long-term interracial mixing. Minority students in integrated schools are less easily targeted for discriminatory treatment and are subject to the same expectations as whites. Students who are culturally different, however, require special teaching sensitivities and strategies, and this means segregating such students into their own tracks and classrooms.

American schools exhibit several signs of deterioration. First, test scores, although imperfect measures of achievement, have declined, except in the case of inflated results from some exams. Student apathy reigns in many classrooms, the dropout rate remains high, and school violence has escalated. Schools in Japan, in contrast, boast of high achievement from their homogeneous and hard-working student body. Japanese culture emphasizes proper behavior over academics and regards success as not simply the result of innate ability but discipline and perseverence. Explanations for failure lie in the individual, not the schools, where children are expected to adjust to the schools. These attitudes contrast with American values. Because we stress hope for equal educational opportunity, our schools do not encourage students to plan their academic careers from an early age, as does the Japanese system. And due to the American aversion to elitism, we do not support our academically talented students as much as we could. However, Japanese schools have their own flaws, including early demoralization among students, and they are experiencing increasing violence and dropout rates.

Efforts to reform American schools have taken several forms. Perhaps most importantly, teacher effectiveness must be improved. One proposed solution is to improve the school's organizational climate to help teachers fulfill their potential. Competency tests strive to guarantee teacher quality, but they also raise difficult issues. Other efforts focus on teacher training, certification, and increased pay. Educational reforms also include empowering parents, including home schooling, more parental participation in the school, and voucher plans on open enrollment. Allowing parents to choose their children's schools is popular but raises many questions. Minimum competency exams aim to raise expectations for students, but these tests have been counterproductive in some ways. A national examination may upgrade educational standards in all states. Schools can also arrange more effective classroom environments through several reforms.

			Key Terms
hidden curriculum	correspondence principle	credentialism	

13

Chapter

POPULATIONS AND COMMUNITIES

Sometime during 1991 the world's population passed the 5.4 billion mark and the United Nations Population Fund expects the total to zoom to 6.4 billion by the year 2001. Even *if* global funding for family planning and contraceptives doubles before then and *if* the number of couples in developing countries using contraception increases by nearly 50 percent by the end of the 1990s, the world's population will *still* surge to 10 billion by 2050, begin to level off, and stabilize at about 11.6 billion by 2150. Much of this growth will occur in the "megacities" of underdeveloped countries, led by Mexico City, with 25 million people, and Sao Paulo, Brazil, with 22 million. These numbers conjure up images of an earth sagging in its orbit and huge cities bursting with masses of poor people. Such distressing predictions are increasingly common in **demography,** the scientific study of the size, composition, and movements of populations. In this chapter, we first consider the problem of world population growth, and then focus on the populations of two specific countries. We conclude with a look at various kinds of communities.

Demography: the scientific study of the size, distribution, and composition of populations.

WAR, PESTILENCE, AND FAMINE: WAS MALTHUS RIGHT?

Too many mouths to feed and too little food—this is the dire scenario Thomas Robert Malthus (1766–1834) pondered in his *Essay on the Principle of Population* (1798). Malthus observed that food supply increases in an arithmetic progression (1, 2, 3, 4, 5 . . .), whereas population increases geometrically (1, 2, 4, 8, 16 . . .). From this he reasoned that the world food supply would always lag behind population growth. Even if agricultural production improved, it would simply stimulate more population growth. Malthus opposed artificial birth control measures on religious grounds, advocating instead "preventive checks" such as sexual restraint and late marriage. He held out little hope that such checks would be employed, especially among the lower-class masses, and predicted that population would eventually be curbed by nature's "positive checks"—"war, pestilence, and famine." Were his predictions accurate?

Malthus lived at a time in history when the world population had just begun to explode, soon to reach the 1 billion mark (see Figure 13-1). Since then, the population trajectory has resembled that of an accelerating rocket, one that will not begin to tail off until well into the twenty-first century.

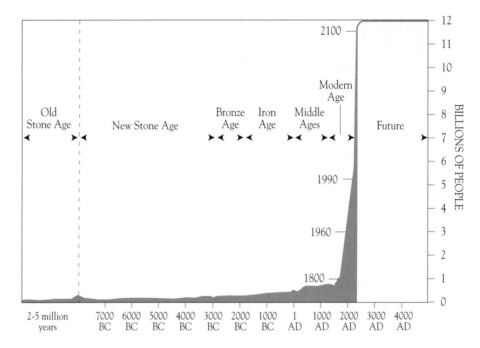

Figure 13-1

WORLD POPULATION GROWTH THROUGH HISTORY

The world's population began to skyrocket during Malthus' lifetime, in the 1800s. The end of this explosive growth is barely in sight.

Source: Joseph McFalls, Jr., "Population: A Lively Introduction," *Population Bulletin*, Vol. 46, No. 2 (Washington, DC: Population Reference Bureau, Inc., 1991).

Table 13-1 compares some of the factors that explain such dramatic demographic growth. To put it simply, a large number of births offset by relatively few deaths and little emigration equals a mushrooming population. The resulting growth rate of poorer countries like Mexico and India is around 2 percent, compared to an average of 0.5 percent for developed nations like the United States and Japan.

Like that of Malthus, our own lifetime may be remembered as a critical demographic period. In fact, current trends may determine whether world population, which increases by about 250,000 every day, triples or merely doubles before it reaches a plateau (Sadik, 1991). Each year over 10 million people, mostly children, die of starvation, while over 80 million are born. Unless such growth is brought under strict control in the fast-growing poor countries, Malthusian catastrophes seem inevitable.

So far, disaster has largely been held in check in developed countries. There, widespread famine and pestilence have been averted by social and technological advances unforeseen by Malthus. The machine technologies of the Industrial Revolution produced a plethora of goods for the masses. Agricultural improvements such as the McCormick reaper, the grain driller, insecticides, fertilizers, and even tractors with lights (enabling night and day harvesting) boosted food production beyond anyone's foretelling. In Europe, many couples decided to limit their family size, and developing contraceptive technology made such choices easier to fulfill. Medical advances prevented much of the pestilence predicted by Malthus.

Since the 1960s, however, some have pointed to the so-called Third World as the stage upon which Malthusian horrors will be played out. They note that during the next 35 years, 95 percent of the world's population growth will take place in less developed nations, where already scant resources will be spread even more thinly. In Nepal, Bangladesh, Burma, and Ethiopia, for example, an equal distribution of the gross national product would give each person less than $200 per year, in contrast to about $9,000 in Austria and Japan and $13,000 in the United States.

SELECTED FACTORS IN POPULATION GROWTH, 1990

Population Growth Factors	United States	Japan	Mexico	India
Fertility rate: the annual number of live births per 1,000 women of childbearing age.	1.85	1.61	3.43	3.78
Crude birth rate: the annual number of births per 1,000 total population.	14.9	10.6	29.0	30.0
Crude death rate: the annual number of deaths per 1,000 total population.	8.7	6.8	4.9	10.5
Infant mortality rate (an age-specific death rate): the annual number of deaths of children under age 1 per 1,000 live births.	10.4	4.5	32.7	89.4
Life expectancy rate: the average number of years a person born in a specific year can expect to live.	75.6	79.3	71.8	57.7
Projected population growth rate: the difference between numbers of births and deaths, and migrants entering and leaving the population.	0.7	0.3	2.1	1.8

Table 13-1

Source: U.S. Bureau of the Census.

To some extent, the suffering Malthus foresaw has become reality. Malnutrition is prevalent in undeveloped countries, where one in four children die before the age of 5. Demographers report that at least one-half of the world's population go to bed hungry each night. People born in the poorest nations can expect to live only 40 or 50 years, while those in richer countries typically live into their 70s. Such low **life expectancy rates** indicate bare subsistence, as do the high **infant mortality rates** in undeveloped nations, which are often 10 times those in developed nations. Other statistical indicators of population processes gone awry are the surging **fertility rates** and the nearly doubly high **crude death rates** and **crude birth rates** in undeveloped countries. (See Figure 13-2.) Such a picture of masses of people being born and dying in abject poverty provides substantial demographic evidence that Malthus was right.

The case of Kenya illustrates what such growth means in people's lives (Ozanni, 1990). There the average woman has 6.7 children, and the nation's population is expected to soar from 22 million to 37 million in the next decade. Farmers overwork the shrinking farms; schools and health clinics are tremendously overcrowded. Unemployment drives young people to the cities, which are becoming urban pressure cookers of hunger and pollution.

As populations expand, deforestation leads to environmental dangers such as flooding and soil erosion. Unchecked demands for firewood and building materials as well as additional farmlands have led Thailand to ban logging. Although it also relies on timber exports, Malaysia is considering following suit. In India and Java, exploding populations are overfarming the soil. Brazilian farmers in need of new land have

Life expectancy rate: the average number of years a person born in a specific year can expect to live.

Infant mortality rate: the annual number of deaths of children under age 1, per 1,000 live births.

Fertility rate: the annual number of live births per 1,000 women of childbearing age.

Crude death rate: the annual number of deaths per 1,000 total population.

Crude birth rate: the annual number of births per 1,000 total population.

Average children per woman

More than 5.5

3.5–5.4

2.5–3.4

Less than 2.5

Figure 13-2

FERTILITY RATES AROUND THE WORLD

Because of the momentum of their fertility rates, the developing nations, largely in the South, will continue to grow much faster than the more developed countries in the foreseeable future.

Source: *Population Today* (January 1992), Population Reference Bureau.

Demographic transition theory: the theory that initially small, stable populations experience substantial growth and restabilization through a three-stage decline in death rates and, later, birth rates.

destroyed millions of acres of rainforest. To the Malthusian prediction of mass starvation, we can add environmental catastrophe as well in some of these countries.

Demographic Transition

Like other developed nations, the United States went through a stage of large population increases, yet experienced no demographic calamity. **Demographic transition theory** (Thompson, 1929) explains how initially small, stable populations can experience booming growth and eventually stabilize again (see Figure 13-3). In the first stage, high fertility rates are offset by high mortality rates due to natural causes such as disease and periodic starvation. The population explosion occurs in the second stage as increased food supplies, public health measures, and medical advances diminish death rates. The birth rates fall later, only after changes in social values regarding family size and birth control. During this stage of high birth rates and falling death rates, the population increases. The increase continues until the third and final stage, when birth rates fall to the level of the death rates.

Today's developed nations suffered little as they moved through the demographic transition. Death rates declined slowly as technologies developed over a century or so. Meanwhile, industrializing economies produced enough food, clothing, shelter, medical care, and other benefits to sustain improvements in living standards. Population growth proceeded relatively slowly and painlessly.

Having long ago reached the stage of low fertility, several developed nations have continued to experience declining fertility rates to the point that they are now below

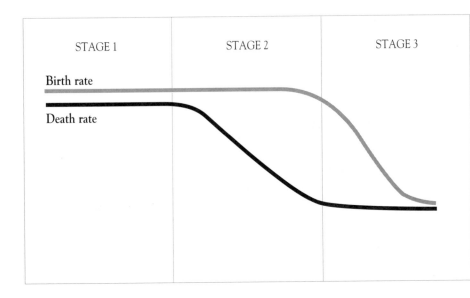

Figure 13-3

DEMOGRAPHIC TRANSITION

According to the demographic transition theory, preindustrial societies (Stage 1) exhibit high death and birth rates, and thus maintain a stable population size. With the advent of modernization, the death rate typically declines while the birth rate remains high (Stage 2). In Stage 3, the birth rate also falls, and the population approaches stability again. The area between the birth and death rate lines represents population growth.

replacement level. In the process, such countries have undergone what Dirk van de Kaa (1987) labels a "second demographic transition." Most noticeably, the populations of Germany, Austria, Denmark, and Hungary will decline if these low fertility rates stabilize. Former East Germany experienced a startling 50 percent decline before reunification (Haub, 1991). Spain also reports a slipping birth rate. Such demographic shifts typically elicit fear of reduced national strength. Smaller populations translate into fewer young people to consume, work, defend the nation, and support the older generation. Some European countries have responded with "pronatalist" policies aimed at increasing birth rates. Romania and Hungary, for example, have made contraceptives and abortions more difficult to obtain. Tax breaks, pension enhancements, offers of medical care and child care, and other childbearing incentives have generated little enthusiasm among young couples in such nations, for whom the lure of careers (especially for women) and individualistic life styles overshadow the benefits of parenting.

In contrast, developing nations today proceed into the second, high-growth stage of demographic transition with breathtaking speed and usually without corresponding economic development. Since World War II, immunization vaccines, antibiotics, malaria-fighting insecticides, and improved public health technologies have been introduced into developing countries in the short space of only one or two decades. Mortality rates have accordingly plummeted—after all, death-fighting measures meet little cultural resistance. Pronatal values, however, developed over centuries and are well-entrenched, and therefore birth rates will remain high for generations. The resulting gap between lowered death rates and high birth rates in the developing world has produced burgeoning populations. Although fertility rates in developing nations peaked in the late 1960s, the large number of women still entering childbearing age will probably sustain demographic momentum well into the late 1990s.

Zero population growth (ZPG), which indicates a stable population, remains only a faint, distant hope for most developing nations today. ZPG is reached when the number of births and immigrants is equal to or less than the number of deaths and emigrants. Fertility rates have declined in some countries, but even if such trends persist for the next century, population projections are sobering. By the year 2100, for

Zero population growth (ZPG): a state of no growth in a population, in which the number of births and immigrants is equal to or less than the number of deaths and emigrants.

example, Nigeria could have half a billion citizens, equal to the population of the entire African continent in 1982. There would be 10 people to every hectare of farmland, compared to a 3-to-1 ratio in France today (Sadik, 1991). Such nations must race against time to reach ZPG before disaster unfolds.

A Critical Perspective

Forestalling Malthusian predictions is not simply a matter of generating more wealth and cutting back on population. It is also a matter of equalizing the global distribution of goods and services. Some densely populated countries like the Netherlands and Japan have relatively few resources and little poverty, whereas South America and Africa are less densely populated, possess tremendous natural resources, but suffer massive poverty. Why? One reason is exploitation. In many poor countries, a small elite accumulates most of the national wealth for its own benefit by exploiting the natural resources and the people's labor. This powerful class, moreover, often enjoys financial aid from the U.S. government and multinational corporations. Also, wealthy nations consume many times more resources than does the undeveloped world. This leaves us with a picture of the rich of the world combining forces to exploit the poor.

Conflict theorists argue that a global capitalist elite directs the world's resources into investment that enriches the few rather than improving living conditions for the masses. Furthermore, capitalist economies require large populations. More people at home and abroad means expanding consumer markets as well as a cheap and docile labor force. From this perspective, overpopulation results not simply from numerical factors but from the requirements of a powerful business elite.

Will Malthus's predictions be realized? In some cases, such as Ethiopia, the future has already visited us. But developing nations and regions are not all alike; some have undergone more rapid socioeconomic changes and achieved considerable success with family planning programs. East Asia and China have an annual population growth rate of 1.3 percent, compared to 2.3 percent for South Asia, 2.1 percent for Latin America and 3.0 percent for Africa (U.S. Bureau of the Census, 1990). Such figures suggest that Malthusian visions will haunt nations that fail to effect the social/economic changes that hasten the plunge of birth rates (see Table 13-2).

Research Box

Using Garbage to Second-Guess the Census

The Constitution directs the United States Census Bureau to count all citizens every 10 years. Though the Bureau does an admirable job regarding most people, it undercounts homeless people, illegal aliens, and those living in ghettoes. To explore ways of reducing this undercounting, the Bureau turned to the University of Arizona's Garbage Project, which after more than two decades of study has established linkages between behavior patterns of households and their garbage (Rathje and Murphy, 1992).

The most reliable correlations were derived from plastic. Every individual, regardless of sex or age, generates about the same amount of plastic garbage. The researchers found that household size could be calculated, without questioning the family the usual way, by multiplying the weight of plastic garbage collected from them over a five-week period by 0.2815. In a neighborhood of 100 households, this equation is accurate within a range of ±2.5 percent, which is better than the Bureau's own projections in some localities.

Counting subpopulations presents greater difficulties. Infants are easily counted by multiplying the number of diapers disposed of over a five-week period by 0.01506. The researchers tried using discarded razors, cosmetics, toy packages, male contraceptives, cigar butts, and other "markers" for sex and age, but none were as accurate as diapers for babies.

The project researchers concluded that garbage analysis would not improve on the census count in well-to-do neighborhoods, which render extremely accurate counts. "But there is not much doubt that estimates derived from garbage could provide a usable snapshot of low-income neighborhoods" (p. 54). □

POPULATION CONTROL POLICIES: IS THERE ANY HOPE?

The world population grows by a quarter of a million every day. In a 15-week semester, approximately 26 million new people will inhabit the earth—as many as in New York City and Chicago combined. Even with a more equitable redistribution of the world's resources, clearly the globe can support only a finite number of people. The two most effective strategies for reversing the slide down the Malthusian slope are population control and economic development.

Birth Control

Birth control measures today take two forms: voluntary family planning and government coercion. Each offers some hope but not a simple solution.

Family planning has existed since ancient times in the form of abstinence, infanticide, and abortion. During this century, however, improved sterilization methods and condoms were introduced. New forms of contraception have become available,

A NEW WORLD EMERGING

Region	Population Size, 1990 (in millions)	Population Growth Rate, 1985–1990
World	5,292	1.7%
Africa	642	3.0%
Latin America	448	2.1%
North America	276	0.8%
Asia	3,113	1.9%
Europe	498	0.2%
Pacific Islands	27	1.5%

Table 13-2

Source: *1990 Demographic Yearbook*, New York: United Nations, 1992, page 141.

including the intrauterine device (IUD), "the Pill," and time-release implants for women (and perhaps someday for men). Use of these technologies, however, is lowest in many of the poorest and fastest-growing regions of the world. We can better understand this resistance to contraception from the perspective of cultural relativism.

In some societies, a large family affirms masculinity and femininity, bestows prestige on the household, and supplies farm workers. Recent surveys in the African nations of Mali, Burundi, Liberia, Senegal, and Togo found that women still hope to bear six or seven children (Freedman, 1990). Moreover, some religions (such as Catholicism and Hinduism) forbid artificial interference in propagation. Another difficulty is that women often have little control over their own fertility. Husbands in many undeveloped countries have traditionally demanded large families, especially many sons. Empowering women regarding childbearing decisions would thus seem to be a key element in any strategy to decrease population growth (Lappe and Collins, 1986). An important consideration is that in many poor nations, with no publicly financed social security system, children often serve as the parents' retirement system. Birth control devices also cost money, and when people make less than $200 per year, as they do in some countries, few are willing to pay even the smallest amount for contraceptives. Even heavy government subsidization of contraceptives often proves inadequate in overcoming centuries-old pronatalist values. All these factors increase the likelihood of runaway population in many countries on the periphery.

A recent doubling in the number of televisions in the developing world offers a new tactic to promote contraception (Hagerman, 1991). The integration of birth control messages into popular TV shows has resulted in a substantial increase in the use of family planning clinics.

Despite such successes, however, the widespread reluctance of couples to limit their family size has prompted some governments to institute population control programs. In the 1970s, India coerced several million men to have vasectomies. Not surprisingly, this forced sterilization program aroused large-scale objections, and voluntary programs were substituted. India then resumed its march toward overtaking China as the world's most populous nation, probably around the middle of the 21st century.

China provides a fascinating and important example of how many of the obstacles to population control can be overcome by far-reaching, persistent, and coercive government effort. State-sponsored programs beginning in the 1970s have caused a faster decline in population growth rate than in any other large developing country. At first, the government encouraged people to marry later and to have fewer children with greater spacing between the birth of each child. Later, it strongly urged couples to have only one child. Now the state not only provides free birth control devices, but uses a carrot-and-stick approach to convince people to limit the size of their families. The government rewards parents who have only one child with free hospital care for their child's delivery, free medical care and education for the child, salary bonuses, and special housing opportunities. Children without siblings receive educational and occupational benefits. For parents who do not cooperate, official reprimands are followed by pay cuts for those who have a third child. Abortions are encouraged and common even late in pregnancy. Many couples prefer a son so strongly that they may drown a first-born daughter to try again for a son.

Other overpopulated countries may find China's program morally objectionable or politically unfeasible. Those that try such drastic measures may achieve little or no success without a powerful, strongly integrated, centralized state apparatus. Even in totalitarian China, many rural families still persist in having more babies than the

Many governments have established population control programs in an effort to avoid the crush of overpopulation.

government deems proper. This strong pronatal attitude among rural couples, along with international condemnation of the heavy use of abortion and female infanticide, pressured the government to relax its one-child pressures in the late 1980s. Predictably, the birth rate quickly rose.

Economic Development

A second population control strategy focuses on economic development. This approach assumes that as a nation's standard of living rises, people willingly limit their family size in accordance with changing social values. Industrialization displaces people from farms, where children are seen as productive assets. As fewer families rely on agriculture for their livelihood, children instead come to be perceived as economic liabilities.

Economic development undoubtedly has an impact on fertility. Demographers estimate that while birth control programs account for anywhere from 10 percent to nearly half of birth rate declines in developing countries (Keyfitz, 1989), economic growth accounts for most of the remainder. Indeed, while most developing countries by now have some type of national family planning program, the most successful are those where social and economic development has been most rapid (Freedman, 1990). For example, Asia's "little dragons"—Singapore, Hong Kong, Taiwan, and South Korea—experienced explosive population growth between 1960 and 1980 but still managed to quadruple per capita wealth. Two reasons for their prosperity are adaptability to social and economic changes and development of human capital through education, health care, and nutrition. These nations are now approaching ZPG along with the United States and other industrialized nations.

An obvious limitation to economic development as a population control strategy is the elusiveness of the means. While presumably all nations on the periphery struggle to industrialize and increase technological progress, resources must often be diverted simply to feed the relentless surge of humanity.

Is there hope for stabilizing world population growth? Considerable barriers face attempts to develop effective birth control and economic development policies. Without monumental social changes and unexpected scientific breakthroughs in food production and contraception, increasing numbers of people will painfully probe the limits of the globe's capacity to support them.

Critical Thinking Box

Are We Ready for Eugenics?

Ever since Sir Francis Galton coined the term "eugenics" in the late 19th century, the notion of improving human genetic stock has incited fierce controversy. According to Daniel Kevles (1992), the eugenics movement currently enjoys a revival of interest and funding.

The idea behind eugenics is simple: Increase the proportion of "good" genes and decrease that of "bad" ones. Since the American Eugenics Society's "Fitter Family" state fair contests in the 1920s, "positive eugenics" policies have encouraged couples with "desirable" genetic traits to produce more offspring. In 1984, for example, Singapore began offering incentives to well-educated women to have more children and encouraged less-educated (and presumably less intelligent) women to have themselves sterilized. In 1988, several Chinese provinces instituted "negative eugenics" policies that banned marriages between mentally deficient people unless they were sterilized. Two years later, the United States launched its 15-year, $3 billion Human Genome Project. Europe and Japan established similar but smaller efforts. The goal of these programs is to create rough maps of the human gene code. Potential benefits include new diagnostic techniques and "preventive medicine," which would alert individuals with genetic vulnerabilities to protect themselves (for example, with diet and self-monitoring) and to choose sterilization and adoption. Millions of dollars in medical costs could be saved, giving nations with such technology a competitive edge in terms of human resources. On a more personal level, some couples would want the opportunity to use genetic analysis of embryos to select the most "fit" to bring to term.

Despite such benefits, however, eugenics raises deeply troubling ethical questions. During World War II, millions of "genetically inferior" peoples were exterminated in Nazi concentration camps. Those camps could be characterized as a huge eugenics experiment to improve human stock using government coercion. This may not represent a realistic fear today, but it is easy to imagine U.S. taxpayers, enraged over skyrocketing health care costs, demanding that gene mapping be used to identify and "incapacitate" individuals who might produce genetically deficient—and extremely expensive—children. Employers and medical insurance companies might rely on such techniques to screen out applicants with inborn weaknesses. And, of course, abortion would become an even more widely used tool to weed out undesirable embryos.

Technologies are developing quickly to fully realize the potential benefits and dangers of eugenics. What restrictions, if any, would you impose on genetic research and on the applications of its results? ■

A DEMOGRAPHIC CONTRAST OF TWO COUNTRIES

Personally visiting a country familiarizes one with its people and culture, but to come closer to a full knowledge of a society requires a macrosociological perspective. Demography provides such an overview. It helps us understand, for example, the Japanese phenomenon of renting a young couple with a baby to fill in for the son who never visits. Japan's current elderly generation had few children, and many of their sons and daughters are too busy to visit parents anyway. The solution: hiring actors to stage fake—but apparently satisfying—family reunions. In Japan's past, with high birth rates, large families, and less emphasis on national economic production, such rented families would have been ludicrous.

Population Composition and Life Opportunities

A demographic overview of the populations of the United States and Mexico similarly reveals some of the forces that produce contrasting life opportunities in these two nations.

An Overview: Population Pyramids   Figure 13-4 contrasts Mexico's child-centered, fast-growing population with the relatively stable, slow-growing society of the United States. **Population pyramids** depict the proportions of the sexes and age

Population pyramid: a figure depicting the proportions of the sexes and age groups in a society.

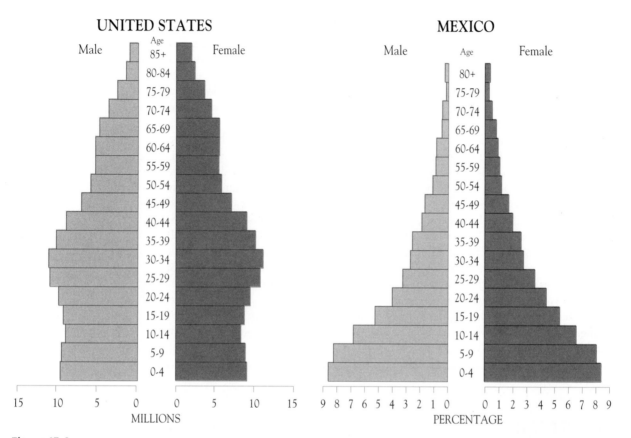

UNITED STATES

Male   Female

MEXICO

Male   Female

MILLIONS

PERCENTAGE

Figure 13-4

POPULATION PYRAMIDS OF THE UNITED STATES AND MEXICO

Population pyramids offer at a glance information about a society's recent demographic history, growth rate, dependency ratio, and sex ratio.

Source: U.S. Bureau of the Census, with special thanks to Patricia M. Rowe and John Matthew Reed, Center for International Research.

Fecundity: the potential number of children an average woman can bear.

groups in a society, with males and females on either side, younger age groups at the bottom, and the old at the top. Mexico's bottom-heavy pyramid indicates a preponderance of infants and children, suggesting that women in that society are closer to reaching **fecundity**—the potential number of children an average woman can bear—than are women in a society like the United States with a small-base pyramid.

Large-base pyramids tell us more than a country has a high birth rate. For example, it is likely that industrialization, if it has taken place at all, is limited or recent since children become economic liabilities in developed economies. Also, women in such societies usually have low labor-force participation. Mexico did not begin industrializing until several decades into this century, and traditional values have prevented most women from entering the workforce.

Both Mexico and the United States experienced population booms after World War II that lasted until the mid- to late 1960s. Still, Mexico's annual growth rate of 2.0 percent contrasts sharply with the 0.9 percent of the United States. In fact, if such low birth rates continue in this country, we will reach ZPG in only a few decades. In that case, the U.S. population pyramid will be more rectangular in shape, with the age levels all approximately the same size.

The Consequences of ZPG   Zero population growth has a long-term impact on a society's values and opportunities. A ZPG society, for example, is likely to be less child-centered and devote more of its resources and attention to older citizens. Health care and other social services important to the elderly rank higher in a stable population's priorities. Low birth rates mean women devote less time to childbearing and presumably more to careers. Fewer new workers entering the work force translates into a labor shortage. Older workers are needed on the job longer, limiting the promotion opportunities of younger workers.

The Dependency Ratio   Population pyramids also indicate the **dependency ratio** of a society, the proportion of people of nonworking age (under 15 and over 65) compared to people of working age. This ratio provides one measure of a nation's economic health: the more nonworkers who depend on one worker, the more vulnerable they and the economy are. Poor countries typically have about one worker per dependent person, leaving relatively few adults to care for the children and the elderly. Widespread hunger lurks just around the corner when so many people depend on so few to feed them. Mexico's population has a higher proportion of children (38 percent) than does the United States (22 percent), but the dependency ratios are not so different due to the larger percentage of people over 65 in the U.S. (13 percent) than in Mexico (4 percent).

Dependency ratio: the proportion of people of nonworking age (under 15 and over 65) in a population.

Sex Ratios   The higher the proportion of men to women in a society, the higher the **sex ratio.** The population pyramids of Mexico and the United States show no obvious imbalance in the sexes' proportions. The ratio of men to women in the United States is 94 (that is, 94 men for every 100 women); in Mexico the number is 96.

Not all pyramids are so symmetrical. Germany's pyramid shows relatively few males due to the tremendous losses of World War II. The United Arab Emirates has an unusually high sex ratio because of the large number of male migrants (without their families) brought into the country to work in the oil fields. Such an imbalance has obvious implications for mate availability but less obvious implications for women's other opportunities. With a high sex ratio, women are more likely to marry and to find that mothering and homemaking roles are highly valued in society (Guttentag and Secord, 1983). Also, female labor force participation is typically low (Pampel and Tanaka, 1986), as are divorce and women's literacy rates (South and Trent, 1987).

Sex ratio: the proportion of men to women in a population.

The U.S. Baby Boom Cohort   The bulge in the United States' population pyramid indicates an especially large **birth cohort,** or people born within the same time frame. This swelling of the birth rate between 1946 and 1964 resulted from huge numbers of people returning from World War II military service to start families. Also contributing to the "baby boom" was widespread economic prosperity, which produced enough high-paying jobs to enable many wives to stay out of the labor force. The post-war culture likewise strongly emphasized domesticity for women and large families.

Birth cohort: people born within the same time frame.

Like other large cohorts, the baby boom generation exerted strains on the nation's institutions—its schools, juvenile courts, and eventually its social security system—but the strains were felt mostly by those born late in the cohort. Late baby boomers faced limited opportunities—an already flooded labor market, lower pay, and high unemployment rates—that led to delayed marriage and childbearing. They also encountered inflated housing costs and accounted for higher crime rates. Men born near the end of such a population boom, because of their tendency to look for mates several years younger, have fewer mating choices in the following "baby bust" cohort. (See Figure 13-5.)

The differences between early and late "boomers" are lessening (Russell, 1991). With older boomers entering the "empty nest" phase as their children leave home, and younger members of the cohort stabilizing their family and career activities, the

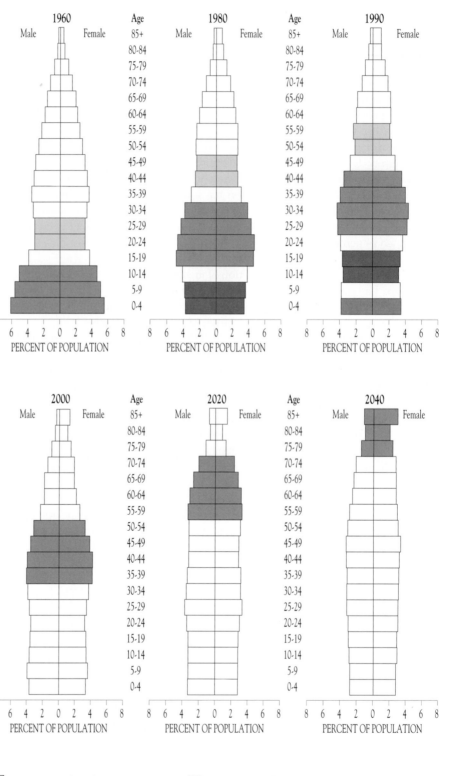

Figure 13-5

U.S. POPULATION PYRAMIDS, 1960–2040: THE BABY BOOM AND ITS ECHO

The large baby boom birth cohort will continue to have a significant impact on the U.S. population picture for some time.

Source: Leon F. Bouvier and Carol J. De Vita, "The Baby Boom—Entering Midlife," *Population Bulletin*, Vol. 46, No. 3 (Washington, DC: Population Reference Bureau, Inc. 1991).

Depression Cohort, born 1930-1939

Baby-boom Cohort, born 1946-1964

Baby-bust Cohort, born 1970-1979

Baby-boom Echo Cohort, born 1985-1995

income gap between the two segments has narrowed. Largely because men's incomes (and to a lesser extent, women's) tend to increase as they enter middle age, the younger boomers now earn 79 percent the income of older cohort members, up from 72 percent in 1984. The home-ownership gap has also diminished: The rate of ownership for younger boomers increased from about one-half that of older cohort members in the mid-1980s to approximately two-thirds the rate of the older segment in the early 1990s.

In Mexico, each succeeding generation faces difficulties similar to those of late boomers in the United States. Until the slackening birth rate produces smaller generations, children born in Mexico will enter a society already crowded with competitors.

Patterns of Migration

Demographers study the movements of human populations as well as their composition. Indeed, as one demographer notes, "Our species is distinguished by the distance and frequency of its moves" (du Toit, 1990, p. 305). While the growth rate and age distribution of Mexico contrasts sharply with that of the United States, the population redistribution patterns of the two countries are quite similar, especially with respect to internal **migration.**

Migration: the movement of people from one area to another, usually with the intention of establishing a new residence.

Rural-to-Urban Migration   Cities have always acted as population magnets, but rural-to-urban migration increased in Mexico early this century largely because of land reforms that displaced masses of peasants. Moving to the cities in search of jobs became a means of survival as it has in many other developing countries. Migration into the cities surged in the 1950s despite the inadequacy of urban facilities, services, and jobs. About 1,000 people move to Mexico City alone each day. Desperate people in the countryside see no other alternative—except migration to the United States.

Rural-to-urban migration in Mexico and other developing nations exhibits several patterns (du Toit, 1990). One is "chain migration," in which young adult males (and increasingly, females) establish a "link" in the destination, followed by dependent spouses, children, and parents. This contingent in turn serves as the urban contact for kin or pseudo-kin (such as other members of the village of origin), who use them as a homing device and source of information, orientation, and temporary aid. In the "push–pull" model of migration, economic hardship and lack of excitement provide the "push" for villagers, especially those whose households are deprived relative to their neighbors (Stark and Taylor, 1991); possible jobs and entertainment in the city provide the "pull." The circulation model depicts migrants who go to cities but do not always stay. Movement to cities is sometimes followed by movement back to the village; migrants may circulate between the two with no commitment to either. Much of the migration to cities in Mexico in recent decades has been of this temporary type, a coping strategy to generate earnings for the support of relatives in the home village.

In the United States, people have tended since Colonial times to migrate from outlying, rural areas to cities. The flow increased to a torrent in the mid-1800s, more than a century before Mexico experienced similar patterns of migration in conjunction with its own industrialization. For several decades, however, people in the United States have generally been moving outward from the urban cores toward the fringes of metropolitan areas. In the 1970s, in fact, nonmetropolitan growth was slightly faster than urban growth for the first time in U.S. history, largely because of jobs created by the booming oil industry and farming prosperity. Much of this migration was urban overflow into outlying small towns. This "suburban creep" largely accounted for the 11.3 percent nonmetropolitan growth rate in the 1980s, compared to only 6.1 percent for urban areas.

Demographers have discovered some undercurrents in this rural-to-urban population flow. Rural areas remain overwhelmingly white. Generally speaking, they hold less attraction for minorities, especially Native Americans, who benefit more by migration to urban areas (Jensen and Tienda, 1989). Age is another factor. Rather than flee urban areas altogether, many people moved into the original suburbs years ago and stayed there into their old age. In fact, by 1977 a majority of the elderly had settled in suburbs, where many are now in need of special government services (Golant, 1990).

Migration Between Regions   Another dimension of internal migration involves population movement from one region of a country to another. Mexico experienced nothing analogous to the U.S. population shift during the 1970s and 1980s from the older industrial centers of the northeastern and northcentral states—the "Frost Belt"—to the "Sunbelt" states of the West and South, especially Florida, California, and Texas. Lured by weaker unions and lower labor costs, businesses flocked to these regions, bringing with them tax revenues, jobs, and, at least in urban areas, prosperity (Lyson, 1989). The subsequent increase in population has given these states proportionally more influence in national politics. The frenetic pace of this Sunbelt growth is not expected to continue.

International Migration   Patterns of international migration—movement between countries—reveal Mexico and the United States as almost mirror images of each other, one a source of migration and the other a destination. The "push" of domestic economic hardship in Mexico combined with the "pull" of economic opportunity in the United States has lured millions of Mexican people to their northern neighbor. This case illustrates the worldwide flow of people from poor nations to rich ones, which has increased in recent decades due to improvements in communication and transportation. In fact, a 1993 United Nations Population Fund study estimated that at least 100 million people live in some country other than the one of their birth.

The Mexican migration to the United States has produced complaints that migrants are displacing U.S. citizens from jobs, depressing wage levels, and sending much of their earnings back home. (Most migrants do indeed take jobs, jobs the natives often refuse, and many businesses depend on migrants' willingness to work for substandard wages.) Another fear is based on the sheer number of migrants, many of whom are illegally in the country, uncountable, and very difficult to deter.

Garrett Hardin (1991) recommends that all nations restrict such migration, with an eye for population control. Fast-growing, poor nations might become more serious about population policies, he argues, if deprived of this convenient safety valve. Certainly the United States, whose immigration accounts for nearly half of its annual population growth, could more quickly approach ZPG. On the other hand, immigrants have long been a source of new talent and energy for the United States. Similarly, Western Europe has seen the need to import immigrant labor for decades to supplement its aging populations. These non-European, often nonwhite workers, however, have elicited resentment and discrimination in the host nations. From the conflict perspective, these developed countries are exploiting the valuable labor of their poorer neighbors. International migration restrictions would benefit the developing nations, who often lose many of their brightest citizens to richer nations. This

Today's international migration has reached a scale previously unknown among humans. Over 100 million people have moved from their homeland, and this mass of migrants now includes many women and teenage girls searching for employment so as to support their families back home.

"brain drain" of the most educated and skilled individuals to the comforts and security of developed countries has been going on for decades. In any event, it will not be easy to restrict the centuries-old movement of people across borders, especially when "pushes" and "pulls" continue to exert strong effects.

While migration from Mexico to the United States is fueled by economics, especially by the desire for better jobs and higher living standards, other factors are at work in many instances of international population movement. For example, religious and ethnic persecution, war, and political oppression are all partly responsible for the massive dislocations of people in former Yugoslavia.

This demographic overview of the United States and Mexico illustrates the kind of changing population patterns that exist in many other countries, some enjoying the advantages of a well-educated, relatively content, stabilizing population and others struggling against wave after wave of the hungry, poor, and oppressed.

Using Demography to Pinpoint Markets

Research Box

Of all the fields of sociology, demographics has perhaps the most lucrative applications. Cheryl Russell (1991) offers one illustration in her picture of the huge group of consumers between the ages of 25 and 44. Baby boomers are an appealing marketing target due to their overall affluence. Members of this cohort are typically engrossed in childrearing, paying for a mortgage, and saving for retirement and their children's college education. Rather than luxury and self-indulgence, these practical, family-oriented consumers are more interested in quality and value. Looking ahead, this large cohort will begin to produce many empty nesters and widows in the next few decades.

A similar application of demographics predicts and pinpoints the market for contact lenses (Exter, 1988). One marketing research company has found that many adults are switching from eyeglasses to contact lenses. Furthermore, young adults are more likely to wear contact lenses than are older people, and women are more likely to do so than men. Also, those with college experience generally prefer contact lenses over eyeglasses. Using the contact-lens usage rate for each of these groups, and factoring in the changing age, sex, and education characteristics of the population, it is easier to market the product. Similar predictions are made for other consumer markets, often with the large baby boom cohort in mind. □

THREE CITIES, THREE URBAN AGES

The world population explosion parallels a dramatic surge in **urbanization,** the process in which increasing proportions of people become concentrated in cities and suburbs. Like the population explosion, large-scale urbanization occurred very recently relative to the span of human existence. Until the last century or so, the world's few cities were pinpoints in an overwhelmingly rural landscape, most with relatively few people. In the approaching twenty-first century, however, more than half of the world's massive population will reside in urban areas.

Urbanization: the process in which increasing proportions of the population become concentrated in cities and suburbs.

Despite its long agricultural heritage, the United States is not immune to this global trend. In 1990, the Census Bureau reported that for the first time more than half of all Americans live in large metropolitan centers rather than in small cities or rural areas. As we will see, the bulk of that growth has occurred in the suburban fringes of the urban areas, where most of us seek the age-old benefits of the countryside along with the excitement, opportunities, and services of the city.

Today's new kind of urban area represents the latest evolutionary form of urbanization. The world's first cities were relatively small, tightly packed, and intensely focused. In the nineteenth century, industrialization produced enormous urban populations centered around dominating centers. Today's urban areas resemble growing amoebas with several nuclei. The following description of three cities provides an overview of this evolutionary process. It also offers some clues as to where we are headed next.

The Preindustrial City: Teotihuacan, Mexico

The first cities arose around 5,000 years ago in Mesopotamia, the land watered by the Tigris and Euphrates rivers, in what is today part of Iraq. The valleys of the Indus River in Pakistan, the Nile in Egypt, and the Yellow River in China also sprouted cities about this time. These ancient settlements, each of which had several thousand inhabitants, represented not simply an increase in population density but a new form of social existence. **Urbanism** connotes a way of life in cities characterized by increased social differentiation and stratification. Why did this new way of life arise in these few places after millennia of rural existence?

Urbanism: a way of life in cities characterized by increased social differentiation and stratification.

The prime requirement of urbanization is the ability to produce a surplus: A society must generate enough food and other necessary goods to allow a sector of the population to provide services and luxury items. As Gideon Sjoberg (1960) explains, the earliest urban sites enjoyed the three necessary conditions for surplus production: a climate and soil suitable for large-scale agriculture, advanced technology (such as irrigation and the iron plow), and a well-organized power structure. At the same time, most preindustrial cities were limited in size by relatively inefficient food production techniques, poor food transportation and storage systems, and lack of sanitation facilities and public health measures. Babylon, for example, covered only a little over three square miles. Most cities until the 1800s contained fewer than 20,000 people.

The first city in the New World, Teotihuacan, was unusually large, encompassing at its peak over 100,000 people and more than eight square miles (Kandell, 1988). It arose in the Valley of Mexico during the first century B.C. near spring waters that sustained irrigation projects. Other than its unusual size, its spatial arrangements and social structure closely resembled the cities of the Old World, and it serves as a useful illustration of the first evolutionary phase of urbanization.

Spatial Arrangement   Like most ancient and medieval cities, Teotihuacan employed walls for defense and demarcation of the various city districts. In this case, rather than bounding the city perimeter the walls enclosed the temples, palaces, and granaries of the city's central citadel. This sacred quarter incorporated the city's political and religious powers. Main thoroughfares radiated from this center, with narrow secondary streets serving the several thousand stone and mudbrick houses of craftsmen, merchants, and warriors. The neighborhoods were well-defined, displaying one of the basic processes of urbanization: ecological differentiation of activities (MacKensie, 1925). In Teotihuacan, as in most preindustrial cities, some districts were given

Preindustrial cities offered a
new way of life: urbanism.

over to specific crafts—pottery, weaving, and so on. Similarly, streets in medieval
cities were usually dominated by particular occupations, sometimes even kinship
groups.

Segregation   The spatial arrangement of Teotihuacan also illustrates the clear
social-class segregation of early cities. In such a closely packed environment, the two
social classes were not separated by great distances, but the elite lived comfortably in
the center while the lower classes' shabby residences fanned outward. The occupations
of some of the poor required access to the outlying rural lands, or they produced
unpleasant smells or sights that required as much distancing as possible from the upper
classes. The elite clustered around the city's facilities and enjoyed greater protection
from invasion.

The Industrial City: Chicago, 1860–1920

By the early 1800s, most urban areas still had fewer than 5,000 inhabitants, and in many ways functioned similarly to preindustrial cities like Teotihuacan. Even in the larger commercial cities, people clustered tightly around the centers' stores, manufacturing shops, transportation facilities, and political structures. Rich and poor still lived in separate neighborhoods, but they were so closely situated to each other that a great deal of social integration was still possible. By mid-century, however, a new urban form quickly evolved as one of the most visible dimensions of the Industrial Revolution. This type of city was large, organized around specialized factory production, and characterized by a relatively open class system.

Industrial cities grew rapidly, attracting people from rural areas and assimilating masses of immigrants. Only about 20 percent of those in the United States lived in urban areas of any kind, including small towns, by the beginning of the Civil War. The enormous growth of cities doubled that percentage by century's end. Chicago represents an excellent example of a city coming of age during this period of rapid economic and social change. In 1860, it had around 100,000 citizens; by 1920, despite the great fire of 1871, that figure rose to 2.7 million. Chicago doubled in size during the 1880s alone. What spurred such furious growth?

Like most cities, old as well as modern, Chicago grew largely because of its advantageous location. Situated at the juncture of the Great Lakes system and the Mississippi River basin, it dominates the main natural arteries of the Midwest. As Blake McKelvey (1963) points out, industrial cities expanded near mineral resources, at water power or transportation sources, at destination points for immigrants, at railroad centers, and at major breaks in transportation routes where goods had to be transferred—for example, from ships to rail cars. David Meyer (1990) observes that those

Industrial cities mushroomed into populations of millions of people tightly packed around a dominating city center featuring tall buildings and mass transit.

cities in a position to control economic exchange in regional markets were more likely to emerge as industrial giants.

A succession of transportation innovations emerged in response to the great need to disperse huge urban populations. Beginning in the 1830s, horse-drawn omnibusses, steam-powered commuter trains, bridges, and ferries allowed the upper and middle classes to work downtown and reside in the less congested, quieter outlying districts. Chicago built the nation's largest cable car system in the 1800s and, like most other surging industrial cities, embraced the electrified trolley by the turn of the century. Subways followed in some cities; Chicago and others constructed elevated tracks.

Chicago also boasted the first skyscraper fashioned of steel and light masonry in 1885. The subsequent tall office structures, apartment buildings, and tenements helped Chicago and other industrial cities grow upward as well as outward. Multi-family residences such as those mushrooming along Chicago's Gold Coast became acceptable for middle-class and even wealthy families. The shabby, rickety tenements quickly became slums to entrap the poor, especially immigrants, as a pool of cheap labor for the nearby factories.

Segregation   The social segregation evident in preindustrial cities continued in places like nineteenth-century Chicago, but in a different form. As the city spread outward because of the liberating effects of mass transit in the late 1800s, the social classes, races, and ethnic groups became separated by greater distances. Black ghettoes and ethnic enclaves emerged in the city center, while the suburbs were overwhelmingly middle-class. The suburban neighborhoods themselves were clearly ranked according to the income levels of their inhabitants. This geographical distancing contributed to greater social distance and the anonymity so characteristic of urban life today.

Another new feature of the industrial city was its relatively open power structure. The preindustrial city had been characterized by long ancestral lines of elite families who presided over a rigid class structure. Chicago was ruled by a powerful elite, but the city's dynamic growth constantly created entryways into the inner circle. Dizzying economic and physical expansion translated into opportunities for social mobility that were rare in preindustrial cities.

Spatial Arrangement   As Chicago's industrial growth peaked near 1920, it spawned the study of human ecology at the University of Chicago. Robert Park and Ernest Burgess (1921) postulated that human behaviors affect the city's spatial arrangements and vice versa. Along with their colleagues at "the Chicago School," they created models depicting the various zones of homogeneous land use in their city. (See Figure 13-6.)

The concentric zone model fit Chicago quite well, as it did other cities that grew quickly during the industrial era. The central zone of the model contains the central business district: shops, government buildings, and businesses. Radiating outward from this zone are a transitional zone of low-income housing mixed with business and light industry, working-class residential neighborhoods, middle-class areas of apartments and homes, and the outlying suburban zones first inhabited by the well-to-do.

Burgess noted that each of these zones was continually expanding outward, explaining the relentless sprawl of cities like Chicago, which absorbed its streetcar suburbs like Hyde Park, Woodlawn, and Pullman in the late 1890s. This expansion was fueled by ecological **invasion:** new populations or activities coming into an area. As factories invaded Chicago at the end of the nineteenth century, for example, land values in the city center shot up; residences were leveled and replaced by

Invasion: new populations or activities coming into an area.

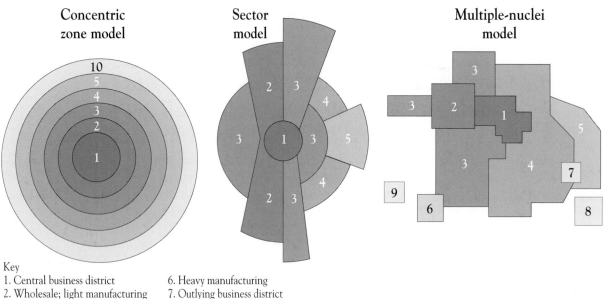

Concentric zone model

Sector model

Multiple-nuclei model

Key
1. Central business district
2. Wholesale; light manufacturing
3. Low-class residential
4. Middle-class residential
5. High-class residential
6. Heavy manufacturing
7. Outlying business district
8. Residential suburb
9. Industrial suburb
10. Commuters' zone

Figure 13-6

MODELS OF URBAN STRUCTURE

Sociologists describe three basic forms of urban structure. The concentric zone model describes a business core and other rings that reach outward to more affluent residential neighborhoods. The sector model is based on transportation arteries. The multiple-nuclei model focuses on land uses and costs.

Source: Reprinted from "The Nature of Cities," by Chauncy D. Harris and Edward L. Ullman in volume 242 (November 1945), p. 13, of *Annals of the American Academy of Political and Social Science.* Copyright, 1945, by The American Academy of Political and Social Science. All rights reserved.

Succession: the process in which one population or activity displaces another in an area.

skyscrapers. When this invasion was more or less complete, the new population or activity having replaced the former one, **succession** had occurred.

The concentric zone model did not accurately describe many other cities, especially those which grew to prominence during the era of the automobile. Homer Hoyt (1939) noted that some cities had developed from a central business district but, instead of concentric circles, the growth patterns took the form of sectors extending outward from the center. These wedge-shaped sectors generally followed transportation arteries. Secondary business districts radiated outward along streetcar lines. Warehouse districts formed along railway lines and trucking routes.

Still other cities seemed to have no single center. Chauncy Harris and Edward Ullman (1945) developed the multiple-nuclei model to depict cities with several centers of specialized districts: a number of business districts, one or more concentrations of government buildings, several areas of heavy industry, and so on. Each nucleus forms around the facilities and economic conditions it requires. For example, industrial districts form near transportation facilities. High-income residential nuclei cluster near such attractions as waterfront and beautiful trees, and away from factories and slums. Warehouses collect on large parcels of inexpensive land near transportation arteries.

The Postindustrial City: New Metropolitan Areas

As the old industrial cities like Chicago peaked in size and dominance around 1920, countertrends were already at work creating the urban form that would succeed and supplant them. Factories in search of cheaper land, lower taxes, more pliant government policies, and less commuting for their skilled workers, relocated away from the city core. Commercial and residential areas followed. In the first two decades of the twentieth century, this dispersion of the industrial city's population began to create increasingly self-sufficient communities on the metropolitan outskirts.

In some cases, the resulting suburbs or satellite cities resisted annexation by the sprawling industrial metropolis and became independent entities, acorns taking root in the shadow of the mother tree. Even when absorbed, these outlying districts were metropolitan centers in their own right. New cities, in other words, emerged around old industrial centers which then often became, like Newark, New Jersey, just one of many local centers.

After about 1945, the old industrial cities began to show visible signs of decline. Chicago lost 400,000 jobs between 1947 and 1977. Detroit lost 600,000 people between 1950 and 1980, Cleveland about one-third its population, St. Louis nearly half. Meanwhile, a new urban form was evolving, a decentralized urban area alternately labelled, among other things, slurb, spread city, sprawl, urban field, and others. The U.S. Census Bureau uses the term **metropolitan area** to refer to an area with a large population nucleus along with any adjoining communities economically and socially integrated into that central area.

The modern urban landscape also includes the **megalopolis,** a huge conglomeration of two or more metropolitan areas. The "BosWash" megalopolis stretches along the northeast coast of the United States from Boston to Washington, DC. Others are found along the Great Lakes, the southeastern Florida coast, the California coast, Southeast England, and the Rhine Valley in Germany.

What causes this sprawling decentralization? Since the nineteenth century, people have sought the tranquility, clean air, lower crime levels, and spaciousness of low-density living in the city's outskirts. More recent technological developments have further weakened the magnetic pull of the city. The automobile, for example, helped fill in the spaces between the urbanizing lines of mass transit. So did improvements in humbler technologies like well-drilling, septic tank construction, and rural electrification.

Metropolitan area: an area with a large population nucleus and any adjoining communities economically and socially integrated into that central area.

Megalopolis: a huge conglomeration of two or more metropolitan areas.

Today's postindustrial cities, free to sprawl because of automobiles and telecommunications, have formed vast collages of mixed land usages.

The trucking industry similarly freed commercial and industrial areas from the grip of the city core and rail lines.

A less visible, but equally influential, technology is telecommunications. Computers increasingly facilitate the substitution of face-to-face communication. Fax machines, teleconferencing, national electronic bulletin boards, and other innovations free workers to seek remote workplaces and residences. Large numbers of data manipulation and analysis jobs have located in small towns and suburban fringes as businesses set up shop wherever their skilled workers desire to live and work. The emerging information and services society is not shackled to the urban core. Today's new businesses do not usually depend on a nearby rail line, docks, or mines—only a phone line for electronically transmitted information and a road for truck deliveries. Computers also free consumers from downtown commercial areas: Electronic shopping and banking are becoming commonplace. The attraction of the urban core's museums and concert halls likewise weakens in the face of electronic storage and transmission of top-quality entertainment and the promise of "virtual reality" simulations.

Government policies encouraged this urban decentralization for several decades after World War II. The federal government subsidized new suburban housing and funded highway construction. Local communities lured businesses with low tax rates and other incentives. The large numbers of Social Security–supported retirees added to the demand for housing and services away from the crumbling urban core.

The women's liberation movement has also facilitated urban decentralization. Developers realized by the 1970s the advantage of putting jobs in the suburbs, where legions of well-educated women resided (Garreau, 1991).

Spatial Arrangement   The postindustrial city encompasses hundreds of square miles, and lacks definable boundaries or a single dominant core (Fishman, 1990). Within this milieu, residents tend to measure distance in terms of minutes rather than miles. Each person's mental construct of "city" corresponds to his or her usual destinations: job, church, recreation, and so on. Distinctions between residential, industrial, and commercial zones are increasingly blurred. The modern city resembles a vast grid—of shopping malls, industrial parks, and housing developments—rather than concentric rings or neat sectors. As open spaces are swallowed up by this sprawling urban landscape, critics worry that "The new city seems to be an environment as out of control as the old metropolis" (Fishman, p. 44).

Segregation   African Americans and other minorities have joined the trek to the suburbs, especially since the 1970s. In many metropolitan areas, blacks are moving to the suburbs at rates equal to or greater than those of whites. Minorities still often find themselves in segregated neighborhoods, however. Hispanics in the Northeast are likely to be concentrated in isolated pockets of poverty, as are blacks outside the West (Massey and Eggers, 1990). Blacks typically move into aging suburbs abandoned by whites, illustrating the invasion–succession processes (Stahura, 1988). Still, signs of progress can be discerned. Whites still prefer limited contact with blacks, but increasingly they agree when questioned that African Americans might be acceptable neighbors (Massey and Gross, 1991). Peter Wood and Barrett Lee (1991) see neighborhood racial invasion–succession as less inevitable now than it was several decades ago. Whites are less likely to move out of a neighborhood when blacks move in.

Gentrification: the restoration of a neglected urban neighborhood by middle- and upper-middle-class newcomers.

Researchers have identified several segregation patterns in today's cities. Similar to the formation of a megalopolis, "extreme poverty tracts" typically enlarge and overlap to form larger poor areas (Greene, 1991). The process of **gentrification** typically involves the restoration of a crumbling, neglected neighborhood of former elegance. These old homes offer not only the charm of fine woodwork, gracious high ceilings, and quaint architectural facades, but their location affords convenience to the surviving attractions of downtown, especially some high-level jobs. These islands of middle- and upper-middle-class comfort, however, are usually surrounded by a sea of poverty. The resentments and fears inherent in this social gap often produces hatred and violence (Sleeper, 1982; Taylor and Covington, 1988).

As the population and functions of the postindustrial city decentralize, we can expect power to likewise spread out to small towns and rural areas. *Convergence theory* holds that telecommunications and the emerging service sector are erasing urban–rural differences and increasing the freedom of both businesses and individuals to locate where they please (Frey, 1987). Other researchers note, however, that managerial and professional occupations, as well as services that control the operations of other industries, are still heavily concentrated in metropolitan areas (Cook and Beck, 1991). The computer networks that determine the flow of information are likewise centered in large cities (Hepworth, 1990). Power, it seems, will diffuse only when decision makers abandon the major metropolitan areas.

This third, postindustrial form of the city undoubtedly does not represent the final evolutionary stage. While we can only guess at what will follow, we see next how the spatial dispersion of the city has already blurred traditional distinctions between urban and community living.

A COMPARISON OF LIFE IN URBAN, SUBURBAN, AND RURAL COMMUNITIES

Stereotypes often impair our efforts to judge and evaluate. The image of the dysfunctional, crime-ridden, frenetic city, for example, might hide from us the rich exuberance and exciting opportunities urban life has to offer. Condescending stereotypes of suburban life as "bedroom communities composed of self-satisfied lawn-rakers and smug backyard barbecuers" (Rybczynski, 1992, p. 110) can affect our own assessment. Do we expect rural communities to offer quietude and folksy intimacy or closed-minded neighbors and old tires dumped on our property? The research of social scientists can help us move beyond such stereotypes in evaluating the three basic types of communities.

Urbanism Analyzed

Sociologists began to analyze the emerging sense of community in cities over a century ago, beginning with Ferdinand Tönnies's *Community and Society* in 1887.

A New Kind of Community   Tönnies created two models to contrast life in rural communities with that in the new large cities. Small towns and villages are typically characterized by a **gemeinschaft,** in which social relations are based on intimacy, cooperation, and emotional satisfaction. Shared values and life style help cement the bonds among community members and provide a clear set of behavioral guidelines;

Gemeinschaft: a model of community social relations characterized by intimacy, cooperation, and emotional satisfaction.

everyone knows which behaviors are proper and which will be considered outrageous. People are held in check by the informal sanctions imposed by kin and neighbors. Gossip and the withholding of respect act as formidable deterrents. The delinquent child finds that virtually all the adults in the community act as overseers. Along with the social controls, however, comes social support. Members of the *gemeinschaft* identify with others in the community and stand ready to lend a hand. In short, the well-being of the group as a whole takes precedence over the rights or wants of the individual.

Gesellschaft: a model of community social relations characterized by individual life style freedom and impersonal, formal, competitive relationships.

The urban environment, in contrast, is likely to be characterized by a **gesellschaft.** In this type of society, relationships are more impersonal. Social cohesion is based not on the sameness of the members but their interdependence. Secondary relationships rather than kin networks meet most of the individual's needs. Life style choices are not confined to tradition, and behaviors are held in check only by formal laws and enforcement agencies. Since these controls are relatively easy to circumvent, those in a *gesellschaft* enjoy considerable personal freedom. Moreover, one's neighbors are likely to be seen as competitors who seek advantages rather than willing helpers. Formal contracts replace reciprocity in economic dealings. For better or worse, contemporary society has shifted from a *gemeinschaft* to a *gesellschaft.*

Emile Durkheim, another contemporary observer of the late nineteenth-century transition from rural to urban life, discerned changing types of social solidarity. People in preindustrial communities hold similar occupations and share a strong collective conscience, or system of basic values and norms that overwhelms individuality. Just as molecules of an inorganic substance are united in the inanimate body, members of such societies work together as part of an integrated whole. Durkheim labeled this form of community cohesion **mechanical solidarity.** Based on homogeneity, tradition, and consensus, this type of solidarity is found only in the few simple societies not yet engulfed by the tide of global urbanization.

Mechanical solidarity: community cohesion based on collective conscience, homogeneity, tradition, and consensus.

Organic solidarity: community cohesion based on specialization and interdependence.

As societies urbanize and develop a more complex division of labor, community cohesion is increasingly based on specialization and interdependence. **Organic solidarity** resembles a living organism in that each organ is specialized and somewhat autonomous, performing its own different function. The urbanized society of the United States is obviously characterized by organic solidarity.

Strangers and Stress   Louis Wirth's classic 1938 essay "Urbanism as a Way of Life" extended the view of Tönnies that population size strongly affects people's patterns of behavior. A large population size, according to Wirth, means increased human interaction and relationships characterized by anonymity, superficiality, and competition. Those who live in cities may thus have many acquaintances but few deep social ties. Wirth also blamed urban population density for greater social friction, the predominance of formal control mechanisms, and segregation. He pointed out that city people experience close physical contact but considerable social distance. Finally, he noted that the heterogeneity of urban life creates instability, insecurity, and depersonalization in social relations.

Other researchers have likewise perceived a link between a city's population size and its sense of community. Near the turn of the century, Georg Simmel contended that the sheer number of strangers encountered in an urban environment forces city dwellers to maintain a protective aloofness. And Stanley Milgram (1972) describes how this stressful sensory or psychic overload results in the city resident's frozen face focused on some middle distance.

But there is more to a city than the size or density of its population. Urban crime rates are more than double those of rural areas; the difference in violent offenses is even greater. High crime rates, however, do not result merely from large concentrations of people. Rodney Stark (1987) identifies several characteristics of urban life related to crime, including poverty, mixed land use, transience, and dilapidation. Such conditions do not by themselves cause crime but are likely to prompt responses that lead to crime: moral cynicism among the residents, more opportunities and greater motivation to commit crime, and decreased neighborhood control. Ralph Taylor and Jeanette Covington (1988) found the upsurge of crime in Baltimore, Maryland, linked to two variables: (1) the relative deprivation felt by poor residents in gentrifying neighborhoods, and (2) family breakdown in emerging underclass neighborhoods.

The dreariness of urban life pervades some neighborhoods where unemployment hovers at around 80 percent and adult volunteers must guard the perimeter of the schoolyard each day so children can play safely during recess. Added to this is the surge in homelessness that has blighted American cities since the 1980s. Another indication of urban decay is the abandonment of inner cities by supermarkets following their middle-class customers to the suburbs, leaving the poor with higher grocery prices. Growing numbers of Asian Americans and Hispanics compete with blacks in these desperate neighborhoods, heightening ethnic tensions. Drugs, unsupervised children, and cutbacks in federal funding during the 1980s have all contributed to the deterioration of many inner-city communities.

Opportunities, Friendships, and Excitement   We would be guilty of stereotyping, however, if we failed to note the positive aspects of urban life. For one thing, city living is not inherently stressful and unstable. Life expectancy is higher for metropolitan populations (Potter and Galle, 1990). Also, cities generally offer more social services, better health care, and safer water and sewer systems. And studies have found no significant differences in the suicide rates of urban and rural areas (Schroeder and Beegle, 1953; Lester and Frank, 1990).

Other researchers question the Tönnies–Durkheim–Simmel–Wirth thesis that a larger population size inevitably produces lower levels of community attachment. Of

Urban residents do not necessarily suffer alienation, stress, and loneliness.

course, personal relationships can be intense and intimate in a densely populated environment. Herbert Gans (1982) found strong community loyalty and cohesion in ethnic neighborhoods of large cities. Bartolomeo Palisi and Claire Canning (1983) observe that urbanites visit friends as much as or more than people in suburban or rural environments. Claude Fischer (1976, 1982) notes that a large population enables those who share a subculture to gather enough people to maintain the shops, churches, and other supportive elements of their distinctive way of life. Such diversity enriches and enlivens the urban experience.

Fischer (1981) also questions the stereotype of anonymous, lonely urban dwellers. He contends that those who live in the city have no fewer social ties than rural residents and that urbanites' distrust of "foreign" groups or people is limited to the public, not the private, sphere. Urban people seem colder because they deal with strangers more frequently, but not differently, than those in rural communities.

Other research supports this line of reasoning. Karen Franck (1980) studied two groups of migrants: those who moved to New York City and those who moved to a town with a population of 31,000. Seven months after the transition, the two groups of newcomers were similar as to the number of friendships they established and the frequency of contact with those friends. The only difference was that the New Yorkers found a greater barrier of mistrust and fear to overcome and greater initial difficulty in forming friendships. Similarly, John Kasarda and Morris Janowitz (1974) found that residents who remain in densely populated neighborhoods long enough to form stable, dependable relationships can penetrate the anonymity of city life.

Mark Baldassare (1982) suggests that some urban stress results from lack of resources rather than high population density. He describes a typical urban neighborhood in which many residents are renters who, with little capital and several children, feel unable to control events in their crowded locale. Such an environment is likely to exhibit high strain and low satisfaction—but the same results might be expected in a rural area with similar lack of resources and control.

In view of such research, we can conclude that urban life is not necessarily characterized by alienation, emotional stress, and loneliness. If cities are not as bad as their reputation, are suburbs the paradise many of us seem to think?

Suburban Living

Intellectuals have long criticized life in the suburbs as blandly homogeneous and its residents as anxiously conformist. Yet, beginning with the construction of Llewellyn Park in 1857 just outside New York City, millions of people have sought the promise of the best of both urban and rural environments. The first suburbs housed those wealthy enough to make commuting feasible. The streetcar later gave the middle classes access to the suburban dream. The automobile helped create the heterogeneous, populous suburbs of today. The 1970 census revealed that for the first time more people lived in the metropolitan areas outside central cities than anywhere else. The 1990 census fixed the number of suburbanites at 46.2 percent of the U.S. population.

As more people have joined the exodus to the suburbs, however, the problems of urban life have tagged along: nightmarish traffic congestion during commuting hours, economic segregation created by the abandonment of inner cities, and social isolation in air-conditioned homes and cars perhaps worse than the supposedly alienating city neighborhood.

In response to the resulting disappointment with suburbia, urban planners are now designing instant small-town environments in new or retrofitted suburbs. Andres

Suburbanites often find they are isolated from their neighbors in their homes and cars.

Duany and Elizabeth Plater-Zyberk (1992) have spearheaded this development. Local planners and zoning boards, they contend, designed suburbs for cars, not people, thus destroying civic life and community. Partly because the elements of the town migrated to the suburbs at different times (first residences, then stores, then offices), suburban development segregated these elements. Also, typical suburban layouts, based on collector streets connecting one area with another, virtually guarantee that residents use their cars to go everywhere. The result is not only social isolation but the paradox of traffic jams in low-density environments. Duany and Plater-Zyberk use straight-line road grids to diffuse the traffic in communities. Trees, building-size limits, and other techniques create public space "that draws people out from their private realms to stroll and loiter with their neighbors" (p. 39).

Several "instant small towns" planned along these lines have recently broken ground, attesting to a widespread disillusionment with suburban life. A common feature is a hub containing a supermarket, stores, elementary schools, and other essentials, all within walking distance of the entire neighborhood. The goals of such projects as Seaside (in Florida's panhandle), Kentlands (Gaithersburg, Md.), and Montgomery Village (Princeton, N.J.) are both convenience and a sense of community.

At least two problems, however, have already surfaced in these planned environments. First, most lack easy access to workplaces or mass transit. Second, houses in such developments often carry a sizable price tag, often eliminating the working and even middle classes from these supposedly diverse, "small-town" environments. Furthermore, while the tight packing of residences may facilitate walking, it runs counter to the widespread American preference for large homes and larger yards (Saltzman, 1990).

Beyond the planned suburban community, cohousing offers an escape from the "single-family fortresses, with their porchless exteriors and fenced-in yards, that now define most suburbs" (Streisand, 1992, p. 82). In perhaps a dozen places in the United States, groups of people have designed and constructed clusters of single-family homes on communal property in such a way as to reduce privacy but maximize a sense of community. Typically, cohousing developments are centered around a common house where meals are shared and child care and recreation are centered.

Rural Life: A Nonromantic View

Ironically, although for over 200 years people in the United States have tended to migrate to metropolitan areas, they have all the while romanticized rural life as clean, moral, and healthful. However, life in the country was never as idyllic as imagined by those trapped in sooty industrial cities or today's chaotic urban areas, and today it is not as identifiably rural, either.

Tönnies's *gesellschaft*, Durkheim's organic solidarity, and other descriptions of urbanism increasingly apply to virtually all of modern society's landscapes, from the piney woods to the asphalt jungle. From the 1920s to the 1970s, the number of people living in rural areas (including small towns) declined. In the last two decades, rural populations have grown, but they have also become more urbanized. Much of this "rural" expansion has consisted of urbanites staying one step ahead of encroaching metropolitan sprawl. Also, telecommunications have broadcast urban tastes, attitudes, and values into the countryside.

Just as evidence has mounted that the large, dense populations of cities do not automatically lead to anonymity and loneliness, recent research challenges the assumption that a smaller population translates into stronger social bonds. For example, Willis Goudy (1990) found that the longer people have lived in a community, and the greater their freedom to select social ties, the more positively they evaluate their local attachments. This is not surprising, but as we have seen, Kasarda and Janowitz (1974) identify the same variables at work in the city.

This is not to say, however, that urban areas exhibit as much social cohesion as rural ones. The same determinants of community attachment may operate in both environments, but they are usually more prevalent in areas that are still essentially rural. Thus, insofar as rural communities have more cohesion, we can expect crime rates to be lower. Research results by Gregory Kowalski and Don Duffield (1990) "indicate that the traditional bond of group cohesion assumed to be associated with the rural environment and its residents continues to have an inhibiting effect on homicide in the United States" (p. 76). As urban migrants and telecommunications invade this rural setting, however, such "inhibiting effects" are likely to diminish, narrowing rural–urban differences in crime rates.

Many living in outlying areas watch with chagrin as the quaintness and solidarity of their communities disappear under wave upon wave of urban immigration. As we would expect, small towns that are rocked by extremely rapid population growth lose some of their "rural" cohesion. In their study of one small Western town that experienced a "boom" during the 1980s, Ralph Brown, H. Reed Geertsen and Richard Krannich (1989) found that considerable social disruption accompanied rapid expansion. Moreover, the small-town, preboom feelings of satisfaction with community services and attachment to neighbors did not return during the subsequent bust phase of the growth cycle.

The contrasts between urban, suburban, and rural living have become muted by demographic and technological changes. Accordingly, social-class level, age, race, geographical stability, and other variables take on more importance in determining an individual's quality of life.

Saving Public Places or Hassling the Homeless?

The early 1990s saw a heightened interest in cleaning up city streets across the United States. This cleaning, however, had less to do with rubbish than with panhandlers and vagrants. John Leo (1992) describes the controversy revolving around this movement.

On the one hand, do such programs illustrate once again the persecution of society's victims? Do not poor and homeless people have the right to ask for money? The enterprising youngsters who clean windshields at red lights are merely trying to earn a few dollars in a society that offers them no alternatives. Critics charge that our society has no more compassion; those who once gave beggars money and contributed to charitable causes are now turning mean, and want to obliterate the specter of down-and-out, homeless people. The clean-up programs represent nothing less than a war on the poor.

On the other hand, James Q. Wilson and George Kelling (1982) contend that these new public attitudes are a recognition of the "broken window" theory of social decay. When broken windows are not fixed, or graffiti is not removed, they say, a signal is sent to residents that no one cares about social conditions any more. Morale erodes, vandalism becomes common, properties deteriorate. Criminals, drug dealers, and prostitutes ply their trades openly, and the neighborhood quickly disintegrates. From this perspective, clean-up efforts are entirely justified—in fact, necessary—if a community wants to arrest its slide into social decay. Of course, this argument could also be used to rationalize or justify oppression.

Which view do you think best characterizes these clean-up campaigns: residents merely salvaging their public places from deterioration or making war on the poor? ■

SUMMARY

We can investigate predictions like those of Thomas Robert Malthus using *demography*, the scientific study of the size, distribution, and composition of populations. His belief that population growth would outrun the world's food supply seems to be born out, at least in part, by recent trends. While social and technological advances have averted demographic catastrophe in developed nations, undeveloped countries are already experiencing the effects of overpopulation: low *life expectancy rates* (the average number of years a person born in a specific year can be expected to live), and high *infant mortality rates* (the annual number of deaths of children under age 1 per 1,000 live births), *fertility rates* (the annual number of live births per 1,000 women of childbearing age), *crude death rates* (the annual number of deaths per 1,000 total population), and *crude birth rates* (the annual number of births per 1,000 total population), as well as environmental dangers. *Demographic transition theory* explains how initially small, stable populations experience substantial growth and restabilization through a three-stage decline in death rates and, later, birth rates. Some developed nations have experienced declining fertility rates to the point they are now below replacement level, but many developing nations today move quickly into the high-growth stage of transition. Consequently, they will take a long time to reach *zero population growth* (ZPG), a state of no growth in a population in which the number of births and immigrants is equal to or less than the number of deaths and emigrants. Conflict theorists argue that we should focus our attention less on overpopulation than on the exploitation that keeps these nations poor and in fact encourages excessive growth.

One strategy for dealing with population growth is birth control. Despite technological breakthroughs, contraceptive use is lowest in many of the fastest-growing nations due to gender-role notions, perceived costs and risks, and so on. Government birth control programs have been successful in China. A second approach focuses on social and economic development, assuming that as a nation's standard of living rises, values will change toward a smaller family size.

A nation's *population pyramid* depicts the proportions of the sexes and age groups in a society. Mexico's pyramid shows that society's greater biological potential for fertility, or *fecundity*, and that Mexico will take longer than the United States to reach ZPG, the consequences of which include a labor shortage and a larger proportion of elderly people. The proportion of people of nonworking age, or *dependency ratio*, in Mexico is increased by its large number of children, as it is in America by the growing percentage of people over 65. Both these countries have a balanced proportion of men to women, or *sex ratio*. The U.S. population pyramid shows a large *birth cohort* of people born between 1946 and 1964: the "baby boom." People born late in this cohort have faced reduced opportunities, although this effect is lessening. Mexico and the United States exhibit similar patterns of rural-to-urban *migration*, or movement of people from one area to another, usually with the intention of establishing a new residence. The flood of people from Mexico's countryside into its cities is explained by "chain migration," the "push–pull" model, and the circulation model. U.S. internal migration has recently been outward from urban cores, and from the northeastern and northcentral states to the South and West. Between these two nations we see a pattern found all over the world: the flow of people from poor countries to rich ones. Migration from Mexico to the United States has elicited some fears, and, in fact, restriction of such international movements of people might influence population control efforts.

Another relatively recent development in the human experience is *urbanization*, the process in which increasing proportions of the population become concentrated in cities and suburbs. Preindustrial cities like Teotihuacan, Mexico, arose due to surplus production but were still limited in size. They used walls for defense and a clear spatial demarcation of neighborhoods. Residents in these early cities were segregated by class. Industrial cities like Chicago that arose in the late 1800s through early 1920s centered around a dominating city core. They grew due to good location, transportation innovations, and new building techniques. As these cities grew and spread, attracting huge numbers of people from rural areas and other countries, social classes were separated by greater distances but opportunities for social mobility expanded. Industrial cities took the form of (1) concentric zones, (2) cores with sectors radiating outward along transportation lines, or (3) multiple nuclei, with several centers of specialized districts. In a process called *succession*, new populations or activities would move into an area (*invasion*), replacing the existing ones. These industrial cities gradually decentralized, so much so that many of us now live in a *metropolitan area*, which refers to a large population nucleus along with any adjoining communities economically and socially integrated into it. In fact, many metropolitan areas have merged with others, forming a *megalopolis*. The postindustrial landscape is the result of many factors, including the automobile, telecommunications, government policies, and the women's liberation movement. It has vague boundaries and spreads over hundreds of square miles. Its shape and zones are indefinite. Racial and ethnic segregation persists, and large poverty tracts have formed. Old neighborhoods are sometimes restored by *gentrification*, but this process also produces some problems. Although rural–urban differences are narrowing, the major metropolitan areas remain centers of power.

In evaluating *urbanism*, a way of life in cities characterized by increased social differentiation and stratification, we can use two concepts of Ferdinand Tönnies. His *gemeinschaft* model describes social relations in a small town as intimate, cooperative, and based on emotional satisfaction. In a city, we are more likely to find a *gesellschaft*, characterized by impersonal, formal, competitive relationships and greater life style freedom for individuals. Likewise, Emile Durkheim explained that preindustrial communities are held together by collective conscience, homogeneity, tradition, and consensus, what he called *mechanical solidarity*. In urbanization, this gives way to *organic solidarity*, in which a stricter division of labor creates more individuality for the community members and cohesion is based on specialization and interdependence. Louis Wirth contended that the city's large population creates anonymity, superficiality, and competition. While the urban environment contributes to aloofness, crime, and an overall dreariness in the inner city, it also offers better services and facilities than rural areas, and densely populated neighborhoods can support lively ethnic communities. Nearly half of Americans live in suburbs, which increasingly suffer from their own problems. Planners are designing instant "small-town" environments, and cohousing attracts those in search of a sense of community. Rural populations have grown recently, but while these areas have become increasingly urbanized, they still feature more social cohesion than urban areas. This cohesion is usually lost during "boom" times.

Key Terms

demography	zero population	invasion
life	growth (ZPG)	succession
expectancy rate	population pyramid	metropolitan area
infant	fecundity	megalopolis
mortality rate	dependency ratio	gentrification
fertility rate	sex ratio	gemeinschaft
crude death rate	birth cohort	gesellschaft
crude birth rate	migration	mechanical solidarity
demographic	urbanization	organic solidarity
transition theory	urbanism	

14
Chapter

SOCIAL CHANGE

"Thinking sociologically" means more than thinking only about our own society. The appliances, automobiles, and foods we buy that are produced in Mexico, Korea, Peru, and elsewhere abroad are just one sign of how our life styles and opportunities are increasingly tied to developments on other continents. At least part of the reason that the U.S. share of the world gross national product has declined from about 50 percent in the late 1940s to below 16 percent today lies in the rise of "prickly and tough new nations . . . small, formerly weak powers" (Rosecrance, 1990). Moreover, social forecasters predict that because 95 percent of the growth in the world's workforce occurs in developing countries, more Americans will move across national boundaries in search of new job opportunities. We will have to compete, however, with better educated workers in these lands: The developing countries' share of the world's college students will mushroom from 23 percent in 1970 to 60 percent in the year 2000 (Johnston, 1991). Along with this growing competition, most of the world's nations continue to rapidly increase their relative size while our own population stabilizes. And we have seen in recent years how political changes in a place as distant as Eastern Europe (following the collapse of the Soviet Union) can radically alter our military objectives and budget. Clearly, a global perspective is in our own best interests.

In this chapter, we use a global perspective to consider differences over time occurring in parts of a society or culture—what is called **social change.** We first focus on those nations that do not yet pose serious economic threats to the United States because they have not fully industrialized and are largely poor (though some will not remain so for long).

Social change: differences over time that occur in parts of a society or culture.

IS SOCIAL CHANGE GOOD FOR DEVELOPING NATIONS?

Many of us might first assume that the answer is obviously "yes," but a moment's reflection reveals that the question requires a judgment on the value of change in these mostly poor countries. Cultural relativism and social change theory are useful tools in making such a judgment.

All too easily, Americans view change in undeveloped countries ethnocentrically, regarding the modern, Western world as the standard by which other cultures should be judged. We easily assume that others show "progress" by becoming like us, especially when we compare the United States with a country as different as Bangladesh. For example, 117 infants out of 1,000 die in that developing nation, compared to only 10 in the United States. A newborn can expect to live 53 years in Bangladesh or nearly 76 in our own country. The average person in Bangladesh consumes energy equivalent to 44 tons of coal, while the average American consumes over 10,000 tons. Bangladesh has 10 newspaper copies for every 1,000 people; the United States has nearly 26 times as many. Fewer than 5 television receivers exist for every 100,000 people in Bangladesh; the same number of Americans have over 800.

The people in Bangladesh might welcome lower infant mortality rates, longer life expectancies, and more energy consumption, televisions, and newspaper circulation as a sign of progress, but not necessarily. More newspapers and televisions might dispense information that leads to a questioning and breakdown of traditional values. Higher energy consumption would be accompanied by more pollution and materialism. Longer life expectancies and lower infant mortality rates would exacerbate population pressures. Change is not always beneficial, and change in the direction of our own culture might legitimately be viewed by people of other countries as disastrous.

From the perspective of cultural relativism, change is not desirable everywhere. Each option must be evaluated in terms of how it affects a particular culture. What works in a developed country may not work in, for example, Bangladesh or Iraq. Immediately after the Persian Gulf War in 1991, some analysts viewed a democratically elected government as a dangerously unstable alternative to dictator Saddam Hussein. Even such a seemingly attractive option as democracy may benefit one society but not another.

It is difficult to simply list which changes are beneficial for developing countries. First, different nations have different priorities regarding natural resources, government reform, economic change, and so on. Ethiopia needs political reform more than anything else, while India must face its greatest challenge: population control. Nations also have different levels of needs: Some are well on the road to development while others have not even begun. Saudi Arabia, for example, has only required time to effectively utilize its wealth, while Uganda is still mired in political and economic confusion. Second, change has several different faces. Depending on the perspective from which it is viewed, the same change in the same society can lead to greater complexity, inevitable death, possible chaos, or perhaps justice.

The Evolutionary Theory of Social Change

Evolutionary perspective: the view that social change moves from simple to complex, from traditional to modern.

From the **evolutionary perspective,** social change generally moves from simple to complex, from traditional to modern. This view is one of sociology's oldest: Auguste Comte, for example, contended that societies evolve through stages of thinking toward the scientific method. The advent of Charles Darwin's theory on biological evolution boosted the widespread popularity of this perspective in the nineteenth century. Herbert Spencer similarly argued that societies follow the law of "survival of the fittest," and that superior forms eventually evolve toward perfection.

Unilinear evolutionary perspective: the discredited view that social change occurs along only one path, that of "advanced" cultures.

These nineteenth-century theorists assumed that all cultures eventually evolve along the same path blazed by "advanced" Western nations. This **unilinear evolutionary perspective** supported ethnocentric beliefs among Westerners and justified exploitation of nations deemed to need the guiding hand—and control—of "superior" peoples. Few, however, actually studied other societies, relying instead on the accounts of tourists and travelers. This view fell from fashion in the early twentieth century as new anthropological knowledge on quickly disappearing "primitive" cultures throughout the world exposed flaws in the old evolutionary theories. By the middle of the 1920s, they no longer served as useful sociological tools—or so it seemed.

Over the last several decades, evolutionary theory has been revived in a modified form. It has always been obvious that some sequence of social development exists, that some changes occur in an orderly way. A political empire, for example, cannot be built until a people learn how to produce a surplus of wealth. Algebra cannot develop before the concept of zero is invented. New evolutionary theories have returned to the entirely plausible notion that social change occurs sequentially, in a definite direction. They employ a **multilinear evolutionary perspective** that recognizes more than one course of social change. Cultures move along different paths as they evolve; however, they generally do so in a parallel direction.

Multilinear evolutionary perspective: the view that cultures move along different paths as they change, although generally in a parallel direction.

But is such evolution or "development" progress? A contrast between the frenzied, dissatisfied life of many Americans and that of "primitive" people—with no deadlines, no career decisions, no final exams—suggests that developing nations may simply be trading one set of problems for another. Or consider the physical fitness of Australian aborigines before and after the arrival of civilization: "Although malnutrition—a condition brought about by the disappearance of game as a result of civilization—has left many present-day Arunta potbellied, in their natural state they have the strong chest, arms, and thighs of a long-distance runner. For them a trek of one hundred miles on foot is common" (Pinney, 1968, p. 221). Clearly, "development" is not synonymous with progress.

It is easy—and ethnocentric—to assume that social change is good for people whose cultures are not modern or "advanced." The consequences of change, however, cannot always be considered progress.

Cyclical Theories

Cyclical perspective: the view that social change takes the form of repeating phases of a cycle.

From the **cyclical perspective,** social change appears as inevitable repetition of the same few phases of a cycle, and so is predictable but not necessarily beneficial. One type of cycle is that of a pendulum swinging—for example, from political liberalism to conservatism, or from parenting permissiveness to restrictiveness. We can thus imagine a developing nation changing from an anti-Western, isolationist state to a pro-modern, open-door state—and perhaps back again. It is difficult to predict whether this change is beneficial, only that it is likely to occur again.

Another type of cycle is that of rising and falling waves, which Oswald Spengler (1926) saw in the birth, growth, maturity, decay, and death of a culture. This view presents a pessimistic outlook for an American society that seems to be, according to some historians, past its peak or even in decline. In contrast, a developing nation like South Korea would be situated near the beginning of such a cycle, with a long period of growth and maturation ahead of it. Social change, then, can easily be seen as desirable for an undeveloped nation, but perhaps the beginning of the end for a developed one.

Whether a nation is rich or poor, its eventual decay is not unavoidable or uncontrollable, according to Arnold Toynbee (1946), whose predictions were more firmly based on research than those of Spengler. Toynbee believed cultural decline can be avoided, though not without a struggle. This struggle is based on challenge from the global environment, to which the culture responds. During times of challenge, he argued, cultures can grow toward perfection or else edge closer to collapse. Faced with economic competition from Japan, Germany, and other nations, the United States may thus stand at the brink of either decline or renewal. In the less developed world, Nigeria and Ethiopia have responded to the challenges of development in strikingly different ways. Nigeria has produced the largest black elite of university-trained professionals in Africa, and the nation is positioning itself for eventual prosperity. Ethiopia's "revolutionary socialism," in contrast, has helped turn what is potentially Africa's breadbasket into one of the world's poorest nations. The ascendence or decline of such societies seems to depend on how they deal with crises.

Functionalist Theory

Functionalist theory of change: the theory that social systems tend toward stability.

The **functionalist theory of change** focuses on potential disruptions, rather than benefits, of social systems. From this perspective, society is a system of interrelated parts, each one contributing to the healthy functioning of the overall system. Change inherently threatens the system's stability.

Equilibrium theory: the theory that a change in one part of a social system requires compensatory adjustments elsewhere.

Talcott Parsons' **equilibrium theory,** a version of this functionalist perspective, holds that a change in one part of a social system requires compensatory adjustments elsewhere. In African societies, for example, postcolonial development has disrupted the old cohesive bonds of family and tribe, but new bonds arising in ethnic and religious associations, sports clubs, women's groups, trade unions, and farm cooperatives have counterbalanced these changes (Appiah, 1991). As long as society maintains what Parsons (1964) called a "moving equilibrium" that ensures the continued performance of vital social functions, it will not be harmed by change.

Cultural lag: when one part of a culture does not change at the same pace as others, causing incompatibility and disequilibrium.

Sometimes the various parts of a culture do not change at the same rate, resulting in what William Ogburn (1922) called **cultural lag.** In complex modern societies, this usually involves the technology speeding ahead, leaving the values and organizational forms unable to maintain the necessary equilibrium. In other words, nonmaterial

The design of the ladies' bicycle has not changed despite the change in women's clothing fashions and other norms. This is a case of cultural lag.

change is slower than material progress. This lag may take the form of trivial incongruities such as "ladies" bicycles designed to accommodate riders wearing skirts, a rarity nowadays. Other cases are more important, such as the growing incompatibility between the traditional notion of "family" and changes in contraceptive technology, the economy (two paychecks are necessary in many households), and reproductive procedures that allow the freezing of sperm and eggs. We also see a gap between the proliferation of stepfamilies and cohabiting couples on the one hand and laws regarding parental rights and responsibilities on the other. Uneven change, often brought on by economic development, can threaten the smooth functioning of the overall system.

Following the lead of Parsons, functionalists worry about a developing nation's **differentiation,** an underlying pattern of change in which one part of the social system splits into two or more new parts. For example, the family of a premodern society eventually differentiates into several parts such as religion, economy, and government, each of which performs some of the family's traditional functions as society develops. The difficulty lies in integrating or coordinating these new parts to achieve a new equilibrium.

From this perspective, then, the desirability of social change depends on how fast and extensive it is, and how well society can adjust. Gradual development can lead to an improved equilibrium, sudden changes can lead to dislocations and suffering, mass starvation and alienation.

Differentiation: an underlying pattern of change in which one part of a social system fragments into two or more parts.

Conflict Theory

When Dorothy looks behind the curtain, she discovers that the Wizard of Oz is not what he appeared to be. Conflict theorists likewise claim to sweep aside the functionalist explanation to reveal that society is less than a smoothly functioning system.

Conflict theory of change: the theory that conflict is constant and the key to causing social change.

Instead of a healthy equilibrium, the **conflict theory of change** depicts constant tension in an unjust society that cries out for change.

Karl Marx described conflict as the key to fundamental changes throughout history. He argued that each form of society develops out of economic upheaval within previous forms. In each historical stage, according to Marx, the status quo embodies the interests of the exploitative ruling class over those of the lower classes—whether they are slaves, serfs, or workers. The struggle between oppressors and oppressed leads to the next stage along the evolutionary path. The contradictions and conflict within this new stage give rise to the next, and so on, until a classless communist society is eventually created. This Marxist perspective encourages poor people—say, in a developing nation—to view themselves as potential agents of revolutionary change and thus harbingers of a new social justice. Change in this view is a necessary revolutionary tool.

Ralf Dahrendorf's version of the conflict perspective points to an unequal distribution of power as the cause of tension and conflict (1973). In developed as well as undeveloped societies, some group always feels dissatisfied with the balance of power and wants change. This is evident, for example, in the Philippines, where the government has struggled for years with communist rebels who have played on the unrest of a disillusioned and poverty-stricken people. As long as some elements of the population are unhappy, social change will occur: Those without power want more, while those with power strive to keep what they have.

Tensions and conflict can foment on a global scale, according to *world systems theory* (see Chapter 10). This view describes an ongoing clash between modern industrial societies (the "core") and those that are less developed (the "periphery"). The core exploits the periphery as sources of raw materials and new markets. Developing nations that enter the global economy usually find a "zero sum game" in which there is a fixed amount of wealth, with core nations gaining at the expense of the periphery.

Constant struggle may seem like a distinctly undesirable condition to most of us, but in the eyes of desperately poor nations on the periphery it can look full of promise. Bridging the gap between core and periphery, however, presents a host of difficulties. Nigeria, for example, is one of the few developing nations in Africa making progress toward establishing a stable economy and democratic government, but only after the turmoil of six military coups and the assassination of three heads of state (Harden, 1991).

Returning to our original question, is social change generally good for developing nations? As viewed through the lens of cultural relativism, the answer depends on which social change perspective is used, and of course the situation of each country. Thinking through this question sociologically, in other words, requires the exercise of caution and the careful application of social change theory to any particular nation.

Critical Thinking Box

What's Wrong with This Analogy?

Functionalists see the continuing adjustment in society as analogous to what goes on in living organisms. Both the human body and a developing nation, they argue, make up systems trying to maintain equilibrium. The body's organs are like the major institutions of society, each working to promote the overall health and stability of the system. And the society seeks stability just as the body each morning is basically the same as it was the morning before, with only a few minor changes—a few hairs lost, some new skin cells added. The organs have all been active in maintaining this state of health. The organism is designed to cope with gradual changes such as maturation and aging, but outside agents such as germs or bullets can disrupt its equilibrium. Similarly, modern Western ideas can wreak havoc in a traditional culture.

This analogy, however, can only be carried so far. How so? ■

MODERNIZATION IN AFRICA: ARE ITS FRUITS WORTH THE COSTS?

Modernization, a process that occurs in all developing societies, describes the evolution of modernizing societies as they move from a simple, agrarian form toward a complex, industrial one. Using Africa as an example of this "Westernization," we see that it brings tremendous disruptions as well as increased opportunities. On balance, is Africa better off now than before modernization?

Modernization: the process of urbanization and industrialization, often involving "Westernization."

Economy

Improvements in material well-being make up the most dramatic, visible fruits of modernization. In general, more goods are produced per person, making possible a higher standard of living. In fact, developing nations have recently increased their share of the world's industrial output by 400 percent, and their food production has tripled. This translates into more televisions, motor vehicles, and other goods. Such

Modernization usually brings a higher standard of living, at least for some.

societies use more natural resources, and learn to do so more efficiently. Transportation becomes more convenient, and modern comforts such as air conditioning are less uncommon.

As African nations convert to free-market economies, more jobs are created, especially in housing construction and the manufacturing of clothing and household goods. Small businesses, as well as the chronically overstaffed civil service, offer precious opportunities for upward social mobility. Africa's middle class, however, remains "meager, perhaps five percent of the population in many countries" (Klitgaard, 1991, p. 40).

While the gap between rich and poor in a country may eventually become smaller due to greater opportunities and more wealth to distribute, this leveling by no means occurs swiftly or with certainty. The well-entrenched upper classes often take advantage of the new conditions to become wealthier and stronger. Africa's widespread corruption (nothing unique to the developing world) is a favorite means for self-aggrandizement; government officials demand bribes for bestowing informal favors or else wield bureaucratic red tape arbitrarily.

Another downside to industrialization is that while it creates some new job slots, overpopulation and the growing dominance of corporate farming operations dislocate many peasant farmers. At the same time, labor-saving technologies eliminate many jobs for urban workers. In the face of such unemployment pressures, skilled workers emigrate to other nations in search of opportunities, resulting in a costly shortage of talent at home.

Government

The political ramifications of modernity are less predictable. Power tends to become centralized as governments control more social functions. African nations often require concentrated power to unify the disparate ethnic and tribal allegiances. Somalia offers a tragic illustration of the results of decentralized power. There, clan divisions produced paralyzing chaos that triggered United Nations intervention. And

Modernization has brought violence as central governments attempt to fill the void left by traditional governing bodies.

ironically, while elections become more common in Africa, effective government remains elusive. For example, after Francisco Macias Nguema was elected president of Equatorial Guinea in the 1960s, he proceeded to imprison and murder his political opponents; outlaw competing political parties; abolish the constitution; shut down churches and libraries; stop the publication of all books, newspapers, and magazines; and declare himself president for life (Klitgaard, 1991). So, while Africans have increasing say in who governs, their chosen rulers all too frequently must be driven from office at gunpoint.

Social Relations

A century ago, Emile Durkheim observed that modernization involves increasing specialization or division of labor, wherein social relations become more impersonal, less intimate, and based largely on material interests and contract rather than tradition. Similarly, Ferdinand Tönnies lamented the transition from *gemeinschaft* to *gesellschaft* caused by urbanization. By this shift he meant that the intimate, familiar social interactions typical of small rural communities gradually give way to an impersonal mass society based on formal controls, privacy, self-interest rather than cooperation, and little sense of commonality. Africa's modernization experience has not yet forged a society of faceless bureaucrats and isolated, lonely strangers. Associations based on tribal, ethnic, and religious allegiances envelop and integrate many Africans. Through these civic associations, Africans are bound together as they perform many of the functions that lie within the domain of the state bureaucracy, from financing and staffing schools to maintaining "public" roads to furnishing equipment for "government" hospitals to managing old people's homes and orphanages. Along with these associations, "sports clubs, market-women's groups, professional organizations, trade unions, and farm cooperatives" become vital in maintaining civil society (Appiah, 1991). Most people in developing societies are not so lucky; rather than remain woven into the social fabric of a village, modernization often thrusts them into an urban throng of strangers.

Education

Long cherished in the Western world as a means of personal fulfillment and social progress, education becomes accessible for more people in modernizing societies. In the 1980s, for example, Indonesia first offered universal elementary schooling; significantly, the Department of Education now makes up the largest department in the government. Social trends, however, rarely proceed smoothly: In Africa, primary school enrollment dropped during the 1980s, and many schools lack books, desks, and chalkboards anyway. According to a 1990 United Nations report, Africa's school enrollment rates are the lowest of all the continents: 76 percent of children attend elementary school, and only 25 percent move on to secondary school. Even as education expands in many developing nations, often there are too few appropriate jobs for graduates, or else colleges turn out philosophers and lawyers rather than the agronomists and engineers the country needs. Furthermore, colleges are plagued by a "brain drain" of professors and intellectuals (caused by low salaries and political unrest) and poor preparation of students, as seen in one engineering professor's course at the University of Dar-es-Salaam that begins with a demonstration of how a bolt fits into a nut (Hiltzik, 1990).

Religion

Africa's religious profile, like that of other modernizing regions, shows the homogenizing influences of outside proselytizers and missionaries. Traditional and tribal institutions tend to be overwhelmed by major religions such as Christianity and Islam. Muslim fundamentalism has found especially fertile ground in many parts of Africa recently. Even insulated, developing China is experiencing a self-propagating wave of Christianity.

Family

Families in modernizing nations usually undergo shock waves of change. Partly due to equalizing gender roles, Africans marry at later ages, thus extending the premarital stage. Elders are losing control over the young, especially the females, and the number of premarital pregnancies and abortions has mushroomed. Modernization has not yet swept away all African family values: Except for the tiny middle-class, urban, Westernized, and Christianized populations, large families are still desirable, children still bring parents prestige, extended family ties still predominate, and polygamy continues to flourish (Lauras-Lecoh, 1990). One major feature of family life that has changed, however: the freedom young people now enjoy. Modernization offers young people education, jobs, and the opportunity to travel, thus freeing them from the watchful authority of elders.

As in other developing regions, the results of modernization are mixed for African women. Though the new market economies offer women greater employment opportunities and competitive wages, they receive on average less pay than men for similar work and remain for the most part confined to less productive and lower-paid jobs such as personal services and labor-intensive manufacturing. Nonetheless, as women gain access to jobs, they shrug off the authority of husbands and clans. Sometimes such independence is legally sanctioned, as seen in a 1976 law in Kenya giving women the right to inherit their husbands' estates, protection from physical spousal abuse, the power to sue and to borrow money, and protection from being forced into marriage by their family.

However, increasing economic independence does have its costs for African women (Hartnagel and Mizanuddin, 1986; Cox, 1990). Many still carry the burden of large families, and they increasingly find themselves abandoned by husbands who migrate far afield to take advantage of new job opportunities. Moreover, new rights gained may clash with ancient traditions. As one elderly Kenyan woman working in a field declared, "Our sisters in the past have decided that women will be in charge of the food. That cannot be changed. It is our right, and we will never let a man take it from us" (quoted in Shah, 1988). And in Eritrea, while some women have boldly removed the shawls from their faces in their husbands' presence, others still have their clitoris forcibly removed and vaginas sewn nearly shut to prevent them from "wandering" and to increase men's pleasure.

Cities

As job and educational opportunities lead to greater geographical mobility and multinational corporations drive peasants off their land, many in modernizing nations are uprooted. Explosive growth results in booming cities, where people seek scarce jobs,

As part of the modernization process, masses of peasants stream into the cities looking for work. They usually crowd into sprawling slums.

schools, and social services. In Africa, the Nigerian city of Lagos is now larger than Chicago, and Kinshasa, Zaire, has grown to about the size of Dallas. In other continents, modernization has given birth to some of the world's largest and fastest-growing cities: By the year 2000, Mexico City will likely be the world's largest city, followed by Sao Paulo, Brazil (U.S. Bureau of the Census, 1990).

Unfortunately, this swelling of urban areas generally occurs where abject poverty is worst: Desperate people perceive no better alternative, and they stream into starving, disease-ridden slums. In South America, "barrios" and shantytowns have appeared on steep, almost uninhabitable mountainsides, where bathroom facilities are lacking and foul water has to be carried in to the hovels. In these areas, garbage becomes a source of food.

Deviance

Uprooted individuals, booming cities, and infusions of new values combine in modernizing regions like Africa to produce rising tides of deviance. Confusion and permissiveness fill the vacuum left by the collapse of old norms. Desperate poverty drives many to prostitution and theft, while the modern outside world introduces the corrupting influence of bribery and narcotics trafficking. Economic dislocation is causing African towns to be increasingly populated by delinquent gangs of abandoned children, a troubling sight found in many cities in other developing regions as well.

Still, this trend in Africa is no more uniform than any other in the modernization process. While in Nigeria "urban armed robbery and banditry on the highways have become accepted inconveniences," in Ghana deviance can be controlled largely through traditional means: "Disputes in urban as well as in rural areas [are] likely to end up in arbitration between the heads of families or in the courts of 'traditional' chiefs and queen-mothers" (Appiah, 1991, p. 29).

Health

Modernization brings changes in diets and behavior patterns that often mean less exercise, more alcohol, processed foods, and stress.

Are Africans at least healthier because of modernization? We would expect so, though reliable statistics are not readily available. Public health usually improves with modernization: Child death rates have been cut by half in most of the developing world, and more than 70 percent of newborns are now immunized. Infectious disease rates generally decline dramatically. However, Africa's mortality rates are the highest in the world, and its average life expectancy—54 years for women, 50 for men—is the lowest. Furthermore, the importation of Western diets and behaviors brings with it an array of health problems, including a higher incidence of cardiovascular disease, cancer, and strokes. Elevated arterial blood pressure has been linked to the life style stresses of developing societies (Dressler et al., 1987). Alcohol and drug abuse, with all their attendant health problems, have also risen dramatically.

Have the benefits of these extensive social changes in Africa been worth the costs? As we might expect, people more quickly accept those aspects of modernization that cause the least amount of pain and disruptions. Thus Africans, like other developing peoples, say "yes" to jobs, comforts, and conveniences, but "maybe later" to bureaucratic control and the ideal of monogamous, nuclear families. Most would probably say that only some aspects of modernization have been worth the costs, and that some of the costs have indeed been considerable.

HOW DOES CHANGE OCCUR IN DEVELOPING NATIONS? THE CASE OF JAPAN

Until the late 1800s, Japan was rich in history and tradition but neither wealthy nor powerful like the United States or the countries of industrialized Europe. Japan's development over the past century and a half illustrates how social change occurs in developing nations.

Perry's voyage forced Japan to open its doors to social changes.

In 1853, Commodore Matthew Perry's four "black ships" sailed into Japanese waters with a message from U.S. President Millard Fillmore demanding that Japan open itself to trade with the United States. Like most unindustrialized nations, Japan had little choice in the face of the developed world's overwhelming military might. Japanese leaders decided—again, a typical response in such situations—to begin a crash course in Westernization.

Behind this decision lay several factors that help determine the process of social change in developing nations today. First, the Japanese attitude toward newness changed from a centuries-long one of fear and mistrust to, in this as in many cases, eager anticipation. Japanese leaders saw rapid modernization as the only way to become powerful and prosperous like the West.

The weakening structural unity of Japan also played a role. Even though Japan's power elite had imposed cultural isolation on the nation for several centuries, increasingly frequent visits from European traders, explorers, and missionaries beginning in the early 1800s weakened social integration. Another breach in Japan's isolationism resulted from the granting of official permission in 1720 to study European books. As in other developing countries, once the culture's fabric begins to unravel, loose ends become more likely to snag on some change agent. In this case, that agent was Commodore Perry.

A third determinant of social change in Japan was its superb access to sea routes, an advantage it shared with Great Britain. Countries with favorable physical environments experience change more rapidly and beneficially. In fact, natural resources are one factor that help distinguish the prosperous developing societies from those languishing in poverty: Nations blessed with oil reserves (Saudi Arabia), rich soil (Argentina), precious metals (Republic of South Africa), or great forests (Brazil) have achieved fast-paced development while those lacking adequate fuel, water, and minerals face a political and economic disadvantage. Of course, environment alone cannot determine a country's course of development. Japan, for example, possesses few minerals and scarce arable land. Likewise, Singapore and Hong Kong have enjoyed spectacular economic success despite the fact that both must import drinking water.

Diffusion

Diffusion: the spread or transmission of elements from one culture to another.

The case of Japan, whose isolation from Western cultures prevented modernization until the mid-1800s, shows that contact with other cultures serves as the catalyst for most social change. This intercultural contact produces **diffusion,** the spreading or transmission of elements from one culture to another. Anything that promotes such contact—trade, war, royal intermarriage, missionaries—stimulates social change. Once Perry helped break Japan's self-imposed isolation, her great potential for diffusion accelerated Westernization. Cities like Jerusalem or New York City and countries like Japan or Great Britain that are situated along major trade routes and have many cultural contacts historically have been in the forefront of social change.

Developing countries bombarded with offerings from other cultures to some extent become clones of the more advanced nations. Historian James McClain describes Japan's early embrace of anything Western: "By the end of the 1870s short haircuts had replaced the topknot, men wore gold watches, carried black rolled umbrellas, and dressed in knitted underwear" (1987, p. 157). Japan quickly acquired a railroad, gas lights, the telegraph, beer halls, coffee shops, and even a taste for beef.

Convergence: a growing similarity among cultures brought on by modernization.

No matter where modernization occurs, its most obvious consequence is this **convergence,** or a growing similarity among cultures. Travelers can encounter the same clothing, food, architecture, and automobiles in Nairobi as they do in Mexico City. Recent marketing efforts by U.S. companies have helped spread tobacco use throughout the developing world. Brand names such as Coca Cola and Sony can now be

The Japanese quickly accepted Western goods and behaviors that were compatible with their own culture.

found in nearly any city. Budweiser and bluejeans have become commonplace today in Japan.

But the spread of brand names and modern technologies is neither automatic nor smooth. Firstly, because diffusion is selective, not all aspects of modernity are accepted by developing nations. Late nineteenth-century Japan admittedly showed little discrimination in its imitation of Western styles and fashions. As one government official wrote in 1874, "Clothing, customs, even all kinds of crafts and scholarly pursuits—there is nothing which we are not today taking from the West" (McClain, p. 157). Still, Western religions made few inroads into Shinto and Buddhism even at the height of Japan's frenzied Westernization, nor did Japanese forego their tradition of collectivist, extended family forms. Similarly, a fundamentalist Muslim nation like Saudi Arabia may accept Western technology but not clothing fashions or drinking habits, or allow its women to drive cars.

Compatibility largely determines the extent of cultural diffusion. Japan readily accepted baseball in 1873 because, in their view, it coincided with their traditional values of loyalty, order, perseverance, and honor. "Batters," McClain observes, "were likened to samurai swordsmen" (p. 159). The nation embraced the sport so enthusiastically that in the first official (though amateur) match-up with an American team in 1896, the Japanese won 29–4.

Rarely, if ever, is a new trait accepted without some alteration. Japan completely revised its law codes in 1890 along Western lines but retained such distinctly Japanese notions as oligarchic rule by elder statesmen, respect for the nobility and military, and a divine emperor. When Malayans accepted Islam in the 1400s, "they blended the ways of Islam with the familiar rites and customs of older faiths. Noblemen retained their Hindu titles; Buddhist rituals remained a part of everyday living" (*Wilson Quarterly*, 1987, p. 49). This adaptation was not made when the United States imported professional soccer in the 1980s. Efforts to change the rules to allow more scoring and satisfy fans' demand for more explosive excitement failed, and consequently the receiving culture largely rejected the new element.

One rather unusual aspect of Japan's intense period of modernization a century ago is that diffusion virtually occurred in only one direction. Usually when two cultures meet, both change, but the United States and Europe in the late 1800s showed little interest in anything Japanese. Representatives of modern nations often bring home ideas and goods from less technologically advanced societies, from dances (such as the lambada and tango) to foods (tacos and salsa) to religions (Islam is now estimated as one of the ten largest in the United States). Nevertheless, developing nations usually get more than they give in their contact with more advanced nations, and this was clearly the case with Japan in the nineteenth century.

Diffusion can cause unanticipated, sometimes devastating problems in developing nations when cultural traits are adopted piecemeal. Bottle-feeding, for example, which offers less immunity and nutrition to infants, is sometimes accepted as an alternative to breastfeeding in undeveloped countries. Also, the importation of modern public health practices can send population growth rates skyrocketing as they dramatically reduce infant mortality.

Invented in the late 1200s in England, eyeglasses diffused with breathtaking speed. By 1290 they were worn by French nobility, and were seen in court society in Egypt by 1300 and in China by 1310 (Drucker, 1993).

Innovation

Not all social change originates outside a nation, even a developing one. Internally produced additions to the cultural storehouse are called **innovations.** While drawing heavily on Chinese culture for centuries, Japan also created Shinto, a religious faith

Innovation: the addition of new, internally produced elements to a culture, or such an element itself.

Besides incompatibility and opposition from vested interests, there is another reason why innovations may not cause social change. This reason is illustrated in the case of the Ancient Greeks, who knew about steam power and used the principle in small models. But this new power source caused no social change. The Greeks, with sufficient slave and animal power, certainly had no industrial revolution or any other significant change due to this innovation. What then, is the third prerequisite for innovation to produce social change?

Invention: the creation of a new cultural element, or such an element itself.

Discovery: the awareness of a cultural element that has already existed, or such an element itself.

based on ancestor and nature worship, and a system of military government headed by a Seiitaishogun ("barbarian-subduing great general"). In modern history, however, Japan has established a reputation for mastery of diffusion and adaptation.

Sociologists differentiate between two types of innovation. **Invention** is the creation of a new cultural element, while **discovery** is the awareness of a cultural element that has already existed. The former is more likely to be deliberate, the latter unplanned. Either type of innovation can lead to social change, as shown by the invention of the cotton gin. This device enabled plantation owners to plant and clean lowland cotton, allowing the "cotton kingdom" to spread to more parts of the South and West and thus help precipitate the Civil War.

A society that allows or promotes social innovations opens itself to potentially profound changes. Japan's creation of a shogunate altered its political history, ushering in an era of civil wars that culminated in a rigidly stratified feudal society lasting from the 1600s until the beginning of modernization. The reverberation of innovation is illustrated in our own society by the women's liberation movement, which wrought an entire package of consequences. It infused the economy with millions of new workers, caused more fathers to become involved in parenting, encouraged freer expression of sex within and outside marriage, and shrank the pool of competent prospective schoolteachers. As noted earlier, new educational and employment opportunities for African women have triggered increases in premarital sex and marital breakups.

Innovation does not guarantee social change in a developing nation. The new idea or technology may remain "on the shelf," causing little impact on the culture. As with diffusion, compatibility is a prerequisite. For example, Japan's revised constitution of 1946 provided for equality of the sexes, but the "new family" it hoped to create did not materialize in most parts of the country because of its incompatibility with traditional values. Similarly, around much of the developing world contraceptive technology encounters resistance from cultures that value large families. Also, innovation must not challenge the position of powerful vested interests. Threatened by numerous farmers' movements in the 1930s demanding more protectionist government policies, the Japanese urban industrial elite countered by insisting that agriculture was the principal basis of nationhood and that farmers should view hard work and sacrifice as patriotic and sacred duty.

Social Movements

A **social movement** is an organized attempt to promote or resist some social change. Such large-scale efforts clearly can affect the transformation of developing or developed nations.

Social movement: an organized attempt to promote or resist some social change.

The power of social movements can be explained partly by the participants' sense of morality and justice. Those involved are passionately motivated to right what they perceive as some wrong, which is evident in the wild eyes, straining necks, and flashing teeth of faces at a protest demonstration. Not surprisingly, social movements can sometimes shake the course of societies.

Social movements blossom fairly easily in developed societies whenever people become aware of some problem and organize efforts to solve it. Since the beginning of modernization in Japan, social movements have sprouted over international affairs,

Innovations can send waves of change through a culture. The innovation of affordable home air conditioning helped strip the South of its unique regional charm, most obviously in its architecture. Southern houses today are built to conserve conditioned air rather than to ventilate. Gone are the raised foundations, twelve-foot-high ceilings, tall windows, and verandas. Besides this, the South's cooled factories invigorated the economy and drew a diverse invasion of people from the North and other countries, thus ending the region's cultural isolation. Also, as has happened elsewhere, neighbors retreated to their cooled homes rather than visit over the fence (Arsenault, 1984).

family values, agricultural policies, labor, the environment, and other concerns. Movements for labor unions, animals' rights, legal abortion, gay rights, and women's liberation make up just some of the topics that have proliferated in our own society.

Social movements do not generally arise in preindustrial, premodern societies, where tradition dominates and innovation is seen as threatening or mysterious. Throughout Japanese history, various leaders exerted control over the people, and few if any movements arose among the people themselves. Those in a tightly controlled society who see some need for organized collective action to solve a problem tend to express their discontent by forming a religious movement promising hope for the oppressed. For example, defeated and confined to reservations by the late 1800s, some North American Plains Indian tribes believed that participating in the frenzied Ghost Dance would enable them to reinstate their way of life and drive the whites away. Today in many developing nations, Islam acts as the agent focusing opposition to the encroachment of Western culture. In others, notably in South and Central America, Jesuits have served as galvanizing social reform agents.

Once a society starts down the path of modernization, social movements become more common and are more likely to be secular and political rather than religious. For example, an antiforeign movement arose in Japan in the 1890s to resist the nation's unabashed imitation of the West; one critic observes that Japan "had learned the decadence of the Roman Empire without first attaining its pinnacle of glory" (McClain, p. 158). Of course, such movements will not likely emerge in societies with autocratic governments, where people are not permitted to openly criticize the established order or form associations to promote changes.

A fountainhead of social movements in developing nations springs from discontent or social strain. Such movements arise when many people collectively define an unjust or unacceptable situation as a social problem. In the latter half of the 1800s Japan perceived a seeming inferiority of their culture relative to the West; the modernization movement was the perceived solution.

Many people in the undeveloped world have endured impoverishment for generations, but social movements there rarely explode. Why? One reason lies in the absence of **relative deprivation,** discontent that occurs when people perceive their living standards as lower than others' or their own in the past. Exposed to the baubles and gadgets of the West, the once complacent Japanese suddenly felt "backward," and resolved to close the gap with the industrialized nations through the modernization movement. Not until outsiders came did Japan see a need for the telegraph and railroads. Today, people in undeveloped countries who get a "taste of the good life" through advertising or an influx of new consumer items are more likely to join a social movement. Relative deprivation is especially likely to arise when improvements are lost or are perceived as inadequate. As one writer puts it, "Students of revolution have long noted that trouble comes not from the depths of misery but from the appetite that grows with better eating" (Landes, 1989, p. 26).

The Japanese government of the late 1800s faced the same challenge as governments of the developing world today: raising living standards without raising people's expectations too high. The goal becomes to maintain a constant rise in living standards without letting reality slip too far behind expectations. A widening gap between expectations and reality always raises the danger that a radical social movement may arise. Japan made the transition relatively easily in this respect; living standards for the most part gradually rose, at least for urbanites.

The Japanese case illustrates another prerequisite of social movements: Deprivation must be a shared experience, uniting people with a common interest (Tilly,

Relative deprivation: discontent that occurs when people perceive their living standards as lower than others' or their own in the past.

In most parts of the developing world today, discontent based on deprivation festers in abundance. The plight of many children in the developing world is an agonizing example. In Peru, abondoned children flee to Lima to avoid being conscripted by rebel groups or the army. Once they reach the cities, the children are easily exploited via prostitution or sink into drug addiction. The picture is similar in other Latin American countries: millions of children living in the streets, being used for cheap labor, sold, imprisoned, or kidnapped. A human rights activist warns that these children "will certainly not stay forever on the sidelines, meekly staring at the rich as they tuck into the feast" (Esquivel, 1991, p. 33).

1978). Feelings of cultural inferiority were widespread in Japan after the first shock of exposure to the West, and the nation was united in its resolve to change what it saw as an intolerable state of affairs. Without such widespread, spontaneous support, Japan's modernization movement would not have been possible.

According to **resource mobilization theory,** the rise of a social movement often requires more than frustrated individuals acting on shared discontent. First, like-minded individuals must be integrated into their community through professional associations, labor unions, civic groups, and religious organizations. In late nineteenth-century Japan, such associations were still intact and strong. Second, the associations involved must gain sufficient control of skilled leaders, money, loyalties, facilitating laws, and goods. These assets can be acquired by attracting more converts, evoking a greater commitment on the part of existing members, or collaborating with other organizations, which expand communication networks, offer new leaders, and provide value consensus or loyalty. In Japan's case, these goals were easily met since government supported the entire movement.

Unless the government is oppressive, economic development usually leads to more social movements. Terry Boswell and William Dixon (1990) point out that as a nation's economy grows it also generates more social resources—such as extensive communications networks, labor unions, and other organizations—that make such movements likely. During the last few decades, an increasingly prosperous Japan has seen a proliferation of social movements emerging from student and worker associations.

This groundswell of protest has occurred in other developed nations, including the United States. In fact, today it seems that every group has its own social movement through which it airs its grievances. The professionalization of social movement

Resource mobilization theory: the theory that resources must be activated to fulfill a nation's potential for social change.

Social movements today can produce protest demonstrations that are larger, more frequent, and more peaceful than in previous decades, largely due to the more professional management of social movement organizations.

organizations explains in part this heightened activism (Staggenborg, 1988). Because charitable foundations contributed heavily to such organizations in the late 1960s, many activists found career opportunities in what might be called the "social movement field." These career activists formed a network linking an expanding array of social movement organizations that cooperate more effectively on particular issues, which also explains why protest demonstrations today involve greater number of participants than in the past. Moreover, because foundation funding has diminished since the 1970s, professional organizers rely on a new source of funding: large memberships. Social movement professionals thus have turned to protest demonstrations as a resource. Frequent and well-publicized gatherings serve to maintain and stimulate support and recruit new members, provided that they hold little risk of arrest or injury. Thus, demonstrations by social movement organizations have become more frequent, larger in scale, and less violent than in previous decades (Everett, 1992).

Without activist leaders, many movements would never get off the ground. While the potential for a movement may exist, "mobilizers" must motivate people at the individual level in political groups, churches, informal friendship networks, and so on, as well as forge links among various organizations. They must coordinate and integrate groups with overlapping interests, gathering resources and managing public relations. Mobilizers must also shape members' perceptions, "developing a common frame of meaning to interpret the issue at stake" (Gerhards and Rucht, 1992, p. 559). Without such professionals working behind the scenes, social movements would not engage our attention as effectively as they do today.

Social movement organizations provide valuable support for local grass-roots protest groups. One such group formed during the 1980s in Texarkana, Texas, to call attention to chemical contamination of the Carver Terrace neighborhood (Capek, 1993). Having failed to win a government buyout for their community, it sought help from other communities with similar problems and from other organizations. In 1989, national activists organized a "National Grass-roots Conference on Environmental Justice" in Carver Terrace that brought in prominent activists from around the country. In this way, the local group learned from experienced activists how to use protest effectively, how to attract media attention, and what kind of support they could expect from other organizations. With their help, the Carver Terrace group staged a protest that attracted international attention, and they eventually won five million dollars for a federal buyout and relocation. While the national environmental movement provided direct help to the Carver Terrace protesters, this neighborhood group in turn inspired local activists elsewhere, thus helping to mobilize resources for the larger movement. This case shows the importance of career activists and networks among social movement organizations.

Sometimes the impetus for social change comes from outside a society altogether. Change agents from other cultures can provide the necessary resources for social movements and also help mobilize those resources. For decades, communist agents were planted in countries around the world to foment social movements that would ultimately lead to revolutions, which became especially evident in Angola and several nations in Central America. Similarly, agents from the United States attempted to establish prodemocracy social movements in countries such as Nicaragua and Afghanistan. However, when the use of such outside agents becomes known, as in Japan, it usually works to the detriment of social movements (Frank and Fuentes, 1989).

Types of Movements   The kind of change generated by any given social movement depends on its goals and methods. At least four types of movements can be discerned that, together, illustrate the various ways they can reshape societies.

Some movements target just one aspect of a society for change, supposedly for the better. Japan's student movements of the 1960s and 1970s sought to influence specific government policies and international issues such as the Security Treaty of 1960. Various Japanese "citizens' movements" focused on national concerns like the presence of American military bases and relations with Vietnam. Today, "local residents' movements" respond to local issues such as a polluting factory, plans for a nuclear plant, or noise from a nearby airport. Such one-issue campaigns that seek to improve, not destroy, society are called *reform movements*. They generally limit themselves to advancing the interests of only some segments of society, as was the case in Japan's farmers' and labor movements and the U.S. civil rights movement in the 1960s.

Reform movements usually employ legal means and work within the existing system, at least after they have managed to gain access to the formal power structure. Japan's student movement never gained that access. It successfully shut down Tokyo University in 1968–1969, but its use of violence kept the movement on the outside of the political power structure, and the movement is politically irrelevant today. In Mexico, the galvanizing issue for a succession of social movements since 1968 has been "collective resistance" against the one-party state. These movements have unsuccessfully tried to work within the political system to win more democratic reform (Monsivais, 1990). An example of a reform movement that has achieved success through legal means is that for equal employment opportunity in the United States, which has worked hand in glove with the federal government (Burstein, 1991).

Social change is sometimes impeded by countermovements, or *resistance movements*, that arise to prevent further change or to reverse changes already made. An example is Japan's aforementioned antiforeign movement of the 1890s, which arose in reaction to decades of Westernization.

Such "backlash" movements can be reactionary or regressive when their goal requires a return to the past and substitution of old institutions and values for current ones. Classic examples in the United States are the Ku Klux Klan, which seeks a return to a segregated society, and the antiabortion and antinuclear movements. Elsewhere, the militaristic, anticommunist New Christian Right, which campaigns against feminism, homosexual rights, and abortion, has become a force in many nations (Jorstad, 1987; Diamond, 1989).

Sometimes social movements aim to change neither society nor the political structure but individuals, to bring about an inward, personal transformation. Some of these *expressive movements* seek emotional satisfaction or new identities for their members. In the 1970s, as Japan began moving into the postindustrial age, many intellectuals promoted the Nihonjin-ron, or "debate on being Japanese," through which Japanese "might begin to understand ourselves and regain our identity" (McClain, p. 160). The Unification Church of the "Moonies" and the Hare Krishna movement are also examples. Other expressive movements seek to establish a utopian society for their members, hoping that the example they set will bring change in the broader society.

Japan's "Red Army" aims to overthrow existing institutions and replace them with new ones. It seeks not reform but total, radical change. Like other *revolutionary movements*, the Red Army has strong, charismatic leaders who demand great dedication from the members. In developing nations, such movements may show us the shape of things to come: The national governments of the Soviet Union, the Peoples Republic of China, and the United States all began with revolutionary social movements.

Terrorism: organized, politically motivated violence directed against government or high-visibility targets in such a way as to conceal the identity and location of those perpetrating the act(s).

Terrorism Revolutionary movements like the Red Army that are thwarted in their goals may resort to **terrorism:** organized, politically motivated violence directed against government or high-visibility targets in such a way as to conceal the identity and location of those perpetrating the act(s) (Gibbs, 1989). We are all familiar with terrorists' tactics: hijacking, bombing, kidnapping, and assassinating key figures. Terrorists justify even the most heinous of such acts on the grounds that their ultimate objective is morally compelling. Furthermore, the murder of innocents can be rationalized easily in cultures where the value of human life is considered collectively.

Many well-known groups use terrorism: the Palestinian Liberation Organization, the Shining Path of Peru, the Irish Republican Army, to name a few. They achieve publicity through their manipulation of the mass media. Publicity justifies the violence; it gives the groups' political views worldwide attention and greater importance than they could otherwise obtain. For those who feel an overwhelming need to change the world but who feel powerless to do so through established political channels, terrorism offers a glimmer of success. Rarely, however, will terrorism generate much social change beyond extra security measures instituted at airports and on behalf of wealthy or high-profile political targets.

In sum, the example of Japan shows that as societies begin to develop, diffusion, innovation, and social movements combine to produce social change. As changes occur, they make others more likely, and the process accelerates. We can thus expect

Terrorist organizations see the need to work outside established political channels and use outrageous acts to attract attention to their cause.

today's developing societies to undergo the often bewildering rate of change experienced by both Japan and the United States.

We now return full circle to the sociological perspective introduced in the first chapter. Throughout this text, we have looked beyond common sense notions that, for example, change equates with progress. We have used several perspectives to explore the various facets of the change process. We might now reflect on how such global changes close off some pathways in our personal lives and lead us into new ones—taking us off to war on the one hand but breaking up military communities on the other, creating new jobs and eliminating others, and bringing into our homes vegetables from Chile and appliances from Korea. The sociological perspective enables us to see more of the richness and complexity of the social world.

Why Do People Join Social Movements?

During the 1960s and 1970s, Americans became accustomed to news broadcasts of protestors around the world being attacked or counterattacked by waves of baton-swinging, helmeted riot police. The apparent benefits of participation in social movements sometimes seem insufficient to explain why members willingly suffer beatings, imprisonment, and humiliation for the group cause. According to the *stage model* (Hirsch, 1986), people join social movements for different reasons and at different levels of involvement depending on the stage of the movement's development. As a social movement grows, it may offer different kinds of incentives, from economic self-interest to social solidarity to political power. At any point in its history, a social movement can attract a mixture of people who have different reasons for joining. Another rationale is that in socially disorganized settings, confused and impulsive people likely seek security and feelings of righteousness in the movement (Turner and Killian, 1987). While this may explain some participation, other movements, particularly political protests, are often carefully planned by close-knit groups of committed individuals.

Eric Hirsch searched for the basis of such dedication during the 1981–1985 divestment protest movement at Columbia University (Hirsch, 1990). Several hundred students staged a "sit-in" in 1985 to demand that the university divest itself of stock in companies doing business in racist South Africa. The sit-in lasted three weeks, during which students endured freezing rain, missed classes, exams, and study time, lost primary relationships with nonprotesters, and faced the threat of expulsion.

Hirsch used several methods to discover why these students made such a commitment, most of them for the first time. He spent hours each day observing the participants, discussing the protest with them and others. He read all leaflets and press reports on the demonstration. He later conducted 19 extensive interviews, of about one and one-half hours each, with students who had participated. Hirsch also distributed a survey to the dormitory mailboxes of a random sample of the college's students (his return rate was 60 percent).

From the information he collected, Hirsch discovered that the sit-in participants did not make their commitment on the basis of isolated individual cost/benefit calculations but on political solidarity. Several processes within the group mobilized the students: consciousness raising (through rap sessions, forums, and teach-ins), collective empowerment (manipulating a large number of demonstrators into a stand-off confrontation to convince them that a protest might work), polarization (the protest members saw their own welfare tied to the group's fate as it confronted a surprisingly stern response from the university) and group decision making.

Five months after the protest, the university divested.   □

SUMMARY

We use a global sociological perspective in considering whether *social change*, or differences over time that occur in parts of a society or culture, is good for developing nations. From an ethnocentric point of view, the answer is clearly "yes": Those nations benefit from becoming more like us, but using cultural relativism, we note that societies have different needs and that the value of change depends on one's theoretical perspective. From the *evolutionary perspective*, social change moves from simple to complex. According to the nineteenth century's *unilinear evolutionary perspective*, all cultures change along the path of "advanced" Western nations, but social scientists have since abandoned this viewpoint. Instead, they now use a *multilinear evolutionary perspective* which assumes that cultures move along different paths as they change, although generally in a parallel direction. This direction, however, may not necessarily result in progress. From the *cyclical perspective*, social change takes the form of repeating phases of a cycle, like those of a pendulum or rising and falling waves, although social decline cannot necessarily be avoided or controlled. The *functionalist theory of change* holds that social systems tend toward stability. *Cultural lag* results when one part of a culture, usually the technology, changes faster than the rest of the culture, causing incompatibility and disequilibrium According to *equilibrium theory*, a change in one part of a social system requires compensatory adjustments elsewhere. This adjustment is necessary partly because of *differentiation*, an underlying pattern of change in which a social system fragments into two or more new parts. According to the *conflict theory of change*, conflict is constant and the key causing social change. Karl Marx observed that change based on economic conflict has historically fueled social progress. Ralf Dahrendorf argues that an unequal distribution of power creates the tensions underlying change. According to world systems theory, conflict arises from the exploitation of countries on the periphery by core nations.

Societies undergoing *modernization* move from simple agrarian forms toward urban, industrial, "Western" ones. Africa demonstrates how this process increases economic well-being and raises the standard of living. It may also narrow class inequalities and create new job opportunities. Power tends to become centralized in modernizing nations, but in Africa democratic reforms often end with violence. Modernization tends to make social relations more impersonal, less intimate, and contractual, though Africa's traditional associations have allayed this tendency. Education becomes more accessible, but quality is uneven in modernizing areas like Africa, and it does not always lead to higher productivity. Tribal religions must compete with invading faiths, and families must adjust to changes in gender roles and family controls. Women find more job opportunities but often at the low end of the labor market, and their new freedoms often bring them into conflict with other traditions and responsibilities. Cities in modernizing nations attract many uprooted people, who often create vast slums. Deviance flourishes in the confusion of modernization. Public health usually improves, but new diets and behaviors lead to a different range of risks and diseases.

Japan's experience shows how developing societies change. Before it could begin to modernize, Japan had to adopt less conservative attitudes toward newness, abandon its strong cultural cohesion, and take advantage of its physical environment. As with other societies, foreign contact played the key role in Japan's success. Such contact facilitates the spread or transmission of elements from one culture to another, or *diffusion*. Modernization leads to *convergence*, a growing similarity among affected cultures. Diffusion, however, is selective; new elements are rejected unless they are compatible with the receiving culture, and even when they are accepted they are usually altered to fit the receiving way of life. Intercultural contact benefits both developed and undeveloped societies, but the piecemeal adoption of cultural traits can cause problems. The addition of new, internally produced elements to a culture, or *innovation*, also effects change. When the innovation is a new creation, it is an *invention*; when it is a new awareness of something that has already existed, the innovation is a *discovery*. Innovations can lead to profound social changes, but only if they are culturally compatible and do not challenge vested interests.

Change also results from *social movements*, organized attempts to promote or resist some social change. Such collective efforts do not usually develop in premodern societies where tradition dominates, but social discontent may be expressed as a religious movement. Once a society begins to develop, social movements typically emerge, especially if people feel *relative deprivation*—that their living standards are lower than others' or their own in the past. Such feelings are likely to arise when improvements are lost or are perceived as inadequate. Social movements are also formed on the basis of shared discontent. According to *resource mobilization theory*, resources must be activated to fulfill a nation's potential for social change. That is, frustrated individuals must be integrated into their community and their organizations must possess adequate assets before they can take action. A growing economy facilitates this mobilization of resources. Social movements sometimes result from instigation by outsiders, but they are increasingly guided by professional activists who effectively use protest to recruit members, generate assets, and form networks.

Social movements take several forms. Reform movements aim to improve, not destroy society. They usually focus on one issue and try to work within the existing system. Resistance movements try to prevent further change or reverse changes already made. Expressive movements seek to bring about an inward, personal transformation of their members. Revolutionary movements aim to overthrow existing institutions and replace them with new ones. *Terrorism* is organized, politically motivated violence directed against government or high-visibility targets in such a way as to conceal the identity and location of those perpetrating the act(s). Terrorists seek publicity and attention, but rarely generate much social change.

Key Terms

social change	cyclical perspective	innovation
evolutionary perspective	functionalist theory of change	invention
unilinear evolutionary perspective	equilibrium theory	discovery
multilinear evolutionary perspective	cultural lag	social movement
	conflict theory of change	relative deprivation
	modernization	resource mobilization theory
	diffusion	terrorism

GLOSSARY

Absolute poverty: lack of an income adequate to provide necessary food, clothing, and shelter.

Accommodation: the process by which a minority group lives side by side with the majority and adapts to the mainstream culture without embracing it.

Acculturation: the process by which a minority group accepts the culture of the dominant group.

Achieved status: a social position acquired through a person's actions.

Ageism: social attitudes and stereotypes that devalue old age and the elderly.

Amalgamation: the blending of subcultures to produce a new culture and, through intermarriage, a new population.

Androgyny: the absence of cultural definitions of femininity or masculinity; including characteristics of both genders.

Animism: the belief in spiritual forces and souls.

Anomie: a state of confusion or normlessness.

Anticipatory socialization: the process of learning to perform a particular role with the expectation of assuming that role in the future.

Ascribed status: a social position assigned by factors beyond the individual's control, such as biology or the passage of time.

Assimilation: integration or absorption of a minority culture into the dominant culture.

Authoritarian: a form of government in which the state controls only the political system.

Authority: legitimate, formal power based on socially recognized status; in politics, power regarded as legitimate or appropriate.

Autocracy: form of government in which power rests in the hands of one person or a few people.

Bilateral descent: tracing ancestry through both parents.

Biological determinism: the tendency to explain human behaviors in terms of genetic or other biological factors; also known as biological reductionism.

Biological universals: the biological features found in all members of the species.

Birth cohort: people born within the same time frame.

Birth rate differential: the tendency for upper-class people to have fewer children than lower-class people.

Bourgeoisie: Marx's term for the class of individuals who own the means of production; the capitalist class.

Bureaucracy: a type of formal organization based on hierarchy, division of labor, and rules.

Capitalism: economic system in which the means of production are privately owned; market forces determine production and distribution.

Capitalist patriarchy: the interaction of capitalism with male supremacy that results in the occupational subordination of women.

Caste: a stratum in a closed system of stratification in which social mobility is not allowed.

Coercive organization: an organization in which membership is not a matter of personal choice.

Collective behavior: relatively unstructured, unpredictable, spontaneous, and short-lived behaviors shared by people.

Competition: regulated struggle for limited rewards.

Conflict: interaction aimed at destroying or neutralizing opponents.

Conflict theory of change: the theory that conflict is constant and the key to causing social change.

Control group: used for comparison in an experiment, the group that should be similar in all relevant respects to the experimental group except that it does not receive the independent variable.

Convergence: a growing similarity among cultures brought on by modernization.

Cooperation: a form of exchange in which people combine their efforts toward a common goal.

Corporatism: form of advanced capitalism in which top labor and business leaders negotiate wage and price agreements at the national level.

Correlation: a mathematically measurable association between two or more variables.

Correspondence principle: that the organization of the schools mirrors that of the workplace.

Counterculture: a subculture that in some way(s) stands in opposition to the mainstream culture.

Credentialism: the demand for ever-higher educational levels that are irrelevant or unnecessary for actual job performance; a means of restricting job competition to only those from advantaged backgrounds.

Crowd: a relatively unstructured, short-lived gathering of people who share a common focus for their attention.

Crude birth rate: the annual number of births per 1,000 total population.

Crude death rate: the annual number of deaths per 1,000 total population.

Cult: a usually small religious group headed by a charismatic leader offering an innovative belief system outside the cultural mainstream.

Cultural lag: when one part of a culture does not change at the same pace as others, causing incompatibility and disequilibrium.

Cultural pluralism: the coexistence of ethnic groups with some degree of mutual respect and tolerance for one another's cultures.

Cultural relativism: the viewpoint through which we judge other cultures relative to how they meet the needs of their people.

Culture: a learned, shared, integrated way of life.

Culture of poverty: a way of life embodying fatalism, apathy, and other attitudes that perpetuate social and economic disadvantages.

Cyclical perspective: the view that social change takes the form of repeating phases of a cycle.

De facto segregation: separation and exclusion of a minority group based on custom, tradition, and personal choice.

De jure segregation: legally sanctioned separation and exclusion of a minority group.

Democracy: form of government in which power rests in the hands of the governed.

Demographic transition theory: the theory that initially small, stable populations experience substantial growth and restabilization through a three-stage decline in death rates and, later, birth rates.

Demography: the scientific study of the size, distribution, and composition of populations.

Denomination: a large, wealthy, respected, tolerant religious organization.

Dependency ratio: the proportion of people of nonworking age (under 15 and over 65) in a population.

Dependency theory: the theory that the penetration of foreign capital undermines the economies of developing countries.

Dependent variable: in an experiment, the effect or result presumably caused by the independent variable.

Desocialization: unlearning the behavior patterns associated with old roles.

Determinism: the assumption that every phenomenon has a cause.

Deviance: behavior that violates mainstream norms.

Differential association: the notion that delinquency can be culturally transmitted, depending on the balance of illegitimate and legitimate attitudes a person learns from his or her associations.

Differentiation: an underlying pattern of change in which one part of a social system fragments into two or more parts.

Diffusion: the spread or transmission of elements from one culture to another.

Discovery: the awareness of a cultural element that has already existed, or such an element itself.

Discrimination: differential, unequal treatment of people based solely on their group membership.

Dual labor market: a segregated labor market in which workers in the primary sector enjoy advantages that those in the secondary sector do not.

Dual labor market theory: the theory that there is an advantageous "core" job sector with superior worker benefits, as contrasted with a "periphery" sector with lower pay, less security, poorer benefits, and fewer opportunities for advancement.

Dysfunction: the negative consequence or effect a part has for the whole social system.

Egalitarianism: when applied to the family, the equal sharing of power between spouses.

Ego: the logical, conscious portion of the personality responsible for balancing the demands of the id with the superego.

Empirical data: information based on observation and experience.

Equilibrium theory: the theory that a change in one part of a social system requires compensatory adjustments elsewhere.

Ethnic group: a socially defined group distinguished by its nationality or distinctive way of life.

Ethnic identification: feelings of closeness and shared interests among members of an ethnic group.

Ethnocentrism: the belief that one's own way of life is superior and properly serves as the standard by which all others are judged.

Evangelism: a revivalistic, "old-time," Protestant-based movement that seeks to establish a personal relationship with Christ through conversion, ardent worship, and an appeal to the primary authority of the Bible.

Evolutionary perspective: the view that social change moves from simple to complex, from traditional to modern.

Exchange: a reciprocal transaction involving the giving and repayment of benefits and punishments.

Experiment: a research design in which relevant variables are manipulated and controlled in order to test a hypothesis.

Experimental group: the group to which the independent variable is applied in an experiment.

Expressive role: usually associated with femininity, this set of expectations focuses on providing emotional support and social integration.

Extended family: those related by blood.

Fads: folkways followed briefly and by only a small group of people.

Family: group of people related by blood, marriage, or adoption who form an economic and household unit.

Fashions: folkways describing some life style matter; longer than fads, they define what is tasteful and respectable.

Fecundity: the potential number of children an average woman can bear.

Fertility rate: the annual number of live births per 1,000 women of childbearing age.

Folkways: norms defining proper but not required behaviors.

Formal organization: a social structure purposefully established to efficiently accomplish a specific, large-scale task.

Formal sanctions: official rewards and punishments applied by authorized agents or people occupying specialized social-control roles.

Function: the positive consequence or effect a part has for the whole social system.

Functionalism (or structural functionalism): a perspective that assumes society is comprised of interrelated parts which contribute to its stability and maintenance.

Functionalist theory of change: the theory that social systems tend toward stability.

Fundamentalism: an antimodern, antisecular approach to religion based on a literal interpretation of scripture and a return to "original truth."

Gemeinschaft: a model of community social relations characterized by intimacy, cooperation, and emotional satisfaction.

Gender: social status based on culturally determined distinctions of men and women; a set of personality traits associated with being female or male.

Gender identity: self-conception as a female or male.

Gender role socialization: the process by which males and females are taught behavior and attitudes considered appropriate to their sex.

Gender roles: behavior patterns considered appropriate for each sex.

Generalized other: Mead's term for an integrated view of the attitudes and expectations of society as a whole.

Genocide: extermination or annihilation of a racial or ethnic group.

Gentrification: the restoration of a neglected urban neighborhood by middle- and upper-middle-class newcomers.

Gesellschaft: a model of community social relations characterized by individual life style freedom and impersonal, formal, competitive relationships.

Government: those who occupy positions of power in the state, and the institutions they form.

Group: two or more people who interact recurrently within a structured situation, and who share a common purpose or goal and a consciousness of membership.

Hidden curriculum: the largely middle-class values and standards of behavior implicitly and explicitly taught in school but not part of the formal curriculum.

Homogamy: the tendency of people to select marriage partners of similar social backgrounds.

Human capital: the potential to contribute to society, usually measured in terms of educational level, skills, and work experience; acquired capabilities for contributing to the economy.

Hypothesis: a statement depicting the expected relationship between two or more variables; an informed guess about such a relationship.

Id: the innate, unconscious portion of the personality; it represents selfish desires and drives.

Ideology: a set of ideas or beliefs that explains and justifies social arrangements.

Independent variable: in an experiment, the suspected cause.

Infant mortality rate: the annual number of deaths of children under age 1 per 1,000 live births.

Inference: reasoning from the known to the unknown.

Influence: informal power based on personal attributes.

Informal sanctions: rewards and punishments applied by people with no special authority.

In-group: those people with whom we identify or feel part of.

Innovation: the addition of new, internally produced elements to a culture, or such an element itself.

Institutionalized discrimination: unequal treatment of minority group members based on entrenched social policies and customs; may be unintentional.

Institutions: widely-shared, relatively stable, standardized solutions for society's major tasks.

Instrumental role: usually associated with masculinity, this set of expectations focuses on performing tasks and achieving goals.

Interest groups: voluntary associations that attempt to influence political policies for the benefit of their members.

Intergenerational mobility: social mobility between generations, usually measured by comparing one's own class level with that of one's parents.

Internalization: the process by which people make society's norms their own.

Intragenerational mobility: social mobility within one's own lifetime.

Invasion: new populations or activities coming into an area.

Invention: the creation of a new cultural element, or such an element itself.

Latent functions: unintended, unrecognized, or unexpected effects or consequences of social elements.

Laws: formalized norms put in writing and publicly decreed by authorities.

Life expectancy rate: the average number of years a person born in a specific year can expect to live.

Macrosociological: a perspective that studies society as a whole or its basic patterns or systems.

Magic: a set of beliefs and practices intended to control natural and supernatural forces.

Majority group: that part of a population that controls access to cultural, political, and economic resources; the dominant group.

Mana: a supernatural force thought to exist within certain beings or objects.

Manifest functions: intended consequences or goals of social elements.

Mass behavior: reaction by widely separated people to the same stimulus, though in individual ways.

Mass hysteria: a form of collective behavior involving persecutions, widespread acceptance of unlikely stories, or symptoms of physical illness, usually stemming from fear and stress.

Mass media: means of communication directed at large numbers of people.

Master status: the status that determines more than any other how people respond to one another.

Material culture: concrete, physical, human-made parts of a way of life.

Matriarchy: family system placing authority in the hands of women.

Matrilineal: tracing ancestry through the mother.

Mechanical solidarity: community cohesion based on collective conscience, homogeneity, tradition, and consensus.

Medicalization: a trend in which the medical establishment increases its control over ever more parts of society.

Megalopolis: a huge conglomeration of two or more metropolitan areas.

Meritocracy: a system in which merit or ability determines one's place in the social hierarchy.

Metropolitan area: an area with a large population nucleus along with any adjoining communities economically and socially integrated into that central area.

Microsociological: a perspective that focuses on interactions among individuals.

Middleman minorities: minority groups limited to serving society's needs at mid-level occupations.

Migration: the movement of people from one area to another, usually with the intention of establishing a new residence.

Minority group: a culturally or physically distinct population subset whose members are assigned subordinate status and given less access to social resources than the dominant majority group.

Mob: a type of active crowd, aroused and emotional, with a focus or specific target for its violence.

Modernization: the process of urbanization and industrialization, often involving "Westernization."

Monogamy: one spouse per person at any one time.

Mores: serious norms defining behaviors considered essential to society's survival.

Multilinear evolutionary perspective: the view that cultures move along different paths as they change, although generally in a parallel direction.

Multinational corporations (MNCs): business organizations that transcend national boundaries, with branches and facilities in many countries.

Nonmaterial culture: abstract parts of a way of life, including beliefs, traditions, and customs.

Norms: behavioral guidelines or rules.

Nuclear family: one or two parents and their unmarried offspring.

Objectivity: maintaining clear, undistorted, and accurate perceptions free of emotions or biases.

Oligarchy: rule by the few.

Organic solidarity: community cohesion based on specialization and interdependence.

Out-group: those people with whom we do not identify or feel part of.

Panic: irrational, collective flight from some perceived threat.

Parkinson's Law: in a bureaucracy, workers will use all available time to complete a given task.

Patriarchy: family system placing authority in the hands of the husband or, in the case of the extended family, the eldest male of the household.

Patrilineal: tracing ancestry through the father.

Peer groups: interacting groups of equals, usually of the same age or sex status.

Peter Principle: in a bureaucracy, workers tend to rise to their level of incompetence.

Politics: the process through which people gain and use power.

Polyandry: form of polygamy in which the wife has more than one husband.

Polygamy: marriage form involving several spouses for either the husband or the wife.

Polygyny: form of polygamy in which the husband has more than one wife.

Population pyramid: a figure depicting the proportions of the sexes and age groups in a population.

Poverty line: an official line designating the minimum income needed to feed, house, and clothe a family.

Power: the ability to impose one's will.

Power elite: a unified group of several hundred individuals who exert great control over government, business, and military affairs.

Prejudice: an emotional, rigid attitude that prejudges people on the basis of their group membership.

Prestige: honor, respect, and admiration accorded an individual.

Primary deviance: behavior that violates social norms but evokes no societal reaction to define the behaver as deviant.

Primary group: a group based on expressive ties; it tends to be small, cooperative, intimate, and person-centered.

Profane: dealing with the ordinary, commonplace, and secular.

Proletariat: Marx's term for the exploited working class in a capitalist society.

Public: a large, dispersed population of people with some shared interest or purpose.

Race: a population with a common genetic heritage and distinctive physical features.

Racism: belief in the innate inequality of races; the notion that differences in individual and cultural achievements are determined by race.

Random assignment: using chance to sort units of study into experimental and control groups.

Recidivism: the tendency of released inmates to return to prison.

Redlining: the practice in which banks and other lending institutions refuse to qualify low-income groups, often minorities, for home mortgages, thereby excluding those groups from certain neighborhoods.

Reference groups: groups or social units a person uses for self-evaluation.

Relative deprivation: insufficient income to afford what others have; discontent that occurs when people perceive their living standards as lower than others' or their own in the past.

Religion: a system of beliefs and practices shared by a people as they relate themselves to the supernatural.

Representative sample: a subset of the target population that reflects the characteristics of that larger population.

Repression: the process of forcing unwanted impulses, feelings, or memories to the unconscious level.

Resocialization: the process by which the individual learns new values and behaviors in place of older ones.

Resource mobilization theory: the theory that resources must be activated to fulfill a nation's potential for social change.

Reverse discrimination: preferential treatment given to minorities at the expense of the majority group.

Reverse socialization: the process in which the supposed targets of socialization influence the supposed socializers.

Riot: a type of active crowd, aroused and emotional, with no focus or specific target for its violence.

Ritualism: rigid conformity to an organization's rules to the point of forgetting or ignoring the organization's goals.

Role: the set of behaviors expected of a person occupying a particular status.

Role conflict: a clash of two or more roles.

Role set: several roles related to one status.

Role strain: conflict between several demands within a single role.

Role taking: mentally assuming the perspective of another person, enabling us to look at ourselves from others' point of view.

Rumors: stories of an unknown source passed from one person to another.

Sacred: out-of-the-ordinary beliefs and practices that inspire awe and reverence.

Sanctions: rewards and punishments aimed at regulating behaviors.

Scapegoating: placing the blame for one's own misfortune on someone else.

Secondary deviance: behavior that results from society labeling a person as deviant for earlier behavior.

Secondary group: a group based on impersonal, goal-oriented, instrumental relationships.

Sect: a usually small religious organization at odds with larger society that claims sole legitimacy.

Segregation: physical isolation and social exclusion of a minority group from the dominant group.

Self: the individual's organized set of beliefs, dispositions, values, and interests; one's awareness of what kind of person she or he is.

Self-image: the total perceptions of one's body and personality, capabilities, and other qualities.

Separatism: desire for cultural distance from the dominant group.

Sex ratio: the proportion of men to women in a population.

Sexism: the prejudiced belief that males are innately superior to females.

Sexual division of labor: the separation of work into distinct specializations deemed appropriate for males and females.

Significant others: persons whose affection, approval, and judgment are especially important in the development of the self.

Social change: differences over time that occur in parts of a society or culture; "socio-cultural change" is perhaps more accurate, but is less often used.

Social class: a stratum of individuals sharing similar amounts of wealth, power, and prestige; according to Marxists, *class* refers to people of similar positions or levels of control in the economy.

Social control: rules and actions aimed at regulating human behavior.

Social differentiation: the process of categorizing individuals according to personal attributes.

Social distance: the degree to which we feel a differentness or sense of otherness.

Social interaction: people responding to one another's actions.

Social movement: an organized attempt to promote or resist some social change.

Social network: the web of social relationships that link us directly or indirectly to other people and groups.

Social stratification: institutionalized social inequality, in which social patterns determine the allocation of social rewards.

Social structure: stable, predictable, patterned social relationships.

Social system: a set of interdependent parts.

Socialism: economic system in which the means of production are collectively owned; the state directs production and distribution.

Socialization: the process by which humans learn the behaviors and beliefs appropriate for their social surroundings.

Socialization agents: the people, groups, and organizations responsible for the molding of individuals.

Society: a large population, usually enduring at least several generations and sharing a territory and a way of life.

Sociobiology: the study of animal and human behavior patterns that stresses the central importance of evolved, genetic influences.

Sociological imagination: the ability to perceive relationships between personal experience and the broader social environment.

Sociology: the scientific study of human society and social behaviors.

Spatial mismatch hypothesis: that the shift of low-skill jobs to the suburbs accounts for the high unemployment rates of minorities in the inner cities.

Split labor markets: the condition in which members of some groups are paid less than other workers for the same work; a means of driving down wage levels.

State: an institution that claims a monopoly on the use of physical force within its territory.

Status: a person's recognized social position.

Status inconsistency: a condition in which one holds substantially different rankings in various status hierarchies.

Stereotypes: fixed generalizations about all members of a group or category.

Structural mobility: widespread changes in class status caused by changes in society, especially the economy.

Structural theory of poverty: the theory that poverty is largely built into the patterns and policies of society and the economy.

Subculture: a distinct way of life shared by a subset of society that has some aspects of the mainstream, dominant culture.

Succession: the process in which one population or activity displaces another in an area.

Superego: the portion of the personality dedicated to controlling the id and gaining social approval; it functions as the moral conscience.

Symbolic racism: espousing racial equality but blaming other races' lack of success on their supposed innate inferiority.

Symbols: stimuli that represent things or ideas; having no inherent meaning, they must be learned.

Terrorism: organized, politically motivated violence directed against government or high-visibility targets in such a way as to conceal the identity and location of those perpetrating the act(s).

Theories: logical, well-supported explanations about how facts are related.

Total institutions: institutions which monitor and regulate all aspects of the inmates' lives.

Totalitarianism: form of autocracy in which the state uses its concentrated political power to totally shape the lives of its citizens.

Trained incapacity: excessive reliance on established procedure to the point that adaptability is impaired.

Underclass: a persistently poor, economically and socially isolated social stratum.

Unilinear evolutionary perspective: the discredited view that social change occurs along only one path, that of "advanced" cultures.

Urbanism: a way of life in cities characterized by increased social differentiation and stratification.

Urbanization: the process in which increasing proportions of the population become concentrated in cities and suburbs.

Value consensus: an underlying, widespread agreement on a group's goals and the proper means of achieving them.

Values: shared, persisting standards about what is good, right, moral, or desirable.

Variables: characteristics that vary from one individual, group, or time to another.

Vertical mobility: movement up or down the social ladder.

Voluntary association: an organization in which membership is optional and not remunerative.

World systems theory: the theory that developed societies (the "core") exploit the less developed nations (the "periphery") for their resources, labor, and markets.

Zero population growth (ZPG): a state of no growth in a population, in which the number of births and immigrants is equal to or less than the number of deaths and emigrants.

REFERENCES

ABRAMOWITZ, ALAN I. 1991. Incumbency, campaign spending, and the decline of competition in U.S. House elections. *The Journal of Politics*, **53**, February, pp. 34–56.

ACOCK, ALAN C. AND VERN L. BENGTSON. 1980. Socialization and attribution processes: Actual versus perceived similarities among parents and youth. *Journal of Marriage and the Family*, **42**, pp. 501–515.

ADAMIC, LOUIS. 1944. *A nation of nations*. New York: Harper and Brothers.

ADER, ROBERT, NICHOLAS COHEN, AND DAVID FELTON. 1990. *Psychoneuroimmunology*. 2d ed. San Diego: Academic Press.

AGNEW, ROBERT. 1990. Adolescent resources and delinquency. *Criminology*, **28**, pp. 535–558.

————. 1991. A longitudinal test of social control theory and delinquency. *Journal of Research in Crime and Delinquency*, **28**, May, pp. 126–156.

————. 1992. Foundation for a general strain theory of crime and delinquency. *Criminology*, **30**, February, pp. 44–87.

AGUIRRE, BENIGNO E., FREDRIC D. WOLINSKY, JOHN NIEDERAUER, VERNA KEITH, AND LIH-JIUAN FANN. 1989. Occupational prestige in the health care delivery system. *Journal of Health and Social Behavior*, **30**, September, pp. 315–329.

AIDA, YUKIE AND TONI FALBO. 1991. Relationships between marital satisfaction, resources, and power strategies. *Sex Roles*, **24**, January, pp. 43–56.

AKARD, PATRICK J. 1992. Corporate mobilization and political power: The transformation of U.S. economic policy in the 1970s. *American Sociological Review*, **57**, October, pp. 597–615.

ALBA, RICHARD AND MITCHELL CHAMLIN. 1983. A preliminary examination of ethnic identification among whites. *American Sociological Review*, **48**, April, pp. 240–247.

ALBA, RICHARD AND REID GOLDEN. 1986. Patterns of ethnic marriage in the United States. *Social Forces*, **65**, pp. 202–223.

ALBA, RICHARD AND GWEN MOORE. 1982. Ethnicity in the American elite. *American Sociological Review*, **47**, June, pp. 373–383.

ALBRECHT, STAN AND TIM HEATON. 1984. Secularization, higher education, and religiosity. *Review of Religious Research*, **26**, pp. 43–58.

ALDRICH, NELSON. 1993. The upper class, up for grabs. *The Wilson Quarterly*, **17**, Summer, pp. 65–72.

ALEXANDER, KARL, MARTHA COOK, AND EDWARD MCDILL. 1978. Curriculum tracking and educational stratification: Some further evidence. *American Sociological Review*, **43**, February, pp. 47–66.

ALEXANDER, KARL AND AARON PALLAS. 1983. Private schools and public policy: New evidence on cognitive achievement in public and private schools. *Sociology of Education*, **56**, October, pp. 170–182.

ALEXANDER, PAMELA C., SHARON MOORE, AND ELMORE R. ALEXANDER III. 1991. What is transmitted in the intergenerational transmission of violence? *Journal of Marriage and the Family*, **53**, August, pp. 657–668.

ALFORD, RICHARD D. 1987. *Naming and identity: A cross-cultural study of personal naming practices*. New Haven, Conn.: HRAF Press.

ALLAN, EMILIE A. AND DARRELL J. STEFFENSMEIER. 1989. Youth, underemployment, and property crime: Differential effects of job availability and job quality on juvenile and young adult arrest rates. *American Sociological Review*, **54**, February, pp. 107–123.

ALLEN, MICHAEL P. AND PHILIP BROYLES. 1989. Class hegemony and political finance: Presidential campaign contributions of wealthy capitalist families. *American Sociological Review*, **54**, April, pp. 275–287.

———. 1991. Campaign finance reforms and the presidential campaign contributions of wealthy capitalist families. *Social Science Quarterly*, **72**, December, pp. 738–750.

ALLMAN, WILLIAM. 1993. The mating game. *U.S. News & World Report*, July 19, pp. 57–63.

ALTENHOF, J. C. 1984. Influence of item characteristics on male and female performance on SAT-math, unpublished doctoral dissertation, City University of New York.

ALWIN, DUANE. 1991. Family of origin and cohort differences in verbal ability. *American Sociological Review*, **56**, October, pp. 625–638.

AMANO, IKUO. 1989. The dilemma of Japanese education today. In James J. Shields, Jr. (ed.), *Japanese Schooling*. University Park, Penn.: The Penn State University Press.

AMATO, PAUL R. 1987. Family processes in one-parent, stepparent, and intact families: The child's point of view. *Journal of Marriage and the Family*, **49**, pp. 327–337.

AMATO, PAUL R. AND BRUCE KEITH. 1991. Parental divorce and adult well-being: A meta-analysis. *Journal of Marriage and the Family*, **53**, February, pp. 43–58.

AMBRY, MARGARET. 1992. Childless chances. *American Demographics*, April, p. 55.

———. 1993. Receipts from a marriage. *American Demographics*, February, pp. 30–37.

AMERICAN ASSOCIATION OF UNIVERSITY WOMEN. 1992. How schools shortchange girls. *EPIEgram*, **18**, March, pp. 1, 18.

AMES, KATRINE, CHRISTOPHER SULAVIK, NADINE JOSEPH, LUCILLE BEACHY, AND TODD PARK. 1992. Domesticated bliss. *Newsweek*, March 23, pp. 62–63.

ANDERSON, D. AND P. COLLINS. 1989. The impact on children's education: Influences on cognitive development. In S. Landers, "Watching T.V. children do learn." *Monitor (American Psychological Association)*, March, p. 25.

ANDERSON, ELIJAH. 1989. Sex codes and family life among poor inner-city youths. *Annals of the American Academy of Political and Social Science*, **501**, January, pp. 59–78.

ANDERSON, LORIN W. AND LEONARD PELLICER. 1990. Synthesis of research on compensatory and remedial education. *Educational Leadership*, **48**, September, pp. 10–15.

ANDERSON, STEPHEN A., CANDYCE S. RUSSELL, AND WALTER R. SCHUMM. 1983. Perceived marital quality and family life-cycle categories: A further analysis. *Journal of Marriage and the Family*, **45**, pp. 127–139.

ANDERSSON, BENGT-ERIK. 1989. Effects of public day-care: A longitudinal study. *Child Development*, **60**, pp. 857–866.

———. 1992. Effects of day-care on cognitive and socioemotional competence of thirteen-year-old Swedish schoolchildren. *Child Development*, **63**, pp. 20–36.

ANDRES, G. 1985. Business involvement in campaign finance: Factors influencing the decision to form a corporate PAC. *Political Science*, **18**, pp. 215–219.

ANDREWS, D. A., IVAN ZINGER, ROBERT D. HOGE, JAMES BONTA, PAUL GENDREAU AND FRANCIS T. CULLEN. 1990. Does correctional treatment work? A clinically relevant and psychologically informed meta-analysis. *Criminology*, **28**, pp. 369–392.

ANNANDALE, ELLEN. 1989. Proletarianization or restratification of the medical profession? The case of obstetrics. *International Journal of Health Services*, **19**, pp. 611–634.

ANTONOVSKY, AARON. 1987. *Unravelling the mystery of health*. San Francisco: Jo Sey-Bass.

APPIAH, KWAME ANTHONY. 1991. Altered states. *The Wilson Quarterly*, **15**, Winter, pp. 20–32.

AQUILINO, WILLIAM S. AND KHALIL R. SUPPLE. 1991. Parent–child relations and parent's satisfaction with living arrangements when adult children live at home. *Journal of Marriage and the Family*, **53**, February, pp. 13–27.

ARCHER, DANE AND ROSEMARY GARTNER. 1984. *Violence and crime in cross-national perspective*. New Haven, Conn.: Yale University Press.

ARGYLE, MICHAEL, MANSUR LALLJEE, AND MARK COOK. 1968. The effects of visibility on interaction in a dyad. *Human Relations*, **12**, pp. 3–17.

ARIES, P. 1962. *Centuries of childhood*. Harmondsworth: Penguin Books.

ARMINEN, ILKKA. 1990. The genesis of self-consciousness and its debt to the other: The case of Alcoholics Anonymous, paper presented at the 12th World Congress of Sociology, co-sponsored by the International Sociological Association and held in Madrid, Spain. July 9–13.

ARSENAULT, RAYMOND. 1984. The cooling of the South. *The Wilson Quarterly*, **8**, Summer, pp. 150–159.

ARTHUR, JOHN. 1991. Development and crime in Africa: A test of modernization theory. *Journal of Criminal Justice*, **19**, pp. 499–513.

ASCH, SOLOMON. 1955. Opinions and social pressure. *Scientific American*, **193**, November, pp. 31–55.

ASELTINE, ROBERT, JR., AND RONALD KESSLER. 1993. Marital disruption and depression in a community sample. *Journal of Health and Social Behavior*, **34**, September, pp. 237–251.

ASTONE, NAN AND SARA MCLANAHAN. 1991. Family structure, parental practices, and high school completion. *American Sociological Review*, **56**, June, pp. 309–320.

ATKINSON, PAUL. 1984. Training for certainty. *Social Science and Medicine*, **19**, pp. 949–956.

AUKETT, RICHARD, JANE RITCHIE, AND KATHRYN MILL. 1988. Gender differences in friendship patterns. *Sex Roles*, **19**, July, pp. 57–66.

BABCHUK, NICHOLAS AND HUGH P. WHITT. 1990. R-order and religious switching. *Journal for the Scientific Study of Religion*, **29**, pp. 246–254.

BACHMAN, JERALD G., LLOYD D. JOHNSTON, AND PATRICK M. O'MALLEY. 1987. *Monitoring the future questionnaire responses from the nation's high school seniors, 1986*. Ann Arbor, Mich.: University of Michigan Institute for Social Research.

BAHR, HOWARD. 1987. Ups and downs: Three Middletown families. *The Wilson Quarterly*, **11**, Winter, pp. 128–135.

BAILEY, J. MICHAEL AND RICHARD C. PILLARD. 1991. A genetic study of male sexual orientation. *Archives of General Psychiatry*, **48**, December, pp. 1089–1096.

BAILEY, THOMAS. 1993. Can youth apprenticeship thrive in the United States? *Educational Researcher*, **22**, April, pp. 4–10.

BAILEY, THOMAS AND ROGER WALDINGER. 1991. Primary, secondary, and enclave labor markets: A training systems approach. *American Sociological Review*, **56**, August, pp. 432–445.

BAILEY, WILLIAM C. 1990. Murder, capital punishment, and television: Execution publicity and homicide rates. *American Sociological Review*, **55**, October, pp. 628–633.

BAINBRIDGE, WILLIAM SIMS. 1978. *Satan's power*. Berkeley and Los Angeles, Calif.: University of California Press.

———. 1990. Explaining the church member rate. *Social Forces*, **68**, pp. 1287–1298.

BALDASSARE, MARK. 1982. The effects of neighborhood density and social control on resident satisfaction. *The Sociological Quarterly*, **23**, Winter, pp. 95–105.

BALDWIN, LAURA-MAE, HEIDI L. HUTCHINSON, AND ROGER A. ROSENBLATT. 1992. Professional relationships between midwives and physicians: Collaboration or conflict? *American Journal of Public Health*, **82**, February, pp. 262–264.

BALES, ROBERT F. 1953. The equilibrium problem in small groups. In Talcott Parsons, Robert F. Bales, and Edward A. Shils, (eds.), *Working papers in the theory of action*. Glencoe, Ill.: Free Press.

BALKWELL, JAMES W. 1990. Ethnic inequality and the rate of homicide. *Social Forces*, **69**, September, pp. 53–70.

————. 1991. From expectations to behavior: An improved postulate for expectation states theory. *American Sociological Review*, **56**, June, pp. 355–369.

BALTZELL, E. DIGBY. 1964. *The Protestant establishment: Aristocracy and caste in America*. New York: Random House.

BANDURA, ALBERT. 1990. Selective activation and disengagement of moral control. *Journal of Social Issues*, **46**, pp. 27–46.

BANDURA, ALBERT AND R. H. WALTERS. 1963. *Social learning and personality development*. New York: Holt, Rinehart and Winston.

BARKER-BENFIELD, J. 1979. Sexual surgery in the late nineteenth century. In C. Dreifus (ed.), *Seizing our bodies*. New York: Vintage.

BARLING, JULIAN, STEPHEN BLUEN, AND VERNE MOSS. 1990. Type A behavior and marital dissatisfaction: Disentangling the effects of achievement striving and impatience-irritability. *The Journal of Psychology*, **124**, pp. 311–319.

BARNETT, L. R. 1986. Bulimarexia as symptom of sex-role strain in professional women. *Psychotherapy: Theory, Practice, and Research*, **23**, pp. 311–315.

BARON, JAMES N. AND ANDREW E. NEWMAN. 1990. For what it's worth: Organizations, occupations, and the value of work done by women and nonwhites. *American Sociological Review*, **55**, April, pp. 155–175.

BARR, ROBERT AND KEN PEASE. 1990. Crime placement, displacement and deflection. In Michael Tonry and Norval Morris (eds.), *Crime and justice: An annual review of research*. Vol. 12. Chicago: University of Chicago Press.

BARRINGER, HERBERT, DAVID TAKEUCHI, AND PETER XENOS. 1990. Education, occupational prestige and income of Asian Americans. *Sociology of Education*, **63**, January, pp. 27–43.

BART, P. B. 1972. Depression in middle-age women. In V. Gornick and B. K. Moran (eds.), *Women in sexist society*. New York: New American Library.

BARZUN, JACQUES. 1991. *Begin here: The forgotten conditions of teaching and learning*. Chicago: University of Chicago Press.

BASSOFF, E. S. AND G. V. GLASS. 1982. The relationship between sex roles and mental health: A meta-analysis of twenty-six studies. *The Counseling Psychologist*, **10**, pp. 105–112.

BATES, TIMOTHY. 1985. Entrepreneur human capital endowments and minority business viability. *Journal of Human Resources*, **20**, pp. 540–554.

————. 1990. Entrepreneur human capital inputs and small business longevity. *Review of Economics and Statistics*, **72**, pp. 551–559.

BAVELAS, ALEX. 1953. Communication patterns in task-oriented groups. In Dorwin Cartwright and Alvin Zander (eds.), *Group Dynamics*. New York: Harper and Row.

BAYDAR, NAZLE AND JEANNE BROOKS-GUNN. 1991. Effects of maternal employment and child-care arrangements on preschoolers' cognitive and behavioral outcomes: Evidence from the children of the National Longitudinal Survey of Youth. *Development Psychology*, **27**, November, pp. 932–945.

BECK, E. M. AND STEWART TOLNAY. 1990. The killing fields of the deep South: The market for cotton and the lynching of blacks, 1882–1930. *American Sociological Review,* **55**, August, pp. 526–539.

BECK, MELINDA AND JEANNE GORDON. 1991. A dumping ground for granny. *Newsweek,* December 23, p. 64.

BECK, SCOTT H., BETTIE S. COLE, AND JUDITH A. HAMMOND. 1991. Religious heritage and premarital sex: Evidence from a national sample of young adults. *Journal for the Scientific Study of Religion,* **30**, pp. 173–180.

BECKER, BETSY JANE. 1990. Item characteristics and gender differences on the SAT-M for mathematically able youths. *American Educational Research Journal,* **27**, Spring, pp. 65–87.

BECKER, GARY. 1985. The allocation of effort, specific human capital, and the differences between men and women in earnings and occupations. *Journal of Labor Economics,* **3**, pp. S33–58.

BECKER, HOWARD. 1963. *Outsiders.* New York: Free Press.

BECKER, HOWARD AND BLANCHE GEER. 1958. The fate of idealism in medical school. *American Sociological Review,* **23**, pp. 50–56.

BECKMAN, HOWARD B. AND RICHARD M. FRANKEL. 1984. The effect of physician behavior on the collection of data. *Annals of Internal Medicine,* **101**, pp. 692–696.

BEER, JOHN. 1989. Relation of divorce to self-concepts and grade point averages of fifth-grade school children. *Psychological Reports,* **65**, pp. 104–106.

BELANGER, SARAH AND MAURICE PINARD. 1991. Ethnic movements and the competition model: Some missing links. *American Sociological Review,* **56**, August, pp. 446–457.

BELL, DANIEL. 1973. *The coming of post-industrial society.* New York: Basic Books.

———. 1976. *The cultural contradictions of capitalism.* New York: Basic Books.

BELLAH, ROBERT N. 1967. Civil religion in America. *Daedalus,* **96**, pp. 1–21.

BELLAS, MARCIA. 1993. Faculty salaries: Still a cost of being female? *Social Science Quarterly,* **74**, March, pp. 62–71.

BELSKY, JAY. 1988. The effects of infant day care reconsidered. *Early Childhood Research Quarterly,* **3**, pp. 235–272.

———. 1990. Parental and nonparental child care and children's socioemotional development: A decade in review. *Journal of Marriage and the Family,* **52**, pp. 885–903.

BELSKY, JAY AND MICHAEL ROVINE. 1990. Patterns of marital change across the transition to parenthood: Pregnancy to three years postpartum. *Journal of Marriage and the Family,* **52**, February, pp. 5–19.

BENBOW, CAMILLA. 1988. Sex differences in mathematical reasoning ability in intellectually talented preadolescents. *The Behavioral and Brain Sciences,* **11,** June, pp. 169–183.

BENN, R. 1986. Factors promoting secure attachment relationships between employed mothers and their sons. *Child Development,* **57**, pp. 1224–1231.

BENNETT, N. G., A. K. BLANC, AND D. E. BLOOM. 1988. Commitment and the modern union: Assessing the link between premarital cohabitation and subsequent marital stability. *American Sociological Review,* **53**, pp. 127–138.

BENNETT, RICHARD R. 1991. Development and crime: A cross-national, time-series analysis of competing models. *The Sociological Quarterly,* **32**, pp. 343–363.

BENNETT, RICHARD R. AND LOUISE SHELLEY. 1985. Crime and economic development: A longitudinal cross-national analysis. *Annales de Vaucresson,* **22**, pp. 13–32.

BENNETT, STEPHEN EARL. 1991. Left behind: Exploring declining turnout among non-college young whites, 1964–1988. *Social Science Quarterly,* **72**, June, pp. 314–333.

BENSON, MICHAEL L. AND ELIZABETH MOORE. 1992. Are white-collar and common offenders the same? An empirical and theoretical critique of a recently proposed general theory of crime. *Journal of Research in Crime and Delinquency*, **29**, August, pp. 251–272.

BERG, IVAR. 1970. *Education and jobs: The great training robbery*. New York: Praeger.

BERGER, PETER. 1979. *The heretical imperative: Contemporary possibilities of religious affirmation*. New York: Doubleday.

BERK, RICHARD A., ALEC CAMPBELL, RUTH KLAP, AND BRUCE WESTERN. 1992. The deterrent effect of arrest in incidents of domestic violence: A Bayesian analysis of four field experiments. *American Sociological Review*, **57**, October, pp. 698–708.

BERKMAN, LISA AND S. LEONARD SYME. 1979. Social networks, host resistance, and mortality: A nine-year follow-up study of Alameda County residents. *American Journal of Epidemiology*, **109**, pp. 186–204.

BERNARD, THOMAS J. 1990. Angry aggression among the "truly disadvantaged." *Criminology*, **28**, pp. 73–95.

BERRY, J. M., M. STORANDT, AND A. COYNE. 1984. Age and sex differences in somatic complaints associated with depression. *Journal of Gerontology*, **39**, pp. 465–467.

BIBLARZ, TIMOTHY J. AND ADRIAN E. RAFTERY. 1993. The effects of family disruption on social mobility. *American Sociological Review*, **58**, February, pp. 97–109.

BICKERTON, DEREK. 1990. *Language and species*. Chicago: University of Chicago Press.

BIELBY, WILLIAM AND JAMES BARON. 1984. A woman's place is with other women: Sex segregation within organizations. In Barbara Reskin (ed.), *Sex segregation in the workplace*. Washington, D.C.: National Academy Press.

BIELBY, WILLIAM T. AND DENISE D. BIELBY. 1989. Family ties: Balancing commitments to work and family in dual-earner households. *American Sociological Review*, **54**, pp. 776–789.

———. 1992. I will follow him: Family ties, gender-role beliefs, and reluctance to relocate for a better job. *American Journal of Sociology*, **97**, March, pp. 1241–1261.

BILLINGHAM, ROBERT E. AND KATHLEEN R. GILBERT. 1990. Parental divorce during childhood and use of violence in dating relationships. *Psychological Reports*, **66**, pp. 1003–1009.

BINSTOCK, R. 1985. The oldest old: A fresh perspective of compassionate ageism revisited? *Milbank Memorial Fund Quarterly*, **63**, Spring, pp. 420–451.

BIRD, CHLOE E. AND ALLEN M. FREMONT. 1991. Gender, time use, and health. *Journal of Health and Social Behavior*, **32**, June, pp. 114–129.

BIRKET-SMITH, KAJ. 1971. *Eskimos*. New York: Crown.

BISHOP, JOHN H. 1989. Is the test score decline responsible for the productivity growth decline? *American Economic Review*, **79**, March, pp. 178–197.

BISNAIRE, LISE M. C., PHILIP FIRESTONE, AND DAVID RYNARD. 1990. Factors associated with academic achievement in children following parental separation. *American Journal of Orthopsychiatry*, **60**, January, pp. 67–76.

BLACK, DONALD. 1983. Crime as social control. *American Sociological Review*, **48**, February, pp. 34–45.

BLACKBURN, R. 1978. Psychopathy, arousal and the need for stimulation. In R. D. Hare and D. Schalling (eds.), *Psychopathic behavior: Approaches to research*. Chichester, England: John Wiley and Sons.

BLACKLEY, PAUL R. 1990. Spatial mismatch in urban labor markets: Evidence from large U.S. metropolitan areas. *Social Science Quarterly*, **71**, March, pp. 39–52.

BLAIR, SAMPSON LEE AND MICHAEL P. JOHNSON. 1992. Wives' perceptions of the fairness of the division of household labor: The intersection of household and ideology. *Journal of Marriage and the Family*, **54**, August, pp. 570–581.

BLAKE, J. 1989. *Family size and achievement*. Berkeley, Calif.: University of California Press.

BLAKE, JUDITH. 1985. Number of siblings and educational mobility. *American Sociological Review*, **50**, February, pp. 84–94.

BLAKE, ROBERT AND JANE S. MOUTON. 1982. Theory and research for developing a science of leadership. *The Journal of Applied Behavioral Science*, **18**, pp. 275–291.

BLANCHARD-FIELDS, FREDDA, LORNE SULSKY, AND SUSAN ROBINSON-WHELEN. 1991. Moderating effects of age and context on the relationship between gender, sex role differences, and coping. *Sex Roles*, **25**, pp. 645–660.

BLAU, FRANCINE AND MARIANNE FERBER. 1991. Career plans and expectations of young women and men. *The Journal of Human Resources*, **26**, Fall, pp. 581–607.

BLAU, JUDITH AND PETER M. BLAU. 1982. The cost of inequality: Metropolitan structure and violent crime. *American Sociological Review*, **47**, pp. 114–129.

BLAU, PETER. 1977. *Inequality and heterogeneity: A primitive theory of social structure*. New York: Free Press.

BLAU, PETER, TERRY BLUM, AND JOSEPH SCHWARTZ. 1982. Heterogeneity and intermarriage. *American Sociological Review*, **47**, pp. 45–62.

BLAU, PETER AND OTIS DUNCAN. 1967. *The American occupational structure*. New York: John Wiley and Sons.

BLAU, PETER AND JOSEPH SCHWARTZ. 1984. *Crosscutting social circles*. Orlando, Fla.: Academic Press.

BLOOMFIELD, BRIAN P. 1989. On speaking about computing. *Sociology*, **23**, pp. 409–426.

BLUM, TERRY. 1985. Structural constraints on interpersonal relations. *American Journal of Sociology*, **91**, pp. 511–521.

BLUMER, HERBERT. 1939. Collective behavior. In Robert E. Park (ed.), *Principles of sociology*. New York: Barnes and Noble.

———. 1951. Collective behavior. In Alfred McClung Lee (ed.), *New Outline of the principles of sociology*. New York: Barnes and Noble.

———. 1969. *Symbolic Interactionism*. Englewood Cliffs, N.J.: Prentice-Hall.

BODOVITZ, KATHY AND BRAD EDMONSON. 1991. Asian American. *American Demographics Desk Reference*, July, pp. 16–18.

BOGGIANO, ANN AND MARTY BARRETT. 1991. Gender differences in depression in college students. *Sex Roles*, **25**, pp. 595–605.

BOHANNON, JUDY ROLLINS. 1991. Religiosity related to grief levels of bereaved mothers and fathers. *Omega*, **23**, pp. 153–159.

BOHM, ROBERT. 1991. American death penalty opinion, 1936–1986: A critical examination of the Gallup Polls. In R. Bohm (ed.), *The death penalty in America: Current research*. Cincinnati, Ohio: Anderson.

BOLLEN, KENNETH AND DAVID PHILLIPS. 1982. Imitative suicides: A national study of the effects of television news stories. *American Sociological Review*, **47**, December, pp. 802–809.

BOOTH, ALAN AND PAUL AMATO. 1991. Divorce and psychological stress. *Journal of Health and Social Behavior*, **32**, December, pp. 396–407.

BOOTH, ALAN AND JOHN EDWARDS. 1985. Age at marriage and marital stability. *Journal of Marriage and the Family*, **47**, pp. 67–75.

BOOTH, ALAN AND D. WAYNE OSGOOD. 1993. The influence of testosterone on deviance in adulthood: Assessing and explaining the relationship. *Criminology*, **31**, pp. 93–117.

BOOTH, ALAN AND L. WHITE. 1980. Thinking about divorce. *Journal of Marriage and the Family*, **42**, pp. 605–616.

BORNSCHIER, VOLKER AND CHRISTOPHER CHASE-DUNN. 1985. *Transnational corporations and underdevelopment*. New York: Praeger.

BOSE, CHRISTINE E. AND PETER H. ROSSI. 1983. Gender and jobs: Prestige standings of occupations as affected by gender. *American Sociological Review*, **48**, pp. 316–330.

BOSK, CHARLES. 1980. Occupational rituals in patient management. *New England Journal of Medicine*, **303**, pp. 71–76.

BOSWELL, TERRY AND WILLIAM DIXON. 1990. Dependency and rebellion: A cross-national analysis. *American Sociological Review*, **55**, August, pp. 540–559.

BOURDIEU, PIERRE. 1977. Cultural reproduction and social reproduction. In Jerome Karabel and A. H. Halsey (eds.), *Power and ideology in education*. Oxford: Oxford University Press.

———. 1989. Social space and symbolic power. *Sociological Theory*, **7**, pp. 14–25.

BOWERS, WILLIAM AND GLENN PIERCE. 1980. Deterrence on brutalization: What is the effect of executions? *Crime & Delinquency*, **26**, pp. 453–484.

BOWLES, SAMUEL AND HERBERT GINTIS. 1976. *Schooling in capitalist America: Educational reform and the contradictions of economic life*. New York: Basic Books.

BOX, STEVEN. 1987. *Recession, crime and punishment*. New York: Barnes and Noble.

BOYD, ROBERT. 1990. Black and Asian self-employment in large metropolitan areas: A comparative analysis. *Social Problems*, **37**, May, pp. 258–272.

BRADBURY, KATHARINE. 1990. The changing fortunes of American families in the 1980s. *New England Economic Review*, July–August.

BRADSHAW, YORK. 1988. Reassessing economic dependency and uneven development: The Kenyan experience. *American Sociological Review*, **53**, October, pp. 693–708.

BRADY, DAVID AND KENT TEDIN. 1976. Ladies in pink: Religion and political ideology in the anti-ERA movement. *Social Sciences Quarterly*, **65**, pp. 564–575.

BRAITHWAITE, JOHN. 1993. Transnational regulation of the pharmaceutical industry. *The Annals of the American Academy of Political and Social Science*, **525**, January, pp. 12–30.

BRAUS, PATRICIA. 1992. What workers want. *American Demographics*, **14**, August, pp. 30–37.

BRAVERMAN, H. 1974. *Labor and monopoly capital*. New York: Monthly Review Press.

BRAY, J. T. 1988. Children: Development during early remarriage. In E. M. Herrington and J. D. Arasteh (eds.), *Impact of divorce, single parenting, and stepparenting on children*. Hillsdale, N.J.: Erlbaum.

BREAULT, K. D. 1986. Suicide in America: A test of Durkheim's theory of religious and family integration, 1933–1980. *American Journal of Sociology*, **92**, November, pp. 628–656.

———. 1988. Beyond the quick and dirty: Problems associated with analyses based on small samples or large ecological aggregates: Reply to Gerard. *American Journal of Sociology*, **93**, pp. 1479–1486.

BREMS, C. AND M. JOHNSON. 1989. Problem-solving appraisal and coping style: The influence of sex-role orientation and gender. *The Journal of Psychology*, **123**, pp. 187–194.

BREZNITZ, ZVIA AND TRACY SHERMAN. 1987. Speech patterning of natural discourse of well and depressed mothers and their young children. *Child Development*, **58**, April, pp. 395–400.

BRINT, STEVEN. 1984. New class and cumulative trend explanations of the liberal political attitudes of professionals. *American Journal of Sociology*, **90**, July, pp. 30–71.

BRODY, E. M. 1990. *Women in the middle: Their parent-care years*. New York: Springer.

BRODY, E. M., N. P. DEMPSEY, AND R. A. PRUCHNO. 1990. Mental health of sons and daughters of the institutionalized aged. *The Gerontologist*, **30**, pp. 212–219.

BRODY, E. M., S. J. LITVIN, C. HOFFMAN, AND M. H. KLEBAN. 1992. Differential effects of daughters' marital status on their parent-care experiences. *The Gerontologist*, **32**, pp. 58–67.

BRODY, GENE H., EILEEN NEUBAUM, AND REX FOREHAND. 1988. Serial marriage: A heuristic analysis of an emerging family form. *Psychological Bulletin*, **103**, pp. 211–222.

BRODY, JANE. 1981. Male hormones tied to aggresive acts. *New York Times*, March 7.

BRONFENBRENNER, URIE. 1966. Socialization and social class through time and space. In Reinhard Bendix and Seymour M. Lipset (eds.), *Class, status and power*. New York: Free Press.

BROOKS, CLARK. 1989. Plain in the reign of beauty. *Los Angeles Herald Examiner*, October 30.

BROVERMAN, I. 1979. In P. Bunkle (ed.), *Woman in New Zealand society*. Auckland, New Zealand: George Allen and Unwin.

BROWN, CHARLES. 1980. Equalizing differences in the labor market. *Quarterly Journal of Economics*, **94**, pp. 113–134.

BROWN, RALPH B., H. REED GEERTSEN, AND RICHARD S. KRANNICH. 1989. Community satisfaction and social integration in a boom town: A longitudinal analysis. *Rural Sociology*, **54**, pp. 568–586.

BROWNLEE, SHANNON AND ELIZABETH PEZZULLO. 1992. A cure for sexism: Women doctors herald a kinder, gentler way to practice medicine. *U.S. News & World Report*, March 23, pp. 86–89.

BRUCE, STEVE. 1990. *A house divided: Protestantism, schism, and secularization*. New York: Routledge.

BRUDERL, JOSEF, PETER PREISENDORFER, AND ROLF ZIEGLER. 1992. Survival chances of newly founded business organizations. *American Sociological Review*, **57**, April, pp. 227–242.

BRUDERL, JOSEF AND RUDOLF SCHUSSLER. 1990. Organizational mortality: The liabilities of newness and adolescence. *Administrative Science Quarterly*, **35**, pp. 530–547.

BUCHKO, AARON A. 1992. Employee ownership, attitudes, and turnover: An empirical assessment. *Human Relations*, **45**, pp. 711–733.

BULLOCK, CHARLES AND SUSAN MACMANUS. 1990. Structural features of municipalities and the incidence of Hispanic council members. *Social Science Quarterly*, **71**, December, pp. 665–681.

BUMPASS, LARRY AND JAMES A. SWEET. 1972. Differential in marital stability: 1970. *American Sociological Review*, **37**, pp. 754–766.

————. 1989. National estimates of cohabitation. *Demography*, **26**, November, pp. 615–627.

BUMPASS, LARRY, JAMES A. SWEET, AND ANDREW CHERLIN. 1991. The role of cohabitation in declining rates of marriage. *Journal of Marriage and the Family*, **53**, November, pp. 913–927.

BURAWOY, MICHAEL. 1985. *The Politics of production: Factory regimes under capitalism and socialism*. New York: Verso.

BURAWOY, MICHAEL AND PAVEL KROTOV. 1992. The Soviet transition from socialism to capitalism: Worker control and economic bargaining in the wood industry. *American Sociological Review*, **57**, February, pp. 16–38.

BURGER, JERRY. 1984. Desire for control, locus of control, and proneness to depression. *Journal of Personality*, **52**, pp. 71–89.

BURGOON, JUDEE K. 1991. Relational message interpretations of touch, conversational distance, and posture. *Journal of Nonverbal Behavior*, **15**, Winter, pp. 233–258.

BURKETT, STEVEN R. AND DAVID A. WARD. 1993. A note on perceptual deterrence, religiously based moral condemnation, and social control. *Criminology*, **31**, pp. 119–132.

BURSTEIN, PAUL. 1991. Reverse discrimination cases in the federal courts: Legal mobilization by a counter movement. *The Sociological Quarterly*, **32**, pp. 511–528.

BURSTIN, HELEN R., STUART LIPSITZ, AND TROYER BRENNAN. 1992. Socioeconomic status and risk for substandard medical care. *Journal of American Medical Association*, **268**, November 4, pp. 2383–2387.

BURTON, MICHAEL AND JOHN HIGLEY. 1987. Elite settlements. *American Sociological Review*, **52**, June, pp. 295–307.

BUSS, DAVID M. 1990. Unmitigated agency and unmitigated communion: An analysis of the negative components of masculinity and femininity. *Sex Roles*, **22**, pp. 555–567.

BUTLER, ROBERT N. 1987. Ageism. *Encyclopedia of Aging*. New York: Springer.

BUTLER, W. E. 1992. Crime in the Soviet Union: Early glimpses of the true story. *British Journal of Criminology*, **32**, Spring.

CAHILL, SPENCER. 1989. Fashioning males and females: Appearance management and the social reproduction of gender. *Symbolic Interaction*, **12**, Fall, pp. 281–298.

CALASANTI, TONI M. AND CAROL A. BAILEY. 1991. Gender inequality and the division of household labor in the United States and Sweden: A socialist-feminist approach. *Social Problems*, **38**, February, pp. 34–53.

CALISTRO, PADDY. 1988. In the land of the obsessed. *Los Angeles Times*, January 17.

CALLAHAN, DANIEL. 1987. *Setting limits: Medical goals in an aging society*. New York: Simon and Schuster.

———. 1990. *What kind of life: The limits of medical progress*. New York: Simon and Schuster.

CAMPBELL, KAREN AND BARRETT LEE. 1990. Gender differences in urban neighboring. *The Sociological Quarterly*, **31**, pp. 495–512.

CAN, LE THAC. 1991. Higher education reform in Vietnam, Laos, and Cambodia. *Comparative Education Review*, **35**, February, pp. 170–176.

CANAVAN, MARGARET M., WALTER J. MEYER, III, AND DEBORAH C. HIGGS. 1992. The female experience of sibling incest. *Journal of Marital and Family Therapy*, **18**, pp. 129–142.

CANTOR, MURIEL. 1987. Popular culture and the portrayal of women: Content and control. In Beth Hess and Myra Ferree (eds.), *Analyzing gender: A handbook of social research*. Newbury Park, Calif.: Sage.

CAPEK, STELLA M. 1993. The "environmental justice" frame: A conceptual discussion and an application. *Social Problems*, **40**, February, pp. 5–22.

CAPLOW, THEODORE, HOWARD BAHR, AND BRUCE CHADWICK. 1983. *All faithful people: Change and continuity in Middletown's religion*. Minneapolis, Minn.: University of Minneapolis Press.

CAPORAEL, LINDA. 1976. Ergotism: The Satan loosed in Salem? *Science*, **192**, April 2, pp. 21–26.

CAREY, GREGORY. 1992. Twin imitation for antisocial behavior: Implications for genetic and family environment research. *Journal of Abnormal Psychology*, **101**, pp. 18–25.

CARLSON, SUSAN M. 1992. Trends in race/sex occupational inequality: Conceptual and measurement issues. *Social Problems*, **39**, August, pp. 268–278.

CARNEVALE, ANTHONY. 1991. *America and the new economy*. Alexandria, Va.: The American Society for Training and Development.

CARPENTER, P. G. AND J. A. FLEISHMAN. 1987. Linking intention and behavior: Australian students' college plans and college attendance. *American Educational Research Journal*, **24**, pp. 79–105.

CARSON, DAVID K., LINDA M. GERTZ, MARY ANN DONALDSON, AND STEPHEN A. WONDER-LICH. 1991. Intrafamilial sexual abuse: Family-of-origin and family-of-procreation characteristics of family adult victims. *The Journal of Psychology*, **125**, pp. 579–597.

CASLER, L. 1965. The effects of extra tactile stimulation on a group of institutionalized infants. *Genetic Psychology Monographs*, **71**, pp. 137–175.

CHAGNON, N. A. 1968. Yanomamo social organization and warfare. In M. Fried, M. Harris, and R. Murphy (eds.), *War: The anthropology of armed conflict and aggression*. New York: Natural History Press.

CHAIKEN, JAN M. AND MARCIA CHAIKEN. 1982. *Varieties of criminal behavior*. Santa Monica, Calif.: Rand Corporation.

CHANCE, NORMAN A. 1966. *The Eskimo of North Alaska*. New York: Holt, Rinehart and Winston.

CHARLES, MARIA. 1992. Cross-national variation in occupational segregation. *American Sociological Review*, **57**, August, pp. 483–502.

CHEN, C. AND D. H. UTTAL. 1988. Cultural values, parents' beliefs, and children's achievement in the United States and China. *Human Development*, **31**, pp. 351–358.

CHERLIN, ANDREW. 1990. Recent changes in American fertility, marriage, and divorce. *The Annals of the American Academy of Political and Social Science*, **510**, July, pp. 145–154.

CHERLIN, ANDREW AND FRANK FURSTENBERG. 1988. The changing European family. *Journal of Family Issues*, **9**, pp. 291–297.

CHILD, IRWIN, HERBERT BARRY, AND MARGARET BACON. 1965. Sex differences. *Journal of Studies on Alcohol*, **3**, Supplement, pp. 49–61.

CHIRICOS, THEODORE G. 1987. Rates of crime and unemployment: An analysis of aggregate research evidence. *Social Problems*, **34**, pp. 187–212.

CHIRICOS, THEODORE G. AND MIRIAM A. DELONE. 1992. Labor surplus and punishment: A review and assessment of theory and evidence. *Social Problems*, **39**, November, pp. 421–436.

CHOMSKY, NOAM. 1957. *Syntactic structures*. The Hague: Mouton.

CHRISTENSEN, BRYCE J. 1992. In sickness and in health: The medical costs of family meltdown. *Policy Review*, Spring, pp. 70–73.

CLARK, ROGER. 1992. Economic dependency and gender differences in labor force sectoral change in non-core nations. *The Sociology Quarterly*, **33**, pp. 83–98.

CLARK-NICOLAS, PATRICIA AND BERNADETTE GRAY-LITTLE. 1991. Effect of economic resources on marital quality in black married couples. *Journal of Marriage and the Family*, **53**, August, pp. 645–655.

CLARKE-STEWART, K. ALISON. 1987. In search of consistencies in child-care research. In Deborah Phillips (ed.), *Quality in day care*. Washington, D.C.: NAEYC.

———. 1989. Infant day-care: Maligned or malignant? *American Psychologist*, **44**, pp. 266–273.

CLAUSEN, A. W. 1987. Poverty in the developing countries. In J. A. Frieder and D. A. Lake (eds.), *International political economy: Perspectives on global power and wealth*. New York: St. Martin's Press.

CLAWSON, DAN AND ALAN NEUSTADTL. 1989. Interlocks, PACs, and corporate conservatism. *American Journal of Sociology*, **4**, January, pp. 749–773.

CLIFFORD, WILLIAM. 1976. *Crime control in Japan*. Lexington, Mass.: D. C. Heath.

CLINARD, MARSHALL AND DANIEL ABBOTT. 1973. *Crime in developing countries: A comparative perspective*. New York: John Wiley.

CLOWARD, RICHARD AND LLOYD OHLIN. 1960. *Delinquency and opportunity*. New York: The Free Press.

COATES, WENDY, DETRICH JEHLE, AND ERIC COTTINGTON. 1989. Trauma and the full moon: A waning theory. *Annals of Emergency Medicine*, **18**, July, pp. 763–765.

COCHRAN, JOHN, LEONARD BEEGHLEY, AND WILBUR BOCK. 1988. Religiosity and alcohol: An exploration of reference group theory. *Sociological Forum*, **3**, Spring, pp. 256–276.

COHEN, ALBERT. 1955. *Delinquent boys*. New York: Free Press.

COHEN, BEN-ZION, RUTH EDEN, AND AMNON LAZAR. 1991. The efficacy of probation versus imprisonment in reducing recidivism of serious offenders in Israel. *Journal of Criminal Justice*, **19**, pp. 263–270.

COHEN, CARL I., HAL ONSERUD, AND CHARLENE MONACO. 1992. Project rescue: Serving the homeless and marginally housed elderly. *The Gerontologist*, **32**, pp. 466–471.

COHEN, CARL I., J. A. TERESI, D. HOLMES, AND E. ROTH. 1988. Survival strategies of older homeless men. *The Gerontologist*, **28**, pp. 58–65.

COHEN, JERE. 1987. Parents as educational models and definers. *Journal of Marriage and the Family*, **49**, May, pp. 339–351.

COHEN, LAWRENCE AND MARCUS FELSON. 1979. Social change and crime rate trends: A routine activities approach. *American Sociological Review*, **44**, pp. 588–607.

COHEN, LAWRENCE AND RICHARD MACHALEK. 1988. A general theory of expropriative crime: An evolutionary ecological approach. *American Journal of Sociology*, **94**, November, pp. 465–501.

COHN, STEVEN F., STEVEN E. BARKAN, AND WILLIAM A. HALTEMAN. 1991. Punitive attitudes toward criminals: Racial concensus or racial conflict? *Social Problems*, **38**, May, pp. 287–296.

COLEMAN, JAMES. 1993. The rational reconstruction of society: 1992 Presidential Address. *American Sociological Review*, **58**, February, pp. 1–15.

COLEMAN, JAMES, ERNEST Q. CAMPBELL, CAROL J. HOBSON, JAMES MCPARTLAND, ALEXANDER M. MOOD, FREDERIC D. WEINFELD, AND ROBERT L. YORK. 1966. *Equality of educational opportunity*. Washington, D.C.: U.S. Government Printing Office.

COLEMAN, JAMES, THOMAS HOFFER, AND SALLY KILGORE. 1981. Public and private schools, report to the National Center for Education Statistics by the National Opinion Research Center, University of Chicago. March.

COLEMAN, LERITA M., LEE JUSSIM, AND JERRY L. ISAAC. 1991. Black students' reactions to feedback conveyed by white and black teachers. *Journal of Applied Social Psychology*, **21**, pp. 460–481.

COLEMAN, MARILYN AND LAWRENCE H. GANONG. 1990. Remarriage and stepfamily research in the 1980s: Increased interest in an old family form. *Journal of Marriage and the Family*, **52**, November, pp. 925–940.

COLLEY, LINDA. 1992. Women and political power. *The Wilson Quarterly*, **16**, Spring, pp. 50–58.

COLLINS, RANDALL. 1980. *The credential society*. New York: Academic Press.

———. 1985. *Three sociological traditions*. New York: Oxford University Press.

COLLINS, RANDALL AND MICHAEL MAKOWSKY. 1978. *The discovery of society*. 2d ed. New York: Random House.

CONGER, RAND D., GLEN H. ELDER, JR., FREDERICK O. LORENZ, KATHERINE J. CONGER, RONALD L. SIMONS, LES B. WHITBECK, SHIRLEY HUCK, AND JANET N. MELBY. 1990. Linking economic hardship to marital quality and instability. *Journal of Marriage and the Family*, **52**, August, pp. 643–656.

CONRAD, PETER AND JOSEPH SCHNEIDER. 1980. *Deviance and medicalization: From badness to sickness*. St. Louis: Mosby.

CONTRATTO, S. 1984. Mothers. In M. Lewin (ed.), *The shadow of the past: Psychology portrays the sexes*. New York: Columbia University Press.

CONWAY, M. 1986. PACs and congressional elections in the 1980s. In A. Ciglar and B. Loomis (eds.), *Interest group politics*. Washington, D.C.: Congressional Quarterly Press.

COOK, ANNABEL AND DONALD BECK. 1991. Metropolitan dominance versus decentralization in the Information Age. *Social Science Quarterly*, **72**, June, pp. 284–298.

COOL, LINDA. 1980. Ethnicity and aging: Continuity through change for elderly Corsicans. In C. L. Fry (ed.), *Aging in culture and society*. Brooklyn, N.Y.: J. F. Bergin.

COOLEY, CHARLES H. 1909. *Social organization*. New York: Charles Scribner.

COONEY, TERESA M. AND DENNIS P. HOGAN. 1991. Marriage in an institutionalized life course: First marriage among American men in the twentieth century. *Journal of Marriage and the Family*, **53**, February, pp. 178–190.

COOPERSMITH, STANLEY. 1967. *The antecedents of self-esteem*. San Francisco: Freeman.

COOPERSTOCK, R. AND H. L. LENNARD. 1979. Some social meanings of tranquiliser use. *Sociology of Health and Illness*, **1**, pp. 331–347.

CORCORAN, MARY AND GREG J. DUNCAN. 1985. *Why do women earn less?* Institute for Social Research, University of Michigan.

CORNFIELD, MICHAEL. 1992. How to read the campaign. *The Wilson Quarterly*, **16**, Spring, pp. 38–46.

CORZINE, JAY, JAMES CREECH, AND LIN CORZINE. 1983. Black concentration and lynchings in the South: Testing Blalock's power threat hypothesis. *Social Forces*, **61**, March, pp. 774–796.

COSTANTINI, EDWARD. 1990. Political women and political ambition: Closing the gender gap. *American Journal of Political Science*, **34**, August, pp. 741–770.

COTTON, JEREMIAH. 1989. Opening the gap: The decline in black economy indications in the 1980s. *Social Science Quarterly*, **70**, December, pp. 803–819.

COTTON, PAUL. 1993. Women physicians target barriers. *Journal of American Medical Association*, **269**, February 24, p. 965.

COURTNEY, ALICE AND THOMAS WHIPPLE. 1983. *Sex stereotyping in advertising*. Lexington, Mass.: Lexington Books.

COVERMAN, SHELLEY. 1985. Explaining husbands' participation in domestic labor. *The Sociological Quarterly*, **26**, pp. 81–97.

COWAN, PHILIP A., CAROLYN P. COWAN, AND GERTRUDE HEMING. 1989. From parent adaptation in pregnancy to children's adaptation in kindergarten, paper presented in a symposium chaired by Joy Osofsky at the biennial meeting of the Society for Research in Child Development, Kansas City, Mo. April.

COWGILL, DONALD. 1985. *Aging around the world*. Belmont, Calif.: Wadsworth.

COX, ELIZABETH. 1990. Gender sensitive strategies for poverty identification and alleviation in Papua, New Guinea, paper presented at the 12th World Congress of Sociology, co-sponsored by the International Sociological Association and held in Madrid, Spain. July 9–13.

CRAIN, ROBERT L. AND RITA E. MAHARD. 1983. The effect of research methodology on desegregation-achievement studies. *American Journal of Sociology*, **88**, pp. 839–854.

CRAWFORD, MARY AND MARGO MACLEOD. 1990. Gender in the college classroom: An assessment of the 'chilly climate' for women. *Sex Roles*, **23**, pp. 101–122.

CRENSHAW, EDWARD. 1991. Foreign investment as a dependent variable: Determinants of foreign investment and capital penetration in developing nations, 1967–1978. *Social Forces*, **69**, June, pp. 1169–1182.

CRISPELL, DIANE. 1991. Women's earning gap is closing—slowly. *American Demographics*, **13**, February, p. 14.

CROCKENBERG, SUSAN AND CINDY LITMAN. 1990. Autonomy as competence in two-year-olds: Maternal correlates of child compliance, noncompliance, and self-assertion. *Developmental Psychology, 26,* pp. 961–971.

———. 1991. Effects of maternal employment on maternal and two-year-old child behavior. *Child Development, 62,* pp. 930–953.

CROMWELL, PAUL F., BEN R. ABADIE, J. T. STEPHENS, AND MARILEE KYLER. 1989. Hair mineral analysis: Biochemical imbalances and violent criminal behavior. *Psychological Reports, 64,* pp. 259–266.

CROZIER, MICHEL. 1964. *The bureaucratic phenomenon.* Chicago: University of Chicago Press.

CRUTCHFIELD, ROBERT D. 1989. Labor stratification and violent crime. *Social Forces, 68,* December, pp. 489–512.

CRUTCHFIELD, R., M. GEERKEN, AND W. GOVE. 1982. Crime rates and social integration: The impact of metropolitan mobility. *Criminology, 20,* pp. 467–478.

CSIKSZENTMIHALYI, MIHALY. 1975. *Beyond boredom and anxiety: The experience of play in work and games.* San Francisco: Jossey-Bass.

CULLEN, FRANCIS T., SANDRA EVANS SKOVRON, JOSEPH E. SCOTT, AND VELMER S. BURTON, JR. 1990. Public support for correctional treatment: The tenacity of rehabilitative ideology. *Criminal Justice and Behavior, 17,* March, pp. 6–18.

CULLINGFORD, CEDRIC. 1984. *Children and television.* New York: St. Martin's Press.

CUMMING, ELAINE, L. R. DEAN, D. S. NEWELL, AND I. MCCAFFREY. 1960. Disengagement, a tentative theory of aging. *Sociometry, 23,* pp. 23–35.

CURLEE, J. 1969. Alcoholism and the empty-nest. *Bulletin of the Menninger Clinic, 33,* pp. 165–171.

CURRIE, ELLIOTT. 1989. Confronting crime: Looking toward the twenty-first century. *Justice Quarterly, 6,* pp. 5–25.

———. 1991. Crime in the market society: From bad to worse in the nineties. *Dissent, 38,* Spring, pp. 254–259.

CURRY, G. DAVID AND IRVING A. SPERGEL. 1992. Gang involvement and delinquency among Hispanic and African-American adolescent males. *Journal of Research in Crime and Delinquency, 29,* August, pp. 273–291.

CURTISS, SUSAN. 1977. *Genie: A psycholinguistic study of a modern-day "wild-child."* New York: Academic Press.

CUTLER, STEPHEN AND RAYMOND COWARD. 1992. Availability of personal transportation in households of elders: Age, gender, and residence differences. *The Gerontologist, 32,* pp. 77–81.

CZIKO, GARY. 1992. The evaluation of bilingual education. *Educational Researcher, 21,* March, pp. 10–15.

DAHL, ROBERT. 1961. *Who governs? Democracy and power in an American City.* New Haven, Conn.: Yale University Press.

DAHRENDORF, RALF. 1973. Toward a theory of social conflict. In E. Etzioni-Halevy and A. Etzioni (eds.), *Social Change.* New York: Basic Books.

DALPHIN, JOHN. 1982. *The persistence of social inequality in America.* Cambridge, Mass.: Schenckman.

DARLEY, JOHN AND MARK ZANNA. 1982. Making moral judgments. *American Scientist, 70,* pp. 515–521.

DARNTON, NINA AND PAT WINGERT. 1992. A split verdict on America's marital future. *Newsweek,* January 13, p. 52.

DAVIDSON, BASIL. 1969. *The African genius.* Boston: Little, Brown.

DAVIS, E. G. 1971. *The first sex*. New York: Putman.

DAVIS, KINGSLEY. 1947. Final note on a case of extreme isolation. *American Journal of Sociology*, **52**, March, pp. 432–437.

DAVIS, KINGSLEY AND WILBERT MOORE. 1945. Some principles of stratification. *American Sociological Review*, **10**, April, pp. 242–249.

DAVIS, MARADEE A., JOHN M. NEUHAUS, DEBORAH J. MORITZ, AND MARK R. SEGAL. 1992. Living arrangements and survival among middle-aged and older adults in the NHANES 1 epidemiologic follow-up study. *American Journal of Public Health*, **82**, March, pp. 401–406.

DAVIS, NANCY AND ROBERT ROBINSON. 1988. Class identification of men and women in the 1970s and 1980s. *American Sociological Review*, **53**, February, pp. 103–112.

DAWSON, DEBORAH A. 1991. Family structure and children's health and well-being: Data from the 1988 National Health Interview Survey on Child Health. *Journal of Marriage and the Family*, **53**, August, pp. 573–584.

DAWSON, DON. 1988. The rational subordination of women's leisure under patriarchal capitalism. *Society and Leisure*, **11**, Fall, pp. 397–411.

DAYMONT, THOMAS AND PAUL ANDRISANI. 1988. Why women earn less than men: The case of recent college graduates. *Industrial Relations Research Association 35th Annual Proceedings*, Spring, pp. 425–435.

DEAUX, K. AND J. ULLMAN. 1982. Hard-hatted women: Reflections on blue-collar employment. In H. Bernardin (ed.), *Women in the work-force*. New York: Praeger.

DELGADO-GAITON, CONCHA. 1987. Cultural meaning systems. In Richard Shweder and Robert LeVine (eds.), *Culture theory*. Cambridge, England: Cambridge University Press.

DELUCA, H. R., THOMAS J. MILLER, AND CARL F. WIEDEMANN. 1991. Punishment vs. rehabilitation. A proposal for revising sentencing practices. *Federal Probation*, **55**, September, pp. 37–45.

DEMARIS, ALFRED AND K. VANINADHA RAO. 1992. Premarital cohabitation and subsequent marital stability in the United States: A reassessment. *Journal of Marriage and the Family*, **54**, February, pp. 178–190.

DEMO, DAVID. 1992. Parent–child relations: Assessing recent changes. *Journal of Marriage and the Family*, **54**, February, pp. 104–117.

DENTZER, SUSAN. 1991. The vanishing dream. *U.S. News & World Report*, April 22, pp. 30–43.

DESAI, SONALDE AND LINDA J. WAITE. 1991. Women's employment during pregnancy and after the first birth: Occupational characteristics and work commitment. *American Sociological Review*, **56**, August, pp. 551–566.

DEVAUS, DAVID AND IAN MCALLISTER. 1987. Gender differences in religion. *American Sociological Review*, **52**, pp. 472–481.

DEVOS, G. (ed.). 1973. *Socialization for achievement: Essays on the cultural psychology of the Japanese*. Berkeley, Calif.: University of California Press.

DEVOS, G. 1983. Achievement, motivation and intra-family attitudes in immigrant Koreans. *Journal of Psychoanalytic Anthropology*, **6**, pp. 25–71.

DIAMOND, SARA. 1989. *Spiritual warfare: The politics of the Christian Right*. London: Pluto Press.

DIDERICHSEN, FINN. 1993. Market reforms in Swedish health care: A threat to or salvation for the universalistic welfare state? *International Journal of Health Services*, **23**, pp. 185–188.

DIMAGGIO, PAUL J. AND WALTER W. POWELL. 1983. Iron cage revisited: Institutional isomorphism and collective rationality in organizational fields. *American Sociological Review*, **48**, April, pp. 147–160.

DIPRETE, THOMAS AND DAVID GRUSKY. 1990. Structure and trend in the process of stratification for American men and women. *American Journal of Sociology*, **96**, July, pp. 107–143.

DISHION, T. J., G. R. PATTERSON, M. STOOLMILLER, and M. L. SKINNER. 1991. Family, school, and behavioral antecedents to early adolescent involvement with antisocial peers. *Developmental Psychology*, **27**, pp. 172–180.

DODGE, KENNETH. 1990. Development of psychopathology in children of depressed mothers. *Developmental Psychology*, **26**, January, pp. 3–6.

DOHERTY, WILLIAM J. AND RICHARD H. NEEDLE. 1991. Psychological adjustment and substance use among adolescents before and after a parental divorce. *Child Development*, **62**, pp. 328–337.

DOMHOFF, G. WILLIAM. 1990. *The power elite and the state*. New York: Aldine de Gruyter.

————. 1992. American state autonomy via the military? Another counterattack on a theoretical delusion. *Critical Sociology*, **18**, pp. 9–56.

DONEGAN, J. 1978. *Women and men midwives*. Westport, Conn.: Greenwood Press.

DONENBERG, GERI AND LOIS HOFFMAN. 1988. Gender differences in moral development. *Sex Roles*, **18**, June, pp. 701–717.

DONLEY, J. 1986. *Save the midwife*. Auckland, New Zealand: New Woman's Press.

DONNELLY, DENISE AND DAVID FINKELHOR. 1992. Does equality in custody arrangement improve the parent–child relationship? *Journal of Marriage and the Family*, **54**, November, pp. 837–845.

DONOVAN, ROBERT AND RAY SCHERER. 1992. Politics transformed. *The Wilson Quarterly*, **16**, Spring, pp. 19–33.

DOTY, PAMELA, KORBIN LIU, AND JOSHUA WIENER. 1985. An overview of long-term care. *Health Care Financing Review*, **6**, pp. 69–78.

DOUGHERTY, KEVIN J. 1992. Community colleges and baccalaureate attainment. *Journal of Higher Education*, **63**, March/April, pp. 188–214.

DOWD, JAMES AND VERN BENGSTON. 1978. Aging in minority populations: An examination of the double jeopardy hypothesis. *Journal of Gerontology*, **33**, pp. 427–436.

DOWNS, ANTHONY. 1966. *Inside bureaucracy*. Boston: Little, Brown.

DOYLE, DANIEL P. AND DAVID F. LUCKENBILL. 1991. Mobilizing law in response to collective problems: A test of Black's theory of law. *Law & Society Review*, **25**, pp. 103–114.

DREMAN, SOLLY, EMDA ORR, AND ROY ALDOR. 1990. Sense of competence, time perspective, and state-anxiety of separated versus divorced mothers. *American Journal of Orthopsychiatry*, **60**, January, pp. 77–85.

DRESSLER, WILLIAM, JOSÉ DOS SANTOS, PHILIP GALLAGHER, JR., AND FERNANDO VITERI. 1987. Arterial blood pressure and modernization in Brazil. *American Anthropologist*, **89**, June, pp. 398–409.

DREW, PAUL AND ELIZABETH HOLT. Complainable matters: The use of idiomatic expressions in making complaints. *Social Problems*, **35**, October, pp. 398–417.

DRUCKER, PETER. 1993. *Post-capitalist society*. New York: Harper Collins.

DUANY, ANDRES AND ELIZABETH PLATER-ZYBERK. 1992. The second coming of the American small town. *The Wilson Quarterly*, **16**, Winter, pp. 19–48.

DULL, DIANA AND CANDACE WEST. 1991. Accounting for cosmetic surgery: The accomplishment of gender. *Social Problems*, **38**, February, pp. 54–70.

DUNCAN, GREG J. AND SAUL D. HOFFMAN. 1985. A reconsideration of the economic consequences of marital dissolution. *Demography*, **22**, November, pp. 485–497.

DUNCAN, GREG, TIMOTHY SMEEDING, and WILLARD ROGERS. 1992. The incredible shrinking middle class. *American Demographics*, **14**, May, pp. 34–38.

DUNN, J. 1988. Relations among relationships. In S. W. Duck (ed.), *Handbook of personal relationships*. New York: Wiley.

DURHAM, ALEXIS M. 1989. Rehabilitation and correctional privatization: Observations on the 19th century experience and implications for modern corrections. *Federal Probation*, **53**, March, pp. 43–52.

DURKHEIM, EMILE. 1950 (1895). *The rules of sociological method*. French ed. New York: Free Press.

———. 1951 (1897). *Suicide*. New York: Free Press.

———. 1965 (1915). *The elementary forms of religious life*. New York: Free Press.

———. 1938. *The rules of sociological method*. Trans. Sarah A. Solovay and John H. Mueller. New York: Free Press.

DU TOIT, BRIAN. 1990. People on the move: Rural–urban migration with special reference to the Third World. *Human Organization*, **49**, Winter, pp. 305–319.

DWORETZ, STEVEN. 1987. Before the age of reason: Liberalism and the media socialization of children. *Social Theory and Practice*, **13**, Summer, pp. 187–218.

DYCHTWALD, KEN. 1989. *Age wave: The challenges and opportunities of an aging America*. Los Angeles: Jeremy Tarcher.

EAGLY, ALICE H. AND BLAIR T. JOHNSON. 1990. Gender and leadership style: A meta-analysis. *Psychological Bulletin*, **108**, pp. 233–256.

EAKINS, BARBARA AND GENE EAKINS. 1976. Verbal turn-taking and exchange in faculty dialogue. In Betty Dubios and Isabel Crouch (eds.), *The sociology of the languages of American women*. San Antonio, Texas: Trinity University Press.

EARLY, JOHN D. AND JOHN F. PETERS. 1990. *The population dynamics of the Mucajai Yanomama*. New York: Academic Press.

EASTERLIN, RICHARD A. 1978. The economics and sociology of fertility: A synthesis. In Charles Tilley (ed.), *Historical studies of changing fertility*. Princeton, N.J.: Princeton University Press.

———. 1987. *Birth and fortune: The impact of numbers on personal welfare*. Chicago: University of Chicago Press.

EASTON, DAVID. 1965. *A system: Analysis of political life*. New York: Wiley.

EDER, DONNA AND STEPHEN PARKER. 1987. The cultural reproduction of gender: The effect of extracurricular activities on peer-group culture. *Sociology of Education*, **60**, July, pp. 200–213.

EDIN, KATHRYN. 1991. Surviving the welfare system: How AFDC recipients make ends meet in Chicago. *Social Problems*, **38**, November, pp. 462–473.

EDWARDS, JOHN N. 1991. New conceptions: Biosocial innovations and the family. *Journal of Marriage and the Family*, **53**, May, pp. 349–360.

EDWARDS, RICHARD. 1979. *Contested terrain*. New York: Basic Books.

EGAN, JANET M. 1989. Graduate school and the self. *Teaching Sociology*, **17**, April, pp. 200–207.

EGELAND, BYRON, DEBORAH JACOBVITZ, AND ALAN SROUFE. 1988. Breaking the cycle of abuse. *Child Development*, **59**, pp. 1080–1088.

EGERTON, JOHN. 1974. *The Americanization of Dixie: The southernization of America*. New York: Harper & Row.

EGGEBEEN, DAVID AND DANIEL LICHTER. 1991. Race, family structure, and changing poverty among American children. *American Sociological Review*, **56**, December, pp. 801–817.

EGLIN, RICHARD. 1978. The oligopolistic structure and competitive characteristics of direct foreign investment in Kenya's manufacturing sectors. In Raphael Kaplinsky (ed.), *Readings on the multinational corporation in Kenya*. Nairobi, Kenya: Oxford University Press.

EHRENREICH, B. AND D. ENGLISH. 1978. *For her own good: 150 years of the experts' advice to women*. London: Pluto Press.

EISENSTEIN, ELIZABETH. 1979. *The printing press as an agent of change*. New York: Cambridge University Press.

EKEH, PETER. 1974. *Social exchange theory: The two traditions*. Cambridge, Mass.: Harvard University Press.

EKLAND-OLSON, SHELDON, WILLIAM R. KELLY, AND MICHAEL EISENBERG. 1992. Crime and incarceration: Some comparative findings from the 1980s. *Crime and Delinquency*, **38**, July, pp. 392–416.

ELDER, GLEN H., JR. 1974. *Children of the Great Depression: Social change in life experience*. Chicago: University of Chicago Press.

―――. 1985. Perspectives on the life course. In Glen H. Elder, Jr. (ed.), *Life course dynamics*. Ithaca, N.Y.: Cornell University Press.

ELLIS, LEE. 1991. Monoamine oxidase and criminality: Identifying an apparent biological marker for antisocial behavior. *Journal of Research in Crime and Delinquency*, **28**, May, pp. 227–251.

ELLISON, CHRISTOPHER G. 1991. Identification and separatism: Religious involvement and racial orientations among black Americans. *The Sociological Quarterly*, **32**, pp. 477–494.

―――. 1992. Are religious people nice people? Evidence from the National Survey of black Americans. *Social Forces*, **71**, December, pp. 411–430.

ELLISON, CHRISTOPHER G. AND DAVID A. GAY. 1989. Black political participation revisited: A test of compensatory, ethnic community, and public arena models. *Social Science Quarterly*, **70**, March, pp. 101–119.

ELLISON, CHRISTOPHER G., DAVID A. GAY, AND THOMAS A. GLASS. 1989. Does religious commitment contribute to individual life satisfaction? *Social Forces*, **68**, pp. 100–123.

ELLISON, CHRISTOPHER G. AND DARREN E. SHERKAT. 1993. Conservative Protestantism and support for corporal punishment. *American Sociological Review*, **58**, February, pp. 131–144.

ELLWOOD, D. T. 1986. The spatial mismatch hypothesis: Are there teenage jobs missing in the ghetto? In R. B. Freeman, H. J. Holzer (eds.), *The black youth employment crisis*. Chicago: University of Chicago Press.

EMERSON, RICHARD M. 1976. Social exchange theory. *Annual Review of Sociology*, **2**, pp. 335–362.

EMERY, ROBERT E. 1982. Interparental conflict and the children of discord and divorce. *Psychological Bulletin*, **92**, pp. 310–330.

―――. 1989. Family violence. *American Psychologist*, **44**, pp. 321–328.

EMERY, ROBERT E. AND DANIEL O'LEARY. 1984. Marital discord and child behavior problems in a non-clinic sample. *Journal of Abnormal Child Psychology*, **12**, pp. 411–420.

ENDERSBY, JAMES W. AND MICHAEL C. MUNGER. 1992. The impact of legislator attributes on union PAC campaign contributions. *Journal of Labor Research*, **13**, Winter, pp. 79–97.

ENGELS, FRIEDRICH. 1974 (1845). *The condition of the working class in England*. Moscow: Progress Publishers.

ENSMINGER, MARGARET AND ANITA SLUSARCICK. 1992. Paths to high school graduation or dropout: A longitudinal study of a first-grade cohort. *Sociology of Education*, **65**, April, pp. 95–113.

ENTWISLE, DORIS AND KARL ALEXANDER. 1992. Summer setback: Race, poverty, school composition and mathematics achievement in the first two years of school. *American Sociological Review*, **57**, February, pp. 72–84.

ERICKSON, KAI. 1966. *Wayward puritans*. New York: Wiley.

ERIKSON, ERIK. 1959. *Identity and the life cycle*. New York: International Universities.

———. 1963. *Childhood and society*. New York: Norton.

———. 1968. *Identity, youth, and crisis*. New York: Norton.

———. 1982. *The life cycle completed*. New York: Norton.

ESKILSON, ARLENE AND MARY GLENN WILEY. 1987. Parents, peers, perceived pressure and adolescent self-concept: Is a daughter a daughter all of her life? *The Sociological Quarterly*, **28**, pp. 135–145.

ESQUIVEL, ADOLPHO PEREZ. 1991. The time bomb of child poverty. *World Press Review*, **38**, March, pp. 32–33. Originally published in *Le Monde Diplomatique*.

ETZIONI, AMITAI AND THOMAS DIPRETE. 1979. The decline of confidence in America: The prime factors. *Journal of Applied and Behavioral Science*, **15**, pp. 520–526.

EVANS, PETER. 1979. *Dependent development: The alliance of multinational, state, and local capital in Brazil*. Princeton, N.J.: Princeton University Press.

EVERETT, KEVIN. 1992. Professionalization and protest: Changes in the social movement sector, 1961–1983. *Social Forces*, **70**, pp. 957–975.

EWEN, STUART AND ELIZABETH EWEN. 1982. *Channels of desire: Mass images and the shaping of American consciousness*. New York: McGraw-Hill.

EXTER, THOMAS. 1988. Options for opticians. *American Demographics*, **10**, pp. 38, 40, 42, 43.

FALSEY, BARBARA AND BARBARA HEYNS. 1984. The college channel: Private and public schools reconsidered. *Sociology of Education*, **57**, April, pp. 111–122.

FALUDI, SUSAN. 1991. *Backlash: The undeclared war against American women*. New York: Crown.

FARBER, NAOMI. 1990. The significance of race and class in marital decisions among unmarried adolescent mothers. *Social Problems*, **37**, February, pp. 51–63.

FARBER, S. L. 1981. *Identical twins reared apart*. New York: Basic Books.

FARKAS, GEORGE, ROBERT GROBE, DANIEL SHEEHAN, AND YUAN SHUAN. 1990. Cultural resources and school success: Gender, ethnicity, and poverty groups within an urban school district. *American Sociological Review*, **55**, February, pp. 127–142.

FARKAS, GEORGE, DANIEL SHEEHAN, AND ROBERT P. GROBE. 1990. Coursework mastery and school success: Gender, ethnicity, and poverty groups within an urban school district. *American Educational Research Journal*, **27**, Winter, pp. 807–827.

FARLEY, REYNOLDS AND WALTER ALLEN. 1987. *The color line and the quality of life in America*. New York: Russell Sage.

FARRELL, RONALD. 1989. Cognitive consistency in deviance causation: A psychological elaboration of an integrated systems model. In Steven Messner, Marvin Krohn, and Allen Liska (eds.), *Theoretical integration in the study of deviance and crime: Problems and prospects*. Albany, N.Y.: State University of New York Press.

FARRINGTON, DAVID. 1977. The effects of public labeling. *British Journal of Criminology* **17**, pp. 112–125.

FEAGIN, JOE R. 1975. *Subordinating the poor: Welfare and American beliefs*. Englewood Cliffs, N.J.: Prentice-Hall.

———. 1991. The continuing significance of race: Antiblack discrimination in public places. *American Sociological Review*, **56**, February, pp. 101–116.

FEINGOLD, ALAN. 1992. Sex differences in variability in intellectual abilities: A new look at an old controversy. *Review of Educational Research*, **62**, Spring, pp. 61–84.

FELSON, MARCUS. 1987. Routine activities and crime prevention in the developing metropolis. *Criminology*, **25**, pp. 911–932.

FELSON, RICHARD AND MARY ZIELINSKI. 1989. Children's self-esteem and parental support. *Journal of Marriage and the Family*, **51**, August, pp. 727–735.

FERRARO, KATHLEEN J. 1989. Policing woman battering. *Social Problems*, **36**, February, pp. 61–74.

FERRARO, KENNETH. 1989. Reexamining the double jeopardy to health thesis. *Journal of Gerontology: Social Sciences*, **44**, pp. S14–16.

FERRARO, KENNETH F. AND TAMMY SOUTHERLAND. 1989. Domains of medical practice: Physicians' assessment of the role of physician extenders. *Journal of Health and Social Behavior*, **30**, June, pp. 192–205.

FERRI, ELSA. 1984. *Stepchildren: A national study*. Atlantic Highlands, N.J.: Humanities.

FESTINGER, LEON. 1954. A theory of social comparison processes. *Human Relations*, **7**, pp. 114–140.

FIEDLER, FRED. 1967. *A theory of leadership effectiveness*. New York: McGraw-Hill.

FIJNAUT, CYRILLE. 1990. Organized crime: A comparison between the United States of America and Western Europe. *British Journal of Criminology*, **30**, Summer, pp. 321–340.

FILER, RANDALL. 1985. Male–female wage differences: The importance of compensating differentials. *Industrial and Labor Relations Review*, **38**, pp. 426–437.

———. 1989. Occupational segregation, compensating differentials, and comparable worth. In R. Michael, H. Hartmann, and B. O'Farrell (eds.), *Pay equity: Empirical inquiries*. Washington, D.C.: National Academy Press.

FINE, MARK A. AND LAWRENCE A. KURDEK. 1992. The adjustment of adolescents in stepfather and stepmother families. *Journal of Marriage and the Family*, **54**, November, pp. 725–736.

FINE, MICHELLE. 1991. *Framing dropouts: Notes on the politics of an urban public high school*. Albany, N.Y.: State University of New York Press.

FINKE, ROGER AND RODNEY STARK. 1986. Turning pews into people: Estimating 19th century church membership. *Journal for the Scientific Study of Religion*, **25**, pp. 180–192.

———. 1988. Religious economies and sacred canopies: Religious mobilization in American cities. *American Sociological Review*, **53**, pp. 41–49.

FINKELHOR, D. 1980. Sex among siblings: A survey report on prevalence, variety and effects. *Archives of Sexual Behavior*, **4**, pp. 171–194.

FINLEY, NANCY J. 1991. Political activism and feminist spirituality. *Sociological Analysis*, **52**, pp. 349–362.

FINN, JEREMY D. AND CHARLES M. ACHILLES. 1990. Answers and questions about class size: A statewide experiment. *American Educational Research Journal*, **27**, Fall, pp. 557–577.

FINN, JEREMY D. AND DEBORAH COX. 1992. Participation and withdrawal among fourth-grade pupils. *American Educational Research Journal*, **29**, Spring, pp. 141–162.

FINN, ROBERT. 1985. Origins of speech. *Science Digest*, August, pp. 53–54, 64.

FIORENTINE, ROBERT. 1987. Men, women, and the premed persistence gap: A normative alternatives approach. *American Journal of Sociology*, **92**, March, pp. 1118–1139.

FIREBAUGH, GLENN. 1992. Growth effects of foreign and domestic investment. *American Journal of Sociology*, **98**, July, pp. 105–130.

FIREBAUGH, GLENN AND KENNETH DAVIS. 1988. Trends in antiblack prejudice, 1972–1984. *American Journal of Sociology*, **94**, September, pp. 251–272.

FISCHER, CLAUDE. 1976. *The urban experience*. New York: Harcourt Brace Jovanovich.

————. 1981. The public and private worlds of city life. *American Sociological Review,* **46,** June, pp. 306–316.

————. 1982. *To dwell among friends: Personal networks in town and city.* Chicago: University of Chicago Press.

FISCHER, DAVID H. 1978. *Growing old in America.* New York: Oxford University Press.

FISHBEIN, DIANA H. 1990. Biological perspectives in criminology. *Criminology,* **28,** pp. 27–71.

FISHBEIN, DIANA H., D. LOZOVSKY, AND J. H. JAFFE. 1989. Impulsivity, aggression, and neuroendocrine responses to serotonirgic stimulation in substance abusers. *Biological Psychiatry,* **25,** pp. 1049–1066.

FISHMAN, PAMELA. 1980. Conversational insecurity. In H. Giles, W. Robinson and P. Smith (eds.), *Language: Social psychological perspective.* New York: Pergamon.

FISHMAN, ROBERT. 1990. Megalopolis unbound. *The Wilson Quarterly,* Winter, pp. 25–45.

FITZPATRICK, KEVIN AND SEAN-SHONG HWANG. 1992. The effects of community structure on opportunities for interracial contact. *The Sociological Quarterly,* **33,** pp. 51–61.

FITZPATRICK, KEVIN AND WILLIAM C. YOELS. 1992. Policy, school structure, and sociodemographic effects on statewide high school dropout rates. *Sociology of Education,* **65,** January, pp. 76–93.

FIVUSH, ROBYN. 1989. Exploring sex differences in the emotional content of mother–child conversations about the past. *Sex Roles,* **20,** June, pp. 675–691.

FLOGE, LILIANE. 1989. Changing household structure, child-care availability, and employment among mothers of pre-school children. *Journal of Marriage and the Family,* **51,** February, pp. 51–63.

FLYNN, J. R. 1987. The rise and fall of Japanese IQ. *Bulletin of British Psychological Society,* **40,** pp. 459–464.

FORD, AMASA, MARIE R. HAUG. PAUL K. JONES. ANN W. ROY, AND STEVEN J. FOLMAN. 1990. Race-related differences among elderly urban residents: A cohort study, 1975–1984. *Journal of Gerontology: Social Sciences,* **45,** pp. S163–171.

FOREHAND, REX, MICHELLE WIERSON, AMANDA MCCOMBS THOMAS, ROBERT FAUBER, LISA ARMISTEAD, TRACY KEMPTON, AND NICHOLAS LONG. 1991. A short-term longitudinal examination of young adolescent functioning following divorce: The role of family factors. *Journal of Abnormal Child Psychology,* **19,** pp. 97–111.

FORM, WILLIAM, ROBERT KAUFMAN, TOBY PARCEL, AND MICHAEL WALLACE. 1988. The impact of technology on work organization and work outcomes. In George Farkas and Paula England (eds.), *Industries, firms, and jobs: Sociological and economic approaches.* New York: Plenum.

FORST, EDMUND, JR., AND ROSE MARIE HEALY. 1991. Correlations among religion, commitment, and volunteer participation. *Psychological Reports,* **69,** p. 1224.

FOSSETT, MARK AND JILL KIECOLT. 1989. The relative size and minority populations and white racial attitudes. *Social Science Quarterly,* **70,** December, pp. 820–835.

FOST, DAN. 1991. American Indians in the 1990s. *American Demographics,* **13,** December, pp. 26–34.

FOSTER, GLADYS PARKER. 1991. Cultural relativism and the theory of value: The educational implications. *The American Journal of Economics and Sociology,* **50,** July, pp. 257–267.

FOSTER, JOHN L. 1990. Bureaucratic rigidity revisited. *Social Science Quarterly,* **71,** June, pp. 223–238.

FOSTER, MICHELLE. 1989. It's cookin' now: A performance analysis of the speech events in an urban community college. *Language in Society,* **18,** pp. 1–29.

FOWERS, BLAINE J. 1991. His and her marriage: A multivariate study of gender and marital satisfaction. *Sex Roles*, **24**, pp. 209–221.

FRANCK, KAREN. 1980. Friends and strangers: The social experience of living in urban and non-urban settings. *Journal of Social Issues*, **36**, pp. 52–71.

FRANK, ANDRE G. 1972. *Lumpenbourgeoisie, lumpendevelopment: Dependence, class, and politics in Latin America*. New York: Monthly Review Press.

FRANK, ANDRE G. AND MARTA FUENTES. 1989. Ten theses about social movements. Trans. Javier Saenz. *Revista Mexicana de Sociologia*, **51**, October–December, pp. 21–43.

FRANK, S. J., A. M. MCLAUGHLIN, AND A. CRUSCO. 1984. Sex role attributes, symptom distress, and defensive style among college men and women. *Journal of Personality and Social Psychology*, **47**, pp. 182–192.

FRAZIER, CHARLES E., DONNA M. BISHOP, AND JOHN C. HENRETTA. 1992. The social context of race differentials in juvenile justice dispositions. *The Sociological Quarterly*, **33**, pp. 447–458.

FREEDMAN, RONALD. 1990. Family planning programs in the Third World. *The Annals of the American Academy of Political and Social Science*, **510**, July, pp. 33–43.

FREEMAN, LINTON C. 1992. The sociological concept of "group": An empirical test of two models. *American Journal of Sociology*, **98**, July, pp. 152–166.

FREIDSON, ELIOT. 1970. *Profession of medicine: A study of the sociology of applied knowledge*. New York: Dodd, Mead.

FRENCH, RUTH. 1968. *The dynamics of health care*. New York: McGraw-Hill.

FREUDENBURG, WILLIAM R. AND ROBERT EMMETT JONES. 1991. Criminal behavior and rapid community growth: Examining the evidence. *Rural Society*, **56**, pp. 619–645.

FREY, WILLIAM. 1987. Migration and depopulation of the metropolis: Regional restructuring on rural renaissance. *American Sociological Review*, **52**, pp. 240–257.

FRIEDAN, BETTY. 1963. *The feminine mystique*. Harmondsworth, Penguin.

FRIEDMAN, LYNN. 1989. Mathematics and the gender gap: A meta-analysis of recent studies on sex differences in mathematical tasks. *Review of Educational Research*, **59**, Summer, pp. 185–213.

FRIEZE, IRENE. 1990. Perceived and actual discrimination in the salaries of male and female managers. *Journal of Applied Social Psychology*, **20**, January, pp. 46–67.

FULLER, THEODORE, JOHN EDWARDS, SANTHAT SERMSI, AND SAIRUDEE VORAKITPHOKATORN. 1993. Gender and health: Some Asian evidence. *Journal of Health and Social Behavior*, **34**, September, pp. 252–271.

FUNG, K. K. 1991. One good turn deserves another: Exchange of favors within organizations. *Social Science Quarterly*, **72**, September, pp. 443–463.

FUNK, RICHARD AND FERN WILLITS. 1987. College attendance and attitude change: A panel study, 1970–1981. *Sociology of Education*, **60**, October, pp. 224–231.

FURSTENBERG, F. F., JR., S. P. MORGAN, AND P. D. ALLISON. 1987. Paternal participation and children's well-being after marital dissolution. *American Sociological Review*, **52**, pp. 695–701.

GALANTER, MARC. 1990. Cults and zealous self-help movements: A psychiatric perspective. *American Journal of Psychiatry*, **147**, May, pp. 543–551.

GAMORAN, ADAM. 1987. The stratification of high school learning opportunities. *Sociology of Education*, **60**, July, pp. 135–155.

———. 1992. The variable effects of high school tracking. *American Sociological Review*, **57**, December, pp. 812–828.

GAMORAN, ADAM AND MARK BERENDS. 1987. The effects of stratification in secondary schools: Synthesis of survey and ethnographic research. *Review of Educational Research,* **57**, Winter, pp. 415–435.

GAMORAN, ADAM AND ROBERT D. MARE. 1989. Secondary school tracking and educational inequality: Compensation, reinforcement or neutrality? *American Journal of Sociology,* **94**, March, pp. 1146–1183.

GAMSON, WILLIAM. 1968. *Power and discontent.* Homewood, Ill.: Dorsey.

GANS, HERBERT. 1982. *The urban villagers.* New York: Free Press.

GARET, MICHAEL AND BRIAN DELANY. 1988. Students, courses, and stratification. *Sociology of Education,* **61**, April, pp. 61–77.

GARFINKEL, HAROLD. 1967. *Studies in ethnomethodology:* Englewood Cliffs, N.J.: Prentice-Hall.

GARREAU, JOEL. 1991. *Edge city: Life on the new frontier.* New York: Doubleday.

GARTNER, ROSEMARY. 1990. The victims of homicide: A temporal and cross-national comparison. *American Sociological Review,* **55**, pp. 92–106.

GECAS, VIKTOR AND MICHAEL SCHWALBE. 1986. Parental behavior and adolescent self-esteem. *Journal of Marriage and the Family,* **48**, pp. 37–46.

GECAS, VIKTOR AND MONICA SEFF. 1989. Social class, occupational conditions, and self-esteem. *Sociological Perspectives,* **32**, Fall, pp. 353–364.

———. 1990. Families and adolescents: A review of the 1980s. *Journal of Marriage and the Family,* **52**, November, pp. 941–958.

GEE, ELLEN M. AND JEAN E. VEEVERS. 1990. Religious involvement and life satisfaction in Canada. *Sociological Analysis,* **51**, pp. 387–394.

GEER, DOUGLAS, RICHARD POTTS, JOHN WRIGHT, AND ALETHA HUSTON. 1982. The effects of television commercial form and commercial placement on children's social behavior and attention. *Child Development,* **53**, June, pp. 611–619.

GERHARDS, JURGEN AND DIETER RUCHT. 1992. Mesomobilization: Organizing and framing in two protest campaigns in West Germany. *American Journal of Sociology,* **3**, November, pp. 555–595.

GERRITY, MARTHA, JO ANNE EARP, AND ROBERT DEVELLIS. 1992. Uncertainty and professional work: Perceptions of physicians in clinical practice. *American Journal of Sociology,* **97**, January, pp. 1022–1051.

GERSTEL, NAOMI. 1988. Divorce and kin ties: The importance of gender. *Journal of Marriage and the Family,* **50**, pp. 209–219.

GIBBS, JACK P. 1989. Conceptualization of terrorism. *American Sociological Review,* **54**, June, pp. 329–340.

GILBERT, DENNIS AND JOSEPH KAHL. 1987. *The American class structure.* 3d ed. Chicago: Dorsey.

GILBERT, L. A. 1985. *Men in dual career families: Current realities and future prospects.* Hillsdale, N.J.: Erlbaum.

GILES-SIMS, JEAN AND D. FINKELHOR. 1984. Child abuse in stepfamilies. *Family Relations,* **33**, pp. 407–414.

GILFORD, ROSALIE. 1984. Contrasts in marital satisfaction throughout old age: An exchange theory analysis. *Journal of Gerontology,* **39**, pp. 325–333.

GILOVICH, THOMAS. 1991. The "hot hand" and other illusions of everyday life. *The Wilson Quarterly,* **15**, Spring, pp. 52–59.

GINSBERG, B. E. AND B. F. CARTER. 1987. *Premenstrual syndrome: Ethical and legal implications in a biomedical perspective.* New York: Plenum.

GIRARD, CHRIS. 1988. Church membership and suicide reconsidered: Comment on Breault. *American Journal of Sociology,* **93**, pp. 1471–1479.

GITLIN, TODD. 1983. *Inside prime time*. New York: Pantheon.

GLASS, JENNIFER. 1990. The impact of occupational segregation on working conditions. *Social Forces*, **68**, March, pp. 779–796.

GLASS, JENNIFER AND VALERIE CAMARIGG. 1992. Gender, parenthood, and job–family compatibility. *American Journal of Sociology*, **98**, July, pp. 131–151.

GLASTRIS, PAUL. 1993. Life among the 'meritocrats'. *U.S. News & World Report*, August 30/September 6, pp. 30–33.

GLENN, NORVAL D. 1991. The recent trend in marital success in the United States. *Journal of Marriage and the Family*, **53**, May, pp. 261–270.

———. 1992. What does family mean? *American Demographics*, June, pp. 30–37.

GLENN, NORVAL D. AND SARA MCLANAHAN. 1982. Children and marital happiness: A further specification of the relationship. *Journal of Marriage and the Family*, **44**, pp. 63–72.

GLENN, NORVAL D. AND C. N. WEAVER. 1981. The contribution of marital happiness to global happiness. *Journal of Marriage and the Family*, **43**, pp. 161–168.

GLICK, PAUL. 1989. Remarried families, stepfamilies, and stepchildren. *Family Relations*, **38**, pp. 24–27.

GLICK, PETER. 1991. Trait-based and sex-based discrimination in occupational prestige, occupational salary, and hiring. *Sex Roles*, **25**, pp. 351–378.

GLICK, PETER C. AND S. LIN. 1986. Recent changes in divorce and remarriage. *Journal of Marriage and the Family*, **48**, pp. 737–747.

GLICK, PETER, C. ZION, AND C. NELSON. 1988. What mediates sex discrimination in hiring decisions? *Journal of Personality and Social Psychology*, **55**, pp. 178–186.

GOFFMAN, ERVING. 1959. *The presentation of self in everyday life*. Garden City, N.Y.: Doubleday.

———. 1961. *Asylums: Essays on the social situation of mental patients and other inmates*. Garden City, N.Y.: Doubleday.

———. 1963. *Behavior in public places*. Glencoe, Ill.: Free Press.

———. 1967. *Interaction ritual: Essays on face-to face behavior*. New York: Aldine.

GOLANT, STEPHEN. 1990. The metropolitanization and suburbanization of the U.S. elderly population: 1970–1988. *The Gerontologist*, **30**, pp. 80–88.

GOLD, MARTHE R. AND PETER FRANKS. 1990. The social origin of cardiovascular risk: An investigation in a rural community. *International Journal of Health Services*, **20**, pp. 405–416.

GOLDENBERG, NAOMI R. 1979. *Changing of the gods: Feminism and the end of traditional religions*. Boston: Beacon.

GOLDSCHEIDER, FRANCES K. AND CALVIN GOLDSCHEIDER. 1991. The intergenerational flow of income: Family structure and the status of black Americans. *Journal of Marriage and the Family*, **53**, May, pp. 499–508.

GOLDSCHEIDER, FRANCES K. AND LINDA J. WAITE. 1986. Sex differences in the entry into marriage. *American Journal of Sociology*, **92**, pp. 91–109.

GOLDSTEIN, ARNOLD. 1992. Testimony in hearing before the subcommittee on elementary, secondary, and vocational education of the Committee on Education and Labor, House of Representatives, Bronx, New York. May 4, 1992.

GOOD, KENNETH WITH DAVID CHANOFF. 1991. *Into the heart*. New York: Simon & Schuster.

GOODMAN, SHERRYE AND ELIZABETH BRUMLEY. 1990. Schizophrenic and depressed mothers: Relational deficits in parenting. *Developmental Psychology*, **26**, January, pp. 31–39.

GORDON, DAVID, RICHARD EDWARDS, AND MICHAEL REICH. 1982. *Segmented work, divided workers*. New York: Cambridge University Press.

GORDON, MARGARET A. AND DANIEL GLASER. 1991. The use and effects of financial penalties in municipal courts. *Criminology*, **29**, pp. 651–676.

GORDON, MILTON. 1964. *Assimilation in American life*. New York: Oxford University Press.

GORE, SUSAN, ROBERT ASELTINE, JR., AND MARY ELLEN COLTON. 1992. Social structure, life stress and depressive symptoms in a high school-aged population. *Journal of Health and Social Behavior*, **33**, June, pp. 97–113.

GORTMAKER, STEVEN, CHARLES SALTER, DEBORAH WALKER, AND WILLIAM DIETZ, JR. 1990. The impact of television on mental aptitude and achievement: A longitudinal study. *Public Opinion Quarterly*, **54**, Winter, pp. 594–604.

GOTTFREDSON, MICHAEL R. AND TRAVIS HIRSCHI. 1990. *A general theory of crime*. Stanford, Calif.: Stanford University Press.

GOUDY, WILLIS, J. 1990. Community attachment in a rural region. *Rural Sociology*, **55**, pp. 178–198.

GOVE, WALTER R., SUZANNE ORTEGA, AND CAROLYN STYLE. 1989. The maturational and role perspectives on aging and self through the adult years: An empirical evaluation. *American Journal of Sociology*, **94**, March, pp. 1117–1145.

GOVE, WALTER R. AND HEE-CHOON SHIN. 1989. The psychological well-being of divorced and widowed men and women: An empirical analysis. *Journal of Family Issues*, **10**, pp. 122–144.

GOVE, WALTER R., CAROLYN B. STYLE, AND MICHAEL HUGHES. 1990. The effect of marriage on the well-being of adults: *Journal of Family Issues*, **11**, pp. 4–35.

GRAF, DOYLE. 1987. Roper study of the premium class. *The Public Pulse*. The Roper Organization, Inc.

GRAMMER, KARL. 1990. Strangers meet: Laughter and nonverbal signs of interest in opposite-sex encounters. *Journal of Nonverbal Behavior*, **14**, Winter, pp. 209–236.

GRANOVETTER, MARK. 1973. The strength of weak ties. *American Journal of Sociology*, **78**, pp. 1360–1380.

GRANT, PETER R. 1991. Ethnocentrism between groups of unequal power under threat in intergroup competition. *The Journal of Social Psychology*, **131**, pp. 21–28.

GRASMICK, HAROLD G. AND ROBERT J. BURSICK, JR. 1990. Conscience, significant others, and rational choice: Extending the deterrence model. *Law & Society Review*, **24**, pp. 837–861.

GRASMICK, HAROLD G., ROBERT J. BURSIK, JR., AND BRUCE J. ARNEKLEV. 1993. Reduction in drunk driving as a response to increased threats of shame, embarrassment, and legal sanctions. *Criminology*, **31**, pp. 41–67.

GRASMICK, HAROLD G., ROBERT J. BURSIK, JR., AND JOHN K. COCHRAN. 1991. 'Render unto Caesar what is Caesar's.' Religiosity and taxpayers' inclinations to cheat. *The Sociology Quarterly*, **32**, pp. 251–266.

GRASMICK, HAROLD G., ELIZABETH DAVENPORT, MITCHELL B. CHAMLIN, AND ROBERT J. BURSIK, JR. 1992. Protestant fundamentalism and the retributive doctrine of punishment. *Criminology*, **30**, pp. 21–45.

GRASMICK, HAROLD G., KARYL KINSEY, AND JOHN K. COCHRAN. 1991. Denomination, religiosity and compliance with the law: A study of adults. *Journal for the Scientific Study of Religion*, **30**, pp. 99–107.

GRASMICK, HAROLD G., CHARLES R. TITTLE, ROBERT J. BURSIK, JR., AND BRUCE J. ARNEKLEV. 1993. Testing the core empirical implications of Gottfredson and Hirschi's general theory of crime. *Journal of Research in Crime and Delinquency*, **30**, February, pp. 5–29.

GRASMICK, HAROLD G., LINDA PATTERSON WILCOX, AND SHARON R. BIRD. 1990. The effects of religious fundamentalism and religiosity on preference for traditional family norms. *Sociological Inquiry*, **60**, November, pp. 352–369.

GRAYSON, DONALD K. 1990. Donner Party deaths: A demographic assessment. *Journal of Anthropological Research*, **46**, Fall, pp. 223–243.

GREELEY, ANDREW M. 1977. *The American Catholic*. New York: Basic Books.

———. 1989a. *Religious change in America*. Cambridge, Mass.: Harvard University Press.

———. 1989b. Protestant and Catholic: Is the analogical imagination extinct? *American Sociological Review*, **54**, August, pp. 485–502.

GREENE, RICHARD. 1991. Poverty concentration measures and the urban underclass. *Economic Geography*, **67**, July, pp. 240–253.

GREENGARD, S. 1990. Doctor's orders: Why don't patients do what their physicians say? *American Medical News*, February 9, pp. 37–42.

GREENGLASS, E. R., K. L. PANTONY, AND R. J. BURKE. 1988. A gender-role perspective on role conflict, work stress, and social support. *Journal of Social Behavior and Personality*, **3**, pp. 317–328.

GREENHAUS, J. H., A. G. BEDEIAN, AND K. W. MOSSHOLDER. 1987. Work experience, job performance, and feelings of personal and family well-being. *Journal of Vocational Behavior*, **31**, pp. 200–215.

GREENSTEIN, THEODORE, N. 1990. Marital disruption and the employment of married women. *Journal of Marriage and the Family*, **52**, August, pp. 657–676.

GREENWOOD, PETER WITH ALLAN ABRAHAMSE. 1982. *Selective incapacitation*. Santa Monica, Calif.: Rand Corporation.

GRENIG, JAY E. 1991. The dismissal of employees in the United States. *International Labour Review*, **130**, pp. 569–581.

GROSSMAN, DAVID, CAROL MILLIGAN, AND RICHARD DEYO. 1991. Risk factors for suicide attempts among Navajo adolescents. *American Journal of Public Health*, **81**, July, pp. 870–874.

GROSSMAN, HILDRETH, PATRICIA SALT, CAROL NADELSON, AND MALKAH NOTMAN. 1987. Coping resources and health responses among men and women medical students. *Social Science and Medicine*, **25**, pp. 1057–1062.

GROVES, BETSY MCALISTER, BARRY ZUCKERMAN, STEVEN MARANS, AND DONALD J. COHEN. 1993. Silent victims: Children who witness violence. *Journal of the American Medical Association*, **269**, January 13, pp. 262–264.

GRUBB, W. NORTON AND ROBERT WILSON. 1989. Sources of increasing inequality in wages and salaries, 1960–80. *Monthly Labor Review*, **112**, April, pp. 3–13.

GRUSKY, DAVID B. AND THOMAS A. DIPRETE. 1990. Recent trends in the process of stratification. *Demography*, **27**, November, pp. 617–637.

GUELZOW, MAUREEN G., GLORIA W. BIRD, AND ELIZABETH H. KOBALL. 1991. An exploratory path analysis of the stress process for dual-career men and women. *Journal of Marriage and the Family*, **53**, February, pp. 151–164.

GUEST, AVERY, NANCY LANDALE, AND JAMES MCCANN. 1989. Intergenerational occupational mobility in the late 19th century in the United States. *Social Forces*, **68**, December, pp. 351–378.

GUISINGER, SHAN, P. COWAN, AND D. SCHULDBERG. 1989. Changing parent and spouse relations in the first years of remarriage of divorced fathers. *Journal of Marriage and the Family*, **51**, pp. 445–456.

GUR, RUBEN C. 1991. Gender differences in age effect on brain atrophy measured by magnetic resonance imaging. *Proceedings of the National Academy of Sciences of the United States of America*, **88**, April 1, pp. 2845–2849.

GURR, TED R. 1981. Historical trends in violent crimes: A critical review of the evidence. *Crime and Justice: An Annual Review of Research*, **3**, pp. 295–353.

GUSTAFSSON, ROLF A. 1989. Origins of authority: The organization of medical care in Sweden. *International Journal of Health Services*, **19**, pp. 121–133.

GUTEK, B. AND B. MORASCH. 1982. Sex ratios, sex-role spillover, and sexual harassment of women at work. *Journal of Social Issues*, **38**, pp. 55–74.

GUTIERREZ, ROBERTO AND ROBERT SLAVIN. 1992. Achievement effects of the nongraded elementary school: A best evidence synthesis. *Review of Educational Research*, **62**, Winter, pp. 333–376.

GUTMANN, D. 1987. *Reclaimed powers: Toward a new psychology of men and women in later life*. New York: Basic Books.

GUTTENTAG, MARCIA AND PAUL SECORD. 1983. *Two many women? The sex ratio question*. Beverly Hills, Calif.: Sage.

HAAS, JENNIFER S., STEVEN UDVARHELYI, CARL N. MORRIS, AND ARNOLD M. EPSTEIN. 1993. The effect of providing health coverage to poor uninsured pregnant women in Massachusetts. *Journal of American Medical Association*, **269**, pp. 87–91.

HACHEN, DAVID S., JR. 1992. Industrial characteristics and job mobility rates. *American Sociological Review*, **57**, February, pp. 39–55.

HADAWAY, C. KIRK, PENNY LONG MARLER, AND MARK CHAVES. 1993. What the polls don't show: A closer look at U.S. church attendance. *American Sociological Review*, **58**, December, pp. 741–752.

HADWIGER, DAVID. 1992. Money, turnout, and ballot measure success in California cities. *Western Political Quarterly*, **45**, June, pp. 539–558.

HAFEN, B. Q. and M. J. BROG. 1983. *Alcohol*. New York: West.

HAFFEY, MARTHA AND PHYLLIS MALKIN COHEN. 1992. Treatment issues for divorcing women. *Families in Society*, March, pp. 142–148.

HAGAN, JOHN. 1989. *Structural criminology*. New Brunswick, N.J.: Rutgers University Press.

———. 1990. Clarifying and extending power-control theory. *American Journal of Sociology*, **95**, January, pp. 1024–1037.

HAGE, DAVID, DON BOROUGHS, AND ROBERT BLACK. 1992. Hidden monopolies. *U.S. News & World Report*, February 3, pp. 42–48.

HAGERMAN, ERIK. 1991. As the Third World turns. *World Watch*, September–October.

HALABY, CHARLES. 1988. Action and information in the job mobility process: The search decision. *American Sociological Review*, **53**, February, pp. 9–25.

HALADYNA, THOMAS, SUSAN BOBBIT NOLEN, AND NANCY S. HAAS. 1991. Raising standardized achievement test scores and the origins of test score pollution. *Educational Researcher*, **20**, June–July, pp. 2–7.

HALL, EDWARD T. 1966. *The hidden dimension*. Garden City, N.Y.: Doubleday.

HALL, G. STANLEY. 1904. *Adolescence: Its psychology and its relation to physiology, anthropology, sociology, sex, crime, religion, and education*. New York: D. Appleton.

HALL, R. M. and B. R. SANDLER. 1982. *The classroom climate: A chilly one for women? Project on the status and education of women*. Washington, D.C.: Association of American Colleges.

HALL, ROBERTA, DONI WILDER, PAMELA BODENROEDER, AND MICHAEL HESS. 1990. Assessment of AIDS knowledge, attitudes, behaviors, and risk levels of Northwestern American Indians. *American Journal of Public Health*, **80**, July, pp. 875–877.

HALLIN, DANIEL C. 1992. Sound bite democracy. *The Wilson Quarterly*, **16**, Spring, pp. 34–37.

HALLINAN, MAUREEN T. AND AAGE SORENSEN. 1987. Ability grouping and sex differences in mathematics achievement. *Sociology of Education*, **60**, April, pp. 63–72.

HAMER, DEAN, STELLA HU, VICTORIA MAGNUSON, NAN HU, AND ANGELA PATTATUCCI. 1993. A linkage between DNA markers on the X chromosome and male sexual orientation. *Science*, **261**, July 16, pp. 321–327.

HAMER, JOHN. 1972. Aging in a gerontocratic society: The Sidamo of southwest Ethiopia. In D. O. Cowgill and L. D. Holmes (eds.), *Aging and modernization*. New York: Appleton-Century Crofts.

HAMILTON, MYKOL C. 1988. Using masculine generics: Does generic 'he' increase male bias in the user's imagery? *Sex Roles*, **19**, pp. 785–799.

HAMILTON, MYKOL C. AND N. M. HENLEY. 1982. Detrimental consequences of generic masculine usage, paper presented at the meeting of the Western Psychological Association, Sacramento, Calif., April.

HANNAN, MICHAEL. 1989. Competitive and institutional processes in organizational ecology. In Joseph Berger and Morris Zelditch, Jr. (eds.), *Sociological theories in progress*. Newbury Park, Calif.: Sage.

HANSON, SANDRA L. AND THEODORA OOMS. 1991. The economic costs and rewards of two-earner, two-parent families. *Journal of Marriage and the Family*, **53**, August, pp. 622–634.

HANUSHEK, ERIC A. 1989. Expenditures, efficiency, and equity in education: The federal government's role. *American Economic Review*, **79**, May, pp. 46–51.

HARDEN, BLAINE. 1991. A bright spot. *The Wilson Quarterly*, **15**, Winter, pp. 38–39.

HARDIN, GARRETT. 1991. Conspicuous benevolence and the population bomb. *Chronicles*, October.

HARE, PAUL. 1981. Group size. *American Behavioral Scientist*, **24**, May/June, pp. 695–708.

HAREVEN, TAMARA K. AND KANJI MASAOKA. 1988. Turning points and transitions: Perceptions of the life course. *Journal of Family History*, **13**, pp. 271–289.

HARKINS, STEPHEN G. AND KATE SZYMANSKI. 1989. Social loafing and group evaluation. *Journal of Personality and Social Psychology*, **56**, pp. 934–941.

HARLOW, H. F. AND M. K. HARLOW. 1962. Social deprivation in monkeys. *Scientific American*, November, pp. 137–147.

HARRIS, CHAUNCY D. AND EDWARD L. ULLMAN. 1945. The nature of cities. *Annals of the American Academy of Political and Social Science*, **242**, pp. 7–17.

HARRIS, MARVIN. 1971. *Culture, man, and nature*. New York: Crowell.

HARRIS, T. GEORGE AND DANIEL YANKELOVICH. 1989. What good are the rich? *Psychology Today*, April, pp. 34–39.

HARRISON, LAWRENCE E. 1992. *Who prospers: How cultural values shape economic and political success*. New York: Basic Books.

HARRISON, LAWRENCE E. AND R. PASSERO. 1975. Sexism in the language of elementary textbooks. *Science and Children*, **12**, pp. 22–25.

HART, C. W. M. AND ARNOLD R. PILLING. 1960. *The Tiwi of North Australia*. New York: Holt, Rinehart and Winston.

HARTMANN, HEIDI. 1981. The family as the locus of gender, class, and political struggle: The example of housework. *Signs*, **6**, pp. 366–394.

HARTNAGEL, TIMOTHY AND MUHAMMAD MIZANUDDIN. 1986. Modernization, gender role convergence, and female crime. *International Journal of Comparative Sociology*, **27**, pp. 1–14.

HAUB, CARL. 1991. Fertility plunges in eastern Germany. *Population Today*, **19**, November, p. 4.

HAUSER, ROBERT AND JOHN LOGAN. 1992. How not to measure intergenerational occupational persistence. *American Journal of Sociology*, **97**, May, pp. 1689–1711.

HAUSER, ROBERT AND WILLIAM SEWELL. 1985. Birth order and educational attainment in full sibships. *American Educational Research Journal*, **22**, pp. 1–23.

HAWKINS, DARRELL. 1987. Beyond anomalies: Rethinking the conflict perspective on race and criminal punishment. *Social Forces*, **65**, March, pp. 719–745.

HAYWARD, MARK. 1990. Work and retirement among a cohort of older men in the United States, 1966–1983. *Demography, 27*, August, pp. 337–356.

HEALY, JANE. 1991. *Endangered minds: Why our children don't think.* New York: Simon & Schuster.

HEATH, JULIA AND DAVID CISCEL. 1988. Patriarchy, family structure, and the exploitation of women's labor. *Journal of Economic Issues, 22*, September, pp. 781–794.

HEATH, SHIRLEY BRICE. 1982. Questioning at home and at school: A comparative study. In G. D. Spindler (ed.), *Doing the ethnography of schooling.* New York: Holt, Rinehart and Winston.

HEATON, TIM B. 1984. Religious homogamy and marital satisfaction reconsidered. *Journal of Marriage and the Family, 46*, pp. 729–733.

———. 1991. Time-related determinants of marital dissolution. *Journal of Marriage and the Family, 53*, May, pp. 285–295.

HEATON, T. B., S. L. ALBRECHT, AND T. K. MARTIN. 1985. The timing of divorce. *Journal of Marriage and the Family, 47*, pp. 631–633.

HECKATHORN, DOUGLAS D. 1990. Collective sanctions and compliance norms: A formal theory of group-mediated social control. *American Sociological Review, 55*, June, pp. 366–384.

HEISE, LORI. 1989. The global war against women. *The Washington Post,* April 9, pp. B1, B4.

HELGESON, VICKI S. 1990. The role of masculinity in a prognostic predictor of heart attack severity. *Sex Roles, 22*, pp. 755–774.

HENGGELER, SCOTT AND CHARLES BORDUIN. 1981. Satisfied working mothers and their preschool sons. *Journal of Family Issues, 2*, pp. 322–335.

HENIG, JEFFREY R. 1990. Choice in public schools: An analysis of transfer requests among magnet schools. *Social Science Quarterly, 71*, March, pp. 69–82.

HENLEY, N. M., B. GRUBER, AND L. LERNER. 1984. Effects of sex-biased language on attitudes and self-esteem, paper presented at a meeting of the Southern California Language and Gender Interest Group, Los Angeles, Calif. October.

HEPWORTH, MARK E. 1990. Planning for the information city: The challenge and response. *Urban Studies, 27*, August, pp. 537–558.

HERRENKOHL, ELLEN, ROY HERRENKOHL, AND LORI TOEDLER. 1983. Perspectives on the intergenerational transmission of abuse. In David Finkelher, Richard Gelles, Gerald Hotaling, and Murray Straus (eds.), *The dark side of families: Current family violence research.* Newbury Park, Calif.: Sage.

HERRING, CEDRIC, JAMES S. HOUSE, AND RICHARD P. MERO. 1991. Racially based changes in political alienation in America. *Social Science Quarterly, 72*, March, pp. 123–134.

HERRNSON, PAUL S. 1992. Campaign professionalism and fundraising in congressional elections. *The Journal of Politics, 54*, August, pp. 859–870.

HERSHORN, MICHAEL AND ALAN ROSENBAUM. 1985. Children of marital violence: A closer look at the unintended victims. *American Journal of Orthopsychiatry, 55*, pp. 260–266.

HESS, ROBERT D. AND HIROSHI AZUMA. 1991. Cultural support for schooling: Contrasts between Japan and the United States. *Educational Researcher, 20*, December, pp. 2–8, 12.

HETHERINGTON, E. M. 1989. Coping with family transitions: Winners, losers, and survivors. *Child Development, 60,* pp. 1–18.

HICKS, ALEXANDER AND WILLIAM PATTERSON. 1989. On the robustness of the left corporatist model of economic growth. *Journal of Politics, 51*, pp. 662–675.

HIGLEY, JOHN AND MICHAEL BURTON. 1982. Predicting marital and career success among dual-worker couples. *Journal of Marriage and the Family*, **44**, pp. 53–62.

————. 1989. The elite variable in democratic transitions and breakdowns. *American Sociological Review*, **54**, February, pp. 17–32.

HILTZIK, MICHAEL. 1990. Higher education in the depths in Africa. *Los Angeles Times*, May 29.

HIRSCH, ERIC. 1986. The creation of political solidarity in social movement organizations. *The Sociological Quarterly*, **27**, September, pp. 373–387.

————. 1989. Sacrifice for the cause: Group processes, recruitment, and commitment in a student social movement. *American Sociological Review*, **55**, April, pp. 243–254.

HIRSCHHORN, LARRY. 1984. *Beyond mechanization: Work and technology in a postindustrial age*. Cambridge, Mass.: MIT Press.

HIRSCHI, TRAVIS. 1969. *Causes of delinquency*. Berkeley, Calif.: University of California Press.

HIRSCHI, TRAVIS AND MICHAEL GOTTFREDSON. 1989. The significance of white-collar crime for a general theory of crime. *Criminology*, **27**, pp. 359–364.

————. 1993. Commentary: Testing the general theory of crime. *Journal of Research in Crime and Delinquency*, **30**, February, pp. 47–54.

HIRSCHMAN, CHARLES AND MORRISON WONG. 1986. The extraordinary educational attainment of Asian-Americans: A search for historical evidence and explanations. *Social Forces*, **65**, pp. 1–27.

HITCHENS, CHRISTOPHER. 1992. Voting in the passive voice: What polling has done to American democracy. *Harper's Magazine*, **284**, April, pp. 45–52.

HOCHSCHILD, ARLIE. 1989. *The second shift*. New York: Viking.

HODGE, ROBERT AND STEVEN LAGERFELD. 1987. The politics of opportunity. *The Wilson Quarterly*, **11**, Winter, pp. 109–127.

HODGES, HAROLD. 1964. *Social stratification*. Cambridge, Mass.: Schenkman.

HODGES, W. F. 1986. *Interventions for children of divorce*. New York: Wiley.

HODSON, RANDY. 1978. Labor in the monopoly, competitive, and state sectors of production. *Politics and Society*, **8**, pp. 429–480.

HOEBEL, E. ADAMSON. 1960. *The Cheyennes: Indians of the Great Plains*. New York: Holt, Rinehart and Winston.

————. 1966. *Anthropology: The study of man*. New York: McGraw-Hill.

HOELTER, JON AND LYNN HARPER. 1987. Structural and interpersonal family influences on adolescent self-conception. *Journal of Marriage and the Family*, **49**, February, pp. 129–139.

HOFFMAN, SAUL D. AND GREG J. DUNCAN. 1988. What are the economic consequences of divorce? *Demography*, **25**, November, pp. 641–645.

HOGAN, DENNIS AND TAKASHI MOCHIZUKI. 1988. Demographic transitions and the life course: Lessons from Japanese and American comparisons. *Journal of Family History*, **13**, pp. 291–305.

HOGE, ROBERT D. AND THEODORE COLADARCI. 1989. Teacher-based judgments of academic achievement: A review of literature. *Review of Educational Research*, **59**, Fall, pp. 297–313.

HOLDEN, GEORGE W. AND KATHY L. RITCHIE. 1991. Linking extreme marital discord, child rearing, and child behavior problems: Evidence from battered women. *Child Development*, **62**, pp. 311–327.

HOLLAND, MAX. 1991. Citizen McCloy. *The Wilson Quarterly*, **15**, Autumn, pp. 22–42.

HOLLOWAY, RALPH L., JR. 1992 (October 1969). Culture: A human domain. *Current Anthropology*, **33**, Supplement, pp. 47–59.

HOLMES, H. ET AL. 1980. *Birth control and controlling birth*. New Jersey: Humana Press.

HOMANS, GEORGE. 1961. *Social behavior: Its elementary forms*. New York: Harcourt Brace Jovanovich.

HOSSLER, DON AND FRANCES STAGE. 1992. Family and high school experience influences on the postsecondary educational plans of ninth-grade students. *American Educational Research Journal*, **29**, Summer, pp. 425–451.

HOULIHAN, MARGARET M., JOAN JACKSON, AND TIM R. ROGERS. 1990. Decision making of satisfied and dissatisfied married couples. *The Journal of Social Psychology*, **130**, pp. 89–102.

HOUT, MICHAEL. 1988. More universalism, less structural mobility: The American occupational structure in the 1980s. *American Journal of Sociology Behavior*, **93**, May, pp. 1358–1400.

HOWARD, R. C. 1984. The clinical EEG and personality in mentally abnormal offenders. *Psychological Medicine*, **14**, pp. 569–580.

HOWELL, JOSEPH T. 1973. *Hard living on clay street*. Garden City, N.Y.: Doubleday.

HOWES, CAROLLEE. 1990. Can the age of entry and the quality of infant child care predict adjustment in kindergarten? *Developmental Psychology*, **26**, pp. 292–303.

HOYT, HOMER. 1939. *The structure and growth of residential neighborhoods in American cities*. Washington, D.C.: Federal Housing Administration.

HOYT, LYNNE A., EMORY L. COWEN, JOANNE L. PEDRO-CARROLL, AND LINDA J. ALPERT-GILLIS. 1990. Anxiety and depression in young children of divorce. *Journal of Clinical Child Psychology*, **19**, pp. 26–32.

HUBERT, NANCY, THEODORE WACHS, PATRICIA PETERS-MARTIN, AND MARY JANE GANDOUR. 1982. The study of early temperament: Measurement and conceptual issues. *Child Development*, **53**, June, pp. 571–600.

HUGHEY, A. M. 1990. The incomes of recent female immigrants to the United States. *Social Science Quarterly*, **71**, June, pp. 383–390.

HUGICK, LARRY. 1992. Public opinion divided on gay rights. *The Gallup Poll Monthly*, **321**, June, pp. 2–5.

HUMPHRIES, CRAIG. 1991. Corporations, PACs, and the strategic link between contributions and lobbying activities. *Western Political Quarterly*, **44**, pp. 353–372.

HUNDLEBY, JOHN AND G. WILLIAM MERCER. 1987. Family and friends as social environments and their relationship to young adolescents' use of alcohol, tobacco, and marijuana. *Journal of Marriage and the Family*, **49**, February, pp. 151–164.

HUNT, EARL AND FRANCA AGNOLI. 1991. The Whorfian hypothesis: A cognitive psychology perspective. *Psychological Review*, **98**, pp. 377–389.

HUNTINGTON, SAMUEL. 1992. How countries democratize. *Political Science Quarterly*, **106**, pp. 579–589.

HUSEN, TORSTEN AND ALBERT TUIJNMAN. 1991. The contribution of formal schooling to the increase in intellectual capital. *Educational Researcher*, **20**, October, pp. 17–25.

HWANG, SEAN-SHONG AND STEVE MURDOCK. 1991. Ethnic enclosure on ethnic competition: Ethnic identification among Hispanics in Texas. *The Sociological Quarterly*, **32**, pp. 469–476.

HYDAN, GORAN. 1983. *No shortcuts to progress: African development management in perspective*. Berkeley, Calif.: University of California Press.

HYDE, JANET SHIBLEY. 1981. How large are cognitive gender differences? *American Psychologist*, **36**, pp. 892–901.

HYDE, JANET SHIBLEY, ELIZABETH FENNEMA, AND SUSAN J. LAMON. 1990. Gender differences in mathematics performance: A meta-analysis. *Psychological Bulletin*, **107**, March, pp. 139–155.

IANNACCONE, LAURENCE R. 1990. Religious practice: A human capital approach. *Journal for the Scientific Study of Religion*, **29**, pp. 297–314.

IDLER, ELLEN L. 1987. Religious involvement and the health of the elderly: Some hypotheses and an initial test. *Social Forces*, **66**, pp. 226–238.

IDLER, ELLEN L. AND STANISLAV KASL. 1992. Religion, disability, depression, and the timing of death. *American Journal of Sociology*, **97**, January, pp. 1052–1079.

ILIFFE, JOHN. 1983. *The emergence of African capitalism*. Minneapolis, Minn.: University of Minnesota Press.

IMERSHEIN, ALLEN W., PHILIP C. ROND III, AND MARY P. MATHIS. 1992. Restructuring patterns of elite dominance and the formation of state policy in health care. *American Journal of Sociology*, **97**, January, pp. 970–993.

INVERARITY, J. AND D. MCCARTHY. 1988. Punishment and social structure revisited: Unemployment and imprisonment in the United States. *Sociological Quarterly*, **29**, pp. 263–279.

IRWIN, JOHN. 1985. *The jail: Managing rabble in American society*. Berkeley, Calif.: University of California Press.

IZZO, R. L. AND R. R. ROSS. 1990. Meta-analysis of rehabilitative programs for juvenile delinquents. *Criminal Justice and Behavior*, **17**, pp. 134–142.

JACKLIN, CAROL, JANET DIPIETRO, AND ELEANOR MACCOBY. 1984. Sex-typing behavior and sex-typing pressure in parent/child interaction. *Archives of Sexual Behavior*, **13**, October, pp. 413–425.

JACOBS, DAVID. 1985. Unequal organizations or unequal attainments? *American Sociological Review*, **50**, April, pp. 166–180.

JACOBS, JERRY. 1989a. Long-term trends in occupational segregation by sex. *American Journal of Sociology*, **95**, July, pp. 160–173.

———. 1989b. *Revolving doors: Sex segregation and women's careers*. Stanford, Calif.: Stanford University Press.

JACOBSON, J. L., R. L. TIANEEN, D. E. WILLE, AND D. M. AYTCH. 1986. Infant–mother attachment and early peer relations. In E. Mueller and C. Cooper (eds.), *Process and outcome in peer relations*. New York: Academic Press.

JAMES, DAVID R. 1989. City limits on racial equality: The effects of city–suburb boundaries on public-school desegregation, 1968–1976. *American Sociological Review*, **54**, December, pp. 963–985.

JANIS, IRVING. 1972. *Victims of groupthink*. Boston: Houghton Mifflin.

JENCKS, CHRISTOPHER S., SUSAN BARTLETT, MARY CORCORAN, JAMES CROUSE, DAVID EAGLESFIELD, GREGORY JACKSON, KENT MCCLELLAND, PETER MUESER, MICHAEL OLNECK, JOSEPH SCHWARTZ, SHERRY WARD, AND JILL WILLIAMS. 1979. *Who gets ahead? The determinants of economic success in America*. New York: Basic Books.

JENCKS, CHRISTOPHER S., M. SMITH, H. ACKLAND, M. J. BANE, D. K. COHEN, H. GINTIS, B. HEYNS, AND S. MICHAELSON. 1972. *Inequality: A reassessment of the effect of family and schooling in America*. New York: Basic Books.

JENKINS, CRAIG AND AUGUSTINE KPOSOWA. 1990. Explaining military coups d'etat: Black Africa, 1957–1984. *American Sociological Review*, **55**, December, pp. 861–875.

JENSEN, ARTHUR. 1980. *Bias in mental testing*. New York: Free Press.

JENSEN, LARRY, REA J. NEWELL, AND TOM HOLMAN. 1990. Sexual behavior, church attendance, and permissive beliefs among unmarried young men and women. *Journal for the Scientific Study of Religion*, **29**, pp. 113–117.

JENSEN, LEIF AND MARTA TIENDA. 1989. Nonmetro minority families in the United States: Trends in racial and ethnic economic stratification, 1959–1986. *Rural Sociology*, **54**, pp. 509–532.

JOHNSON, COLLEEN L. AND LILLIAN TROLL. 1992. Family functioning in late late life. *Journal of Gerontology*, **47**, pp. 566–572.

JOHNSON, DAVID R., TEODORA O. AMOLOZA, AND ALAN BOOTH. 1992. Stability and developmental change in marital quality: A three-wave panel analysis. *Journal of Marriage and the Family*, **54**, August, pp. 582–594.

JOHNSON, PERRY M. 1992. Setting the record straight: Methvin's incarceration argument doesn't hold up under scrutiny. *Corrections Today*, April, pp. 199–200.

JOHNSON, W. AND M. MINTON. 1982. The economic choice in divorce: Extended or blended family? *Journal of Divorce*, **5**, pp. 101–113.

JOHNSTON, JANET, ROBERTO GONZALEZ, AND LINDA CAMPBELL. 1987. Ongoing post-divorce conflict and child disturbance. *Journal of Abnormal Child Psychology*, **15**, pp. 493–509.

JOHNSTON, J. R., L. E. G. CAMPBELL, AND S. S. MAYES. 1985. Latency children in post-separation and divorce disputes. *Journal of the American Academy of Child Psychiatry*, **24**, pp. 563–574.

JOHNSTON, WILLIAM B. 1991. Global work force 2000: The New World labor market. *Harvard Business Review*, March–April.

JONES, BARBARA H. AND KATHLEEN MCNAMARA. 1991. Attitudes toward women and their work roles: Effects of intrinsic and extrinsic religious orientations. *Sex Roles*, **24**, pp. 21–29.

JORSTAD, ERWIN. 1987. *The new Christian Right, 1981–1988*. Lewiston, N.Y.: Edwin Mellen Press.

JOURILES, E. N., C. M. MURPHY, AND K. D. O'LEARY. 1989. Interspousal aggression, marital discord, and child problems. *Journal of Consulting and Clinical Psychology*, **57**, pp. 453–455.

JUDIS, JOHN. 1991. Twilight of the gods. *The Wilson Quarterly*, **15**, Autumn, pp. 43–55.

JULIAN, TERESA W., PATRICK C. MCKENRY, AND KEVIN ARNOLD. 1990. Psychosocial predictors of stress associated with the male midlife transition. *Sex Roles*, **22**, pp. 707–722.

JUNG, CARL. 1958. *Psyche and symbol*. New York: Anchor.

KAGAN, SPENCER. 1986. Cooperative learning and sociocultural factors in schooling. In *Beyond language*. Los Angeles: California State University, Evaluation, Dissemination, and Assessment Center.

KAIN, J. F. 1968. Housing segregation, Negro employment, and metropolitan decentralization. *Quarterly Journal of Economics*, **82**, May, pp. 175–197.

KALLEBERG, ANNE AND AAGE SORENSEN. 1979. The sociology of labor markets. *Annual Review of Sociology*, **5**, pp. 35–79.

KALMIJN, MATTHIJS. 1991a. Status homogamy in the United States. *American Journal of Sociology*, **97**, September, pp. 496–523.

———. 1991b. Shifting boundaries: Trends in religious and educational homogamy. *American Sociological Review*, **56**, December, pp. 786–800.

KALMUSS, DEBRA. 1984. The intergenerational transmission of marital aggression. *Journal of Marriage and the Family*, **46**, pp. 11–19.

KALMUSS, DEBRA, ANDREW DAVIDSON, AND LINDA CUSHMAN. 1992. Parenting expectations, experiences, and adjustment to parenthood: A test of the violated expectations framework. *Journal of Marriage and the Family*, **54**, August, pp. 516–526.

KALTER, NEIL. 1987. Long-term effects of divorce on children: A developmental vulnerability model. *American Journal of Orthopsychiatry*, **57**, pp. 587–601.

KAMERMAN, SHEILA B. AND ALFRED J. KAHN. 1989. The possibilities for child and family policy: A cross-national perspective. *Proceedings of the Academy of Political Science*, **37**, pp. 84–98.

KANDEL, ELIZABETH AND SARNOFF A. MEDNICK. 1991. Perinatal complications predict violent offending. *Criminology*, **29**, pp. 519–529.

KANDELL, JONATHAN. 1988. *La Capital: Biography of Mexico City*. New York: Random House.

KANIN, EUGENE. 1985. Date rapists: Differential sexual socialization and relative deprivation. *Archives of Sexual Behavior*, **14**, June, pp. 219–231.

KANTROWITZ, BARBARA AND JOHN MCCORMICK. 1992. A head start does not last. *Newsweek*, January 27, pp. 44–45.

KAPLAN, HOWARD. 1989. Health, disease, and the social structure. In Howard Freeman and Sol Levine (eds.), *Handbook of medical sociology*. 4th ed. Englewood Cliffs, N.J.: Prentice-Hall.

KAPLAN, HOWARD B. AND ROBERT J. JOHNSON. 1991. Negative social sanctions and juvenile delinquency: Effects of labeling in a model of deviant behavior. *Social Science Quarterly*, **72**, March, pp. 98–122.

KARABEL, J. 1984. Status group struggle, organizational interests, and the limits of institutional autonomy: The transformation of Harvard, Yale, and Princeton, 1918–1940. *Theory and Society*, **13**, pp. 1–40.

KAREN, DAVID. 1990. Toward a political-organizational model of gatekeeping: The case of elite colleges. *Sociology of Education*, **63**, October, pp. 227–240.

KARIYA, TAKEHIKO AND JAMES E. ROSENBAUM. 1987a. Market and institutional mechanisms for the high school to work transition, paper presented at the annual meeting of the American Sociological Association, Chicago.

————. 1987b. Self-selection in Japanese junior high schools: A longitudinal study of students' educational plans. *Sociology of Education*, **60**, July, pp. 168–180.

KARLSEN, CAROL. 1989. *The devil in the shape of a woman*. New York: W. W. Norton.

KARP, DAVID. 1988. A decade of reminders: Changing age consciousness between fifty and sixty years old. *The Gerontologist*, **28**, pp. 727–738.

KARP, DAVID AND WILLIAM YOELS. 1976. The college classroom: Some observations on the meanings of student participation. *Sociology and Social Research*, **60**, July, pp. 421–439.

KASARDA, JOHN. 1989. Urban industrial transition and the underclass. *The Annals of the American Academy of Political and Social Science*, **501,** January, pp. 26–47.

KASARDA, JOHN AND MORRIS JANOWITZ. 1974. Community attachment in mass society. *American Sociological Review*, **39**, June, pp. 328–339.

KATZ, LAWRENCE AND LAWRENCE SUMMERS. 1989. Industry rents: Evidence and implications. *Brookings Papers on Economic Activity*, Special issue, pp. 209–275.

KAUFMAN, JOAN AND DANTE CICCHETTI. 1989. Effects of maltreatment on school-age children's socioemotional development. *Developmental Psychology*, **25**, pp. 516–524.

KAUFMAN, JOAN AND EDWARD ZIGLER. 1987. Do abused children become abusive parents? *American Journal of Orthopsychiatry*, **57**, pp. 186–192.

KAUS, MICKEY. 1990. For a new equality. *The New Republic*, May 7, pp. 18–27.

KEIGHER, SHARON AND SADELLE GREENBLATT. 1992. Housing emergencies and the etiology of homelessness among the urban elderly. *The Gerontologist*, **32**, pp. 457–465.

KEITH, VERNA AND CEDRIC HERRING. 1991. Skin tones and stratification in the black community. *American Journal of Sociology*, **97**, November, pp. 760–778.

KELLEY, MARYELLEN R. 1990. New process technology, job design, and work organization: A contingency model. *American Sociological Review*, **55**, April, pp. 191–208.

KELLSTEDT, LYMAN, JOHN GREEN, JAMES GUTH, AND CORWIN SMIDT. (1993, July). *Religious traditions and religious commitments in the U.S.A.* Paper prepared for the 22nd International Conference of the International Society for the Sociology of Religion, Budapest, Hungary.

KELLY, J. B. AND J. S. WALLERSTEIN. 1976. The effects of parental divorce: Experiences of the child in early latency. *American Journal of Orthopsychiatry*, **46**, pp. 20–32.

KELLY, RITA MAE, MICHELLE SAINT-GERMAIN, AND JODY HORN. 1991. Female public officials: A different voice? *The Annals of the American Adademy of Political and Social Science*, **515**, May, pp. 77–87.

KENEALY, PAMELA, NEIL FRUDE, AND WILLIAM SHAW. 1991. Teacher expectations as predictors of academic success. *The Journal of Social Psychology*, **131**, April, pp. 305–306.

KENNEDY, LESLIE W. AND STEPHEN W. BARON. 1993. Routine activities and a subculture of violence: A study of violence on the street. *Journal of Research in Crime and Delinquency*, **30**, February, pp. 88–112.

KERCKHOFF, ALAN C. 1989. On the social psychology of social mobility processes. *Social Forces*, **68**, September, pp. 17–25.

KESSLER, RONALD. 1979. Stress, social status, and psychological distress. *Journal of Health and Social Behavior*, **20**, pp. 259–272.

KEVE, PAUL W. 1992. The costliest punishment—a corrections administrator contemplates the death penalty. *Federal Probation*, **56**, March, pp. 11–15.

KEVLES, DANIEL. 1992. Controlling the genetic arsenal. *The Wilson Quarterly*, **16**, Spring, pp. 68–76.

KEY, V. O., JR. 1964. *Politics, parties, and pressure groups*. 5th ed. New York: Thomas Y. Crowell.

KEYFITZ, NATHAN. 1989. The growing human population. *Scientific American*, **261**, September, pp. 118–126.

KICK, EDWARD AND GARY LAFREE. 1985. Development and the social context of murder and theft. In *Comparative Social Research: Deviance*. Greenwich, Conn.: JAI Press.

KIECOLT, K. JILL AND HART M. NELSEN. 1991. Evangelicals and party realignment, 1976–1988. *Social Science Quarterly*, **72**, September, pp. 552–569.

KIELCOLT-GLASER, JANICE, LAURA FISHER, PAULA OGROCKI, JULIE STOUT, CARL SPEICHER, AND RONALD GLASER. 1987. Marital quality, marital disruption, and immune function. *Psychosomatic Medicine*, **49**, pp. 13–34.

KILBOURNE, JEAN. 1992. Beauty and the beast of advertising. In Paula Rothenberg (ed.), *Race, class, and gender in the United States*. 2d ed. New York: St. Martin's Press.

KILGORE, SALLY B. 1991. The organizational context of tracking in schools. *American Sociological Review*, **56**, April, pp. 189–203.

KITSON, GAY C. AND LESLIE A. MORGAN. 1990. The multiple consequences of divorce: A decade review. *Journal of Marriage and the Family*, **52**, November, pp. 913–924.

KLEBAN, MORTON H., ELAINE M. BRODY, CLAIRE B. SCHOONOVER, AND CHRISTINE HOFFMAN. 1989. Family help to the elderly: Perceptions of sons-in-law regarding parent care. *Journal of Marriage and the Family*, **51**, pp. 303–312.

KLEMKE, LLOYD. 1978. Does apprehension for shoplifting amplify or terminate shoplifting activity? *Law and Society Review*, **12**, pp. 391–403.

KLINE, MARSHA, JANET R. JOHNSTON, AND JEANNE M. TSCHANN. 1991. The long shadow of marital conflict: A model of children's postdivorce adjustment. *Journal of Marriage and the Family*, **53**, May, pp. 297–309.

KLITGAARD, ROBERT. 1991. Adjusting to African realities. *The Wilson Quarterly*, **15**, Winter, pp. 33–43.

KLUEGEL, JAMES R. 1987. Macro-economic problems: Beliefs about the poor and attitudes toward welfare spending. *Social Problems*, **34**, pp. 82–99.

———. 1990. Trends in whites' explanations of the black–white gap in socioeconomic status, 1977–1989. *American Sociological Review*, **55**, August, pp. 512–525.

KNOKE, DAVID AND FRANZ URBAN PAPPI. 1991. Organizational action sets in the U.S. and German labor policy domains. *American Sociological Review*, **56,** August, pp. 509–523.

KNUPFER, GENEVIEVE. 1982. Problems associated with drunkenness in women: Some research issues. In *Special population issues*. Rockville, Md.: National Institute on Alcohol Abuse and Alcoholism.

KODRAS, JANET E. AND IRENE PADAVIC. 1993. Economic restructuring and women's sectoral employment in the 1970s: A spatial investigation across 380 U.S. labor market areas. *Social Science Quarterly*, **74**, March, pp. 10–26.

KOEPPEL, BARBARA. 1989. A company town decays. *The Progressive*, **53,** pp. 12–13.

KOHN, MELVIN L., ATSUSHI NAOI, CARRIE SCHOENBACH, CARMI SCHOOLER, AND KAZIMIERZ SLOMCZYNSKI. 1990. Position in class structure and psychological functioning in the United States, Japan, and Poland. *American Journal of Sociology*, **95**, January, pp. 964–1008.

KORNHAUSER, RUTH. 1978. *Social sources of delinquency*. Chicago: University of Chicago Press.

KOSTERS, MARVIN H. 1990. Be cool, stay in school. *The American Enterprise*, **1**, March/April, pp. 60–62.

KOUTROULIS, G. 1990. The orifice revisited: Portrayal of women in gynaecological texts. *Community Health Studies*.

KOWALSKI, GREGORY S. AND DON DUFFIELD. 1990. The impact of the rural population component on homicide rates in the United States: A county-level analysis. *Rural Sociology*, **55**, pp. 76–90.

KRAFT, CHRISTINE. 1991. What makes a successful black student on a predominately white campus? *American Educational Research Journal*, **28**, Summer, pp. 423–443.

KRAHN, HARVEY, TIMOTHY HARTNAGEL, AND JOHN GARTRELL. 1986. Income inequality and homicide rates: Cross-national data and criminological theories. *Criminology*, **24**, pp. 269–295.

KRAMER, RITA. 1991. *Education school follies: The miseducation of America's teachers*. New York: Free Press.

KRAUSE, ELLIOTT A. 1977. *Power & illness: The political sociology of health and medical care*. New York: Elsevier.

KRAUSE, NEAL M. 1987. Stress in racial differences in self-reported health among the elderly. *The Gerontologist*, **27**, pp. 72–76.

KREFT, ITA. 1993. Using multilevel analysis to assess school effectiveness: A study of Dutch secondary schools. *Sociology of Education*, **66**, April, pp. 104–129.

KROHN, M. D. 1978. A Durkheimian analysis of international crime rates. *Social Forces*, **57**, pp. 654–670.

KRUGMAN, PAUL R. 1992. Disparity and despair. *U.S. News & World Report*, March 23, pp. 54–56.

KRUTTSCHNITT, CANDACE AND MAUDE DORNFELD. 1991. Childhood victimization, race, and violent crime. *Criminal Justice and Behavior*, **18**, December, pp. 448–463.

KUMAR, USHA. 1991. Life stages in the development of the Hindu woman in India. In Lenore Adler (ed.), *Women in cross-cultural perspective*. New York: Praeger.

KURDEK, LAWRENCE A. 1990. Divorce history and self-reported psychological distress in husbands and wives. *Journal of Marriage and the Family*, **52**, August, pp. 701–708.

————. 1991. Marital stability and changes in marital quality in newlywed couples: A test of the contextual model. *Journal of Personal and Social Relationships*, **8**, pp. 27–48.

KURDEK, L. A. AND J. P. SCHMITT. 1986. Relationship quality of partners in heterosexual married, heterosexual cohabiting, and gay and lesbian relationships. *Journal of Personality and Social Psychology*, **51**, pp. 711–720.

KUTNER, NANCY AND DONNA BROGAN. 1991. Sex stereotypes and health care: The case of treatment for kidney failure. *Sex Roles*, **24**, March, pp. 279–290.

LACHMANN, RICHARD. 1990. Class formation without class struggle: An elite conflict theory of the transition to capitalism. *American Sociological Review*, **55**, June, pp. 398–414.

LAMKE, LEANNE K. 1989. Marital adjustment among rural couples: The role of expressiveness. *Sex Roles*, **21**, pp. 579–590.

LAMONT, MICHELE. 1987. Cultural capital and the liberal political attitudes of professionals. *American Journal of Sociology*, **92**, May, pp. 1501–1505.

LAND, KENNETH C., GLENN DEANE, AND JUDITH R. BLAU. 1991. Religious pluralism and church membership: A spatial diffusion model. *American Sociological Review*, **56**, April, pp. 237–249.

LANDALE, NANCY AND AVERY GUEST. 1990. Generation, ethnicity, and occupational opportunities in late 19th century America. *American Sociological Review*, **55**, April, pp. 280–296.

LANDES, DAVID. 1989. Rich country, poor country. *The New Republic*, **201**, November 20, pp. 23–27.

LANGDON, STEVEN W. 1978. The multinational corporation in Kenya political economy. In Raphael Kaplinsky (ed.), *Readings on the multinational corporation in Kenya*. Nairobi, Kenya: Oxford University Press.

LAPPE, FRANCIS M. AND JOSEPH COLLINS. 1986. *World hunger: Twelve myths*. New York: Grove Press.

LARSON, DAVID B., KIMBERLY A. SHERRILL, JOHN S. LYONS, FREDERIC C. CRAIGIE, JR., SAMUEL B. THIELMAN, MARY A. GREENWOLD, AND SUSAN S. LARSON. 1992. Associations between dimensions of religious commitment and mental health reported in the American Journal of Psychiatry and Archives of General Psychiatry: 1978–1989. *American Journal of Psychiatry*, **149**, April, pp. 557–559.

LARSON, ERIK. 1992. Watching Americans watch TV. *The Atlantic Monthly*, **269**, March, pp. 66–80.

LARZELERE, ROBERT E. AND GERALD R. PATTERSON. 1990. Parental management: Mediator of the effect of socioeconomic status on early delinquency. *Criminology*, **28**, pp. 301–313.

LASCH, CHRISTOPHER. 1979. *The culture of narcissism*. New York: Warner Books.

LATANE, BIBB, KIPLING WILLIAMS, AND STEPHEN HARKINS. 1979. Many hands make light the work: The causes and consequences of social loafing. *Journal of Personality and Social Psychology*, **37**, pp. 822–832.

LAUER, ROBERT H., JEANETTE C. LAUER, AND SARAH T. KERR. 1990. The long-term marriage: Perceptions of stability and satisfaction. *International Journal of Aging and Human Development*, **31**, pp. 189–195.

LAURAS-LECOH, THERESE. 1990. Family trends and demographic transition in Africa. *International Social Science Journal*, **42**, November, pp. 475–491.

LAUREAU, ANNETTE. 1987. Social class differences in family–school relationships: The importance of cultural capital. *Sociology of Education*, **60**, April, pp. 73–85.

LAVEIST, THOMAS. 1989. Linking residential segregation with the infant mortality race disparity in U.S. cities. *Sociology and Social Research*, **73**, pp. 90–94.

———. 1990. Simulating the effects of poverty on the race disparity in post-neonatal mortality. *Journal of Public Health Policy*, **11**, pp. 463–473.

————. 1992. The political empowerment and health status of African-Americans: Mapping a new territory. *American Journal of Sociology*, **97**, January, pp. 1080–1095.

LAVINE, LINDA. 1982. Parental power as a potential influence on girls' career choice. *Child Development*, **53**, June, pp. 658–663.

LEAVITT, GREGORY C. 1992. General evolution and Durkheim's hypothesis of crime frequency: A cross-cultural test. *The Sociological Quarterly*, **33**, pp. 241–263.

LE BON, GUSTAV. 1960 (1895). *The crowd: A study of the popular mind.* New York: Viking.

LEE, BARRETT A., DAVID W. LEWIS, AND SUSAN HINZE JONES. 1992. Are the homeless to blame? A test of two theories. *The Sociological Quarterly*, **33**, pp. 535–552.

LEE, GARY R. AND CONSTANCE L. SHEHAN. 1989. Retirement and marital satisfaction. *Journal of Gerontology: Social Sciences*, **44**, pp. S226–230.

LEE, VALERIE AND ANTHONY BYRK. 1988. Curriculum tracking as mediating the social distribution of high school achievement. *Sociology of Education*, **61**, pp. 78–94.

————. 1989. A multilevel model of the social distribution of high school achievement. *Sociology of Education*, **62**, July, pp. 172–192.

LEE, VALERIE AND KENNETH FRANK. 1990. Students' characteristics that facilitate the transfer from two-year to four-year colleges. *Sociology of Education*, **63**, July, pp. 178–193.

LEESON, J. AND J. GRAY. 1978. *Women and medicine.* London: Tavistock.

LEICHT, KEVIN T. 1989. On the estimation of union threat effects. *American Sociological Review*, **54**, December, pp. 1035–1047.

LEIGH, PAUL AND ROGER FOLSOM. 1984. Estimates of the value of accident avoidance at the job depends on the concavity of the equalizing differences curve. *Quarterly Journal of Economics and Statistics*, **24**, pp. 56–66.

LEMANN, NICHOLAS. 1991. The other underclass. *The Atlantic*, **268**, December, pp. 96–111.

LEMERT, EDWIN. 1967. *Human deviance, social problems, and social control.* Englewood Cliffs, N.J.: Prentice-Hall.

LEMPERS, JACQUES D., DANIA CLARK-LEMPERS, AND RONALD SIMONS. 1989. Economic hardships, parenting, and distress. *Child Development*, **60**, February, pp. 25–39.

LENNANE, J. AND J. LENNANE. 1973. Alleged psychogenic disorders in women: A possible manifestation of sexual prejudice. *New England Journal of Medicine*, February 8.

LENSKI, GERHARD. 1966. *Power and privilege: A theory of social stratification.* New York: McGraw-Hill.

LEO, JOHN. 1992. Fighting for our public spaces. *U.S. News & World Report*, February 3, p. 18.

LERNER, MICHAEL A. 1982. The elite meet in retreat. *Newsweek*, August 2, pp. 21–22.

LESTER, DAVID AND MICHAEL FRANK. 1990. Suicide and homicide in rural areas: A study of Arkansas. *Psychological Reports*, **66**, p. 426.

LESTER, M. L. AND D. H. FISHBEIN. 1987. Nutrition and neuropsychological development in children. In R. Tarter, D. H. Van Thiel, and K. Edwards (eds.), *Medical neuropsychology*, New York: Plenum.

LEVIN, JEFFREY S. AND HAROLD VANDERPOOL. 1987. Is frequent religious attendance really conducive to better health? Toward an epidemiology of religion. *Social Science and Medicine*, **24**, pp. 589–600.

LEVINSON, D. 1977. The mid-life transition: A period of adult psychosocial development. *Psychiatry*, **40**, pp. 99–111.

LEVINSON, DANIEL J., CHARLOTTE DARROW, EDWARD KLEIN, MARIA LEVINSON, AND BRAXTON MCKEE. 1978. *The seasons of a man's life.* New York: Knopf.

LEVY, FRANK AND RICHARD MICHEL. 1986. An economic bust for the baby boom. *Challenge, 29*, March–April, pp. 33–39.

LEWIS, MICHAEL. 1992. *Shame: The exposed self.* New York: Free Press.

LEWIS, OSCAR. 1966. *La vida: A Puerto Rican family in the culture of poverty.* San Juan, Puerto Rico, and New York: Random House.

LICHTER, DANIEL T. 1990. Delayed marriage, marital homogamy, and the mate selection process among white women. *Social Science Quarterly, 71*, December, pp. 802–811.

LIEBERMAN, PHILIP. 1991. *Uniquely human: The evolution of speech, thought, and selfless behavior.* Cambridge, Mass.: Harvard University Press.

LIEBERSON, STANLEY AND ELEANOR O. BELL. 1992. Children's first names: An empirical study of social taste. *American Journal of Sociology, 98*, November, pp. 511–554.

LIEM, RAMSAY AND JOAN LIEM. 1978. Social class and mental illness reconsidered: The role of economic stress and social support. *Journal of Health and Social Behavior, 19*, pp. 139–156.

LIN, CHIN-YAU CINDY AND VICTORIA FU. 1990. A comparison of child-rearing practices among Chinese, immigrant Chinese, and Caucasian-American parents. *Child Development, 61*, pp. 429–433.

LIN, NAN AND WEN XIE. 1988. Occupational prestige in urban China. *American Sociological Review, 93*, January, pp. 793–832.

LINTON, RALPH. 1942. Age and sex categories. *American Sociological Review, 7*, 589–603.

LIPSET, SEYMOUR M. 1959. Some social requisites for democracy: Economic development and political legitimacy. *American Political Science Review, 53*, March, pp. 69–105.

————. 1963. *The first new nation: The United States in historical and comparative perspective.* New York: Basic Books.

————. 1982. Social mobility in industrial societies. *Public Opinion, 5*, June–July, pp. 41–44.

————. 1985. *The continental divide: The values and institutions of the United States and Canada.* Los Angeles: Routledge.

LIPSET, SEYMOUR M., MARTIN TROW, AND JAMES COLEMAN. 1956. *Union democracy.* New York: Free Press.

LITOFF, J. 1986. *The American midwife debate.* Westport, Conn.: Greenwood Press.

LITTLEPAGE, GLENN E. 1991. Effects of group size and task characteristics on group performance: A test of Steiner's model. *Personality and Social Psychology Bulletin, 17*, August, pp. 449–456.

LIZOT, JACQUES. 1985. *Tales of the Yanomami: Daily life in the Venezuelan forest.* Trans. Ernest Simon. Cambridge, England: Cambridge University Press.

LLOYD, BARBARA, GERARD DUVEEN, AND CAROLINE SMITH. 1988. Social representations of gender and young children's play: A replication. *The British Journal of Developmental Psychology, 6*, March, pp. 83–88.

LO, CELIA AND GERALD GLOBETTI. 1991. Parents noticing teenage drinking: Evidence from college freshmen. *Sociology and Social Research, 76*, October, pp. 20–27.

LOBEL, T. E. AND G. L. WINCH. 1986. Different defense mechanisms among men with different sex-role orientations. *Sex Roles, 15*, pp. 215–220.

LOEBER, ROLF AND MAGDA STOUTHAMER-LOEBER. 1986. Family factors as correlates and predictors of juvenile conduct problems and delinquency. In M. Tonry and N. Morris (eds.), *Crime and justice: An annual review of research.* Vol. 7. Chicago: University of Chicago Press.

LONDON, BRUCE. 1988. Dependence, distorted development, and fertility trends in non-core nations: A structural analysis of cross-cultural data. *American Sociological Review,* **53**, pp. 606–618.

LONDON, BRUCE AND THOMAS ROBINSON. 1989. The effect of international dependence on income inequality and political violence. *American Sociological Review,* **54**, April, pp. 305–308.

LONDON, BRUCE AND DAVID SMITH. 1988. Urban bias, dependence, and economic stagnation in non-core nations. *American Sociology Review,* **53**, pp. 454–463.

LONDON, BRUCE AND BRUCE WILLIAMS. 1988. Multinational corporate penetration, protest, and basic needs provision in non-core nations: A cross-national analysis. *Social Forces,* **66,** pp. 747–773.

———. 1990. National politics, international dependency, and basic needs provision: A cross-national study. *Social Forces,* **69**, December, pp. 565–584.

LONG, B. C. 1989. Sex-role orientation, coping strategies, and self-efficacy of women in traditional and nontraditional occupations. *Psychology of Women Quarterly,* **13**, pp. 307–324.

LONGORIA, THOMAS, ROBERT WRINKLE, and J. L. POLINARD. 1990. Mexican-American voter registration and turnout: Another look. *Social Science Quarterly,* **71**, June, pp. 356–361.

LORENZ, FREDERICK O., RAND D. CONGER, RONALD L. SIMON, LES B. WHITBECK, AND GLEN H. ELDER, JR. 1991. Economic pressure and marital quality: An illustration of the method variance problem in the causal modeling of family processes. *Journal of Marriage and the Family,* **53**, May, pp. 375–388.

LOSCOCCO, KARYN A. AND ARNE L. KALLEBERG. 1988. Age and the meaning of work in the United States and Japan. *Social Forces,* **67**, December, pp. 337–356.

LOUNSBURY, MARY AND JOHN BATES. 1982. The cries of infants of differing levels of perceived temperamental difficultness. *Child Development,* **53**, June, pp. 677–686.

LOVELL, MADELINE, THUANGO TRAN, AND CHI NGUYEN. 1987. Refugee women: Lives in transition. *International Social Work,* **30**, October, pp. 317–325.

LUCKMANN, THOMAS. 1990. Shrinking transcendence, expanding religion? *Sociological Analysis,* **50**, pp. 127–138.

LUKER, KRISTIN. 1984. *Abortion and the politics of motherhood.* Los Angeles: University of California Press.

LUNDBERG, FERDINAND. 1937. *America's Sixty Families.* New York: Vanguard.

LYND, ROBERT S. AND HELEN M. LYND. 1937. *Middletown in Transition.* New York: Harcourt Brace.

LYNN, R. 1977. The intelligence of the Japanese. *Bulletin of the British Psychological Society,* **30**, pp. 69–72.

LYSON, THOMAS A. 1989. *Two sides to the sunbelt.* New York: Praeger.

MABRY, MARCUS, JEANNE GORDON, LINDA DENWORTH, AND CLARA BINGHAM. 1990. The new teacher corps: Alternative training programs stir a revolution in the classroom. *Newsweek,* July 16, pp. 62–63.

MACCOBY, ELEANOR. 1990. Sex, a social category. *Actes de la recherche en sciences sociales,* **83**, June, pp. 16–26.

MACCOBY, ELEANOR AND CAROL JACKLIN. 1974. *The psychology of sex differences.* Stanford, Calif.: Stanford University Press.

MACDERMID, SHELLEY M., TED L. HUSTON, SUSAN M. MCHALE. 1990. Changes in marriage associated with the transition to parenthood: Individual differences as a function of sex-role attitudes and changes in the division of household labor. *Journal of Marriage and the Family,* **52,** May, pp. 475–486.

MACEWEN, KARYL E. AND JULIAN BARLING. 1991. Effects of maternal employment experiences on children's behavior via mood, cognitive difficulties, and parental behavior. *Journal of Marriage and the Family,* **63,** August, pp. 635–644.

MACFARQUHAR, EMILY. 1992. *Fighting over the dream. U.S. News & World Report,* May, p. 34.

MACKENSIE, R. D. 1925. The scope of human ecology. *Publications of the American Sociological Society,* **20.**

MACKEY, SANDRA. 1987. *The Saudis: Inside the desert kingdom.* Boston: Houghton Mifflin.

MACLAREN, PETER. 1980. *Cries from the corridor.* Toronto: Methuen.

MACLEOD, JAY. 1987. *Ain't no making it.* Boulder, Colo.: Westview Press.

MACY, MICHAEL W. 1990. Learning theory and the logic of critical mass. *American Sociological Review,* **55,** December, pp. 809–826.

MAIN, GLORIA L. 1991. An inquiry into when and why women learned to write in colonial New England. *Journal of Social History,* **24,** Spring, pp. 579–584.

MAJORIBANKS, KEVIN. 1991. Relationship of children's ethnicity, gender, and social status to their family environments and school-related outcomes. *The Journal of Social Psychology,* **131,** February, pp. 83–91.

MALATESTA, CAROL AND JEANNETTE HAVILAND. 1982. Learning display rules: The socialization of emotion expression in infancy. *Child Development,* **53,** August, pp. 991–1003.

MALTHUS, THOMAS ROBERT. 1976 (1798). *Essay on the principles of population.* Ed. Phillip Appleman. New York: Norton.

MANDELBAUM, DAVID. 1988. *Women's seclusion and men's honor: Sex Roles in North India, Bangladesh, and Pakistan.* Tucson, Ariz.: University of Arizona Press.

MANNING, WILLIAM AND WILLIAM O'HARE. 1988. The best metros for Asian-American businesses. *American Demographics,* **10,** pp. 35–37.

MANSFIELD, PHYLLIS M., PATRICIA BARTHALOW KOCH, JULIE HENDERSON, JUDITH VICARY, MARGARET COHN, AND ELAINE YOUNG. 1991. The job climate for women in traditionally male blue-collar occupations. *Sex Roles,* **25,** pp. 63–73.

MANTZICOPOULOS, PANAYOTA AND DELMONT MORRISON. 1992. Kingergarten retention: Academic and behavioral outcomes through the end of second grade. *American Educational Research Journal,* **29,** Spring, pp. 182–198.

MAPLE, SUE A. AND FRANCES K. STAGE. 1991. Influences on the choice of math/science major by gender and ethnicity. *American Educational Research Journal,* **28,** Spring, pp. 37–60.

MARCIANO, TERESA. 1987. Families and religions. In Marvin Sussman and Suzanne Steinmetz (eds.), *Handbook of marriage and the family.* New York: Sage.

MARE, ROBERT AND MEEI-SHENN TZENG. 1989. Fathers' ages and the social stratification of sons. *American Journal of Sociology,* **95,** July, pp. 108–131.

MARTIN, DAVID. 1982. Revived dogma and new cult. *Daedalus,* **111,** Winter, pp. 53–71.

MARTIN, JOHN D., GARLAND E. BLAIR, ROBERT NEVELS, AND JOYCE H. FITZPATRICK. 1990. A study of the relationship of styles of loving and marital happiness. *Psychological Reports,* **66,** pp. 123–128.

MARTIN, STEVEN, ROBERT ARNOLD, AND RUTH PARKER. 1988. Gender and medical socialization. *Journal of Health and Social Behavior,* **29,** December, pp. 333–343.

MARTIN, TERESA AND LARRY BUMPASS. 1989. Recent trends in marital disruption. *Demography,* **26,** pp. 37–51.

MARX, KARL. 1977 (1867). *Capital.* Vol. 1. New York: Vintage Books.

MARX, KARL AND FREDRICH ENGELS. 1963 (1848). *The communist manifesto.* (D. Ryazanoff, Ed.). New York: Russell and Russell.

MASHETER, CAROL. 1991. Postdivorce relationships between ex-spouses. The roles of attachment and interpersonal conflict. *Journal of Marriage and the Family,* **53**, February, pp. 103–110.

MASLAND, TIM, ROD NORDLAND, MELINDA LIN, AND JOSEPH CONTRERAS. 1992. Slavery. *Newsweek,* **119**, May 4, pp. 30–39.

MASON, TODD AND SCOTT TICER. 1988. TV evangelists are looking for a few miracles. *Business Week,* February 1, p. 32.

MASSEY, DOUGLAS S. 1990. American apartheid: Segregation and the making of the underclass. *American Journal of Sociology,* **96**, September, pp. 332–357.

MASSEY, DOUGLAS S. and NANCY A. DENTON. 1988. Suburbanization and segregation in United States metropolitan areas. *American Journal of Sociology,* **94**, November, pp. 592–626.

MASSEY, DOUGLAS S. AND MITCHELL EGGERS. 1990. The ecology of inequality: Minorities and the concentration of poverty, 1970–1980. *American Journal of Sociology,* **95**, March, pp. 1153–1188.

MASSEY, DOUGLAS S. AND ANDREW GROSS. 1991. Explaining trends in racial segregation, 1970–1980. *Urban Affairs Quarterly,* **27**, September, pp. 13–35.

MASTEKAASA, ARNE. 1992. Marriage and psychological well-being: Some evidence on selection into marriage. *Journal of Marriage and the Family,* **54**, November, pp. 901–911.

MASTERS, M. AND G. KEIM. 1985. Determinants of PAC participation among large corporations. *Journal of Politics,* **47**, pp. 1158–1173.

MATON, KENNETH. 1989. Community settings as buffers of life stress? Highly supportive churches, mutual help groups, and senior centers. *American Journal of Community Psychology,* **17**, pp. 203–232.

MATSUEDA, ROSS L. 1989. The dynamics of moral beliefs and minor deviance. *Social Forces,* **68**, December, pp. 428–457.

MATSUEDA, ROSS L., ROSEMARY GARTNER, IRVING PILIAVIN, AND MICHAEL POLAKOWSKI. 1992. The prestige of criminal and conventional occupations: A subculture model of criminal activity. *American Sociological Review,* **57**, December, pp. 752–770.

MATTES, J. A. AND M. FINK. 1987. A family study of patients with temper outbursts. *Journal of Psychiatric Research,* **21**, pp. 249–255.

MATTHEWS, J. 1984. *Good and mad women.* Sydney: George Allen and Unwin.

MATTHEWS, SARAH H. AND TENA TARLER ROSNER. 1988. Shared filial responsibility: The family as the primary caregiver. *Journal of Marriage and the Family,* **50**, pp. 185–195.

MAUSS, ARMAND L. AND PHILIP L. BARLOW. 1991. Church, sect, and scripture: The Protestant Bible and Mormon sectarian retrenchment. *Sociological Analysis,* **52**, pp. 397–414.

MAYER, KARL AND URS SCHOEPFLIN. 1989. The state and the life course. *Annual Review of Sociology,* **15**, pp. 187–209.

MAYNARD, DOUGLAS W. 1991. Interaction and asymmetry in clinical discourse. *American Journal of Sociology,* **97**, September, pp. 448–495.

MCCARTHY, BELINDA R. 1991. Social structure, crime, and social control: An examination of factors influencing rates and probabilities of arrest. *Journal of Criminal Justice,* **19**, pp. 19–29.

MCCARTHY, BILL AND JOHN HAGAN. 1992. Mean streets: The theoretical significance of situational delinquency among homeless youths. *American Journal of Sociology*, **98,** November, pp. 597–627.

MCCLAIN, JAMES. 1987. Mr. Ito's dance party. *The Wilson Quarterly*, **11**, Winter, pp. 154–160.

MCCLELLAND, KENT AND CHRISTOPHER HUNTER. 1992. The perceived seriousness of racial harassment. *Social Problems*, **39**, February, pp. 92–107.

MCCORD, JOAN. 1991. Family relationships, juvenile delinquency, and adult criminality. *Criminology*, **29**, pp. 397–417.

MCCORMICK, JOHN. 1991. A class act for the ghetto. *Newsweek*, December 23, pp. 62–63.

MCCUBBIN, HAMILTON AND JOAN PATTERSON. 1982. Family adaptation to crisis. In Hamilton McCubbin, A. Elizabeth Cauble, and Joan Patterson (eds.), *Family stress, coping, and social support*. Springfield, Ill.: Charles C. Thomas.

MCCULLUM, PAMELA. 1989. Turn allocation in lessons with North American and Puerto Rican students. *Anthropology and Education Quarterly*, **20**, pp. 133–156.

MCHALE, SUSAN M. AND ANN D. CROUTER. 1992. You can't always get what you want: Incongruence between sex-role attitudes and family work roles and its implications for marriage. *Journal of Marriage and the Family*, **54**, August, pp. 537–547.

MCKELVEY, BLAKE. 1963. *The urbanization of America*. New Brunswick, N.J.: Rutgers University Press.

MCKENRY, P., K. ARNOLD, T. JULIAN, AND J. KUO. 1987. Interpersonal influences on the well-being of men at mid-life. *Family Perspective*, **21**, pp. 225–233.

MCKNIGHT, JOHN. 1985. Health and empowerment. *Canadian Journal of Public Health*, **76**, Supplement, pp. S37–S38.

MCLANAHAN, SARA. 1985. Family structure and the reproduction of poverty. *American Journal of Sociology*, **90**, pp. 873–901.

MCLANAHAN, SARA AND KAREN BOOTH. 1989. Mother-only families: Problems, prospects, and politics. *Journal of Marriage and the Family*, **51**, August, pp. 557–580.

MCLANAHAN, SARA AND LARRY BUMPASS. 1988. Intergenerational consequences of family disruption. *American Journal of Sociology*, **94**, pp. 130–152.

MCLANAHAN, SARA AND IRWIN GARFINKEL. 1986. *Single mothers and their children*. Washington, D.C.: Urban Institute Press.

MCLANAHAN, S. S. AND A. B. SORENSEN. 1985. Life events and psychological well-being over the life course. In G. H. Elder (ed.), *Life course dynamics*. Ithaca, N.Y.: Cornell University Press.

MCLEOD, JANE D. AND RONALD C. KESSLER. 1990. Socioeconomic status differences in vulnerability to undesirable life events. *Journal of Health and Social Behavior*, **31**, June, pp. 162–172.

MCPHAIL, CLARK. 1989. Blumer's theory of collective behavior: The development of a non-symbolic interaction explanation. *The Sociological Quarterly*, **30**, pp. 401–423.

MCPHERSON, J. MILLER. 1981. A dynamic model of voluntary affiliation. *Social Forces*, **59**, pp. 705–728.

MEAD, GEORGE HERBERT. 1934. *Mind, self, and society*. Chicago: University of Chicago Press.

MEAD, MARGARET. 1930. *Growing up in New Guinea*. New York: William Morrow.

———. 1935. *Sex and temperament in three primitive societies*. New York: Dell.

MEDNICK, BIRGITTE R., ROBERT L. BAKER, AND LINN E. CAROTHERS. 1990. Patterns of family instability and crime: The association of timing of the family's disruption with subsequent adolescent and young adult criminality. *Journal of Youth and Adolescence*, **19**.

MEEKS, S., L. L. CARSTENSEN, B. TAMSKY, T. L. WRIGHT, AND D. PELLEGRINI, 1989. Age differences in coping: Does less mean worse? *International Journal of Aging and Human Development*, **282**, pp. 127–140.

MEHAN, HUGH. 1992. Understanding inequality in schools: The contribution of interpretive studies. *Sociology of Education*, **65**, January, pp. 1–20.

MEHAN, HUGH, ALMA HETWECK, AND J. LEE MEIHLS. 1985. *Handicapping the handicapped: Decision making in students' careers*. Stanford, Calif.: Stanford University Press.

MEHRABIAN, ALBERT. 1989. Marital choice and compatibility as a function of trait similarity–dissimilarity. *Psychological Reports*, **65**, p. 1202.

MEIER, ROBERT, STEVEN BURKETT, AND CAROL HICKMAN. 1984. Sanction, peers, and deviance: Preliminary models of a social control process. *Sociological Quarterly*, **25**, pp. 67–82.

MENAGHAN, ELIZABETH. 1983. Marital stress and family transitions: A panel analysis. *Journal of Marriage and the Family*, **45**, pp. 371–386.

MERCER, JANE. 1974. *Labeling the mentally retarded*. Berkeley, Calif.: University of California Press.

MERCY, JAMES AND LALA STEELMAN. 1982. Familial influence on the intellectual attainment of children. *American Sociological Review*, **47**, August, pp. 532–542.

MERTENSMEYER, C. AND M. COLEMAN. 1987. Correlates to inter-role conflict in young rural and urban parents. *Family Relations*, **36**, pp. 425–429.

MERTON, ROBERT K. 1938. Social structure and anomie. *American Sociological Review*, **3**, October, pp. 672–682.

———. 1940. Bureaucratic structure and personality. *Social Forces*, **18**, pp. 560–568.

———. 1968. Manifest and latent functions. In Robert K. Merton (ed.), *Social theory and social structure*. New York: Free Press.

———. 1976. *Sociological ambivalence*. New York: Free Press.

MESSNER, STEVEN F. 1986. Television violence and violent crime: An aggregate analysis. *Social Problems*, **33**, pp. 218–235.

———. 1989. Economic discrimination and societal homicide rates: Further evidence on the cost of inequality. *American Sociological Review*, **54**, August, pp. 597–611.

MESSNER, STEVEN F. AND REID M. GOLDEN. 1992. Racial inequality and racially disaggregated homicide rates: An assessment of alternative theoretical explanations. *Criminology*, **30**, August, pp. 421–447.

MEYER, DAVID R. 1990. The rise of the industrial metropolis: The myth and the reality. *Social Forces*, **68**, March, pp. 731–752.

MEYER, JOHN W. 1986. The self and the life course: Institutionalization and its effects. In Aage B. Sorensen, Franz E. Weinert, and Lonnie R. Sherrod (eds.), *Human development and the life course: Multidisciplinary perspective*. Hillsdale, N.J.: Erlbaum.

MICHAUD, STEPHEN AND HUGH AYNESWORTH. 1983. *The only living witness*. New York: Linden Press.

MICHELS, ROBERT. 1915. *Political parties*. Glencoe, Ill.: Free Press.

MICKELSON, ROSLYN ARLIN. 1990. The attitude-achievement paradox among black adolescents. *Sociology of Education*, **63**, January, pp. 44–61.

MIETHE, TERANCE D. 1991. Citizen-based crime control activity and victimization risks: An examination of displacement and free-rider effects. *Criminology*, **29**, pp. 419–437.

MILARDO, ROBERTO. 1987. Changes in social networks of women and men following divorce: A review. *Journal of Family Issues*, **8**, pp. 78–96.

MILES, STEVEN H. AND ALLISON AUGUST. 1990. Courts, gender, and the right to die. *Law, Medicine, and Health Care*, **18**, Spring/Summer, pp. 85–95.

MILGRAM, STANLEY. 1972. The experience of living in cities. *Science,* **167**, pp. 1461–1468.

MILLER, ANNETTA, KAREN SPRINGEN, AND DODY TSIANTAR. 1992. Now: The brick wall. *Newsweek*, August 24, pp. 54–56.

MILLER, W. B. 1958. Lower-class culture as a generating milieu of gang delinquency. *Journal of Social Issues,* **14**, pp. 5–19.

MILLS, BELEN AND ANN STEVENS. 1985. Employed and nonemployed mothers: Differences in parental child-rearing practices. *Early Child Development and Care,* **22**, pp. 181–194.

MILLS, C. WRIGHT. 1956. *The power elite*. New York: Oxford University Press.

MILLS, D. QUINN. 1985. Seniority versus ability in promotion decisions. *Industrial and Labor Relations Review,* **38**, pp. 421–425.

MIRANNE, ALFRED AND MICHAEL GEERKEN. 1991. A test of Greenwood's predictive scale. *Criminology,* **29**, pp. 497–518.

MIROWSKY, JOHN AND CATHERINE E. ROSS. 1984. Mexican culture and its emotional contradictions. *Journal of Health and Social Behavior,* **25**, pp. 2–13.

———. 1986. Social patterns of distress. *Annual Review of Sociology,* **12**, pp. 23–45.

———. 1992. Age and depression. *Journal of Health and Social Behavior,* **33**, September, pp. 187–205.

MISHLER, ELIOT. 1984. *The discourse of medicine: Dialectics of medical interviews*. Norwood, N.J.: Ablex.

MOCHIZUKI, KAZUHIRO. 1989. The present climate in Japanese junior high schools. In James J. Shields, Jr. (ed.), *Japanese schooling*. University Park, Penn.: Penn State University Press.

MODEL, SUZANNE. 1992. The ethnic economy: Cubans and Chinese reconsidered. *The Sociological Quarterly,* **33**, pp. 63–82.

MODELL, JOHN, F. FURSTENBERG, AND T. HERSHBERG. 1976. Social change and transitions to adulthood in historical perspective. *Journal of Family History,* **1**, pp. 7–32.

MOEN, PHYLLIS, DONNA DEMPSTER-MCCLAIN, AND ROBIN WILLIAMS, JR. 1992. Successful aging: A life-course perspective on women's multiple roles and health. *American Journal of Sociology,* **97**, May, pp. 1612–1638.

MOEN, PHYLLIS AND KAY B. FOREST. 1990. Working parents, workplace supports, and well-being: The Swedish experience. *Social Psychology Quarterly,* **53**, pp. 117–131.

MOLM, LINDA D. 1990. Structure, action, and outcomes: The dynamics of power in social exchange. *American Sociological Review,* **55**, June, pp. 427–447.

———. 1991. Affect and social exchange: Satisfaction in power-dependence relations. *American Sociological Review,* **56**, August, pp. 475–493.

MOLNAR, JANICE M., WILLIAM R. RATH, AND TOVAH P. KLEIN. 1990. Constantly compromised: The impact of homelessness on children. *Journal of Social Issues,* **46**, pp. 109–124.

MONK-TURNER, ELIZABETH. 1983. Sex, educational differentiation, and occupational status: Analyzing occupational differences for community and four-year college entrants. *The Sociological Quarterly,* **24**, pp. 393–404.

———. 1990. The occupational achievements of community and four-year college entrants. *American Sociological Review,* **55**, October, pp. 719–725.

MONSIVAIS, CARLOS. 1990. From '68 to Cardenismo: Toward a chronicle of social movements. *Journal of International Affairs,* **43**, Winter, pp. 385–393.

MONTEMAYOR, RAYMOND. 1984. Maternal employment and adolescents' relations with parents, siblings, and peers. *Journal of Youth and Adolescence,* **13**, pp. 543–557.

MONTEPARE, J. M. AND L. ZEBROWITZ-MCARTHUR. 1987. Perceptions of adults with child-like voices in two cultures. *Journal of Experimental Social Psychology*, **23**, pp. 331–349.

MOORE, JOAN. 1989. Is there a Hispanic underclass? *Social Science Quarterly*, **70**, June, pp. 265–284.

————. 1991. *Going down to the barrio: Homeboys and homegirls in charge*. Philadelphia: Temple University Press.

MOOREHOUSE, MARTHA J. 1991. Linking maternal employment patterns to mother–child activities and children's school competence. *Developmental Psychology*, **27**, March, pp. 295–303.

MORALES, ARMANDO. 1982. The Mexican-American gang member: Evaluation and treatment. In Rosina Becerra, Marvin Karno, and Javier Escobar (eds.), *Mental health and Hispanic Americans*. New York: Grune and Stratton.

MORASH, MERRY AND LILA RUCKER. 1990. A critical look at the idea of boot camp as a correctional reform. *Crime & Delinquency*, **36**, April, pp. 204–222.

MORGAN, MYFANWY. 1980. Marital status, health, illness, and service use. *Social Science and Medicine*, **14A**, pp. 633–643.

MORGAN, S. PHILIP, DIANE LYE, AND GRETCHEN CONDRAN. 1988. Sons, daughters, and divorce: Does the sex of children affect the risk of marital disruption? *American Journal of Sociology*, **94**, pp. 110–129.

MORGAN, WILLIAM. 1983. Learning and student life quality of public and private school youth. *Sociology of Education*, **56**, October, pp. 187–202.

MOSHER, WILLIAM D., LINDA B. WILLIAMS, AND DAVID P. JOHNSON. 1992. Religion and fertility in the United States: New patterns. *Demography*, **29**, May, pp. 199–214.

MULKEY, LYNN, ROBERT L. CRAIN, AND ALEXANDER HARRINGTON. 1992. One-parent households and achievement: Economic and behavioral explanations of a small effect. *Sociology of Education*, **65**, January, pp. 48–65.

MULLEN, BRIAN, CYNTHIA SYMONS, LI-TZE HU, AND EDUARDO SALAS. 1989. Group size, leadership behavior, and subordinate satisfaction. *The Journal of General Psychology*, **116**, pp. 155–169.

MULLER, THOMAS. 1984. *The fourth wave: California's newest immigrants—a summary*. Washington, D.C.: Urban Institute Press.

MUNGAS, D. 1983. An empirical analysis of specific syndromes of violent behavior. *Journal of Nervous and Mental Disease*, **171,** pp. 354–361.

MURAKAMI, YOSHIO. 1989. Bullies in the classroom. In James J. Shields, Jr. (ed.), *Japanese schooling*. University Park, Penn.: Pennsylvania State University Press.

MURRAY, CHARLES A. 1984. *Losing ground*. New York: Basic Books.

MURRAY, CHARLES A. AND RICHARD J. HERRNSTEIN. 1992. What's really behind the SAT score decline? *The Public Interest*, **106**, Winter, pp. 32–56.

MUTCHLER, JAN E. AND JEFFREY A. BURR. 1989. *A resource-based model of living among the unmarried elderly*. Washington, D.C.: U.S. Bureau of the Census.

————. 1991. Racial differences in health and health care service utilization in later life: The effect of socioeconomic status. *Journal of Health and Social Behavior*, **32**, December, pp. 342–356.

NATRIELLO, GARY, AARON PALLAS, AND KARL ALEXANDER. 1989. On the right track? Curriculum and academic achievement. *Sociology of Education*, **62**, April, pp. 109–118.

NEAL, ARTHUR, THEODORE GROAT, AND JERRY WICKS. 1989. Attitudes about having children: A study of 600 couples in the early years of marriage. *Journal of Marriage and the Family*, **51**, May, pp. 313–328.

NECKERMAN, KATHRYN AND JOLEEN KIRSCHENMAN. 1991. Hiring strategies, racial bias, and inner-city workers. *Social Problems*, **38**, November, pp. 433–447.

NEE, VICTOR. 1991. Social inequities in reforming state socialism: Between redistribution and markets in China. *American Sociological Review*, **56**, June, pp. 267–282.

NEFF, JAMES. 1984. Race differences in psychological distress: The effects of SES, urbanicity, and measurement strategy. *American Journal of Community Psychology*, **12**, pp. 337–351.

NEIGHBORS, HAROLD W., JACQUELINE JACKSON, PATRICIA BOWMAN, AND GERALD GURIN. 1983. Stress coping and black mental health: Preliminary findings from a national study. *Prevention in Human Services*, **2**, p. 125.

NETTLES, SAUNDRA MURRAY. 1991. Community involvement and disadvantaged students: A review. *Review of Educational Research*, **61**, Fall, pp. 379–406.

NEUGARTEN, BERNICE. 1973. Patterns of aging: Past, present, and future. *Social Service Review*, **47**, pp. 571–580.

NEUHOUSER, KEVIN. 1992. Democratic stability in Venezuela: Elite concensus on class compromise? *American Sociological Review*, **57**, February, pp. 117–135.

NEWMANN, FRED M., ROBERT A. RUTTER, AND MARSHALL S. SMITH. 1989. Organizational factors that affect school sense of efficacy, community, and expectations. *Sociology of Education*, **62**, October, pp. 221–238.

NEWPORT, FRANK. 1979. The religious switcher in the United States. *American Sociological Review*, **44**, August, pp. 528–552.

Newsweek. 1990. The 21st century family, Special Issue, Winter/Spring, p. 18.

NICHOLS, P. 1987. Minimal brain dysfunction and soft signs. In D. Tupper (ed.), *Soft neurological signs*. New York: Grune and Stratton.

NIEHOFF, BRIAN P. AND DEBRA J. MESCH. 1990. Effects of reward structures on academic performance and group processes in a classroom setting. *The Journal of Psychology*, **125**, pp. 457–467.

NOVACK, DENNIS H., GRETCHEN VOLK, DOUGLAS A. DROSSMAN, AND MACK LIPKIN, JR. 1993. Medical interviewing and interpersonal skills teaching in U.S. medical schools: Progress, problems, and promise. *Journal of American Medical Association*, **269**, April 28, pp. 2101–2105.

OAKES, JEANNIE. 1985. *Keeping track: How schools structure inequality*. New Haven, Conn.: Yale University Press.

———. 1992. Can tracking research inform practice? *Educational Researcher*, **21**, May, pp. 12–21.

O'BRIEN, ROBERT. 1989. Relative cohort size and age-specific crime rates: An age-period-relative-cohort-size model. *Criminology*, **27**, pp. 57–67.

———. 1991. Sex ratios and rape rates: A power-control theory. *Criminology*, **29**, pp. 99–113.

O'BRYANT, SHIRLEY. 1988. Sibling support and older widows' well-being. *Journal of Marriage and the Family*, **50**, February, pp. 173–183.

O'CONNOR, PAT. 1991. Women's experience of power within marriage. An inexplicable phenomenon? *The Sociological Review*, **39**, November, pp. 823–842.

OFFER, DANIEL, ERIC OSTROV, KENNETH HOWARD, AND ROBERT ATKINSON. 1988. *The teenage world: Adolescents' self-image in ten countries*. New York: Plenum.

OGBU, J. U. 1978. *Minority education and caste: The American system in cross-cultural perspective*. New York: Academic Press.

OGBURN, WILLIAM F. 1922. *Social change*. New York: Huebsch.

O'HARE, WILLIAM. 1986. The eight myths of poverty. *American Demographics*, May, pp. 22–25.

O'HARE, WILLIAM P. AND BRENDA CURRY-WHITE. 1992. *The rural underclass: Examination of multiple-problem populations in urban and rural settings*. Washington, D.C.: Population Reference Bureau.

O'HARE, WILLIAM P., KELVIN M., POLLARD, TAYNIA L. MANN, AND MARY M. KENT. 1991. African Americans in the 1990s. *Population Bulletin, 46*, July, pp. 2–38.

OLECKNO, WILLIAM A. AND MICHAEL J. BLACCONIERE. 1991. Relationship of religiosity to wellness and other health-related behaviors and outcomes. *Psychological Reports, 68*, pp. 819–826.

OLIVER, PAMELA AND GERALD MARWELL. 1988. The paradox of group size in collective action: A theory of the critical mass II. *American Sociological Review, 53*, February, pp. 1–8.

OLNECK, MICHAEL AND KI-SEOK KIM. 1989. High school completion and men's incomes: An apparent anomaly. *Sociology of Education, 62*, July, pp. 193–207.

OLSON, JOSEPHINE E., IRENE H. FRIEZE, AND ELLEN G. DETLEFSEN. 1990. Having it all? Combining work and family in a male and a female profession. *Sex Roles, 23*, November, pp. 515–525.

OLSON, MANCUR. 1965. *The logic of collective action*. Cambridge, Mass.: Harvard University Press.

OLSON, PAULETTE. 1990. The persistence of occupational segregation: A critique of its theoretical underpinnings. *Journal of Economic Issues, 24*, March, pp. 161–171.

O'MALLEY, PATRICK AND JERALD BACHMAN. 1983. Self-esteem: Change and stability between ages 13 and 23. *Developmental Psychology, 19*, pp. 257–268.

O'REILLY, BRIAN. 1990. How much does class matter? *Fortune*, July 30, pp. 123–124.

OSGOOD, NANCY, BARBARA BRANT, AND AARON LIPMAN. 1990. *Suicide among the elderly in long-term care facilities*. Westport, Conn.: Greenwood Press.

OSTERMAN, PAUL. 1991a. Gains from growth? Poverty in a full employment economy. In Christopher Jencks and Paul Peterson (eds.), *The urban underclass*. Washington, D.C.: Brookings Institute.

———. 1991b. Welfare participation in a full employment economy: The impact of neighborhood. *Social Problems, 38*, November, pp. 475–491.

OZANNI, JULIAN. 1990. Kenya fights its baby boom. *World Press Review, 37*, July, p. 67.

PALAMARA, FRANCES, FRANCIS CULLEN, AND JOANNE GERSTEN. 1986. The effect of police and mental health intervention on juvenile deviance: Specifying contingencies in the impact of formal reaction. *Journal of Health and Social Behavior, 27*, pp. 90–105.

PALISI, BARTOLOMEO AND CLAIRE CANNING. Urbanism and social psychological well-being: A cross cultural test of three theories. *Sociological Quarterly, 24*, pp. 527–543.

PALLAS, AARON, GARY NATRIELLO, AND EDWARD MCDILL. 1989. The changing nature of the disadvantaged population: Current dimensions, future trends. *Educational Researcher, 18*, June–July, pp. 16–22.

PALMER, HELEN T. AND JOANN LEE. 1990. Female workers' acceptance in traditionally male-dominated blue-collar jobs. *Sex Roles, 22*, pp. 607–625.

PALMER, RUTH. 1991. Sustained effects evaluations of a Chapter 1 program. *Early Child Development and Care, 73*, pp. 73–86.

PALMER, T. 1975. Martinson revisited. *Journal of Research in Crime and Delinquency, 12*, pp. 133–152.

PALMORE, ERDMAN B. 1981. *Social patterns in normal aging: Findings from the Duke longitudinal study*. Durham, N.C.: Duke University Press.

———. 1990. *Ageism: Negative and positive*. New York: Springer.

PAMPEL, FRED AND KAZUKO TANAKA. 1986. Economic development and female labor force participation. *Social Forces, 64*, pp. 599–619.

PANITCH, LEO. 1986. *Working class politics in crisis*. London: Verso.

PARCEL, TOBY AND CHARLES MUELLER. 1989. Temporal change in occupational earnings attainment, 1970–1980. *American Sociological Review*, **54**, August, pp. 622–634.

PARIS, SCOTT G., THERESA LAWTON, JULIANNE TURNER, AND JODIE ROTH. 1991. A developmental perspective on standardized achievement testing. *Educational Researcher*, **20**, June–July, pp. 12–20.

PARK, R. D., K. B. MACDONALD, A. BEITEL, AND N. BHAVNAGRI. 1988. The role of the family in the development of peer relationships. In R. Peters and R. McMahan, (eds.), *Social learning systems: Approaches to marriage and the family*. New York: Brunner-Mazel.

PARK, ROBERT E. 1930. Collective behavior. In Edwin Seligman (ed.), *Encyclopedia of the social sciences*. New York: Macmillan.

PARK, ROBERT E. AND ERNEST BURGESS. 1921. *Human Ecology*. Chicago: University of Chicago Press.

PARKER, R. N. AND A. V. HORWITZ. 1986. Unemployment, crime, and punishment. *Criminology*, **24**, pp. 751–774.

PARKINSON, C. NORTHCOTE. 1957. *Parkinson's Law*. Boston: Houghton Mifflin.

PARMER, S. NORMAN. 1987. The British legacy. *The Wilson Quarterly*, **11**, Winter, pp. 54–79.

PARSONS, JACQUELYNNE, TERRY ADLER, AND CAROLINE KACZALA. 1982. Socialization of achievement attitudes and beliefs: Parental influences. *Child Development*, **53**, pp. 310–321.

PARSONS, TALCOTT. 1958. Definition of health and illness in the light of American values and social structure. In E. G. Jaco (ed.), *Patients, physicians, and illness*. New York: Free Press.

———. 1964. (1951). *The social system*. New York: Free Press.

PARSONS, TALCOTT AND ROBERT F. BALES. 1955. *Family socialization and interaction process*. Glencoe, Ill.: Free Press.

PASLEY, KAY AND VIKTOR GECAS. 1984. Stresses and satisfactions of the parental role. *Personal and Guidance Journal*, **2**, pp. 400–404.

PASLEY, KAY AND MARILYN IHINGER-TALLMAN. 1984. Stress in remarried families. *Family Perspective*, **16**, pp. 181–190.

PATE, ANTONY M. AND EDWIN E. HAMILTON. 1992. Formal and informal deterrents to domestic violence: The Dade County spouse assault experiment. *American Sociological Review*, **57**, October, pp. 691–697.

PATERNOSTER, RAYMOND. 1987. The deterrent effect of the perceived certainty and severity of punishment: A review of the evidence and issues. *Justice Quarterly*, **4**, pp. 173–217.

PATTERSON, E. BRITT. 1991. Poverty, income inequality, and community crime rates. *Criminology*, **29**, pp. 755–770.

PATTERSON, GERALD R. 1982. *Coercive family process*. Eugene, Oreg.: Castalia.

PATTERSON, GERALD AND LEW BANK. 1989. Some amplifying mechanisms for pathologic processes in families. In M. Gunnar and E. Thelen (eds.), *Systems and development: Minnesota symposia on child psychology*, **22**. Hillsdale, N.J.: Lawrence Erlbaum.

PATTERSON, ORLANDO. 1991. *Freedom in the making of Western culture*. New York: Basic Books.

PAYEFF, BEVERLY. 1989. Looking at the power of image. *Nashua Telegraph*, September 29.

PEAK, LOIS. 1991. *Learning to go to school in Japan: The transition from home to preschool life*. Berkeley, Calif.: University of California Press.

PEARSON, JESSICA AND NANCY THOENNES. 1990. Custody after divorce: Demographic and attitudinal patterns. *American Journal of Orthopsychiatry*, **60**, April, pp. 233–249.

PECK, JONATHAN AND CLEMENT BEZOLD. 1992. Health care and AIDS. *The Annals of the American Academy of Political and Social Sciences*, **522**, July, pp. 130–139.

PEEK, CHARLES, N. BELL, T. WALDREN, AND G. SORELL. 1988. Patterns of functioning in families of remarried and first couples. *Journal of Marriage and the Family*, **50**, pp. 699–708.

PEEK, CHARLES W. AND SHARON BROWN. 1980. Sex prejudice among white Protestants: Like or unlike ethnic prejudice. *Social Forces*, **59**, pp. 169–185.

PEEK, CHARLES W., GEORGE D. LOWE, AND L. SUSAN WILLIAMS. 1991. Gender and God's word: Another look at religious fundamentalism and sexism. *Social Forces*, **69**, June, pp. 1205–1221.

PEREZ, LISANDRO. 1986. Cubans in the United States. *Annals of the American Academy of Political and Social Science*, **487**, September, pp. 126–137.

PESCOSOLIDO, BERNICE A. 1990. The social context of religious integration and suicide: Pursuing the network explanation. *The Sociological Quarterly*, **31**, pp. 337–357.

PESCOSOLIDO, BERNICE A. AND SHARON GEORGIANNA. 1989. Durkheim, suicide, and religion: Toward a network theory of a suicide. *American Sociological Review*, **54**, February, pp. 33–48.

PETER, LAURENCE J. AND RAYMOND HULL. 1969. *The Peter principle*. New York: Morrow.

PETERS, JOHN F. 1985. Adolescents as socialization agents to parents. *Adolescence*, **2**, Winter, pp. 921–933.

PETERSEN, LARRY AND ANITA ROY. 1985. Religiosity, anxiety, and meaning and purpose: Religion's consequences for psychological well-being. *Review of Religious Research*, **27**, pp. 49–62.

PETERSEN, TROND. 1992. Individual, collective, and systems rationality in work groups: Dilemmas and market-type solutions. *American Journal of Sociology*, **98**, November, pp. 469–510.

PETERSON, CANDIDA. 1990. Husbands' and wives' perceptions of marital fairness across the family life cycle. *International Journal on Aging and Human Development*, **31**, pp. 179–188.

PETERSON, CYNTHIA D., DONALD H. BAUCOM, MARY JANE ELLIOTT, AND PAMELA AIKEN FARR. 1989. The relationship between sex role identity and marital adjustment. *Sex Roles*, **21**, pp. 775–787.

PETERSON, JAMES L. AND NICHOLAS ZILL. 1986. Marital disruption, parent–child relationships, and behavior problems in children. *Journal of Marriage and the Family*, **48**, pp. 295–307.

PETERSON, PAUL E. 1990–91. The rise and fall of special interest politics. *Political Science Quarterly*, **105**, Winter, pp. 539–556.

PETERSON, PENELOPE L. AND ELIZABETH FENNEMA. 1985. Effective teaching, student engagement in classroom activities, and sex-related differences in learning mathematics. *American Educational Research Journal*, **22**, Fall, pp. 309–335.

PETERSON, RICHARD. 1989. *Women, work, and divorce*. Albany, N.Y.: State University of New York Press.

PETERSON, RICHARD R. 1989. Firm size, occupational segregation, and the effects of family status on women's wages. *Social Forces*, **68**, December, pp. 397–414.

PETERSON, RICHARD R. AND KATHLEEN GERSON. 1992. Determinants of responsibility for child-care arrangements among dual-earner couples. *Journal of Marriage and the Family*, **54**, August, pp. 527–536.

PFEFFER, JEFFREY AND JAMES BARON. 1988. Taking the workers back out: Recent trends in the structuring of employment. In Barry Staw and L. L. Cummings (eds.), *Research in organizational behavior*. Greenwich, Conn.: JAI Press.

PHILIPS, SUSAN. 1982. *The invisible culture: Communication in classroom and community on the Warm Springs Indian Reservation*. New York: Longman.

PHILLIPS, B. S. 1957. A role theory approach to adjustment in old age. *American Sociological Review*, **22**, pp. 212–217.

PHILLIPS, D. A. 1987. Socialization of perceived academic competence among highly competent children. *Child Development*, **58**, pp. 1308–1320.

PHILLIPS, GERALD M. AND J. ALFRED JONES. 1991. Medical compliance: Patient or physician responsibility? *American Behavioral Scientist*, **34**, July/August, pp. 756–767.

PHILLIPS, MARGARET. 1991. A hedgehog proposal. *Crime & Delinquency*, **37**, October, pp. 555–574.

PIETTE, JOHN D., JOHN A. FLEISHMAN, MICHAEL D. STEIN, VINCENT MOR, AND KENNETH MAYER. 1993. Perceived needs and unmet needs for formal services among people with HIV disease. *Journal of Community Health*, **18**, February, pp. 11–23.

PIHL, R. O. ET AL. 1982. Psychotropic drug use by women: Characteristics of high consumers. *International Journal of Addictions*, **17**, p. 259.

PIIRTO, REBECCA. 1991. New women's revolution. *American Demographics*, **13**, April, p. 6.

PILISUK, MARK. 1982. Delivery of social support: The social inoculation. *Journal of Orthopsychiatry*, **52**, pp. 20–30.

PINNEY, ROY. 1968. *Vanishing tribes*. New York: Crowell.

PLECK, J. H. 1983. Husband's paid work and family roles: Current research issues. In H. Lopata and J. H. Pleck (eds.), *Research in the interweave of social roles: Families and jobs*. Greenwich, Conn.: JAI Press.

PLOMIN, R., K. NITZ, AND D. C. ROWE. 1990. Behavioral genetics and aggressive behavior in childhood. In M. Lewis and S. M. Miller (eds.), *Handbook of developmental psychopathology*. New York: Plenum.

POLIT, DENISE AND TONI FALBO. 1987. Only children and personality development: A quantitative review. *Journal of Marriage and the Family*, **49**, May, pp. 309–325.

POLLARD, KEVIN. 1993. Faster growth, more diversity in U.S. projections. *Population Today*, **21**, February, pp. 3, 10.

POLLNER, MELVIN. 1989. Divine relations, social relations, and well-being. *Journal of Health and Social Behavior*, **30**, March, pp. 92–104.

PONTELL, HENRY N. AND KITTY CALAVITA. 1993. White-collar crime in the Savings and Loan scandal. *The Annals of the American Academy of Political and Social Science*, **525**, January, pp. 31–45.

POPENOE, DAVID. 1991. Family decline in the Swedish welfare state. *The Public Interest*, **102**, Winter, pp. 65–77.

POPKIN, SAMUEL. 1991. *The reasoning voter: Communication and persuasions in presidential campaigns*. Chicago: University of Chicago Press.

PORTER, ROSALIE P. 1990. *Forked tongue: The politics of bilingual education*. New York: Basic Books.

PORTES, ALEJANDRO AND ROBERT BACH. 1985. *Latin journey: Cubans and Mexican immigrants in the United States*. Berkeley, Calif.: University of California Press.

POTTER, LLOYD AND OMER GALLE. 1990. Residential and racial mortality differentials in the South by cause of death. *Rural Sociology*, **55**, pp. 233–244.

POWELL, BRIAN AND LALA CARR STEELMAN. 1989. The liability of having brothers: Paying for college and the sex composition of the family. *Sociology of Education*, **62**, April, pp. 134–147.

POWERS, CHARLES B., PATRICIA A. WISOCKI, AND SUSAN K. WHITBOURNE. 1992. Age differences and correlates of worrying in young and elderly adults. *The Gerontologist*, **32**, pp. 82–88.

PREISENDORFER, PETER AND THOMAS VOSS. 1990. Organizational mortality of small firms: The effects of entrepreneurial age and human capital. *Organization Studies*, **11**, pp. 107–129.

PROVENCE, SALLY AND ROSE LIPTON. 1962. *Infants in institutions*. New York: International Universities Press.

PUTALLAZ, MARTHA. 1987. Maternal behavior and children's sociometric status. *Child Development*, **58**, April, pp. 324–340.

QUINNEY, RICHARD. 1970. *The social reality of crime*. Boston: Little, Brown.

RACHLIN, VICKI AND JAMES HANSEN. 1985. The impact of equity or egalitarianism on dual-career couples. *Family Therapy*, **13**, pp. 151–164.

RAFFERTY, YVONNE AND MARYBETH SHINN. 1991. The impact of homelessness on children. *American Psychologist*, **46**, November, pp. 1170–1179.

RAINVILLE, R. E. AND J. G. GALLAGHER. 1990. Vulnerability and heterosexual attraction. *Sex Roles*, **23**, July, pp. 25–32.

RAKESTRAW, JENNIE F. AND DONALD RAKESTRAW. 1990. Home schooling: A question of quality, an issue of rights. *The Educational Forum*, **55**, Fall, pp. 67–76.

RANK, MARK R. 1989. Fertility among women on welfare: Incidence and determinants. *American Sociological Review*, **54**, April, pp. 296–304.

RANSDELL, ERIC. 1992. Africa's trek to freedom. *US News & World Report*, August 10, pp. 28–31.

RATHJE, WILLIAM AND CULLEN MURPHY. 1992. Garbage demographics. *American Demographics*, May, pp. 50–54.

RAUDENBUSH, STEPHEN W., BRIAN ROWAN, AND YUK FAI CHEONG. 1992. Contextual effects on the self-perceived efficacy of high school teachers. *Sociology of Education*, **65**, April, pp. 150–167.

RAWLINGS, STEVE W. 1992. Household and family characteristics. *Current Population Reports*, Series P20, No. 467. Washington, D.C.: U.S. Government Printing Office. March.

REED, KIMBERLY. 1991. Strength of religious affiliation and life satisfaction. *Sociological Analysis*, **52**, pp. 205–210.

REGISTER, CHARLES AND DONALD WILLIAMS. 1990. Wage effects of obesity among young workers. *Social Science Quarterly*, **11**, March, pp. 130–141.

REHBERG, RICHARD AND EVELYN ROSENTHAL. 1978. *Class and merit in the American high school: An assessment of the revisionist and meritocratic arguments*. New York: Longman.

REICH, ROBERT. 1991. *The work of nations: Preparing ourselves for 21st century capitalism*. New York: Alfred A. Knopf.

REINARDY, JAMES R. 1992. Decisional control in moving to a nursing home: Postadmission adjustment and well-being. *The Gerontologist*, **32**, pp. 96–103.

REISS, IRA L. 1980. *Family systems in America*. 3d ed. New York: Holt, Rinehart and Winston.

RELMAN, ARNOLD. 1992. What market values are doing to medicine. *The Atlantic Monthly*, **269**, March, pp. 99–106.

RENNER, CRAIG AND VICENTE NAVARRO. 1989. Why is our population of uninsured and underinsured persons growing? The consequences of the deindustrialization of the United States. *International Journal of Health Services*, **19**, pp. 433–442.

REYNOLDS, ARTHUR J. 1991. Early schooling of children at risk. *American Educational Research Journal*, **28**, Summer, pp. 392–427.

RICHE, MARTHA FARNSWORTH. 1991. We're all minorities now. *American Demographics*, **13**, October, pp. 26–34.

———. 1993. New research illuminates immigration controversies. *Population Today*, **21**, September, p. 3.

RIDDELL, SHEILA. 1989. Exploiting the exploited? The ethics of feminist educational research. In Robert Burgess (ed.), *The Ethics of Educational Research*. New York: Falmer Press.

RIDGEWAY, CECILIA. 1987. Nonverbal behavior, dominance, and the basis of status in task groups. *American Sociological Review*, **52**, October, pp. 683–694.

RIDGEWAY, CECILIA AND JOSEPH BERGER. 1986. Expectations, legitimation, and dominance behavior in task groups. *American Sociological Review*, **51**, October, pp. 603–617.

RIDGEWAY, CECILIA AND DAVID DIEKEMA. 1989. Dominance and collective hierarchy formation in male and female task groups. *American Sociological Review*, **54**, February, pp. 79–93.

RIDGEWAY, CECILIA AND CATHRYN JOHNSON. 1990. What is the relationship between socioemotional behavior and status in task groups? *American Journal of Sociology*, **95**, March, pp. 1189–1212.

RINDFUSS, RONALD, GARY SWICEGOOD, AND RACHEL ROSENFELD. 1987. Disorder in the life course: How common does it matter? *American Sociological Review*, **52**, December, pp. 785–801.

RITTER, JEAN, RITA CASEY, AND JUDITH LANGLOIS. 1991. Adults' responses to infants varying in appearance of age and attractiveness. *Child Development*, **62**, February, pp. 68–82.

ROBBINS, CYNTHIA. 1989. Sex differences in psychosocial consequences of alcohol and drug abuse. *Journal of Health and Social Behavior*, **30**, March, pp. 117–130.

ROBBINS, THOMAS. 1988. *Cults, converts, and charisma*. New York: Sage.

ROBERTS, LESLIE. 1989. Disease and death in the New World. *Science*, December 8, pp. 1245–1247.

ROBERTSON, JOAN AND RONALD SIMONS. 1989. Family factors, self-esteem, and adolescent depression. *Journal of Marriage and the Family*, **51**, February, pp. 125–138.

RODRIGUEZ, LUIS. 1993. *Always running*. Willimantic, Conn.: Curbstone Press.

RODRIQUEZ, RICHARD. 1982. *Hunger of memory*. Boston: David Godine.

ROGERS, JOHN D. 1989. Theories of crime and development: An historical perspective. *Journal of Developmental Studies*, **25**, April, pp. 314–328.

ROGERS, JOSEPH W. 1989. The greatest correctional myth: Winning the war on crime through incarceration. *Federal Probation*, **53**, September, pp. 21–28.

ROKEACH, MILTON AND SANDRA J. BALL-ROKEACH. 1989. Stability and change in American value priorities, 1968–1981. *American Psychologist*, **44**, May, pp. 775–784.

ROLLINS, BOYD AND KENNETH CANNON. 1974. Marital satisfaction over the family life cycle: A reevaluation. *Journal of Marriage and the Family*, **356**, pp. 271–283.

RONCEK, DENNIS W. AND PAMELA A. MAIER. 1991. Bars, blocks, and crimes revisited: Linking the theory of routine activities to the empiricism of "hot spots." *Criminology*, **29**, pp. 725–737.

RONCEK, DENNIS W. AND MITCHELL A. PRAVATINER. 1989. Additional evidence that taverns enhance nearby crime. *Sociology and Social Research*, **73**.

ROOF, WADE CLARK. 1978. *Community and commitment*. New York: El Sevier.

———. 1982. America's voluntary establishment: Mainline religion in transition. *Daedalus*, **111**, Winter, pp. 165–184.

———. 1992. The baby boom's search for God. *American Demographics*, **14**, December, pp. 50–57.

ROOS, PATRICIA. 1981. Sex stratification in the workplace: Male–female differences in returns to occupation. *Social Science Research*, **10**, pp. 195–224.

ROSE, STEPHEN. 1986. *The American profile poster*. New York: Pantheon.

ROSECRANCE, RICHARD. 1990. Must America decline? *The Wilson Quarterly*, **14**, Autumn, pp. 67–83.

ROSEN, PAUL M. AND BARENT W. WALSH. 1989. Patterns of contagion in self-mutilation epidemics. *American Journal of Psychiatry*, **146**, May, pp. 656–658.

ROSENBERG, S. AND M. FARRELL. 1981. *Men at midlife*. Boston: Auburn House.

ROSENFIELD, SARAH. 1989. The effects of women's employment: Personal control and sex differences in mental health. *Journal of Health and Social Behavior*, **30**, March, pp. 77–91.

———. 1992. The costs of sharing: Wives' employment and husbands' mental health. *Journal of Health and Social Behavior*, **33**, September, pp. 213–225.

ROSENHOLTZ, SUSAN J. AND CARL SIMPSON. 1990. Workplace conditions and the rise and fall of teachers' commitment. *Sociology of Education*, **63**, October, pp. 241–257.

ROSENTHAL, ALVIN, KEITH BAKER, AND ALAN GINSBURG. 1983. The effect of language background on achievement level and learning among elementary school students. *Sociology of Education*, **56**, October, pp. 157–169.

ROSENTHAL, MARILYN. 1971. Rumors in the aftermath of the Detroit riot. In Irving Louis Horowitz and Mary Symons Strong (eds.), *Sociological realities*. New York: Harper and Row.

ROSENTHAL, ROBERT AND LENORE JACOBSEN. 1968. *Pygmalion in the classroom*. New York: Holt, Rinehart and Winston.

ROSOW, IRVING. 1973. The social context of the aging self. *The Gerontologist*, **3**, pp. 82–87.

ROSS, CATHERINE E. 1990. Religion and psychological distress. *Journal for the Scientific Study of Religion*, **29**, pp. 236–245.

———. 1991. Marriage and the sense of control. *Journal of Marriage and the Family*, **53**, November, pp. 831–838.

ROSS, CATHERINE E. AND JOHN MIROWSKY. 1989. Explaining the social patterns of depression. Control and problem solving—or support and talking? *Journal of Health and Social Behavior*, **30**, pp. 206–219.

ROSS, SANDRA AND JEFFREY JACKSON. 1991. Teachers' expectations from black males' and black females' academic achievement. *Personality and Social Psychology Bulletin*, **17**, February, pp. 78–82.

ROSSELL, CHRISTINE. 1990. The carrot or the stick for school desegregation policy? *Urban Affairs Quarterly*, **25**, March, pp. 474–499.

ROSSI, ALICE. 1965. Naming children in middle-class families. *American Sociological Review*, **30**, pp. 499–513.

ROTHERAM-BORUS, MARY JANE, CHERYL KOOPMAN, AND ANKE EHRHARDT. 1991. Homeless youths and HIV infection. *American Psychologist*, **46**, November, pp. 1188–1197.

ROTHMAN, STANLEY AND ROBERT LERNER. 1988. Television and the communications revolution. *Society*, **26**, November/December, pp. 64–70.

ROWE, DAVID C. 1986. Genetic and environmental components of antisocial behavior: A study of 265 twin pairs. *Criminology*, **24**, pp. 513–532.

ROWE, DAVID C. AND BILL L. GULLEY. 1992. Sibling effects on substance use and delinquency. *Criminology*, **30**, May, pp. 217–233.

RUBIN, LILLIAN. 1983. Blue-collar marriage and the sexual revolution. In Arlene Skolnick and Jerome Skolnick (eds.), *Family in transition*. 4th ed. Boston: Little, Brown.

RUBIN, LINDA AND SHERRY BORGERS. 1990. Sexual harassment in universities during the 1980s. *Sex Roles*, **23**, October, pp. 397–410.

RUGGIE, MARY. 1992. The paradox of liberal intervention: Health policy and the American welfare state. *American Journal of Sociology*, **97**, January, pp. 919–944.

RULE, WILMA. 1990. Why more women are state legislators. *The Western Political Quarterly*, **43**, June, pp. 437–447.

RUSSELL, CHERYL, 1991. On the baby-boom bandwagon. *American Demographics*, **13**, May, pp. 24–31.

RUSSELL, J. G. 1991. Narratives of denial: Racial chauvinism and the black other in Japan. *Japan Quarterly*, **38**, pp. 416–428.

RUTTER, MICHAEL AND HENRI GILLER. 1983. *Juvenile delinquency: Trends and perspective*. New York: Guilford Press.

RYAN, WILLIAM. 1971. *Blaming the victim*. New York: Random House.

RYBCZYNSKI, WITOLD. 1992. Should suburbs be designed? *The Atlantic Monthly*, January, pp. 109–112.

RYFF, CAROL. 1985. The subjective experience of life-span transitions. In Alice Rossi (ed.), *Gender and the life course*. Hawthorne, N.Y.: Aldine.

RYSCAVAGE, PAUL AND PETER HENLE. 1990. Earnings inequality accelerates in the 1980s. *Monthly Labor Review*, **113**, December, pp. 3–16.

RYTINA, NANCY. 1981. Occupational segregation and earnings differences by sex. *Monthly Labor Review*, **194**, pp. 49–53.

RYTINA, STEVE. 1992. Scaling the intergenerational continuity of occupation: Is occupational inheritance ascriptive after all? *American Journal of Sociology*, **97**, May, pp. 1658–1688.

SADIK, NAFIS. 1991. World population continues to rise. *The Futurist*, **25**, March–April, pp. 9–14.

SAKAMOTO, ARTHUR AND MEICHU D. CHEN. 1991. Inequality and attainment in a dual labor market. *American Sociological Review*, **56**, June, pp. 295–308.

SALTMAN, RICHARD B. 1991. Emerging trends in the Swedish health system. *International Journal of Health Services*, **21**, pp. 615–623.

SALTZMAN, AMY. 1990. The quest for community. *U.S. News & World Report*, April 9, pp. 75–76.

———. 1991. Wooed by the classroom. *U.S. News & World Report*, February 4, pp. 68–69.

SALZINGER, SUZANNE, RICHARD S. FELDMAN, MURIEL HAMMER, AND MARGARET ROSARIO. 1993. The effects of physical abuse on children's social relationships. *Child Development*, **64**, pp. 169–187.

SAMPSON, ROBERT J. 1987. Urban black violence: The effect of male joblessness and family disruption. *American Journal of Sociology*, **93**, pp. 348–382.

SAMPSON, ROBERT J. AND W. BYRON GROVES. 1989. Community structure and crime: Testing social-disorganization theory. *American Journal of Sociology*, **94**, January, pp. 774–802.

SAMPSON, ROBERT J. AND JOHN H. LAUB. 1990. Crime and deviance over the life course: The salience of adult social bonds. *American Sociological Review*, **55**, October, pp. 609–627.

SAMUELSON, ROBERT J. 1992. How our American dream unraveled. *Newsweek*, March 2, pp. 32–39.

SANCHIRICO, ANDREW. 1991. The importance of small-business ownership in Chinese-American educational achievement. *Sociology of Education*, **64**, October, pp. 293–304.

SANDERS, JIMY. 1991. New structural poverty? *The Sociological Quarterly*, **32**, pp. 179–199.

SANDERS, JIMY AND VICTOR NEE. 1987. Limits of ethnic solidarity in the enclave economy. *American Sociological Review*, **52**, December, pp. 745–773.

SANDERS, JOSEPH AND LEE HAMILTON. 1992. Legal cultures and punishment repertoires in Japan, Russia, and the United States. *Law & Society Review*, **26**, pp. 117–138.

SANDOMIRSKY, SHARON AND JOHN WILSON. 1990. Processes of disaffiliation: Religious mobility among men and women. *Social Forces*, **68**, pp. 1211–1229.

SANTIAGO, ANNE AND MARGARET WILDER. 1991. Residential segregation and links to minority poverty: The case of Latinos in the United States. *Social Problems*, **38**, November, pp. 492–515.

SAPIR, EDWARD. 1929. The status of linguistics as a science. *Language*, **5**, pp. 207–214.

SAPP, STEPHEN AND WENDY HARROD. 1989. Social acceptability and intentions to eat beef. *Rural Sociology*, **54**, Fall, pp. 420–438.

SAURER, M. KAYE AND RICHARD M. EISLER. 1990. The role of masculine gender role stress in expressivity and social support network factors. *Sex Roles*, **23**, pp. 261–271.

SCANZONI, J. 1972. *Sexual bargaining: Power politics in the American marriage*. Englewood Cliffs, N.J.: Prentice-Hall.

SCARR, S., J. LANDE, AND K. MCCARTNEY. 1989. Child care and the family: Compliments and interactions. In J. S. Lande, S. Scarr, and N. Guzenhauser (eds.), *Caring for children: Challenge to America*. Hillsdale, N.J.: Erlbaum.

SCASE, RICHARD AND ROBERT GOFFEE. 1982. *The entrepreneurial middle class*. London: Croom Helm.

SCHAFER, ROBERT B. AND PAT M. KEITH. 1990. Matching by weight in married couples: A life cycle perspective. *The Journal of Social Psychology*, **130**, pp. 657–664.

SCHIAVI, R. C., A. THEILGAARD, D. R. OWEN, AND D. WHITE. 1984. Sex chromosome anomalies, hormones, and aggressivity. *Archives of General Psychiatry*, **41**, pp. 93–99.

SCHILLER, BRADLEY. 1973. Empirical studies of welfare dependency: A survey. *The Journal of Human Resources*, **8**, Supplement, pp. 19–32.

SCHMIDT, KAREN. 1993. Old no more. *U.S. News & World Report*, March 8, pp. 66–73.

SCHNAIBERG, ALLAN AND SHELDON GOLDENBERG. 1986. From empty nest to crowded nest: Some contradictions in the returning-young-adult syndrome, paper presented at the annual meeting of the American Sociological Association, New York. August.

———. 1989. From empty nest to crowded nest: The dynamics of incompletely launched young adults. *Social Problems*, **36**, June, pp. 251–269.

SCHOEN, ROBERT. 1992. First unions and the stability of first marriages. *Journal of Marriage and the Family*, **54**, May, pp. 281–284.

SCHOENBORN, CHARLOTTE AND BARBARA WILSON. 1988. Are married people healthier? Health characteristics of married and unmarried U.S. men and women, paper presented at the annual meeting of the American Public Health Association, Boston.

SCHROEDER, W. W. AND J. A. BEEGLE. 1953. Suicide. *Rural Sociology*, **18**, pp. 45–52.

SCHROF, JOANNIE. 1992. Wedding bands made of steel. *U.S. News & World Report*, April 6, pp. 62–63.

SCHUDSON, MICHAEL. 1984. *Advertising, the uneasy persuasion*. New York: Basic Books.

SCHULTZ, JANE E. 1992. The inhospitable hospital: Gender and professionalism in Civil War medicine. *Signs: Journal of Women in Culture and Society*, **17**, pp. 363–392.

SCHULTZ, NOEL C., CYNTHIA L. SCHULTZ, AND DAVID H. OLSON. 1991. Couple strengths and stressors in complex and simple stepfamilies in Australia. *Journal of Marriage and the Family*, **53**, August, pp. 555–564.

SCHWAB, REINHOLD AND KAY UWE PETERSEN. 1990. Religiousness: Its relation to loneliness, neuroticism, and subjective well-being. *Journal for the Scientific Study of Religion*, **29**, pp. 335–345.

SCHWALBE, MICHAEL AND CLIFFORD STAPLES. 1986. Class position, work experience, and health. *International Journal of Health Services*, **16**, pp. 583–602.

SCHWARTZ, BARRY. 1974. Waiting, exchange, and power. *American Journal of Sociology*, **79**, January, pp. 841–870.

SCHWARTZ, LITA LINZER. 1979. Cults: The vulnerability of sheep. *USA Today*, **108**, July, pp. 22–24.

SCULLY, D. AND P. BART. 1973. A funny thing happened on the way to the orifice: Women in gynaecology textbooks. In J. Ehrenreich (ed.), *The cultural crisis of modern medicine*. New York: Monthly Review Press.

SEAGRAVES, ROBERT T. 1980. Marriage and mental health. *Journal of Sex and Marital Therapy*, **6**, pp. 187–198.

SECHREST, DALE K. 1989. Prison "boot camps" do not measure up. *Federal Probation*, **53**, September, pp. 15–20.

SEELEY, DAVID. 1984. Home-school partnership. *Phi Delta Kappan*, **65**, pp. 383–393.

SEMYONOV, MOSHE AND YINON COHEN. 1990. Ethnic discrimination and the income of majority-group workers. *American Sociological Review*, **53**, February, pp. 107–114.

SEWELL, WILLIAM H. 1971. The inequality of opportunity for higher education. *American Sociological Review*, **36**, pp. 793–808.

SEWELL, WILLIAM H., ARCHIBALD O. HALLER, AND ALEJANDRO PORTES. 1969. The educational and early occupational attainment process. *American Sociological Review*, **34**, pp. 82–92.

SEXTON, CHRISTINE AND DANIEL PERLMAN. 1989. Couples' career orientation, gender role orientation, and perceived equity as determinants of marital power. *Journal of Marriage and the Family*, **51**, November, pp. 933–941.

SHACHAR, RINA. 1991. His and her marital satisfaction: The double standard. *Sex Roles*, **25**, pp. 451–467.

SHADE, BARBARA. 1982. Afro-American cognitive style: A variable in school success? *Review of Educational Research*, **52**, Summer, pp. 219–244.

SHAH, REENA. 1988. Kikuyu tradition ties women to life of servitude. *St. Petersburg Times*, April 25.

SHAPIRO, JOSEPH P. 1992. The elderly are not children. *U.S. News & World Report*, January 13, pp. 26–28.

SHAPIRO, LAURA. 1990. Guns and dolls. *Newsweek*, May 28, pp. 56–65.

SHAPIRO, SUSAN. 1990. Collaring the crime, not the criminal: Reconsidering the concept of white-collar crime. *American Sociological Review*, **55**, June, pp. 346–365.

SHARP, S. 1986. Folk medicine practices: Women as keepers and carriers of knowledge. *Women's Studies International Forum*, **9**, pp. 243–249.

SHAVIT, YOSSI AND DAVID FEATHERMAN. 1988. Schooling, tracking, and teenage intelligence. *Sociology of Education*, **61**, January, pp. 42–51.

SHAW, CLIFFORD R. AND HENRY D. MCKAY. 1929. *Delinquency areas*. Chicago: University of Chicago Press.

SHAW, DANIEL AND ROBERT EMERY. 1987. Parental conflict and other correlates of the adjustment of school-age children whose parents have separated. *Journal of Abnormal Child Psychology*, **15**, pp. 269–281.

SHEEHY, GAIL. 1982. *Pathfinders*. New York: Bantam Books.

SHELLEY, LOUISE. 1981. *Crime and modernization*. Carbondale, Ill.: Southern Illinois University Press.

SHELTON, BETH ANNE. 1990. The distribution of household tasks: Does wife's employment status make a difference? *Journal of Family Issues*, **11**, pp. 115–135.

SHERBOURNE, CATHY DONALD AND RON D. HAYS. 1990. Marital status, social support, and health transitions in chronic disease patients. *Journal of Health and Social Behavior*, **31**, December, pp. 328–343.

SHERKAT, DARREN E. 1991. Leaving the faith: Testing theories of religious switching using survival models. *Social Science Research*, **20**, pp. 171–187.

SHERMAN, LAWRENCE AND RICHARD BERK. 1984. The specific deterrent effects of arrest for domestic assault. *American Sociological Review*, **49**, pp. 261–272.

SHERMAN, LAWRENCE W., PATRICK R. GARTIN, AND MICHAEL E. BUERGER. 1989. Hot spots of predatory crime. Routine activities and the criminology of place. *Criminology*, **27**, pp. 27–55.

SHIBLEY, MARK A. 1991. The southernization of American religion. Testing a hypothesis. *Sociological Analysis*, **52**, pp. 159–174.

SHRUM, WESLEY, NEIL CHEEK, JR., AND SAUNDRA HUNTER. 1988. Friendship in school: Gender and racial homophily. *Sociology of Education*, **61**, October, pp. 227–239.

SILVEIRA, J. 1980. Generic masculine words and thinking. In C. Kramarae (ed.), *The voices and words of women and men*. Oxford: Pergamon Press.

SIMMEL, GEORG. 1950. *The sociology of Georg Simmel*. Ed. and trans. Kurt H. Wolff. New York: Free Press.

SIMMONS, LEO. 1960. Aging in pre-industrial societies. In C. Tibbits (ed.), *Handbook of social gerontology*. Chicago: University of Chicago Press.

SIMON, ROBIN. 1992. Parental role strains, salience of parental identity, and gender differences in psychological distress. *Journal of Health and Social Behavior*, **33**, March, pp. 25–35.

SIMPSON, SALLY S. AND CHRISTOPHER S. KOPER. 1992. Deterring corporate crime. *Criminology*, **30**, August, pp. 347–376.

SINGHAL, UMA AND NIHAR MRINAL. 1991. Tribal women of India: The Tharu women. In Leonore Adler (ed.), *Women in cross-cultural perspective*. New York: Praeger.

SJOBERG, GIDEON. 1960. *The preindustrial city, past and present*. New York: Free Press.

SKERRY, PETER. 1992. E Pluribus Hispanic? *The Wilson Quarterly*, **16**, Summer, pp. 62–73.

SLATER, PHILIP E. 1955. Role differentiation in small groups. In A. Paul Hare, Edgar F. Borgatta, and Robert F. Bales (eds.), *Small groups: Studies in social interaction*. New York: Knopf.

———. 1976. *The pursuit of loneliness*. Boston: Beacon.

SLAVIN, ROBERT E. 1987. Ability grouping and student achievement in elementary schools: A best-evidence synthesis. *Review of Educational Research*, **57**, Fall, pp. 293–336.

SLEEPER, JIM. 1982. Neighborhood gentrification: More inequality than meets the eye. *Dissent*, Spring, pp. 169–175.

SMALL, GARY W., MICHAEL W. PROPPER, EUGENIA T. RANDOLPH, AND SPENCER ETH. 1991. Mass hysteria among student performers: Social relationship as a symptom predictor. *American Journal of Psychiatry*, **148**, September, pp. 1200–1205.

SMELSER, NEIL. 1963. *Theory of collective behavior*. New York: Free Press.

SMIRCICH, LINDA AND GARETH MORGAN. 1982. Leadership: The management of meaning. *The Journal of Applied Behavioral Science*, **18**, pp. 257–273.

SMITH, DOUGLAS AND PATRICK GARTIN. 1989. Specifying specific deterrence: The influence of arrest on future criminal activity. *American Sociological Review*, **54**, February, pp. 94–105.

SMITH, MARY LEE. 1991. Put to the test: The effects of external testing on teachers. *Educational Researcher*, **20**, June–July, pp. 8–11.

SMITH, MICHAEL. 1990. What is new in "new structuralist" analyses of earnings? *American Sociological Review*, **54**, December, pp. 827–841.

SMITH-LOVIN, LYNN AND CHARLES BRODY. 1989. Interruptions in group discussions: The effects of gender and group composition. *American Sociological Review*, **54**, June, pp. 424–435.

SMOCK, PAMELA AND FRANKLIN D. WILSON. 1991. Desegregation and the stability of white enrollments: A school-level analysis, 1968–1984. *Sociology of Education*, **64**, October, pp. 278–292.

SMOLE, W. J. 1976. *The Yanomamo Indians: A cultural geography*. Austin, Texas: University of Texas Press.

SNOW, CATHERINE E., WENDY BARNES, JEAN CHANDLER ET AL. 1991. *Unfulfilled expectations: Home and school influence on literacy*. Cambridge, Mass.: Harvard University Press.

SNOW, DAVID A. AND RICHARD MACHALEK. 1984. The sociology of conversion. *Annual Review of Sociology*, **10**, pp. 167–190.

SOLOMON, JOLIE. 1993. The fall of the dinosaurs: Competing in the '90s. *Newsweek*, February 8, pp. 42–44.

SORAUF, FRANK J. 1992. Politics and money. *American Behavioral Scientist*, **35**, July, pp. 725–734.

SORENSEN, ANNAMETTE. 1983. Women's employment patterns after marriage. *Journal of Marriage and the Family*, **45**, pp. 311–321.

SOUTH, SCOTT J. 1985. Economic conditions and the divorce rate. *Journal of Marriage and the Family*, **47**, pp. 31–41.

———. 1991. Sociodemographic differentials in mate selection preferences. *Journal of Marriage and the Family*, **53**, November, pp. 928–940.

SOUTH, SCOTT J. AND STEVEN MESSNER. 1986. Structural determinants of intergroup association: Interracial marriage and crime. *American Journal of Sociology*, **91**, May, pp. 1409–1430.

SOUTH, SCOTT J. AND GLENNA SPITZE. 1986. Determinants of divorce over the marital life course. *American Sociological Review*, **51**, pp. 583–590.

SOUTH, SCOTT J. AND STEWART E. TOLNAY. 1992. Relative well-being among children and the elderly: The effects of age group size and family structure. *The Sociological Quarterly*, **33**, pp. 115–133.

SOUTH, SCOTT J. AND KATHERINE TRENT. 1987. Sex ratios and women's roles: A cross-national analysis, paper presented at the annual meeting of the Population Association of America.

SOUTH, SCOTT J. AND WEIMAN XU. 1990. Local industrial dominance and earnings attainment. *American Sociological Review*, **55**, August, pp. 591–599.

SPENCER, J. WILLIAM AND KRISS A. DRASS. 1989. The transformation of gender into conversational advantage: A symbolic interactionist approach. *The Sociological Quarterly*, **30**, Fall, pp. 363–383.

SPENGLER, OSWALD. 1926. *The decline of the West*. New York: Alfred A. Knopf.

SPILERMAN, SEYMOUR AND TORMOD LUNDE. 1991. Features of educational attainment and job promotion aspects. *American Journal of Sociology*, **97**, November, pp. 689–720.

SPINRAD, WILLIAM. 1991. Charisma: A blighted concept and an alternative formula. *Political Science Quarterly*, **106**, pp. 295–311.

SPITZ, RENÉ. 1945. Hospitalization: An inquiry into the genesis of psychiatric conditions in early childhood. In A. Freud (ed.), *The psychoanalytic study of the child*. New York: International Universities Press.

SPITZE, G. 1988. Women's employment and family relations: A review. *Journal of Marriage and the Family*, **50**, pp. 595–618.

STACK, STEVEN. 1982. Suicide: A decade review of the sociological literature. *Deviant Behavior*, **4**, pp. 41–66.

———. 1984. The effect of suggestion on suicide, paper presented at the 79th annual meeting of the American Sociological Society, San Antonio, Texas. August.

———. 1990. New micro-level data on the impact of divorce on suicide, 1959–1980: A test of two theories. *Journal of Marriage and the Family*, **52**, February, pp. 119–127.

STAGGENBORG, SUZANNE. 1988. The consequences of professionalization and formalization in the pro-choice movement. *American Sociological Review*, **53**, August, pp. 585–606.

STAHL, SIDNEY AND MONTY LEBEDUN. 1974. Mystery gas: An analysis of mass hysteria. *Journal of Health and Social Behavior*, **15**, March, pp. 44–50.

STAHURA, JOHN. 1988. Changing patterns of suburban racial composition, 1970–1980. *Urban Affairs Quarterly*, **23**, March, pp. 448–460.

STAMPP, KENNETH. 1989 (1956). *The peculiar institution*. New York: Vintage.

STARK, LEONARD P. 1991. Traditional gender role beliefs and individual outcomes: An exploratory analysis. *Sex Roles*, **24**, pp. 639–649.

STARK, ODED AND J. EDWARD TAYLOR. 1991. Migration incentives, migration types: The role of relative deprivation. *The Economic Journal*, **101**, September, pp. 1103–1178.

STARK, RODNEY. 1987. Deviant places: A theory of the ecology of crime. *Criminology*, **25**, pp. 893–909.

STARK, RODNEY AND WILLIAM SIMS BAINBRIDGE. 1980. Networks of faith: Interpersonal bonds and recruitment to cults and sects. *American Journal of Sociology*, **85**, pp. 1376–1395.

———. 1985. *The future of religion*. Berkeley, Calif.: University of California Press.

———. 1987. *A theory of religion*. New York: Peter Lang.

STARR, PAUL. 1982. *The social transformation of American medicine*. New York: Basic Books.

STARR, RAYMOND H., JR. 1988. Physical abuse of children. In Vincent B. Van Hasselt, Randall L. Morrison, Alan S. Bellack, and Michel Hersen (eds.), *Handbook of family violence*. New York: Plenum.

STATTIN, HAKAN AND GUNNAR KLACKENBERG. 1992. Discordant family relations in intact families: Developmental tendencies over 18 years. *Journal of Marriage and the Family*, **54**, November, pp. 940–956.

STEARNS, LINDA AND CHARLOTTE COLEMAN. 1990. Industrial and local labor market structures and black male employment in the manufacturing section. *Social Science Quarterly*, **71**, June, pp. 285–298.

STEEH, CHARLOTTE AND HOWARD SCHUMAN. 1992. Young white adults: Did racial attitudes change in the 1980s? *American Journal of Sociology*, **98**, September, pp. 340–367.

STEELE, CLAUDE M. 1992. Race and the schooling of black Americans. *The Atlantic Monthly*, **269**, April, pp. 68–78.

STEELMAN, LALA AND JOHN DOBY. 1983. Family size and birth order as factors on the IQ performance of black and white children. *Sociology of Education*, **56**, April, pp. 101–109.

STEELMAN, LALA CARR AND BRIAN POWELL. 1989. Acquiring capital for college. *American Sociological Review*, **54**, pp. 844–855.

STEFFENSMEIER, DARRELL J. 1989. On the causes of "white-collar" crime: An assessment of Hirschi and Gottfredson's claims. *Criminology*, **27**, November, pp. 345–357.

STEFFENSMEIER, DARRELL J., EMILIE A. ALLAN, MILES HARER, AND CATHY STREIFEL. 1989. Age and the distribution of crime. *American Journal of Sociology*, **94**, January, pp. 803–831.

STEFFENSMEIER, DARRELL J. AND MILES D. HARER. 1991. Did crime rise or fall during the Reagan presidency? The effects of an "aging" U.S. population on the nation's crime rate. *Journal of Research in Crime and Delinquency*, **28**, August, pp. 330–359.

STEFFENSMEIER, DARRELL J., CATHY STREIFEL, AND EDWARD S. SHIHADEH. 1992. Cohort size and arrest rates over the life course: The Easterlin hypothesis reconsidered. *American Sociological Review*, **57**, June, pp. 306–314.

STEIGER, THOMAS L. AND MARK WARDELL. 1992. The labor reserve and the skill debate. *The Sociological Quarterly*, **33**, pp. 413–433.

STEIL, JANICE. 1983. Marriage: An unequal partnership. In B. Wolman and G. Stricker, (eds.), *The handbook of family and marital therapy*. New York: Plenum.

STEIL, JANICE AND KAREN WELTMAN. 1991. Marital inequality: The importance of resources, personal attributes, and social norms on career valuing and the allocation of domestic responsibilities. *Sex Roles*, **24**, pp. 161–179.

STEIN, LEONARD I. 1967. The doctor–nurse game. *Archives of General Psychiatry*, **16**, pp. 699–703.

STEIN, LEONARD I., DAVID T. WATTS, AND TIMOTHY HOWELL. 1990. Sounding board: The doctor–nurse game revisited. *The New England Journal of Medicine*, **322**, February, pp. 546–549.

STEINBERG, LAURENCE, JULIE ELMEN, AND NINA MOUNTS. 1989. Authoritative parenting, psychosocial maturity, and academic success among adolescents. *Child Development*, **60**, December, pp. 1424–1436.

STEINBERG, LAURENCE AND SUSAN SILVERBERG. 1986. The vicissitudes of autonomy in early adolescence. *Child Development*, **57**, pp. 841–851.

STEINER, I. D. 1972. *Group process and productivity*. Orlando, Fla.: Academic Press.

STEINMETZ, GEORGE AND ERIK OLIN WRIGHT. 1989. The fall and rise of the petty bourgeoisie: Changing patterns of self-employment in the postwar United States. *American Journal of Sociology*, **94**, March, pp. 973–1018.

STEMPEL, GUIDO, AND JOHN WINDHAUSER, 1991. *The media in the 1984 and 1988 presidential campaigns: Contributions to the study of mass media and communications*. Westport, Conn.: Greenwood Press.

STEPAN-NORRIS, JUDITH AND MAURICE ZEITLIN. 1991. "Red" unions and "bourgeois" contracts? *American Journal of Sociology*, **96**, March, pp. 1151–1200.

STETS, JAN E. 1991. Cohabiting and marital aggression: The role of social isolation. *Journal of Marriage and the Family*, **53**, August, pp. 669–680.

STEVENS, DENNIS J. 1992. Research note: The death sentence and inmate attitudes. *Crime and Delinquency*, **38**, April, pp. 272–279.

STEVENS, GILLIAN AND GRAY SWICEGOOD. 1987. The linguistic context of ethnic endogamy. *American Sociological Review*, **52**, February, pp. 73–82.

STEVENS-LONG, J. 1984. *Adult life*. Palo Alto, Calif.: Mayfield.

STEVENSON, H. W. AND H. AZUMA. 1983. IQ in Japan and the United States: Methodological problems in Lynn's analysis. *Nature*, **306**, pp. 291–292.

STEVENSON, HAROLD W. AND SHIN-YING LEE. 1990. Contexts of achievement: A study of American, Chinese, and Japanese children. Chicago: University of Chicago Press.

STEYN, ANNA. 1987. The peer group as reference group in the behavior of the adolescent with reference to sexual behavior. *The South African Journal of Sociology*, **18**, August, pp. 88–94.

STILLE, ALEXANDER. 1992. No blacks need apply. *The Atlantic Monthly*, **269**, February, pp. 28–38.

STOKES, RANDALL AND ANDY ANDERSON. 1990. Disarticulation and human welfare in less developed countries. *American Sociological Review*, **55**, February, pp. 63–74.

STOLZENBERG, ROSS. 1990. Ethnicity, geography, and occupational achievement of Hispanic men in the United States. *American Sociological Review*, **55**, February, pp. 143–154.

STONE, DONALD. 1981. Social consciousness in the human potential movement. In Thomas Robbins and Dick Anthony (eds.), *In Gods we trust: New Patterns of religious pluralism in America*. New Brunswick, N.J.: Transaction.

STONE, LAWRENCE. 1990. *Road to divorce: England 1530–1987*. London: Oxford University Press.

STONE, ROBYN, GAIL L. CAFFERATA, AND JUDITH SANGL. 1987. Caregivers of the frail elderly: A national profile. *The Gerontologist*, **27**, pp. 616–626.

STOPER, EMILY. 1991. Women's work, women's movement: Taking stock. *Annals of the American Academy of Political and Social Science*, **515**, May, pp. 151–162.

STOUT, DANIEL AND RUSSELL MOURITSEN. 1988. Prosocial behavior in advertising aimed at children. *The Southern Speech Communication Journal*, **53**, Winter, pp. 159–174.

STRAUS, MURRAY A. AND RICHARD J. GELLES. 1986. Societal change and change in family violence from 1975 to 1985 as revealed by two national surveys. *Journal of Marriage and the Family*, **48**, pp. 465–479.

———. 1988. How violent are American families? Estimates from the National Family Violence Resurvey and other studies. In G. T. Hotaling, D. Finkelhor, J. T. Kirkpatrick, and M. A. Straus (eds.), *Family abuse and its consequences: New directions in research*. Beverly Hills, Calif.: Sage.

STRAUS, MURRAY A. AND STEPHEN SWEET. 1992. Verbal/symbolic aggression in couples: Incidence rates and relationships to personal characteristics. *Journal of Marriage and the Family*, **54**, May, pp. 346–357.

STREISAND, BETSY. 1992. Creating an instant extended family. *U.S. News & World Report*, April 6, pp. 82–83.

SUE, STANLEY AND SUMIE OKAZAKI. 1990. Asian-American educational achievements. A phenomenon in search of an explanation. *American Psychologist*, **45**, pp. 913–920.

SUITOR, J. JILL. 1991. Marital quality and satisfaction with the division of household labor across the family life cycle. *Journal of Marriage and the Family*, **53,** February, pp. 221–230.

SULLINS, ELLEN S. 1991. Emotional contagion revisited: Effects of social comparison and expressive style on mood convergence. *Personality and Social Psychology Bulletin*, **17**, April, pp. 166–174.

SULLIVAN, DEIDRE. 1991. Targeting souls. *American Demographics*, **13**, October, pp. 42–46, 56–57.

SUMNER, WILLIAM G. 1906. *Folkways*. New York: Ginn.

SUTHERLAND, E. H. 1940. White-collar criminality. *American Sociological Review*, **5**, February, pp. 1–12.

SUTHERLAND, EDWIN H. AND DONALD R. CRESSEY. 1960. *Principles of criminology*. 6th ed. Philadelphia: Lippincott.

SUTTON, ROSEMARY E. 1991. Equity and computers in the schools: A decade of research. *Review of Educational Research,* **61,** Winter, pp. 475–503.

SWACKER, MARJORIE. 1975. The sex of speaker as a sociolinguistic variable. In Barrie Thorne and Nancy Henley (eds.), *Language and sex: Difference and dominance.* Rawley, Mass.: Newbury House.

SZASZ, THOMAS AND MARC HOLLENDER. 1956. The basic models of the doctor–patient relationship. *Archives in Internal Medicine,* **97,** pp. 585–592.

TAGLIACOZZO, DAISY AND HANS MAUKSCH. 1979. The patient's view of the patient's role. In E. Gartly Jaco (ed.), *Patients, physicians, and illness.* 3d ed. New York: Free Press.

TAMIR, LOIS. 1982. Men at middle age: Developmental transitions. *Annals of the American Academy of Political and Social Science,* **464,** November, pp. 47–56.

TAYLOR, RALPH AND JEANETTE COVINGTON. 1988. Neighborhood changes in ecology and violence. *Criminology,* **26,** pp. 553–573.

TAYLOR, ROBERT AND LINDA CHATTERS. 1988. Church members as a source of informal social support. *Review of Religious Research,* **30,** pp. 193–202.

TEACHMAN, JAY D. 1991. Who pays? Receipt of child support in the United States. *Journal of Marriage and the Family,* **53,** August, pp. 759–772.

TELLES, EDWARD. 1992. Residential segregation by skin color in Brazil. *American Sociological Review,* **57,** April, pp. 186–197.

TELLES, EDWARD AND EDWARD MURGUIA. 1990. Phenotypic discrimination and income differences among Mexican Americans. *Social Science Quarterly,* **71,** December, pp. 682–696.

———. 1992. The continuing significance of phenotype among Mexican Americans. *Social Science Quarterly,* **73,** March, pp. 120–122.

TENNER, EDWARD. 1989. Talking through our hats. *Harvard Magazine,* **91,** May/June, pp. 21–26.

THARP, ROLAND AND RONALD GALLIMORE. 1988. *Rousing minds to life: Teaching, learning, and schooling in social context.* Cambridge, England: Cambridge University Press.

THOMAS, A., S. CHESS, AND H. G. BIRCH. 1970. The origin of personality. In R. C. Atkinson, (ed.), *Contemporary personality: Readings from Scientific American.* San Francisco: W. H. Freeman.

THOMAS, CHER CARRIE AND ROSS TARTELL. 1991. Effective leadership: Evaluations of the next generation of workers. *Psychological Reports,* **69,** pp. 51–61.

THOMAS, ELIZABETH. 1959. *The harmless people.* New York: Knopf.

THOMAS, PATRICIA. 1979. Targets of the cults. *Human Behavior,* **8,** March, pp. 58–59.

THOMPSON, KENNETH. 1991. Transgressing the boundary between the sacred and the secular/profane: A Durkheimian perspective on a public controversy. *Sociological Analysis,* **52,** pp. 277–291.

THOMPSON, MAXINE SEABORN, DORIS ENTWISLE, KARL ALEXANDER, AND JANE SUNDIUS. 1992. The influence of family composition on children's conformity to the student role. *American Educational Research Journal,* **29,** Summer, pp. 405–424.

THOMPSON, VICTOR. 1961. *Modern organizations.* New York: Knopf.

THOMPSON, WARREN. 1929. Population. *American Journal of Sociology,* **34,** pp. 959–975.

THOMSON, ELIZABETH AND UGO COLELLA. 1992. Cohabitation and marital stability: Quality or commitment? *Journal of Marriage and the Family,* **54,** May, pp. 259–267.

THOMSON, ELIZABETH, SARA S. MCLANAHAN, AND ROBERTA BRAUN-CURTIS. 1992. Family structure, gender, and parental socialization. *Journal of Marriage and the Family*, **54**, May, pp. 368–378.

THORNBERRY, TERENCE P., MARVIN D. KROHN, ALAN J. LIZOTTE, AND DEBORAH CHARD-WIERSCHEM. 1993. The role of juvenile gangs in facilitating delinquent behavior. *Journal of Research in Crime and Delinquency*, **30**, February, pp. 55–87.

THORNTON, ARLAND. 1991. Influence of marital history of parents on the marital and cohabitational experiences of children. *American Journal of Sociology*, **96**, January, pp. 868–894.

THORNTON, ARLAND, WILLIAM G. AXINN, AND DANIEL H. HILL. 1992. Reciprocal effects of religiosity, cohabitation, and marriage. *American Journal of Sociology*, **3**, November, pp. 628–651.

THORNTON, BILL, RACHEL LEO, AND KIMBERLY ALBERG. 1991. Gender role typing, the superwoman ideal, and the potential for eating disorders. *Sex Roles*, **25**, pp. 469–484.

TICKAMYER, ANN AND KATHLEEN BLEE. 1990. The racial convergence thesis in women's intergenerational occupation mobility. *Social Science Quarterly*, **71**, December, pp. 711–728.

TIENDA, MARTA, SHELLEY SMITH, AND VILMA ORTIZ. 1987. Industrial restructuring, gender segregation, and sex differences in earnings. *American Sociological Review*, **52**, April, pp. 195–210.

TILLY, CHARLES. 1978. *From mobilization to revolution*. Reading, Mass.: Addison-Wesley.

TIMBERLAKE, MICHAEL AND KIRK WILLIAMS. 1984. Dependence, political exclusion, and government repression: Some cross-national evidence. *American Sociological Review*, **49**, February, pp. 141–146.

TIPTON, STEVEN M. 1982. *Getting saved from the sixties: Moral meaning in conversion and cultural change*. Berkeley, Calif.: University of California Press.

TITTLE, CHARLES AND MICHAEL WELCH. 1983. Religiosity and deviance: Toward a contingency theory of constraining effects. *Social Forces*, **61**, March, pp. 653–682.

TOBY, JACKSON. 1957. Social disorganization and stake in conformity: Complimentary factors in the predatory behavior of hoodlums. *Journal of Criminal Law, Criminology, and Police Science*, **48**, pp. 12–17.

TOBY, JACKSON AND DAVID ARMOR. 1992. Carrots or sticks for high school dropouts? *The Public Interest*, **106**, Winter, pp. 76–90.

TOCH, THOMAS, NANCY LINNON, AND MATTHEW COOPER. 1991. Schools that work. *U.S. News & World Report*, May 27, pp. 58–66.

TOCH, THOMAS AND TED SLAFSKY. 1991. The great college tumble. *U.S. News & World Report*, June 3, p. 50.

TOFFLER, ALVIN. 1970. *Future shock*. New York: Bantam Books.

TOLBERT, PAMELA S. AND ALICE A. OBERFIELD. 1991. Sources of organizational demography. Faculty sex ratios in colleges and universities. *Sociology of Education*, **64**, October, pp. 305–315.

TOLNAY, STEWARD AND E. M. BECK. 1992. Racial violence and black migration: The American South, 1910 to 1930. *American Sociological Review*, **57**, February, pp. 103–116.

TOMASHEVICH, GEORGE. 1981. Aging and the aged in various cultures. In G. Falk, U. Falk, and G. V. Tomashevich (eds.), *Aging in America and other cultures*. Saratoga, Calif.: Century Twenty One.

TOMPKINS, DWIGHT EDWARD. 1991. An argument for privacy in support of the choice of home education by parents. *Journal of Law and Education,* **20**, Summer, pp. 301–323.

TÖNNIES, FERDINAND. 1903 (1887). *Gemeinschaft und Gesellschaft* [Community and society]. (Charles Loomis, trans. and ed.). New York: Harper & Row.

TOWNSEND, BICKLEY AND KATHLEEN O'NEIL. 1990. American women get mad. *American Demographics,* **12**, August, pp. 26–32.

TRENT, KATHERINE AND SCOTT SOUTH. 1989. Structural determinants of the divorce rate: A cross-societal analysis. *Journal of Marriage and the Family,* **51**, May, pp. 391–404.

TROYER, RONALD. 1989. Chinese social organization. In Ronald Troyer, John Clark, and Dean Rojek (eds.), *Social control in the People's Republic of China.* New York: Praeger.

TSCHANN, JEANNE, JANET JOHNSTON, MARSHA KLINE, AND JUDITH WALLERSTEIN. 1989. Family process and children's functioning during divorce. *Journal of Marriage and the Family,* **51**, pp. 431–444.

TSCHANN, JEANNE, JANET JOHNSTON, AND JUDITH WALLERSTEIN. 1989. Resources, stresses, and attachment as predictions of adult adjustment after divorce: A longitudinal study. *Journal of Marriage and the Family,* **51**, pp. 1033–1046.

TURNBULL, COLIN. 1972. *The mountain people.* New York: Simon & Schuster.

TURNER, BYRAN S. 1989. Ageing, status politics, and sociological theory. *The British Journal of Sociology,* **40**, December, pp. 588–606.

TURNER, LENLEY CRAIG. 1992. The case for intensive supervision probation. *Corrections Today,* **154**, April, pp. 142–144.

TURNER, RALPH AND LEWIS KILLIAN. 1987. *Collective Behavior.* Englewood Cliffs, N.J.: Prentice-Hall.

TWITO, T. J. AND M. A. STEWART. 1982. A half-sibling study of aggressive conduct disorder. *Neuropsychobiology,* **8**, pp. 144–150.

UEDA, REED. 1989. False modesty. *The New Republic,* July 3, pp. 16–17.

UEHARA, EDWINA. 1990. Dual exchange theory, social networks, and informal social support. *American Journal of Sociology,* **96**, November, pp. 521–557.

UHLENBERG, PETER. 1987. How old is "old age"? *The Public Interest,* Summer.

UHLENBERG, PETER, TERESA COONEY, AND ROBERT BOYD. 1990. Divorce for women after midlife. *Journal of Gerontology: Social Sciences,* **45**, pp. S3–11.

ULBRICH, PATRICIA M., GEORGE J. WARHEIT, AND RICK S. ZIMMERMAN. 1989. Race, socioeconomic status, and psychological distress: An examination of differential vulnerability. *Journal of Health and Social Behavior,* **30**, March, pp. 131–146.

UMBERSON, DEBRA. 1989. Relationships with children: Explaining parents' psychological well-being. *Journal of Marriage and the Family,* **51**, pp. 999–1012.

UMBERSON, DEBRA, CAMILLE WORTMAN, AND RONALD KESSLER. 1992. Widowhood and depression: Explaining long-term gender differences in vulnerability. *Journal of Health and Social Behavior,* **33**, March, pp. 10–24.

U.S. Bureau of the Census. 1989. *Statistical abstract of the United States.* Washington, D.C.: U.S. Government Printing Office.

———. 1990. *Statistical abstract of the United States.* Washington, D.C.: U.S. Government Printing Office.

———. 1991. *Statistical abstract of the United States.* 111th ed. Washington, D.C.: U.S. Government Printing Office.

USEEM, MICHAEL. 1984. *The inner circle: Large corporations and the rise of business political activity in the U.S. and U.K.* New York: Oxford University Press.

UTTAL, D. H., M. LUMMIS, AND H. W. STEVENSON. 1988. Low and high mathematics achievement in Japanese, Chinese, and American elementary-school children. *Developmental Psychology*, **24**, pp. 335–342.

VAN DE KAA, DIRK J. 1987. *Europe's second demographic transition*. Washington, D.C.: Population Reference Bureau.

VANDELL, DEBORAH L. 1989. Child care: Does it have long-term effects? Paper presented at the biennial meeting of the Society for Research in Child Development, Kansas City.

VANDELL, DEBORAH L. AND M. A. CORASANITI. 1990. Variations in early child care: Do they predict subsequent social, emotional, and cognitive differences? Unpublished manuscript, University of Wisconsin, Madison.

VANDELL, DEBORAH AND KATHY WILSON. 1987. Infants' interactions with mother, sibling, and peer: Contrast and relations between interaction systems. *Child Development*, **58**, February, pp. 176–186.

VANFOSSEN, BETH, JAMES JONES, AND JOHN SPADE. 1987. Curriculum tracking and status maintenance. *Sociology of Education*, **60**, April, pp. 104–122.

VANNOY, DANA AND WILLIAM W. PHILLIBER. 1992. Wife's employment and quality of marriage. *Journal of Marriage and the Family*, **54**, May, pp. 387–398.

VAUGHAN, JAMES, JR. 1964. The religion and world view of the Marghi. *Ethnology*, **3**, pp. 380–397.

VEBLEN, THORSTEIN. 1922. *The instinct of workmanship*. New York: Huebsch.

VELEZ, WILLIAM. 1989. High school attrition among Hispanic and non-Hispanic white youths. *Sociology of Education*, **62**, April, pp. 119–133.

VEMER, ELIZABETH, M. COLEMAN, L. GANONG, AND H. COOPER. 1989. Marital satisfaction in remarriage: A meta-analysis. *Journal of Marriage and the Family*, **51**, pp. 713–725.

VERBRUGGE, LOIS M. 1989. The twain meet: Empirical explanations of sex differences in health and mortality. *Journal of Health and Social Behavior*, **30**, September, pp. 282–304.

VEROFF, JEROME, ELIZABETH DOUVAN, AND RICHARD KULKA. 1981. *The inner American: A self-portrait from 1957 to 1976*. New York: Basic Books.

VIGIL, JAMES DIEGO. 1988. *Barrio gangs: Street life and identity in Southern California*. Austin, Tex.: University of Texas Press.

VILA, BRYAN J. AND LAWRENCE E. COHEN. 1993. Crime as strategy: Testing an evolutionary ecological theory of expropriative crime. *American Journal of Sociology*, **98**, January, pp. 873–912.

VILLEMEZ, WAYNE J. AND WILLIAM P. BRIDGES. 1988. When bigger is better: Differences in the individual-level effect of firm and establishment size. *American Sociological Review*, **53**, April, pp. 237–255.

VINOVSKIS, MARIS A. 1992. Schooling and poor children in 19th-century America. *American Behavioral Scientist*, **35**, January/February, pp. 313–329.

VIRKKUNEN, M., J. DE JONG, J. PARTKKO, F. K. GOODWIN, AND M. LINNOILA. 1989. Relationship of psychobiological variables to recidivism in violent offenders and impulsive fire setters. *Archives of General Psychiatry*, **46**, pp. 600–603.

VISHER, CHRISTY, A., PAMELA K. LATTIMORE, AND RICHARD L. LINSTER. 1991. Predicting the recidivism of serious youthful offenders using survival models. *Criminology*, **29**, pp. 329–361.

VOLD, G. B. AND T. J. BERNARD. 1986. *Theoretical criminality*. New York: Oxford University Press.

VOYDANOFF, PATRICIA. 1988. Women, work, and family: Bernard's perspective on the past, present, and future. *Psychology of Women Quarterly*, **12**, pp. 269–280.

VUCHINICH, SAMUEL, REGINA VUCHINICH, E. MAVIS HETHERINGTON, AND GLENN CLINGEMPEEL. 1991. Parent–child interaction and gender differences in early adolescents' adaptation to stepfamilies. *Developmental Psychology*, **27**, pp. 618–626.

WACQUANT, LOIC AND WILLIAM J. WILSON. 1989. The cost of racial and class exclusion in the inner city. *Annals of the American Academy of Political and Social Science*, **501**, January, pp. 8–25.

WAITE, LINDA. 1980. Working wives and the family cycle. *American Journal of Sociology*, **86**, pp. 272–294.

WAITZKIN, HOWARD. 1989. A critical theory of medical discourse: Ideology, social control, and the processing of social context in medical encounters. *Journal of Health and Social Behavior*, **30**, June, pp. 220–239.

WAITZKIN, HOWARD AND BARBARA WATERMAN. 1974. *The exploitation of illness in capitalist society*. Indianapolis: Bobbs-Merrill.

WALKER, S. 1989. *Sense and nonsense about crime: A policy guide*. Pacific Grove, Calif.: Brooks/Cole.

WALLACE, JOHN AND JERALD BACHMAN. 1991. Explaining racial/ethnic differences in adolescent drug use. *Social Problems*, **38**, August, pp. 333–357.

WALLACE, PAMELA M. AND IAN H. GOTLIB. 1990. Marital adjustment during the transition to parenthood: Stability and predictors of change. *Journal of Marriage and the Family*, **52**, February, pp. 21–29.

WALLACE, STEVEN. 1990. Race versus class in the health care of African-American elderly. *Social Problems*, **37**, November, pp. 517–534.

WALLER, WILLARD AND REUBEN HILL. 1951. *The family*. New York: The Dryden Press.

WALLERSTEIN, IMMANUEL M. 1974. *The modern world system: Capitalist agriculture and the origins of the European world economy in the sixteenth century*. New York: Academic Press.

WALLERSTEIN, JUDITH AND SANDRA BLAKESLEE. 1989. *Second chances: Men, women, and children a decade after divorce*. New York: Tichnor and Fields.

WALLERSTEIN, JUDITH AND JOAN B. KELLY. 1980. *Surviving the breakup: How children and parents cope with divorce*. New York: Basic Books.

WALTERS, GLENN D. 1992. A meta-analysis of the gene–crime relationship. *Criminology*, **30**, pp. 595–611.

WALTERS, GLENN D. AND THOMAS W. WHITE. 1989. Heredity and crime: Bad genes or bad research? *Criminology*, **27**, pp. 455–482.

WANDERSEE, WINIFRED D. 1988. *On the move: American women in the 1970s*. Boston: Twayne.

WARNER, LLOYD AND PAUL LUNT. 1941. *The social life of a modern community*. New Haven, Conn.: Yale University Press.

WARR, MARK. 1993. Age, peers, and delinquency. *Criminology*, **31**, pp. 17–40.

WARREN, MARTIN AND SHELD BERKOWITZ. 1969. The employability of AFDC mothers and fathers. *Welfare in Review*, **7**, July/August, pp. 1–7.

WASIK, BARBARA HANNA, CRAIG T. RAMEY, DONNA M. BRYANT, AND JOSEPH J. SPARLING. 1990. A longitudinal study of two early intervention strategies: Project CARE. *Child Development*, **61**, pp. 1682–1696.

WATANABE, SUSUMU. 1991. The Japanese quality control circle: Why it works. *International Labour Review*, **130**, pp. 57–77.

WATARU, KURITA. 1990. School phobia. *Japan Quarterly*, **37**, July/September, pp. 298–303.

WATERS, HARRY. 1982. Life according to TV. *Newsweek*, December 6, pp. 136–140.

WATSON, JOHN S. 1991. Religion as a cultural phenomenon, and national mortality rates from heart disease. *Psychological Reports*, **69**, pp. 439–442.

WEAKLIEM, DAVID L. 1990. Relative wages and the radical theory of economic segmentation. *American Sociological Review*, **55**, August, pp. 574–590.

WEATHERFORD, M. STEPHEN. 1991. Mapping the ties that bind: Legitimacy, representation, and alienation. *The Western Political Quarterly*, **44**, June, pp. 251–276.

WEAVER, CHARLES N. AND MICHAEL D. MATTHEWS. 1990. Work satisfaction of females with full-time employment and full-time housekeeping: 15 Years later. *Psychological Reports*, **66**, pp. 1248–1250.

WEBER, MAX. 1947. *The theory of social and economic organization*. Trans. Talcott Parsons. Glencoe, Ill.: Free Press.

———. 1958 (1904). *The Protestant ethic and the spirit of capitalism*. Trans. Talcott Parsons. New York: Scribner.

———. 1978 (1921). *Economy and society*. Eds. Guenter Roth and Claus Wittich. New York: Bedminister.

WEBSTER-STRATTON, CAROLYN. 1989. The relationship of marital support, conflict, and divorce to parent perceptions, behaviors, and childhood conduct problems. *Journal of Marriage and the Family*, **51**, May, pp. 417–430.

WEGENER, BERND. 1991. Job mobility and social ties: Social resources, prior job, and status attainment. *American Sociological Review*, **56**, February, pp. 60–71.

WEHLAGE, GARY, GREGORY SMITH, AND PAULINE LIPMAN. 1992. Restructuring urban schools: The new futures experience. *American Educational Research Journal*, **29**, Spring, pp. 51–93.

WEINBERG, SAMUEL. 1987. The self-fulfillment of the self-fulfilling prophecy. *Educational Researcher*, **16**, December, pp. 28–37.

WEIS, JOSEPH G. 1986. Issues in the measurement of criminal careers. In Alfred Blumstein, Jacqueline Cohen, Jeffrey A. Roth, and Christy A. Visher (eds.), *Criminal careers and "career criminals."* Vol. 2. Washington D.C.: National Academy Press.

WEISBURD, DAVID, ELLEN F. CHAYET, AND ELIN J. WARING. 1990. White-collar crime and criminal careers: Some preliminary findings. *Crime & Delinquency*, **36**, July, pp. 342–355.

WEISNER, THOMAS AND HELEN GARNIER. 1992. Nonconventional family life-styles and school achievement: A 12-year longitudinal study. *American Educational Research Journal*, **29**, Fall, pp. 605–632.

WEITZMAN, LENORE J. 1985. *The divorce revolution: The unexpected social and economic consequences for women and children in America*. New York: Free Press.

———. 1988. Women and children last: The social and economic consequences of divorce law reforms. In S. M. Dornbusch and M. H. Strober (eds.), *Feminism, children, and the new families*. New York: Guilford Press.

WELCH, FINIS. 1987. A reconsideration of the impact of school desegregation programs on public school enrollment of white students, 1968–1976. *Sociology of Education*, **60**, October, pp. 215–221.

WELCH, MICHAEL R., CHARLES R. TITTLE, AND THOMAS PETEE. 1991. Religion and deviance among adult Catholics: A test of the "moral communities" hypothesis. *Journal for the Scientific Study of Religion*, **30**, pp. 159–172.

WELSH, PATRICK. 1991. A teacher's view. *The Wilson Quarterly*, Summer, pp. 77–87.

WEST, CANDACE. 1984. *Routine complications: Troubles with talk between doctors and patients*. Bloomington, Ind.: Indiana University Press.

WESTBURY, IAN. 1992. Comparing American and Japanese achievement: Is the United States really a low achiever? *Educational Researcher*, **21**, June–July, pp. 18–24.

WESTERMANN, TED AND JAMES BURFEIND. 1991. *Crime and justice in two societies: Japan and the United States*. Pacific Grove, Calif.: Brooks/Cole.

WESTERN, BRUCE. 1991. A comparative study of corporatist development. *American Sociological Review*, **56**, June, pp. 283–294.

WEXLER, HARRY K., GREGORY P. FALKIN, AND DOUGLAS S. LIPTON. 1990. Outcome evaluation of a prison therapeutic community for substance abuse treatment. *Criminal Justice and Behavior*, **17**, March, pp. 71–92.

WHEATON, BLAIR. 1990. Life transitions, role histories, and mental health. *American Sociological Review*, **55**, April, pp. 209–223.

WHEELER, GERALD. 1978. *Counter-deterrence: A report on juvenile sentencing and effects of prisonization*. Chicago: Nelson-Hall.

WHEELER, STANTON, DAVID WEISBURD, NANCY BODE, AND ELIN WARING. 1988. White-collar crime and criminals. *American Criminal Law Review*, **25**, pp. 331–357.

WHITBECK, LES B. AND VIKTOR GECAS. 1988. Value attribution and transmission between parents and children. *Journal of Marriage and the Family*, **50**, pp. 829–840.

WHITE, G. S. 1980. Physical attractiveness and courtship progress. *Journal of Personality and Social Psychology*, **39**, pp. 660–668.

WHITE, KEVIN. 1991. The sociology of health and illness. *Current Sociology*, **39**, Autumn, pp. 1–116.

WHITE, LYNN AND ALAN BOOTH. 1985. The transition to parenthood and marital quality. *Journal of Family Issues*, **6**, pp. 435–449.

WHITE, LYNN AND JOHN N. EDWARDS. 1990. Emptying the nest and parental well-being: An analysis of national panel data. *American Sociological Review*, **55**, April, pp. 235–242.

WHITE, LYNN AND BRUCE KEITH. 1990. The effect of shift work on the quality and stability of marital relations. *Journal of Marriage and the Family*, **52**, May, pp. 453–462.

WHITE, S. G. AND C. HATCHER. 1984. Couple complementarity and similarity: A review of the literature. *American Journal of Family Therapy*, **12**, pp. 15–25.

WHITEHEAD, BARBARA D. 1993. Dan Quayle was right. *The Atlantic Monthly*, **271**, April, pp. 47–84.

WHITEHEAD, J. T. AND S. P. LAB. 1989. A meta-analysis of juvenile correctional treatment. *Journal of Research in Crime and Delinquency*, **26**, pp. 276–295.

WHITLEY, B. E., JR. 1984. Sex role orientation and psychological well-being: Two meta-analyses. *Sex Roles*, **12**, pp. 207–225.

WHITMAN, DAVID AND DORIAN FRIEDMAN. 1992. Busing's unheralded legacy. *U.S. News & World Report*, April 13, pp. 63–65.

WHITSETT, DONI AND HELEN LAND. 1992. Role strain, coping, and marital satisfaction of stepparents. *Families in Society*, **73**, February, pp. 79–92.

WHITTLE, JEFF, JOSEPH CONIGLIARO, C. B. GOOD, AND RICHARD LOFGREN. 1993. Racial differences in the use of invasive cardiovascular procedures in the Department of Veterans Affairs medical system. *The New England Journal of Medicine*, **329**, August 26, pp. 621–627.

WHORF, BENJAMIN L. 1956. *Language, thought, and reality: Selected writings of Benjamin Lee Whorf*. Ed. J. B. Carroll. Cambridge, Mass.: MIT Press.

WIDOM, CATHY. 1989. The cycle of violence. *Science*, **244**, April 4, pp. 160–166.

WIERSMA, UCO J. AND PETER VAN DEN BERG. 1991. Work–home role conflict, family climate, and domestic responsibilities among men and women in dual-earner families. *Journal of Applied Social Psychology*, **21**, pp. 1207–1217.

WIJNBERG, MARION H. AND THOMAS HOLMES. 1992. Adaptation to divorce: The impact of role orientation on family life-cycle perspectives. *Families in Society*, **73**, March, pp. 159–167.

WILENSKY, HAROLD AND LOWELL TURNER. 1987. *Democratic corporatism and policy linkages*. Berkeley, Calif.: Institute of International Studies.

WILLIAMS, ALLEN AND SUZANNE ORTEGA. 1990. Dimensions of ethnic assimilation. An empirical appraisal of Gordon's typology. *Social Science Quarterly*, **71**, December, pp. 697–710.

WILLIAMS, CHRISTINE L. 1992. The glass escalator: Hidden advantages for men in the 'female' professions. *Social Problems*, **39**, August, pp. 253–267.

WILLIAMS, KIRK. 1992. Social source of marital violence and deterrence: Testing an integrated theory of assaults between partners. *Journal of Marriage and the Family*, **54**, August, pp. 620–629.

WILLIAMS, KIRK AND RICHARD HAWKINS. 1986. Perceptual research on general deterrence: A critical review. *Law and Society Review*, **20**, pp. 545–572.

WILLIAMS, RHYS H. AND N. J. DEMERATH III. 1991. Religion and political process in an American city. *American Sociological Review*, **56**, August, pp. 417–431.

WILLIAMS, ROBIN, JR. 1970. Social order and social conflict. *Proceedings of the American Philosophical Society*, **114**, June, pp. 217–225.

WILSON, E. O. 1975. *Sociobiology*. Cambridge, Mass.: Belknap Press.

WILSON, FIONA. 1992. Language, technology, gender, and power. *Human Relations*, **45**, pp. 883–904.

WILSON, JAMES Q. AND GEORGE KELLING. 1982. Broken windows. *The Atlantic Monthly*, **249**, March, pp. 29–38.

WILSON, KENNETH AND JANET BOLDIZAR. 1990. Gender segregation in higher education: Effects of aspirations, mathematics achievement, and income. *Sociology of Education*, **63**, January, pp. 62–74.

WILSON, KENNETH AND ALEJANDRO PORTES. 1980. Immigrant enclaves: An analysis of the labor market experience of Cubans in Miami. *American Journal of Sociology*, **86**, pp. 295–319.

The Wilson Quarterly, 1987. Monsoon country. Winter, pp. 47–53.

WILSON, WILLIAM JULIUS. 1978. *The declining significance of race*. Chicago: University of Chicago Press.

———. 1987. *The truly disadvantaged: The inner city, the underclass, and public policy*. Chicago: University of Chicago Press.

———. 1989. The ghetto underclass: Social science perspectives. *Annals of the American Academy of Political and Social Science*, **501**, January, pp. 182–191.

———. 1991. Poverty, joblessness, and family structure in the inner city: A comparative perspective, paper delivered at Chicago Urban Poverty and Family Life Conference, sponsored by the University of Chicago's Graduate School of Public Policy and the Social Science Research Council. October.

WIMBERLY, DALE W. 1991. Transnational corporate investment and food consumption in the Third World: A cross-national analysis. *Rural Sociology*, **56**, pp. 406–431.

WINEBERG, HOWARD. 1992. Childbearing and dissolution of the second marriage. *Journal of Marriage and the Family*, **54**, November, pp. 879–887.

WINFIELD, IDEE, RICHARD T. CAMPBELL, ALAN C. KERCKHOFF, DIANE EVERETT, AND JERRY M. TROTT. 1989. Career processes in Great Britain and the United States. *Social Forces*, **68**, September, pp. 284–308.

WOLFE, LEE. 1987. Enduring cognitive effects of public and private schools. *Educational Researcher*, **16**, May, pp. 5–11.

WOO, DEBORAH. 1989. The gap between striving and achieving: The case of Asian American women. In *Making waves*. Asian Women United of California: Beacon Press.

WOOD, PETER AND BARRETT LEE. 1991. Is neighborhood racial succession inevitable? *Urban Affairs Quarterly*, **26**, June, pp. 610–620.

WRIGHT, ERIK OLIN. 1985. *Classes*. London: New Left.

WRIGHT, ERIK OLIN AND DONMOON CHO. 1992. The relative permeability of class boundaries to cross-class friendships. *American Sociological Review*, **57**, February, pp. 85–102.

WRIGHT, ERIK OLIN, DAVID HACHEN, CYNTHIA COSTELLO, AND JOEY SPRAGUE. 1982. The American class structure. *American Sociological Review*, **47**, December, pp. 709–726.

WRIGHT, STUART A. 1991. Reconceptualizing cult coercion and withdrawal: A comparative analysis of divorce and apostasy. *Social Forces*, **70**, September, pp. 125–145.

WUTHNOW, ROBERT. 1989. *The struggle for America's soul: Evangelicals, liberals, and secularism*. Grand Rapids, Mich.: W. B. Eerdmans.

YANG, PEI-LIN, VIVIAN LIN, AND JAMES LAWSON. 1991. Health policy reform in the People's Republic of China. *International Journal of Health Services*, **21**, pp. 481–491.

YANKELOVICH, DANIEL. 1981. *New rules: Searching for self-fulfillment in a world turned upside-down*. New York: Random House.

YEATTS, DALE, THOMAS CROW, AND EDWARD FOLTS. 1992. Service use among low-income minority elderly: Strategies for overcoming barriers. *The Gerontologist*, **32**, pp. 24–32.

YEDIDIA, MICHAEL, JUDITH BARR, AND CAROLYN BERRY. 1993. Physicians' attitudes toward AIDS at different career stages: A comparison of internists and surgeons. *Journal of Health and Social Behavior*, **34**, September, pp. 272–284.

YOGEV, S. 1986. Relationships between stress and marital satisfaction among dual-earner couples. *Women and Therapy*, **5**, pp. 313–330.

YOUNG, RUTH AND JOE FRANCIS. 1991. Entrepreneurship and innovation in small manufacturing firms. *Social Science Quarterly*, **72**, pp. 149–162.

YOUNGBLADE, LISA AND JAY BELSKY. 1989. The social and emotional consequences of child maltreatment. In R. Ammerman and Michel Hersen (eds.), *Children at risk: An evaluation of factors contributing to child abuse and neglect*. New York: Plenum.

ZAHN, G. LAWRENCE. 1991. Face-to-face communication in an office setting: The effects of position, proximity, and exposure. *Communication Research*, **18**, December, pp. 737–754.

ZAMBLE, EDWARD AND FRANK PORPORINO. 1990. Coping, imprisonment, and rehabilitation: Some data and their implications. *Criminal Justice and Behavior*, **17**, March, pp. 53–70.

ZEBROWITZ, LESLIE, DANIEL TANENBAUM, AND LORI GOLDSTEIN. 1991. The impact of job applicants' facial maturity, gender, and academic achievement on hiring recommendations. *Journal of Applied Social Psychology*, **21**, April, pp. 525–548.

ZERUBAVEL, EVIATAR. 1981. *Hidden rhythms: Schedules and calendars in social life*. Chicago: University of Chicago Press.

ZILL, NICHOLAS. 1988. Behavior, achievement, and health problems among children in stepfamilies: Findings from a national survey of child health. In E. Mavis Hetherington and J. D. Arasteh (eds.), *Impact of divorce, single parenting, and stepparenting*. Hillsdale, N.J.: Lawrence Erlbaum.

ZIV, AVNER AND ORIT GADISH. 1989. Humor and marital satisfaction. *The Journal of Social Psychology*, **129**, pp. 759–768.

ZWERLING, CRAIG AND HILARY SILVER. 1992. Race and job dismissal in a federal bureaucracy. *American Sociological Review*, **57**, October, pp. 651–660.

NAME INDEX

SUBJECT INDEX

CREDITS

P. 3, © Don Allen Sparks/The Image Bank.   P. 4, © Luis Villot/The Stock Market.
P. 4, © Photo Edit.   P. 7, © Joe Bensen/Stock, Boston.   P. 9, © 1992 Louis
Psihoyos/Contact Press Images.   P. 12, The Bettmann Archive.   P. 12, The
Bettmann Archive.   P. 13, The Bettmann Archive.   P. 14, The Bettmann
Archive.   P. 15, Bettmann.   P. 26, © Michael Newman/Photo Edit.
P. 32, Photos © Kenneth Good. From *Into The Heart: One Man's Pursuit of Love and
Knowledge among the Yanomamo* by Kenneth Good with David Chanoff.
P. 33, Photos © Kenneth Good. From *Into The Heart: One Man's Pursuit of Love and
Knowledge among the Yanomamo* by Kenneth Good with David Chanoff.
P. 36, © Mark Wagner/Tony Stone Images.   P. 38, Photos © Kenneth Good. From
Into The Heart: One Man's Pursuit of Love and Knowledge among the Yanomamo by
Kenneth Good with David Chanoff.   P. 41, © Rick Browne/Photoreporters.
P. 42, Photos © Kenneth Good. From *Into The Heart: One Man's Pursuit of Love and
Knowledge among the Yanomamo* by Kenneth Good with David Chanoff.
P. 44, © 89 Pedro Coll/The Stock Market.   p. 46, © David Young-Wolff/Photo
Edit.   P. 48, © Jon Gray/Tony Stone Images.   P. 50, © Erwin C.
Nielsen/Lightwave.   P. 54, Photos © Kenneth Good. From *Into The Heart: One
Man's Pursuit of Love and Knowledge among the Yanomamo* by Kenneth Good with
David Chanoff.   P. 57, © Robert Caputo/Stock, Boston.   P. 59, © Illustrations by
Jared Schneidman Design.   P. 64, © Flip Chalfant/The Image Bank.
P. 65, © Georg Gerster/Comstock.   P. 67, © Richard Hutching/Photo Edit.
P. 70, UPI/Bettmann.   P. 74, © Oscar Palmquist/Lightwave.   P. 78, © Joel
Gordon 1992.   P. 83, © Paul Conklin/Photo Edit.   P. 84, © David Young-
Wolff/Photo Edit.   P. 89, © Richard Pasley/Stock, Boston.   P. 91, © Sheryl
McNee/Tony Stone Images.   P. 68, © Michael Newman/Photo Edit.
P. 98, © Myrleen Ferguson Cate/Photo Edit.   P. 100, © Myrleen Ferguson/Photo
Edit.   P. 101, © Cliff Feulner/The Image Bank.   P. 102, Courtesy of William C.
NesSmith.   P. 103, Courtesy of William C. NesSmith.   P. 106, © Erik Leigh
Simmons/The Image Bank.   P. 107, © David R. Frazier.   P. 113, © Mary Kate
Denny/Photo Edit.   P. 116, © Bill Robbins/Tony Stone Images.   P. 118, © 1993
Martini & Rossi Corporation.   P. 123, © Joel Gordon 1987.   P. 127, © Sipa
Press/San Jose Mercury.   P. 129, © N. Schiller/The Image Works.
P. 130, Reuters/Bettmann.   P. 139, © 1992 GM Corp.   P. 142, © Joe Sohm/The
Image Works.   P. 144, © Pete Saloutos/Tony Stone Images.   P. 147, © Photo
Edit.   P. 150, UPI/Bettmann.   P. 153, © Starr/Stock, Boston.   P. 154, © Mary
Kate Denny/Photo Edit.   P. 160, © Topham/The Image Works.   P. 161, © Susan
Van Etten/Photo Edit.   P. 163, National Anthropological Archives, Smithsonian
Institution. Neg. # 303-B.   P. 165, Glenbow Archives, Calgary, Canada
(NA-395-1).   P. 165, © Elena Rooraid/Photo Edit.   P. 167, © 1992 GM Corp.
P. 190, © Tony Freeman/Photo Edit.   P. 192, © Joel Gordon 1992.
P. 200, © Don Klumpp/The Image Bank.   P. 203, Reuters/Bettmann.
P. 206, © Charles Moore/Black Star.   P. 208, © Mark Peters/Sipa Press.
P. 209, Reuters/Bettmann.   P. 215, The Bettmann Archive.   P. 217, © Nancy
Brown/The Image Bank.   P. 221, © Don Smetzer/Tony Stone Images.
P. 225, © Nancy Brown/The Image Bank.   P. 227, © Michael Melford/The Image
Bank.   P. 234, © Bill Bachmann/Photo Edit.   P. 237, © 1993 Chanel, Inc.
P. 247, © David Young-Wolff/Photo Edit.   P. 250, © Vic Bider/Photo Edit.
P. 252, © Howard Grey/Tony Stone Images.   P. 254, © Maria Taglienti/The Image